THE CASSELL
SOCCER
COMPANION

THE CASSELL
SOCCER
COMPANION

HISTORY · FACTS · ANECDOTES

DAVID PICKERING

CASSELL

A CASSELL BOOK

First published 1994
by Cassell
Villiers House
41/47 Strand
London
WC2N 5JE

Distributed in the United States
by Sterling Publishing Co., Inc.
387 Park Avenue South, New York,
New York 10016–8810

Distributed in Australia
by Capricorn Link (Australia) Pty Ltd
2/13 Carrington Road, Castle Hill, NSW 2154

British Library Cataloguing-in-Publication Data
A catalogue record for this book is available
from the British Library

ISBN 0–304–34231 9

Typeset by Colset Pty Limited, Singapore

Printed and bound in Great Britain by
Mackays of Chatham PLC, Chatham, Kent

Preface

There have been many fine reference books on soccer, but few which have tried to look at all aspects of the sport that so many people love for so many reasons. What I have set out to do in this Companion is to provide a comprehensive and kaleidoscopic guide to the world of association football. This has entailed drawing on a vast number of different sources, in order to do justice to the astonishing array of themes encompassed by football culture. Entries range from clubs and personalities of the game to technical terms, nicknames, and other topics from the heritage of oddities and curiosities that has accumulated in the course of soccer's colourful history. I have included details of all of the English and Scottish League clubs as well as prominent sides from elsewhere in the world; coverage of national teams; and brief accounts of many respected non-League clubs, together with descriptions and histories of famous grounds. The celebrated players, managers, and other figures who have shaped the game over the years are also discussed in full, while other entries extend coverage to football legends and phraseology. Thus, interspersed with such factually based entries as Manchester United and Stanley Matthews will be found such diverse headings as the Battle of Highbury, 'giant-killer', Hand of God, and 'sick as a parrot'.

I have tried to enliven articles throughout the book by relevant anecdotes and quotations, as well as by statistical information about such matters as record scorelines and, where applicable, extracts from both familiar and less well-known club songs. It is my hope that the book will be of equal interest to the casual armchair enthusiast and to the dedicated fan, regardless of team allegiance, and that the alphabetical organisation and clear cross-referencing will make it easy to use and enjoyable to browse through.

I would like to extend my thanks to members of my family, as well as Roger Edwards, Simon Lee, Richard Penny, Gavin Love, and numerous other friends and contacts, including the clubs themselves, for their invaluable assistance, and to the editors and production staff at Cassell for their co-operation.

David Pickering

A

A's Nickname of the English non-League football club BANSTEAD ATHLETIC, short for Athletic.

abandonment Bringing a game to an end when further play becomes impossible. Power to abandon a match rests with the referee, who is entitled to call off play for any reason (usually because of bad weather or unruly crowd behaviour).

Under the early rules of the game time lost because of abandonment had to be replayed at a later date. This led to some very curious meetings. In late 1888, for instance, a game between Aston Villa and Sheffield Wednesday at Sheffield had to be stopped with just ten minutes remaining because of bad light (with Wednesday leading 3–1). The League was torn as to whether to replay the whole match or to let the result stand – in the end, they decided that the remaining ten minutes would have to be played and accordingly the two teams turned out 15 weeks later to contest the remaining 630 seconds of play (followed by a full-length friendly to placate spectators). Villa won 4–1 and went on to take the Championship.

Similar incidents occurred in matches between Stoke City and Wolverhampton (when a game of five minutes was played) and between Walsall and Newton Heath before the League bowed to public scorn and changed the rules. Under the current laws of the game an abandoned match must be replayed in full, or else the score as it stood at the time of abandonment is accepted as the final result.

Abbey Stadium The home ground of CAMBRIDGE UNITED. The club originally played on Parker's Piece, a small area of recreational ground in the centre of Cambridge, before moving in 1932 to a new base on land known as the Celery Trenches, because it was situated among some vegetable allotments. The running of the club and its ground, now called the Abbey, was carried out for many years in the official headquarters in the Dog and Feathers public house. One area of seating is called the Celery Trenches in honour of the ground's origins.

Abbey United Until 1949, the name of CAMBRIDGE UNITED. It was derived from the Abbey district of the city in which the club has its ground.

Abercorn Former Scottish League football club, which dropped out of the League in 1915. Having been a founder member of the Scottish League, the club – based at Underwood Park and from 1899 at Ralston Park – was eventually overshadowed by neighbouring Paisley.

Aberdare Athletic Former Welsh League club, which dropped out of the League in 1927. Having been a member of the League since 1921, the club played at the Athletic Ground in Ynis; it was eventually replaced in the League by Torquay.

Aberdeen Scottish football club, nicknamed the Dons. Strip: all red with a white trim (replacing a black and gold strip worn until World War II). Formed in 1903 and formerly dubbed the Whites and subsequently the Wasps before acquiring their current nickname, the Dons have enjoyed their greatest period of success in relatively recent times, when they have broken up the hold of the Old Firm on the major Scottish competitions.

The modern club was arrived at through the amalgamation of Orion, Victoria United, and Aberdeen, a team set up in 1881 by a group of teachers that moved permanently to the PITTODRIE stadium in 1899. Having won promotion from the Scottish Second Division after only one season, Aberdeen had to wait until 1955 before they could claim the First Division championship, although some consolation came with success in the Scottish Cup in 1947.

A second Scottish Cup win came in 1970, when Martin Buchan captained the side at the age of only 21, but the truly great era at Pittodrie began ten years later in 1980, with the club capturing the Premier Division championship for the first time. Further Premier Division titles came in 1984 and 1985, together with triumph in the Scottish Cup in 1982, 1983, 1984, 1986, and 1990 and in the Scottish League Cup (won by the Dons twice before, in 1956 and 1977) in 1986 and 1990. In 1991 Aberdeen lost the League championship to Rangers on the very last day of the season. The club also won the Dryborough Cup in 1971 and 1980.

Aberdeen's most glorious moment to date was, however, in 1983, when the side registered a 2–1 victory over Real Madrid in the final of the European Cup Winners' Cup, a triumph that constituted – with their capture of the Scottish Cup ten days later – a unique double in British football. Among the fans who rejoiced in this achievement was one George Dixon, who had recently emigrated to Australia; determined to follow his team's progress in the European Cup, he rang his mother in Scotland and asked her to put the radio next to the telephone so he could hear the match commentary. The call cost him £220, but he considered it worth every penny. Many attribute Aberdeen's remarkable run of success in the 1980s to the efforts of manager Alex Ferguson.

Aberdeen enjoyed their record victory in 1923, when they beat Peterhead 13–0; they suffered their worst defeat in 1965 when they lost 8–0 to Celtic. Willie Miller holds the record for League appearances with the club, having played in 556 matches for them between 1973 and 1990. *See also* DUG-OUT.

> When I was a lad, a tiny wee lad,
> My mother said to me,
> 'Go see the Dons, the glorious Dons,
> Down at Pittodrie',
> They call them the heavenly dancers,
> Superb in attack and defence,
> I'll never forget that wonderful sight,
> I've been a supporter ever since.
>
> Supporters' song, to the tune of 'The Northern Lights of Old Aberdeen'

Abide with Me English hymn, with words by Rev. Henry Francis Lyte (1793–1847) and music by William Henry Monk (1823–89), which has been associated with the FA Cup Final for many years. First sung at Lyte's funeral in 1847, the hymn has frequently been heard at big public gatherings of various kinds ever since. It was first sung at a Cup Final at the suggestion of the FA Secretary Sir Frederick Wall, who knew it to be the favourite hymn of George V, who attended the Finals on more than one occasion.

Abingdon Town English non-League football club, nicknamed Over the Bridge. Strip: yellow with green trim shirts, green with yellow trim shorts, and yellow socks. Founded in 1870 and based at the Culham Road ground in Abingdon, the club play in the Isthmian League.

AC Delco Cup Competition for non-League members of the Isthmian League. It began life as the Isthmian League Cup in 1975, when it was won by Tilbury. It acquired its present name in 1986.

Academy, The Original name of the Argentine football club RACING.

Academy of Soccer Nickname acquired by WEST HAM UNITED in the late 1950s, when the team won promotion from the Second Division. The nickname referred to the regular training discussions held by Malcolm Allison, Frank O'Farrell, John Bond, and Noel Cantwell, in which they developed such concepts as attacking fullbacks.

Accies The nickname (derived from the club's full name) of HAMILTON ACADEMICAL.

Accrington Stanley (1) Former English football club, nicknamed the Old Reds, which has acquired almost mythical status since resigning from the League in 1962. The Old Reds had already broken up once before in their troubled history. Having been a founder member of the League, Accrington FC resigned from the League in 1893 after just five years of existence when the club was accused of paying one of its players and finally disbanded in 1896.

The team revived, however, in the shape of amateur club Stanley Villa, who bought up the defunct team's home, PEEL PARK, in 1919 and acquired League status in 1921. Attracting crowds of up to 20,000 the team prospered and in 1955 was even selected for coverage on television (long before many First Division sides had been seen). Another curiosity of their history occurred in the 1950s when they became the first club in the English League to field a team entirely composed of Scots.

The reasons for Accrington Stanley's demise were financial and can be traced to a combination of low gates and the club's shortsighted opposition to the establishment of a supporters' club. Worries off the field were mirrored by the club's poor performance on it: of the 33 games they played in the 1961–62 season, they won just five, drew eight, and lost 20, conceding 60 goals to the 19 they had scored themselves. The final game was played in a snowstorm at Gresty Road in March 1962 against Crewe Alexandra; Crewe won 4–0 and two days later it was revealed that Stanley owed £60,000 and could no longer continue. An attempt to launch a last-hour rescue under the slogan 'Save Stanley' failed.

The club's name is now universally identified with football failure. When, during their last season, 71-year-old Sylvester Bickerton was invited for a trial, wags confessed they were not in the least surprised. Peel Park, their home for so many years, is now little more than wasteland.

(2) English non-League football club, nicknamed the Reds, founded in 1968 as successor to the infamous Accrington Stanley League side. Strip: all red. Based at the Livingstone Road Ground in Accrington, the club play in the Northern Premier League.

action replay During a televised match, the instant replaying of film showing a particularly exciting moment, usually in slow motion so that commentators can analyse the incident in detail. Many viewers are grateful for the opportunity to see a goal or other crucial development they may have missed; others fret that while the replay is being shown they are missing further live action. Occasional overuse of the action replay has led disgruntled viewers to complain of 'action replay disease' among television producers. *See also* TELEVISION.

> *Strangely, in slow motion replay, the ball seemed to hang in the air for even longer.*
>
> David Acfield
>
> *We don't always get from slow motion the pace at which they play.*
>
> John Barrett

Adders Nickname of the English non-League football club ATHERSTONE UNITED, from the club's full name.

Addicks A former nickname of CHARLTON ATHLETIC. *See also* HADDICKS; VALIANTS.

Ademir, Marques Menezes (1924–   ) Brazilian centre-forward, who was considered one of the finest attacking players of the immediate post-war period. He was the leading goalscorer in the 1950 World Cup; at home he played for Vasco da Gama.

admission charge The price of admission to a ground has always been a source of grievance among supporters, whatever its level. At the first FA Cup Final (1872) the entrance price of one shilling was enough to lead to speculation that the low size of the crowd (just 2000) was a direct result of the high cost of admission.

In the early history of the game there was no admission charge as such but spectators were expected to put donations in a hat that was passed round. This system had its drawbacks, however, and the risk of dishonesty as well as the reliance upon the crowd's generosity after a poor performance led to the introduction of turnstiles at all grounds relatively quickly. The League set a minimum charge for all matches, but at various times attempts have been made to circumvent this, usually in times of economic hardship when the local supporters genuinely could not afford to come in.

For many years it was possible for supporters to gain free admission at half time or to be allowed in without payment by assisting to clear the pitch of snow. It was also customary for women to be admitted free of charge, but this idea had lost favour with clubs by the late 19th century when it was realized that a substantial proportion of crowds were in fact female. Special discounts or free admission for women have been reintroduced from time to time, particularly in recent years (as at Meadowbank in the early 1980s) in an attempt to woo family audiences.

Fans attending a game in the early years of the 20th century generally paid sixpence (2.5 pence) to get in. By 1948 the price had risen to around one shilling three pence and by the 1960s to five shillings. In 1980 fans could expect to pay an average of £1.56 to get in, although taking inflation into account it was generally slightly less expensive to see a match in the 1980s than it had been in the 1960s. Charges are, however, increasing rapidly towards the end of the century as the costs of ground improvements to meet the Government's stricter safety rules are passed on to supporters.

Prices vary widely from one club to another. In 1986, for example, a season ticket to watch Albion Rovers cost £15 whereas a ticket to sit at a single Wimbledon match cost £13. In the first season of the Premier League in 1992–93, the most expensive admission charges were those at

Stamford Bridge, where the cheapest adult seats were priced at £20.

advantage, playing the The rule that allows a referee to exercise his discretion in permitting play to continue after a foul has been committed. Normally the clause is only brought into play when an interruption in proceedings would be to the benefit of the team guilty of the foul.

advertising *See* SPONSORSHIP.

AEK Athens Greek football club, nicknamed the Harem Girls. AEK (short for Athletiki Enosis Konstantinopoulos) were founded in 1924 and rank among the top three Greek sides; they play at the NEA FILADELPHIA stadium in Athens.

Afghanistan A member of the Asian Confederation of FIFA since 1948, the Afghan national team has yet to win a place in the World Cup Finals. Strip: all white with red trim.

African Champions Cup International competition founded in 1964 under the aegis of the Confederation of African Football to provide an African equivalent of the European Cup. Dogged by lack of financial resources, indiscipline on the pitch, and political problems, the competition has somehow been successfully staged every year since 1964, with the exception of 1965. It has been dominated in recent years by teams from North Africa, notably Egypt (with five wins), although clubs from Cameroon have also won the competition several times.

African Cup Winners' Cup International competition founded in 1975 in imitation of the equivalent European tournament. Like the African Champions Cup, the competition has in recent times seen the emergence of several strong North African sides, with a string of victories by Egyptian teams in the 1980s and further wins by clubs from Algeria and Tunisia.

African Nations Cup International competition established in 1957 by the Confederation of African Football. From humble beginnings, with just three sides competing in the inaugural contest, the Cup quickly attracted many more countries, although political unrest has frequently led to disruption. Held on a biannual basis, the cup has been won most often by Ghana, with a total of four wins; Egypt has won three times.

Ageless Wonder Nickname bestowed by admiring fans upon the great English forward Stanley MATTHEWS in reference to his lengthy career in first-class football (*see also* DRIBBLE, WIZARD OF).

> *Last night I had the strangest dream*
> *I've never had before*
> *Stan Matthews on the wing for Stoke*
> *At the age of 84.*

Keele University students' rag record (1964)

agent An intermediary who negotiates various business agreements as a representative of a player or other individual, usually in exchange for a commission. The role of the agent in football took on a new prominence in 1978, when the players won a legal battle giving them greater freedom of contract. Agents themselves argue that their presence protects their clients from exploitation by unscrupulous clubs and allows players themselves to concentrate on their game. Others regard their activities as a blight on football itself, putting financial reward before the good of the game and pushing up transfer fees to unreasonable, even immoral, limits. Eric Hall, one of the best known football agents, had no qualms in admitting (1989) the lengths he would go to in the interests of his clients: 'I have no morals when it comes to dealing with my clients. I would deal with the devil to get the best deal for them.'

Managers and others more closely involved in the day-to-day running of the game frequently bewail the damaging influence of such dealings. In 1988, Bobby Gould, manager of Wimbledon, observed: 'It used to be the wives who affected players, now it's the agents.'

Graham TAYLOR, while manager of Watford in 1983, probably spoke for the majority of his colleagues when he put his feelings very plainly: 'Agents do nothing for the good of football. I'd like to see them lined up against a wall and machine-gunned . . . some accountants and solicitors with them.'

air crashes Although air travel is statistically safer than many other forms of transport, football has inevitably suffered its share of air disasters over the years. Although the Munich air crash is usually the first such disaster to come to the minds of British fans, other nations have suffered similar traumas. Italy remembers the Superga air crash of 1949, involving Torino, while Chilean football still recalls the day in 1961 when the entire Green Cross team perished in an air crash and Bolivian fans mourn the 19 players representing The Strongest who died in an air crash in the Andes in 1969. More recent disasters have included the loss in 1987 of the 18 members of the Peruvian Alianza club when their plane crashed into the sea off Lima, the crash in 1989 that cost 15 Surinamese players connected with Dutch clubs their lives, and the destruction of Zambia's promising World Cup squad in an air crash off Libreville, Gabon, in 1993 (with the loss of 17 players).

Airdrieonians Scottish football club, nicknamed the Diamonds. Strip: white shirts decorated with a red diamond, with white shorts and red socks. Also nicknamed the Waysiders, the club have always lived in the shadow of the Old Firm in nearby Glasgow.

Airdrieonians' golden period lay back in the 1920s, although they have seen a revival in their fortunes in recent times. Formed in 1878, the Diamonds first went on the pitch as Excelsior, becoming Airdrieonians in 1881. Until 1892, when Broomfield Park became their permanent base, they shared Old Mavisbank, a cricket field, as their first home. The club was admitted to the League in 1894, to Division II, and went on to take the Division II championship in 1903, 1955, and 1974. The great team of the 1920s, with whom future Rangers star Bob McPhail and Hughie GALLACHER played, captured the Scottish Cup in 1924; the club also finished runners-up in the First Division championship four years in succession (1922–26).

In 1980 Airdrie returned to the limelight when they won promotion to the Premier League, but were relegated after two seasons. They were runners-up in the Scottish Cup in 1975 and 1992 and won the Scottish Spring Cup in 1976.

The club enjoyed their record victory in 1894, when they beat Dundee Wanderers 15–1; they suffered their worst defeat in 1959 when they lost 11–1 against Hibernian. Paul Jonquin holds the record for League appearances with the club, having played in 523 matches between 1962 and 1979.

Ajax Dutch football club named after the daring (though slow-witted) hero of Homer's *Iliad*, who went mad and killed himself after losing a contest against Odysseus over the armour of the dead Achilles. Strip: red and white shirts, white shorts, and red and white socks. Formed in 1900, Ajax are the most successful football club in Dutch history. The club, which has been based at the DE MEER STADIUM in Amsterdam since 1934 (although there are plans to move to a new ground elsewhere in the city), first tasted Championship success in 1918 and again in 1919, largely due to the guidance of the talented British trainer Jack Reynolds, who arrived in 1915 and remained with Ajax throughout the halcyon days of the 1930s, when the club added a further five League titles to its tally (1931, 1932, 1934, 1937, and 1939).

The club's domination of football in Holland continued after World War II with League titles in 1947, 1957, 1960, 1966, 1967, 1968, 1970, 1972, 1973, 1977, 1979, 1980, 1982, 1983, 1985, 1990, and 1993. Ajax have also experienced Cup success many times since 1917. International honours have included the European Cup (1971, 1972, and 1973), the European Cup Winners' Cup (1987), the Super Cup (1972 and 1973), and the World Club Championship (1972).

The team's remarkable run of victories under manager Rinus Michels in the 1960s and 1970s was the product of its adoption of the theory of TOTAL FOOTBALL, which also characterized the play of their longtime rivals Feyenoord. Among the many stars to appear for the team in the early 1970s were Johan Neeskens, Rudi Krol, and Johan CRUYFF, who was acquired by the team's British manager Vic Buckingham.

Albania The Albanian national team, which was affiliated to FIFA in 1932, have yet to win a place in the World Cup Finals. Strip: all red.

Albert, Florian (1941–) Hungarian centre-forward, who was hailed as one of the finest attacking players in European football in the 1960s. Spearheading the Ferencváros attack at home, he scored 32 goals in 75 games for his country and proved a devastating force in the 1962 and 1966 World Cups. He won four championship medals and was highest scorer in the Hungarian League in three seasons. In 1967 he became the only Hungarian to be voted European Footballer of the Year. A knee injury in 1969 effectively ended his career.

Albion Abbreviated form of the name of numerous British football clubs, notably Brighton and Hove Albion, Stirling Albion, and West Bromwich Albion. Albion was the ancient and poetical name for Great Britain, probably from the white (Latin *albus*) cliffs that face France, but possibly from the Celtic *alp*. Albion or Albany may originally have been the Celtic name of all Great Britain.

According to legend, a giant son of Neptune named Albion discovered the country and ruled over it for 44 years, lending it his own name. Another derivation concerns the story of the 50 daughters of the King of Syria (the eldest of whom was named Albia), who were all married on the same day and murdered their husbands on their wedding night. As punishment, they were set adrift in a ship, which eventually fetched up on the coast of Britain (where they duly found new native husbands). Alternatively, in his *Poly-Olbion* (1613), the poet Michael Drayton names Albion as a Roman who became the first Christian martyr in Britain.

The use of the name by so many British clubs was presumably inspired by the Victorian sentiment for romantic patriotism.

Albion Rovers Scottish football club, nicknamed the Wee Rovers. Strip: yellow shirts with a red trim, red and yellow shorts, and yellow socks. Formed in 1882, the club has suffered by comparison with more illustrious neighbours in Airdrie and Motherwell and has hit the headlines just three times in its long history.

Having joined the Scottish Second Division in 1903, the Wee Rovers moved up to the First Division after World War I and first attracted widespread attention when they were runners-up in the Scottish Cup in 1920, reaching the final after defeating Rangers in the semi-finals. The second time that they brought glory to CLIFTONHILL PARK, their home ground in Coatbridge, was in 1934, when the club captured the Division II championship (having been relegated in 1923) by just one point. It was not until 1989 that they were able to repeat this feat, and even then the celebrations were short-lived, with relegation following a year later.

The Albion Rovers enjoyed a record 12–0 win against Airdriehill in 1887; they suffered their worst defeat in 1946, when they lost 9–0 against St Johnstone. Murdy Walls holds the record for League appearances with the club, having played in 399 matches between 1921 and 1936.

alcoholic 'My name is Jimmy Greaves. I am a professional footballer. And I am an alcoholic.' The words with which Jimmy GREAVES officially announced to the world that he had a drink problem. The admission, which was printed on the front of his autobiography *This One's On Me* (1979), won Greaves praise for his frankness and courage in facing his difficulty publicly.

In *It's a Funny Old Life* (1990), the second volume of his autobiography, he reflected that even with the help of Alcoholics Anonymous he would never cease to be an alcoholic:

> I will always be an alcoholic . . . The important thing is that I must be a non-drinking alcoholic – a drunk who doesn't drink. The only way I can do that is not have a drink today. That's the simple rule I must follow for the rest of my life.

At the other end of the scale, Wilf Dixon, later to become a professional with Aldershot and a respected trainer and assistant manager, began his career before World War II with a club called Silksworth IOGT (Independent Order of Good Templars), every member of which was a professed teetotaller.

Aldershot English football club, nicknamed the Shots, which was a member of the League from 1932 to 1992. Strip: red shirts and socks with a royal blue trim and blue shorts with a red trim. Formed in 1926 at the instigation of a local newsagent, Aldershot have failed to capture a major honour despite the occasional respectable showing in the League and the FA Cup, in which they did at least reach the fifth round in 1933 and 1979. It was not until 1973 that the club won promotion to the Third Division, and three years later were relegated; in 1987 they returned to the Third Division but were again relegated after two years, after which the deep financial problems at the RECREATION GROUND intensified.

In July 1990, Aldershot were wound up as a going concern, but days later won a reprieve when Spencer Trethewy, a 19-year-old property developer and supporter of the club, invested £200,000. This last-minute rescue was not enough, however, to lift the team's play: in November 1990 they slumped to a record 10–1 defeat against Southend. The club finally resigned from the League for financial reasons in March 1992, making them the first side to do so since Accrington Stanley in the early 1960s. Aldershot Town currently play in the Isthmian League.

The most remarkable sides ever fielded by the Shots were those seen during World War II, when the team included a number of players posted to the town on military service. Among those to don Aldershot shirts were such stars as Matt BUSBY, Denis Compton, Stan CULLIS, Tommy LAWTON, Wilf Mannion, Joe MERCER, Cliff Britton,

Wilf Copping, Jimmy Hagan, and Frank SWIFT, who between them just about comprised a full international side.

Aldershot enjoyed record victories by a margin of seven goals in 1958, when they beat Gateshead 8–1, and in 1931, when they beat Chelmsford 7–0. Murray Brodie holds the record for League appearances with the club, having played in 461 games between 1970 and 1983.

You're so bad, you're worse than Aldershot.

Taunt from fans to Luton players (1988)

Ale House Brawlers Nickname bestowed upon SOUTHAMPTON in the 1970s by Bill SHANKLY. Shankly's description followed a particularly bruising encounter between the Saints and his own Liverpool side and stuck to the team for some years.

Alex Alternative nickname of CREWE ALEXANDRA, which is thought to have been taken from the name of the pub – the Alexandra – where the initial meetings of the club were held, although another explanation suggests a patriotic link with Princess Alexandra. *See also* RAILWAYMEN.

Alfreton Town English non-League football club, nicknamed the Reds. Strip: red and white striped shirts, black shorts, and red socks. Founded in 1959 and based in North Street, Alfreton, the Reds play in the Northern Premier League.

Algeria The Algerian national team made their first appearance in the World Cup Finals in 1982, when they distinguished themselves by beating a strong West German team 2–1; in 1986 they became the first African nation to qualify for the finals of two successive World Cups. Subsequent honours have included victory in the African Nations Cup in 1990. Stars of the side in recent years have included Rabah Madjer. Strip: green shirts, white shorts, and red socks.

Ali Sami Yen Stadium The home ground in Istanbul of the Turkish football club GALATASARAY. Galatasaray first emerged as the strongest Turkish football club in the 1960s, when their ground (first developed in the 1940s) was substantially updated. Events in the ground's history have included a near tragedy in the opening game at the refurbished stadium in 1964, when 70 people were injured as a safety barrier collapsed after a small fire had broken out.

Allchurch, Ivor (1929–) Welsh inside-forward, nicknamed the Golden Boy, who was a star with Swansea, Newcastle United, Cardiff, and Wales in the 1950s and 1960s. He scored 251 goals in his first-class career and was widely respected for his skills both as a scorer and as a passer of the ball. He made 692 League appearances and collected a record 68 caps with Wales. He was a key player in the Welsh campaign that took the national side to the quarter-finals of the World Cup in 1958. His brother Len also played for Wales as well as for Swansea, Sheffield United, and Stockport County.

You could do nothing but admire him.

Ron Greenwood

Allgood, Johnny Nickname of the English forward John GOODALL.

Alliance Premier League *See* CONFERENCE, THE.

Alloa Scottish football club, nicknamed the Wasps. Strip: black-trimmed gold shirts and socks and black shorts. Formed in 1883, the club has spent many years in both the First and Second Scottish divisions since joining the League in 1921.

Having moved to their permanent home at RECREATION PARK in 1895, Alloa enjoyed their earliest major success in 1922 when their inaugural season in the League resulted in the club becoming the first team to be promoted to the First Division under the new system of automatic relegation for the least successful side in the top division. Unfortunately a year later they were back in the Second Division once again, establishing a pattern of fluctuating fortunes that they have followed ever since.

Highlights of the years since then have included four seasons since 1975 when the club has finished as runner-up in the Second Division championship. In 1964 the team won fame in a somewhat different sphere when they took on the role of the fictional Tannochbrae team in an episode of the successful television series 'Doctor Finlay's Casebook'.

Popular players with the club have included Wee Willy Crilley, who proved a prolific goalscorer in the early 1920s; John White, and Tommy Hutchinson. The club's record win stands at 9–2 against Forfar Athletic in 1933; their worst defeats came in matches against Dundee in 1947 and against Third Lanark in 1953, on both occasions losing 10–0.

all-seater A stadium in which seating is provided for every spectator, as stipulated by the UK Government as a result of the recommendations made by the TAYLOR REPORT following the HILLSBOROUGH DISASTER in 1989. The report recommended that all First and Second Division Football League grounds be converted to all-seating by 1994, with remaining grounds to follow suit by 1999. Second (now First) Division grounds have subsequently been reprieved. Taylor's recommendation was backed up by similar rulings from both UEFA and FIFA, although the cost involved and the effect the change would have upon traditions cherished by spectators for over 100 years led to agonized protest from both fans and clubs alike. The Government responded by allocating funds towards the conversion of grounds, but left the clubs with an enormous shortfall to make up. Many fans have speculated that this cost will be passed on to them through increases in ticket prices and that many grounds will eventually be forced to close.

Leading the field in the conversion to all-seater stadia have been Aberdeen, who made their Pittodrie home the first all-seater stadium in the UK back in 1978. By virtue of gradual introduction and a healthy bank balance due to success in Europe, the club escaped many of the traumas other clubs have since experienced in the course of such conversion. The first all-seater ground in England was Highfield Road (1981).

Many supporters say they wouldn't stand for all-seater stadiums.

Guy Michelmore

all-ticket A match at which admission is only permitted on production of a valid ticket, rather than by payment at the turnstiles. The first such match – a home international between Scotland and England – was played at Cathkin Park on 17 March 1884; Scotland won 1–0. FA Cup Finals have been run on a strictly all-ticket basis since the near-disaster of the 1923 White Horse Final at Wembley.

Altafini, José (1938–) Brazilian-born forward, dubbed Mazzola, who won praise playing for Palmeiras, AC Milan, Napoli, Juventus, Brazil and Italy. He was one of Brazil's key players in the World Cup of 1958 in Sweden and in all won a total of eight caps for Brazil and six for Italy. After he moved to Italy, he reverted to the name Altafini in order to avoid confusion with the Mazzola footballing family already well

known in that country. He ended his career with two Italian championship titles with Juventus in 1973 and 1975.

Altrincham English non-League football club, nicknamed the Robins. Strip: red and white striped shirts, black shorts, and red socks. Founded in 1891 and based at the Moss Lane ground in Altrincham, the club were founder members of the Alliance Premier League in 1979. They were winners of the FA Trophy in 1978 and 1986, in which year they also joined the ranks of noted giant-killers with a 2–1 win over First Division Birmingham City.

Altrincham are the Manchester United of non-league soccer.

Tommy Docherty (1987)

Alvechurch English non-League football club, nicknamed the Church. Strip: gold shirts, black shorts, and gold socks. Founded in 1929 and based at Lye Meadow in Alvechurch (southwest of Birmingham), the Church play in the Southern League. Stars with the club have included centre-forward Alan Smith, who went on to play for Leicester City, Arsenal, and England in the late 1980s.

Alvechurch attracted attention in 1971 when they were involved in an unusually protracted contest with Oxford City to decide the outcome of a qualifying round of the FA Cup. The two teams met initially at Lye Meadow and drew 2–2. The second meeting, at Oxford, resulted in a 1–1 draw and the third, at Birmingham, in another 1–1 draw. No goals were scored in the fourth game, at Oxford, or in the fifth, again at Oxford. With both teams exhausted and fans suggesting annual reunions of all those supporters who had seen all the games, the saga finally ended in the sixth meeting, at Villa Park, when Alvechurch won 1–0; they were, however, knocked out in the next round by Aldershot. In all 660 minutes of football had been played to decide the outcome.

Amancio, Amaro Valela (1939–) Spanish forward, who was a star with Real Madrid from 1962 to 1976. Acclaimed for his dribbling skills, he won more than 40 international caps and played a major role in the Spanish side that won the European Nations Championship in 1964 and in Real's 1966 European Cup victory.

Amateur Cup Former FA competition for amateur clubs that was founded in 1893.

Run on a knock-out basis, the competition offered great glory to the winners, who from 1949 played the Final at Wembley, often in front of huge crowds (100,000 in 1953). The first Final, between Old Carthusians and Casuals, was won 2–1 by the Old Carthusians; the side had previously also won (1881) the FA Cup itself, making it the first team to win both competitions.

The competition soon became the most prestigious for amateur sides outside the FA Cup. Public school teams figured prominently in the early history of the Cup; subsequent sides to make their mark in the tournament included Bishop Auckland, Pegasus, and Hendon. Bishop Auckland in fact appeared in the Final on 18 occasions and won the Cup itself ten times. The Amateur Cup finally came to an end in 1974 when the distinction between amateur and professional was dropped by the FA. Its place was taken by The VASE.

It was during an Amateur Cup game in 1967 between Highgate United and Enfield that four players were seriously injured and another actually killed when they were struck by lightning.

Amateur Era The term by which the early history of the FA is often known. Back in the 1860s all clubs were amateurs and money played a relatively small role in the development of the national game. By 1885, however, pressure for the recognition of professionalism was irresistible and the idealistic Amateur Era came to an end, though tensions between paid and unpaid players were to continue for many decades (*see* AMATEUR SPLIT).

> *The admission into the amateur ranks of professional football players is possibly the beginning of the end in an important social movement . . . the first effect of the change will be to make the Rugby game the aristocratic one, and the Association game will probably die out in the South of England, where it is already declining in favour.*
>
> *The Manchester Guardian* (1884)

amateur football Strictly, football that is played for reasons other than financial reward. Originally, of course, all football was played on an amateur basis and it is still true that far more games are played week in week out on an amateur rather than a professional footing.

It was on an amateur basis that such immortal sides as the Wanderers and the Royal Engineers fought the first FA Cup Final in 1872 and amateur players also contested the first internationals between England and Scotland. For much of the subsequent early history of the professional game, amateur teams competed side by side with paid players, often inflicting heavy defeats (as in the case of Corinthians, who had a particularly outstanding record in the FA Cup before World War II). On an individual basis, amateur players figured in the England side until World War II. The last man to appear for England while playing with an amateur side (Dulwich Hamlet) was Edgar Kail in 1929.

The legalization of professionalism in 1885 signalled the inevitable split in the game that grew steadily wider in the 20th century; precisely, it dates from 1907 when, at a meeting at the Holborn Restaurant, the amateurs approved the establishment of an Amateur Football Association. For many years the issue of payment and the conflicting interests of money and sportsmanship created dissension between the authorities governing both types of game (*see* AMATEUR SPLIT; BROKEN TIME; PENALTY; SHAMATEURISM). These arguments continued even after 1974, when the distinction between amateur and professional was finally dropped by the FA, notably in relation to the Olympic Games.

The FA Cup remains the best opportunity for semi-professional sides to make their mark on the professional game (*see* GIANTKILLER).

> *Amateurism and good sportsmanship . . . for this club one is valueless without the other and, if either is surrendered, even in the present difficult world, in the cause of success, the time has surely been reached for the club's life, at least at senior level, to be brought to a close. Euthanasia must come before corruption.*
>
> Corinthians centenary brochure (1983)

After 1974 many former amateur leagues found ways to adapt successfully under the new regime, as in the case of the Isthmian League. The amateur game received a big boost in the 1960s when Sunday Football was officially sanctioned by the FA and has managed to distance itself from crowd violence and decline in behaviour on the field that have plagued professional football in recent years.

Amateur Football Alliance Administrative organization established in 1907 (as the Amateur Football Defence Federation) to promote amateur football in England. At a time when football was being increasingly dominated by professional teams, it was felt necessary to protect the amateur game and in particular to focus opposition to the FA's decision to let professional sides join local football associations. The argument over local football associations was settled in 1913 but further trouble arose in 1928 when the AFA and its counterparts in Scotland, Wales, and Ireland resigned from FIFA over the issue of broken time (they did not rejoin until 1946).

The question of defining 'amateurism' remained central to the Alliance's activities until 1974, when the FA effectively abolished the distinction. The Alliance continues to oversee the running of a long list of amateur competitions, including the Amateur Football Alliance Senior Cup and the Arthur Dunn Cup.

Amateur Split The division between some amateur clubs and the professional sides that led to a number of amateur teams breaking away from the FA in 1906 and setting up their own administrative organization a year later. The split was a consequence of growing professionalism in the game and a forlorn attempt to protect the integrity of the amateur game. Led by the county associations of Surrey and Middlesex, the amateurs refused to contemplate the affiliation of professional clubs, but found themselves excluded from FA competitions and increasingly isolated. The rift was finally mended in 1913 and the FA emerged from the affair with new authority. *See also* AMATEUR FOOTBALL ALLIANCE.

Ambassador of Football Nickname of the English full-back Eddie HAPGOOD, in reference to his diplomatic behaviour as England captain in the 1930s.

Ambrosiana-Inter The name under which the Fascists forced the Italian football club Internazionale to play in the 1930s and 1940s. The club's original name was deemed to reflect Marxist thinking and the authorities instructed a change to a name more in tune with nationalist sympathies (Saint Ambrogio is the patron saint of Milan). With World War II over, the side wasted no time in reverting to their famous original title.

American Soccer League US football organization, which has proved one of the more enduring professional soccer leagues that have been established in the USA. Founded in 1921, the ASL covers the eastern seaboard of the USA and somewhat against expectations survived the upheaval that followed the establishment and subsequent demise of the NASL. The ASL did, in fact, fold in the late 1920s but was revived in 1931 and was again renewed in 1988. Only in its early years, however, did it win significant national attention. Since the collapse of the NASL in 1985 the ASL has co-ordinated soccer activity on the east coast, providing a possible springboard for a new national league.

Anderlecht Belgian football club, titled in full the Royal Sporting Club Anderlechtois (or RSC Anderlecht). Strip: all white with a violet trim. Formed in 1908, the club emerged as the dominant Belgian club only after World War II, winning its first Belgian League championship in 1947.

Anderlecht spent many years in the Third Division before reaching the First Division in 1935 and subsequently (based at the new VANDEN STOCK STADIUM in Brussels) establishing themselves as Belgium's strongest team. Among the stars who emerged after the war were goalkeeper Josef Mermans and subsequently Jan Mulder, Arie Haan, and Robbie Rensenbrink. The club consolidated its first success with 14 national titles between 1947 and 1968 and at one point in 1964 the entire Belgian national squad consisted of Anderlecht players.

In international competition Anderlecht have been equally successful, winning the European Cup Winners' Cup in 1976 and 1978 with the aid of prolific goalscorer Van der Elst; their appearance in the Final of 1977 (which they lost 2–0 against Hamburg) made Anderlecht the first team to reach three consecutive Finals in the competition. The team has also notched up victories in the UEFA Cup (1983) and the Super Cup (1976 and 1978).

Much of the credit for the team's remarkable run of victories in the 1960s rests with manager Pierre Sinibaldi.

Andover English non-League football club, nicknamed the Lions. Strip: red and black shirts, black shorts, and red socks. Founded in 1883 and based at the Portway Stadium in Andover, the Lions played in the Southern League, but left it in 1993.

Andrade, José (1901–) Uruguayan midfielder, who is often remembered as the first great black footballer. A right-half, he played a key role in the victorious Uruguayan Olympic campaigns of 1924 and 1928 and in 1930 figured in the Uruguayan squad that won the first World Cup tournament. At home, he played for Bella Vista, Nacional, Peñarol, Atlanta, and Wanderers.

Anfield The home ground of the English football club LIVERPOOL. One of the most famous grounds in the UK, Anfield began life somewhat unusually as the home of another First Division side, Everton. In 1892, however, an argument between Everton and the owner of the ground led to Everton leaving for a new home elsewhere, upon which John Houlding, the owner, founded Liverpool AFC (the club's initial rent of Anfield was just £100 per annum).

Notable features of the ground include the Kop, rebuilt in 1928, which is crowned by a tall white flagpole. This flagpole was originally the top mast of the *Great Eastern*, Brunel's huge iron ship, which had been broken up in the Mersey docks in 1888 after serving her last years as a floating advertisement for a department store and as a funfair in the Liverpool Exhibition of 1887.

The vivid colour of the seats in the Anfield Road Stand, which range from orange to violet and emerald green, were deliberately chosen after manager Bob PAISLEY complained that the red shirts of his players rendered them almost invisible when seen against the background of the red seats that were originally installed there.

Another feature of the ground is the set of wrought-iron gates – the so-called Shankly Gates – dedicated to the legendary Bill SHANKLY, the manager who built Liverpool up into the most feared side in modern football. Spectators pass through these gates to reach the Main Stand; it was here that supporters tied scarfs and piled flowers in memory of those who died during the Hillsborough disaster in 1989:

The saddest and most beautiful sight I have ever seen.

Kenny Dalglish

The surrounding area is less than picturesque and more than one band of visiting supporters have voiced their reactions to the relatively run-down character of the district in which Anfield lies. Portsmouth fans claim credit for the best known of these observations, an adaptation of the song 'My Liverpool Home' first heard in 1980:

In your Liverpool slums, in your Liverpool slums,
You look in the dustbin for something to eat,
You find a dead rat and you think it's a treat,
In your Liverpool slums.

The partisan atmosphere of Anfield has always been a big advantage for the home team. Among the teams to be particularly affected by it has been Tottenham Hotspur, who failed to win a single game at Anfield between 1912 and the 1984–85 season. *See also* YOU'LL NEVER WALK ALONE.

Anfield Iron Nickname of the English footballer Tommy SMITH.

Anfield Rap Title of a pop song associated with Liverpool that became a top ten hit in 1988. Its lyrics were the work of the players themselves, who were invited to 'send themselves up'. Part of the lyrics referred to the showers of bananas that greeted the appearance of black star player John BARNES:

I come from Jamaica,
My name is John Barnes,
When I do my thing,
The crowd go bananas.

After one such banana-throwing incident involving Everton fans, an admirably unruffled Barnes wryly observed: 'Some fruit and vegetable dealers did very well'.

Angels (1) Nickname of several football clubs around the world. Among the most illustrious clubs to share the nickname are Sweden's GOTHENBURG.

(2) The three angels of TOTTENHAM HOTSPUR, who are traditionally supposed to bring the team good luck. An example of an enduring football superstition, the role of the three angels is often portrayed by supporters in fancy dress. Three is also considered a lucky number for the club.

Angels with Dirty Faces Nickname of the gifted and formidable inside-forward line, comprising Antonio Angelillo, Humberto Maschio, and Omar SIVORI, that spearheaded Argentina's attack in the 1950s. The trio acquired their nickname after they came to Italy to play for such teams as Juventus.

angling A defensive technique that involves a defender moving to reduce the area vulnerable to a potential attack by the opposing team.

Anglo-Italian Cup International competition founded, with the Anglo-Italian Cup Winners' Cup, in 1969 when Swindon Town's Third Division status prevented them from playing in the Fairs Cup even though they had captured the English League Cup. Swindon won the Anglo-Italian League

Cup Winners' Cup in 1969 and the Anglo-Italian Cup in 1970. In 1976 the new Anglo-Italian Tournament provided an outlet to Europe for prominent non-League teams. In 1992 the competition was revived, Cremonese beating Derby County in the Final at Wembley.

Anglo-Scottish Cup Competition founded in 1976 as a replacement for the Texaco Cup. Competed for by both English and Scottish clubs, the Cup went north of the border on only one occasion, in 1980 when it was won by St Mirren. The Scottish clubs withdrew in 1981 and the Cup was reorganized as the GROUP CUP.

Anglo-Scottish football See BRITISH LEAGUE CUP; CORONATION CUP.

Angola The Angolan national team, which was affiliated to FIFA in 1980, have yet to appear in the World Cup Finals. Strip: red shirts, black shorts, and red socks.

Annfield Park The home ground of the Scottish football club STIRLING ALBION. Before the establishment of Stirling Albion in 1945, football in Stirling was centred on Forthbank Park, which was the home of a side called King's Park. In 1940, however, the ground was badly damaged when a stray German plane dropped a single bomb on it – the only bomb, in fact, to fall on Stirling during World War II. A new ground was then agreed upon, though the felling of oak trees to clear the chosen site caused some controversy with conservationists.

Initially there were no stands and officials sat in two Albion lorries (hence the name Stirling Albion), although the players themselves had dressing-rooms in nearby Annfield House, an 18th-century mansion (now derelict). The ground has since been much improved, but in return for help from the council the club had to agree in 1987 to install artificial turf (for wider community use). Grass had, however, been restored by 1992.

Memorable episodes in the ground's history have included a half-time break in April 1954, when the crowd was entertained by the US television cowboy Roy Rogers, complete with Dale Evans and his horse, Trigger.

Antigua The Antiguan national team, affiliated to FIFA in 1970, have yet to appear in the World Cup Finals. Perhaps the most famous name to appear on the rosta of their national squad is that of Viv Richards, best known for his achievements on the cricket pitch in the 1980s. Strip: gold shirts with black shorts and socks.

Antognoni, Giancarlo (1954–) Italian midfielder, who was one of the strongest members of the Italian national squad in the 1970s and early 1980s. Celebrated for his skill at taking free kicks, he recovered from injury in 1981 to excel in Italy's 1982 World Cup campaign. At home he played exclusively with Fiorentina.

appearances The record number of appearances by any player in the Football League is 930, notched up by goalkeeper Peter SHILTON. Of these, he appeared 286 times for Leicester City, 110 times for Stoke City, 202 times for Nottingham Forest, 188 times for Southampton, and 144 times for Derby County between 1966 and 1991. He also holds the record for caps won as a member of the England team, with a total of 125 appearances, and a record of over 1200 appearances in all types of senior matches.

The record number of League appearances for one club belongs to John Trollope, who played 770 times for Swindon Town between 1960 and 1980. The record for the most consecutive League appearances is held by Harold Bell, who appeared 401 times without a break for Tranmere Rovers between 1946 and 1955. The Scottish forward Tommy Walker and the English player Dick Habbin both turned out for a total of 48 League matches in a single season, in 1946–47 and 1974–75 respectively; in 1980 Walker became the first Scot to be honoured with an OBE for his service to the game.

The record number of FA Cup appearances is held by Ian Callaghan, who turned out for Liverpool 79 times, Swansea City 7 times, and Crewe Alexandra twice, making a grand total of 88 appearances. Some careers end early with injury; others go on for decades – Bobby Collins, of Celtic, Everton, Leeds, Bury, Morton, and Oldham Athletic enjoyed the longest career of them all, making 653 appearances over a record 22 seasons. See also CAP; ONE-CLUB MAN.

apprentice See TRAINEE.

Arbroath Scottish football club, nick-named the Red Lichties. Strip: maroon shirts and socks with white shorts. The club was founded in 1878 by some rugby enthusiasts and hit the headlines for the first – and virtually only – time in 1885, when they scored a victory of 36–0 over Bon

Accord (a side from Aberdeen), which remains a record for senior football. Apparently, the match was so one-sided that the Arbroath goalkeeper spent most of it smoking a pipe.

Based at GAYFIELD PARK, Arbroath joined the League in 1921 and finished runners-up in the Second Division four times (1935, 1959, 1968, and 1972). Star players have included Dave Easson, who was noted for his prolific goalscoring ability (he scored 45 times in the 1958–59 season alone).

Their worst defeat came in 1949, when they lost 8–0 against Kilmarnock. Tom Cargill holds the record for League appearances for the club, having played in 445 matches between 1966 and 1981.

Ardiles, Osvaldo (1952–   ) Argentinian midfielder who became a favourite with British crowds after transferring to Tottenham Hotspur in 1978. Ardiles attracted international attention after playing a major role in Argentina's World Cup victory in 1978 (he won 42 caps in all). Shortly afterwards he was brought to the UK after being released from his previous club, Huracan of Buenos Aires (he began his career with Instituto Cordoba). He played an important part in Tottenham's FA Cup triumph in 1981 despite much speculation that he, like other imports from South America at the time, would find English football too physical – as reflected in a Spurs team pop song that reached number five in the charts that year:

> Ossie's going to Wembley.
> His knees have gone all trembly.

'Ossie's Dream' (1981)

Mistrust of how such exotic transplants would fare in a hardy climate were also shared by English players. Liverpool's Tommy SMITH, for instance, observed of Ardiles: 'I think Spurs ought to buy a good stock of cotton wool for such posers. They can't expect not to be tackled just because Argentina won the World Cup.'

The doubts were proved ill-founded, and in 1982 Ardiles helped to take Spurs to the Final once more, but was then obliged to drop out of the team for a while when the Falklands War between the UK and Argentina broke out. He was loaned to Paris St Germain until it was considered acceptable to allow him back into the Tottenham side, where the fact of his nationality was tactfully forgotten by both players and crowds alike.

Ardiles figured in Tottenham's UEFA Cup Winners' Cup win over Anderlecht in

1984 and eventually transferred to Blackburn Rovers on a temporary basis in 1988, subsequently joining Queen's Park Rangers before finally retiring as a player and being appointed manager of Swindon Town in 1989. Here he successfully lifted the team's fortunes and qualified them for a place in the First Division, but a financial scandal linked to Lou Macari, the previous manager, led to the side losing its right to promotion. Since then he has been employed as manager of Newcastle United, West Bromwich Albion, and – from 1993 – of his old club Tottenham Hotspur.

> *He was everywhere. It was like trying to tackle dust.*

Joe Royle, manager of Oldham (1988)

Ardwick The name under which MANCHESTER CITY played football on joining the Football Alliance in 1891. The club, which were formed from the merger of West Gorton St Mark's and Gorton Athletic in 1887, prospered in its first season in the Alliance, which then became the new Second Division, and finished in fifth place. In 1893, however, Ardwick suffered a dramatic decline and ended the season in 13th position and in a state of near-bankruptcy. At this point enterprising members of the Manchester Football Association took over and the club were reformed at the Hyde Road ground, this time as Manchester City FC.

Arena The former home ground of the Italian football club INTERNAZIONALE, in Milan. The Arena, built in the early 19th century, claims to be the oldest venue in the world ever to have staged first-class football. It was erected during the rebuilding of Milan in the first decade of the century and was opened by Napoleon himself in 1807. Also used to stage mock battles and other military displays, it first hosted a football match around 1908, when Internazionale were formed. Subsequent landmarks there have included the first match played by the Italian national team, in 1910 (against France), the execution of eight Italian partisans by the Nazis during World War II, and a friendly between Internazionale (who left the stadium in 1947) and Brazil in 1960. It still hosts women's and youth football among other sporting events.

Argentina The Argentinian national team have one of the most illustrious records in international football, with two World Cup victories to their credit (1978 and 1986) as well as a long list of wins in the South American Championship. Argentina were runners-up in the very first World Cup (1930) and again finished in second place in 1990 (when the Final was marred by much ill-feeling on the pitch). The 1978 World Cup victory was largely the work of the inspired manager Cesar Menotti. Undisputed star of the 1986 World Cup triumph was Diego MARADONA (see HAND OF GOD); celebrated players from earlier eras included Alfredo DI STEFANO, José Manuel Moreno, and Omar SIVORI. Argentina qualified for the 1994 World Cup in America. Strip: blue and white striped shirts, black shorts, and white socks.

Aristocrats of European Football Nickname sometimes bestowed upon the Italian football club AC MILAN, reflecting their status as one of the most senior European sides as well as the patronage they enjoy of some of Milan's wealthiest citizens. See also OLD MAN.

Armadale Former Scottish League football club, which dropped out of the League in 1932. Having joined the League in 1921, the club (based at Volunteer Park) now plays in the West Lothian League – as Armadale Thistle.

Armfield, Jimmy (1935–) English right-back, who distinguished himself with both Blackpool (making a record 568 appearances) and England (winning 43 caps). Voted the best right-back in the 1962 World Cup, he subsequently went into management before opting for a career as a radio journalist. In 1993 he was recalled by the FA to investigate new structures for international appointments.

Army Cup Prestigious Cup competition for British army teams. The tournament is often remembered for the 1948 Cup Final replay between the Royal Armoured Corps and a Royal Artillery side, which witnessed the deaths of two players when they were struck by lightning during the game at Aldershot. No one was sure what had attracted the fatal bolt, though some of those present blamed the referee's whistle and a waterpipe close to the pitch. The Cup was shared, with each team enjoying possession of it for six months. Other tournaments contested by teams from the armed forces include fixtures organized by the Amateur Football Alliance. The World Military Championships provide an opportunity for teams drawn from the armed forces to play on an international basis. See also FOOTBALLERS' BATTALION; ROYAL ENGINEERS.

Arsenal English football club, nicknamed the Gunners. Strip: red shirts with white sleeves, white shorts, and red socks with a white trim. This strip replaced an all-red scheme formerly used by the club until 1933 (back in 1895 a strip of red and light blue stripes was also briefly experimented with). Founded in 1886, the club was initially called Dial Square after one of the workshops at the Royal Arsenal; subsequently, until 1891 it played under the title Royal Arsenal.

Prime mover in the foundation of the club was Fred Beardsley, a former Nottingham Forest player, who managed to persuade his old club to donate some red shirts and a ball for the use of the Arsenal enthusiasts. The team played at a number of local venues, including a former pig farm, before acquiring the Invicta Ground in Plumstead in 1890. The club took professional status (1891) as Woolwich Arsenal (nicknamed the Woolwich Reds after their red shirts) and in 1893 won election to the Second Division, later purchasing their own ground, Manor Field, where they had previously played before moving to the Invicta Ground.

In 1904 the club won promotion to the First Division but were faced with increasing debts and in 1910 were forced into liquidation. Property developer Henry Norris then stepped in, at first suggesting a merger with Fulham; then, when the team were relegated in 1913 (setting an all-time record for failure with only one home win) and faced with even deeper financial problems, recommended starting from scratch at a new venue in North London, at Highbury (see HIGHBURY STADIUM). The arrival of a new professional club in Highbury caused much controversy, with objections from the existing teams in the area and a campaign against the move was led by Islington Borough Council. Nonetheless the move went through and The Arsenal, as the side was rechristened in 1914 and remained until 1927 when the 'The' was dropped, set about building up a local following.

World War I brought further financial hardship and in 1919, when plans were announced to expand the First Division by two clubs, Norris had no qualms in using his wealth to secure one of the places for The Arsenal, even though they had only finished in fifth place in the Second Division. The club has never left the First Division since then, a record in the English

League. Norris dropped out of football in 1925 after being found guilty of financial irregularities, including the unsanctioned use of a chauffeur, and being suspended by the FA. Before he went, however, he pulled a last masterstroke, bringing the great manager Herbert CHAPMAN to Highbury and thereby paving the way for Lucky Arsenal's great successes of the 1930s.

The Gunners won the First Division championship in 1931, 1933, 1934, 1935, 1938, and subsequently in 1948, 1953, 1971, 1989, and 1991 (when they were undefeated at home, lost only one away match – and also had two points deducted after a brawl on the field against Manchester United). They also won the FA Cup in 1930, 1936, 1950, 1971, 1979, and 1993 and the League Cup in 1987 and 1993 (thus completing a unique Cup double). Other titles have included the European Fairs Cup in 1970. Their greatest moment to date was perhaps the League and Cup double in 1971, which they achieved by the narrowest of margins (they won the League championship by a crucial goal in the final match thanks to the efforts of Ray Kennedy). Chairman Denis Hill-Wood was in no doubt that it was their finest hour: 'It seems ridiculous when I look at all that silverware, but also very wonderful. I believe that the present team is the greatest that has ever represented Arsenal.'

Despite their record of success in the 1980s and early 1990s, critics of the club still remained, many of them accusing the team of boring play. Stars with the contemporary side include strikers Anders Limpar, Ian Wright, and Paul Merson. Predecessors ranged from centre-forward Ted Drake in the 1930s, Joe MERCER in the 1950s, Peter Storey and Alan BALL in the 1960s, and subsequently Charlie George, Liam BRADY, Frank Stapleton, and Pat JENNINGS.

The Gunners enjoyed their record win back in 1896, when they beat Loughborough Town 12–0; this was revenge for their worst defeat, suffered in another game against Loughborough Town in 1896, when they lost 8–0. David O'Leary holds the record for the most League appearances with the club, having played in 558 matches between 1975 and 1993.

I remember that as a boy, there was only one club for me – Arsenal.

Ferenc Puskas, *Captain of Hungary* (1955)

We were boring when I played, we were boring in the Thirties and no doubt we'll be called boring in the next decade. I

don't mind as long as the trophies keep coming.

George Graham

See also GOOD OLD ARSENAL.

Arsenal tube station A station on the London Underground railway network that was named in honour of Arsenal football club in 1932. This extraordinary publicity coup was the brainwave of manager Herbert CHAPMAN, who was eager to exploit any means of advertising the club's presence. The London Transport organization took several weeks to mull over his suggestion that their Gillespie Road station should be renamed after the newly successful club nearby but finally gave way under pressure from the redoubtable manager.

Arthur Scargill of Football, The Nickname bestowed in 1983 by Alan Mullery upon Gordon Taylor, the Secretary of the PROFESSIONAL FOOTBALLERS' ASSOCIATION, acknowledging his naturally combative and controversial character (reminiscent of miners' leader Arthur Scargill himself).

Arthurlie Former Scottish League football club, which dropped out of the League twice (in 1915 and 1929). The club first joined the League in 1901 and again in 1923 and continues in minor leagues at its base at Dunterlie Park in Barrhead.

artificial turf See ASTROTURF; PLASTIC PITCH.

Aruba The Aruban national team, which was affiliated to FIFA in 1988, has yet to make an appearance in the World Cup Finals. Strip: yellow shirts, blue shorts, and yellow and blue socks.

Ash Wednesday football See SHROVE-TIDE FOOTBALL.

Ashbourne football See SHROVETIDE FOOTBALL.

Ashford Town English non-League football club, nicknamed the Nuts and Bolts. Strip: white with green trim. Founded in 1930 and based at the Homelands ground in Ashford, the club play in the Southern League.

Ashington Former English football League club, which dropped out of the League in 1929. Based at Portland Park (now the home of a team of the same name), Ashington joined the League in 1912 and were eventually replaced by York City. Ashington is perhaps more famous among football fans as the home town of the Milburn family, whose members included 'Wor Jackie' MILBURN and the CHARLTON brothers.

Ashton Gate The home ground of BRISTOL CITY. Ashton Gate belonged originally to the Bedminster club, but when Bedminster and Bristol City merged in 1904 the ground became the permanent home of the Robins. There used to be two main stands at the ground, but both of these suffered from bombing during World War II and new stands were erected in the 1950s. A further stand, the Dolman Stand, was opened in 1970 and named after a past chairman of the club, Harry Dolman. The cost of this stand very nearly bankrupted the club, which was in fact wound up some years later after a dramatic slide down to the bottom of the Fourth Division. Plans for the ground to be shared with Bristol Rovers failed to become reality in 1986. Home fans congregate in the Enclosure (popularly dubbed the Chicken Run).

Asian Cup International competition founded by the Asian Football Confederation in 1956 to promote footballing contact at a national level in Asia. The competition is held every four years and is the region's most prestigious tournament, second only to the World Cup.

assist A move made by a player that effectively creates a goal-scoring opportunity. Under the rules of the NASL, a point was awarded to a player's personal record for every instance of play that led to a goal being scored. Crediting such assists was designed to give a more accurate reflection of a player's abilities and achievements than was given by the number of goals (two points) scored alone.

Associate Members Cup See FOOTBALL LEAGUE TROPHY.

associated schoolboy See TRAINEE.

Association Football The formal name for the game of soccer, to distinguish it from rugby football and other related sports. It is so called because the game was first organized into a system of local football associations who dictated rules etc.

Aston Villa English football club, nicknamed Villa, or the Villans. Strip: claret and blue, with white shorts (though there was a recent experiment with a purple and pink strip likened by one journalist to a summer pudding). Founded in Birmingham in 1874 (according to legend during a meeting of cricketing enthusiasts underneath a street-corner gaslight), the club had their first home at the Aston Lower Grounds amusement park, sharing the billing with trick-cyclists, lacrosse players, cricketers, and others. The first match, against Aston Brook St Mary's rugby team, was an odd affair, with one half of the match being rugby and the other half soccer. In 1876 the club moved to a field in Perry Barr, and rapidly built up a strong reputation and a large local following before returning (1897) to the Lower Grounds and building a permanent home, VILLA PARK.

Villa joined the League in 1888 and were soon recognized as one of the best teams in the country, winning the First Division championship in 1894, 1896, 1897, 1899, 1900, and 1910. The club also recorded early success in the FA Cup, winning in 1887, 1895, 1897, 1905, 1913, and 1920 (see LITTLE TIN IDOL). The extraordinary run of success in the last decade of the 19th century, which included in 1897 a prized double (making them only the second club to achieve this), confirmed Villa's reputation as the leading English football club.

Among the illustrious names associated with Villa at this time were the chairman, William MCGREGOR, who founded the League itself, dribbler George Ramsay, centre-forward Archie Hunter (who died at the age of 35), Howard Spencer, James Crabtree, winger Charlie Athersmith (who played one game in the rain carrying an umbrella), and captain John Devey, who led the team in all of its first five Championship seasons. Unfortunately Villa's triumphant record petered out as the years went by and, despite the efforts of such players as Billy Walker and Pongo Waring in the 1930s, the club ended up being relegated to the Second Division in 1936. Subsequently Villa moved between the top two divisions, winning the Second Division championship in 1938 and 1960 (when Joe MERCER was in control), the FA Cup in 1957, and the League Cup in its first year in 1961. Ultimately, however, Villa sank down into the Third Division (1970–72), remaining there until Ron Saunders restored the club to the top flight.

There followed the club's greatest period of success since the early years of the century with two League Cup titles (1975 and 1977), the First Division championship in 1981 (when they called on the services of just 14 players), the European Cup in 1982, and the Super Cup in 1983. Notwithstanding this revival in the club's fortunes, Villa spent a further season in the Second Division in 1987–88, although another revival saw them among the leading teams in the inaugural year of the Premier League.

Well-known contemporary supporters of the famous club include violinist Nigel Kennedy. Recent triallists for the team have included the son of prime minister John Major in 1990.

The Villans enjoyed a record 13–0 win against Wednesbury Old Athletic in 1886; they suffered their worst defeat in 1889, when they lost 8–1 against Blackburn Rovers. Charlie Aitken holds the record for League appearances with the club, having played in 561 matches between 1961 and 1976.

> If there is a club in the country which deserves to be dubbed the greatest (and the matter is one of some delicacy) few will deny the right of Aston Villa to share the highest niche of fame with even the most historic of other aspirants. For brilliancy and, at the same time, for consistency of achievement, for activity in philanthropic enterprise, for astuteness of management and for general alertness, the superiors of Aston Villa cannot be found.

William McGregor

Astroturf Tradename of a man-made playing surface developed in the USA in the 1960s and subsequently experimented with by several footballing nations. The first Astroturf pitch – the forerunner of all subsequent plastic pitches – was laid in Houston's Astrodome indoor ball park, which also lent its name to the new surface. It soon proved its suitability as an all-weather surface possessing most of the qualities offered by grass (although the pitch at the Astrodome itself withered badly from the lack of sunlight coming through glass panels overhead). The success of Astroturf did much to promote the campaign for plastic pitches in the UK.

Atatürk Stadium The home ground, in Izmir, of the Turkish football club Karşiyaka. Built in 1971 and named after the founder of modern Turkey, the Atatürk stadium is the biggest and most advanced ground in the country and is considered lucky for the national team.

Athenian League Former Amateur Football league that was founded in England in 1912. Distinguished member clubs included Barnet, Kingstonian, Southall, and Wimbledon. The league was finally disbanded in 1984 in the wake of the abolition of the distinction between amateur and professional status in the game ten years earlier.

Atherstone United English non-League football club, nicknamed the Adders. Strip: red and white shirts, with red shorts and socks. Founded in 1979 and based at Sheepy Road in Atherstone, the Adders play in the Southern League.

Athletic The name of numerous football clubs around the world. Examples in the UK are Charlton Athletic, Oldham Athletic, Wigan Athletic, Forfar Athletic, Dunfermline Athletic, and (until 1980) Alloa Athletic. Elsewhere Spain's Athletic Bilbao and Atlético Madrid are among the notable clubs sharing the same name. Both these Spanish clubs originally adopted the English spelling of the word in homage to the Englishmen who first promoted the game in Spain; when the Fascists came to power in the 1930s, however, the clubs were obliged to adopt the Spanish spelling – although Bilbao eventually reverted to the English original. The name usually reflects the origins of a club as an athletic or sporting club, or the use of their ground as a venue for athletics.

Athletic Bilbao Spanish football club, which has long been one of the dominant Spanish sides. Strip: red and white striped shirts, with black shorts and socks. The club, founded in 1898 and thus the oldest club in the country, was given its Anglicized name in recognition of the training given to early Spanish footballers in England. The team, which traditionally exercised a policy of using only Basque players, has won eight League Championships but also has a glorious record in the Spanish Cup competition, with 23 victories to its credit. The club is based at the SAN MAMÉS STADIUM in Bilbao.

Atkinson, Ron (1939–   ) English manager, nicknamed Big Ron. Big Ron, an extrovert with a reputation for building stylish teams, had a distinguished playing career before going into management. As wing-half and captain of Oxford United he played over 600 games before hanging up his boots in 1971. Subsequently he became as famous for his bluff personality as for his successful management of such clubs as West Bromwich Albion, Atlético Madrid, Manchester United, with whom he captured two FA Cups in the early 1980s, Sheffield

Wednesday, with whom he won the League Cup and promotion in 1991, and Aston Villa.

His flamboyance has won him many friends among the fans; in the late 1980s supporters of Sheffield Wednesday even took to wearing Elvis-style spectacles in imitation of those donned by their hero. Revelations about an extra-marital affair in 1984 and the controversial circumstances under which he left Manchester United and Sheffield Wednesday were among the various incidents in his turbulent career to attract massive media attention.

It's bloody tough being a legend.

Ron Atkinson (1983)

As far as he's concerned, he is God. There's nobody big enough to tell him what to do.

Margaret Atkinson, his wife

Atlético Madrid Spanish football club; one of the main contenders behind Real Madrid and Barcelona. Strip: red and white striped shirts, blue shorts, and red socks with white trim. Founded in 1903, Atlético have generally languished in the shadow of the two big clubs, but still have an illustrious record, with eight League championships to their credit and six wins in the Spanish Cup. Based at the VICENTE CALDERÓN STADIUM in Madrid, the team has also distinguished itself in international competition, winning the European Cup Winners' Cup in 1962 and the World Club Championship in 1974.

Australia The Australian national team has played a relatively minor role in international competition, though occasionally surfacing in the major tournaments. Australian football's golden hour was in 1974, when the team dubbed the Socceroos qualified for the World Cup Finals for the first time. They lost their first two games (against the two Germanies) but then managed a draw with Chile before going out of the competition. Strip: gold shirts with green trim, green shorts, and white socks with green and gold trim.

Austria The Austrian national side has a distinguished history in international competition and was once universally regarded as the strongest side in the world. Having played the first official international outside Britain (beating Hungary 5–0 in 1902), Austria prospered under the leadership of manager Hugo MEISL and coach Jimmy HOGAN and came to dominate the world game in the 1920s and early 1930s (see WUNDERTEAM). The side lost only two of 27 games between 1931 and 1934, when they unexpectedly failed to crown their success with victory in the World Cup (coming fourth). The 1938 World Cup campaign was subverted by the Nazis, who obliged leading Austrian players to turn out for Germany, but another illustrious Austrian side emerged after the war. Spearheaded by such stars as Ernst OCWIRK and Gerhard HANAPPI, the team reached the semi-finals of the World Cup in 1954 but then declined and Austria have since failed to progress beyond the second stage of any World Cup Finals series. Particularly embarrassing was a 1–0 defeat in 1990 against the Faroe Islands in a European Championship qualifier. Strip: white shirts, with black shorts and socks.

Aveley English non-League football club, nicknamed the Millers. Strip: royal blue shirts with white shorts and socks. Founded in 1927 and based at the Mill Field ground in Aveley, the Millers play in the Isthmian League.

away A match that is played at a venue other than the home ground of the team concerned. A team that plays 'away from home' has the obvious disadvantage of facing unfamiliar surroundings and a largely hostile crowd, possibly at the end of a very long journey. On one day in 1937, for instance, there was not a single away win in a total of 35 FA Cup and League matches.

Some sides, however, respond to the pressure an away fixture imposes and find inspiration in the automatic assumption that their best play cannot be expected of them. In the 1938–39 season, Sheffield United were performing so much better away from home than they were in Sheffield that the management took the novel step of taking the team on a lengthy coach journey before each home fixture in an attempt to improve their performance: the ruse worked and the side won promotion to the First Division.

Teams from geographically remote parts are especially vulnerable to the hardships of prolonged travelling, as are their visitors. Swansea Town were once called upon to make a 400 mile journey between fixtures in Plymouth and Newcastle while the longest journey involving non-League teams in the FA Cup was probably that undertaken by Folkestone when they were drawn against Stockton in 1951–52.

Failure to perform well at away fixtures is particularly resented by a team's supporters, who may have travelled a long way to follow their club's fortunes. When Hibernian ended the 1990–91 season without an away win, the only senior club in the UK to do so, one fan was moved to observe:

> Hibs have sixty-six players on their books – that's a team for every day of the week except Saturday.

The problems of getting to away fixtures have caused many players and managers nightmares in the past. The vagaries of the weather and transport systems have all had their influence and every club has its memories of delayed arrivals and missing stars. When a West Bromwich Albion player missed the train back in 1897 a special train consisting of an engine and one coach was hired to get him to the match in time (at a cost of £50); the railways have, however, generally proved less amenable in latter years. Other players have been whisked to matches on chartered aircraft after missing team coaches or trains. On one occasion the plane carrying a Wolverhampton Wanderers player to Sheffield got hopelessly lost and arrived unannounced at an RAF airfield in Worksop to the consternation of the groundstaff and the plane's occupants alike. Fear of flying led one player, Alfred Broadbent of Notts County, to turn down an offer to join the England team in the West Indies (the invitation was never repeated).

Coach travel is the conventional mode of transport for contemporary players on the way to domestic fixtures, but coaches have thrown up horror stories of their own: in 1981 East Stirling had a nightmare of a journey when no fewer than three coaches broke down on their way to play Montrose.

Other players have relied on their own transport to get them to matches safe and sound – Bob Crompton of Blackburn Rovers is thought to have been the first to drive himself to fixtures in his own vehicle back in 1908 – but cars have proved equally unreliable. In 1941 nine members of the Bristol City side got lost on their way by car to Southampton; their places eventually had to be filled by a soldier, a schoolmaster, a spectator, their opponents' trainer, and five Southampton reserves (who must have lacked motivation to win). When the missing players finally arrived it was too late to go on the field. An attempt to smuggle one of their number on to the pitch by disguising him with a coating of mud so that he would be confused with those already playing failed to work. Southampton won 5–2; one of the scorers against them was their own trainer.

away-goals rule A method of deciding the result of a match when the teams are level on aggregate after a replay, as employed in European competitions. Until the 1960s such situations were settled by the toss of a coin, which always went down very badly with the losing team and not a lot better with the team that won. The tossing of a coin to decide a close-fought battle between Linz and Dynamo Zagreb in a preliminary-round tie of the 1963–64 European Cup Winners' Cup when the two teams were level at 2–2 after the replay, prompted a change in the rules (Linz won).

In the 1965–66 competition the away-goals rule was first employed, with the honours going to the team that had scored the most goals away from home. Satisfyingly, Dynamo Zagreb themselves benefited from this change in the rules at an early stage of the 1966–67 Fairs Cup competition, when application of the away-goals rule for the first time in the tournament's history allowed them to progress to the next round after drawing 4–4 with Dunfermline Athletic; they went on to win the competition.

Aylesbury United English non-League football club, nicknamed the Ducks. Strip: green and white hooped shirts, white shorts, and green socks. Founded by a merger of the Printing Works and Night Schools clubs in 1897, Aylesbury moved to a new home on the Buckingham Road in 1986 and in 1988 won promotion to the GM Vauxhall Conference but were relegated after just one season. That same year they captured the headlines when, as winners of the Southern League, they played a friendly at their new ground against England, who were preparing for the 1988 European Championships; England won 7–0.

Ayr United Scottish football club, nicknamed the Honest Men. Strip: white shirts with black sleeves and black socks and shorts. Founded in 1910, the Honest Men have spent most of their history in the Scottish Second Division; they enjoyed their heyday in the 1960s and 1970s under manager Ally Macleod.

The modern team is descended from Ayr FC and Ayr Parkhouse, both of which played in the Second Division in the first decade of the century. Having acquired a permanent home at SOMERSET PARK (Ayr FC's base since 1888), the club went on to capture the Second Division championship in 1912, 1913, 1928 (after a season during which Jimmy Smith scored no less than 66 League goals), 1937, 1959, 1966, and 1988. Ayr United enjoyed their record victory in

1952, when they beat Dumbarton 11–1; this was, incidentally, the first double-figure score to be reached in the Scottish League Cup (strange to relate, the return match two weeks later resulted in a 1–1 draw). On other occasions Ayr has lost by a record 9–0, against Rangers in 1929, Hearts in 1931, and Third Lanark in 1954. Ian McAllister holds the record for League appearances with the club, having played in 371 matches between 1977 and 1990.

Ayresome Park The home ground of the English football club MIDDLESBROUGH. Opened in 1903, when Boro were already a First Division side, Ayresome Park was considered one of the best grounds of its time and parts of it remain much as they were at the start. It soon became an acknowledged venue for occasional international matches as well as amateur events and the regular professional matches. Its capacity was enlarged in the 1930s when the team were enjoying a long run (1929–54) in the First Division; even so on occasion the gates had to be locked to prevent the ground from overflowing.

Three World Cup matches were played here in 1966 (including appearances by the so-called Diddy Men from North Korea), although the decline in Boro's fortunes by then had rendered Ayresome Park a somewhat less glamorous venue. In 1981 a gate at the ground collapsed at the end of a match against Manchester United, killing two people. The cost of making further safety improvements in recent years, coupled with the club's continued lack of success, have raised question marks over the future of both team and venue; in 1986 Boro had to play at Hartlepool's ground for a time as Ayresome Park had been put in the hands of the official receiver.

Azteca The huge football stadium that serves as Mexico's most important international venue. Major matches hosted at the massive Azteca Stadium have included the 1986 World Cup Final between Argentina and West Germany.

B

back A player who operates in a defensive position towards the rear of the team's formation. *See also* FULL-BACK; HALF-BACK.

back four A group of four players, usually two FULL-BACKS and two central defenders, who have responsibility for the defence.

> *No footballer of talent should play in the back four.*
>
> Malcolm Allison (1975)

Back Home The title of a pop song recorded by the England World Cup squad in 1970. One of the more successful such efforts, it actually reached number one in the charts.

back of the net Informally, the area of the goal behind the goal line, into which the whole of the ball must pass for a goal to be scored.

back pass A pass in which the ball is played safely back to a team mate. The prevalence of such 'safe' play in recent years has robbed football of much of its spectator appeal, and when the Premier League was established in 1992 one of the first reforms insisted upon was the outlawing of back passes to the goalkeeper. More radical critics, such as Clive THOMAS, have suggested banning the use of such passes altogether within a team's own half. In practice, the reform has turned out to have the side-effect of encouraging keepers to kick the ball as far as they can upfield or directly into touch rather than to defenders close by.

back to square one Back to where one started from. This is one of the few soccer phrases that has passed into the general language. It was popularized in the early days of broadcast commentaries on football matches when, in order to make the course of the game easier to follow, a diagram of the pitch, divided into numbered squares, was printed in the *Radio Times*. While one commentator described the action another in the background called out the square into which the ball had passed. The play would

return to square one, in the centre of the pitch, after a goal was scored.

The system was first employed in 1927 when the very first radio broadcast of a football game, involving Arsenal and Sheffield United at Highbury, was transmitted. The experiment was a success and soon an audience of ten million listened in to the broadcasts. Among the commentators who became familiar to the new audience during this period was Derek 'Uncle Mac' McCulloch – later famous as a broadcaster of programmes for children – whose job it was to call out the square numbers. The system had, however, been dropped by 1940.

It is probable that the saying 'back to square one' was derived from earlier usage in various board games but it was its adoption by the football commentators that made it a stock catchphrase of the 20th century.

backheel A pass in which the ball is kicked backwards with the heel to a team mate behind. The move is fraught with danger as the person backheeling often has little idea of who is standing behind him and many goals have been given away by incautious passes of this kind. The move can, of course, also be highly effective.

Badgers Nickname of the English non-League football club EASTWOOD TOWN, in reference to the club colours.

Baggies Nickname of the English football club WEST BROMWICH ALBION. Probably a reference to the baggy shorts the players once wore, this is the nickname preferred by local fans.

Bahamas The Bahamas joined FIFA in 1968 but have yet to make much impact in international competition. Strip: yellow shirts, black shorts, and yellow socks.

Bahrain Bahrain joined FIFA in 1966 but have still to establish a strong international reputation. Strip: white shirts, red shorts, and red and white socks.

Bailey, N.C. *See* PRINCE OF THE HALF-BACKS.

Bairns Nickname of the Scottish football club FALKIRK. It has its origins in the old saying 'Better meddle wi' the Devil than the Bairns o' Falkirk'. In a similar vein, the club's motto, 'Touch 'ane, touch 'a' reminds opponents that members of the Bairns will spring to each other's aid if threatened.

Bairnsford Britannia Original name of EAST STIRLINGSHIRE.

Bald Eagle Nickname of the football manager Jim SMITH, in reference to his thinning hair.

Baldock Town English non-League football club, nicknamed the Reds. Strip: red shirts, white shorts, and red socks. Founded in 1889 and based at the Norton Road ground in Baldock, the Reds play in the Southern League.

ball A host of regulations govern the type and condition of ball that may be used in modern professional soccer. Although virtually any roughly round object was acceptable to participants in rudimentary versions of the game in centuries gone by (including inflated sheep's bladders and even hogs' heads), the laws of football now dictate that the ball must be spherical with a circumference of 68–71 cm (27–28 in) – as agreed in 1872 – and be cased in leather or other approved material; it must also weigh no more than 453 grams and no less than 396 grams at the start of a game.

As time went by leather balls were discarded in favour of plastic versions that picked up less mud and water and the old laced varieties were replaced by valve balls. In the 1950s, with the increased use of floodlighting, white balls (and then black and white patterned balls) were first introduced (although the ball used in the 1966 World Cup Final was still all-brown). In fact, white balls had been experimented with much earlier and there is a record of one being used in a testimonial match in 1892: in this case it was simply a regulation brown leather ball repeatedly dipped in whitewash.

If the referee authorizes it, the ball can be replaced during play, either because it has been damaged or because changes in the light mean that a ball of a different colour would be preferable.

Modern match footballs are expensive items. Colchester United were so fed up with losing balls amounting to a total of £700 a year when they were kicked into nearby gardens that in 1987 they put up a net to catch them (they were subsequently obliged to take it down when the neighbours objected). Luton Town have acted similarly in the early 1990s. Peter Knowles of Wolverhampton Wanderers once kicked the ball out of Portsmouth's stadium in joy after scoring a goal; to his chagrin, he later had to stump up £7.10s for a replacement. In 1985 Reading player Trevor Senior was equally dismayed when, instead of receiving the match ball as a memento of a hat-trick against Cardiff City, as was customary, he was told he could have the ball only if he paid for it – the asking price: £40.

The rewards for success in having a make of ball accepted for a major competition are considerable: Slazenger, who provided 111 balls for the 1966 World Cup, benefited enormously from the prestige the competition brought them. The choice of ball in a World Cup Final was a major issue back in 1930, when Argentina and Uruguay failed to agree whose ball should be used. In the end a coin was tossed – the Argentinian ball was used in the first half (which ended with Argentina leading 2–1) and the Uruguayan ball in the second (with Uruguay emerging the victors with a scoreline of 4–2). *See also* BURST BALLS.

> *Am I so round with you as you with me.*
> *That like a football you spurn me thus?*
> *You spurn me hence, and he will spurn me*
> *　hither;*
> *If I last in this service you must case me in*
> *　leather.*
>
> William Shakespeare, *Comedy of Errors* (1590)

> *The trouble that day was that they used an orange-coloured ball. Eric Caldow and I were afraid to kick it and Billy McNeill was afraid to touch it.*
>
> Bobby Shearer, Scotland defender, after a 9–3 defeat by England (1961)

Ball, Alan (1947–) English midfielder, who was a star of the victorious 1966 England World Cup campaign. Aged just 21 when he appeared in the 1966 triumph, Ball was renowned for his tireless and imaginative style of play, which contributed greatly to the team's success. At home he played for Blackpool, Everton, and Arsenal and was famous for his adoption of fashionable white boots. After retiring as a player, with a total of 72 caps, he has worked as a coach and manager at several clubs.

ball boy A young boy or girl whose job it is to retrieve the ball after it has gone out of play. The first ball boys are thought to have been the two small boys employed by Chelsea in the early years of the 20th century to emphasize the bulk of their star goalkeeper William 'Fatty' FOULKE. It is not unheard of for keen ball boys to rise to stardom themselves in their later years: Arsenal's Perry Groves, who played a key role in setting up the winning goal in the 1987 League Cup Final was present as a ball boy in the FA Cup Final of 1980.

ball control The ability to direct the movement of the ball at all times, one of the essential skills of all players. Many players pride themselves on their skill at juggling with the ball and have even turned their talent to practical use off the pitch. In 1991, the South Korean player Huh Nam Jin managed to keep a regulation football in the air without it once touching the ground for a total of 17 hours, 10 minutes and 57 seconds (*see also* HEADER) to establish a world record. A Czech player called Jan Skorkovsky, meanwhile, managed to juggle the ball with his feet without it touching the ground once while running a distance of over 26 miles in the Prague City marathon of 1990.

> While I was in Rio a photographer asked me to juggle a ball on the Copacabana beach. I felt so embarrassed – we were surrounded by kids who could juggle the ball so much better than me.
>
> John Barnes

ballon d'or *See* GOLDEN BALL.

Bamber Derisive epithet beloved by football crowds who apply it to any player or other personality connected with the game who is suspected of being 'too clever for his own good'. Derived from the name of Bamber Gascoigne, presenter of the TV quiz 'University Challenge', it has been directed at virtually every player who has an O Level to his credit. In particular, Liverpool stars Brian Hall and Steve Heighway (both of whom had been to university) were widely known as 'Little Bamber' and 'Big Bamber' respectively in the 1970s.

Among the most highly qualified players to have pursued a career in professional football was Ronnie Mitchell, left-half with Berwick Rangers: he held a BSc and a PhD and was a lecturer in mathematics at the University of St Andrews (possibly an advantage when it came to calculating

angles and weighing the chances to score). Such players remain, however, the exception rather than the rule.

> He's incredibly loyal. Ask him to jump off the stand roof and he'd do it. But he's as thick as two short planks. He always grabbed the quiz book on our coach trips so that he could ask the questions. That way he didn't have to answer.
>
> Arnie Reed, Wealdstone physiotherapist, of Vinny Jones (1988)

> I prefer players not to be too good or clever at other things. It means they concentrate on football.
>
> Bill Nicholson (1973)

> The failure to understand the physical and mental strains on a professional is behind the widely held belief that footballers are stupid.
>
> Johan Cruyff (1973)

> What they say about footballers being ignorant is rubbish. I spoke to a couple yesterday and they are quite intelligent.
>
> Raquel Welch

banana shot An attacking shot in which the ball is intended to describe a sharp curve (like that of a banana) in the air. A risky shot to attempt at the best of times, it is of particular relevance in corner kicks, when it offers virtually the only way of scoring a goal with a direct shot.

Bandito, El Nickname of the English footballer Nobby STILES.

Bangladesh Bangladesh joined FIFA in 1974 but have yet to make much impact in international competition. Strip: orange shirts, white shorts, and green socks.

Bangor City Welsh non-League football club, nicknamed the Citizens. Strip: royal blue. Founded in 1876 and based at the stadium in Farrar Road, Bangor, the club play in the Konica League of Wales. In 1962 Bangor, having won the Welsh Cup that year, nearly pulled off one of the most remarkable giant-killing acts ever when they won the first leg of their European Cup Winners' Cup tie against the mighty Italian club Napoli 2–0. The Italians won their home leg 3–1 and only narrowly secured victory in the play-off at Highbury with a scoreline of 2–1.

Bank of England Nickname of the SUNDERLAND side that was a dominant force in

English football in the 1940s and 1950s, when the team included such famous names as Len SHACKLETON, Trevor Ford, Billy BINGHAM, and Stan Anderson. The nickname reflected not only the strength of the team, but also the huge amounts of money that had been spent to bring it together in an attempt to emulate prewar success.

Ironically, the side is often remembered for its most embarrassing failure, which occurred on 29 January 1949 in a fourth round FA Cup meeting with the non-League part-timers Yeovil Town. Foxed by Yeovil's notorious sloping pitch, the strength of Yeovil's local support, and by fog, the Bank of England side fell apart and ended up losing the game 2–1 in what has remained one of the most celebrated instances of giant-killing ever recorded. Yeovil's chances of winning the match had been put at 5000–1 by the bookmakers.

> Occasionally a bugle sounded. Whether Sunderland thought it sounded the retreat I don't know.
>
> 'Argus', Sunderland Echo, match report (1949)

Yeovil Town went on to play Manchester United in front of a crowd of 81,565 but history was not to repeat itself: they lost 8–0.

Bankies Nickname of the Scottish football club CLYDEBANK.

Banks, Gordon (1937–) English goalkeeper, nicknamed Banks of England, who was for many years considered the finest keeper in the world. Banks began his career with Chesterfield in 1955 and subsequently played for Leicester City (1959–67), Stoke City (1967–72), and England. His performances for England made him a legend with English fans, who considered their goal as well protected as the money in the Bank of England when Banks was between the posts. He was beaten only three times in the victorious 1966 World Cup campaign and four years later saved an apparently unstoppable shot from the great PELÉ in the same competition. Even Pelé had to admit the English keeper's save had left him dumbfounded: 'At that moment I hated Gordon Banks more than any man in soccer. But when I cooled down I had to applaud him with my heart. It was the greatest save I had ever seen.'

Having won a total of 73 caps, Banks lost the sight of one eye in a car crash. He then spent two seasons in the USA where, despite his disability, he was voted Most Valuable

Goalkeeper in the North American League, although Banks himself had his reservations about the experience: 'I felt like a circus act when I was playing in America. Roll up, roll up, roll up to see the greatest one-eyed goalkeeper in the world.'

bans See SUSPENSIONS.

Banstead Athletic English non-League football club, nicknamed the A's. Strip: amber shirts with black trim, black shorts and socks. Founded in 1944 and based at Merland Rise in Tadworth, Surrey, the A's – short for Athletic – play in the Isthmian League.

Bantams Nickname of the English football club BRADFORD CITY, in reference to the team colours (resembling those of a bantam chicken).

Barbados Barbados joined FIFA in 1968 but have yet to establish themselves as a major international side. Strip: royal blue shirts with gold trim, gold shorts, and royal blue socks with gold trim.

Barcelona Spanish football club, which ranks alongside Real Madrid as the country's leading side. Strip: red and blue striped shirts, with blue shorts and socks. Founded in 1899 by a Swiss enthusiast named Joan Gamper, Barcelona played their first match against a team of British sailors. The club experienced hard times before and during the Spanish Civil War, when it became a focus of resistance to the Franco regime; it was even forcibly closed down for a period back in the 1920s after fans whistled during a royal march played at half time.

Based at the NOU CAMP stadium since 1957, Barcelona have won the Spanish League title 12 times and the Cup 22 times. Their international trophies include the European Cup Winners' Cup in 1979, 1982, and 1989, the Fairs Cup in 1958, 1960, and 1966, the European Cup in 1992, and the Super Cup in 1989. Supporters of the club – which claims to be the largest in the world – include Pope John Paul II, who was granted honorary membership during a visit to Spain in 1982.

Barking English non-League football club, nicknamed the Blues. Strip: blue shirts and socks with white shorts. Founded in 1880 and based at Mayesbrook Park, the Blues play in the Isthmian League.

barmy army Popular nickname applied to

various large groups of football supporters, sometimes by themselves.

Barnes English football club that was founded in Barnes, London, in 1862 by the footballing pioneer Ebenezer Cobb MORLEY. Based at the Limes Field, Mortlake, the club played a significant role in the development of the game, meeting Richmond in what was the first game to be played under the first set of laws adopted by the FA. Notable members of this famous club included Morley himself (captain), Robert Willis, and R.G. Graham, who together were the first three Secretaries of the FA. In the years that followed many players with the club joined various old boys' teams while Barnes themselves participated in their last FA Cup tournament in the 1886–87 season.

Barnes, John (1963–   ) Jamaican-born English forward, who won acclaim as one of the finest English strikers of the 1980s. Variously nicknamed the Black Heighway, Digger, and Tarmac, he began his professional career with Watford in 1981 and made his first appearance in the England team in 1983. Subsequently (although his international career never took off as his domestic career did) he collected more than 50 caps for his country. He transferred to Liverpool in 1987 and a year later won the PLAYER OF THE YEAR award.

Highlights of the 1980s included a brilliant goal against Brazil in 1984 and his part in three FA Cup Finals. A great stylist, his presence revitalized the Liverpool team in the late 1980s, although opposing fans made him a target of racist criticism (see ANFIELD RAP). Barnes himself won many friends with his relaxed attitude to such prejudice, remarking that he was only there 'to bring some colour to the team'.

> Having a priest cane him every weekend . . . I thought: 'That'll be good for him'.
>
> Colonel Ken Barnes, Jamaican Defence Force, his father (1988)

Barnet English football club, nicknamed the Bees. Strip: amber shirts, with black shorts and socks. Founded in 1888, the Bees – based at the Underhill Stadium – turned professional in 1965 and won promotion to the Fourth Division in 1991, having triumphed in the Conference. Previous honours included the FA Amateur Cup title (1946).

The club's brief history in the League has not been a happy one. Highly publicized arguments between the somewhat eccentric chairman Stan Flashman and manager Barry Fry combined with mounting debts, which grew even larger through fines imposed for financial irregularities, traumatized the 1992–93 season. Yet the Club won promotion to the Second Division. Flashman eventually resigned, and Fry moved to Southend. The FA allowed many of the players to leave on a free transfer, as they had not been paid, and a patched together squad face a bleak future in the League.

Notable players with the club over the years have included Jimmy GREAVES, who appeared for the Bees at the end of his playing career.

> We're dreaming of a nine point Christmas,
> Just like the ones we used to know,
> Where the goalposts glisten,
> And children listen,
> To hear the West Bank in full flow.
>
> Supporters' song, to the tune of 'White Christmas' (1985)

Barnsley English football club, nicknamed the Tykes. Strip: red shirts with white trim, white shorts, and red socks. Also nicknamed the Reds and the Colliers, the club began life in 1887, when they were founded by the Rev. Tiverton Preedy as the church team Barnsley St Peter's. They changed to their present name a year after joining the League in 1898 and have since spent more time in the Second Division than any other club.

Based at the Oakwell ground in Barnsley, the club have visited all three of the lower divisions but never yet reached the top flight. Nonetheless, they reached the FA Cup Final in 1910 (losing to Newcastle United) and subsequently overcame all other opposition to win the Cup itself in 1912 (see BATTLING BARNSLEY). The club's fortunes ebbed in the 1960s and 1970s with repeated financial crises and periods spent in the Fourth Division but they were restored to the Second Division in 1981.

Stars with the team over the years have included such distinguished names as Danny BLANCHFLOWER, Tommy Taylor, and David Currie. Famous fans include television personality Michael Parkinson.

The Tykes have enjoyed record victories of 9–0 on two occasions, against Loughborough Town in 1899 and against Accrington Stanley in 1934; they suffered their worst defeat, also with a scoreline of 9–0, against Notts County in 1927. Barry Murphy holds the record for League appearances with the team, having played in 514 matches between 1962 and 1978.

From the green, green grass of Oakwell,
To the shores of Sicily,
We will fight, fight, fight for Barnsley,
Till we win the Football League.
To hell with Manchester,
To hell with Liverpool,
We will fight, fight, fight for Barnsley,
Till we win the Football League.

Supporters' song, to the tune of 'Halls of Montezuma'

Barrow English non-League football club, nicknamed the Bluebirds. Strip: white shirts and socks with navy blue shorts. Founded in 1901, the club (based at the Holker Street ground) joined the League in 1921 but dropped out of it in 1972 when their eleventh application for re-election was refused and their place was taken by Hereford. Recent honours have included the FA Trophy (1990).

One of the most memorable matches involving Barrow was a fixture against Kettering Town in 1979: not only did the Bluebirds whitewash their opponents 4–0, but all four goals were scored by the same person – Colin Cowperthwaite. The first of Cowperthwaite's four goals came after just 3.58 seconds of play.

Back in 1937 Barrow anticipated the signings of players from Argentina that was to dominate the English transfer market in the late 1970s when they bought the Argentinian half-back Augustus Corpa and the inside-left Casco Rinaldi.

Barry Town Welsh non-League football club, nicknamed the Linnets. Strip: green shirts, navy blue shorts, and green socks. Founded in 1923 and based at Jenner Park in Barry, the Linnets play in the Welsh Abacus League.

Barton Rovers English non-League football club, nicknamed Rovers. Strip: white shirts with blue shorts and socks. Founded in 1898 and based at Sharpenhoe Road in Barton-le-Cley, Bedford, Barton Rovers play in the Isthmian League.

Baseball Ground The home ground of the English football club DERBY COUNTY. The club's first home was at Derby's Racecourse Ground, home of the county cricket team, but in 1895 the Rams settled on a permanent move to the Baseball Ground nearby, having already played some games there. One consequence of the move was that some gipsies camping there were obliged

to vacate the site: as they left it is said that one of them laid a curse on the ground. Although the effects of this curse were less than clear, memories of it were still sufficiently strong in 1946 for Derby's captain to seek out a gipsy encampment and have the curse lifted shortly before the team's appearance in the FA Cup Final that year – Derby won 4–1.

The ground itself had been developed in the 1880s as a recreation area for foundry workers. In 1889 the owner of the foundry had visited the USA and been so impressed with the game of baseball that he had determined to promote the game among his own workers at their ground. Baseball continued to be played at the ground for some years after Derby County moved in and various noted football clubs sent baseball teams to play there, among them sides from Aston Villa and Orient. Derby County bought the ground outright in 1924 and set about completely rebuilding it. The ground suffered bomb damage during World War II but the club still refused offers of new homes elsewhere. In 1990 access to the ground was greatly improved when BR opened the Ramsline Halt station a few hundred yards away specifically for the benefit of fans.

Bashley English non-League football club, nicknamed The Bash. Strip: yellow and black striped shirts with black shorts and socks. Founded in 1947 and based at the Bashley Recreation ground, The Bash play in the Southern League.

Basingstoke Town English non-League football club, nicknamed Stoke. Strip: blue shirts with gold trim, with blue shorts and socks. Founded in 1896 and based at the Camrose Ground in Basingstoke, Stoke play in the Isthmian League.

Bastin, Cliff (1912–) English footballer, nicknamed 'Boy' Bastin, who was one of the stars of the Lucky Arsenal side that dominated English football during the 1930s. Born in Devon, Bastin was one of the key figures in Chapman's team, playing a major role in demolishing the defences of all other leading sides despite his youth – hence his nickname. He had won virtually every major honour offered in the domestic game before he was 21. When the outstanding Austrian Wunderteam of Hugo MEISL lost to Italy in the semi-finals of the 1934 World Cup, the famous manager had no doubt what his team had lacked to win the competition: Boy Bastin himself.

bath, to take an early To leave the field of play prematurely, through injury, being sent off, etc. and to retire to the players' dressing-rooms for a post-match bath. A phrase beloved of sports commentators on both sides of the Atlantic (and in the UK particularly associated with the rugby commentator Eddie Waring), the phrase is now commonly heard in many non-sporting contexts.

Bath City English non-League football club, nicknamed City. Strip: black and white striped shirts, black shorts, and black and white socks. City (based at TWERTON PARK) were founded in 1889 and play in the Conference, but have never won promotion to the League.

Bathgate Former Scottish League football club, which dropped out of the League in 1928. Based at Mill Park, West Lothian, the club joined the League in 1921.

Battle of Berne Nickname given to a notorious World Cup match between Hungary and Brazil that took place in Berne, Switzerland, in the quarter-finals of the 1954 competition. The emotions of the players involved in the match were so heated that play was frequently interrupted by clashes between them, culminating in a full-scale brawl in the dressing-rooms afterwards. Three players (Santos and Tozzo of Brazil and Boszik of Hungary) were sent off. Hungary won the game but lost the Final against West Germany six days later.

Battle of Highbury Nickname given to a legendary and bruising encounter that took place between England and Italy, then world champions, at Highbury in 1934. This most famous of interwar internationals saw England overcome the all-conquering Italians 3–2. Seven of the English players came from the same club, Arsenal (whose home ground was, of course, Highbury); the captain was also one of the Arsenal men and even the commentary was provided by a figure with a strong Arsenal link – ex-manager George Allison.

The match had been eagerly awaited by English fans, with advance publicity for the event describing it as 'the most important football match that has been played anywhere in the world since the Great War', and victory in the contest was considered a matter of intense national pride in both England and Fascist Italy.

When the star Italian centre-half Luisito Monti had to leave the field with a broken

toe, the rest of the Italian side – thinking his injury was the result of foul play – became increasingly physical in their game. English captain Eddie HAPGOOD suffered a broken nose and for a time it seemed the game would disintegrate into open warfare, although tempers did eventually cool. Part of the reason behind the furiosity of the Italian attack may have lain in the fact that the players were promised huge sums of money, cars, and exemption from military service if they won.

The English players themselves admitted that the Italian assault had almost provoked them into similar retaliation, Hapgood commenting afterwards that it was difficult to 'play like a gentleman when somebody closely resembling an enthusiastic member of the Mafia is wiping his studs down your legs'.

Battle of Santiago A notorious ill-tempered match in the 1962 World Cup Finals that involved the national teams of Chile and Italy. The crowd and a massive television audience saw the Chilean player Leonel Sanchez throw a punch at Italy's Humberto Maschio, which broke the latter's nose. The referee and the two linesmen, however, failed to witness the blatant foul and Chile emerged victors with a 2–0 scoreline to the outrage of viewers around the world.

Battle of Turin A widely condemned outbreak of violence that marred the progress of England in the European Championship of 1980. The trouble began during a match between England and Belgium in Turin on 12 June 1980. When the Belgians scored an equalizing goal, Italian fans present launched into a barrage of taunts directed at the English supporters, who responded with an all-out attack that only subsided with the intervention of Italian riot police using tear gas and batons. After a five-minute stoppage due to goalkeeper Ray Clemence being blinded by the gas, the game itself ended in a 1–1 draw.

The FA was fined £8000 by UEFA and English football authorities roundly condemned the English hooligan element. Margaret Thatcher had no hesitation in describing the whole event as 'a disgraceful embarrassment'. It has been suggested that the bitterness stirred up at this match was a precursor to the violence that preceded the Heysel Stadium disaster in 1985.

Battling Barnsley Nickname of the BARNSLEY line-up that won the FA Cup in 1912.

The nickname reflected the hard campaign the team had to wage before triumphing in the competition. In all they played 12 games on their route to the trophy, of which six were 0–0 draws, five were victories by the narrow margin of one goal, and the remaining match was a 3–1 win against Birmingham. The final itself was also a long drawn-out affair, with the single winning goal (scored by Harry Tufnell) coming in the last minute of extra time in the replay against West Bromwich Albion.

Baxter, Jim (1939–) Scottish forward, nicknamed Slim Jim, who emerged as a Scottish folk-hero playing for Rangers and the national side in the 1960s. Baxter began his career with Raith Rovers in 1957 and subsequently joined Rangers in 1960, in which year he won the first of 34 caps for Scotland. Highlights of his career in the 1960s included his two goals in Scotland's 2–1 triumph over England in 1963 (at the end of which he left the pitch with the ball tucked up his shirt) and his exceptional contribution to the Scottish 3–2 victory over World Cup winners England in 1967.

Inspired by Baxter, Rangers clinched three League championships and reached three Scottish Cup Finals and four League Cup Finals. He transferred to Sunderland in 1965 and later (1967) moved to Nottingham Forest before returning two years later to Rangers. His efforts south of the border were less sensational and he lost his playing edge and put on weight as he indulged freely in such extra-curricular activities as alcohol and sex. He retired in 1970 to take over a public house in Glasgow.

I overdid it.

Jim Baxter, on breaking his leg against Rapid Vienna (1964)

Bay Nickname of a number of British clubs with a seaside location, among them the Welsh non-League football club COLWYN BAY and the English non-League football club WHITLEY BAY.

Bayern Munich German football club, which is considered by many the leading modern side in the country. Strip: all red. Founded in 1900, it was not until the 1960s that the club first established itself as a dominant force in German football (with a single League Championship in 1932 and one Cup win in 1957). It all changed, however, when the club joined the Bundesliga in 1963, with the team capturing the League title in 1969, 1972, 1973, 1974, 1980,

1981, 1985, 1986, 1987, 1989, and 1990 as well as the Cup in 1966, 1967, 1969, 1971, 1982, 1984, and 1986. On the international stage, the side won the European Cup in 1974, 1975, and 1976, the European Cup Winners' Cup in 1967, and the World Club Championship in 1976. Stars with the side in their golden era have included Sepp MAIER, Franz BECKENBAUER, Gerd MÜLLER, Karl-Heinz RUMMENIGGE, and Lothar MATTHAÜS.

Bears Nickname of the English non-League football club CONGLETON TOWN.

Beasant, Dave (1959–) English goalkeeper, nicknamed Lurch, who established himself as one of the finest keepers in the modern game while manning the Wimbledon goal in the 1980s. Celebrated as the first keeper to save a penalty in an FA Cup Final (when he stopped a shot by Liverpool's John Aldridge in the course of the 1988 Final, which Wimbledon won 1–0), he was also the first goalkeeper to captain an FA Cup-winning side at Wembley. Subsequently he also played for Newcastle United and Chelsea (from 1988).

I was a bit disappointed. I should have caught it really.

Dave Beasant, of his save in the FA Cup Final (1988)

Beaujoire The home ground of the French football club NANTES, who moved into the Beaujoire stadium – one of the best in France – in 1984 after outgrowing their old home, the Marcel Saupin stadium. One of the two main stands is named after the writer Jules Verne, who hailed from the Nantes area. It is also a major venue for rugby.

Beavers Nickname of the English non-League football club HAMPTON, in reference to the team's home at Beveree Stadium.

Beazer Homes League *See* SOUTHERN LEAGUE.

Beckenbauer, Franz (1945–) German footballer, nicknamed The Kaiser, who exercised a profound influence over the development of team tactics in the 1960s and 1970s and has been rated among the world's most successful footballers of all time. Born in Munich, Beckenbauer joined Bayern Munich in 1958 and reached the first team in 1963. He made his international debut for West Germany in 1965 and a year later played in the World Cup Final against England. Subsequently he helped Bayern Munich capture the European Cup in 1967, reached the World Cup semi-finals in 1970, took over the captaincy of West Germany in 1971, led his country to victory in the European Championship and won the European Footballer of the Year award (1972), earned winners' medals in both the European Cup and the World Cup (1974), and won the European Cup again in 1975 and once more in 1976, in which year he was made European Footballer of the Year for a second time.

In 1977 he moved to the US team Cosmos, transferring to Hanover in 1982 (as West Germany's highest-paid player), and returning to Cosmos in 1983. He retired as a player in 1984 and took up the post of manager of West Germany, seeing them through to the semi-finals of the World Cup in 1986 and securing the Cup itself in 1990 (becoming the first man both to captain and to manage World Cup-winning teams). Later that year he was appointed coach of Marseille and then joined the technical staff there.

Beckenbauer's extraordinary record of success has much to do with his philosophy of football, based on remorseless attacking play and intelligent use of a sweeper – the strategy often called total football. Perhaps his finest hour was in 1972, when West Germany's triumph in the European Championship was constructed very much around his own brilliance (some of his later teams were accused of being too cautious and defensive). As a player he was particularly effective in the role of sweeper, although he had to battle for a long time before he was allowed to develop the tactic of mounting attacks from deep within his own defence. When he moved to the USA he encountered similar difficulties:

> Tell the Kraut to get his ass up front. We don't pay a million for a guy to hang around in defence.
>
> Cosmos executive (1977)

Bedworth United English non-League football club, nicknamed the Greenbacks. Strip: green shirts, white shorts, and green socks. Founded in 1896, the club are based at the Oval in Bedworth and play in the Southern League.

Bees Nickname of several football clubs that sport striped shirts (usually yellow or amber and black). They include BARNET, BRENTFORD, and TROWBRIDGE TOWN.

Beith Former Scottish League football club, which dropped out of the League in 1926. Based at Bellsdale Park in Ayrshire (where the side still plays), Beith enjoyed just three years in the top flight, having joined the League in 1923.

Belfast Celtic Former Northern Irish football team that was once one of the most powerful sides in the whole of Ireland. The team, based at CELTIC PARK in Belfast, won the Irish League on no fewer than 14 occasions but eventually resigned from the League in 1949 following a riot at Windsor Park during a game with rivals Linfield. A Celtic player's leg was broken during the violence instigated by a sectarian mob and the directors of the club swore that the team (which was identified strongly with the Catholic community) would never again play in front of an Irish crowd. The team still exists as a limited company and holds the occasional commemorative dinner.

Belgium The Belgian national team have traditionally languished in the shadow of such neighbours as Germany and the Netherlands, but have on occasion emerged to make their mark in international competition. Winners of the Olympic football title in 1920, the side participated in the very first World Cup tournament back in 1930 but were humbled 3–0 by the USA and subsequently failed to progress far in the Finals of 1934 and 1938. They recorded their first Finals win in 1970 while in 1982 the team got as far as the quarter-finals. The 1986 competition saw Belgium surprise the experts by getting into the semi-finals – though they finished in fourth place after a 2–0 defeat against Argentina. Belgium also finished third in the European Championship in 1972 and second in 1980. Belgium qualified for the 1994 World Cup in America. Strip: red shirts with tricolour trim, red shorts, and red socks with tricolour trim.

Belize Belize joined FIFA in 1986 but the national team has yet to make much impact in international competition. Strip: blue shirts with red and white trim, white shorts, and blue socks.

Belle Vue The home ground of DONCASTER ROVERS. Rovers moved to Belle Vue in 1922 with the supporters themselves doing the lion's share of the construction work necessary. The unusually large pitch is famous for its high-quality grass, which in the 1970s was the object of an unsuccessful approach by the managers of Wembley, who offered the club £10,000 for the pitch. Curious features of the ground include the 'Pigeon Box', a box high in the roof of one of the stands in which an owl once nested; according to local superstition, Doncaster would win if the owl came out of the box during the course of the game. The box now houses a video camera.

bench Collectively, the manager and other senior officials of a football club. During the course of a match these luminaries commonly watch the game from a bench at the side of the pitch, often placed within a dugout. Substitutes also sit on the bench as they await a possible order to go on to the field of play.

benefit A match, the proceeds of which go to a specific named person (usually a player nearing retirement), club, charity, or other worthy cause. Usually, the player named has been with the club concerned for at least ten years.

Benfica Portuguese football club, nicknamed the Eagles. Strip: red shirts, white shorts, and red socks. Founded in 1904 by Cosme Damião (who had learnt the game from British immigrants), Benfica are Portugal's most successful team, having won the League championship 29 times and the Cup 24 times. Based at the STADIUM OF LIGHT in Lisbon, they have also notched up two famous victories in the European Cup, winning it in 1961 and 1962. Stars with the team during the great era of the 1960s included the incomparable EUSÉBIO. He, along with other noteworthy players and supporters, have been honoured with the 'rank' of Golden Eagle.

E Pluribus Unum *(All for one).*

Benfica club motto

Benin Benin joined FIFA in 1962 but have yet to make much impact in international competition. Strip: all green.

Berkhamsted Town English non-League football club, nicknamed the Lilywhites. Strip: white shirts, with black shorts and socks. Founded in 1895 and based at the Broadwater ground in Berkhamsted, the Lilywhites play in the Isthmian League.

Bermuda Bermuda joined FIFA in 1962 but have yet to make much impact in international competition. Strip: royal blue shirts, with white shorts and socks.

Bernabeu The home ground of the Spanish football club REAL MADRID. Situated in the most exclusive district of Madrid, the Bernabeu Stadium – then called the Chamartin Stadium – became Real's home in 1924, but was subsequently devastated during the Spanish Civil War.

Santiago Bernabeu, a lawyer and Franco supporter, became club president in 1943 and oversaw the complete rebuilding of the ground, which reopened in 1947 and was finally named in his honour in 1955. Failing to get financial help from the banks, Bernabeu drew on the club's devoted fans by selling bonds worth £200,000 within the space of just a few hours, enabling work on the ground to proceed.

The stadium has staged more internationals than any other Spanish venue. The complex includes such curious facilities as a team chapel and the club's fabulous trophy room, visited by a quarter of a million fans every year. The stadium is also famous for the Ultra Sur stand where some of the most partisan – and often unruly – fans in Europe congregate.

Berwick Rangers English football club, nicknamed the Borderers. Strip: black and gold shirts, with black shorts and socks. Founded in 1881, the Borderers are technically an English club based on English soil – they began as a member of the Northumberland Association – but the side eventually joined the Scottish League in 1951 and is now the only English-based team that takes part in Scottish competitions.

Based at Shielfield Park since 1919, the Borderers have only a modest record, their greatest success being their Second Division championship in 1979. Their most remarkable single result, however, came in the Scottish Cup in 1967, when they performed a giant-killing act against Rangers, whom they beat 1–0. Other newsworthy moments in their history have included the appointment of George Deans as chairman at the age of just 21.

The Borderers enjoyed their record victory in 1965, when they beat Forfar Athletic 8–1; they suffered their worst defeat at the hands of Hamilton Academical, against whom they lost 9–1 in 1980. Eric Tait holds the record for League appearances with the Borderers, having played 435 games with them between 1970 and 1987; by the time he reached a total of 50 games that year, he had played in every position on the field, including that of goalkeeper, and had filled the roles of captain, caretaker-manager, and substitute.

Bescot Stadium The home ground of the English football club WALSALL. Bescot Stadium replaced Fellows Park as Walsall's base in 1990 after years of impassioned debate. The Saddlers moved into their longtime home in Hillary Street back in 1896 and named it Fellows Park around 1930 in honour of the club's chairman H.L. Fellows, making it one of just three League grounds to be named after individuals (*see also* DEAN COURT; NINIAN PARK).

An unprepossessing ground, it was nonetheless cherished by Walsall's supporters and when plans for a move were discussed in the mid-1980s there was much furore over the topic. Ideas of moving in with Wolverhampton Wanderers at MOLINEUX and with Birmingham City at ST ANDREW'S had to be dropped, as was an even more eccentric plan for all three clubs to operate from Fellows Park itself. The fans wielded considerable influence over events through the Save Walsall Action Group and the ground's future looked secure when Terry Ramsden, a London businessman, flew in by helicopter and bought the club outright. The optimism was premature, however, and in 1990 Walsall began a new life half a mile away from their traditional home (now a supermarket), at the recently built stadium at Bescot.

Best, George (1946–) The brilliant Northern Ireland-born forward, who is included by most experts among the most talented players ever to appear on a football pitch. Born in Belfast, Best turned professional with Manchester United in 1963 and three years later established a worldwide reputation when he spearheaded his club's comprehensive 5–1 victory over Benfica in Lisbon. Danny BLANCHFLOWER went so far as to declare him the equal of FINNEY and MATTHEWS:

> Basically, Best makes a greater appeal to the senses than the other two. His movements are quicker, lighter, more balletic . . . he has ice in his veins, warmth in his heart, and timing and balance in his feet.

Best was a tremendous showman on the pitch and thrilled crowds with his mastery of the ball, defying massed defences and scoring apparently impossible goals after typically indulging in a dazzling display of dribbling. He loved to taunt defenders into committing themselves to a tackle, which he would then evade with ease, and jealously kept possession of the ball until a chance to shoot presented itself (leading many fans to accuse him of selfishness). Joe MERCER

called him a 'football freak' and Jimmy GREAVES described him as 'the greatest footballer of my lifetime, and I include the likes of Pelé, Di Stefano, Puskas, Eusébio, Maradona, Cruyff, Matthews and Finney in that assessment'. (Best himself considered Di Stefano the finest player he had ever seen).

In combination with Denis LAW and Bobby CHARLTON there were few teams that could resist the Manchester United onslaught in the mid-1960s. Having played a crucial role in the club's League championship title in 1965, Best helped regain the title in 1967 and in 1968 won the ultimate accolade of Footballer of the Year and – scoring in the team's European Cup triumph that year – also European Footballer of the Year. Other highlights of his career included a run of six goals in a match against Northampton Town in 1970 on his first appearance after suspension following a confrontation with a referee.

In 1971 Best's Irish background led to threats on his life and a year later, after further clashes with the footballing authorities, he announced his retirement. In 1973 he made a brief comeback with his old club, but two years later he transferred to Stockport County and then to the US team Los Angeles Aztecs and to Cork Celtic. Stints with Fulham (1976–77), Fort Lauderdale (1978), Hibernian (1979), San José Earthquakes (1980), and Bournemouth (1983) followed before his final retirement.

While with Fulham he set an unusual record, playing in all four home countries in the space of just ten days with matches for Northern Ireland in Belfast and for Fulham away to Cardiff and St Mirren and at home to Crystal Palace. In all he collected 37 caps playing for Northern Ireland.

Best's outstanding skills won him many admirers, but his mercurial temperament and weakness for alcohol brought him repeated difficulties with the football authorities. (He once confessed that while in the USA he had got himself a house by the sea but, as the route to the beach went through a bar, he had never once reached the shore). Problems in his personal life impinged increasingly upon his performance on the field and many speculated that the pressures of the game effectively destroyed his talent. Still more have regretted that he never had the opportunity to display his skill on a wider stage in the World Cup Finals. In 1980 he sought treatment for alcoholism and in 1985 his chequered private life brought him a spell in Ford Open Prison; as recently as 1991 he was still getting into trouble, on one occasion for swearing on the early evening chat show 'Wogan'.

Former colleagues responded to the scandals surrounding Best's name in different ways. The journalist Geoffrey Green saw El Beatle and his troubles as a symbol of his time, calling him 'a cult for youth, a new folk hero, a living James Dean who is a rebel with a cause'. His mother on the other hand scolded him for his wild ways even as she offered to help him overcome his weakness for alcohol, threatening 'I'll cut off his legs and put him in the circus if he lets me down'. Sir Matt BUSBY, Best's ex-boss, acknowledged the difficulties of working with United's golden boy, but was inclined to forgive his waywardness: 'We had our problems with the wee feller, but I prefer to remember his genius.'

Best Goalkeeper in the World Nickname bestowed upon the English goalkeeper Peter SHILTON. Shilton was regularly described in this way after he transferred to Nottingham Forest in 1977 and the No.1 shirt in the England team became his personal property. Other contenders for the title would have to include Gordon BANKS, who was Shilton's predecessor in the England goal; a bid might also be put forward for the Irish keeper Pat JENNINGS and the Soviet keeper Lev YASHIN among others.

betting *See* POOLS.

Bhoys Nickname of the Scottish football club CELTIC.

bicycle kick A shot in which the player kicks the ball over his head, using both feet. One of the more spectacular shots in the tactical repertoire, it is also somewhat risky given the player's limited view of his target and the danger of injury involved in such a violent manoeuvre. The first player to win acclaim for his mastery of the bicycle kick was LEONIDAS DA SILVA of Brazil. *See also* SCISSOR KICK.

Big Ben Nickname of the Scottish centre-half Willie WOODBURN.

Big Five The five leading English professional football clubs who were at the centre of controversial negotiations to set up a SUPER LEAGUE in the mid-1980s. The clubs, Arsenal, Everton, Liverpool, Manchester United, and Tottenham Hotspur, aimed to secure greater influence over the national game and a larger share of the profits,

threatening the welfare of many smaller clubs at a time when crowds were falling and football was wracked by the trauma of the Heysel Stadium disaster and difficulties surrounding television coverage. In 1986 an uneasy compromise was reached, with the First Division clubs attaining a greater say as well as a larger share of football revenue, among other reforms. *See also* BIG TEN.

Big Jack Nickname of the English footballer Jack CHARLTON.

Big Man Nickname of the great Scottish manager Jock STEIN.

Big Ron Nickname of the English manager Ron ATKINSON.

Big Swifty Nickname of the celebrated English goalkeeper Frank SWIFT.

Big Ten The ten clubs that threatened a breakaway from the Football League in the late 1980s. Comprising the Big Five with the addition of Aston Villa, Newcastle, Nottingham Forest, Sheffield Wednesday, and West Ham, the Big Ten were courted by ITV in an attempt to counter the offers being made to the League by newly arrived British Satellite Broadcasting (BSB). The issue caused enormous controversy, threatening the disintegration of the League itself. Eventually the ITV offer was accepted (but to include the whole of the League) and the threat of reformation of the game in the UK temporarily receded. *See* SUPER LEAGUE.

Billericay Town English non-League football club, nicknamed Town. Strip: yellow shirts, with black shorts and socks. Founded in 1880 and based at the New Lodge ground in Billericay, the club play in the Isthmian League. Billericay are the most successful side in the history of the FA Vase competition, having won three times (1976, 1977, and 1979).

Billy The white police horse which became a national celebrity after the FA Cup Final of 1923, the first to be played at Wembley (*see* WHITE HORSE FINAL). Immortal as a legend of English football, Billy himself lived on until 15 December 1930, when he died at the age of 20.

Billy the Fish Eponymous hero of a comic strip series in *Viz*, a cult comic for adults that enjoyed widespread popularity in the late 1980s. Billy the Fish Thomson, born half man and half fish, is the leading star of

Fulchester United and the central character in most of the adventures experienced by the club. A parody of the footballing stories of children's comics, the series began in 1983 and became one of the most successful featured in *Viz*, eventually spawning a television cartoon version.

Billy's escapades since 1983 have included being kidnapped, killed (twice), and being revealed to be the father of manager Tommy Brown's baby. Among other stars of the team are Brown Fox (a buxom Red Indian squaw), Professor Wolfgang Schnell (who calculates every shot mathematically), and blind 84-year-old Rex Findlay (with his guide dog Shep).

> *As team manager my job has not been an easy one. I've been sacked, slandered in the gutter press, I've suffered a fatal heart attack, been kidnapped and taken to Mars, undergone a sex change operation and travelled back through time to caveman days. But that's football.*
>
> Tommy Brown, *The Viz Billy the Fish Football Yearbook* (1990)

Bilston Town English non-League football club. Strip: tangerine shirts, black shorts, and tangerine socks. Founded in 1895 and based at the Queen Street ground in Bilston, the club play in the Southern League.

Bimbo Nickname of the great Austrian forward Franz BINDER.

Binder, Franz Austrian forward who played for Sturm 19, St Polten, and Rapid Vienna and won 20 caps with Austria and nine caps with Germany after the two teams were merged in the 1930s. His career total of 1006 goals in just 756 games between 1930 and 1950 earned him the accolade of first European footballer to score 1000 goals in first-class football.

Bingham, Billy (1931–) Northern Ireland-born winger and manager, who is particularly celebrated for his long association with the Northern Ireland national team. Born in Belfast, Bingham made his debut with Glentoran and quickly attracted the attention of the English club Sunderland, which acquired his services in 1950. A year later Bingham made his first appearance for Northern Ireland and in 1958 he played a crucial role in the campaign that took the team to the quarter-finals of the World Cup. That same year he transferred to Luton, with whom he reached the FA

Cup Final in 1959. He joined Everton in 1960 and won the League championship with them in 1963 before moving to Port Vale. Having won 56 caps, he moved into management (at Southport) in 1965 and three years later was appointed manager of Plymouth Argyle and Northern Ireland. Two years later he became manager of Greece and in 1973 he took over Everton. He returned to Greece in 1977, but was back in the UK (at Mansfield Town) in 1978 and in 1980 was reappointed manager of Northern Ireland. Under Bingham's stewardship, the Northern Ireland squad reached the last 12 in the World Cup in 1982 and qualified for the Finals once more in 1986. He retired in 1993.

Binos Nickname of the Scottish football club STIRLING ALBION, derived from 'Albion'.

Birmingham and District League English football league, founded in 1889 and one of the two oldest leagues still operating. Now known as the Banks's Brewery League, it was dominated in its early years by the reserve teams of several League clubs but in more recent times has seen the rise of such sides as Kidderminster Harriers (holders of six championships) and Halesowen Town and Tamworth (both winners in five seasons).

Birmingham City English football club, nicknamed the Blues. Strip: royal blue shirts and socks with white trim and white shorts. Founded in 1875 by cricketing enthusiasts associated with Trinity Church, Bordesley, the Blues have a relatively undistinguished record, enjoying their best season to date back in 1956, when they finished sixth in the First Division. Success in both the League and the FA Cup has eluded their grasp and for much of their existence the Blues have been overshadowed by their neighbours Aston Villa. Fans of Birmingham City have had to learn to live with repeated disappointment, as reflected in a wry comment by Blues fan and comedian Jasper Carrott – a director of the club – in 1978: 'You lose some, you draw some.'

The club began life as Small Heath and did well in their early seasons in the League, moving to their permanent home at ST ANDREW'S in 1906, when they also changed their name to Birmingham City. In the 1920s the Blues began an 18-year stay in the First Division and in 1931 they reached the FA Cup Final, only to lose to West Bromwich Albion. Runners-up in the FA

Cup in 1956, Birmingham reached the Final of the Fairs Cup in both 1960 and 1961, losing on both occasions. Other honours have included the League Cup in 1963 and the Leyland Daf Cup in 1991. In 1989 the club tasted life in the Third Division for the first time in their history.

Famous names associated with Birmingham have numbered amongst them centre-forward Joe Bradford and goalkeeper Harry Hibbs in the 1920s and 1930s, Jeff Hall and Trevor Smith in the 1950s, and Trevor FRANCIS and Bob Latchford in the 1970s.

The club's record victory stands at 12–0 against Walsall Town Swifts in 1892; their record defeat was sustained in 1930, when they lost 9–1 to Sheffield Wednesday. Frank Womack holds the record for League appearances with the Blues, having played in 491 games between 1908 and 1928.

> All through life it's a long, long road,
> There'll be joys and sorrows too,
> As we journey on, we will sing this song,
> For the boys in Royal Blue.
> We're often partisans, la, la, la,
> We will journey on, la, la, la,
> Keep right on to the end of the road,
> Keep right on to the end.

Supporters' song (1956)

Biscuitmen A former nickname of the English football club READING, usually called the Royals. The nickname refers to the fact that the club's home ground is close to the factory of Huntley and Palmers, the biscuit manufacturers. Somewhat ironically, in 1982 the authorities at Reading decided that they would no longer provide the referee and linesmen with their traditional biscuits at half time, as an economy measure.

Bishop Auckland English non-League football club, nicknamed the Bishops. Strip: light and dark blue. Founded in 1886 (as Auckland Town), the club (based at the Kingsway ground) emerged as the most successful amateur side in postwar football, winning the Amateur Cup on a record ten occasions (surprisingly they have never won the FA Trophy). Stars with the side (many of whom were nationally known in the team's great days) have included wing-half 'Bob' Hardisty in the 1950s. The club play in the Northern Premier League.

Bishop's Stortford English non-League football club, nicknamed the Bishops. Strip: blue and white striped shirts with blue shorts and socks. The Bishops – based at

the George Wilson Stadium – joined the Isthmian League in 1971, were relegated in 1978, and rejoined in 1981. In 1974 the side won the very last Final of the FA Amateur Cup.

Bites Yer Legs Nickname of the English footballer Norman HUNTER.

Black, The Man in See MAN IN BLACK.

Black and Blues Nickname of the Italian football club INTERNAZIONALE, in reference to the team colours.

Black Arabs Former nickname of BRISTOL ROVERS, in reference to the black shirts they once wore.

Black Diamond Nickname of the great Brazilian centre-forward LEONIDAS DA SILVA.

Black Heighway Nickname of John BARNES, likening him to a former Liverpool star, Steve Heighway.

Black Octopus Nickname of the Soviet goalkeeper Lev YASHIN.

Black Panther Nickname of the Portuguese striker EUSÉBIO Ferreira da Silva.

Black Pearl Nickname of the great Brazilian inside-forward PELÉ.

Black Watch See EVERTON.

Blackburn Rovers English football club, nicknamed the Blue and Whites. Strip: blue and white halved shirts, white shorts, and blue socks. Founded in 1875, the club began life as Blackburn Grammar School Old Boys and turned professional in 1880, after which they established themselves as one of the most powerful sides of the pre-World War I era.

They made their first appearance in an FA Cup Final in 1882, when they lost 1–0 to the Old Etonians, to the great chagrin of their supporters, who had been confident of victory – as expressed by a local poet in a somewhat premature celebration of the expected win:

> The English Cup, by brilliant play
> From Cockney land they brought away;
> Let's hope in Blackburn it will stay
> To cheer the Blackburn Rovers.

Similar sentiments were expressed in a song taken up on the day by the Cup Final crowd:

All hail, ye gallant Rover lads!
Etonians thought you were but cads:
They've found a football game their dads
By meeting Blackburn Rovers.

In the event, just two more seasons were to elapse before the fans were able to celebrate FA Cup victory, with Blackburn capturing the trophy in 1884 and going on to regain it in 1885 and 1886 to complete the hat-trick; they also won it in 1890 (the year in which they settled at EWOOD PARK), 1891, and once more in 1928.

1891 witnessed one of the more curious games in the team's history, when they met Burnley in miserable weather in December that year. After the second of two fights on the pitch Rovers called it a day and the whole team except veteran goalkeeper Herby Arthur left the field. This left Arthur to face the entire Burnley team alone. He countered the first attack by successfully appealing for offside and then held on to the ball for so long (having no one to pass it to) that the referee finally gave in and stopped the match; the club later apologized for the episode, explaining that their players had been too cold to continue, and the stalwart Arthur was given a benefit match two days afterwards.

Trips by huge crowds of Rovers supporters to the south were memorable affairs, with brass bands, fireworks, and parties, to the bemusement of their opponents. For many years the team gave their supporters every reason to treat matches as grand occasions, adding to their tally of Cup wins the First Division championship in 1912 and 1914 (when the team was led by the still-revered full-back Bob Crompton). After the war, however, the club's fortunes declined and Blackburn have never equalled their early success since. Relegation came for the first time in 1936, although the team did stage something of a comeback in the 1950s with the likes of winger Ronnie Clayton, full-back Bill Eckersly, and centre-forward Tommy Briggs in the side.

Honours in more recent times have included the Second Division championship in 1939, the Third Division title in 1975, and the Full Members' Cup in 1987. A return to form under Kenny DALGLISH in the early 1990s saw the team safely into the Premier League when it was set up in 1992; the club also set a new record in transfer fees, acquiring Southampton's Alan SHEARER for £3.6 million.

Blackburn enjoyed their record victory back in 1884, when they beat Rossendale 11–0; their record defeat was in 1933, when they lost 8–0 against Arsenal. Derek Fazackerley holds the record for League appearances for the club, having played in 596 games between 1970 and 1986. Burnley are considered the club's arch-rivals by most fans:

> Now I've followed the Rovers for many a year
> And I've spent all my money on football and beer
> But I've one aim in life before I am gone
> That's to follow Blackburn Rovers in Division One.
> And it's no, nay, never, no, nay, never no more
> Will we play Burnley bastards, no, never, no more.

Supporters' song, to the tune of 'The Wild Rover'

Blackheath Former English football club, which was at the centre of the controversy over hacking in the 1860s. As one of the clubs that were founder members of the FA, Blackheath stoutly defended the principle that hacking was indispensable to the enjoyment of the game and maintained that criticisms that such a practice was barbaric were beneath contempt. The weight of opinion was against Blackheath, however, and when the FA agreed to ban hacking the team withdrew in high dudgeon. Subsequently the side became one of the early pioneers of the rugby code and in 1871 were themselves instrumental in banning hacking from soccer's sister game.

Blackpool English football club, nicknamed the Seasiders. Strip: tangerine shirts with navy and white trim, white shorts, and tangerine socks with white tops. Founded in 1887 at a meeting at the Stanley Arms Hotel by old boys of St John's School, Blackpool joined the League in 1896 and had several homes before finally settling at BLOOMFIELD ROAD in 1899 (in which year they failed to win re-election to the League, although they applied successfully once more the following year). They spent the next 30 years in the Second Division, then won the Second Division title (largely through the efforts of striker Johnny Hampson) to join the First Division, where they were to spend much of their subsequent history (1930–33, 1937–67, and 1970–71).

The club's golden era was in the 1940s when star players included the great Stanley MATTHEWS and Stan MORTENSEN, who spearheaded a number of campaigns that culminated in the side clinching their only FA Cup title (1953), in what was dubbed thereafter the MATTHEWS FINAL, as well as appearances as losing finalists in the Finals of 1948 and 1951. The team were also runners-up in the League championship in 1956.

Other honours have included reaching the semi-finals of the League Cup in 1962 and victory in the Anglo-Italian Cup in 1971 (and runners-up position in 1972). Successors to Matthews and Mortensen in the 1960s and 1970s numbered amongst them Jimmy ARMFIELD, Alan BALL, and Ray Charnley. The club has enjoyed less glory in recent years, having spent time since 1978 exclusively in the bottom two divisions.

The Seasiders enjoyed their record victory back in 1948, when they beat Preston North End 7–0; they have suffered record defeats with a scoreline of 10–1 on two occasions, against Small Heath in 1901 and against Huddersfield Town in 1930. Jimmy Armfield holds the record for League appearances with the club, having played in 568 games between 1952 and 1971.

Blackpool Bombshell Nickname of the great English forward Stan MORTENSEN.

Blades Nickname of the English football club SHEFFIELD UNITED, a reference to the city's long history in the manufacture of steel and fine blades. It was also formerly the nickname of the city's other major club, Sheffield Wednesday (now known as the Owls).

Blanchflower, Danny (1926–93) Belfast-born footballer, nicknamed Danny Boy, who led Tottenham Hotspur to victory on numerous occasions in the 1960s and became one of the best-known personalities in the game. Blanchflower began his career with the Irish club Glentoran in 1945 and transferred to Barnsley in 1949 (in which year he also made his debut for Northern Ireland). In 1951 he moved to Aston Villa and finally arrived at Tottenham in 1954, remaining there until his retirement as a player in 1964.

His remarkable tally of victories with Spurs included the League Cup and FA Cup double in 1961, a second FA Cup in 1962, and the European Cup Winners' Cup in 1963. He was made Footballer of the Year in 1958 and 1961 and collected a record 56 international caps. Subsequently he worked as a journalist and briefly as manager of Chelsea and Northern Ireland.

Throughout his career, he attracted praise for both his eloquence and his intelligence. Of his tactics as captain of North-ern Ireland he once remarked, with typical gnomic originality: 'We try to equalize before the others have scored.'

He became particularly renowned for his resolute and serious attitude to life as a whole; an attempt to get him to agree to participate in the television programme 'This Is Your Life', for instance, met with a blank refusal. His frank and uncompromising condemnation of the poor standard of play in the NASL during its brief existence did not go down too well either, especially as he was being employed as a commentator on matches for the CBS Television Network at the time.

> *The great fallacy is that the game is first and last about winning. It's nothing of the kind. The game is about glory. It's about doing things in style, with a flourish, about going out and beating the other lot, not waiting for them to die of boredom.*
>
> Danny Blanchflower

Blaydon Races Traditional English ballad, which has been sung for many years by fans of Newcastle United who have adopted it as their anthem.

blind side The area that lies outside that easily covered by a marker, into which an attacker will attempt to put himself to receive a pass. *See also* CREATE SPACE.

Blokhin, Oleg (1953–) Soviet-born outside-left, who emerged as a major international footballer in the 1970s. A star with Dynamo Kiev, he became the Soviet Union's top goalscorer of all time, with 302 goals, as well as scoring a record 44 goals in an unsurpassed 108 internationals. Voted European Footballer of the Year in 1975, he featured in the World Cups of 1982 and 1986 and in 1988 was allowed to transfer to a Western side, Austria's Vowarts Steyr; he eventually ended his career in Cyprus.

Bloods Nickname of a number of football clubs that have adopted a predominantly red strip. They include the English non-League teams DROYLSDEN and SAFFRON WALDEN.

Bloomer, Steve (1874–1938) English forward, nicknamed Paleface, who is remembered as one of the legendary figures of late-Victorian and Edwardian football. Critics accused him of being too relaxed and selfish as a player, but admirers recognized that this nonchalance masked a brilliant goalscoring talent. Playing for Derby County and Middlesbrough, he was a natural choice for the England team and scored a record 28 goals in just 23 Home Internationals (a total that remained unsurpassed for 50 years). Remarkably, he scored in each of his first ten internationals. His League career, which lasted from 1892 to 1914, was distinguished by an impressive 353 goals in 598 games (292 goals for Derby in 473 matches). Subsequently he worked as a coach in Germany (where he was interned during World War I) and back at Derby.

Bloomfield Road The home ground of the English football club BLACKPOOL. Bloomfield Road belonged originally to the local South Shore team until the Seasiders arrived in 1899 and the two sides were merged. During World War II the ground was used by the RAF as a training centre, after which it witnessed the great deeds of the Matthews era. Its features include its own Kop and the East Stand, nicknamed the 'Scratching Shed'.

Blue, The Nickname of the English non-League football club FRICKLEY ATHLETIC, in reference to the club colours.

Blue and Whites Nickname of the English football club BLACKBURN ROVERS, in reference to the team strip.

Blue Ballet Nickname of the celebrated Colombian team Millionarios between the years 1949 and 1952. Millionarios built up one of the best teams in the world, poaching players from many other countries and operating outside the jurisdiction of FIFA. Based in Bogotá, they dominated the Colombian League, winning the Championship in 1949, 1951, and 1952. Stars with the side included the great forward Alfredo DI STEFANO, who eventually left the club to join Real Madrid in Spain. After Colombia rejoined FIFA the 'Blue Ballet' became one of the great attractions of South American football.

Blue is the Colour Title of a pop song recorded by Chelsea FC in 1972. One of the more successful records, reaching number five in the charts, the tune was adopted by the club's fans and enjoyed a longer life as an unofficial anthem than most other similar attempts.

Blue is the colour,
Football is the game,
We're all together,
And winning is our aim,

So cheer us on through the wind and rain,
For Chelsea, Chelsea is our name.

Bluebirds Nickname of several football clubs that sport a predominantly blue strip. They include the English non-League football club BARROW and the Welsh side CARDIFF CITY.

Blues Nickname of numerous football clubs around the world that have adopted a blue strip. Among the national sides to be popularly dubbed The Blues are Scotland, France, and Italy (the *Azzurri*). Club sides include BARKING, BIRMINGHAM CITY, BURNHAM, BURY TOWN, CARLISLE, CHELSEA, CHESTER CITY, CHESTERFIELD, CROYDON, DUNSTABLE, GAINSBOROUGH TRINITY, HERTFORD TOWN, GRAYS ATHLETIC, IPSWICH TOWN, LANCASTER CITY, LEEK TOWN, LINFIELD, MANCHESTER CITY, MARLOW, METROPOLITAN POLICE, RANGERS, SOUTHEND UNITED, STRANRAER, WARE, WINSFORD UNITED, and WYCOMBE WANDERERS.

Blundell Park The home ground of the English football club GRIMSBY TOWN. Blundell Park is unusual in that it is not actually in the home town of its resident team, being situated in nearby Cleethorpes. Grimsby Town developed the ground in 1899 and it now boasts what is the oldest surviving stand in the League. Local industry is reflected in the name of the Findus Stand, which was partly financed by the frozen fish company, and in the distinctive black and white goal nets, which were donated by a local fishing net company.

boats As in the case of locomotives, there is a long tradition of naming boats – chiefly trawlers – in honour of football clubs. In the 1960s the list of vessels sailing under the names of prominent clubs ran: Aldershot, Barnsley, Blackburn Rovers, Carlisle United, Crystal Palace, Everton, Huddersfield Town, Grimsby Town, Hull City, Nottingham Forest, Notts County, and Real Madrid. The *Notts County* sank in a harbour in Iceland towards the end of the decade, while *Aldershot* and *Everton* were heavily involved in the so-called 'Cod War' with Iceland in 1973.

Boban, Zvonimir (1968–) Yugoslavian-born midfielder, nicknamed Zorro, who emerged as a major talent with Dynamo Zagreb and AC Milan in the late 1980s and early 1990s. Bernard Tapie, owner of the French club Marseille, confidently described him as the 'Maradona of the end of the century'.

Bobby Moore Award English award bestowed upon the League club with the best disciplinary record. The award was renamed in 1993 after the tragically early death from cancer of former England captain Bobby MOORE. *See also* FAIR PLAY AWARD.

Boca Juniors Argentinian football club, which is the most popular in the country. Strip: dark blue shirts with yellow hoop, with dark blue shorts and socks. Founded in 1905 and based at the Bombonera ('Chocolate Box') Stadium in Buenos Aires, the club has won some 17 League championships as well as the South American Cup in 1977 and 1978 and the World Club Championship in 1977.

Boghead Park The home ground of the Scottish football club DUMBARTON. Boghead Park became the team's base as long ago as 1879, when the area was a waterlogged field. It acquired its first stand in 1913 – a structure seating just 80 spectators that was variously dubbed the 'Postage Box' or the 'Hen House'; it was demolished in 1979. Fire destroyed another stand during a game in the 1930s. Elsewhere the so-called Old Stand boasts an ornate roof plundered from a disused railway platform in Ayrshire in the late 1950s.

Bognor Regis Town English non-League football club, nicknamed the Rocks. Strip: white shirts with green trim, green shorts, and white socks. Founded in 1883 and based at Nyewood Lane in Bognor Regis, the Rocks play in the Isthmian League.

Bogotá incident Notorious scandal surrounding England's captain Bobby MOORE that threatened to disrupt the national side's progress in the 1970 World Cup tournament in Mexico. England's hopes of repeating their 1966 triumph in the competition were high and it was expected that other countries would pull out all the stops when it came to facing the English team.

From the very moment of their arrival in Mexico the native press adopted a hostile attitude towards RAMSEY and his men as they conducted their final preparations there and in Colombia and Ecuador. The journalists saw their opportunity when a shopgirl called Clara Padilla, who worked in a jewellery shop in the hotel occupied by the English team in Bogotá (the capital of Colombia), alleged that Bobby Moore had stolen an emerald and diamond bracelet worth £600. Moore strenuously denied any involvement in the matter and the team continued their tour. When the team's plane landed at Bogotá once more on the way to Mexico, the accusation was levelled at Moore again and the team had to go on without their captain, who was detained by the police.

The world's press had a field day as the process of examination and cross-examination went on. Gradually flaws in the allegations came to light and it was discovered that several other notable guests had been accused of similar misdeeds while staying at the hotel – although most of them had paid up to keep the scandal quiet. Moore was released and rejoined his team in Mexico, where he was greeted as a national hero before the competition had even begun.

Bohemians Czech football club, nicknamed the Kangaroos. Strip: green and white. The club was founded in 1905 as Vršovice but acquired its current name in 1926 when members of the team toured Australia and felt the need to be more closely identified with their homeland (Prague being capital of Bohemia before the creation of Czechoslovakia). Bohemians, based at the ground known as the DIMPLE, are famous for their espousal of 'pure' football.

Bökelberg The home ground of the German football club BORUSSIA MÖNCHENGLADBACH. The ground was hastily improved in the 1970s when the home team unexpectedly established themselves as one of the most powerful in the country.

Bolivia The Bolivian national team have generally languished in the shadow of their more illustrious South American neighbours, but have on occasion emerged to take the top honours. The side first took part in the World Cup back in 1930 and reappeared in 1950 (when they lost 8–0 against Uruguay); subsequently they won the South American Championship in 1963. Bolivia qualified for the 1994 World Cup in America. Strip: green shirts with white trim, white shorts with green trim, and green socks.

Bologna Italian football club, nicknamed the Red-Blues. Strip: red and blue striped shirts, blue shorts, and blue socks with red trim. Founded in 1909 and based at the DALL'ARA stadium, Bologna enjoyed their best years in the 1920s and 1930s, when they brought their total of League championships to five; they have since won the

Championship twice more (in 1941 and 1964). The 1964 title was particularly memorable, with a fierce controversy over allegations that Bologna players had taken drugs (accusations that were later dismissed with the restoration of points previously deducted from the club's record) and final victory being gained after a play-off against Internazionale. They can also boast two Cup victories (1970 and 1974).

Bolton Wanderers English football club, nicknamed the Trotters. Strip: white shirts, navy blue shorts, and red socks with blue and white trim. They were called the Reds early on in their history when they wore red and white quartered shirts (subsequently they continued to experiment with different colour schemes – around 1883 they favoured white shirts decorated with red spots, which supposedly had the effect of making players look bigger than they actually were).

The club began life in 1874 as the Christ Church Sunday School team under the teacher Thomas Ogden but subsequently broke from the church after a disagreement with the vicar (their president) in 1877, when they adopted their present name (calling themselves the Wanderers because they had no permanent home ground until 1895).

Wanderers were founder members of the Football League in 1888 and subsequently divided their time exclusively between the top two divisions until the 1970s. The club was heavily involved in the heated debate over professionalism in the 1880s and eventually won its case, with the prohibition against professional players being lifted. On the pitch they reached an FA Cup Final in 1894 and again in 1904 but had to wait until the 1920s for their golden era to begin (with just one Second Division title in 1909 for consolation in the meantime).

Inspired by such star players as David Jack, Joe Smith, and Ted Vizard, Bolton clinched victory in three FA Cup campaigns (1923, 1926, and 1929) while enjoying a 23-year stint in the First Division (1911–33). Remarkably, a total of just 17 different players turned out for the club in the three Finals.

Subsequently the club went into something of a decline, which culminated in 1946 with the deaths of 33 fans at their BURNDEN PARK home (*see* BURNDEN PARK DISASTER). Better times came in the 1950s with the recruitment of Nat LOFTHOUSE and Tommy Banks among others and in 1953 they were FA Cup runners-up once more, losing to Blackpool in the classic MAT-

THEWS FINAL. The Trotters claimed FA Cup victory for a fourth time in 1958, when they overcame Manchester United in the Final, but subsequently drifted down through the divisions over the next 30 years, reaching the bottom level for the first time in 1987 (despite the efforts of players of the calibre of Francis LEE and Freddie Hill).

Wanderers enjoyed their record victory back in 1890, when they beat Sheffield United 13–0; they suffered their worst defeat in 1887, losing 9–1 to Preston North End. Eddie Hopkinson holds the record for League appearances with the club, having played in 519 games between 1956 and 1970. *See also* PIE SATURDAY.

> When I first came into the game, Bolton were the team everybody feared for sheer brute force. Their England international full-back Tommy Banks used to say to Chelsea winger Peter Brabrook: 'If thou tries to get past me, lad, thou will get gravel rash'.
>
> Jimmy Greaves, *This One's On Me* (1979)

Bomber, The Nickname of the West German forward Gerd MÜLLER.

Bonds, Billy English manager who took over West Ham in the late 1990. As a player he joined West Ham in the late 1960s and distinguished himself as a reliable – and formidable – defender:

> If anyone kicked me I used to give Bill a wink and say 'Bonzo! Have you seen what they're doing to me?' Then Bill would sort them out in the next five minutes and I'd have the freedom of the field.
>
> Trevor Brooking, *100 Great British Footballers* (1988)

Bo'Ness Former Scottish League football club, which dropped out of the League in 1932. Based at Newton Park, the side joined the League in 1921; they still exist as a minor league team under the title Bo'Ness United.

Bonetti, Peter (1941–) English goalkeeper, nicknamed The Cat, renowned for his catlike ability to save apparently unreachable shots. On the domestic scene, Bonetti enjoyed a formidable reputation occupying the Chelsea goalmouth over a period of several years, but it is for his part in the England World Cup campaign of 1970 that his name is most often recalled, usually – and somewhat unfairly – with considerable ire.

Bonetti was deputy to Gordon BANKS in

both the 1966 and 1970 tournaments but was never expected to play a major role in events on the field. The crisis came, however, at the quarter-final stage of the 1970 competition when England were due to face West Germany at Leon in Mexico. On the point of leaving for Leon, Banks began to suffer from violent stomach pains; in Leon itself he managed to attend the pre-match meeting but it soon became clear that he would not be able to play in the all-important game. Allegations of 'nobbling' by agents for South American countries – even by the CIA – were rife and in this climate of uproar and consternation, Bonetti found himself in the English goal, having had next to no time to prepare for the ultimate test.

At first all went well and England scored twice, but then everything fell apart when the Cat reacted too slowly to save a shot from BECKENBAUER and minutes later was caught out of position by another shot from Uwe SEELER. Extra time brought the final winning goal, from Gerd MÜLLER, and against all expectations the English team were out of the World Cup. The unfortunate Bonetti had to take the brunt of the blame from the press, although his errors were probably not the only significant factor in England's defeat. *See also* MARX BROTHERS.

bonus The bestowing of some reward over and above the salary due to a player as an incentive for good play. As well as prizes for goals and winning scorelines, players have on occasion even been rewarded for losing less disastrously than was expected – as in the case of the Turkish goalkeeper Alptekin, who in 1980 collected a small cash bonus for only conceding four goals in a match that had been expected to end in complete humiliation for the team.

Sometimes it is the fans themselves who seek to honour a fine performance – in 1953 Arsenal goalkeeper Jack Kelsey was sent £5 from an admiring spectator in gratitude for 'the best save I've ever seen'. From time to time players have been showered with far more lavish gifts than mere cash. As early as the 1910–11 season, players with Morton were given a lamb by a local butcher for every goal scored; centre-forward Tommy Gracie called his Toby and it served loyally as the team's mascot prior to its unexplained premature death in the players' bath.

In 1922 hard man Frank Barson was promised a pub by relegated Manchester United if the team returned to the First Division within five years. The team made it (in 1925) and Barson got his pub in Ardwick;

it proved so busy, however, that after just 15 minutes of business, Barson decided to retire from the hostelry trade and gave the place to his barman.

In 1949 two German village teams were offered bonuses of a bottle of schnapps for every goal scored and the game was not surprisingly distinguished by some fine attacking play: the final scoreline read 25–24. In 1967 players with the Argentinian team Racing received £2000 and a new car after defeating Celtic 1–0 in the World Football Club Championships. In contrast, their luckless opponents were each fined £250 for their ill-tempered behaviour.

The victorious Class of '66 earned a bonus of £1000 for their triumph in the World Cup – and then had to go through a lengthy court case to win exemption from £300 tax on it. When Kuwait qualified for the 1982 World Cup Finals, the Crown Prince offered spectacular bonuses of Cadillacs, villas, plots of land, gold watches, and speedboats to each player, while in 1974 the qualification of Zaïre in the same competition prompted the country's president to promise each player a house, a car, and a holiday. However, the offers were rescinded when Zaïre crashed in all their games, failing to score a single goal.

Among the more unusual bonuses received by British players was the oil well in Canada given to Leeds United player Bill Wainscot; it was donated by an admirer in acknowledgement of a fine goal he had scored during a Canadian tour before World War II. A bonus offered to the Turkish national team by the voluptuous Turkish belly dancer Sether Seniz had a somewhat unsettling effect upon the team. When it was learnt that she would be willing to 'entertain' any member of the team to score a goal in their forthcoming match against West Germany there was a near-revolt by disgruntled defenders.

At the opposite end of the scale, players representing Liberia's Lone Star side in the Africa Cup in 1980 were once offered a negative bonus of the most extreme kind: if they failed to give of their best in a forthcoming game they would all be executed. Fortunately they managed a goalless draw and were spared the firing squad. *See also* BATTLE OF HIGHBURY; DEATH, MATCH OF.

£1 per week should be ample remuneration for the best professional footballer that ever existed.

Football Field, newspaper (1886).

Book, The Nickname of the Welsh referee Clive THOMAS.

booking The taking of a player's name by the referee after the player concerned has committed a serious breach of the laws of the game. If a player is booked twice in the same match he is sent off. Upon booking a player the referee writes the offender's name in a small notebook and holds aloft a yellow card to advise the other players and spectators of the situation. If he offends again he is shown the red card and the yellow card together and ordered off the pitch. After the match the player's name is reported to the relevant authority.

Players can be booked for one of four reasons: for entering or leaving the field of play without permission of the referee, for breaking the laws of the game, for dissenting from the referee's decision, or for ungentlemanly conduct, which can range from foul play to spitting or swearing. After a booking has taken place, play is restarted with a free kick.

It is also possible for a player to be booked while not on the field of play – as Welsh centre-half David Jones discovered in the 1978–79 season when his name was taken for remarks he had made from the trainer's bench. One of the most remarkable instances of a mass booking was in 1975 when a Scottish referee was incensed to hear members of the Glencraig United team taking his name in vain as they indulged in a pre-match chant in their dressing-room. He stormed in and booked all 11 players (and the two substitutes), despite the fact that none of them had yet reached the pitch.

In 1969 during a game between Tongham Youth Club and Hawley one referee went even further: he booked all 22 players on the pitch – and just for good measure added one of the linesmen as well. In 1991 Sheffield United's Vinny JONES set a new record when he was booked for a foul after just five seconds of a match against Manchester City (unrepentant, he was sent off later in the match after another foul).

Bootham Crescent The home ground of YORK CITY. After consulting their fans, York City bought Bootham Crescent from York Cricket Club in 1932. During World War II a bomb caused some damage to the terracing, but otherwise the ground has witnessed few momentous events. It is the only ground in the League to retain a wooden perimeter fence, once a common feature of most grounds.

Boothferry Park The home ground of HULL CITY. Boothferry Park finally replaced Hull City's old ground on Anlaby Road in 1946 after several years of delay, the club having bought the land for the ground back in 1930. Facilities built into the venue at an early stage included its own railway station, called Boothferry Park Halt (opened in 1951), which allows passengers to go through the turnstiles immediately upon leaving the platform. Falling attendances led to the demolition of one stand to make way for a supermarket in 1982. Notable fixtures here over the years have included an international between Northern Ireland and Spain in 1972, played here rather than in Northern Ireland to minimize the risk of violence.

Bootle Former English League football club, which dropped out of the League in 1893. Bootle, based at the Hawthorne Road ground in Liverpool, resigned from the League after just one season, becoming the first side to drop out.

boots Two of the more essential items in the football player's locker. The earliest boots were made of inflexible leather and could cause the wearer great discomfort on being 'broken in'. When, for instance, Wolverhampton Wanderers centre-forward George Hedley split his much-patched boots during the 1908 FA Cup Final against Newcastle United (which Wolves went on to win 3–1) he steadfastly refused to put on a new pair brought out to him by the trainer and carried on with his old pair almost falling off his feet rather than suffer the agony of breaking in the replacements.

Cost was also a problem. In 1893 Tottenham Hotspur nearly lost their amateur status after they provided a player with ten shillings to buy a pair of boots after his own were stolen – the FA suspended the club for two weeks and the player for one week and insisted that the player repay the ten shillings. In the opening years of the 20th century a good pair of boots cost between nine and fourteen shillings.

Subsequent developments over the years have included the use of more supple materials, screw-in studs, and the WHITE BOOTS made famous by such players as Alan BALL and Peter Taylor. In an earlier era Herbert CHAPMAN, later to become the celebrated manager of Huddersfield and Arsenal, played in distinctive yellow boots in the years before World War I.

In 1950 the question of boots led to a major upset in the World Cup when the team representing India, which had qualified for the Finals for the first time, withdrew after they were refused permission to play in bare feet. Remarkably, in the 1930s mighty Celtic once fielded an Egyptian player by the name of Abdul Salim who similarly refused to wear boots and played instead with just bandages wrapped around his feet.

Bordeaux French football club, which emerged as one of the leading French sides of the 1980s. Strip: blue shirts, white shorts, and blue socks. Founded in 1898 and based at the Parc de Lescure in Bordeaux, the team rose to the Second Division in the late 1930s, won the Cup in 1941, and won its first League championship in 1950. The team entered its golden era in 1984 when it won the first of a series of three League titles (1984, 1985, and 1987) as well as the Cup in 1986 and 1987. In international competition, the club reached the semi-finals of the European Cup in 1985 and of the European Cup Winners' Cup in 1987.

Borderers Nickname of the English football club BERWICK RANGERS.

Boreham Wood English non-League football club, nicknamed The Wood. Strip: white shirts, black shorts, and red socks. Founded in 1946 and based at Broughinge Road, The Wood play in the Isthmian League.

Boro Nickname of a number of football clubs with the word 'Borough' in their formal name (or else reflecting a town's borough status). They include FARN-BOROUGH TOWN, GOSPORT BOROUGH, HARROW BOROUGH, MIDDLESBROUGH, NUNEATON BOROUGH, RADCLIFFE BOROUGH, SCARBOROUGH, SOLIHULL BOROUGH, STAF-FORD RANGERS, and STEVENAGE BOROUGH.

Borussia Dortmund German football club, which dominated West German football in the 1950s and 1960s. Strip: yellow shirts, dark brown shorts, and yellow socks. Founded in 1909 and based at the WEST-FALENSTADION in Dortmund, the club won the League championship in 1956, 1957, and 1963 and the Cup in 1965 and 1989. On the international stage, they were also winners of the European Cup Winners' Cup in 1966.

Borussia Mönchengladbach German football club, which enjoyed a golden era in the 1970s. Strip: white shirts with green and blue trim, with white shorts and socks. Founded in 1900 and based at the BÖKEL-BERG Stadium in Mönchengladbach, the club won the League championship in 1970, 1971, 1975, 1976, and 1977 and the Cup in 1960 and 1973. On the international stage the team won the UEFA Cup in 1975 and 1979.

Boss, The *See* MANAGER.

Boston United English non-League football club, nicknamed the Pilgrims. Strip: off-gold shirts, black shorts, and off-gold socks. Founded in 1934 and based at the York Street Ground in Boston, the Pilgrims played in the Alliance Premier League from 1979, being relegated to the Northern Premier League in 1993.

Botafogo Brazilian football club, which ranks as one of the country's leading domestic sides. Strip: black and white striped shirts, with black shorts and socks. Founded in 1904 and based at the General Severiano Stadium in Rio, the club has won 12 League championships and enjoyed a golden era in the 1960s, when its stars included the great GARRINCHA.

Botswana Botswana joined FIFA in 1976 but have yet to make much impact in international competition. Strip: sky blue shirts with white trim, with blue shorts and socks with black and white trim.

Boundary Park The home ground of OLD-HAM ATHLETIC. The first club to be based at Boundary Park was Oldham County, who acquired the land from a brewery in 1896, when a silver spade (preserved at the club) was used to cut the first sod of turf. County folded in 1899 and newly formed Oldham Athletic moved in, but soon left again after an argument about the rent; they returned for good in 1906.

Oddities among the ground's features in the early days included a flat roof that was used both by spectators and by the manager, who ran its length while following play on the pitch. Landmarks in the ground's history have included gale damage in 1927, the arrival of undersoil heating in 1980, and in 1986 the installation of artificial turf; the original turf was relaid as a lawn at a hospital nearby. The grass was soon replaced, however, under an order from the League.

Local legend has it that the covered Chadderton Road End is haunted by a ghost called Fred, a particularly loyal fan who always occupied the same place in the stand, dying there during a match in the 1960s.

AFC Bournemouth English football club, nicknamed the Cherries. Strip: red and black striped shirts, with white shorts and socks. Founded in 1899, the Cherries had their origins in the Boscombe St John's team, which had been formed in 1890. The team, based since 1910 at DEAN COURT, was elected to the Third Division (South) in 1923 and subsequently became the longest-serving member of the division before finally being demoted to the Fourth Division in 1970, where they remained for just one season. They were demoted again in 1975, returned to the Third Division in 1982 and in 1987 succeeded in reaching the Second Division; they returned to the Third Division in 1990.

The club's achievements have included getting through to the sixth round of the FA Cup in 1957 and winning the Associate Members' Cup in 1984. The 1957 Cup run was especially memorable for the giant-killing act the Cherries pulled off against mighty Wolverhampton Wanderers in the fourth round, defeating them 1–0. The winning goal was scored by Reg Cutler, who was also responsible for another moment of drama in the match when he collided with the goalpost and brought the whole goal crashing down. The team also notched up a surprise victory against Tottenham Hotspur before going out to Manchester United.

Otherwise, Bournemouth have enjoyed few moments of glory; the renaming of the club as AFC Bournemouth in 1971 in an attempt at least to head alphabetical lists, was ill-received by the fans. Recent directors of the club have included comedian Jim Davidson.

The club's record victory stands at 11–0 against Margate in 1971, on which occasion Ted McDougall established an FA Cup record by scoring no fewer than nine times. The Cherries suffered their record defeat in 1982, losing 9–0 to Lincoln City. Ray Bumstead holds the record for League appearances with the team, having played in 412 games between 1958 and 1970.

box A small area of seating, often glassed in or otherwise made more comfortable than accommodation elsewhere in a stadium, that is reserved for VIPs or wealthier fans who have paid sometimes very large sums for the privilege of sitting there. One step removed from the atmosphere of the terraces, the occupants of boxes are usually considered with a certain amount of scorn and resentment by the mass of ordinary fans, who often brave the elements with a minimum of shelter. Nonetheless, suites of executive boxes have become a feature of many grounds both in the UK and throughout Europe and the finance produced in this way has helped to keep many a struggling club afloat. The very first such boxes to be installed at an English ground were opened at Old Trafford in the 1960s. The facilities offered in the Old Trafford boxes include a switch that allows the occupants to raise or lower the sound that comes in from outside.

Boy Nickname of the talented English forward Cliff BASTIN.

boys' stand In many football grounds, an area of the terracing or stands reserved for minors, who are often admitted at reduced prices. The existence of such stands more or less ended under the pressures of profit-making, safety changes, and the modernization of leading stadia although the arrival of new family enclosures echoes the tradition. *See* SAFE; FAMILY ENCLOSURE.

Bozsik, Jozsef (1925–) Hungarian right-half, who played a crucial role in the enormously successful Hungarian national team of the early 1950s. A star at home with Honved and winner of 100 caps, he played in the World Cups of 1954 and 1958 and in the Olympics of 1952.

Bracknell Town English non-League football club, nicknamed the Robins. Strip: all red. Founded in 1894 and based at the Larges Lane ground in Bracknell, the Robins play in the Isthmian League.

Bradford City English football club, nicknamed the Bantams. Strip: amber shirts with claret stripes, claret shorts, and amber socks. Founded in 1903, Bradford City were elected to the League before they had even assembled a team (as a result of the soccer establishment's hopes of challenging the hold of rugby in the area) but notwithstanding went on to capture the Second Division championship in 1908 and then continued their progress until they were ranked fifth in the First Division in 1911, the year that they also won the FA Cup.

Unfortunately, the club subsequently declined and have never equalled those early achievements. Relegation in 1922 was followed by a gradual retreat to the Fourth Division, which they finally reached in the 1960s. 1985 saw Bradford back in the Second Division, but the celebrations were brought to a premature end at the close of the season with a disastrous fire at their VALLEY PARADE ground (*see* BRADFORD

FIRE). The trauma had a lasting effect upon the club and there was talk of moving to a new ground, but sentimental attachment and an agreement to modernize Valley Parade dictated that it would remain the club's permanent home.

The Bantams enjoyed their record victory in 1928, when they beat Rotherham 11–1; they suffered their worst defeat in 1961, when they lost 9–1 against Colchester United. Cec Podd holds the record for League appearances for the club, having played 502 times between 1970 and 1984. The club's arch-rivals are Leeds United, taking the place of the now-defunct Bradford Park Avenue team.

> We're Bradford City, the pride of the North,
> We hate Newcastle, and Leeds of course,
> We drink our whisky, and bottles of brown,
> The Bradford boys are in town,
> Na, na, na, na, na, na, na, na, na, na, na, na, na.
>
> Supporters' song, to the tune of 'Just one of those songs'

Bradford fire The blaze at Bradford City's home ground Valley Parade on 11 May 1985 that claimed 56 lives and left 200 people suffering from burns in one of football's most horrific tragedies. The disaster came on a day that was meant to be a celebration of Bradford's success in winning the Third Division championship, with 11,000 fans turning up to see a parade and the presentation of the trophy and to cheer their team on in a late-season match with Lincoln City.

Shortly before half time one of the fans in Block G in the main stand noticed smoke coming up through a crack in the flooring and felt heat on his right leg. Another fan poured the remains of a cup of coffee into the crack while someone else called the police and the fire brigade were notified. No one thought there was anything much to worry about and spectators nearby assumed it was a smoke bomb. Five minutes later the entire stand was ablaze.

The flames, probably the result of a lighted match or discarded cigarette setting fire to the mounds of rubbish that had accumulated over many years beneath the stand, spread faster than a person could run and soon the whole of the roof of the structure was burning, raining timber and molten felt on to spectators. Only the most agile spectators in the path of the flames were able to save themselves, as one later recalled: 'I danced over the seats pursued by flames.'

Fans who tried to escape the inferno by leaving through exits at the back of the stand and through the toilets found gates boarded up and turnstiles locked; others – including one elderly man on fire from head to toe – sought refuge by getting on to the pitch. The young and the old had little chance: among the dead was the club's oldest supporter, Sam Firth, who was aged 86. Television cameras recorded the whole event – to the anger of some of the crowd – and witnessed several acts of bravery as fans and policemen tried to save those at risk.

The causes of the tragedy and the lessons to be learnt from it were investigated in full in the Popplewell Inquiry that followed. Among other observations, the report concluded that had the recommendations of the 'Green Guide' – a government publication on safety matters published back in 1976 – been complied with there would have been no disaster. Among those recommendations was the removal of rubbish from beneath stands: a newspaper found in the debris at Bradford dated back to 1968 and a peanut bar wrapper also found there carried a price in pre-decimal currency. Ironically, the roof of Valley Parade's old Main Stand, which burnt so readily in the fire, had been due for demolition the very next day.

> A carelessly discarded cigarette could give rise to a fire risk.
>
> Letter from West Yorkshire County Council to Bradford City FC (July 1984)

Bradford Park Avenue Former English football club, nicknamed the Stans. Strip: white with green trim. The Stans (or Avenuites) were formed in 1907 by members of Bradford Rugby club, who hoped to emulate the success of Bradford's other senior football team, Bradford City. Based at Park Avenue, the team joined the Football League after just one season, in 1908, and in 1914 began a three-year stint in the First Division.

Their golden era was in the 1930s, when the side was one of the strongest in the Second Division and was generally considered superior to rivals Bradford City. Derby matches between the Avenue and City were much relished by local fans; at the time that the Avenue folded they were ahead by just one win in League fixtures between the two clubs.

The Avenue's fortunes declined after the 1950s and they had to seek re-election to the League five times, finally losing their place in 1970. Subsequently the club were obliged to vacate Park Avenue and to share Valley Parade with City. Bradford Park Avenue finally went out of existence in 1974; the stands at Park Avenue were demolished in 1980.

It could have all been very different though. In 1953 the club was on the search for a new manager and ended up with a shortlist of two names. The Stans chose Norman Kirkman, who stayed for just a year before moving on to jobs as a baker, estate agent, aircraft worker, insurance representative, and travelling salesman. The rejected applicant was Bill SHANKLY.

Stars connected with the side included the great Len SHACKLETON, who spent six seasons (1940–46) with the club and scored over 160 goals, Ron GREENWOOD, who joined the side as a player back in 1945, and Kevin Hector. Among the records held by the club was the less than enviable one of having become the first club to make a 'double drop' through the divisions, when in 1921 they were relegated to the Second Division and a year later were sent down to the Third.

It was while playing with Avenue that Jim Fryatt scored what is the fastest League goal ever recorded, putting his team ahead during a match against Tranmere Rovers in 1964 after just four seconds.

The club was revived in the 1988–89 season and is now based at Bramley Rugby League club:

> Our long-term aim is to get back in the League . . . it won't be a six-month thing – we want to make nice, steady progress. At the moment we have no ground, no manager, and no team.
>
> Bob Robinson, chairman-elect of the revived club (1988)

Brady, Liam (1956–   ) Irish midfielder, who was a pillar of the Republic of Ireland's national squad throughout the 1970s and 1980s. He began his international career in 1974, while he was with Arsenal, and played a key role in the Republic's successes in the World Cup, winning 72 caps in all. Later in his career he also played in Italy for Juventus, Sampdoria, Internazionale, and Ascoli, and managed Celtic.

Braintree Town English non-League football club. Strip: yellow and blue. Founded in 1894 and based at Cressing Road in Braintree, the club play in the Southern League.

Bramall Lane The home ground of SHEF-FIELD UNITED. Bramall Lane existed as a sports venue some time before the Blades were founded in 1889, being originally the home of Sheffield Cricket Club, who leased the ground from the Duke of Norfolk. Until 1973, the football pitch existed alongside the cricket pitch, overlapping by 20 yards. Sheffield FC, the oldest football club in the world, were the first to play football at Bramall Lane (in 1862) and other users included The Wednesday (later Sheffield Wednesday). In 1878 the ground witnessed the first football match played under flood-lighting; other landmarks in Bramall's history have included damage from ten bombs in World War II.

Brazil The Brazilian national team has the most illustrious record of all national sides and remains the most glamorous of the world's teams. Participants in the very first World Cup in 1930, the team has taken part in every World Cup Finals since and have a record of success unequalled by any other nation. Host nation in 1950, they lost 2–1 to Uruguay before an all-time record crowd of 200,000 at the MARACANA Stadium and got as far as the quarter-finals four years later. In 1958 they stormed all the way to the Final and convincingly beat hosts Sweden 5–2. Four years later they repeated the feat, defeating Czechoslovakia 3–1 and – after a disappointing performance in 1966 – won again in 1970, when their 4–1 victory over Italy in the Final meant that they won the Jules Rimet Trophy outright. The team's other honours have included wins in the South American Championship in 1919, 1922, 1949, and 1989. Brazil qualified for the 1994 World Cup in America. Strip: yellow shirts with green trim, blue shorts, and white socks with green and yellow trim.

Brechin City Scottish football club, nick-named City. Strip: red with white trim. Founded in 1906 when the two local teams Hearts and Harp were merged, the name City is something of a misnomer as Brechin itself has a population of around 6500, making it the smallest place in the UK to boast a League team. The club joined the Scottish League in 1929 and won the Division C championship in 1954, and the Division Two title in 1983 and 1990. No player has ever won international honours while based at City's home, GLEBE PARK.

The club's record victory stands at 12–1 against Thornhill in 1926; in 1937–38 City suffered the embarrassment of three successive record defeats against Airdrieonians, Albion Rovers, and Cowdenbeath, all with a scoreline of 10–0. David Watt holds the record for League appearances with the club, having played in 459 matches between 1975 and 1989.

In their long and illustrious history, 1906–86 – or, as they're known here, the wilderness years – records have come easily to Brechin City. They were the first club to dabble in sponsorship, when the people of Brechin offered them money to go to play somewhere else.

Satirical profile, *Only an Excuse*, BBC Radio Scotland (1986)

Bremner, Billy (1942–) Scottish midfielder, who played a key role in Don REVIE's enormously successful Leeds United squad in the early 1970s. Fiery and determined, Bremner joined Leeds in 1959 and made his first appearance for Scotland in 1965. In 1968, forming a brilliant partnership with Johnny GILES, he helped United to victory in both the League Cup and the Fairs Cup and a year later was rewarded with the captaincy. Having led Leeds to the League championship in 1969, he was voted Footballer of the Year in 1970 and went on to enjoy FA Cup victory in 1972. Another League medal followed in 1974 and a year later he won the last of his 54 caps for Scotland.

After a brief period with Hull City, Bremner became player-manager for Doncaster Rovers (1978) and eventually (1985) returned to his old club Leeds as manager. Sacked in 1988, he returned to Doncaster in 1989 for another two years.

Brentford English football club, nicknamed the Bees. Strip: red and white striped shirts, black shorts, and red socks with black tops. Founded in 1889, the club turned professional in 1899 and acquired a permanent home at GRIFFIN PARK in 1904. They collected a shoal of local titles in the last years of the 19th century and in 1929, while in the Third Division, became the only League club to win every single one of their home fixtures (21 in all).

Their resourceful manager in the 1920s was Harry Curtis. On one occasion when the Bees were 2–1 down to Oldham Athletic he seized the opportunity when fog descended and play was temporarily abandoned to herd his team quickly into the bath. When the referee attempted to restart play Curtis protested that the health of his players would be put at risk and the referee had no option but to postpone the match. Fortunately for Curtis, the referee was not around when the team emerged from their bath: many of them were still wearing their boots. Brentford won the replay 4–2.

The team's heyday was in the late 1930s, when the club played (1935–47) in the First Division after a meteoric rise from the Third Division in just three seasons. Brentford returned to the Third Division in 1947, since when their first real significant achievement was a place as runners-up in the Freight Rover Trophy tournament in 1985. In 1992 they were promoted to the Second Division. In the 1960s financial problems threatened a merger with Queen's Park Rangers. Apprentices with the club in the early 1960s included one Rod Stewart, who left in order to pursue a career in pop music.

The club enjoyed their record victory in 1963, when they defeated Wrexham 9–0; they lost by a record 7–0 against Swansea Town in 1924 and by the same margin against Walsall in 1957. Ken Coote holds the record for the most League appearances with 514 games for the club between 1949 and 1964.

Brewers (1) Nickname of the English non-League football club BURTON ALBION, in reference to Burton-on-Trent's long history as a centre of the beermaking industry.

(2) Former nickname of the English football club WATFORD. The nickname was first heard in the 1920s, when Benskins Breweries provided considerable financial support for the club.

bribe scandals From time to time the soccer establishment around the world has been rocked by major scandals involving bribes offered to leading players and clubs. Such nefarious dealings date back to the earliest days when the game began to attract significant amounts of money.

Among the most infamous early examples was the 1913 scandal involving attempts to persuade players for West Bromwich Albion to 'throw' a game – captain Jessie Pennington persuaded the culprit to put the offer of £55 (£5 for each player) on paper and then turned the evidence over to the police; the offender was duly arrested and imprisoned for five months. Another early case was the 1915 bribery scandal involving Manchester United and Liverpool: allegations that a game between them had been fixed so that those concerned could win heavily by gambling on the result led ultimately to nine players being suspended. The players' activities were in direct contravention of an 1892 ban on football club members betting on matches.

Another major bribe scandal hit the British game in 1965 (eight years after the ban was lifted), when a substantial game-fixing network was uncovered by the *Sunday People* newspaper (*see* SOCCER CONSPIRACY CASE). More recently Swindon Town were debarred from taking their place in the First Division in 1990 after they were accused of making 'irregular' payments.

Similar scandals in other countries have included the notorious 1983 Hungarian match-fixing conspiracy, which resulted in no fewer than 260 players and 14 referees being suspended with 75 people being convicted, and another involving the Belgian club Standard Liège in 1984, which implicated the club's most senior officials – including the president and coach. In 1993 French football was shaken to the core when European Cup winners Marseille were accused of match-fixing, threatening punitive relegation of the club in its finest hour. *See also* BONUS.

Bridgnorth Town English non-League football club, nicknamed Town. Strip: blue shirts, white shorts, and blue socks. Founded in 1946 and based at Crown Meadow in Bridgnorth, the club play in the Southern League.

Bridlington Town English non-League football club, nicknamed the Seasiders. Strip: all red. Founded in 1925 and based at the Queensgate ground in Bridlington, the Seasiders play in the Northern Premier League.

Bright Side of Life, Always Look on the Title of supporters' song heard at numerous grounds in the late 1980s. Originally sung by Eric Idle in the Monty Python film *The Life of Brian* (1979), the song's ironic content lent it perfectly to the footballing context, particularly to those occasions when defeat was imminent. Various claims have been made as to which band of supporters first took up the song; among the strongest of these is that of Fulham although it was its repetition by the supporters of Manchester United that established its popularity throughout the UK.

Brighton and Hove Albion English football club, nicknamed the Seagulls. Strip: blue and white striped shirts, blue shorts with red trim, and blue socks. Also nicknamed the Shrimps and the Albion, the club began life in 1900 as successors to the disbanded side Brighton United. Brighton settled permanently at the GOLD-

STONE GROUND in 1902 and joined the League in 1920 as founder members of the Third Division. Promotion to the Second Division did not come until 1958, after which the club moved between all three lower divisions until achieving a place in the First Division (1979–83). Brighton narrowly missed the chance to return to the First Division in 1991, when they lost a play-off match against Notts County.

In terms of honours the Seagulls won the Third Division (South) title in 1958 and the Fourth Division title in 1965, as well as winning the Charity Shield (by beating Aston Villa) in 1910 and finishing runners-up in the FA Cup in 1983 (when they lost the replay against Manchester United by 4–0 after holding them to a draw in the initial game – a feat that had manager Jimmy Melia dancing a soft-shoe shuffle in delight).

Famous names associated with the club have included manager Alan Mullery, defender Mark Lawrenson, and forward Andy Ritchie; comedian Norman Wisdom has also served on the club's board of directors.

Brighton enjoyed their record victory in 1965, when they beat Wisbech 10–1; they suffered their worst defeat in 1958 in their very first Second Division fixture, losing 9–0 to Middlesbrough. Ernie 'Tug' Wilson holds the record for League appearances with the club, having played in 509 games between 1922 and 1936; on two occasions he attempted to complete 100 games in succession, but was foiled both times by injury when on 99. *See also* CELERY SONG.

Good old Sussex by the sea,
Good old Sussex by the sea,
For we're going up,
And we'll win the Cup,
For Sussex by the sea.

Traditional supporters' song, purloined from soldiers of the Sussex Regiment during World War I

Brisbane Road The home ground, in east London, of LEYTON ORIENT. The O's had a number of grounds before Brisbane Road, including a substantial site in Millfields Road (1900–30) and briefly (1930) Wembley itself. The O's proved incapable of attracting the size of crowds that the Wembley owners sought, however, and the club finally moved to Brisbane Road in 1937, replacing Leyton Amateurs. The ground houses the widest pitch in the League.

Bristol City English football club, nick-named the Robins. Strip: red shirts, white shorts, and red socks. The club was formed (as Bristol South End) in 1894 and adopted the present name three years later on turn-ing professional. They merged with Bed-minster in 1901, in which year they joined the League (as members of the Second Divi-sion), and in 1904 they moved to their per-manent home at ASHTON GATE. Two years later the Robins, whose early stars included centre-half Billy Wedlock, captured the Second Division championship and went on to finish as runners-up in the First Division (1907) and losing finalists in the FA Cup (1909).

Bristol City's record since the first decade of the 20th century has been less distin-guished with the team having to wait until the 1970s before a return to the First Divi-sion (1976–80); at other times they have experienced life in all three of the lower divisions (with extinction only narrowly averted during a cash crisis in 1982). Their decline from the top level to the Fourth Division in the early 1980s was spectacular with the club plummeting 86 places in the League in just over three years. Star players with the side over the years have included forward John Atyeo in the 1950s and 1960s. Their honours include the Welsh Cup (1934) and the Freight Rover Trophy (1986).

The club enjoyed their record victory in 1960, when they beat Chichester 11–0; they suffered their worst defeat in 1934, losing 9–0 against Coventry City. John Atyeo holds the record for League appearances with the club, having played in 597 matches between 1951 and 1966. Arch rivals are Bristol Rovers:

> *Drink up thee cider, drink up thee cider,*
> *For tonight we'll merry, merry be,*
> *We went down the Rovers,*
> *To do the bastards over,*
> *So drink up thee cider in the jar.*

Supporters' song

> *It's bad enough to have to go and watch*
> *Bristol City without having things stolen.*

Desmond Vowden QC, passing sentence on man who broke into a City fan's car (1984)

Bristol Rovers English football club, nick-named the Pirates. Strip: blue and white quartered shirts, white shorts, and blue socks with white trim. The club was formed in 1883 as the Black Arabs (because they wore black shirts) and a year later were renamed Eastville Rovers, as which they settled at the Eastville Stadium (home of Harlequin Rugby Club).

Bristol Rovers adopted their present name in 1898 and joined the League in 1920 as founder members of the Third Divi-sion. Since then they have divided their time between the Second and Third divisions. One of their darkest hours was in 1939, when the very existence of the club was threatened by the need to apply for re-election to the League and by the side's sub-stantial debts. Further gloom came in 1963, when two Rovers players were suspended for life after a bribe scandal. Brighter moments were enjoyed in 1951, when the team reached the quarter-finals of the FA Cup and in 1953, when the side captured the Third Division (South) title (they won the Third Division championship again in 1990).

In 1986 the Rovers finally vacated their old home at Eastville (which had been severely damaged by a fire in 1980) and moved outside Bristol to TWERTON PARK, the home of Bath City, to enter into one of the first long-term ground-sharing schemes.

Stars of the side have numbered amongst them strikers Geoff Bradford and Alfie Biggs in the 1950s and goalkeeper Nigel Martyn in the 1980s. Back in the 1920s Eddie HAPGOOD began his illustrious career with the club, but was allowed to drift away in 1925 to non-League Kettering Town and thence to mighty Arsenal.

The Pirates have enjoyed record 7–0 vic-tories against Brighton and Hove Albion (1952), Swansea Town (1954), and Shrews-bury Town (1964); they suffered their big-gest defeat in 1936, when they lost 12–0 against Luton Town. Among other notable matches have been two meetings with Man-chester United (in 1956 and 1972), both of which ended with Rovers emerging con-vincing winners (by 4–0 and 2–1 respec-tively). Rovers can also claim the somewhat dubious honour of being the first League club to have played a match behind bars, having competed against a team of prisoners at Erlestoke Prison in Wiltshire in 1982. Stuart Taylor holds the record for League appearances with the team, having played in 545 games between 1966 and 1980.

British Empire Exhibition Cup British cup tournament that was held in 1938 between a number of English and Scottish teams. The teams that competed for the Cup (which was the same trophy awarded as the British League Cup in 1902) were Aberdeen, Celtic, Heart of Midlothian, Rangers, Brentford, Chelsea, Everton, and

Sunderland; Celtic won, as in 1902, over-powering Everton 1–0 in the final.

British Home Championship *See* HOME INTERNATIONAL.

British League Cup Anglo-Scottish competition that was held in 1902. Sympathy for the victims in the IBROX PARK DISASTER inspired the first of several occasional tournaments arranged specifically for teams from England and Scotland. This first tournament in 1902 was contested by Celtic, Rangers, Everton, and Sunderland, Celtic beating Rangers 3–2 in the Final. *See also* BRITISH EMPIRE EXHIBITION CUP; CORONATION CUP.

broadcasts *See* RADIO; TELEVISION.

Brockville Park The home ground of the Scottish football club FALKIRK. Brockville Park, then just a field, was the very first home of the Bairns when they were formed in 1876. Subsequently they moved to other sites before returning to Brockville Park in 1882 and settling permanently. Notable events in the ground's history have included a fire that destroyed the Grandstand in 1908 and an occasion when a ball kicked out of the ground landed in a railway truck and travelled another 43 miles to Perth before it could be retrieved.

broken time The issue that led to the four British home countries withdrawing from FIFA in 1928. In an era when the FA was still torn over the subject of amateurism, it was inevitable that FIFA's demand that amateurs be paid broken time payments to make up for earnings lost through regular employment would meet an impassioned response. Although such a decision had already been taken by the Olympic Games organizers, under pressure from FIFA, the UK authorities held out, believing that such payments would damage the game irrevocably and lead to the much-despised shamateurism.

Accordingly the four home countries not only backed out of the Olympics but also resigned from FIFA. As a result teams from the UK did not compete in the World Cup competitions of 1930, 1934, and 1938. The rift was finally healed in 1946, although the question of broken time payments remained unresolved for many years, only ceasing to be a contentious issue when the distinction between amateur and professional was dropped in 1974. *See also* AMATEUR FOOTBALL; PROFESSIONALISM.

Bromley English non-League football club, nicknamed the Lilywhites. Strip: white shirts, black shorts, and white socks. Founded in 1892 and based at Hayes Lane in Bromley since 1938, the Lilywhites have played in the Isthmian League since 1952. Previously they had won the Athenian League championship three times; they captured the Isthmian title in 1909, 1910, 1954, and 1961. They also won the FA Amateur Cup three times.

Bromsgrove Rovers English non-League football club, nicknamed the Rovers. Strip: red shirts, black shorts, and red socks. Founded in 1885 and based at the Victoria Ground in Bromsgrove, Rovers play in the Conference.

Broxburn United Former Scottish League football club, which dropped out of the League in 1926. Based at the Sports Park, West Lothian, United first joined the League in 1921.

Clubbe Brugge KV Belgian football club, which enjoyed a golden era in the 1970s. Strip: light and dark blue shirts, light blue shorts, and light and dark blue socks. Founded in 1891 and based at the Olympiastadion in Brugges, the club won the League championship in 1920, 1973, 1976, 1977, 1978, 1980, 1988, 1990, and 1992 and the Cup in 1968, 1970, 1977, and 1986. The team were also losing finalists in the UEFA Cup in 1976 and in the European Cup in 1978 (losing both times to Liverpool).

Brunei Brunei joined FIFA in 1969 but have yet to make much impact in international competition. Strip: gold shirts, black shorts, and gold socks.

Brunton Park The home ground of CARLISLE UNITED. The third home of the Cumbrians, Brunton Park first played host to them in 1909 but in its early years it never inspired much love from those associated with this outpost of the League, which prompted one writer to observe: 'the notion that a ball kicked over the wall would go bouncing until it dropped off the end of the world is hard to shake off'. Bill SHANKLY, who joined the Cumbrians in 1949, wrote the ground off as 'a hencoop, a glorified hencoop', while Pat Waters scorned the Main Stand as a 'big wooden rabbit hutch'. In 1953 the whole of the Main Stand was burnt to the ground and subsequently Brunton Park got a facelift.

Bryn The police dog whose intervention in an end-of-season match at Torquay in 1987 helped settle which of three clubs would become the first to be automatically relegated from the Fourth Division. On the final day of the season Torquay United, Burnley, and Lincoln City were all in danger of relegation. Much depended on Torquay's performance and when they slipped 2–0 behind opponents Crewe Alexandra it seemed likely that they would be the first club to lose their League status under the new system of automatic relegation. They managed to claw one goal back but with only minutes left the task seemed impossible. Then Bryn, a police dog on duty that day, took control of the matter, rushing on to the pitch and biting Torquay star Jim McNichol, scorer of their single goal. The referee called a halt and in the resulting injury time Torquay made one last effort. They surged into attack and in the very last minute scored the equalizer they needed through Paul Dobson. Lincoln City went down on goal difference to the GM Vauxhall Conference and Bryn feasted on a steak donated by the Torquay chairman Lew Pope.

bubbles 'I'm Forever Blowing Bubbles': the unofficial anthem of West Ham. A popular music-hall song of the Victorian era, it was particularly associated in that period with advertisements for Pears soap, in which a small child blows soapy bubbles. As a football song, it was adopted by West Ham supporters on the occasion of the 1923 White Horse Final at Wembley, which their team lost. A recording of the song released in 1975, the year that the team won their second FA Cup title, reached number 31 in the charts.

I'm forever blowing bubbles,
Pretty bubbles in the air,
They fly so high, nearly touch the sky,
Then like my dreams they fade and die.
Fortune's always hiding,
I've looked everywhere,
I'm forever blowing bubbles,
Pretty bubbles in the air.

Buchan, Charlie (1891–1960) English inside-forward, who was a highly effective component of the Lucky Arsenal side created by Herbert CHAPMAN in the late 1920s. He played for Leyton and Sunderland before joining Arsenal in 1925 and won just six caps for England.

Buckingham Town English non-League football club, nicknamed the Robins. Strip: all red. Founded in 1883 and based at Ford Meadow in Buckingham, the Robins play in the Southern League.

Buckley Babes Nickname of the teams assembled by Wolverhampton Wanderers manager Major Frank Buckley in the 1930s, which were notable for the inclusion of several gifted young players. Under Buckley Wolves earned a reputation for thrilling, tireless play and reached the Final of the 1939 FA Cup, losing against expectation to Portsmouth, as well as finishing as runners-up in the League championship in 1938 and 1939. Many of Buckley's discoveries – notably Bryn Jones and John CHARLES – went on to become household names with other clubs.

Buckley himself, who had played at centre-half for Derby County and England, also worked as a manager for Notts County, Hull City, Leeds United, and Walsall (by which time he was well into his seventies). His name is now most often recalled for the much discussed 'monkey gland treatment' Buckley was rumoured to have recommended for his 1939 FA Cup Final side (the 'treatment' consisted, in fact, of inoculations against the common cold).

Bucks Nickname of the English non-League football club BUXTON.

Buddies Nickname of the Scottish football club ST MIRREN, after the nickname (coined during the years of mass emigration to Canada and elsewhere) associated with the inhabitants of Paisley itself.

Budgie Nickname of the English forward Johnny BYRNE.

Bulgaria The Bulgarian national team has regularly qualified for the finals of the major international competitions but has yet to turn qualification into ultimate success. They first qualified for the Finals of the World Cup in 1962 but it was not until their fifth appearance, in 1986, that they progressed beyond the first round. Their other honours included two victories in the Balkan Cup in the 1930s and in the European Youth Championship (1959 and 1969). Bulgaria qualified for the 1994 World Cup in America.

Bull, Steve (1965–) English forward, nicknamed the Tipton Terror, whose career blossomed with Wolverhampton Wanderers in the late 1980s. Having transferred to Wolves from West Bromwich Albion in

1986, he scored an impressive total of 52 goals in the 1987–88 season and became the darling of the Molineux crowd as well as establishing a place in the England squad.

> Hark, now hear the West Bank sing,
> A new king's born today,
> His name is Stevie Bull,
> And he's better than Andy Gray.

Wolves supporters' song

Bully Wee Nickname of the Scottish football club CLYDE, in reference to one of their most celebrated forward line-ups (in which the players concerned were all short in stature but renowned for their toughness).

Bundesliga The German Football League, since 1990 also comprising teams from what was formerly East Germany.

Burkina Faso Burkina Faso joined FIFA in 1964 but have yet to make much impact in international competition. Strip: red shirts, green shorts, and red socks.

Burma Burma joined FIFA in 1947 but have yet to establish themselves as a strong international side. Strip: red shirts, white shorts, and red socks.

Burnden Park The home ground of BOLTON WANDERERS. The Wanderers had a number of homes before they settled at Burnden Park in 1895 (hence the name Wanderers). When the club first arrived the site was no more than a rubbish dump overlooked by a railway; legend has it that the pitch was laid over a foundation of barrels and cotton bales. The venue was soon to play host, however, to the most prestigious event in the football calendar – the FA Cup Final (*see* PIE SATURDAY).

After the 1946 BURNDEN PARK DISASTER, extensive changes were made to ensure that no such catastrophe ever happened again. The area of the ground where the disaster occurred finally disappeared in 1986, when a large section of the Railway End was obliterated to make way for a supermarket. It was Burnden Park that was depicted in L.S. Lowry's famous painting *Going to the Match*; it also featured in a scene from the film *Love Match* (1954), starring Arthur Askey.

Burnden Park disaster Football disaster that occurred at Burnden Park, home of Bolton Wanderers, on 9 March 1946,

resulting in the loss of 33 lives. The tragedy occurred just before a quarter-final Cup-tie against Stoke City, an event that had attracted a large crowd of 85,000 fans to the ground. The turnstiles were soon blocked with people and large numbers of supporters entered the ground through forced doors and over walls and fences. One man present decided to take his son out of the ground and picked a locked door: thousands more rushed in through it. Many spectators fell and were trampled but still more fans entered the ground.

The most serious congestion was in the north-west corner, at the Railway End; as the players came on to the pitch two barriers behind the corner flag collapsed and a mass of people fell forwards, leading to many deaths from crushing and asphyxiation. The game began but was then halted while the bodies were laid out on the pitch. Most of the crowd remained unaware of the fact that many people had been killed and to prevent further trouble the police and the referee decided to continue play; many fans left the ground at the end of the game quite ignorant of the fact that they had been present at what was at the time the worst catastrophe in the history of football. The Moelwyn Hughes Report into the disaster recommended limitations on crowd size and the licensing of grounds.

Burnham English non-League football club, nicknamed the Blues. Strip: blue and white shirts, blue shorts, and white socks. Founded in 1876 and based at Wymers Wood Road, Burnham play in the Southern League.

Burnley English football club, nicknamed the Clarets. Strip: claret shirts with sky blue sleeves, with white shorts and socks (though they played originally in green). Founded in 1881 by members of the disbanded Burnley Rovers rugby team, the Clarets played rugby themselves for a year before deciding to switch to soccer in 1882 at a meeting at the Bull Hotel.

The club was a founder member of the League in 1888, winning the Second Division title in 1898 and their first major honour in 1914, when they captured the FA Cup. Subsequently they rose to the top of the First Division, winning the Championship title in 1921 through the efforts of such outstanding players as half-backs George Halley, Tommy Boyle, and William Watson, and goalkeeper Jerry Dawson (who played in 522 League games from 1907 to 1928 and had no fewer than 47 understudies).

Burnley then went into something of a decline until after World War II, when they returned to First Division glory under the management of Bob Lord and others. Their achievements of the 1940s included the remarkable 1946–47 season in which they let in only 32 goals over a total of 51 games. The club brought the First Division championship to TURF MOOR once more in 1960, when stars of the team included Jimmy Adamson and Jimmy MCILROY, but then embarked on a protracted and disastrous journey down through the divisions (despite picking up the Second Division title in 1973 and the Third Division championship in 1982). In 1987 the club – once one of the strongest in the land – escaped relegation from the League itself by the narrowest of margins, winning their crucial last match of the season.

Burnley enjoyed record victories in 1892, when they beat Darwen 9–0, and in 1909, when they beat Crystal Palace by the same score; they suffered record 10–0 defeats against Aston Villa in 1925 and against Sheffield United in 1929.

It was the worst and the best day of my life.

Brian Miller, Burnley manager, on avoiding relegation in 1987

burst balls It is relatively rare for a ball to burst during play, but such events have been recorded from time to time. The earliest such incident in an FA Cup Final was in 1946, when in the match between Derby County and Charlton Athletic the ball unexpectedly burst as Derby's powerful centre-forward Jack Stamps shot at goal. Stamps had the satisfaction of scoring twice with the new ball and his team won 4–1 (the match was also notable for the fact that it saw the unfortunate Charlton player Bert Turner become the first man to score for both sides in an FA Cup Final). The chances of the ball bursting during the match had been estimated by the referee E.D. Smith as a million to one, yet amazingly one year later exactly the same thing happened in the 1947 Final. There has since been speculation that the two events were due in part to the difficulty in obtaining high quality leather immediately after the war.

Burton Albion English non-League football club, nicknamed the Brewers. Strip: all yellow. Founded in 1950, the Brewers (based at Eton Park) joined the Southern League in 1987. One of the most unusual games involving the club was played in

1985, when Albion met Leicester City – whose stars included Gary LINEKER – in the FA Cup; the match ended 6–1 in City's favour but was disrupted by the crowd on several occasions (with Albion's keeper being injured by missiles) and had to be replayed – behind closed doors (City won 1–0).

Burton United Former English League football club, which dropped out of the League in 1907. Based at Peel Croft, United was formed in 1901 when Burton Swifts (members of the League 1892–1901) and Burton Wanderers (League members 1894–97) merged.

Burundi Burundi joined FIFA in 1972 but have so far failed to make much impact in international competition. Strip: red shirts, white shorts, and green socks.

Bury English football club, nicknamed the Shakers. Strip: white shirts with navy blue shorts and socks. Bury were founded at a meeting at the Old White Horse Hotel in Bury in 1885, as successors to the Bury Wesleyans and Bury Unitarians.

Based since their formation at GIGG LANE, they joined the League (as members of the Second Division) in 1894 and a year later won the title and were rewarded with promotion to the First Division, where they remained until 1912. During this time the club established itself as one of the most powerful in the country, winning the FA Cup in 1900 and 1903 (in which year the Shakers achieved a record Cup Final victory of 6–0 against Derby County).

The club has since failed to repeat these early successes and has spent all its recent history in the bottom two divisions. In an attempt to improve the club's image it was suggested in 1971 that the team's name be changed to Manchester North End but the idea was quietly dropped after it failed to find approval with fans. Notable players in living memory have included midfielder Colin Bell.

Bury enjoyed their record victory back in 1897, when they beat Stockton 12–1; they suffered record defeats of 10–0 on two occasions, against Blackburn Rovers in 1887 and against West Ham in 1983. Norman Bullock holds the record for League appearances with the club, having played in 506 games between 1920 and 1935.

Bury Town English non-League football

club, nicknamed the Blues. Strip: all blue.
Founded in 1872 and based at Ram Meadow, Bury Town play in the Southern
League.

Busby, Sir Matt (1909–94) Scottish-born
manager, who earned a lasting place in
English football history as long-term manager of Manchester United (1945–70).
Busby began his career in football as a
player for Manchester City in 1928 and
won his single Scottish cap in 1933. Subsequently he received an FA Cup winner's
medal with City (1934) before joining Liverpool in 1936. After the war he started a
second career in management by undertaking the daunting task of revitalizing Manchester United, who were faced by a badly
bomb-damaged ground and lack of financial resources.

The Busby miracle at Old Trafford first
bore fruit in 1948, when the side won the
FA Cup and four years later Busby's first
great team won the League championship.
Aware of the need to foster new talent,
Busby then launched a new squad of young
players – dubbed the Busby Babes – who
exceeded all expectations and quickly established themselves as the leading side in
English football with two League titles
(1956 and 1957). After the Munich Air
Crash, in which eight players died and
Busby himself suffered severe injuries, it
seemed the Busby era must come to an
end – but the great manager recovered and
immediately set about building a third great
team around the survivors (who included
Bobby CHARLTON). The new squad collected the FA Cup in 1963 and – inspired
by Charlton, BEST, and LAW – two more
League championships (1965 and 1967) as
well as the ultimate achievement of victory
in the European Cup (1968).

Knighted for his services to football in
1968, Busby eventually stepped down in
1969, but returned to the post of manager
briefly a year later. He accepted a post on
the board in 1971 and later became club
president.

*Matt Busby is a symbol of everything that
is best in our great national game.*

Harold Wilson (1978)

Busby Babes Nickname of the great (and
ultimately tragic) Manchester United side of
the 1950s built by manager Matt BUSBY.
Formed in 1953, they included such burgeoning talents as Roger Byrne, Tommy
Taylor, Eddie Colman, Dennis Viollet,
Liam Whelan, Bobby CHARLTON, and the
brilliant Duncan EDWARDS. The Babes were
soon acknowledged to be an unstoppable
force and the League title came to Old Trafford in both 1956 and 1957, as well as
runners-up honours in the FA Cup of 1957.
Busby himself had to concede: 'In all
modesty, my summing-up of 1955–56 and
1956–57 must be that no club in the country
could live with Manchester United.'

Disaster struck, however, in 1958 with
the Munich Air Crash, in which no fewer
than eight of the Babes – including (15
days later) the immensely gifted Duncan
Edwards – died.

*Maybe we weren't the greatest team in the
world. We may never have become the
greatest. But we were certainly the most
loved. The team had youth, glamour and,
above all, modesty . . . The magic of
United could have died at Munich, but the
emotions that team aroused still draw
in the crowds 20 years after the last
championship.*

Harry Gregg, Manchester United goalkeeper
(1988)

*I may be thought odd, but when I think
of Manchester United, I think of Roger
Byrne, Duncan Edwards and Eddie Colman before the crash, and of Harry Gregg,
Bill Foulkes and Nobby Stiles afterwards.
Best, Law and Crerand were replaceable
somehow. They weren't the heart of the
team.*

Bobby Charlton (1972)

Butragueño, Emilio (1963–   ) Spanish
footballer, nicknamed the Vulture, who
emerged as a major star with Real Madrid.
Renowned for his ability to conjure up goalscoring chances, he made his debut for
Spain against Wales in 1984 and subsequently featured strongly in the 1986 World
Cup, scoring four goals in a 5–1 victory
over Denmark. He was also a key figure in
a run of five victorious Real Madrid League
championship campaigns.

Buxton English non-League football club,
nicknamed the Bucks. Strip: all white.
Founded in 1877, Buxton (based at the
Silverlands ground) have played in the
Northern Premier League since 1973.

byline The white line that runs from the
corner flag to the goalpost.

Byrne, Johnny (1939–   ) English forward, nicknamed Budgie, who was a star with Crystal Palace, West Ham, Fulham, and England in the 1960s. A dapper dresser who was noted for his chirpy personality (hence his nickname), he played a key role in West Ham's victory in the 1964 FA Cup and scored 11 goals in his eight internationals before injury curtailed his career. In all he scored 160 goals in 395 League games.

The Di Stefano of British football.

Ron Greenwood, West Ham manager

C

Caernarfon Town Welsh non-League football club, nicknamed the Canaries. Strip: yellow shirts and socks and green shorts. Founded in 1876 and based at the Oval in Caernarfon, the club play in the Northern Premier League.

Caesar Nickname of the Scottish centre-half Billy MCNEILL.

Cagney of the League Nickname of Alan HARDAKER, secretary of the Football League (1957–79). The nickname was inspired by the similarity between Hardaker's aggressively ebullient character and that of James Cagney's tough film persona (there were also marked similarities in appearance). *See also* ST ALAN OF ST ANNE'S.

calcio The name by which the game of football is popularly known in Italy. It is the only name used for the game that is not in some way derived from the English 'association football'. The original game from which the name comes was the *calcio fiorentino*, a violent version of soccer that was played by the servants of rich families in Renaissance Florence, notably in the Piazza di Santa Croce. Records of such games exist from as early as 1530, when a match was held in defiance of an army of Hapsburg mercenaries then besieging the city. Occasional games played to these ancient rules are still enacted in the square with much pomp and pageantry (in 1980 the European Championships in Rome were opened with a game of *calcio* between two teams in ceremonial dress). It was after watching one of these games in the 17th century, that Count Albemarle returned to England and initiated similar contests at the court of Charles II (*see* ROYALTY).

Camberley Town English non-League football club, nicknamed the Krooners. Strip: all red. Founded in 1969 and based at Krooner Park in Camberley, the club play in the Isthmian League.

Cambodia Cambodia joined FIFA in 1953 but have yet to make much impact in inter-national competition. Strip: blue, white, and red shirts, white shorts, and red socks.

Cambridge City English non-League football club, nicknamed the City Devils. Strip: white shirts and socks with black shorts. Founded in 1908 (as Cambridge Town) after breaking away from Cambridge St Mary's, the City Devils – based at the City Ground – adopted their present name in 1958 when they joined the Southern League.

Cambridge Rules An early set of rules for football players, which was drawn up initially for use in matches between sides from English public schools and universities. Prior to the drawing up of the Cambridge Rules there were frequent clashes over different interpretations of the game, with Rugby School, for instance, allowing handling of the ball at any time (in a version of the game that eventually became rugby football) while Etonian players were forbidden to handle it at all:

> What happens when a game of football is proposed at Christmas among a party of young men assembled from different schools? Alas! ... The Eton man is enamoured of his own rules, and turns up his nose at Rugby as not sufficiently aristocratic; while the Rugbeian retorts that 'bullying' and 'sneaking' are not to his taste, and he is not afraid of his shins, or of a 'maul' or 'scrimmage'. On hearing this the Harrovian pricks up his ears, and though he might previously have sided with Rugby, the insinuation against the courage of those who do not allow 'shinning' arouses his ire, and causes him to refuse to lay with one who has offered it. Thus it is found impossible to get up a game.

Editorial, *The Field* (1861)

In order to simplify matters, players at Cambridge University compiled their own code of rules in 1848; subsequently this code came to be adopted by teams throughout London and the South-East. When Sheffield FC, the first true football club, was founded it too followed the Cambridge

Rules. Ultimately this set of rules was modified (1862) and eventually combined with those regulating the game in the North of England to form the basis of modern Association Football.

Under the Cambridge Rules, goals were scored by kicking the ball between two posts connected by a string, one-handed throw-ins were allowed, and a rudimentary offside rule was observed; handling of the ball was permitted and a touchdown law provided for a free kick at goal after an attacker touched the ball down behind his opponents' goal. Unfortunately not one single copy of the rules has survived. *See also* HACKING.

Cambridge United

Cambridge United English football club, nicknamed United. Strip: amber shirts, black shorts, and amber and black socks. United were founded in 1919 as Abbey United, changing to their present name in 1949 when the team adopted professional ·status. After years in the minor leagues, they were elected to the Fourth Division in 1970 and have subsequently played in all three of the lower divisions (in the Second Division in 1978–84 and again from 1991, being relegated to the Second in 1993).

Their brief League career has brought them the Fourth Division title in 1977 and a Third Division championship in 1991. The 1983–84 season, by contrast, witnessed a sequence of 31 matches without a single win, the longest-ever such run by a League club. Famous names connected with the team have included manager Ron ATKINSON and striker Dion Dublin.

Based at the ABBEY STADIUM in Cambridge, United have enjoyed record victories of 6–0 on two occasions, in 1971 against Darlington and in 1989 against Hartlepool; they have suffered record defeats by the same scoreline against Aldershot (1974), Darlington (1974), and Chelsea (1983). Former captain Steve Spriggs holds the record for League appearances with the team, having played in 416 games between 1975 and 1987.

The team has never enjoyed mass support in the university town and one unidentified fan was moved to observe that 'League football in Cambridge is like having bingo in the Albert Hall'.

We beat the Villa,
And we drew at Coventry,
We drew at home to Manchester City,
And when we beat the Swansea,
We won Division Three,
And we've never lost at Wembley.

Win, win, wherever we may be,
We are the famous CUFC,
And we see you all wherever you may be,
And we'll see you all in the Premier League.

Supporters' song, to the tune of 'Lord of the Dance'

Here one goes, here one goes, here one goes.

Cambridge fans, directed at Wimbledon supporters

Cambuslang Former Scottish League football club. Based at Whitefield Park, south of Glasgow, Cambuslang were League members for just two seasons (1890–92) before disappearing.

Cameroon Cameroon's national team, nicknamed the Indomitable Lions, emerged as one of the strongest African national sides in the 1980s. Qualification for the World Cup Finals in 1982 distinguished them as the leading Black African team and was followed by victory in the African Nations Cup in 1984 and 1988. The 1990 World Cup saw Cameroon create the sensation of the series by progressing as far as the quarter-finals before going out 3–2 to England (without having previously lost a single game and having held eventual winners Italy to a 1–1 draw). Stars of the team included centre-forward Roger Milla. Cameroon qualified for the 1994 World Cup in America. Strip: green shirts, red shorts, and yellow socks.

Canada The Canadian national team has a long if relatively undistinguished history in international competition. They did not appear in the Finals of the World Cup until 1986, when they made a brave showing against some of the leading European teams before going out. Strip: all red.

Canadian Soccer League Canadian football organization, that was founded in 1987 in the wake of the collapse of the NASL. The CSL is the first truly national league to have been established in Canada (though the first game played to FA rules in Canada was as long ago as 1876). Rules followed by the dozen or so CSL members include one stipulating that teams may not field more than three foreign players, thus encouraging the development of home-grown talent. Players in the CSL include several who played for Canada in the 1986 World Cup and first came to prominence in the NASL. CSL clubs also include one of the old NASL teams – Toronto Blizzard. Gates at CSL matches rarely exceed 5000.

Canaries Nickname of a number of football clubs, reflecting either their name or their predominantly yellow strips. They include CAERNARFON TOWN, HITCHIN TOWN, NANTES, and NORWICH CITY.

Canterbury City English non-League football club, nicknamed City. Strip: royal blue and white shirts and socks and royal blue shorts. Founded in 1947 and based at the Kingsmead Stadium, City play in the Southern League.

cap Symbolic cap that is awarded to a player for an appearance in a national side. The first international cap was awarded in 1886, at the suggestion of N.L. Jackson (founder of Corinthians). The first England caps were royal blue and decorated with a rose emblem. Later they were embellished with a tassel, other colours were used and the rose emblem was replaced with the familiar three lions badge. In 1959 England captain Billy WRIGHT became the first British player to win 100 caps (his career total was 105 although strictly speaking it was only 93 because caps in the British Home Championship between 1953 and 1984 were supposed to be given for each series played, rather than for each game).

Peter SHILTON holds the record for England caps, with a total of 125. The first Scot to achieve the feat of collecting 100 caps was Kenny DALGLISH; the first Irishman was goalkeeper Pat JENNINGS in 1983. Exceeding all these, however, was the Peruvian star Hector Chumpitaz, who was capped for his country 150 times between 1963 and 1982.

Ladislav KUBALA, Alfredo DI STEFANO, and Jim Kennaway share the distinction of having won caps for three countries (Kubala for Hungary, Czechoslovakia, and Spain, Di Stefano for Argentina, Colombia, and Spain, and Kennaway for the USA, Canada, and Scotland). Crystal Palace's Vic Rouse, who was capped for Wales in 1959, was the first Fourth Division player to represent his country.

Cape Verde Cape Verde joined FIFA in 1986 but have yet to make much impact in international competition. Strip: all green.

Cappielow Park The home ground, in Greenock, of the Scottish football club MORTON. At first the club played on a field before moving to Gravel Park in 1875 and to their permanent home at Cappielow Park in 1879 (with a brief spell (1882–83) at Ladyburn). Events in the long history of the ground have included the burning down of a new pavilion in 1906, a riot by fans in 1922 in a Championship decider against Celtic, and a further riot in 1930 resulting in the temporary closure of the stadium. One of the terraces is nicknamed the Wee Dublin End in reference to the fact that the area behind it was once a slum inhabited for the most part by poor Irish immigrants.

captain That member of the team to whom responsibility for leadership on the field is delegated. The youngest captains ever appointed include Hereford United's Andy Feeley, who was put in charge of the team in 1979–80 and Port Vale's Clint Boulton, who took over the team in 1964; both players were just 17 years old. Arsenal hold the unusual distinction of having provided captains of all five countries in the British Isles since World War II, in the shapes of Alan BALL (England), Frank McLintock (Scotland), Walley Barnes (Wales), Terry Neill (Northern Ireland), and Liam BRADY (Republic of Ireland). Billy WRIGHT holds the record as captain of England, having performed the role in 90 internationals between 1948 and 1959.

Captain Bob (or Bouncing Czech) Nickname of the millionaire British publisher, businessman, Labour politician and football club speculator, Robert MAXWELL.

Captain Marvel Nickname of the Manchester United and England captain Bryan ROBSON.

captain of the crowd A figurehead for the fans of a particular club, to whom the crowds at cricket and football matches in Victorian days looked for guidance. The most well-known such character was the poet Albert Craig (1849–1909), who fulfilled the role for many years as a fan of Chelsea. His finest hour came in 1908 when Chelsea fans, outraged at a controversial decision by the referee, began to flood on to the pitch. Craig rose and called out: 'Boys, do nothing tonight that you will regret tomorrow. I have been your captain for 20 years, so take my advice and go home'. The angry crowd meekly dispersed and the club sent Craig a grateful letter thanking him for his intervention. *See also* MASCOTS.

Cardiff Arms Park The home of Welsh Rugby Union, which has a unique significance in the history of soccer in that it is the oldest surviving international football ground still in use. Wales made their debut there in 1896, losing 9–1 to England, after which the ground was regularly used for football until 1910, when NINIAN PARK opened. Football returned to Cardiff Arms Park in 1989, when the stadium was once more the leading venue for international football in Wales.

Cardiff City

Welsh football club, nicknamed the Bluebirds. Strip: blue shirts and socks, with white shorts. Founded in 1899, the Bluebirds turned professional in 1910, experiencing life as Riverside (1899–1902) and Riverside Albion (1902–08) before adopting their permanent name.

They moved to their home at NINIAN PARK in the year they turned professional but did not join the League until 1920, when they entered their greatest era to date, inspired by their captain and half-back Fred Keenor. Having won the Welsh Cup back in 1912, Cardiff regained it in 1920, 1922, 1923, 1927, 1928, and 1930 – and subsequently in 1956, 1959, 1964, 1965, 1967, 1968, 1969, 1970, 1971, 1973, 1974, 1976, 1988, and 1993. In 1924 the club narrowly missed winning the League championship itself, losing the title on goal average. FA Cup success followed in 1927, when the Bluebirds beat Arsenal 1–0 in the Final, thus becoming the only club to take the trophy out of England. (Critics of the day might have been excused questioning the validity of this 'Welsh' victory – the victorious team comprised three Welshmen, one Englishman, three Scots, and four Irishmen).

In 1929 the Bluebirds conceded just 59 goals in all, a record for a First Division club, but nonetheless were relegated. A disastrous dive to the bottom of the Third Division (South) followed not long afterwards and the club has since spent many seasons in the lower divisions, with a relatively brief return to the top flight in the 1950s. Most recently the future of the club has been threatened by financial crises.

Cardiff enjoyed their record victory in 1931, when they beat Enfield 8–0; they suffered their worst defeat in 1926, losing 11–2 to Sheffield United. Phil Dwyer holds the record for League appearances with the club, having played in 471 games between 1972 and 1985. Swansea City are the club's traditional arch-rivals:

Who's that team they call the Cardiff,
Who's that team they all adore,

We're the boys in Blue and White,
Pissed and looking for a fight,
And we'll hate the Swansea bastards
evermore.

Supporters' song, to the tune of 'Glory Glory Hallelujah'

Cards

Nickname of the English non-League football club WOKING, in reference to the club colours.

Carey, Johnny

(1919–) Irish footballer, nicknamed Gentleman John, who was a star with Manchester United in the 1940s and 1950s. Renowned for his impeccable manners on the field, Carey (otherwise nicknamed Jackie) was able to apply his talents to virtually any position in the team and captained the side that captured the FA Cup in 1948. He won 36 caps in all and also captained a Rest of Europe side in 1947 as well as teams representing Ireland and Northern Ireland (made eligible for both sides through his army service). He was honoured with the title Footballer of the Year in 1949 and later served as manager of Blackburn Rovers, Everton, Leyton Orient, and Nottingham Forest and also joined the board at Old Trafford.

Carlisle United

English football club, nicknamed the Cumbrians, in reference to the location of the team in Cumbria, or Blues. Strip: blue shirts and socks with white shorts. The club was formed in 1903, when Shaddongate United and Carlisle Red Rose were merged, and joined the Third Division (North) in 1928. The Cumbrians were long-term residents of the bottom two divisions until 1965, when their capture of the Third Division championship brought them promotion. By 1966 they could claim to have appeared in five different divisions in successive seasons.

The club's golden era was in the mid-1970s when Carlisle finally reached the First Division, actually rising to the top of the table briefly in 1974–75. Subsequently they suffered a drastic decline and by 1987 were back in the Fourth Division. Major names associated with the club at BRUNTON PARK have included player and manager Alan Ashman, players Ivor Broadis and Peter Beardsley, and manager (1949–51) Bill SHANKLY.

The club's record victory stands at 8–0 against Hartlepools United in 1928; they suffered their worst defeat in 1939, losing 11–1 to Hull City. Alan Ross holds the record for League appearances with the club, having played in 466 matches between 1963 and 1979.

Carrow Road The home ground of NORWICH CITY. Carrow Road replaced the ground at Rosary Road (*see* NEST, THE) in 1935, having been until then the Boulton Paul Sports Ground. The conversion to a Second Division football ground was, remarkably, achieved in just three months.

Notable events in the ground's history have included a visit by George VI in 1938 (the first time a reigning monarch had watched a Second Division match), the building of two gun emplacements in the car park during World War II (of which one still survives), and a disastrous fire in 1979, when much of the Main Stand was destroyed. Among notable features of the ground is the club's own public house, called The Nest in honour of the Canaries' former home. Carrow Road itself was named after Carrow Abbey, which was built nearby in the 12th century.

Carshalton Athletic English non-League football club, nicknamed the Robins. Strip: white with maroon trim, maroon shorts with white trim, and white socks. Founded in 1903 and based at the War Memorial ground in Carshalton, the club play in the Isthmian League.

Carter, Raich (Horatio Stratton Carter; 1913–) English footballer, frequently described as the finest inside-forward of the 1930s and 1940s. Raich emerged as a leading player of his day while with Sunderland (1932–45), winning admiration for his unparalleled tactical skills and helping them to victory in the League championship in 1936 and (as captain) in the FA Cup in 1937. Having scored 213 goals in 451 League games for the club, he went on to play for Derby County (1945–48), winning another FA Cup winner's medal in 1946, and Hull (1948–52), for whom he filled the role of player-manager. He also made 13 appearances for England (forming a brilliant partnership with Stanley MATTHEWS).

> *He carried empty space around with him like an umbrella.*
> Willie Watson

Casuals Former English non-League football club, which amalgamated with Corinthians in 1939. Strip: chocolate and pink. Founded in 1883, players with the club were initially drawn from Old Boys from Charterhouse, Eton, and Westminster. The club was a founder member of the Isthmian League in 1905 and produced many outstanding players; the Casuals won the FA Amateur Cup in 1936.

Cat, The Nickname of the English goalkeeper Peter BONETTI, who was renowned for his catlike ability to save apparently unreachable shots.

catenaccio A defensive formation (four–three–three) that was pioneered by teams from Italy in the 1960s and subsequently widely employed elsewhere. The formation consisted of four defenders, three midfield players, and three forwards; this arrangement denied attacking space for opponents while still maintaining a strong presence in midfield, one player acting as a sweeper. Named after the Italian word for doorbolt, the *catenaccio* formation developed from the introduction of a four–two–four system used to great effect by Brazil in their victorious World Cup campaign of 1958. It also proved to be an ideal strategy for teams that lacked exceptional wingers, as Alf RAMSEY illustrated in 1966 when he employed it with England's triumphant World Cup squad (*see* WINGLESS WONDERS). Unfortunately this ultra-defensive strategy stifled attacking play and all too often rendered matches boring to watch.

> *Juventus, winner of 15 national titles . . . represents the conservative, traditional style known as* catenaccio *(literally, doorbolt). The emphasis is on tight defense, with the opponent's attacks being used as springboards for counterthrusts and breakaway strikes, by swift forwards.*
> *Time* (1973)

Cathedral, The Nickname of the SAN MAMÉS STADIUM, which is home to the Spanish football club ATHLETIC BILBAO.

Cathkin Park The home ground in Glasgow of the now-defunct Scottish football League club THIRD LANARK. Cathkin Park, only a short distance from HAMPDEN PARK, had a long history as one of the most prestigious footballing venues in Scotland, becoming the home of Third Lanark back in 1872. Over the years that followed it hosted three Scottish Cup Finals before a new Cathkin Park was established nearby in 1903. It all came to an end, however, in 1967 when the Hi-Hi's were wound up in the courts and Cathkin Park was redeveloped as a public park.

caution *See* BOOKING.

Celery song Supporters' song that created something of a furore when it was heard on the terraces at Stamford Bridge in the mid-1980s. The song inspired numerous Chelsea fans to come to matches carrying sticks of celery, which they brandished while the song was in progress; the police, at a time when hooliganism was the prime issue facing the game, decided to interpret such actions as a provocation to violence and promptly arrested several fans trying to bring celery into the ground. It is thought the song originated among fans of Brighton and Hove Albion as the anthem of a band of fans calling themselves the 'Caveman's Crew'; rumour had it that sticks of celery played a major role in initiation ceremonies held by the Crew on Brighton's pier.

> Celery, celery,
> If she don't come, I'll tickle her bum,
> With a stick of celery,
> Celery, celery . . .

Celestos Nickname (meaning 'sky blues') of the Uruguayan national team, in reference to the side's light blue playing strip.

Celtic The pre-eminent Scottish football club, nicknamed the Bhoys, that constitutes one half of the OLD FIRM based in Glasgow. Strip: white shirt with green hoops, with white shorts and socks. Founded in 1888, Celtic's origins lay in the soup kitchens providing sustenance for poor Irish Catholic immigrants in Glasgow's East End. The impoverished Catholic inhabitants who met at the soup kitchens were in November 1887 organized by a priest, Brother Walfrid, into a football team whose aim was to raise money for food and clothes for the children of Glasgow's slums. The team quickly became a focus for Catholic identity and, ultimately, developed as a rival to the dominant Protestant Rangers side.

The enthusiasm with which the club's earliest members pursued their dream was unstoppable. They flouted all the laws governing the amateur status of the game and poached players from all the leading Scottish and English teams, quickly gathering a mass following at the home ground, CELTIC PARK, and seeing their efforts rewarded with the first of a long list of titles and trophies. Celtic captured the First Division championship in 1893, 1894, 1896, 1898, 1905–10, 1914–17, 1919, 1922, 1926, 1936, 1938, 1954, and 1966–74, adding the new Premier Division title in

1977, 1979, 1981, 1982, 1986, and 1988; they were runners-up in the senior division no fewer than 21 times. The club also has a distinguished record in the Scottish Cup, winning it in 1892, 1899, 1900, 1904, 1907, 1908, 1911, 1912, 1914, 1923, 1925, 1927, 1931, 1933, 1937, 1951, 1954, 1965, 1967, 1969, 1971, 1972, 1974, 1975, 1977, 1980, 1985, 1988, and 1989. Other triumphs have included nine League Cup wins.

The great Celtic team of the pre-World War I period is still talked about in Glasgow. Among other particularly cherished memories are the club's many Cup triumphs – its victories in the British Empire Exhibition Cup (1938), the Coronation Cup (1953), and in 1967 the European Cup (*see* LISBON LIONS). The relatively lean period after World War II was transformed in the 1960s by manager Jock STEIN; other notable names connected with the club have included its first manager Willie Maley, forward Patsy GALLAGHER, centre-forward Jimmy McGrory (who established a British record of 550 goals in first-class football), and centre-half Billy MCNEILL (who made a record 486 League appearances for the club between 1957 and 1975). The Bhoys enjoyed their record victory to date in 1895, when they defeated Dundee 11–0; their record defeat came in 1937, when they lost 8–0 against Motherwell.

> Sure it's a grand old team to play for,
> And it's a grand old team to see,
> And if you know your history,
> Then it's enough to make your heart
>   go – oh – oh!
> We don't care what the Rangers say,
> What the hell do they know?
> We only know that there's going to be a
>   show,
> And the Glasgow Celtic will be there.

Supporters' song

Celtic Park or **Parkhead** The home ground of the Scottish football club CELTIC. The first Celtic Park was opened in 1888 but two years later the club was forced to leave when the rent rocketed up from £50 a year to £450 in response to the team's success. A new Celtic Park was then established just two hundred yards away; it was often nicknamed 'Paradise' after one fan remarked that the move was 'like leaving the graveyard to enter Paradise'. The first sod of turf, complete with Irish shamrocks, was laid by the Irish nationalist and MP Michael Davitt, who then recited the following verse:

On alien soil like yourself I am here,
I'll take root and flourish, of that never
    fear.

The sod of turf was stolen shortly afterwards, but the ground did indeed flourish,
staging athletics and cycling as well as football matches. An early experiment with
floodlighting took place at the venue in
1893, but ended because the ball kept
hitting the lights. Other notable events at
the ground over the years have included a
fire that destroyed the Main Stand and
Pavilion in 1904, a Coronation parade in
1911, a mock battle complete with trenches
and explosives during World War I, several
open-air masses, and the inaugural speedway meeting (in 1928).

Features of Celtic Park include a stand
known as the 'Jungle', because its inhabitants are among the roughest and most
'animalistic' in football, and the Rangers
End, which is traditionally given over to
Rangers supporters when the OLD FIRM
meet here. The flying of an Irish tricolour
from one of the ground's flagpoles has long
been a focus of sectarian controversy
between Catholic Celtic and their Protestant
arch-rivals.

Tradition has it that one of the goals is
haunted by the ghost of goalkeeper John
Thomson, who died in 1931 in a collision
with a Rangers forward.

Celts Nickname of the English non-League
football club FARSLEY CELTIC.

Central Africa Central Africa joined FIFA
in 1963, but have yet to establish themselves
as one of the stronger African sides. Strip:
grey-blue shirts, white shorts, and red socks
with yellow trim.

Central Alliance League English football league, which was founded in 1911 and
revived in 1947 after a 22-year break. The
League's early history was overshadowed by
the reserve teams of several League clubs;
more recently it has been dominated by such
sides as Ilkeston Town (champions 1951–
55), Alfreton Town, Belper Town, Clay
Cross MW, Gresley Rovers, Heanor Town,
Matlock Town, and Ransome and Marles.

Central Park The home ground of COW-
DENBEATH. Cowdenbeath moved to Central Park in 1917 from North End Park
(nicknamed the Colliers Den). The ground
witnessed its most prosperous times after
the team reached Division I in 1923, but

subsequently it has had to diversify with
dog racing, speedway, and stock car racing
to stave off financial crisis. The ground's
problems have not been eased in recent
years by gales in 1983 and by a fire started
by vandals in 1985.

Central Stadium (1) Major German football stadium, in Leipzig, which was the foremost venue used by the national team that
represented former East Germany. Begun in
1950, when rubble from the bombed city
was used to create banking for spectators,
the stadium opened in 1956 and staged East
Germany's first football international a year
later. Subsequently it hosted many more
internationals and was also regularly used
by LOKOMOTIVE LEIPZIG.

(2) The popular name of the REPUBLICAN
STADIUM in Kiev, which is the home of
DYNAMO KIEV.

Centre of Excellence A local organization that aims to promote coaching and
training of promising young English players
between the ages of 11 and 14. Over 100
such centres were established by the FA in
the 1980s at professional clubs and elsewhere in an attempt to raise playing standards in general.

centre-forward The player in the central
position in the forward line, who is usually
the team's most accomplished goalscorer.
Though looser modern strategies of play
have tended to mean that the honours are
shared fairly evenly among the attacking
positions, the role of centre-forward remains
the most glamorous and the most sought-
after at all levels of the game. Contenders
for the title of the best centre-forward of all
time would have to include Dixie DEAN.

centre-half or **centre-back** The player
who occupies the central position in the
half-back line or final line of the defence.
Often his most crucial role is to act as a link
between the defence and his team's attacking players. Many captains have played in
this position over the years. Steve Bruce of
Manchester United holds the record for
goals scored in a single season while playing
at centre-half, with a total of 13 in the
1990–91 season; by way of contrast, Eric
Hayward of Port Vale and Blackpool spent
20 years at centre-half and failed to score
once. *See also* STOPPER.

Cestrians Nickname of the English football club CHESTER CITY.

Chad Chad joined FIFA in 1962, left in 1974, and rejoined in 1988 but have yet to make much impact in international competition. Strip: yellow shirts, blue shorts, and yellow socks.

Chalfont St Peter English non-League football club, nicknamed the Saints. Strip: white shirts, with green shorts and socks. Founded in 1926 and based at the Playing Fields in Chalfont St Peter, the club play in the Isthmian League.

Champagne Charlie Nickname of the Scottish player and manager Graeme SOUNESS.

Champions of the World The first club to claim this title was the Scottish team Renton FC, who dominated Scottish competitions back in the 1880s. Having won the Scottish FA Cup in 1888 (their third Final in four years), Renton went on to challenge English FA Cup winners West Bromwich Albion to what was billed as a 'World Championship Decider'. Renton won it with ease, beating Albion 4–1.

Years later, Stan CULLIS, manager of Wolverhampton Wanderers claimed the same title for his own club after they comprehensively defeated Moscow Spartak and Honvéd, two of the most feared sides in the world, at Molineux in 1954. The 3–2 victory against Honvéd caused a sensation, as the Hungarian team included six of the players who had recently cowed the English national side.

Cullis's kick and rush tactics and use of the long pass ('Our players are not encouraged to parade their ability in ostentatious fashion . . . every pass, if possible, should be decisive and long') had overwhelmed the most prestigious clubs in the world. Also relevant was the fact that the waterlogged pitch at Molineux had done much to slow the Hungarians down. Cullis himself had had a hand in this, as Ron ATKINSON, then an apprentice at Wolverhampton, revealed:

On the morning of the match, Stan Cullis sent for me and two of the other apprentices, and told us to go out and water the pitch. We thought he was out of his mind. It was December and it had been raining incessantly for four days. When I watched the match in the evening, I understood what he was up to . . . the pitch was getting heavier and heavier. The mud just wore the Hungarians out.

Cullis's cunning paid off and the press was quick to echo his boast that Wolves were the best in the world. His words were, however, to have a wider impact than anyone had expected. The French sports paper *L'Equipe* took issue with his extravagant claim and turned it into a rallying cry for the long-discussed establishment of the European Cup, which would provide a proper framework for the settlement of such claims.

chants The ritualized chanting by fans of slogans and taunts dates back to the earliest days of the game. In their simplest form chants comprise the repeated shouting of a team's name, a custom that is thought to date from the 1960s when South American crowds hailed their heroes in such a way. Other variations include chanting the score-line over and over as a taunt to the losing side, and synchronized yelling of 'We are the champions', or 'One, two, three, four, who is it that we are for?' – followed by the name of the team concerned. Other famous examples include the POMPEY CHIMES associated with Portsmouth and the HERE WE GO refrain heard universally in the 1980s. Similar chants are heard at grounds throughout the world.

Most people are in a factory from nine till five. Their job may be to turn out 263 little circles. At the end of the week they're three short and somebody has a go at them. On Saturday afternoons they deserve something to go and shout at.

Rodney Marsh (1967)

Chapman, Herbert (1875–1934) English football manager, who became one of the legends of the game as manager of Arsenal in the late 1920s and early 1930s. Born in Sheffield, Chapman began his career as an amateur while working as a mining engineer and eventually turned professional with Northampton in 1901. Subsequently he played for Notts County and Tottenham Hotspur before returning to Northampton as manager. In 1912 he took over at Leeds City, where in 1919 he was embroiled in a scandal involving alleged illegal payments before the war (of which he denied any knowledge). He moved to Huddersfield Town in 1921, winning the FA Cup a year later and two First Division titles.

Chapman arrived at Arsenal in 1925 and over the next nine years transformed the club (often dubbed Lucky Arsenal), winning five League championships and two FA Cup titles (one after beating Chapman's old club Huddersfield in the Final) before World War II ended their great run.

Everyone agreed that the chief credit

for this record belonged to the innovative manager of the Gunners, who was not only a master tactician (*see* STOPPER) but also a great propagandist for the side (*see* ARSENAL TUBE STATION). Other significant ventures during the Chapman era at Arsenal, which combined to change the face of football for ever, included experiments with white balls, numbers on players' shirts, rubber studs, all-weather pitches, and floodlighting.

Then, when it was least expected, after watching a game by the third team in bitter cold at Guildford in January 1934, Chapman succumbed to pneumonia and died. Chapman's premature death while the Gunners were enjoying their greatest hour was a body blow to the club. His memory is perpetuated by an Epstein bust in the club's entrance hall and in the many stories still told of his authoritarian regime and irrepressible imagination; also preserved at Highbury is Chapman's carved chapel seat, given to the club by his church in Yorkshire in 1931. An HC club was even formed in his memory. His influence on the team is still felt and officials at Highbury have reported that the ghost of the celebrated manager still haunts the corridors at the stadium.

> *Chapman knew when to blow you up and when to blow you down, when to be the Big Boss and when to be the Family Friend. He was a genius and that's the fact of it.*
>
> Alec Jackson

Charity Shield FA competition that was founded in 1908. Initially the Charity Shield was competed for by the winners of the League championship and the holders of the Southern League title – although there was no match in 1913 and 1923 because the FA disapproved of the unsporting manner in which the FA Cup Final in those years had been played. During the 1920s the competition was usually fought out between one team of amateurs and another of professionals and the result was not always as predictable as one might expect; in 1926, for instance, a very strong professional side including five international players, incredibly lost 6–3 to the amateurs at Maine Road, to the intense embarrassment of the losing team.

From 1928 onwards the Shield was contested mostly by the winners of the FA Cup and the League champions (not being played in the rare years that a single club won both titles). On almost all occasions the Shield has gone to the League champions.

Notable events in the history of the match have included the 1967 game, when goalkeeper Pat JENNINGS scored, and the 1974 meeting (the first at Wembley), when Billy BREMNER and Kevin KEEGAN became the first Britons to be sent off at Wembley for fighting (resulting in each being banned for five weeks); as they left the field both players tore off their shirts in disgust. Liverpool have won the Charity Shield a record 13 times. Proceeds from the game, which is now played as a curtain-raiser to the new season, go to charity.

Charles, John (1931–   ) Welsh forward, nicknamed the Gentle Giant, whose stature – he weighed nearly 14 stone and was over six feet tall – was matched by his talent as a striker. Born in Swansea, Charles joined Leeds United in 1947 as a junior and graduated to the senior team in 1949, becoming in 1950 the youngest player ever to win a cap with Wales. He participated in securing promotion for Leeds to the First Division in 1956 and a year later was the most prolific goalscorer in the top flight (with a total of 38 goals).

He spent the next five years with Juventus, winning three Italian League championships and two Italian Cups before returning briefly to Leeds in 1962 and then going back out to Roma. He ended his great career back in Wales, joining Cardiff City in 1963 and retiring in 1966.

He was particularly praised for his skill in the air, although he was also renowned for his precise ball control (unusual in a player of his build). He was never sent off or even cautioned in the whole of his career – hence his nickname, first bestowed upon him by admiring Italian fans (as *Il Buon Gigante*).

> *Everything John does is automatic. When he moves into position for a goal chance it is instinctive. Watch me and you will see I am seconds late . . . my feet do not do my thinking for me as they do for a player like John Charles. That is why I can never be as great a footballer as he.*
>
> Danny Blanchflower, *Spurs – The Double* (1961)

Charlton, Bobby (1937–   ) English forward, who became a symbol of all that was good in British football from the 1950s to the 1970s. Charlton's name became a touchstone for foreign supporters, including those who could not speak a word of English, from the 1960s on. Alongside the Queen, tea, and the Beatles he became the quintessence of Englishness in the eyes of the world -- not least for his gentlemanly demeanour and consistent fair play:

> The fact that they accused Bobby Charlton of sheltering me while I 'stole' a bracelet proves I'm innocent. Bobby has never done a dishonest thing in his life.

Bobby Moore, referring to the BOGOTÁ INCIDENT (1970)

A relative of the famous Milburn footballing family (through his mother) and younger brother of the equally distinguished Jack CHARLTON, Bobby Charlton owed his start in football to the efforts of his mother and one of his teachers. His mother, herself the daughter of a goalkeeper, took the closest interest in his progress and coached him herself in a local park. When he was finally seen by a Manchester United scout the response was confident and immediate: 'I don't want to butter you up, Missis, but your boy will play for England before he's twenty-one'. The word quickly got round and the redoubtable Mrs Charlton was besieged by scouts from no fewer than 18 leading clubs:

> They were offering us the world. One fellow offered £800. Another said he'd double whatever was the highest offer we'd had. He didn't even ask what it was . . . I'd be cleaning the fireplace in the morning and I'd look round and there'd be another one standing behind me. There were times when we've had one in the front room and one in the kitchen.

Bobby spent his entire playing career with Manchester United, for whom he first signed in 1954. He won a League championship medal in 1957 and had already attracted much attention as one of the most gifted of the BUSBY BABES when he was injured in the MUNICH AIR CRASH in 1958. That same year, however, he made his debut for England, winning the first of a total of 106 caps. In 1963 he played a major role in Manchester United's FA Cup triumph, as he also did in the club's two League championship victories in 1965 and 1967.

On the international stage, he enjoyed his finest hours in 1966 as a key player in England's World Cup success and in 1968 when he captained the Red Devils to glory in the European Cup; he was also voted European Footballer of the Year in 1966.

By the time of his retirement as a player in 1973, he had scored 247 goals in 754 games; his tally of 49 goals for his national team was also a record. Subsequently he served as manager of Preston North End – for whom he also came out as a player for a short time – and of Wigan before joining his old club United as a member of the board and promoting soccer for children.

> He was idolized from his twentieth year on. There has never been a more popular footballer. He was as near perfection as man and player as it is possible to be.

Sir Matt Busby

Charlton, Jack (1935–) English footballer, brother of Bobby CHARLTON, who enjoyed great success both as a player and subsequently as a manager at international level. One of the most famous players of his era, his nicknames included Big Jack, and The Giraffe on account of his long neck and his prodigious talent in the air.

Jack Charlton was – like his brother – a one-club man throughout his playing career, joining Leeds United in 1952 and remaining with them until he went into management in 1973. The great moments in his career on the field included his central role in England's 1966 World Cup triumph and in victories in the League Cup (1968), Fairs Cup (1968 and 1971), and FA Cup (1972); in 1967 he was voted Footballer of the Year.

As a manager he joined Middlesbrough in 1973, Sheffield Wednesday in 1977, Newcastle United in 1984, and Ireland in 1986, getting the national side into the Finals of the European Championship in 1988 and then into the quarter-finals of the World Cup in 1990. He became an Irish folk hero and even Pope John Paul II was heard to refer to him as 'the boss'.

For fans, the most moving moment in the remarkable history of the Charlton footballing family must have been the emotional embrace the two brothers shared at the final whistle in 1966 when they realized they had helped to win the World Cup for England. More outspoken than his brother, Big Jack's career has not been without moments of controversy, reflecting his belligerent attitude to the game. While still a player, he was sternly reprimanded for making what appeared to be an open threat to certain opponents: 'I've got a little black book in which I keep the names of all the players I've got to get before I pack up playing. If I get half a chance they will finish up over the touchline.'

Rumour had it that in fact the notorious black book contained just two names: Denis LAW claimed that his was one of them. Big Jack himself acknowledged his sometimes unreliable temper in 1973: 'I'm very placid most of the time, but I blow up very quickly. I shout and wave my arms, and my lip twitches. I become incoherent, and I swear. All at the same time.' He was inclined, however, to forgive himself, drily observing: 'Soccer is a man's game; not an outing for namby-pambies.'

Charlton Athletic English football club, nicknamed the Valiants. Strip: red shirts, white shorts, and red socks. The Valiants, otherwise known as the Robins from the team colours or as the Addicks (*see* HADDICKS), were founded in 1905 when several local teams merged. They graduated from minor league football in 1921, when they were elected to the Third Division (South).

Charlton, who are based at The VALLEY, began their life in the Football League quietly enough, but everything changed in the 1930s, when manager Jimmy Seed transformed them into one of the most powerful sides in the land (for a time second only to Arsenal). Under Seed the club won their second Third Division (South) championship in 1935 and a year later won promotion to the top flight, as runners-up in the Second Division.

As residents of the First Division from 1936 to 1957, Charlton were runners-up in the League in 1937 and in the FA Cup in 1946; they went on to win the latter in 1947 after beating Burnley (a victory often recalled for the accident that befell the famous trophy when Seed dropped it and broke the top off the lid). Stars of the side in these golden years included goalkeeper Sam Bartram, who is remembered by many as the 'finest keeper England never had'. It was Bartram who in one wartime match played in thick fog failed to realize that the game had been abandoned and remained loyally at his post until a policeman walked up and informed him that he was now alone on the pitch.

The club slipped back into the Second Division in 1957 and two years later disgruntled directors contemplated adopting a new image by renaming the club London Athletic before eventually changing their minds. In 1972 the team dropped further still down into the Third Division (though one fan was still impressed enough by their form to name her new baby son after the entire squad). In 1986, however, they were back in the First Division for another four-year stint, before again falling back into the Second in 1990.

Honours since the 1950s have been somewhat scarce. The club has also been troubled over the fate of their home ground, which they vacated in 1985 to enter a sharing arrangement at SELHURST PARK, only to return after a long campaign by the fans (*see* VALLEY PARTY).

Remarkable matches in the club's history have included one in 1957, when the side was trailing 5–1 against Huddersfield Town with 28 minutes to go but astonishingly finished 7–6 victors (five of their goals being scored by Johnny Summers). Famous names associated with the club very nearly included Stanley MATTHEWS, whose transfer in 1938 to Charlton was agreed by the two team managers, but blocked by the directors.

The Valiants enjoyed record victories with a margin of seven goals in 1953, when they beat Middlesbrough 8–1, and in 1956, when they beat Burton Athletic 7–0; they suffered their worst defeat in 1959, when they lost 11–1 against Aston Villa. Sam Bartram holds the record for League appearances with the club, having played in 582 games between 1934 and 1956.

> *Many miles have I travelled,*
> *Many games have I seen,*
> *Following Charlton,*
> *My only team,*
> *Many hours have I spent,*
> *In the covered end choir,*
> *Singing, Valley, Floyd Road.*
> *Valley, Floyd Road,*
> *The mist rolling in from the Thames,*
> *My only desire is always to be there,*
> *At Valley, Floyd Road.*

Supporters' song, to the tune of 'Mull of Kintyre'

Ché's Nickname of the Spanish football club VALENCIA, from the familiar form of address used in the region.

Chelmsford City English non-League football club, nicknamed City. Strip: claret and white shirts, white shorts, and claret socks. Formed in 1938 when Chelmsford's amateur club was disbanded, City (based at the Stadium in New Writtle Street and sometimes also called Clarets after their strip) have spent their entire history in the Southern League.

Chelsea English football club, nicknamed the Blues. Strip: royal blue with red and white trim. Founded in 1905, the club owe their existence to the fact that Fulham turned down an offer of the use of the athletics stadium at STAMFORD BRIDGE, prompting the owner to form a new club to use the facilities there.

Acquiring excellent players from other clubs Chelsea – also nicknamed the Pensioners – bludgeoned their way into the League in their first year and prospered with the assistance of such stars as goalkeeper William 'Fatty' FOULKE. The club had to wait many years, however, before it enjoyed further significant success and had to suffer the jibes of more outstanding sides. The club's proximity to London's West End and the frequent use of celebrity stars to improve the side's performance also promoted the glamorous image of the team, which only served to point up its lack of achievement over the decades. The club also became renowned for unpredictability.

Everything changed in the 1950s with the arrival of manager Ted Drake. Drake rejuvenated the side with the inclusion of several young players dubbed DRAKE'S DUCKLINGS and in 1955 Chelsea won the First Division championship. Tommy DOCHERTY revived the team once more when he took over in 1961, after Drake had failed to avoid relegation, and steered the club to success in the League Cup in 1965 (making Chelsea the first London side to win it).

New manager Dave Sexton brought the club success in the FA Cup in 1970 and in the European Cup Winners' Cup in 1971, but subsequently the side went into decline, faced with relegation and financial problems. The arrival of chairman Ken Bates in 1982 restored the club's fortunes – Chelsea won the Second Division championship in 1984 and 1989, and in 1992 were founder members of the Premier League.

Famous supporters include Liverpool star Craig Johnston (who named his daughter Chelsea after the club), the film director and actor Richard Attenborough, who was formerly a director of the club, and prime minister John Major; in 1992 Major's minister David Mellor (soon to resign) denied press allegations that a Chelsea kit had played a part in his highly publicized affair with an actress.

The club's record victory stands at 13–0 against Jeunesse Hautcharage in 1971; their record defeat came in 1953, when they lost 8–1 to Wolverhampton Wanderers. For many years Bob Whittingham's tally of 30 League goals in the 1910–11 season remained unchallenged by any other player for the club; this longest-lived of all individual club records was finally broken in the 1958–59 season when Jimmy GREAVES scored 32. Ron 'Chopper' HARRIS holds the record for League appearances with the club, playing in 655 games between 1962 and 1980.

In recent years (especially in the 1970s) Chelsea's supporters (see SHED, THE) have been among the most notorious in the UK, reserving their worst excesses for their arch-rivals Tottenham Hotspur:

> We went up to Wolves,
> We took their North Bank,
> We came down to Arsenal,
> They're not worth a wank,
> So take my advice:
> There's nothing so nice,
> As kicking the fuck out of Tottenham.

Supporters' song, to the tune of 'Messing About on the River'

Commodore already sponsors Tessa Sanderson, Chelsea FC and a football team, Bayern Munich.
Computer Guardian (1988)

Cheltenham Town English non-League football club, nicknamed the Robins. Strip: red and white shirts, black shorts, and red socks. Founded in 1892 and based at the Whaddon Road ground in Cheltenham, the Robins play in the Southern League.

Chequer, A.H. Pseudonym used by the first man to score a goal in an FA Cup Final (1872). A.H. Chequer was really Morton Peto Betts, a member of the FA committee and one of the architects of the competition itself. Betts scored the only goal of the game, capturing the Cup for Wanderers against all expectations, their opponents the Royal Engineers being considered the stronger side. Betts opted to play under a pseudonym (thought to be an abbreviation for 'A Harrow Chequer') in acknowledgement of the fact that he had begun the tournament as a player for the Harrow Chequers side, which had withdrawn in the first round. Under his own name he also played for West Kent and England.

Cherries Nickname of the English football club AFC BOURNEMOUTH, in reference to their predominantly red team colours.

Chertsey Town English non-League football club, nicknamed the Curlews. Strip: blue and white striped shirts, white shorts, and blue socks. Founded in 1890 and based at the Alwyns Lane ground, the Curlews play in the Isthmian League.

Chesham United English non-League football club, nicknamed United. Strip: claret and blue striped shirts, claret shorts, and blue socks. Founded in 1887 and based at Meadow Park in Chesham, United play in the Isthmian League.

Chester City English football club, nick-named the Cestrians or Blues. Strip: royal blue shirts and socks, with white shorts. Founded in 1884 (in a city famous for its medieval tradition of football), Chester joined the Third Division (North) in 1931 and the new Fourth Division in 1958; it was not until 1975 – when they also appeared in the semi-finals of the League Cup – that they first won promotion. Their honours include the Welsh Cup in 1908, 1933, and 1947. In 1990 they left their home at Sea-land Road, where they had settled in 1906, to move in with non-League Macclesfield at the Moss Rose ground in Macclesfield. Despite the club's lack of major success, it can claim to have launched the careers of at least two prominent players – Ron Davies and Ian RUSH.

Chester enjoyed their record victory in 1936, when they beat York City 12–0; they suffered their worst defeat in 1952, losing 11–2 to Oldham Athletic. Ray Gill holds the record for League appearances with the club, having played for them in 408 games between 1951 and 1962.

Chester reports Two reports into the state of English football, which were compiled by a committee chaired by the distinguished academic and football enthusiast Sir Nor-man Chester (1907–86) in 1966 and 1982. Influential recommendations contained in the first report included the establishment of a Football Levy Board, the creation of a Fifth Division (with a total of 100 clubs), new forms of playing contracts (Chester once compared the buying and selling of players to a slave market), a new category of pro-am player, and revision of disciplinary committees.

The second report suggested a smaller First Division and other changes in the structure of the League, financial measures, and automatic promotion of the top non-League club. The FA disagreed with several of the conclusions of the reports, but as the years passed a substantial number of recom-mendations were reflected in changes in the administration of the game.

Chesterfield English football club, nick-named the Spireites. Strip: blue shirts, white shorts, and white socks (though for the 1890–91 season the team wore distinctive Union Jack shirts). Chesterfield are one of the oldest football clubs in the UK and can be traced back to a side formed as early as 1866, although they did not turn profes-sional until 1891.

Also nicknamed the Blues, the club are

based at the RECREATION GROUND and have been members of the League since 1899, when they joined as Second Division mem-bers (with a single break from 1909 to 1921 when they failed to win re-election). Subse-quently the side experienced life in all three of the lower divisions, being restored to the Second Division on two occasions (1931–33 and 1936–51) but alternating between Divisions Three and Four since then; the closest they came to reaching the First Divi-sion was at the close of the 1946–47 season, when they reached the play-offs but failed to go through.

The club's few honours include the Third Division (North) title in 1931 and 1936, the Fourth Division championship in 1970 and 1985, and the Anglo-Scottish Cup in 1981. Star players with the team over the years have included the goalkeepers Sam Hardy and Gordon BANKS. The club president is the Duke of Devonshire.

The Spireites enjoyed their record victory in 1903, when they beat Glossop 10–0; they suffered their worst defeat in 1987, when they lost by 10–0 against Gillingham. Dave Blakey holds the record for League appear-ances with the club, having played in 613 games between 1948 and 1967.

Chicks Nickname of the English non-League football club DORKING.

Chile The Chilean national team has enjoyed a reputation as one of the strong South American sides for many decades but has still to collect any of the major interna-tional awards, with the exception of a single win in the South American Championship back in 1926. Chile were participants in the very first World Cup in 1930 and reappeared in the Finals in 1950, though it was not until 1962 (when Chile was the host nation) that the team got as far as the semi-finals (losing 4–2 to Brazil and eventually finishing third). More recently, the side were runners-up in the 1987 South American Championship (behind Uruguay). Stars of the team over the years have included Eladio Rojas, Leonel Sanchez, Albert Fouilloux, Carlos Caszely, and goalkeeper Roberto Rojas. Strip: red shirts with white trim, blue shorts, and white socks.

Chin, The Nickname of the English com-mentator and former player and manager Jimmy HILL, in reference to his distinctive profile.

China China joined FIFA in 1931, but have yet to make much impact in international competition. Strip: red shirts, white shorts, and red socks.

chip A short stabbing shot with the foot, in which the ball is kicked from beneath and usually lobbed over an opponent's head in passing to a team mate.

Chippy Nickname of the Irish midfielder Liam BRADY in reference to his well-known weakness for fried chips.

Chirk A small mining village in North Wales, which was the birthplace of Welsh football. Responsibility for the early development of the game in Wales rests with T.E. Thomas, who was the schoolmaster at Chirk and later an administrator of the Welsh FA. His championship of football amongst the coalminers of Chirk was to have far-reaching consequences and no fewer than 49 future Welsh internationals began their careers with Thomas's team. The greatest among them was none other than the near-legendary Billy MEREDITH, who was himself a Chirk coalminer.

Chopper Nickname of the English player Ron HARRIS.

Chorley English non-League football club, nicknamed the Magpies. Strip: black and white striped shirts with black shorts. Founded in 1883 and based at Victory Park, Chorley play in the Northern Premier League.

Christmas Day Match *See* FOOTBALLERS' BATTALION.

Church Nickname of the English non-League football club ALVECHURCH.

circus game A game in which players wear fancy dress, or otherwise indulge in fanciful experimentation with the rules of the game. A feature of charity games and local fêtes, circus games have ranged from matches between 'three-legged' teams to an extraordinary game played in Birkenhead in 1910, when one team played with their arms tied to their sides and without any boots or socks and the other staggered about on six-foot high stilts (the team with tied arms won).

Citizens Nickname of a number of football clubs named City. They include the Welsh non-League football club BANGOR CITY and the English side MANCHESTER CITY.

City Nickname of any football club that has 'City' as part of its name. The first League club to be called City was LINCOLN CITY (1892), although Stoke (not called City until some years later) had joined the League back in 1888. Others include BATH CITY, BRECHIN CITY, CANTERBURY CITY, CHELMSFORD CITY, Toronto City, and WORCESTER CITY.

City Devils Nickname of the English non-League football club CAMBRIDGE CITY.

City Ground The home ground of NOTTINGHAM FOREST. The City Ground is in fact the club's fifth home, its first having been the Forest Racecourse (now home of the Nottingham Goose Fair), from which the club took its name. Between 1890 and 1898, Forest occupied the Town Ground where significant milestones included the first official use of goalnets (1891). Notable events in the present ground's history have included the first use of rounded goalposts (1921), a severe flood in 1947 (when swans were seen swimming over the pitch), and the destruction by fire of the Main Stand during a match against Leeds United in 1968, which led to the hurried evacuation of 34,000 spectators.

Clackmannan Former Scottish League football club, which dropped out of the League in the late 1920s. Based at Chapelhill Park, Clackmannan played in the League for five seasons before dropping out and subsequently being revived as a youth team.

Clapton English non-League football club, nicknamed the Tons. Strip: red and white striped shirts, with black shorts and socks. Founded in 1878 and based at the Old Spotted Dog ground in Forest Gate, London, Clapton play in the Isthmian League.

Clarets Nickname of a number of clubs around the world who have adopted a claret-coloured playing strip. The most prestigious outside the UK include the Swiss club Servette. British sides include BURNLEY.

Class of '66 Nickname of the celebrated England team asembled by Sir Alf RAMSEY that won the World Cup in 1966. England played host to the competition (opened by Elizabeth II) that year and secured final victory after drawing 0–0 against Uruguay, beating Mexico and France 2–0, defeating Argentina 1–0 (through a header by Geoff HURST), beating Portugal 2–1 (Bobby

CHARLTON's two goals giving the team victory over a side that included the great EUSÉBIO), and then meeting West Germany in the Final.

The Germans scored the first goal after 13 minutes, but England, under their captain Bobby MOORE, equalized in the 19th minute with a header from Hurst (in the squad as replacement for injured Jimmy GREAVES). England went ahead with a goal from Martin Peters with just 13 minutes left but a German goal resulting from a controversial free kick meant that the game had to go into extra time (the first time this had happened in a World Cup Final since 1934). With everything in the balance, Ramsey gathered his weary players around him and delivered one of the pithiest rallying cries ever uttered by an England manager: 'You've beaten them once. Now go out and bloody beat them again.'

Alan BALL spearheaded a resurgence in the English attack, providing the chance for Hurst to score. Hurst's shot hit the underside of the crossbar and dropped straight down: the referee allowed the goal after consultation with the Russian linesman in what turned out to be one of the most hotly debated decisions ever made in the history of football. Even photographs and archive film of the shot fail to prove whether a goal should have been allowed or not. Fortunately for Hurst, he was able to make the arguments academic when, with seconds to spare, he completed his hat-trick with a powerful shot – 'I just belted it' – that made the final score 4–2 in England's favour and made Hurst the first man to score three goals in a World Cup final.

England's fans went mad. As Hurst's third goal went in commentator Kenneth Wolstenholme spoke what were to prove the most oft-repeated words of his career: 'There are people on the pitch . . . they think it's all over . . . it is now!'

As the final whistle blew, Jack CHARLTON sank to his knees with relief, Bobby Charlton cried, Ray Wilson slapped the grass, and Nobby STILES danced a jig – all images that have become part of the legends surrounding that day.

In 1985 the Class of '66 was brought together once more to restage their match with West Germany as a fund-raiser on behalf of the victims of the BRADFORD FIRE; England won 6–4, with a 46-year-old Geoff Hurst repeating his famous hat-trick. Nearly 30 years on, the Charltons, Stiles, and Ball are still in the soccer business, Banks runs a corporate entertainment company, Cohen is in the property trade, Hunt works in a haulage business, Hurst is on the payroll of a window company, Peters sells car insurance, and Wilson is an undertaker; only Moore is missing, having died of cancer in early 1993.

Have you ever noticed how we only win the World Cup under a Labour government?

Harold Wilson (1971)

See also JULES RIMET TROPHY; MARX BROTHERS; PICKLES; WINGLESS WONDERS; WORLD CUP WILLIE.

clearance A powerful defensive shot designed to get the ball away from the goal area when the attacking team is threatening to score.

clergymen Just as cricket has boasted a surprising number of enthusiasts from the church, so has football had its ecclesiastical adherents. Not all of them have, of course, been in favour of the game – many of them objecting to it on the grounds that it promoted the breaking of the Christian church's rulings on the Sabbath.

One noted opponent of the game in the 19th century was the Rev. Samuel Ashe, who waged a lengthy campaign against the local football side at Langley Burrell in Wiltshire. Each Sunday he secreted himself behind bushes close to the pitch used by the team and whenever the ball bounced within reach pierced it with a long pin. The team soon learnt to overcome this sabotage by always having a spare ball.

Other members of the cloth, however, have distinguished themselves by their devotion to the game. Canon A. Wellesley Orr regularly held 'Football Services' in his church at Kingston Hill. During these auspicious occasions the church was decorated with football pennants and shirts, goalposts, and corner flags; the sermon itself began with a blast on a referee's whistle.

The Rev. Ben Crockett, a fan of Derby County, steadfastly refused to hold wedding services if they clashed with home fixtures and resisted all attempts at dissuasion. One outraged bride-to-be in 1984 took her grievance to the Archbishop of Canterbury but still the Rev. Crockett did not give in; the marriage eventually had to take place in another church while Derby County beat Plymouth Argyle 3–1. The bride was less than amused: 'They say God's house is always open but in this case only if Derby are playing away.'

It has doubtless been suggested to many a football-mad cleric that his passion for the game threatens to bring his church into disrepute. The accused have, however, supreme authority for their weakness. As far back as the 14th century Pope John XXII granted papal dispensation to one Canon William de Spalding after he was involved in a fatal accident in which another man fell on to the Canon's knife – during a game of football. More directly relevant is the involvement of Pope John Paul II in the game: in his youth he was a goalkeeper with the Polish amateur team Wostyla, while in 1990 he condescended to bless the World Cup itself prior to the Finals that year.

Cardinal Basil Hume, head of the Roman Catholic Church in England, has made no secret of his faith in Newcastle United and confesses to watching television's 'Match of the Day' with positively religious fervour: 'I should rather like the Match of the Day theme tune played at my funeral.'

Eddy Brown, who made his League debut in 1950 and became a star with Preston North End, Southampton, Coventry City, Birmingham City, and Leyton Orient, scoring over 200 goals, was also a Roman Catholic Teaching Brother. He was renowned for his eccentricities, which included shaking hands with corner flags after scoring, quoting Shakespeare in the dressing-room, modelling menswear, and dancing professionally with Geraldo and his Orchestra on television.

Perhaps the most important playing recruit from the church, however, was the Rev. Kenneth Hunt, who played for Oxford University and Wolverhampton Wanderers before World War I; he not only appeared for Oxford City in the 1903 FA Amateur Cup Final and scored a goal for Wolves in the 1908 FA Cup Final but also instructed the great Charlie Buchan in tactical play. A match in 1912–13 involving Hunt and another cleric, the Rev. W.C. Jordan (also of Wolves), remains the only recorded instance of two clergymen playing on the same side in League history.

Cliftonhill Park The home ground of the Scottish football club ALBION ROVERS. Albion Rovers moved to their new home in the grounds of Cliftonhill House in 1919 after spending their early history at two other grounds much affected by gales. The club's modest record and the restricting of crowd numbers due to safety considerations have meant a gradual decline in the ground's condition. Many spectators watch games for free from a grass mound overlooking the pitch, known to paying fans as 'Aberdeen Gate' (the inhabitants of Aberdeen being

traditionally notorious for their reluctance to part with money). Others sit on the 1000 seats acquired from Third Lanark when the club disbanded in 1967.

Cliftonville Northern Ireland football club, nicknamed the Reds. Strip: red. Cliftonville, based at the Solitude ground, are the Belfast club favoured by the city's Republican population and thus arch-rivals of the Loyalist clubs Glentoran and Linfield.

> We are the Cliftonville, the Pride of the North,
> We hate the Glentoran and Linfield of course,
> We drink all the cider and sing till we're hoarse,
> We are the Cliftonville boys.

Supporters' song

Clockwork Nickname of the Austrian centre-half Ernst OCWIRK.

close down To mark an opposing player at very close range so as to limit his opportunities to play the ball.

Clough, Brian (1935–) Controversial English football player and manager, who became the longest-serving manager in contemporary British football (celebrating over 1000 games as manager). Clough began his playing career with Middlesbrough in 1952 and won the first of his two caps for England in 1959. He signed for Sunderland in 1961 and rapidly earned a reputation as a prolific goalscorer (his 254 League goals for the two clubs being a postwar record) but subsequently suffered a serious knee injury and was forced to retire as a player in 1964, to his lasting regret:

> No matter what I do in life I will never find anything to match scoring goals. I fed on goals. Every time I put the ball into the net it was ecstasy. Goals were like a drug.

The obvious next step was to go into management, which Clough immediately did – with characteristic confidence:

> I know I am better than the 500 or so managers sacked since the war. If they had known anything about the game, they wouldn't have been sacked.

In 1965 he was appointed manager of Hartlepools United, where he formed an enduring partnership with Peter Taylor as his right-hand man. The club was going through a lean patch and Cloughie even had to drive the team coach himself, working without a salary for a period, but both men began to attract attention for their dedication and showmanship. Two years later the pair moved to Derby County and worked a minor miracle that led to Derby capturing the League championship in 1972.

Always unpredictable, he and Taylor then transferred themselves to Brighton in 1973, after which Clough went by himself to Leeds United and, after only 44 days there, to Nottingham Forest, where Taylor rejoined him. Subsequently Clough guided the team to victory in the League championship (1978), the European Cup (1979 and 1980), and again in the League Cup in 1989 and 1990 (the year in which Taylor died) – making Clough the only manager apart from Herbert CHAPMAN to win the Championship with two clubs. He announced his retirement as Forest slipped out of the Premier League in 1993.

He was one of the front-runners for the management of England in the late 1970s, but was passed over in favour of Ron GREENWOOD, an event regretted by many who regard him as the best manager the national team never had. He demanded strict discipline from his players and never tempered his forthright views, which earned him a reputation as the most outspoken (and most widely recognized) manager in the League. When he was awarded an O.B.E. for services to football, his wife was quite sure the initials stood for 'Old Big 'Ead'.

Notorious episodes during his career included an occasion when he manhandled Nottingham Forest fans who had invaded the pitch. Malcolm Allison called him a 'Rolls-Royce communist' and throughout his long career he displayed a healthy disrespect for officialdom:

> *I shout my opinion. I yell my contempt. I mean every word of it. But when you talk like that you are a target. I've got to be a winner or they'll cut me to shreds.*

His most venomous comments were reserved for the administrators of English football. His most widely reported remarks about them included: 'There's a seven man board at Derby, and I wouldn't give you twopence for five of them' and 'Football hooligans? Well, there are ninety-two club chairmen for a start.'

He once summed up his unique managerial style thus: 'Say nowt, win it, then – talk your head off.'

Clown, The Nickname of the South African-born goalkeeper Bruce GROB-BELAAR.

Clown Prince of Soccer Nickname of the English footballer Len SHACKLETON.

Club, The Nickname of the German football club IFC NUREMBERG.

Club Kings of the World Nickname bestowed upon the Spanish football club REAL MADRID during their greatest period, in the 1950s.

Clyde Scottish football club, nicknamed the Bully Wee. Strip: white shirts and socks with black shorts. Founded in 1878, the Bully Wee played their first games on the banks of the River Clyde in Glasgow, hence the club's name. For many years their home was Shawfield, originally a trotting track where boxing, athletics, and greyhound races were also staged; in 1986, however, they made a highly controversial move to their great rivals Partick Thistle's ground at FIRHILL PARK. In 1991 they occupied the stadium at Douglas Park in Hamilton; a move to a new ground in Cumbernauld is subsequently planned for later in the 1990s.

The club's golden era was in the 1950s, when the team captured the Scottish Cup on two occasions, in 1955 and 1958 (they had previously won it in 1939). Stars of the side during these years included right-winger John Buchanan, who once scored in 11 successive First Division games in the 1952–53 season. Other honours have included the Second Division titles in 1905, 1952, 1957, 1962, 1973, 1978, 1982, and 1993.

Clyde enjoyed their record victory in 1951, when they beat Cowdenbeath 11–1; they suffered their worst defeat in 1879, losing 11–0 against Dumbarton. Brian Ahern has made a record 428 League appearances with the club.

Clydebank Scottish football club, nicknamed the Bankies. Strip: white shirt with red shoulders trimmed with black, white shorts, and red socks with black tops. Founded in 1965, Clydebank came into being in the wake of the East Stirling Clydebank court case of 1965, although there had previously been two junior clubs that had played under the same name. Having joined the League in 1966, the club soon established a reputation for innovation, deciding, for instance, against having a manager and relying instead upon the coach for guidance, and setting up a lively social club to attract extra revenue. Control of affairs at the club's home of NEW KILBOWIE PARK rests in almost all cases with the Steedman family who were at the centre of the celebrated court battle.

Clydebank won the Second Division championship in 1976 and on reaching the Premier Division in 1977 became the first Scottish club to be promoted in consecutive seasons; they reached the semi-finals of the Scottish Cup in 1990. Their record victory in their short history was in 1977, when they beat Arbroath 8–1; their worst defeat was in 1965, when they lost 9–1 to Gala Fairydean. Jim Fallon holds the record for appearances with the club, having played 620 times with the Bankies between 1968 and 1986.

coach A club official who assists the manager in promoting a team's standard of play. The coach generally confines his attention to matters on the field and is usually responsible for working on the fine points of tactics and footballing skills (though the job often overlaps with those of manager and trainer). Many English clubs did without the services of a coach until after World War II, when the success of English coaches of foreign teams underlined the desirability of having a coach on the staff.

Key figures in the development of organized coaching in the UK included Stanley ROUS and Walter WINTERBOTTOM, who set up a nationwide network of coaches and insisted upon rigorous training sessions and full preparation. The wheel turned full circle in 1984, when the FA set up the National School at LILLESHALL HALL as a national coaching centre (*see also* CENTRE OF EXCELLENCE).

Ironically English coaches had a fundamental impact on the development of the game in several foreign countries, the first English player to undertake such duties abroad probably being the former goalkeeper Charlie Bunyan, who worked as a coach in Sweden. He is remembered as the luckless guardian of the Hyde goal in an FA Cup tie in 1887 when their opponents Preston North End scored no fewer than 26 times. One of his successors in Sweden, George Raynor, took the Swedish national team to glory in the 1948 Olympics and to the runners-up position in the 1958 World Cup; Raynor followed this success with third places in the 1952 Olympics and the 1954 World Cup.

British coaches remain in demand overseas to the present day; Scottish coach Danny McLennan, for instance, had already served as coach of the Philippines, Mauri-tius, Rhodesia, Iran, Bahrain, Iraq, and Jordan when in 1982 he was invited to take up the same post for Saudi Arabia. Eric Jones, once a winger with West Bromwich Albion among other clubs, claimed to have worked in 40 different countries in his capacity as a coach by the 1960s.

> *There is no bad coaching – only bad coaches.*
>
> Anon

> *About thirty grand a year.*
>
> Ian Branfoot, Crystal Palace coach, on the difference between a coach and a manager

Cobblers Nickname of the English football club NORTHAMPTON TOWN, referring to the town's long history of shoe manufacturing.

Coca-Cola Cup *See* LEAGUE CUP.

Cock and Hens Nickname of the Northern Ireland team GLENTORAN.

Colchester United English football club, nicknamed the U's. Strip: navy blue and white striped shirts, navy blue shorts, and white socks. Founded in 1937 as successors to amateur Colchester Town, United made the leap from the Southern League to the Football League itself in 1950. Subsequently they reached the Third Division (South) on three occasions before ultimately losing their League status in 1990, when they finished bottom of the Fourth Division. The club returned to the League after winning the GM Vauxhall Conference in 1992.

Perhaps the greatest moment in their history was the sensational meeting with Leeds United in the fifth round of the FA Cup in 1971. Leeds were then at the peak of their powers and the most powerful team in the country, with every player bar one a member of an international squad. Against all expectations Colchester recorded an amazing 3–2 victory, to join the ranks of the most distinguished giant-killers (at one point they were 3–0 ahead); more predictably they lost in the next round to Everton by 5–0 (*see* GRANDAD'S ARMY).

Based at the LAYER ROAD ground in Colchester, star players in recent years have included Paul McGee, who transferred to Wimbledon in 1990.

> *Layer Road is falling down, falling down, falling down,*
> *Layer Road is falling down, poor old Col U.*
> *Shall we kick it down some more, down*

some more, down some more?
Shall we kick it down some more? Poor old
Col U.

Southend United fans' song

Collier Row English non-League football club. Strip: red shirts with black shorts and socks. Founded in 1929 and based at the Sungate ground in Romford, Collier Row play in the Isthmian League.

Colliers Nickname of the English football club BARNSLEY, in reference to the coal-mining industry of South Yorkshire.

Colne Dynamoes The ill-fated English non-League football club that became famous in the late 1980s, when it seemed set to achieve full League status. The fairy-tale story of Colne Dynamoes began in 1963, when 11 schoolfriends founded their own club. The side prospered and steadily improved until ultimately the Dynamoes triumphed in the FA Vase competition at Wembley in 1988 with a full-time profes-sional team. Winners of the HFS Loans League by a record margin in 1990, it seemed that progress to the Conference and thus to the League was little more than a formality – but difficulties over the issue of grounds led to disillusion and chairman Graham White controversially disbanded the club, saying the struggle was no longer worthwhile.

Colo Colo Chilean football club, nick-named the Wildcats. Strip: white shirts, black shorts, and white socks. Founded in 1925 by players from the Magallenes team and based at the Colo Colo Stadium in Santiago, the club have won 16 League championships since 1937 and are undis-puted as Chile's most successful club.

IFC Cologne German football club, which emerged as one of the leading German sides in the 1960s. Strip: all white. Founded in 1901 and reformed in 1948, IFC Cologne are based at the MÜNGERSDORFER stadium in Cologne and have won three League championships (1962, 1964, and 1978) and the Cup four times (1968, 1977, 1978, and 1983). In international competition they have twice reached the semi-finals of the European Cup and the European Cup Win-ners' Cup and were runners-up in the UEFA Cup in 1986.

Colombia The Colombian national team have often threatened to establish them-selves among the leading South American teams, though so far without realizing dreams of victory in the major tournaments. The Colombians first qualified for the World Cup Finals in 1962, when they almost upset Uruguay before going down 2–1 and then held the Soviet Union to a 4–4 draw before losing 5–0 to Yugoslavia. Stars of the team in the 1980s and 1990s included Carlos VALDERRAMA. Strip: red shirts with tricolour trim, blue shorts, and red socks with tricolour trim. Colombia qualified for the 1994 World Cup in America.

Colossus Nickname of the midfielder Ron YEATS.

colours In the early history of the game, teams were differentiated by the colours of their caps and socks or simply by armbands (as in the case of Queen's Park) before the use of coloured shirts became general. By the time of the first FA Cup Final in 1872, teams had adopted their own distinctive coloured strips, which in many cases have remained essentially the same ever since:

It is a good plan, if it can previously be so arranged, to have one side with striped jerseys of one colour, say red; and the other with another, say blue. This prevents con-fusion and wild attempts to run after and wrest the ball from your neighbour. I have often seen this done, and the invariable apology – 'I beg your pardon, I thought you were on the opposite side'.

Routledge's Handbook of Football (1867)

Even when coloured strips became the order of the day, it was some time before the familiar schemes of some modern clubs and national sides were decided upon: in 1903, for instance, Scotland kitted out its players in Lord Rosebery's racing colours of prim-rose and white hoops.

Strict rules governed what was and what was not permissible in terms of colours and patterns; in particular – until the rules were relaxed in the 1970s – goalkeepers were limited to green, blue, scarlet, and white strips. Landmarks in the history of team strips have included the stipulation that goalkeepers should wear yellow jerseys in international games (1921) and the first use of a stripe down the seams of players' shorts, introduced by Everton.

Referees for many years restricted them-selves to all-black, although new colour schemes introduced by the administrators of the new Premier League in 1992 saw referees appear in a new green strip. Every team has a set of change colours for use when their usual strip resembles that of their opponents too closely; since 1924 it has been obligatory for visiting teams to use their reserve strip when their usual colours coincide with those of their hosts.

On occasion, referees have been slow to realize the risk of confusion; in 1962 blue-clad Coventry City and Southend in a similar strip had been playing for three minutes before the referee noticed the problem and halted play for Coventry to change to red. Commentators too have occasionally been caught out:

> For those watching in black and white, Spurs are in the yellow shirts.

John Motson, TV commentary

Factors that have influenced the adoption of new colour schemes have included the increased use of floodlighting (which led many teams to introduce glossier lighter colours and saw match officials experimenting with fluorescent shirts) and even politics, with Stockport County considering (but eventually rejecting) a new strip at the time of the Falklands War of 1982 when it was realized that County's colours were uncomfortably close to those of the Argentinian national team. The regularity of changes in team strips in recent years and the cost of purchasing replica kits have met with little favour among the fans themselves:

> Come on you blue two-tone hoops with red and white trim and a little emblem on the sleeve and the manufacturer's logo and the sponsors' name across the chest!

When Saturday Comes, parody of supporters' chant

Coluna, Mário (1935–) Portuguese midfielder, born in Mozambique, who was a star with Benfica and Portugal in the 1960s. Having begun his career with Desportivo de Lourenço Marques, he played a key role in Benfica's European Cup victories in 1961 (when he scored the winning goal) and 1962 and in 1966 captained the Portuguese side that made a strong showing in the World Cup. Winner of 73 caps, he ended his career with the French club Lyon.

Colwyn Bay Welsh non-League football club, nicknamed the Bay. Strip: sky blue shirts, maroon shorts, and sky blue socks. Founded in 1885 and based at the Thornton Road stadium in Ellesmere Port, Colwyn Bay play in the Northern Premier League.

Comunale Stadium (1) The home ground, in Florence, of the Italian football club FIO-RENTINA. The ground was known initially as the Comunale Giovanni Berta, in honour of a local Fascist leader, but was renamed after World War II. Features of the ground include Pier Luigi Nervi's first cantilevered roof, the prototype for the design of many stands subsequently built around the world.

(2) The former home ground in Turin of the Italian football club JUVENTUS. Juventus moved into the stadium in 1933, by which time they had already established themselves as the most powerful team in Italy. The stadium, erected under Italy's Fascist regime, was renamed the Benito Mussolini stadium after the dictator, who was present at the opening ceremony. Over the next few years the stadium witnessed World Cup matches, the triumph of Juventus over all comers, and numerous internationals. As the years passed, however, the Comunale (renamed after the war) deteriorated and in 1990 was finally vacated by Juventus and TORINO (who had arrived in 1960) in favour of more sumptious surroundings at the NEW COMUNALE STADIUM nearby.

Concacef Central American football organization, which is a regional equivalent of UEFA. The Concacef Championship, inaugurated as the Central American and Caribbean Championship in 1941, is held every two years and is the basis of a qualifying group in the Olympics football tournament. It includes teams from central America and the West Indies. The Concacef Champion Clubs Cup, inaugurated in 1967, is a prestigious cup competition for clubs from the region.

Concrete Lavvy Pan Nickname of the MEADOWBANK STADIUM in Edinburgh, which is home to MEADOWBANK THISTLE.

Conference, The The GM Vauxhall Conference, which is the most senior of the minor leagues that feed into the Football League itself. Winners of the Conference are (since 1987) automatically promoted to the Third Division (in effect making the Conference an unofficial Fourth Division). The league began life in 1979 as the Alliance Premier League and was subsequently renamed the Gola League. Scarborough were the first team to reach the League proper after capturing the GM Vauxhall Conference title in 1987 and displacing Lincoln City. See also PYRAMID.

conflict and art J.B. Priestley's celebrated

description of the nature of football in his novel *The Good Companions* (1929). Priestley's mythical team was Bruddersford United, an archetypal side representing an equally mythical town in the industrial Midlands: according to the author 'a man who had missed the last home match of t' United had to enter social life on tiptoe in Bruddersford'.

> *To say that these men paid their shillings to watch twenty-two hirelings kick a ball is merely to say that a violin is wood and catgut, that* Hamlet *is so much paper and ink. For a shilling the Bruddersford United AFC offered you Conflict and Art . . .*

Congleton Town English non-League football club, nicknamed the Bears. Strip: white shirts, with black shorts and socks. Founded in 1901 and based at the Booth Street ground in Congleton, the club play in the Northern Premier League.

Congo The Congo joined FIFA in 1962 and rank among the stronger African sides. Their moment of greatest glory came in 1972, when they captured the African Nations Cup. Strip: all red.

Conmebol South American football organization, which is a regional equivalent of UEFA. The Conmebol Championship serves as a qualifying group in the Olympics football tournament.

Copa America South American football tournament that was founded in 1916, when it was contested by Argentina, Brazil, Chile, and Uruguay (the eventual winners). It began as an annual competition but since 1927 has been staged approximately every four years. In 1979 it was reorganized as a knock-out competition, having previously been run on a league basis. Like other international competitions for the South American nations the tournament has been dominated by Argentina, Brazil, and Uruguay.

Copa Libertadores South American football tournament that was founded in 1960. Modelled on the European Cup, the contest involves the two top clubs from each of the ten leading soccer nations on the continent. Over the years the competition has dominated the headlines as much for the corruption and violence linked with it as for the action on the field.

Particularly notorious in the history of the Cup was a heated match between Boca Juniors from Argentina and Sporting Cristal from Peru in March 1971. The game erupted into violence after the Boca Juniors' captain lost his temper after a hard tackle; the resulting battle between the two teams left three players in hospital (one with a fractured skull) and another 16 in prison serving a 30-day sentence (quickly turned into suspended sentences by the authorities fearing riots).

Among other infamous episodes were a twice-suspended match between Peñarol and Santos in 1962 (a result of missiles being thrown from the crowd) and another mass brawl in 1970, this time involving Peñarol and Nacional. The two most successful teams in the history of the competition are Independiente and Estudiantes, both from Argentina.

Corby Town English non-League football club, nicknamed the Steelmen. Strip: white shirts, black shorts, and white socks. Founded in 1948 and based at the Rockingham Triangle Stadium, Corby Town play in the Southern League.

Corinthian League English football league that was founded in 1945. The League comprised a number of London teams but finally expired in 1963 when its member clubs were allowed to join the Athenian League; the most successful sides in the League's 18-year history were Hounslow Town, Maidenhead United, and Walton and Hersham.

Corinthians (1) Celebrated English amateur football team that prides itself on its high playing ideals and long giant-killing record. The club was founded in 1882 at the instigation of N. Lane Jackson, the assistant secretary of the FA and one of the staunchest opponents of professionalism.

Jackson assembled a side consisting entirely of amateurs who had already distinguished themselves with other clubs (mostly in London) and fashioned them into one of the most respected teams in the country. They were soon recognized to be masters of dribbling and the short-passing game, which was often called 'Corinthian-style' in their honour. The Corinthians became a byword for fair play and (despite the fact they refused for many years to compete for any cup or other prize) repeatedly humbled professional sides at home and abroad with ease, as recalled by an Austrian player after the team played in Vienna:

I remember how they walked on to the field, spotless in their white shirts and dark shorts. Their hands in their pockets, sleeves hanging down. Yet there was about them an air of casual grandeur, a haughtiness that was yet not haughty, which seemed intangible. And how they played!

Their most notable victims over the years included Sheffield Wednesday, who lost 2–0 to Corinthians after winning the FA Cup that year, Blackburn Rovers, who were thrashed 8–1 after winning the Cup in 1884, and FA Cup victors Bury, who went down 10–3 in 1903. Twice in the 1890s the England team was entirely composed of players with Corinthians.

Famous players with the team included centre-forward G.O. SMITH, who led the attack from 1893 to 1901, the great all-rounder C.B. Fry (who was also a celebrated cricketer and claimed to have turned down offers of the throne of Albania and an invitation to help set up the Nazi youth movement), and from the line-up of the mid-1920s such players as Freddie Ewer, Frank Hartley, Graham Doggart, Alfred Bower, Howard Baker, and Claude Ashton, all of whom won caps with England.

The team finally condescended to contest the FA Cup in 1922, by which time their great days were drawing to a close; they did, however, manage to notch up another major triumph in 1927, when they were runners-up in the FA Charity Shield competition. After amalgamation with the Casuals in 1939 they also competed in various leagues.

The club continued to represent the highest standards of sportsmanship and won admirers in many countries. The term 'Corinthian', evoking images of the noble sporting ideals of the ancient world, is still revered throughout the game and the team continues to observe its honourable traditions.

Somewhat curiously, the original Corinthians were renowned in Greece and Rome not so much for sporting idealism as for licentious living; the term later acquired sporting relevance when it was revived in the Regency period to describe rowdy horse-racing fans. In Shakespeare's time the word simply denoted a hard-living man:

I am no proud Jack, like Falstaff; but a Corinthian, a lad of mettle, a good boy.

Henry IV, Pt. I, II, iv

(2) Brazilian football club, named in tribute to the celebrated English team that popularized football in South America during an early tour of the continent (1910). Strip: white shirts, black shorts, and white socks. The Brazilian incarnation of the team, based at the São Jorge Park in São Paulo, has won some 20 League championships over the years and are second only to Flamengo in terms of popularity.

Corky Nickname of the Scottish defender George YOUNG, who led Scotland with great success in the 1950s. He acquired his nickname after it was disclosed that during internationals he always carried a 'lucky' champagne cork he had kept from the players' celebration of a Rangers' victory over Morton in the Scottish Cup.

corner kick A kick taken from the corner post after the ball has run out of play behind the goal line. The corner kick was first introduced in 1872, but until 1924 the rules disallowed goals scored directly from such a kick. Billy Alston of St Bernards' scored the first direct goal from a corner kick in 1924; the first in League football was W.H. Smith of Huddersfield Town (in the same season). Alex Cheyne of Aberdeen and Scotland was the first player to score from a corner kick in an international, in a match against England in 1929.

Until 1924 there was no law prohibiting a player taking a corner from kicking the ball more than once before it reached another player but no one had realized the potential this allowed until Everton's Sam Chedgzoy, on taking a corner against Tottenham Hotspur that year, dribbled the ball all the way from the corner flag to score. The laws of the game were hastily changed so that players taking corners could kick the ball just once. Accordingly, players representing Huddersfield Town in 1952 felt they had cause to complain when Tottenham Hotspur's Eddie Bailey took a remarkable corner in which the ball rebounded off the referee's back allowing him to centre it for Len Duquemin to score; the goal was allowed despite protests that Bailey had played the ball twice.

Corner kicks are a regular feature of most games; the first League match in which no corners were awarded to either side did not take place until 1931, when neither Newcastle United nor Portsmouth won one – significantly, the match ended in a goalless draw.

Coronation Cup Anglo-Scottish cup tournament that was held in 1953 to celebrate the accession of Elizabeth II. It involved eight Scottish and eight English teams and was finally won by Celtic, as still celebrated in various songs heard to this day at Celtic Park:

> Said Lizzie to Philip 'They don't stand a chance,
> I'll send up the Gunners to lead them a dance,
> With Celtic defeated, the way will be clear,
> And a cup for the Rangers in my crowning year'.
> But alas for the hopes of our royal true blues,
> The Celts beat the Arsenal, and Manchester too,
> With Hibs in the final – a glorious scene,
> All Hampden was covered in gold, white and green.

Cosmos *See* NEW YORK COSMOS.

Costa Rica The Costa Rican team have had relatively little impact in international competition, but attracted interest in 1990 when they qualified for the World Cup Finals. Victory against Scotland effectively ended the Scottish campaign and ensured Costa Rica's passage to the second round, where they lost 4–1 against Czechoslovakia. Strip: red shirts, blue shorts, and white socks.

Cottagers Nickname of the English football club FULHAM, in reference to the side's home at CRAVEN COTTAGE.

County Nickname of the English football clubs NOTTS COUNTY (also called the Magpies) and STOCKPORT COUNTY.

County Ground The home ground of the English football club SWINDON TOWN. The club's first home was a field next to a quarry in the Old Town area, where Swindon played their first matches in 1881; they moved on fairly quickly, however, after a small boy attending one of the matches fell into the quarry. They finally settled at the County Ground, where there was already a cricket pitch, in 1895. Notable events in the ground's history include a period during World War II when it was used as a prisoner-of-war camp.

Cove English non-League football club. Strip: amber shirts, black shorts with amber stripe, and black socks. Founded in 1897 and based at the Oak Farm Field ground in Farnborough, Cove play in the Isthmian League.

Coventry City English football club, nick-

named the Sky Blues. Strip: sky blue shirts with navy blue trim, sky blue shorts, and sky blue socks. The club was formed in 1883 by workers at Singer's bicycle factory and first played under the title Singer's FC. They acquired their current name in 1898 and a year later settled at their permanent home at HIGHFIELD ROAD.

They finally joined the League in 1919, as members of the Second Division, and subsequently divided their time between the Second and Third Divisions (with one disastrous trip down to the Fourth Division in 1958–59) until 1967, when they established themselves as long-term members of the First Division.

The 1960s were a time of great change and controversy for the club and the period is still referred to in Coventry as the 'Sky Blue era'. Under chairman Derrick Robbins and manager Jimmy HILL the whole image of the team was revitalized and the club acquired a reputation for innovation, with special attention being given to improving relations with supporters. The team played in a new, more striking sky blue strip, which gave rise to the nickname, and the whole Sky Blue concept was expanded to include special Sky Blue trains for travelling fans, Sky Blue radio (to entertain fans before matches), etc.

The team prospered under this invigorating leadership (despite Hill's resignation in 1968) and have several times ranked among the country's leading sides. The climax came in 1987 when, under manager John Sillett, Coventry captured the FA Cup after beating Tottenham Hotspur in the Final. They also reached the semi-finals of the League Cup in 1981 and 1990.

Star players over the years have included forward Clarrie Bourton in the 1930s, centre-half George Curtis and winger Roger Rees in the Sky Blue era, Willie Carr and Tommy Hutchison in the 1970s, and Cyrille Regis, David Speedie, and Terry Butcher in the 1980s.

The club enjoyed their record victory in 1934, when they beat Bristol City 9–0; they suffered their worst defeat in 1930, losing 10–2 against Norwich City. George Curtis holds the record for League appearances, having played in 486 games between 1956 and 1970.

> Let's all sing together,
> Play up Sky Blues,
> While we sing together,
> We will never lose,
> Tottenham or Chelsea,
> United or anyone,

They can't defeat us,
We'll fight 'til the game is won.

'Sky Blue Song', to the tune of the 'Eton Boating Song' (written by the schoolmaster and poet William Johnson Cory in 1865)

cover To take up a position close behind a team mate, thus enabling him to challenge for the ball, knowing that a counter-move will be blocked.

Cowdenbeath Scottish football club, nicknamed Cowden. Strip: royal blue and white shirts and shorts with blue socks. Formed in 1881, Cowdenbeath joined the Scottish Second Division in 1905 and have since spent most of their history in the lower rank, winning the Second Division title in 1914, 1915, and 1939.

The club's golden era was in the early 1930s, when they spent several seasons in the First Division; after winning the Second Division championship in 1939 they were robbed of another stay in the top flight by the outbreak of World War II. Stars at CENTRAL PARK over the years have included Jim Paterson, Alex Venters, and more recently Craig Levein.

Cowden enjoyed their record victory in 1928, beating St Johnstone 12–0; they suffered their worst defeat in 1951, losing 11–1 to Clyde.

Cowlairs Former Scottish League football club, which dropped out of the League in 1895. Based at Springvale Park in Springburn, Glasgow, Cowlairs originally joined the League in 1890.

Crab, The Nickname of the English midfielder Ray WILKINS. Wilkins began his playing career with Chelsea and later joined Manchester United (1979), AC Milan, Paris St Germain, Glasgow Rangers, and Queen's Park Rangers, often playing as captain. He has been much admired for his leadership qualities and won a total of 84 caps for his country. His nickname was bestowed on him, somewhat harshly, by Ron ATKINSON, who criticized him for excessive cautiousness and for always passing the ball sideways: 'He can't run, can't tackle, and can't head the ball. The only time he goes forward is to toss the coin.'

Craven Cottage The home ground of the English football club FULHAM. The Cottagers had a number of homes before finally settling at Craven Cottage in 1894. The land the pitch was laid out on was once part of a hunting estate belonging to Anne Boleyn. Subsequently it was the site of a building actually called Craven Cottage, built by the sixth Baron Craven in 1780 and later used as a hunting lodge by George IV; other occupants of the house included the novelist and politician Edward Bulwer-Lytton, whose historical novels included *The Last Days of Pompeii* (1834). When the site was levelled by the Cottagers in preparation for the laying of the pitch they discovered a mysterious underground passage leading from where the house had stood all the way to the Thames.

Distinctive features of the ground, which was finally opened in 1896, included the unusual multi-gabled 'Rabbit Hutch' stand and the Craven Cottage stand designed in red brick by Archibald Leitch in 1905. Among the most notable events in the ground's history have been the staging of a Home International in 1907 (the first time a club ground other than that at Crystal Palace had been used), bombing of the pitch during World War II, and the only London appearance made by PELÉ (who played there in a friendly against Fulham with his club Santos in 1973).

More recently a protracted dispute in the 1980s over plans to develop the ground and to share it with Chelsea made the headlines. When it was realized (in 1987) that this plan had been changed to allow Queen's Park Rangers to merge with Fulham at Loftus Road, loyal Fulham fans (and a consortium led by ex-player and commentator Jimmy HILL) created a furore and a compromise of limited redevelopment was agreed.

Crawley Town English non-League football club, nicknamed the Reds. Strip: red shirts, red shorts, and white socks. Founded in 1896 and based at Town Mead in Crawley, the club play in the Southern League.

Crazy Gang Nickname of the celebrated WIMBLEDON side of the 1980s and 1990s (*see also* DONS). The club earnt their nickname – a reference to the eccentric comedy team of the 1940s – through the various non-League habits they brought with them on their meteoric rise to the First Division and through the refreshingly unconventional managerial style adopted by such managers as Joe Kinnear, the jovial Irishman who succeeded the disciplinarian Peter Withe in the early 1990s.

Kinnear, a former player with Tottenham Hotspur, raised eyebrows with his relaxed attitude, leading players to the pub rather than to the running track and promoting a more friendly club atmosphere. He even encouraged players to vote for the worst member of the side after each match of the 1991–92 season: the unfortunate player named then had to go to see Chekhov's *Uncle Vanya* (described as 'the most boring play in London') at the National Theatre. The approach seemed to work, with the Dons being admitted to the new Premier League and maintaining their new-found reputation as a major club. *See also* WOMBLES.

create space To evade the attentions of a marker so as to have an opportunity to receive the ball unhindered.

Crewe Alexandra English football club, nicknamed the Railwaymen. Strip: red shirts, white shorts, and red socks. Otherwise nicknamed the Alex, Crewe were founded as a football club by railway workers in 1877, though they had previously met to play rugby and cricket. They distinguished themselves early in their history by reaching the semi-finals of the FA Cup in 1888 but have since spent almost their entire League career in the bottom division (actually dropping out of the League altogether in 1896 and not returning until 1921).

The Railwaymen have the unusual distinction of having been founder members of three divisions (the Second Division, the Third Division (North), and the Fourth Division). Other achievements include a disastrous run of 30 games without a win, notched up in the 1956–57 season. In an attempt to lift the team's game in the 1982–83 season, a local garage offered a car as a reward to any player who scored 30 goals in the season: no one qualified (which was less than surprising considering the team only scored 29 goals in total the previous season).

Star players with the club in relatively recent times have included Liverpool's Rob Jones and England international David Platt. Fans include pop star Rod Stewart.

Based at GRESTY ROAD, Crewe enjoyed their record victory in 1932, when they beat Rotherham United 8–0; they suffered their worst defeat in 1960, losing 13–2 against Tottenham Hotspur (a humiliation witnessed by a record attendance). Tommy Lawry made a record 436 League appearances for the club between 1966 and 1978.

The Railwaymen are the only British or Irish professional football club never to have issued a club song on record.

> We're riding along on the Alexandra
>   Special,
> Woo woo, woo woo,
> Just riding along, singing our song,
> The Alexandra! The Alexandra!

Supporters' song, to the tune of 'Chatanooga Choo Choo'

Cripps, Harry (1941–) English player, nicknamed The Dog, who was an enormously popular star at Millwall in the 1960s and 1970s. Millwall fans applauded the terrier-like enthusiasm with which Cripps committed himself to reckless tackles on opposing players and regarded him as a symbol of the toughness for which the Lions had such a reputation. His various achievements with the club included breaking more legs than any other player in the history of the League.

> Oh 'Arry Boy, the fans, the fans are calling,
> From end to end and down the Cold Blow
>   Lane,
> We want a goal, we need your inspiration,
> Oh 'Arry Boy, you know we love you so,
> Throughout the years you've given us your
>   everything,
> Now in return we give this song to you,
> For what you've done is something quite
>   exceptional,
> We pledge ourselves to you our 'Arry Boy.

Supporters' song, to the tune of 'Danny Boy'

cross A pass in which the ball travels across the field of play, often towards the penalty area to create a chance for another player to score.

crossbar The horizontal bar between the two goalposts, below which the ball must pass for a valid goal to be scored. Such bars became compulsory in 1882, though crossbars had been experimented with as early as 1875. Before that, tape was stretched between the posts at eight feet above the ground – as in the first FA Cup Final in 1872.

The modern crossbar is curved to allow for the effect of gravity, which pulls the middle of the bar down when it is put in position. The exact height of the crossbar is laid down in the rules of the game and is rigidly enforced. Back in 1888 Crewe Alexandra succeeded in challenging the height of the crossbar in their match against the London club Swifts in the fourth round of the FA Cup: Crewe proved that the bar was two inches lower than the rules dictated and Swifts, the home team, were consequently disqualified from the competition.

Particular fury surrounded the fact that Crewe only made their objection when the game (a 2–2 draw) was over – it was subsequently decided that in the future similar complaints would have to be communicated before the start of play; Crewe were knocked out of the tournament in the semi-finals by Preston North End.

As recently as 1989 a professional team, Portsmouth, were embarrassed by a disclosure that a crossbar at Fratton Park had been discovered to be an inch too low.

crossover run A tactical ploy in which two players pass each other from opposite directions in order to confuse the defending markers and create space to receive the ball.

Crows Nickname of the English non-League football club ROYSTON TOWN, in reference to the Royston crow (a species of crow discovered in the Royston area around a hundred years ago and now also immortalized in the name of the local newspaper, the *Royston Crow*).

Croydon English non-League football club, nicknamed the Blues. Strip: all blue. Founded in 1953, the club are based at the Croydon Sports Arena and play in the Isthmian League.

Crusaders Former nickname of the English non-League football club HUNGERFORD TOWN, after a magazine connected with the club.

crush barriers Rigid metal barriers erected at intervals on the terracing in order to prevent sections of the crowd collapsing towards the pitch and crushing those at the lowest level (as happened in the Burnden Park disaster when two such barriers failed). The first crush barriers were installed as long ago as 1896, when they were put in position by Celtic in preparation for a Home International between Scotland and England.

Cruyff, Johan (1947–) Dutch footballer, who was widely considered to be among the game's greats long before his playing career was over. He established his reputation as a brilliant (though occasionally unruly) striker while with Ajax and a year after his first appearance with the side made his debut for the Netherlands (1966). Ajax won the European Cup in 1971, in which year Cruyff's individual contribution was acknowledged with the European Footballer of the Year award. Ajax reclaimed the European Cup in 1972, in which year Cruyff scored 25 goals in the Dutch League, and again in 1973, when Cruyff received his second European Footballer of the Year honour. That same year, he transferred to Barcelona for a record £922,000 and continued to appear for his national side, leading the team as captain in the World Cup Final of 1974, but having to be content with a runners-up medal (and his third European Footballer of the Year award).

Having scored 33 goals in 48 internationals, he announced his retirement as a player in 1978 but subsequently played for the US team Los Angeles Aztecs and for Feyenoord for a time before accepting (1982) the post of coach back at Ajax. Under Cruyff's expert hand the team won the European Cup Winners' Cup in 1987, after which he repeated the feat with his old club Barcelona. A mild heart attack in 1991 brought his active involvement in the game to a stop, at least temporarily.

Cruzeiro Brazilian football club, which emerged as one of South America's leading domestic sides in the 1970s. Strip: blue shirts, with white shorts and socks. Founded (as Palestra Italia) in 1921 and based at the Magalhaes Pinto Stadium in Belo Horizonte, Cruzeiro have won some 19 League championships and the South American Cup in 1976.

Crystal Palace (1) English football club, variously nicknamed the Eagles and the Glaziers. Strip: red and blue shirts with red shorts and socks. The first Crystal Palace football team was founded back in 1861 by staff working at the Great Exhibition in Joseph Paxton's celebrated Crystal Palace and was one of the sides to contest the very first FA Cup in 1871, getting as far as the semi-final. The modern club though, dates back to 1905 and used the Crystal Palace as its first home until 1915, when the army took the site over. Subsequently based at Herne Hill, the Den, and the Nest, the Eagles eventually settled at SELHURST PARK in 1924.

The team joined the League in 1920 and for many years remained a relatively undistinguished resident of the lower divisions (having collected the Third Division title in 1921). The 1960s saw an improvement in the club's fortunes, however, with promotion from the Fourth Division in 1961 culminating in their first visit to the First Division in 1969. After a slump back down to the Third Division in the 1970s the Eagles revived under Terry VENABLES and once more reached the First Division in 1979 before slipping back to the Second Division in 1981. Manager Steve Coppell got them back into the First Division in 1989 and a year later saw his team through to the Final of the FA Cup, losing to Manchester United after a replay in which the Palace players were condemned for their aggressive attitude. Howard KENDALL, manager of Everton, observed of the side: 'Don't expect to play Palace and be able to kiss your girlfriend afterwards.'

In 1992 Palace were founder members of the Premier League but were relegated at the end of the first season. Stars with the team have included forward Johnny BYRNE in the 1960s and striker Ian Wright in the 1980s.

The Eagles enjoyed their record victory in 1959, when they beat Barrow 9–0; they suffered their worst defeat in 1990, losing 9–0 to Liverpool. As the final whistle blew in this disastrous latter game, bemused Palace fans were heard singing (to the tune of 'Guantanamera'): 'Score in a minute, we're going to score in a minute.'

Jim Cannon – for a time captain of the team – holds the record for League appearances with the club, having played in 571 games between 1973 and 1988. It was a period that witnessed little in the way of rewards, as reflected in more than one song heard at Selhurst Park at the time:

When Jim, goes up, to get the FA Cup,
We'll be dead, we'll be dead.

Supporters' song, to the tune of 'Quartermaster's Stores'

(2) The sports ground at Sydenham in south London that was for many years one of the most prestigious homes of English football. The ground was laid just below Paxton's glass palace in what had been the bed of an artificial lake and offered an ideal setting for visiting spectators to stroll about and enjoy picnics before and after the match.

In 1895 the ground hosted the FA Cup Final for the first time; subsequently another 19 Finals were staged at Crystal Palace before World War I, ending a year before the so-called Khaki Cup Final in 1915. Highlights of those years included the 1897 Final between Aston Villa and Everton (won – as in 1895, 1905, and 1913 – by Villa), the 1901 Final in which (after a replay in Bolton) Tottenham Hotspur became the only non-League team to win the Cup, and the 1903 Final in which Bury won by a record margin of 6–0 against Derby County. For one team though, Crystal Palace became

synonymous with disappointment: Newcastle United appeared at the stadium in the Final on no fewer than five occasions between 1905 and 1911, but lost every time.

During World War I the ground was used as a depot, after which it served as the home of the Corinthians for several years. Subsequently it witnessed motor racing before being replaced ultimately by the Crystal Palace athletics stadium.

CSKA Sofia Bulgarian football club, nicknamed the Reds. Strip: red shirts, white shorts, and red socks. Founded in 1948, CSKA are the Bulgarian army team and have been known under a range of different titles over the years. Based at the PEOPLE'S ARMY STADIUM in Sofia, the club are the most successful of all Bulgarian sides, having won nearly 30 League championships and five Cup Finals. The club were re-formed in 1985 in the wake of notorious incidents during the Cup Final, which involved a brawl between the players, and was obliged to play under the name Sredets until they were allowed to revert to the old title in 1989.

Cuba Cuba's national team has played a relatively modest role in international competition but have enjoyed the occasional moment of glory. In 1938 the team qualified for the World Cup Finals for the first time and created one of the sensations of the series when they held Romania to a 3–3 draw and then beat them 2–1 in the replay (though they subsequently crashed 8–0 against Sweden and have not since reappeared in the Finals). Strip: white shirts with red trim, dark blue shorts, and white and red socks.

Cullis, Stan (1915–) English centre-half and manager, who enjoyed a long and highly successful association with Wolverhampton Wanderers. Cullis made his debut for Wolves in 1934 and won the first of 12 England caps in 1938. In 1939 he collected a runners-up medal in the FA Cup before the outbreak of World War II disrupted his career. After the war he was appointed assistant manager of the club, eventually rising to the post of secretary manager in 1948. Confident, determined, and unsparing in his criticism of his players, he led the side to victory in the FA Cup in 1949 and in the League championship in 1954, 1958, and 1959; a second FA Cup followed in 1960. The success of Cullis's controversial kick and rush tactics was undeniable and the team proved its effectiveness against the best of opponents from both the UK and the Continent (*see* CHAMPIONS OF THE WORLD). He finally left Wolves in 1964 and a year later became manager of Birmingham City, where he remained until 1970.

Cumbrians Nickname of the English football club CARLISLE UNITED, in reference to the location of the team in Cumbria.

Cup, The The FA Cup (or its equivalent in virtually all major footballing nations).

Cup fever The fervour and excitement that surrounds the FA Cup competition. The tournament has roused extremes of emotion since its earliest days with its opportunities for small clubs to grab the glory (*see* GIANT-KILLER) and for great clubs to demonstrate their superiority against all and sundry.

In the early days of the competition, when the final three rounds were always played in London, the capital would be invaded by crowds of enthusiastic supporters 'oop for t'cup' from all over the country, often to the bemusement of the inhabitants who nonetheless shared their visitors' enthusiasm. When Darwen were obliged to take the long journey to London on three occasions in 1879 to settle a quarter-final against the Old Etonians, the people of London generously set up a 'London Fund' into which they contributed money to help with Darwen's expenses.

The excitement the Cup can bring is unmatched elsewhere in the British game (and arguably in British sport as a whole) and stories of desperate attempts to get tickets to the all-important Final are legion. Legend has it that an advertisement that appeared in *The Times* shortly before a Cup Final some years ago read: 'Man offers marriage to woman supplying Cup Final ticket for next Saturday. Replies must enclose photograph of ticket.'

Cup magic The long history of unexpected victories, outrageous reversals of fortune, and brilliant individual and team performances that is associated with the FA Cup. The competition has inspired many great sides over the years. The most notable manifestations of Cup magic include the WHITE HORSE FINAL of 1923, the MATTHEWS FINAL of 1953, and Second Division Sunderland's epic 1–0 victory over Leeds United in 1973 (in which Sunderland goalkeeper Jim Montgomery memorably saved a shot by Peter Lorimer). *See also* CUP FEVER; LITTLE TIN IDOL.

Cup medals *See* MEDALS.

cup-tied Term indicating that a player is barred from taking part in a Cup competition with his present team as he has already appeared in it with another club.

Curlews Nickname of the English non-League football club CHERTSEY TOWN.

Curzon Ashton English non-League football club, nicknamed the Curzons. Strip: blue shirts and shorts with white socks. Founded in 1963 and based at the National Park in Ashton-under-Lyne, Lancashire, Curzon Ashton play in the Northern Premier League.

cut out To block a pass between players of the opposing team.

Cyprus Cyprus joined FIFA in 1948 but have yet to establish themselves as a leading side in international competition. Strip: blue shirts, white shorts, and blue socks.

Czechoslovakia Czechoslovakia has a distinguished history in international competition (though the division of the country into two separate states in the early 1990s may lead to a change in fortunes). Representative teams from the area played matches as early as the 1890s but it was not until after World War I that the country established its reputation. The side first participated in the World Cup Finals in 1934 and stormed right through to the Final (which they lost 2–1 despite the heroic efforts of such stars as goalkeeper PLANICKA). They reappeared in the 1938 series but did little further to distinguish themselves until 1962, when they played their second World Cup Final (this time losing 3–1 to Brazil). Similarly successful was their campaign in 1990, which saw the Czechs reach the quarter-finals of the World Cup in Italy thanks to the goals of striker Tomas Skuhravy. Their other honours include the European Championship (1976) and the Olympic football title (1980). Strip: red shirts, white shorts, and blue socks.

Czibor, Zoltan (1929–) Hungarian winger, who was a pillar of the celebrated Hungarian national side that dominated international competition in the early 1950s. He played for Komarom and Ferencváros before joining Honvéd and ultimately moved to Barcelona after the Hungarian Revolution. He won a total of 43 caps for Hungary, scoring 17 goals.

D

Dagenham and Redbridge English non-League football club formed in 1992 by the merging of Dagenham and Redbridge Forest, nicknamed the Reds. Strip: red shirts, blue shorts. The club are based at Victoria Road, Dagenham, and play in the Conference.

Dale Nickname of the English football club ROCHDALE.

Dalglish, Kenny (1951–) Scottish footballer, nicknamed King Kenny, whose success as both player and manager is virtually unrivalled in British football. Dalglish made his debut with Celtic in 1970 and just two years later played a key role in the team's achievement of the League and Cup Double; in the meantime he also won the first of a record total of 102 caps for Scotland (1971) and rapidly built up a reputation for stylish and often dazzling attacking play.

After assisting Celtic in the winning of a further seven major trophies (though ironically he had been a Rangers fan as a boy) he was lured by Bob PAISLEY to Liverpool in 1977 as a replacement for Kevin KEEGAN (who was considered by many to be irreplaceable) and quickly carved himself a niche with the Anfield faithful:

Kenny's from Heaven.

Supporters' banner (1970s)

It was largely through Dalglish's efforts that the team's domination of English (and European) football was maintained, with Liverpool winning the First Division championship nine times between 1977 and 1990, the European Cup in 1977, 1978, 1981, and 1984, four successive League Cups (1981–85), and the FA Cup in 1986 and 1989. He was also awarded the Footballer of the Year title in 1979 and 1983, adding real substance to the club's chairman John Smith's claim that Dalglish was the 'best player the club has signed this century'.

In 1985 he succeeded Joe Fagan as manager and a year later won the first of three Manager of the Year awards as Liverpool won the Double (he scored the goal clinching the League title himself). He retired as a player in 1990 and (totally unexpectedly) announced his departure from Anfield and from football itself before the end of the 1991 season, giving stress as his reason. However, he was soon back in the game, taking over the management of Blackburn Rovers and leading them into the Premier League in 1992.

An intensely private and uncommunicative character – Mike Channon said he had as much personality as a tennis racket – King Kenny does, however, have a reputation for practical joking.

Nine's better.

Kenny Dalglish, on being congratulated on his golf handicap of ten (1991)

I never saw anyone in this country to touch him. I can think of only two who could go ahead of him – Pelé and possibly Cruyff.

Graeme Souness (1988)

Dall'Ara The home ground of the Italian football club BOLOGNA. The stadium was opened (as the Littoriale Stadium) in 1927 with the support of Italy's Fascist regime. In accordance with the political thinking of the time the stadium's design reflected the glorious Roman past, with arches, balconies, and other classical features. Players with Bologna still make use of the neighbouring Portico di San Luca – an ancient four-kilometre covered walkway – for training runs. Reflecting contemporary events, the stadium also housed two statues – one (still extant) celebrating the Italian invasion of Abyssinia and the other depicting Mussolini himself on horseback; this latter statue was later melted down and remodelled to represent two of the partisans who had resisted the Duce's dictatorship.

The stadium was given its current name in 1983 in honour of Renato Dall'Ara, the club's president for over 24 years whose death in the hour of Bologna's Championship triumph in 1964 was much regretted. The ground was greatly improved in the 1980s.

Dalymount Park The home ground, in Dublin, of the Irish football clubs Bohemians and (since 1987) SHAMROCK ROVERS. The ground was opened in 1901 and hosted the first of many internationals in 1904. Subsequently it became the most prestigious of all Irish grounds, staging the Cup Final regularly between 1929 and 1971. Threatened by property developers in the 1980s, it was purchased by the FA of Ireland in 1989.

Danny Boy Nickname (in reference to the popular song of the same title) of the celebrated Belfast-born footballer Danny BLANCHFLOWER.

Dark Blues Nickname of the Scottish football club DUNDEE, in reference to the club colours.

Darlington English football club, nicknamed the Quakers. Strip: white shirts, black shorts, and white socks. The team was founded in 1883 and played for many years as a leading amateur side before joining the League in 1921.

Since 1927 Darlington have spent their entire history in the bottom two divisions, with the exception of the years 1989–90, when they dropped out of the League altogether for a single season before gaining readmittance by winning the GM Vauxhall Conference title. Apart from the Third Division (North) title in 1925 and the Fourth Division championship in 1991, the club have never won a major honour but did enjoy two good runs in the FA Cup (in 1911 and 1958). Famous names associated with the club at their home at the FEETHAMS ground in Darlington have included Cyril Knowles, who managed the team for a period in the 1980s. Another was that of an outside-right called Baden Powell who played for the team in the 1950s (he was not, however, the Baden-Powell who won fame as founder of the Boy Scouts).

Darlington enjoyed their record victory in 1928, when they beat Lincoln City 9–2; they suffered their worst defeat in 1964, when they lost 10–0 to Doncaster Rovers. Ron Greener made a record 442 League appearances with the club between 1955 and 1968.

> Come on the Quaker men, the boys in
>   black and white,
> We cheer them every morning, every after-
>   noon, and night.
> Feethams is our home ground where we
>   score goals galore,

> And now we shout for more, more, more!
> We'll sing Darlington forever,
> We'll sing Darlington forever,
> We'll sing Darlington forever,
> As the Quakers go marching on, on, on.

Supporters' song, to the tune of 'John Brown's Body' (1960s)

Dartford English non-League football club, nicknamed the Darts. Strip: black and white hooped shirts with white shorts and socks. Founded in 1894 and based at the Watling Street ground, Dartford – who play in the Southern League – shared their home with newly promoted Maidstone for a time in the early 1990s. The club fanzine is entitled *At the End of the Tunnel* (in reference to the Dartford Tunnel).

Darwen Former English League football club, which was a League member from 1891 to 1899. Lancashire-based Darwen were one of the most influential and distinguished clubs in the early history of organized football in England. In 1879 the side created a sensation when they forced the Old Etonians to two replays in the quarter-finals of the FA Cup at the Kennington Oval – a rare feat at that time for any team not based in the south of the country. Such was the impact of their resistance to the all-conquering Old Etonians led by Alfred KINNAIRD that fans from London cheerfully contributed to a fund to pay for the impoverished Lancashire club's travelling expenses.

Among their stars were the Glaswegian Fergie Suter and fellow-Scotsman Jimmy Love, who were to become two of the first players ever to be ranked professional (*see* PROFESSIONALISM). In fact, Darwen denied they paid either player, but it was clear that their engagements with the side carried with them certain incidental benefits, such as better jobs and the takings from specially arranged benefit matches.

Based at Barley Bank, Darwen disappeared from the League in 1899 at the end of a season that saw them establish a record for consecutive defeats that has never been passed, with 18 Second Division games in a row going against them. Their 12–0 defeat in a game against West Bromwich Albion in 1892 also set a record scoreline for a First Division match, which has only once been equalled (by Leicester Fosse). Almost equally disastrous was a subsequent 11–1 humiliation against Arsenal in 1932; the Gunners excused themselves on the grounds that Darwen 'could not fail to appreciate that it would have been a slight had we acted otherwise than we did.' Darwen still exist as a non-League side.

Das Antas The home ground, in Oporto, of the Portuguese football club PORTO. Porto moved to Das Antas – the site of a prehistoric graveyard – in the 1950s and enlarged it in the 1970s by lowering the pitch to create an extra level of seating.

De Meer Stadium The home ground of the Dutch football club AJAX in Amsterdam. The stadium was opened in 1934 as the Ajaxstadion but soon acquired the name De Meer after the surrounding district. The F-side area of seating is notorious for its resident hooligan element.

De Vecchi, Renzo Italian defender, nicknamed the Son of God, who was a star with the national side in the years around World War I. A full-back, De Vecchi made up for his lack of physical strength with breathtaking skill and was rewarded with his debut for Italy in 1910 at the tender age of 16. A player with Milan and Genoa, he won 43 caps in all, regularly leading Italy as captain.

dead ball Term used to describe the ball during a suspension in play, as in the moments before a free kick or penalty is taken.

Dean, Dixie (William Ralph Dean; 1907–80) Celebrated English footballer, who is often described as the best centre-forward England has ever produced. One of the great names in English football, Dixie was born in Birkenhead and joined Tranmere Rovers in 1924, rapidly building up a reputation as a supremely talented forward. He was transferred to Everton in 1925, where his career was threatened a year later when he fractured his skull in a motorbike accident. He recovered quickly, however, to consolidate his reputation, appearing both for Everton and on 16 occasions for England (for whom he scored no fewer than 18 goals).

Inspired by Dixie, Everton won the League championship in 1928 and 1932, as well as the FA Cup in 1933. Considered one of the all-time greats, he was much sought after; Herbert CHAPMAN offered Everton 'anything they wanted' for him – but all offers were refused. In 1936 Dixie passed Steve BLOOMER's record of 352 League goals; by the time of his retirement in 1940 (having joined Notts County in 1938 and

Sligo Rovers in 1939) he had scored 379 goals in a total of 437 games. His achievements included scoring a record 60 goals in a single League season (in 39 games for Everton in 1927–28).

He remained one of the most popular and revered personalities in the game after his retirement and finally died at Goodison Park after watching Everton play against Liverpool.

Dean Court Home ground of the English football club AFC BOURNEMOUTH. The Cherries settled at Dean Court, then wasteland, in 1910 at the invitation of Cooper Dean (later the club's president), after whom the ground was named. Features of the ground include the Main Stand, which was originally built as a restaurant for the British Empire Exhibition at Wembley in 1923 and was opened in Bournemouth in 1927, and the so-called Brighton Beach End – an open terrace that acquired its name by virtue of the many pebbles used in its construction.

Death, Match of The notorious match to which players with the Soviet side Start (from Kiev) were invited by the occupying Nazis in August 1942. The Germans had invaded the Soviet Union in 1941 and Kiev suffered great hardship in common with all the other Soviet cities in the grasp of Hitler's forces. Members of the celebrated Dynamo Kiev side joined in the armed struggle against the invaders and many of them were subsequently captured and put to work in the Number One Bakery in Kiev, where they established a new team, Start FC.

In a facile attempt to demonstrate their goodwill towards the beleaguered inhabitants of the city, the Nazi authorities challenged the Start team to a game with a German army side. The Soviet players had little alternative but to accept the challenge and duly beat the invaders 5–3. The humiliation was irritating to the invading forces and Start's next match was against sterner opposition – a side called PGS. Start won 6–0. The Germans still would not admit defeat and arranged another fixture, this time against the Hungarian MSG Wal side – again Start won (5–1), adding a second leg victory of 3–2 for good measure.

By now the team had become a symbol of Ukrainian resistance to the Nazis and in desperation the invaders brought in the top German army side, Flakelf, to cow the half-starved Soviets – undaunted, Start saw Flakelf off with a 2–1 victory. The Nazis, cherishing their Aryan delusions, were incensed and ordered a replay – warning the Ukrainians they would be shot if they did not let the German side win.

The Soviet players were faced with a choice between death and national humiliation. There was only one decision they felt they could make – when they met Flakelf once more the Start players turned the game into such a massacre of their opponents that the referee ended the game early. As the Start team left the pitch they were immediately arrested. Two players were assigned to work duties, another escaped, and the rest were executed at Babi Yar, a ravine into which their bodies – still in football kit – were then thrown. A statue to these tragic football martyrs was subsequently erected at Dynamo Kiev's stadium after the war.

The fact that our team lost must not be regarded as an achievement on the part of members of the Start team.

German match report

deaths Deaths on the field of play are thankfully rare, although not unheard of. The first player to die during a first class match is thought to have been the full-back Sam Wynne, who collapsed as he took a free kick during a fixture between his team Bury and Sheffield United at Bramall Lane in 1927; he died in the dressing-room, as a result of pneumonia, and the match was abandoned.

A number of other players have died some time after their last match as a result of injuries received. As early as 1892, the St Mirren player James Dunlop died from tetanus ten days after cutting his knee on broken glass during a game against Abercorn. Subsequent tragedies have included the deaths of Dai Jones of Manchester City, after sustaining a cut in training in 1902, William Walker of Leith Athletic, after he was accidentally kicked in the stomach in 1907, James Maine of Hibernian, from internal injuries in 1909, Arsenal substitute Bob Benson, from a burst blood vessel in 1916, goalkeeper James Williamson of Dumbarton, from injuries suffered in a match against Rangers in 1921, Port Vale full-back Tom Butler, after a broken arm became septic in 1923, Celtic and Scotland goalkeeper John 'Jock' Thomson, after a collision in 1931, Sam Raleigh of Gillingham, after a similar clash in 1934, Sunderland goalkeeper Jim Thorpe, in 1936 as a result of his exertions combined with a diabetic condition, and West Bromwich Albion's former keeper Billy Richardson during a charity game in 1959.

Deaths actually during play have included those of James Beaumont, who fell into a quarry close to a pitch at Walkley, Sheffield, in 1877, that of Thomas Grice of Ashton who died when his belt buckle pierced his stomach in a fall in 1897, and that of a Spanish player in 1924, when he picked up a live electric cable that had fallen on to the pitch. The Army Cup Final of 1948 was particularly tragic, resulting in the deaths of two players when they were struck by lightning.

Many English professionals lost their lives in the trenches during World War I and another 75 died in World War II, though the rollcall of casualties was short when compared with those of some other countries. One of the more famous victims on the Continent was Alex Villaplane, the former captain of the French World Cup team of 1930, who was executed in 1944 for collaborating with the German invaders. *See also* AIR CRASHES; DEATH, MATCH OF; DISASTERS; SOCCER WAR; SUPER SPURS.

debut A player's first appearance. Stories concerning remarkable debuts are legion. Among the happiest tales are those involving Chelsea's George Hilsdon, who scored five goals on his League debut in the 1906–07 season, Fred Howard, who joined Manchester City in 1913 and celebrated by scoring three goals in the first 13 minutes of a match against Liverpool (adding a fourth later in the game), and Harry Nash, who joined Aston Villa in 1915 and scored three times in his first game; it was not until 1947 – when Ronnie Turnbull of Sunderland scored four – that another player scored a hat-trick on his First Division debut.

Also celebrated was the debut of Wrexham's Bernard Evans in 1954: he scored in his first match, against Bradford City, after just 25 seconds of play. North of the border, John Dyet made his claim on the record books when he made his debut for King's Park in 1930: he scored eight goals in a surprise 12–2 victory over favourites Forfar Athletic. Few players making their first appearance could hope to better the tally of goals scored by 16-year-old Tommy Spratt, however: when he made his debut for the Manchester United fifth team in the 1957–58 season he scored no fewer than 14 times in what turned out to be a 25–0 victory.

At the other end of the pitch, Birmingham City goalkeeper Tony Coton enjoyed his debut in 1980 when, after just 85 seconds of play, he saved a penalty with his first touch of the ball in top-flight football. Similarly, goalkeeper Marc de Clerc had a sensational debut for Aberdeen the same year: after just 22 minutes of play he kicked a clearance that bounced straight past the opposing keeper to score a goal.

On the international stage, many aspiring players must have dreamed of repeating the success of Newcastle's W. Foulkes when he made his debut for Wales in 1951: he scored a goal with his very first kick of the ball. Similarly, Aston Villa's Peter McParland scored for Wales with his first kick in international football just 40 seconds after play began in a match against Ireland in 1954.

Other players have experienced mixed fortunes on their debuts – in 1990 Sean McCarthy's debut for Bradford City was marked by a missed penalty, a goal, and a sending off. Even less happily, other players have not stayed long enough on the field to make any kind of mark at all on their debut. Bert Llewellyn of Northampton Town, for instance, spent only 11 minutes on the pitch before injury ended his debut (and, indeed, his career with the club, although he went on to better things with Walsall).

Unhappiest of all are the stories relating to players whose debuts matched their worst nightmares. Some of the most humiliating debuts have fallen to goalkeepers, who by the nature of their job are vulnerable to the worst embarrassments. Goalkeeper Les Surman of Charlton Athletic made his debut in 1965: he conceded three goals and was never invited to play for the team again. Even worse was the debut of goalkeeper Dennis Murray, who appeared for Crewe Alexandra (one of only two games he played in) in 1951: he let in nine goals. Most unfortunate of all must have been Halifax Town's S. Milton who made his debut in 1934: Halifax's opponents Stockport County got no fewer than 13 goals past him.

Dee, The Alternative nickname of the Scottish football club DUNDEE.

Deepdale The home ground of PRESTON NORTH END. The club settled at Deepdale, originally farmland, in 1875, at the time the club participated in rugby and cricket matches as well as in football. For several years sheep continued to graze on the pitch when it was not in actual use. Features of the ground include the elegant West Stand, built in 1906, stained glass windows (installed in the new boardroom in 1936), and an artificial pitch (1987).

defeats Every club has suffered defeats in their history that still cause embarrassment to the fans. Most sides have at some point

been humiliated by scorelines running into double figures, but few have gone down to a score of 20 goals and above. Most defeats on this scale belong to the early years of football's history when teams were often less equal than they usually are today.

Notable among this select group were Hyde United, who crashed to mighty Preston North End in the first round of the FA Cup back in 1887 with a scoreline of 26–0 (the worst defeat suffered by any club in the FA Cup). Legend has it that Hyde's agony was cruelly prolonged by the fact that the referee lost his watch during the course of the game and did not declare the match over until two hours had gone by.

The highest margin of victory in any first-class match, however, was recorded in 1885 when Bon Accord were thrashed 36–0 by Arbroath in the Scottish Cup – extraordinarily, the same day saw Dundee Harps thrash Aberdeen Rovers by a similar score of 35–0.

The record defeat in an international between the home countries is held by Ireland, who lost 10–0 to England in 1882. Honours in the League Cup are shared between Bury and Fulham, who lost by margins of 10–0 to West Ham (1983) and Liverpool (1986) respectively. In the League, Second Division Newport County and Third Division (North) Halifax Town have both lost by a record 13–0, the former against Newcastle United in 1946 and the latter against Stockport County in 1934. In the First Division, both Darwen and Leicester Fosse lost by a record 12–0, to West Bromwich Albion (1892) and Nottingham Forest (1909) respectively. The Scottish League record is held by Second Division Dundee Wanderers, who lost 15–1 to Airdrieonians in 1894.

No First Division team has contrived to lose all its matches in a season, although some have come close; the record for defeats in a single season for a First Division club is held by Stoke City, who lost 31 of their 42 games in the 1984–85 season. In the lower ranks, Nelson had a disastrous season in 1927–28, losing every one of their 21 Division III (North) matches.

At a different level, Woodward Wanderers of the West Bromwich Youth League set a record in the 1981–82 season that other teams would be hard pressed to beat: they let in 422 goals in just 18 matches.

Yes, we've had bad times at Anfield; one year we came second.

Bob Paisley

See also DARWEN; GIANT-KILLER.

Dell, The Home ground of the English football club SOUTHAMPTON. Until 1898 The Dell was a charming beauty spot around a large pond, but the need for Southampton to find a new home after the County Cricket Ground became too small changed all that. The pond was turned into an underground stream and a well-appointed stadium was erected in its place, complete with team showers and stands, making it the finest non-League venue in the country. Features of the early ground included the back wall of a private house, which occupied a corner of the West Stand until eventual demolition in 1922.

Fire destroyed the East Stand in 1929 just hours after the last home match of the season but it was soon rebuilt. During World War II bombs caused the pitch to flood, while in 1941 another fire damaged the West Stand. After the war the stands were expanded at the Milton Road End by means of innovative extra platforms (now dismantled), which were dubbed the 'Chocolate Boxes' by fans. Landmarks in the ground's more recent history have included the first competitive floodlit match between two League teams in England, played in 1951.

Den, The Until 1993, the home ground, in south London, of the English football club MILLWALL. Millwall had a number of different homes before finally settling at the site (then vegetable gardens) in Cold Blow Lane in 1910. The new home was christened The Den from the outset, in reference to the club's nickname The Lions. Events over the years have included bomb damage during World War II and a record number of temporary closures due to crowd violence – in 1920, 1934, 1947, 1950, and 1978.

The ground's forbidding surroundings and gloomy stands, coupled with the fierce reputation of the club's fans, made it one of the most daunting venues for visiting teams in the entire League. The goals were fitted with unusually close-mesh nets to protect keepers from objects thrown from the terraces. The ground was eventually vacated by the club at the end of the 1992–93 season, when they moved to a new stadium in London's docklands. The last game was marked by a pitch invasion and the theft of balls and goalposts.

Teams hate coming to The Den . . . I remember thinking 'Where is this?' Then you go and have a look at the pitch, which is bumpy, terrible. The away team

dressing-room is a dungeon, no light, no window. The bathrooms are horrible. Then you get out there to face them – the Lions. And they come storming at you and most sides jack it in . . .

Eamon Dunphy, *Only a Game?* (1976)

Usually all teams get at Millwall is the tyres let down on their coaches.

Tommy Docherty (1985)

Denmark The Danish national team has a long history in international competition (the side won the unofficial Olympic football title back in 1896) but has rarely threatened to join the ranks of Europe's top teams. The Danes did not make their first appearance in the World Cup Finals until 1986, when they managed to beat Scotland 1–0, then trounced Uruguay 6–1 and beat West Germany 2–0 before losing 5–1 against Spain. Denmark's greatest moment came in 1992 when they captured the European Championship. Strip: red shirts, white shorts, and red socks.

Dens Park The home ground of the Scottish football club DUNDEE, which lies just 89 steps away from the base of rivals Dundee United at TANNADICE PARK. The two clubs that were finally merged to form Dundee in 1893 had previously played at a number of different grounds, of which Carolina Port was considered the best (its features included the 'Burning Mountain', a constantly smouldering heap of shale). In 1898, however, the new club left Carolina Port and settled permanently at Dens Park, formerly farmland on Dens Road.

The ground was reopened in 1921, with stands designed by Archibald Leitch. When an old stand dating from the club's Carolina Port days burnt down very conveniently shortly afterwards, allowing further improvements to be made with finance provided by the fire insurance, more than one observer had their suspicions – particularly when the groundsman who extinguished the fire (and two others that season) was given the sack for his efforts.

derby A match between two local sides, typically from the same town or city, which has special significance for supporters of both teams. Such teams often consider neighbouring clubs to be their biggest enemies and the local derby can be a focus of great rivalry, sometimes friendly, sometimes vicious, but almost always fierce –

inspiring many sides to their most committed efforts of the season.

I love these derby games. Three tackles have gone in before you can even bring the ball down.

Gordon Lee, Everton manager (1988)

The most celebrated derby occasions include meetings between Manchester City and Manchester United (United narrowly leading in terms of wins), Everton and Liverpool (with Liverpool ahead on wins), Sunderland and Newcastle United, Aston Villa and Birmingham City, Sheffield United and Sheffield Wednesday, Bristol Rovers and Bristol City, Notts County and Nottingham Forest, between the London clubs Arsenal and Tottenham Hotspur, and between the Glasgow teams Celtic and Rangers.

The Glasgow event is perhaps the most intense of all local derbies, reflecting not only club loyalties but also religious sentiment (*see* OLD FIRM). Of the 23 Cup Finals these two teams have fought, particularly notable matches have included the 1909 Scottish Cup Final, when two drawn matches and crowd violence led to the Cup not being awarded to either team.

The most traumatic Manchester derby game was in 1974, when the two home teams met in the last match of the season – Denis LAW scored the only goal (for City) and United were relegated; to rub salt into the wound, Law had formerly been one of United's own stars.

Elsewhere in the world there are numerous other derby combinations. The most well-known include those involving AC Milan and Internazionale, Juventus and Torino, and Roma and Lazio in Italy, FK Austria and Rapid Vienna in Austria, and Ajax and Feyenoord in the Netherlands. In international terms, derby events could be said to include meetings between England and Scotland, Belgium and the Netherlands, and – until unification in 1990 – between the two Germanies.

The original derby was, of course, the famous horserace staged annually at Epsom and named after its founder, the 12th Earl of Derby, who organized the first event in 1780; such was the popularity of this race that the word 'derby' came to be applied to any sporting contest of equal importance. *See also* SOCCER WAR.

Derby County English football club, nicknamed the Rams. Strip: white shirts with black sleeves, black shorts, and white socks with black trim. Derby were founded in 1884 by members of Derbyshire County Cricket Club and originally wore a strip of amber, chocolate, and pale blue (based on the cricket club's team colours).

The team (a founder member of the League in 1888) quickly established itself as one of the leading sides of the day and got as far as the semi-finals of 13 FA Cup competitions between 1895 and 1909; appearances in three FA Cup Finals in this period all ended in defeat, however. The side of the 1920s and 1930s was distinguished by the presence of such players as Sammy Crooks, Hughie GALLACHER, and Jack Bowers, but by the time World War II broke out the club could only claim two Second Division championships (1912 and 1915) as their major titles.

A financial scandal over illegal payments signalled the club's low point in the war years, but things improved on the return of peace with victory in the first postwar FA Cup (1946), with a side spearheaded by Raich CARTER, Peter Docherty, and Jack Stamps. The Rams, who had settled at the BASEBALL GROUND in 1895, continued to be counted among the country's best sides for some years but eventually slumped in the late 1950s all the way down to the Third Division.

The arrival of Brian CLOUGH (with Peter Taylor) as manager in 1967 heralded a golden age in the club's history, with promotion to the First Division in 1969 and victory in the First Division championship in 1972 and again (under new manager Dave MACKAY) in 1975. The 1972 Championship was the closest ever witnessed with Derby clinching the title with just one point more than Leeds, Liverpool, and Manchester City: the team learnt of their triumph after they had completed their season and were relaxing on holiday in Majorca. Stars of the side in these heady days included Colin Todd, Terry Hennessey, Archie Gemmill, Bruce Rioch, Francis LEE, and Kevin Hector.

In the year of the club's centenary, Derby were back in the Third Division, and further troubled with financial woes, which threatened the club's extinction. The publisher Robert MAXWELL saved the Rams from being wound up and by the late 1980s, with a team boasting such talents as Peter SHILTON and Dean Saunders, the team were back in the top flight (though Maxwell himself won few fans among the club's supporters).

The Rams enjoyed their record victory in 1976, beating Finn Harps 12–0 in the UEFA Cup; they suffered their worst defeat in the 1889–90 season, when they lost 11–2 against Everton. Kevin Hector holds the record for League appearances with the team, having played in 486 matches between 1966 and 1982.

Deres Nickname of the English non-League football club ERITH AND BELVEDERE.

Di Stefano, Alfredo (1926–) Argentinian footballer, nicknamed the White Arrow, who is often described as the finest footballer in the history of the game. Born in Buenos Aires, Di Stefano made his debut in 1944, for River Plate, and joined the Colombian side Millionarios three years later. In 1953 he travelled to Europe to join the Spanish club Real Madrid, where his unsurpassed talent was given full rein.

Physically strong as well as a brilliant tactician, Di Stefano rapidly consolidated his reputation as the best player of the world, surpassing even PELÉ in the opinion of many who saw him play. With Di Stefano spearheading the attack, Real won the European Cup in 1956, 1957, 1958, 1959, and 1960 (when he scored a hat-trick in the Final against Eintracht Frankfurt). He won the first of 31 caps for Spain in 1957 and was voted European Footballer of the Year in 1957 and 1959.

The White Arrow transferred to Español in 1964, leaving Real to approach Pelé as his only conceivable replacement (though without success). That same year he retired as a player and accepted the management of Elche. Subsequently he was made manager of Boca Juniors (1969) and then of the Spanish club Valencia (1970), who went on to win the Spanish championship in 1971. He returned to his old club Real Madrid as manager in 1982, but left the post a year later, only to be reappointed in 1990.

Di Stefano's many admirers included such noteworthy figures as George BEST (who thought him the best player he had ever seen) and Matt BUSBY who once named him as the player he would most like to sign for Manchester United:

> He was one of the greatest, if not the greatest footballer I have ever seen. At that time we had forwards and defenders doing separate jobs, but he did everything.

Diadora League See ISTHMIAN LEAGUE.

Diamond Lights Title of pop song recorded by Glenn Hoddle and Chris Waddle in 1987. It reached number 12 in the charts. A follow-up single, 'It's Goodbye', was released later that year but failed to impress.

Diamonds Nickname of the Scottish football club AIRDRIEONIANS, with reference to the team strip.

Dick-Kerr's Nickname of the pioneering English women's football club PRESTON LADIES, in reference to the engineering factory in Preston where many of the players worked.

Diddy Men Nickname bestowed by English fans upon the remarkable team from NORTH KOREA that created one of the sensations of the 1966 World Cup. The North Koreans were noticeably shorter than players with the other national teams (none of them being over five feet, eight inches tall) and were very much the underdogs in the tournament. Predictably they lost their first game (against the Soviet Union) 3–0, though they won much praise for their lively and committed play. Their second match, against Chile, went somewhat better and resulted in a 1–1 draw; they were given little hope, however, against their next opponents – Italy, one of the strongest sides in the competition.

The teams met at Ayresome Park and what followed constituted the biggest upset in the World Cup since England were beaten by the United States back in 1950. Pak Doo Ik stunned the Italian side with a surprise goal and the European team never regained their composure, returning to Italy in disgrace after the match ended in a 1–0 defeat. Fearing retribution from their fans, the Italians arrived home at a secret location at an undisclosed hour in the middle of the night; nonetheless, as they touched down on their home soil they had to brave a hail of tomatoes.

The North Koreans became folk heroes overnight in the north-east and for a time it seemed they might even better their performance, establishing a 3–0 lead over mighty Portugal in the next match. The genius of EUSÉBIO foiled them, however, and Portugal finally won the game 5–3 (Eusébio scoring four times). The Diddy Men (so-called after the comic puppet characters associated with the Liverpudlian comedian Ken Dodd) left the tournament as one of the most popular sides ever to appear in the Finals and could comfort themselves with the knowledge that they were not only the first North Korean side to reach the World Cup Finals but were also the first Asian team to win a game at that stage. Their progress in the 1970 World Cup ended abruptly when they were eliminated after refusing to play Israel.

Didì Playing name of the celebrated Brazilian midfielder Waldir Pereira (1928–), who engineered Brazil's 1958 World Cup win. Having begun his career with Fluminense and Botafogo, Didì transferred to Real Madrid in 1959 but came into conflict there with the resident star Alfredo DI STEFANO and ultimately returned to Botafogo. He was the inspiration behind Brazil's outstanding performances in the World Cup campaigns of 1958 and 1962, winning a total of 72 caps for his country; after the 1958 triumph Didì became a national hero and had three streets and a railway station named in his honour. He was particularly admired for his deadly shooting skills, notably for his unpredictable swerving free kicks and for the deceptive shot that was dubbed the DRY LEAF. His skills were nearly lost to football at an early age, when an injury to his knee almost resulted in amputation. After retiring as a player he managed Peru's national squad in the 1970 World Cup.

Digger Nickname of the Jamaican-born English forward John BARNES, after a character with the same surname in the television soap-opera 'Dallas'.

Dimple, The Nickname of the VRŠOVICE STADIUM, the home ground, in Prague, of the Czech football club BOHEMIANS.

Dinamo Bucharest Romanian football club, which was originally the club of the Securitate secret police. Strip: white shirts, red shorts, and white socks. Founded in 1948 and based at the Dinamo Stadium in Bucharest, the side has won 14 League championships and seven Cup titles. During the golden era of the 1980s when they managed three doubles of victory in both the League and the Cup (1982, 1984, and 1990), the team also distinguished itself in European competition, reaching the semifinals of the European Cup in 1984.

Dinc Nickname of the English non-League football club YEADING.

direct free kick A free kick in which a shot at goal is permissible. A direct free kick may be awarded for handling or when a player has been kicked, tripped, jumped at, charged in a violent manner, charged from behind, struck, held, or pushed.

In 1983 a mistake concerning a direct free kick caused the referee of a match between Wimbledon and Millwall some embarrassment: when the Wimbledon full-back took a direct free kick and kicked the ball into his own net, the ref gave a goal to Millwall (he should have awarded a corner).

director A member of the board controlling a football club. The first paid director was Malcolm MacDonald, a former England forward who was appointed to the board of Fulham in 1981. The average director, however, is a businessman with an interest in (though not always knowledge of) football: in Len SHACKLETON's *Clown Prince of Soccer* (1955), the chapter titled 'The Average Director's Knowledge of Football' consisted of a single blank page. John Cobbold, of Norwich City, gave a hint of some directors' priorities in 1973: 'Of course we're going to continue in Europe. How else can we get our duty-free cigarettes?'

Perhaps significantly a number of celebrated comedians have served on the boards of famous British clubs, among them Tommy Cannon (Rochdale), Jasper Carrott (Birmingham City), Jim Davidson (Bournemouth and Aldershot), Arthur English (Aldershot), Eric Morecambe (Luton Town), Tommy Trinder (Fulham), Charlie Williams (Barnsley), and Norman Wisdom (Brighton and Hove Albion). Peter Sellers was honorary vice-president of Wood Green Town.

> You could put his knowledge of the game on a postage stamp. He wanted us to sign Salford Van Hire because he thought he was a Dutch international.
>
> Fred Ayre, of a director of Wigan Athletic (1981)

> The Villa chairman, Doug Ellis, said he was right behind me. I told him I'd sooner have him in front of me where I could see him.
>
> Tommy Docherty (1970)

> The ideal board of directors should be made up of three men – two dead and the other dying.
>
> Tommy Docherty (1977)

disasters The history of football is marred by a series of disasters on a scale unknown in other sports. The presence of huge crowds in often outdated grounds combined with violence and poor stewarding have contributed to scores of deaths in most major soccer-playing countries.

As far back as 1902 the game witnessed a

mass tragedy when 25 people died in the first IBROX PARK DISASTER, a total that was only exceeded in 1946, when 33 fans died in the BURNDEN PARK DISASTER. Horror of even greater proportions was seen in the 1964 LIMA FOOTBALL DISASTER, when no fewer than 318 died at an international between Peru and Argentina, and again in 1968, when 74 people died in the River Plate Stadium Disaster in Buenos Aires. Ibrox Park was once again the scene of a major disaster in 1971, when 66 fans died at a match between Celtic and Rangers, prompting the authorities to introduce the 1975 Safety of Sports Grounds legislation.

The worst catastrophe in the history of the game, however, occurred in 1982, when an unknown number of people lost their lives at a match between Spartak Moscow and Haarlem in the LENIN STADIUM DISASTER; estimates of the dead range from the original official figure of 69 to the revised total of 340 disclosed by the authorities in 1989.

The BRADFORD FIRE of 1985, which resulted in 56 deaths, exceeded all previous disasters to afflict the game in England and was followed just three weeks later by the notorious HEYSEL STADIUM DISASTER involving Liverpool fans, which resulted in 39 deaths. Subsequent disasters have included the 1988 KATMANDU DISASTER, in which at least 95 died, and the worst catastrophe in the history of the British game, when 95 Liverpool fans died in the HILLSBOROUGH DISASTER of 1989, resulting in wholescale re-evaluation of safety at all major grounds.

Despite all the political pressure and expenditure on venues in the UK and elsewhere, disasters continue to take place. In 1992 a further 16 people lost their lives when a temporary steel stand collapsed at a ground in Corsica after the crowd stamped their feet. See also AIR CRASHES; DEATH, MATCH OF; DEATHS; SOCCER WAR.

Divino, Il Nickname of the Brazilian midfielder Paulo Roberto FALCÃO.

division A grouping of clubs that compete with one another within the structure of a larger league, the winners being eligible for promotion to the rank above and the losers being open to relegation. The Football League in England began with just one division back in 1888, with a second division being added in 1892 (bringing the total to 28 clubs). The Southern League provided the clubs that formed the new Third Division in 1920 and by 1923 there were 88 clubs in the League. The Third Division was

split into North and South divisions until 1958, when nationally based Third and Fourth Divisions were introduced. Further reorganization followed in 1992 with the Premier League becoming the most senior of four divisions and the Conference acting as an unofficial extra division. Ray Straw of Derby County and Coventry City is thought to have been the only man to have played in all six old English divisions (between 1952 and 1960).

Dixie Nickname of the celebrated English centre-forward William Ralph DEAN. Although he was universally known as Dixie even as a child, Dean himself loathed the nickname and preferred to be called Bill. Two explanations are put forward for his nickname: according to the first it was inspired by his dark complexion, of the hue seen in the southern USA (Dixieland); alternatively it dated from childhood games of tag, during which 'Digsie' Dean dug his fingers into the backs of other children when tagging them.

Docherty, Tommy (1928–) Scottish-born manager, nicknamed The Doc, who enjoyed a long and controversial career with a bewildering succession of clubs. The Doc began his career as a player with Celtic in 1948 and subsequently played for Preston North End (1949–58), Arsenal, and (as player-coach and then manager) Chelsea, during which time he collected an FA Cup runners-up medal with Preston (1954) and 25 caps for Scotland (serving in eight matches as captain and in 1971 successfully as manager).

Under his management Chelsea reached the FA Cup Final in 1967, after which he moved to Rotherham United (1967), Queen's Park Rangers (28 days in 1968), Aston Villa (1968), Porto (1970), Hull City (1971), Manchester United (1972), with whom he reached two more FA Cup Finals (in 1976 and 1977), Derby County (1977), Queen's Park Rangers (1979), the Australian club Sydney Olympic (1980), Preston North End (1981), the Australian club South Melbourne (1982), Wolverhampton Wanderers (1984), and Altrincham (1987). Docherty is the first to admit he has enjoyed a rich and varied career as a manager: 'I've had more clubs than Jack Nicklaus.'

Docherty has acquired a reputation for his outspoken and often provocative views, which have frequently been in conflict with those of his superiors. One former Manchester United player summed him up as the 'Hurricane Higgins of football', while an anonymous manager observed dryly of his move to Australia in 1981: 'He's gone 200 years too late'. Notorious incidents in his long and successful career as a manager have included a police investigation into the affairs of Derby County and accusations of perjury (of which he was cleared), prompting him to reflect in 1981: 'I've been in more courts than Bjorn Borg'. Eminently quotable, his most oft-repeated observations include the following (said of Wolverhampton Wanderers in 1985): 'Our strikers couldn't score in a brothel.'

Among his more portentous comments upon the contemporary game has been the following, from 1982: 'It's a rat-race – and the rats are winning.'

The Doc is not unaware of his garrulity, admitting: 'I talk a lot. On any subject. Which is always football.'

Dockers Nickname of the English non-League football club TILBURY, in reference to the area's famous docks.

Dog, The Nickname of the Millwall defender Harry CRIPPS.

dogs Dogs have, on odd occasions, influenced the fortunes of more than one football club. Interference by canine participants is a common enough problem in casual kickarounds in local parks, but less often a factor in the organized game. Nonetheless, there have been a number of infamous occurrences involving four-legged interlopers.

Brentford goalkeeper Chic Brodie had reason to rue the day a dog ran on to the pitch during a match against Colchester in 1970: he collided with it and suffered such extensive damage to his knee that he was obliged to give up his career as a professional player. A more deliberate intervention took place in an extraordinary incident at Stoke-on-Trent in 1985 during a Staffordshire Sunday Cup game between Newcastle Town and Knave of Clubs: an unidentified mongrel saw his opportunity when a shot drifted wide of the Newcastle goal and deftly headed it into the net. Amid much hilarity and confusion the referee decided to allow the goal, to the delight of the Knaves (although Newcastle eventually made up the damage and won 3–2).

Scotland's manager Ally MacLeod also had reason to regret the day a dog approached him after Scotland had just drawn disappointingly 1–1 with Iran in the 1978 World Cup Finals: MacLeod stirred from his depression long enough to give the dog a smile and remark 'Ah, my only friend in the world' – the dog bit him. See also BRYN; PICKLES.

Doig, John Edward (1866–1919) Scottish goalkeeper, nickamed the Prince of Goalkeepers, who kept goal for the immensely successful Team of all the Talents that represented Sunderland in the 1890s. Lured south of the border by Sunderland's manager Tom Watson, Doig excelled for the great English side. He was an instantly recognizable figure, his bald head covered by a cap kept in place by an elastic strap fastened under his chin.

Dolphins Nickname of the English non-League football club POOLE TOWN, in reference to the dolphins frequently seen in the town's bay.

Dominican Republic The Dominican Republic joined FIFA in 1958 but have yet to make much impact in international competition. Strip: navy blue shirts, white shorts, and red socks.

Doncaster Rovers English football club, nicknamed the Rovers. Strip: white shirts with red trim, white shorts with red trim, and white socks with red trim. Doncaster Rovers were founded by Albert Jenkins in 1879, initially to play a game against the Yorkshire Institute for the Deaf. They turned professional in 1885 and joined the League in 1901 as members of the Second Division. They lost their League place in 1903, returned in 1904, dropped out again in 1905, and finally got back in 1923, the year after moving into their permanent home at BELLE VUE.

Rovers have known life in all three of the lower divisions, enjoying their most successful era in the 1950s when they spent eight seasons in the Second Division under manager Peter Doherty and included such star players as goalkeeper Harry Gregg and forward Alick Jeffrey. Since then, however, their activities have been confined to the bottom two divisions (despite the assistance of such managers as Lawrie MCMENEMY, Dave MACKAY, and Billy BREMNER). Mackay despaired of the Rovers team in the late 1980s and at the end of the 1987–88 season put the entire senior squad on the transfer list.

In better times, one of their most remarkable seasons was that of 1946–47, when the club managed to win 18 out of 21 away fixtures, won 72 points, and kept an unblemished defensive record in 20 matches. The team are also noted for the fact that, in the days when two points were given for a win and one for a draw, Rovers were holders of records at both ends of the scale, with totals of 72 points in 1946–47 and of just eight points in 1904–05.

Doncaster enjoyed their record victory in 1964, when they beat Darlington 10–0; they suffered their worst defeat in 1903, losing 12–0 to Small Heath. Fred Emery holds the record for League appearances with the club, having played in 417 matches between 1925 and 1936.

With little to get supporters excited in recent years, fans of the club are noted for their zany humour. Instances of this have included a sequence of events in 1991, which involved fans chanting (for no immediately obvious reason) 'Would you like a piece of cake?' at visiting crowds. The police, fearing a breach of the peace, strove to intervene, but eventually saw the funny side and gave up attempts to arrest the perpetrators; at the next match (at Burnley) scores of fans arrived with real cakes, which they eagerly offered to the bemused policemen on duty at the ground, as they sang a version of John Lennon's 'Happy Christmas (War is Over)':

> And so this is Burnley, and what have we done,
> We've lost here already, would you like a cream bun?

donkey Slang term for a slow or clumsy player, heard frequently from the terraces. Often the insult is conveyed by mass braying from the spectators. The 'hee-haw' chant is thought to have originated among fans of Halifax Town in the 1983–84 season and quickly caught on elsewhere. Back at Halifax's ground the SHAY fans went on to adopt a new animal metaphor by likening players to camels, but this failed to catch on, few critics being able to imitate a camel with any accuracy.

Dons (1) Nickname of the Scottish football club ABERDEEN, in reference to the River Don which meets the sea at the city.

(2) Nickname of the English non-League football club HENDON.

(3) Nickname of the English football club WIMBLEDON.

Doog, The Nickname of the Northern Ireland-born centre-forward Derek DOUGAN.

Doonhamers Nickname of the Scottish football club QUEEN OF THE SOUTH (of Dumfries), being a Celtic variant of the phrase 'down homers'.

Dorchester Town English non-League football club, nicknamed the Magpies. Strip: black and white shirts with black shorts. Founded in 1880 and based at the Avenue Stadium, the club play in the Southern League.

Dorking English non-League football club, nicknamed the Chicks. Strip: green and white hooped shirts with white shorts and socks. Founded in 1880 and based at the Meadowbank ground in Dorking, the Chicks play in the Isthmian League.

Double, The Any one of various tournament-winning combinations that are hailed as an outstanding achievement for the club concerned. The most widely recognized Double is that comprising the FA Cup and the League championship, first won by Preston North End in 1888–89 – the inaugural year of the League itself. The club's victory was emphatic: they did not lose a single game in the course of the Championship and did not concede a goal in their victorious FA Cup campaign (*see* OLD INVINCIBLES).

In 1897 Aston Villa became the second club to achieve the most famous Double of all during a run of five League victories and two FA Cup triumphs. Under the management of Bill Nicholson, Tottenham Hotspur became the first club in the 20th century to clinch both competitions (1961); subsequently Arsenal repeated the feat in 1971 and Liverpool did it once more in 1986.

Other notable doubles have included Manchester United's victory in the European Cup Winners' Cup and the League Cup in 1970 and Arsenal's combination of victory in the FA Cup and the League Cup in 1993. *See also* NEW DOUBLE; TREBLE.

double hat-trick The scoring of six goals in a single match by one player (strictly speaking, in two runs of three consecutive goals without another player from the same side scoring). The first recorded occurrence of a double hat-trick in the League goes back to the 1893–94 season when a player by the name of Southworth scored six of Everton's goals in a 7–1 victory over West Bromwich Albion; he was also the League's top scorer that year. The first double hat-trick in an international match dates from 1930, when Joe Bambrick of Linfield FC and Northern Ireland scored six of his country's goals in a 7–0 win over Wales.

Double hat-tricks are rare in the modern game but not unheard of; in 1961, for instance, Manchester City star Denis LAW scored six in a row against Luton Town but lost his chance to enter the record books when the game was abandoned because of bad weather. The Portuguese player Mascarenhas was another to achieve a double hattrick, scoring six goals in a 16–1 victory by Sporting Lisbon over the Cypriot Apoel Nicosia team in what was the first double hat-trick seen in the European Cup Winners' Cup.

Perhaps most remarkable of all was the double hat-trick of Wilf Minter, a forward for St Albans City in an FA Cup fourth round replay against Dulwich Hamlet in 1922. This outstanding amateur player (who turned down offers to go professional in order to join his father's business) scored no fewer than seven goals (three goals in 12 minutes in the first half and three more in ten minutes in the second half, followed by a last one with four minutes left) but incredibly still ended up on the losing side, the final scoreline reading St Albans 7, Dulwich 8. In recognition of his efforts, Minter was made captain of the team the following week and the band played 'For He's A Jolly Good Fellow' as he appeared on the pitch. He remains the player to score the most goals for the losing side in an FA Cup match.

Dougan, Derek (1938–) Northern Ireland-born centre-forward, nicknamed The Doog, who was one of the most respected British footballers of the 1960s and 1970s. Dougan played for Portsmouth, Blackburn Rovers, Aston Villa, Peterborough, Leicester City, and – most famously of all – for Wolverhampton Wanderers; he also won 43 caps for Northern Ireland. An often difficult character who frequently courted controversy, he was unrivalled in the air and became the first Irishman to score 200 League goals.

He became one of the best-known players in the game in the 1960s, attracting wide publicity for such outrageous acts as appearing in the 1960 FA Cup Final with a completely shaved head. He retired in 1975 but continued to work within the game and in 1982 brought together a last-minute deal to save Wolves from being wound up because of debts. As chairman and chief executive of the club he went on to rebuild the team, which soon returned to the First Division, earning himself a reputation as something of a miracle worker:

I think I could put the country right – but then there are 50 million others who think they could do the same.

Douglas Park The home ground of the Scottish football club HAMILTON ACADEMICAL. The Accies settled at Douglas Park in 1888; notable events in the ground's history have included a fire in 1924 and the arrival (on a temporary basis) of the Clyde team in 1991.

Dover Athletic English non-League football club, nicknamed the Lilywhites. Strip: white shirts with black shorts and socks. Founded in 1983 as a replacement for Dover FC and based at the Crabble Athletic Ground in Dover, the club played in the Southern League until 1993, when they won promotion to the Conference.

Dragons (1) Nickname of the Portuguese football club PORTO.
(2) Nickname of the English non-League football club WIVENHOE TOWN.

Drake's Ducklings The nickname bestowed upon the Chelsea team assembled by manager Ted Drake in the 1950s. The Ducklings were notable for their inclusion of young players trained by the club as part of an ambitious youth scheme; unfortunately, after initial success (which included winning the League title in 1955), the experiment failed to lift Chelsea's fortunes and the decade ended with the club relegated to the Second Division.

draw The ritual in which it is decided which teams will meet which in various competitions, including the World Cup and the FA Cup. The FA Cup draw was originally held in secret, the clubs being paired up after numbered boxwood balls were picked out of a blue velvet bag. The ceremony was first broadcast (on radio) in 1935, when FA Secretary Stanley ROUS was asked to shake the bag a bit in order to produce 'a distinctive and suitable sound'. When the FA draw for the 1961–62 season matched Chesterfield with Doncaster Rovers and then Oldham Athletic in the first two rounds for the second year running it was calculated that the odds against this happening had been 3081 to one.

The draw for the World Cup in 1990 scaled new heights as a global media event, with the film star Sophia Loren playing the principal role. The draw for the qualifying rounds of the 1994 World Cup was held in a similar atmosphere in 1991 at Madison

Square Garden in New York; it was the first time the draw for the tournament was held in the host country.

drawing-room football Derisive term commonly heard among Russian and other continental fans for the kind of unappealing football they see played in indoor stadia when the severity of the weather prevents an outdoor pitch from being used. Indoor football has never caught on in the same way as the traditional outdoor game, though many modern stadia include covered pitches for use in training.

dream. We Have a Dream Title of pop song recorded by the Scotland World Cup squad in 1982, when it reached number five in the charts.

dribble To move forward with the ball at one's feet rather than passing it to another player. Skill at dribbling the ball was considered one of the fine arts of the game in the early history of football and the adoption of a faster passing style of play in the late 19th century was the subject of much controversy, many enthusiasts of the game considering such play unconducive to displays of individual excellence. When most teams concentrated on dribbling the ball steadily forward the emphasis was on attack and typically most players acted as strikers; with the introduction of long passing shots (first perfected by sides from the north of the country) teams had to be reorganized into attack, midfield, and defence.

Even in the fast-moving modern game, certain players have won fame for their skill at dribbling, despite the inevitable objections that such play destroys teamwork and leaves a player open to accusations of 'hogging the ball'; celebrated examples of these have included George BEST, whose disinclination to pass the ball led to team mate Pat Crerand admitting 'There are times when you want to wring his neck'. *See also* PRINCE OF DRIBBLERS; WIZARD OF DRIBBLE.

Droylsden English non-League football club, nicknamed the Bloods. Strip: all red. Founded in 1866 and based at the Butchers Arms ground in Droylsden, Manchester, Droylsden play in the Northern Premier League.

drugs The use of banned substances to improve performance on the field has been an issue in the football establishment since the 1970s, although not to the degree it is in some other sports. The first player to be

punished at World Cup level after a drug test proved positive was Haiti's Ernest Jean-Joseph, who was extradited in 1974; subsequently Scotland's winger Willie Johnston was sent home in disgrace during the country's 1978 World Cup campaign.

Attempts to get players in the UK to agree to voluntary drug testing in 1991 met with some resistance; in 1992 compulsory random testing was introduced, though the football establishment proclaimed it believed the sport was 'clean'. Players elsewhere in the world are similarly keen to dissociate the game from the drug menace; in 1990, when two Uruguayan players were suspended after drug tests proved positive as a result of taking medicine for colds, the players' union called a strike. The suspensions were lifted and the strike was averted. Other players have, however, failed to persuade the authorities to give them the benefit of the doubt (as in the case of Diego MARADONA).

> *After the match an official asked for two of my players to take a dope test. I offered him the referee.*
>
> Tommy Docherty (1985)

dry leaf The dead ball shot perfected by the brilliant Brazilian midfield player DIDÌ in the 1950s. The dry leaf (or *folha seca*) was a deceptive swerving shot that did not carry as far as opponents thought it would. Didì's use of the shot contributed to his country's victory in the World Cups of 1958 and 1962.

Dryborough Cup Shortlived Scottish competition involving the highest-scoring teams in the Scottish League. Modelled on the Watney Cup in England, the Dryborough Cup was first contested in 1971 but never really caught the imagination of the fans and was abandoned in 1981 after it had been staged six times. Celtic appeared in the Final on five occasions but won the trophy just once.

Ducks Nickname of the English non-League football club AYLESBURY UNITED, with reference to the town's Aylesbury duck emblem.

Dudley Town English non-League football club, nicknamed the Robins. Strip: red shirts, white shorts, and black socks. Founded in 1883 and based at the Round Oak Stadium in Brierly Hill, the Robins play in the Southern League.

dug-out A sunken covered pit at the side of a pitch in which team managers, coaches, and other officials can sit during the course of a game. The very first dug-out dates from the early 1920s, when one was created at Aberdeen's Pittodrie home at the request of trainer Donald Colman. Colman (who was also interested in boxing and dance) was anxious to study the footwork of his players and also needed somewhere dry where he could make copious notes on matchdays. The idea spread to other grounds after Everton copied it at Goodison Park a few years later – although the low siting of such pits means that the view to be had from them is less than ideal.

Dukla Prague The football club of the Czech army, founded in Prague in 1948. Strip: all yellow with red trim. Based at the JULISKA stadium in Prague, Dukla have amassed 11 League championships and eight Cup titles (including the double in 1961). The club was named in honour of the village of Dukla, which won renown during World War II for its fierce resistance to the Nazis. In the 1960s the club proved virtually invincible but has never enjoyed massive support because of its links with the army.

Dulwich Hamlet English non-League football club, nicknamed The Hamlet. Strip: navy blue and pink striped shirts with blue shorts and socks. Founded in 1893, Dulwich Hamlet are based at the Champion Hill Stadium in East Dulwich, and play in the Isthmian League. They can boast four Isthmian League championships and have won the FA Amateur Cup four times (1920, 1932, 1936, and 1937).

Dumbarton Scottish football club, nicknamed the Sons. Strip: gold shirts, black shorts, and gold and black socks. Dumbarton were founded in 1872 and soon emerged as one of the dominant sides in the early history of the Scottish League. A founder member of the First Division in 1890, the team shared the League championship with Rangers in 1891 and won it outright in 1892; they also won the Scottish Cup in 1883 and were runners-up in the competition in 1881, 1882, 1887, 1891, and 1897.

Subsequently the club have failed to equal their early achievements, although they did add Second Division titles in 1911 and 1972 and were runners-up in the First Division in 1984. The club, based at BOG-HEAD PARK, came close to extinction in the 1950s, but were saved with local support.

Recent stars to be discovered at Boghead Park have included Graeme Sharp and Murdo MacLeod.

Dumbarton enjoyed their record victory in 1888, when they beat Kirkintilloch 13–1; they have suffered record defeats of 11–1 on two occasions, against Albion Rovers in 1926 and Ayr United in 1952.

Dumbarton Harp Former Scottish League football club, which dropped out of the League in 1925. Based at Meadow Park, Dumbarton Harp lasted just two seasons as a League club, having joined in 1923.

dummy, to sell a To deceive an opponent as to which way the ball will be played, typically by fooling him in making a pass or unexpectedly changing the direction in which the ball is travelling.

Dundee Scottish football club, nicknamed the Dark Blues. Strip: dark blue shirts with red and white trim, white shorts, and blue and white socks. Also nicknamed The Dee, the club were founded in 1893, when the Our Boys and East End teams merged.

Dundee's great days lie in the past. Glory first came to the club's home at DENS PARK in 1910, when the team clinched victory in the Scottish Cup after no fewer than two replays. The golden era followed in the years after World War II, when Dundee acquired Billy Steel from Derby County. Winners of the Second Division championship in 1947, they won the Scottish League Cup in 1952 and again in 1953; subsequently they won the First Division title in 1962, with a team that included such stars as Ian Ure and Alan Gilzean. League Cup victory came again in 1974, but the club went into decline, finally being relegated in 1990, before returning to the Premier Division in 1992.

The side's record victory stands at 10–0, achieved in two matches in 1947, against Alloa and Dunfermline Athletic; the Dark Blues suffered their worst defeat back in 1895, losing 11–0 to Celtic. Doug Cowie holds the record for League appearances with the side, playing in 341 games between 1945 and 1961.

Dundee United Scottish football club, nicknamed the Terrors. Strip: tangerine shirts with black shorts. Founded in 1909 and based at TANNADICE PARK, the Terrors played as Dundee Hibernian until adopting their present name in 1923 (having joined the League in 1910). Their history until relatively recent times was undistinguished, with Second Division titles in 1925 and 1929 their only major honours. Foremost of the club's stars in their early years was centre-forward Duncan Hutchison, who eventually left to join Newcastle United, 300 Dundee United fans travelling to see his debut with his new club as a mark of respect for his skills.

It all changed with the arrival of Jim McLean as manager in 1975 and the club won acclaim in the 1980s as one of the most formidable sides in the whole of Europe. Victory in the Scottish League Cup in 1980 and 1981 was crowned in 1983 with the Premier League championship; they were also runners-up in no fewer than six Scottish Cup competitions (1974, 1981, 1985, 1987, 1988, and 1991) and in international football reached the semi-finals of the European Cup in 1984 and the final of the UEFA Cup in 1987. The 1986–87 season was especially galling, with United losing two Cup Finals within just five days.

Leading stars with United under McLean included Scottish international David Narey and Paul Sturrock. Players from earlier eras included Neil Paterson, usually remembered now as the Oscar-winning author of the screenplay for the film Room at the Top (1960).

Dundee United enjoyed their record victory in 1931, when they beat Nithsdale Wanderers 14–0; they suffered their worst defeat in 1954, losing 12–1 against Motherwell. Dave Narey holds the record for League appearances with the club, having played in 554 matches between 1973 and 1991.

Dunfermline Athletic Scottish football club, nicknamed the Pars. Strip: black and white striped shirts, black shorts, and black socks with red trim.

Dunfermline were founded in 1885 by members of a cricket club and joined the League in 1912. Based at EAST END PARK since their formation, they enjoyed their first golden era in the 1960s, when they won the Scottish Cup twice (1961 and 1968) and were for a time managed by Jock STEIN. Their other honours include the Second Division championship in 1926 and 1986 and the First Division title in 1989 as well as a creditable record in European competition.

Their most nail-biting moment came at the end of the 1958–59 season, when relegation seemed a certainty with just one game to go, against Partick Thistle; however, winger Harry Melrose provided inspiration with six goals and with a 10–1

victory to their credit the team lived on to fight as a First Division side for another year. Other stars of the side have included strikers Charlie Dickson and Alex Edwards in the 1960s.

The Pars enjoyed their record victory in 1930, beating Stenhousemuir 11–2; they suffered their worst defeat in 1947, when they lost 10–0 against Dundee. Bobby Robertson holds the record for League appearances with the club, having played in 360 matches between 1977 and 1988.

It's a great job, apart from Saturday afternoons.

Jocky Scott, on managing Dunfermline (1991)

Dunstable English non-League football club, nicknamed the Blues. Strip: all blue. Founded in 1895 and based at Creasey Park, Dunstable play in the Southern League.

Durham City Former English League football club, which dropped out of the League in 1928. Based at Holiday Park, City joined the League in 1921; their place in the League was eventually taken by Carlisle.

dying swan Tactical ruse used by many unscrupulous players to obtain an advantage by winning a free kick or penalty for an imagined foul. Such dying swan acts, in which the perpetrator does all he can to convince the referee that he has been grievously injured, can – if successful – interrupt the flow of play and relieve pressure on a strained defence. The use of such devices (reminiscent of the prolonged death throes of performers in the ballet Swan Lake – hence the nickname) is particularly associated with teams from the Mediterranean, notably those from Spain and Portugal.

Dykehead Former Scottish League football club, which dropped out of the League in 1926. Based at Parkside in the town of Shotts, Dykehead joined the League in 1923.

Dynamo Nickname of numerous continental teams with Dynamo as part of their name, among them DYNAMO KIEV, Dynamo Minsk, DYNAMO MOSCOW, and Dynamo Tbilisi, all from the former Soviet Union. Others include Dynamo Dresden, DINAMO BUCHAREST, and DYNAMO BERLIN. Several of the Dynamo teams (so called in reference to links with the power industries) were attached to the country's secret police (an association that reduced their popularity to some extent and led to demands for name changes in the wake of the collapse of Communism in the late 1980s). *See also* COLNE DYNAMOES.

Dynamo Berlin German football club, who were the foremost team in East Germany prior to German unification in 1989. Strip: red and white shirts, white shorts, and red socks. Founded in 1949 and based at the FRIEDRICH LUDWIG JAHN STADIUM in Berlin, the side set a new record by winning ten successive League championships between 1979 and 1988. They also won the Cup in 1959, 1988, and 1989. The club's association with the unpopular secret police prompted a name change in 1990 and the team is now known as FC Berlin.

Dynamo Kiev Ukrainian football club, which emerged as one of the leading Soviet teams in the 1960s. Strip: all white with blue trim. Founded in 1927 and based at the Republican Stadium in Kiev, Dynamo won their first League championship in 1961 (breaking Moscow's hold on the top domestic honours) and have since reclaimed it some 11 times. They have also captured the Cup title on nine occasions since 1954, were winners of the Super Cup in 1975, and enjoyed victory in the European Cup Winners' Cup in 1975 and 1986. Stars of the side in recent years have included Oleg BLOKHIN and Igor Belanov.

Dynamo Moscow Russian football club, nicknamed the Policemen. Strip: all white. The club was formed (as Orekhovo) back in 1887 by the English mill owners Clement and Harry Charnock, who advertised in *The Times* for 'engineers, mechanics, and clerks capable of playing football well' while in the process of establishing a mill outside Moscow.

Subsequently the club was embroiled in the revolutionary events of 1917, evading the attentions of the Tsar's secret police but after the Revolution ironically became identified with what was to become the KGB. The club acquired the name Dynamo on being adopted by the Soviet Electrical Trades Union.

The club established its international reputation immediately after World War II, when a tour of the UK created a sensation. Dynamo Moscow made their first British appearance against Chelsea at Stamford Bridge in 1945, where the visitors (clad in unusually long shorts and shirts adorned with a huge letter D) were greeted with laughter as they handed bouquets of flowers to their opponents. The laughter soon changed to awestruck gasps, however, as Dynamo battled heroically with one of England's most respected sides, forcing a 3–3 draw. In all 275,000 fans saw Dynamo on their short tour, during which they humbled Cardiff City 10–1, beat Arsenal (complete with guests Stanley MATTHEWS and Stan MORTENSEN) 4–3, and drew 2–2 with mighty Rangers. Bernard Joy, Arsenal's centre-half, recognized his opponents' style of play:

> Dynamo played brilliant attacking soccer based on the short ground pass . . . this was the style we had given the world earlier in the century and had abandoned in the negative football era of the 1930s. The Russians were but the ghosts of our past glories – the 'Wembley Wizards', the Corinthians, Newcastle's team of all talents and the Invincibles of proud Preston.

Then the club were gone, leaving behind them a startled football establishment realizing how much ground the domestic game had lost during World War II. The abrupt departure of the Dynamo players before a match with a strong representative British team could be arranged fuelled speculation that the tour had been politically motivated:

> The speed of the Russian players and the brilliance of their football showed just how far our players had gone back during the war, but this Moscow Dynamo team was a club in name only. The players had been specially assembled from four towns, were the pick of the players from the whole of Russia, and had been drilled into a brilliant machine sent to this country on a political mission with orders that they must not fail.
>
> Tom Whittaker, *Tom Whittaker's Arsenal Story* (1958)

Their only major international success since that time has been an appearance in the Final of the European Cup Winners' Cup in 1972. George Orwell, in an essay entitled 'The Sporting Spirit', had no doubt that whatever the motivation had been behind the tour of 1945 the furore that greeted the success of the visitors proved only that the old adage that sport promoted goodwill between nations was a fallacy:

> Serious sport has nothing to do with fair play. It is bound up with hatred, jealousy, boastfulness, disregard of all rules and sadistic pleasure in witnessing violence: in other words it is war minus the shooting . . . there are quite enough real causes of

trouble already, and we need not add to them by encouraging young men to kick each other on the shins amid the roars of infuriated spectators.

Dynamo Stadium The home ground of the Russian football clubs CSKA and DYNAMO MOSCOW. Built in 1928 and used to host the Olympics of 1980, the stadium includes among its features a plaque commemorating Russian players who died in World War II.

Dzajic, Dragan (1946–) Yugoslavian-born outside-left, nicknamed the Magic Dragon, who won international respect with the Yugoslavian national team in the 1960s and 1970s. Playing at home for Red Star Belgrade and then with Nice and Bastia, he won a record-breaking total of 85 caps, scoring 23 goals for his country and often fulfilling the role of captain. After retiring as a player he served as manager of his old club Red Star Belgrade.

E

E's Nickname of the English non-League football clubs ENFIELD and EPSOM AND EWELL.

Eagles Nickname of a number of football clubs around the world, among them the Portuguese club BENFICA, CRYSTAL PALACE, and non-League HINCKLEY TOWN.

East End Park The home ground of the Scottish football club DUNFERMLINE ATHLETIC. The club have been based at East End Park throughout their history, with breaks during World War I and World War II, when the pitch was requisitioned by the army. In 1935 the East Stand was improved with wood from the great liner *Mauretania*, which was being broken up in the scrapyards nearby, while the ground as a whole was modernized in the 1960s when the club enjoyed a golden era; this period included a chaotic match in 1968 when 27,816 fans (more than the ground's capacity) came to see the team play Celtic – one man died from injuries sustained in a fall from a vantage point overlooking the pitch.

East Fife Scottish football club, nicknamed the Fifers. Strip: black and gold stripes. Founded in 1903 (as East of Fife), the club joined the League in 1921 and enjoyed their golden era between 1938 and 1954. Highlights of their history have included winning the Scottish Cup in 1938 (making them the only Second Division club ever to achieve this), capturing the Second Division championship (1948), and triumphing in the Scottish League Cup in 1948, 1950, and 1954. Among the stars of the postwar team, based at Bayview Park, were centre-forward Henry Morris, who scored a remarkable total of 62 League and Cup goals in the 1947–48 season.

East Fife enjoyed their record victory in 1937, when they beat Edinburgh City 13–2; they suffered their worst defeat in 1957, losing 9–0 to Hearts. David Clarke holds the record for League appearances with the club, having played in 517 games between 1968 and 1986.

East Germany *See* GERMANY.

East Stirlingshire Scottish football club, nicknamed The Shire. Strip: white shirts and shorts, with black socks. Founded in 1880 and based at FIRS PARK in Falkirk, East Stirlingshire have a relatively undistinguished League record, with just one Second Division championship (1932) to their credit.

The club are best known for the controversy that was stirred up in 1964 when the Steedman family, who controlled the club, effected a merger with the Junior club at Clydebank, thus forming a new side called E.S. Clydebank, which played in the League under this name in the 1964–65 season. After a heated debate in the courts, however, the Steedmans' actions were nullified and East Stirlingshire were revived under their old name back in Falkirk.

East Stirlingshire enjoyed their record victory back in 1888, when they beat Vale of Bannock 11–2; their worst defeat came in 1936, when they went down 12–1 against Dundee United. Gordon Simpson, who played for the club between 1968 and 1980, holds a record 379 League appearances with the team.

Easter Road The home ground of the Edinburgh club HIBERNIAN. Hibs first occupied the Easter Road ground in 1892 when the team were resuscitated after having disbanded in the face of opposition from other local clubs. For a time Hibs considered Easter Road a temporary home, bearing in mind such disadvantages as its sloping pitch. The ground remained little changed for many years and there was just one small stand, nicknamed the 'Eggbox'. The pitch was finally levelled, however, in the 1920s and new stands were built; other facilities added subsequently included one of the first sets of floodlights to be installed at a British club (first used in 1954) and the first electric scoreboard to be erected in Scotland.

Eastern Counties League English football league, which was founded in 1935. Oustanding clubs in the League's history have included Lowestoft Town (who have won it nine times), Tottenham Hotspur's A team (holders of four titles), and Sudbury Town (winners four times).

Eastwood Town English non-League football club, nicknamed the Badgers. Strip: black and white striped shirts, black shorts, and red socks. Founded in 1953 and based at Coronation Park in Eastwood, the Badgers play in the Northern Premier League.

easy Derisive chant heard from supporters at sporting venues throughout the UK and in several other countries when it is perceived that one team is apparently romping away with victory. It was first heard on British football terraces in the 1960s. The Scotland squad enjoyed some success with a pop song called 'Easy, Easy' in 1974, when it reached number 20 in the charts.

Ecuador Ecuador joined FIFA in 1926 but remain one of the less distinguished South American footballing nations; together with Venezuela they are the only side never to have reached the Finals of the World Cup – although the country has produced a number of outstanding individual players. Strip: yellow shirts with blue and red trim, blue shorts, and red socks.

Edgeley Park The home ground of the English football club STOCKPORT COUNTY. Originally the home of Stockport rugby club, Edgeley Park became County's home in 1901, two years after the club had joined the Second Division. Events in the ground's history have included closure in 1921 following violent crowd behaviour, a disastrous fire in 1936 (when the club's records were lost and one player risked his life to save his precious boots), a return to rugby during World War II, and the staging of the World Lacrosse championships in 1978.

Edgware Town English non-League football club, nicknamed Town, or The Wares. Strip: all green. Founded in 1939 and based at the White Lion ground in Edgware, the club play in the Isthmian League.

Edinburgh City Former Scottish League football club, which dropped out of the League in 1949. Based at the Marine Gardens and subsequently at Powderhall Stadium and City Park, City were founded in 1928 with high ambitions to become one of the strongest clubs in the country but left the League in 1949 and eventually disbanded in 1955.

Edwards, Duncan (1936–58) Celebrated

Manchester United and England left-half, who was one of the most regretted victims of the MUNICH AIR CRASH. Called the 'Kohinoor diamond amongst our crown jewels' by Manchester United's assistant manager Jimmy Murphy, Edwards died at the height of his powers. He had made his debut for United in 1952 and acquired professional status a year later. In 1955 he became the youngest player ever to win a full England cap and subsequently he played a key role in the BUSBY BABES team that captured two successive League titles (1956 and 1957), winning praise for his mastery of all aspects of the game as well as for his genial temperament. If he had not died from his injuries two weeks after the Munich air crash many believe he would have become England's captain and would have led the victorious Class of '66. As it was, he won just 18 caps. His death shocked the English football establishment and was particularly keenly felt in the player's birthplace, Dudley, where memorials to him include a stained glass window in the parish church of St Francis (largely paid for by one of United's fans).

If I had to play for my life, and could take one man with me, it would be Duncan Edwards.

Bobby Charlton

Egham Town English non-League football club, nicknamed Town, or The Sarnies. Strip: blue shirts with yellow sleeves, blue shorts, and blue socks with amber trim. Founded in 1896 and based at Tempest Road in Egham, the club play in the Isthmian League.

Egypt The Egyptian national side has long ranked among Africa's strongest sides and for many years were undisputed as the continent's leading team. Winners of the African Nations' Cup in 1957, 1959, and 1986, the Egyptians appeared in the World Cup Finals in 1934 but did not qualify until 1990 – when stars with the team included defender Hani Ramzi. Strip: red shirts, white shorts, and black socks.

Eintracht Frankfurt German football club; one of the country's leading postwar sides. Strip: red and black diagonal striped shirts, with black shorts and socks. Founded in 1899 and based at the Waldstadion in Frankfurt, the club won the League championship in 1959 and the Cup in 1974, 1975, 1981, and 1988. On the international stage the side are remembered for their participation in the 1960 European Cup Final, which saw Real Madrid put the seal on their reputation as Europe's finest club; they also reached the semi-finals of the European Cup Winners' Cup in 1976 and won the UEFA Cup in 1980.

El Salvador El Salvador joined FIFA in 1938 but have yet to play more than a minor role in the major international competitions – though their involvement in the SOCCER WAR of 1970 (in which year they appeared in the Finals of the World Cup for the first time) attracted some attention. They qualified again in 1982 but failed to progress far in the tournament. Strip: all blue.

Electric Eel or **Electric Heels** Nickname of the English forward Stan MORTENSEN.

Elland Road The home ground of the English football club LEEDS UNITED. Elland Road originally belonged to Holbeck rugby club but was acquired by Leeds City in 1904. During World War I it was used by the army for shooting and drill practice and when peace returned it was thought likely that Elland Road would once again become a venue for rugby, the football club having been expelled from the League for refusing to hand over financial accounts after allegations of illegal payments to players had been made. In 1919, however, a new club – Leeds United – was formed and the ground's future as a major football venue was settled.

Events in the history of Elland Road have included a disastrous fire, which destroyed the West Stand in 1956, extensive rebuilding in the 1960s after Don REVIE took over (including the removal of the old open Spion Kop end), the installation of a heated pitch (1971), and (in 1985) the sale of the whole stadium to Leeds City Council as a consequence of the club's mounting debts.

Elm Park The home ground of the English football club READING. Reading settled at Elm Park in 1896 after using a number of different venues in the town since their formation in 1871. Events in the ground's history have included a gale in 1925, which destroyed the main stand, bomb damage in World War II, which razed the club's offices in the town centre, and extensive refurbishment in the 1980s to satisfy the safety authorities. The most embarrassing incident in the ground's life dates from 1986, when the groundsman accidentally sprayed

the pitch with undiluted weedkiller, with the result that all the grass died; somewhat ironically the groundsman's name was Gordon Neate.

Elm Park Disease.

Title of Reading fanzine (1988)

Emley English non-League football club. Strip: sky blue shirts, maroon shorts, and sky blue socks. Founded in 1903 and based at the Emley Welfare Sports Ground, Emley play in the Northern Premier League.

Enfield English non-League football club, nicknamed the E's. Strip: white shirts with blue shorts and socks. Founded in 1893 and acquiring their present name in 1900, Enfield won the Athenian League championship in 1962 and 1963 before joining the Isthmian League. They then won the FA Amateur Cup in 1967 and 1970 and had captured seven Isthmian League championship titles by 1980, when they were admitted to the GM Conference (which they won in their second season and again in 1986). The club now play in the Isthmian League. They have been based at the Southbury Road Stadium since 1936.

England The English national team has the longest history of all national sides, having participated in the very first international of all (a goalless draw against Scotland) back in 1872. Subsequently England emerged as the dominant side among the four home countries in the 1890s and went on to display their superiority over virtually all continental opposition during foreign tours (though these did not take place on a regular basis until the 1920s).

England won the unofficial Olympic football title in 1900 and reclaimed it in 1908 and 1912, but the interwar period saw a sea change in European football and the 1930s witnessed the occasional notable upset (including a 4–3 defeat at the hands of Spain in 1929 and another against Switzerland in 1938). England's decision to withdraw from FIFA in 1920 and again in 1928, however, meant that the national side did not take part in the World Cup until after World War II and the myth of English invincibility was artificially protected by the team's absence from the world's premiere competition.

Everything changed after the war when, at a time when the domestic game was enjoying a golden era, the national team (awash with the talents of such players as MATTHEWS, MORTENSEN, LAWTON, and

FINNEY) confronted a new generation of foreign sides whose tactics had advanced more quickly. A 2–0 defeat against Ireland in 1949 (the England team's first home defeat) was followed by a 6–3 humiliation against Hungary in 1953 (confirmed six months later by a 7–1 away defeat in Hungary) and for the first time the England managers were obliged to rethink their game. A recovery in the mid-1950s compensated for the side's disastrous showing in the 1950 World Cup (when the English team lost to the USA and Spain) and they reached the quarter-finals of the competition in 1954 and again in 1962.

England's victory as host nation in the 1966 World Cup (see CLASS OF '66) revived memories of the days when the team were undisputed champions of the world, but disappointment in the 1970 tournament was followed by disaster as the team failed to qualify for both the 1974 and 1978 tournaments. The side reached the quarter-finals of both the 1982 and 1986 World Cups, suffered humiliation in the 1988 European Championships, but then revived with a spirited performance in the 1990 World Cup, which saw them robbed of an appearance in the Final itself after defeat in a penalty shoot-out in the semi-final against eventual winners West Germany. They failed to qualify for the 1994 finals. Strip: white shirts, royal blue shorts, and white socks. See also BATTLE OF HIGHBURY; BOGOTÁ INCIDENT; WINGLESS WONDERS.

English disease Slang denoting the reputation English fans have overseas for creating trouble at football matches (see HOOLIGANISM). The term was heard with increasing frequency in the 1980s, when escalating violence involving English teams on the Continent led ultimately to the barring of all English teams from European competition.

Before it was redefined for use in football contexts, the term 'English disease' had been taken to refer to a variety of social ailments rightly or wrongly associated with the English race. These included class conflict, troubled industrial relations, economic stagnation, bronchitis (due to the combination of industrial pollution and the damp English climate in the 19th century), and syphilis (which was regarded by the French as a peculiarly English sickness as far back as the 16th century).

We do not believe there will be trouble. Because of the cost of getting here, we expect an upper middle-class sort of per-son, the type who represents the British tradition of education . . . like gentlemen, like an officer trained at Sandhurst. Someone like David Niven.

Guillermo Urquigo, Monterrey police spokesman before England match (1986)

entrance charge See ADMISSION CHARGE.

episkyros An early form of football that was played in ancient Greece. Little is known of the rules that governed this primitive version of the game, in which handling of the ball was permitted.

Epsom and Ewell English non-League football club, nicknamed the E's. Strip: royal blue. Founded in 1917 and based at Merland Rise in Surrey, the club play in the Isthmian League.

Equatorial Guinea Equatorial Guinea joined FIFA in 1986 but have yet to make much impact in international competition. Strip: all red.

Erith and Belvedere English non-League football club, nicknamed the Deres. Strip: blue and white shirts, blue shorts, and white socks. Founded in 1908 and based at the Park View ground in Belvedere, the Deres play in the Southern League.

Escape to Victory Title of one of the more memorable soccer FILMS ever made. Filmed in 1981 by John Huston (and alternatively entitled *Victory* in the USA), the movie was a remake of the Hungarian film *The Last Goal* and featured such major stars of the cinema as Sylvester Stallone, Michael Caine, and Max von Sydow. The plot concerns a team of footballing prisoners-of-war who plan to escape the Nazis during World War II after agreeing to participate in a match against the pick of the soccer stars of the Third Reich. They give up their chance of escape at half-time in order to triumph over their opponents (and a crooked referee) and then manage to escape anyway after the crowd invades the pitch.

The Allied team included real football idols, among them PELÉ, Bobby MOORE, John Wark, and Ossie ARDILES. The remainder of the team was played by members of the Ipswich side. Stallone played the goalkeeper and was surprised at how tough he found football to be, breaking a finger and damaging his knees during filming; on his return to the USA he described himself as a 'walking blood clot'.

In fact, despite the presence of the professional players, the actual football played in the film turned out to be pretty mediocre. Critics were less than enthusiastic about the other aspects of the movie, too.

Ethiopia Ethiopia joined FIFA in 1953 and have on occasion pressed their case to be included among the continent's stronger teams. They were winners of the African Nations Cup in 1961. Strip: green and yellow shirts, yellow and red shorts, and red and green socks.

Eton Wall Game A version of football that was first played at Eton College in the early 18th century. The Wall Game takes place every year on 30th November and is contested by teams of 'Oppidans' (commoners who board in houses in the town) and 'Collegers' (who board in college) on a pitch alongside one of the walls bordering the playing fields. The pitch used is 120 yards long, but only six yards wide. The earliest records of the game go back to 1717. *See also* GOAL.

> *The game of football, as originally played at the Wall at Eton, was the author of every sort and condition of football now played throughout the United Kingdom.*
>
> The Etonian (1884)

European Championship International competition, called the European Nations Cup until 1968, which was established in 1960 as a tournament open to all European countries. The Championship was conceived by the French Football Federation but failed to excite much interest in its early years, with only 17 countries (excluding most of the major footballing nations) taking part in the inaugural year. The first tournament was somewhat disrupted when Spain withdrew from the competition in protest against the involvement of the Soviet Union in the Spanish Civil War back in the 1930s; ironically, the two nations met in the final of the tournament just four years later (Spain won 2–1).

Competed for once every four years, the competition gathered pace towards the end of the 1960s. The only team to win the Championship on more than one occasion is West Germany (1972 and 1980). The Final of 1976, between West Germany and Czechoslovakia, was the first major championship to be decided by a penalty shoot-out (Czechoslovakia won). *See also* BATTLE OF TURIN.

European Cup European Champion Clubs Cup, the international competition founded by UEFA in 1955 that is contested annually by the top European clubs (initially on invitation but later on winning the domestic league). The tournament, long planned by the former French player and later sports journalist Gabriel Hanot, was finally brought into being in response to the boast by Wolverhampton Wanderers manager Stan CULLIS in 1954 that his team were the champions of the world after they beat the mighty Honvéd side from Hungary. Hanot suggested an official championship for European clubs and a year later the first European Cup was won by Real Madrid (who have won it a record six times in all).

After Real Madrid's run of successes came to an end, Italian and British teams dominated the competition in the 1960s, while Dutch, German, and English sides shared the honours in the 1970s, with English teams winning every year from 1977 to 1982. The most successful British team is Liverpool, with a total of four victories. English clubs were barred from the competition from 1985 to 1991 after the HEYSEL STADIUM DISASTER.

> *The European Cup, almost 17 pounds of silver that's worth its weight in gold.*
>
> Brian Moore

European Cup Winners' Cup International competition, founded in 1961, which is contested annually by top European clubs (entry being automatically allowed when a club has won any of the major domestic cup tournaments). Outstanding clubs in the history of the competition have included Barcelona (who won it in 1979, 1982, and 1989), Rangers (who won it in 1972 and reached the Final in 1961 and 1967), AC Milan (who won it in 1968 and 1973), Dynamo Kiev (who won it in 1975 and 1986), and Anderlecht (winners in 1976 and 1978).

European Footballer of the Year The player who – in the opinion of football journalists co-ordinated by the French weekly *France Football* – has excelled above all others in European competition over the past season. The award (colloquially known as the Golden Ball) was first given in 1956, when Stanley MATTHEWS won it. Michel PLATINI is the only player to have won the award three years in a row (1983–85); other winners have included Alfredo DI STEFANO (1957 and 1959), Denis LAW (1964), Bobby CHARLTON (1966),

George BEST (1968), Johan CRUYFF (1971, 1973, and 1974), Franz BECKENBAUER (1972 and 1976), Kevin KEEGAN (1978 and 1979), Karl-Heinz RUMMENIGGE (1980 and 1981), and Marco VAN BASTEN (1988 and 1989).

European Nations Cup *See* EUROPEAN CHAMPIONSHIP.

European Pelé *See* EUSÉBIO.

European Super Cup *See* SUPER CUP.

Eusébio (da Silva Ferreira) (1943–) Mozambican-born footballer, nicknamed the Black Panther, who during the 1960s was recognized as one of the most accomplished forwards of all time. Sometimes called the European Pelé, Eusébio made his debut with the Sporting Club of Lourenço Marques in 1958 and transferred to Benfica in 1961, making his first international appearance the same year only after a major row between Benfica and Sporting Lisbon over which club had the better claim to the young star's services. The argument was so intense, in fact, that the bewildered Eusébio spent several months in hiding in a fishing village in the Algarve until it was settled.

The interest in his talent was justified; in 1962 he scored two goals for Benfica in the European Cup Final against Real Madrid and in 1965 he was voted European Footballer of the Year. In 1966 he became the top scorer in the World Cup competition, although England blunted his attack in the semi-finals when they prevented him from displaying his great ball control and thus reducing him to tears by the end of the game.

Further honours for Eusébio included the Golden Boot award in 1968 and 1973. His international career ended with a knee injury – although he subsequently carried Toronto Metros-Croatia to victory in the Soccer Bowl in 1976 and played for a time in the Portuguese Second Division.

Everton English football club, based in Liverpool, who are nicknamed the Toffees. Strip: royal blue shirts with white trim, white shorts with blue trim, and blue socks with white trim. The club began life as a church team called St Domingo's in 1878. They changed their name to Everton in 1879 and adopted a strip of black shirts with a white sash, earning the nickname the Black Watch (after the dark dressed Highland regiment), before finally adopting their royal blue strip in 1901.

Everton were quick to embrace professionalism and were founder members of the Football League in 1888 (subsequently spending only four seasons lower than the First Division). They soon established themselves as a leading club, finishing as runners-up in the First Division in 1890 and clinching the First Division championship in 1891. Runners-up again in 1895, 1902, 1905, 1909, and 1912, they claimed FA Cup victory in 1906 (as well as being runners-up in 1893, 1897, and 1907) and another First Division title in 1915.

Inspired by Dixie DEAN, another golden era at GOODISON PARK (which succeeded ANFIELD as the club's home in 1892) opened in the 1920s with victory in the League championship in 1928, 1932, and 1939 and another FA Cup triumph in 1933 (*see* SCHOOL OF SCIENCE). Other stars with the team in these halcyon years included Joe MERCER, Tommy LAWTON, and Tommy Jones. In one remarkable run in 1931 the team scored no fewer than 33 goals in just four games (with victories of 9–3 against Sheffield Wednesday, 8–1 against Newcastle United, 7–2 against Chelsea, and 9–2 against Leicester City).

Less was achieved in the postwar years and it was not until 1963, with a team constructed by manager Harry Catterick around the talents of Alan BALL, Howard KENDALL, and Colin Harvey, that the club won their next major honour, with their sixth First Division championship. Victory followed in the FA Cup in 1966 (with the runners-up position in 1968) and a seventh League championship in 1970.

Few honours came Everton's way in the 1970s, with the exception of an appearance as losing finalists in the League Cup in 1977 and a place in the record books as the first League club to complete 3000 First Division matches (achieved in 1980). The Toffees reclaimed their place at the top of the League in the mid-1980s, however, under manager Howard Kendall, who committed himself to constructing an entirely fresh side. He was rewarded with two First Division championships (1985 and 1987) and the runners-up position in the year in between as well as a fourth FA Cup (1984) and the runners-up position in the competition in 1985 and 1986. Other honours included victory in the European Cup Winners' Cup (1985) as well as a runners-up position in the League Cup in 1984 and in the League Super Cup in 1986.

Kendall left the club in 1987 in order to take over at Athletic Bilbao, but the good times went on with appearances in the Finals of the FA Cup and the Simod Cup in 1989, after which Kendall returned. With players of the calibre of Peter Reid, Andy Gray, Gary LINEKER, and goalkeeper Neville Southall in the side, few opponents relished a visit to Goodison Park:

> *Facing them on Saturday is like going into hospital for an operation; you would rather not do it but the doctor says you must.*
>
> Howard Wilkinson, Sheffield Wednesday manager (1988)

The club enjoyed their record victory back in 1890, when they beat Derby County 11–2; they suffered their worst defeat in 1958, losing 10–4 against Tottenham Hotspur. Another high score was registered in 1931 when the team beat Southport 9–1; to celebrate Dixie Dean gave the name Nina to his daughter, who was born on the same day. Ted Sagar holds the record for League appearances with the club, having played in 465 games between 1929 and 1953. Fans of the club include controversial political figure Derek Hatton. Neighbours Liverpool are inevitably the club's arch-rivals:

> *We hate Bill Shankly, we hate St John,*
> *But most of all we hate Big Ron,*
> *And we'll hang the Kopites one by one,*
> *On the banks of the Royal Blue Mersey.*
> *To hell with Liverpool and Rangers too,*
> *We'll throw them all in the Mersey,*
> *And we'll fight, fight, fight with all our*
> *   might,*
> *For the lads in the Royal Blue jerseys.*
>
> Supporters' song, to the tune of 'The Halls of Montezuma'

There is, incidentally, another football team called Everton in Chile. *See also* MOONLIGHT DRIBBLERS; TOFFEEOPOLIS.

Ewood Park The home ground of the English football club BLACKBURN ROVERS. Blackburn had a number of different homes before finally settling at Ewood Park in 1890. Among their earlier grounds was a farmer's field, which came complete with drainage pool (or 'cow-pit') in the middle of the pitch (which the enterprising players covered over with planks and turf).

Already the winners of four FA Cups, the team attracted large crowds to the new ground. When Darwen visited Ewood Park not long after it had been opened, however, their supporters vented their outrage at the fact that the home side had seen fit to field only three first-team players against them by making their mark on the venue, tearing out

the goalposts, breaking windows, and ruining carpets.

Subsequent events in the history of Ewood Park have included an early experiment with floodlighting in 1892, the collapse of a stand (with five injuries) in 1896, extensive improvements in 1906, 1913, 1928, and 1975, and a fire in 1984. The archetypal northern setting of the ground, complete with tramlines, mill, and traditional turnstiles, made it the natural choice for the filming of one of the nostalgic Hovis television advertisements in the 1980s.

Exeter City English football club, nicknamed the Grecians. Strip: red and white striped shirts, black shorts, and red socks with white stripes. The club were founded in a rugby stronghold in 1904 when St Sidwell's United and Exeter United merged; the club turned professional in 1908 after a meeting at the Red Lion Hotel approving such a move.

The club joined the Third Division in 1920 and have since enjoyed a relatively undistinguished history, their only major title being the Fourth Division championship in 1990. Stars with the team over the years have included goalkeeper Dick Pym and forward Cliff BASTIN.

The Grecians' record victory stands at 9–1 against Aberdare in 1927; they suffered their worst defeat in 1948, when they lost 9–0 to Notts County. Arnold Mitchell holds the record for League appearances with the club, having played in 495 matches between 1952 and 1966. The club's arch-rivals are Plymouth Argyle.

Exiles Nickname of the Welsh non-League football club NEWPORT, in reference to their location beyond the English border.

extra time An additional period of play that is ordered by the referee when at the end of normal playing time both sides are level and a result from the match is required. Usually comprising two halves of 15 minutes each, extra time was first played in an FA Cup Final back in 1875, when the Royal Engineers and the Old Etonians drew 1–1 (the Royal Engineers won the replay 2–0). Five years later a decision to play extra time in the Final between Nottingham Forest and Sheffield led to Forest winning the title after Sheffield refused to go on.

The first World Cup Final to go into extra time was played between Italy and Czechoslovakia in 1934; Italy won the match. The first European Cup Final to be decided in extra time was played in 1958 between Real Madrid and AC Milan; Real Madrid won 3–2.

Extra time may also be played to make up for stoppages during the initial 90 minutes. Referee Clive THOMAS once added on a grand total of 45 minutes worth of extra time when he oversaw a Boys Club match; the game was played on top of a Welsh mountain and the time had been lost when the ball rolled down the slope each time it went out of play. Other long drawn-out matches have included a Cup tie between Stockport County and Doncaster Rovers in 1946: fans went home for tea as extra time went on and on (a result had to be reached that day) – when they came back, the two teams were still at it and when finally the referee called it a day because of bad light (with the score 4–4) a grand total of 203 minutes of football had been completed. Stockport won the replay 4–0.

The longest first-class game ever played, however, took place in 1962, when Santos and Peñarol met in the Copa Libertadores. With extra time added and numerous interruptions in play, the match finally ended (with a scoreline of 3–3) at one o'clock in the morning after three and a half hours. *See also* LONGEST GAME.

F

F-side The notorious section of the terraces at the DE MEER STADIUM in Amsterdam that is home to the most violent supporters of the Dutch club AJAX.

FA The FOOTBALL ASSOCIATION.

FA Amateur Cup *See* AMATEUR CUP.

FA Challenge Trophy FA cup competition, which was founded in 1969. It is competed for by professional and semi-professional teams not members or associate members of the Football League. The first tournament was won by Macclesfield in 1970. The most successful sides in the competition's history are Scarborough and Telford United, who have both won it three times. Recent winners include Wycombe Wanderers (1991 and 1993). The abolition of the distinction between professional and amateur teams in 1974 strengthened the competition and it is now fiercely fought out by 200 of the best non-League sides with the Final being staged at Wembley. The trophy itself was presented to the FA in 1905 by Sir Ernest Cochrane, a barrister who hoped to promote an international competition between England and teams representing Canada and the United States; the idea never got off the ground.

FA Challenge Vase FA cup competition that was founded in 1974 as a replacement for the Amateur Cup, being aimed at less prominent non-League sides. Hoddesdon Town were the first winners, beating Epsom 2–1. Subsequently the Essex club Billericay Town won the Cup on no fewer than three occasions during the 1970s and Halesowen Town and Stamford each made three Final appearances. Among more recent winners are Guiseley, who beat Gresley Rovers 3–1 in a classic Final that was settled only after a replay (the first match ending level at 4–4) in 1991.

FA Charity Shield *See* CHARITY SHIELD.

FA Cup The FA Challenge Cup, often referred to simply as 'The Cup', which is the oldest knock-out competition in the world. The FA Cup was established in 1871 under the aegis of the Football Association and was modelled in part upon a competition run on similar lines at Harrow School. FA secretary Charles William Alcock had been to Harrow and it was he who realized that the knock-out system would work just as well on a national basis. Accordingly he put the idea forward at a meeting of the FA in the offices of the *Sportsman* newspaper off Ludgate Hill, London on 20 July 1871 and it was agreed (as recorded in the minutes): 'That it is desirable that a Challenge Cup should be established in connection with the Association for which all clubs belonging to the Association should be invited to compete.'

Only 15 sides from the membership of 50 entered the first competition, as many members feared such a tournament would lead to unwelcome rivalry between the clubs; they were BARNES, Civil Service, CRYSTAL PALACE, Clapham Rovers, Hitchin, MAIDENHEAD, MARLOW, QUEEN'S PARK, Donington Grammar School, Hampstead Heathens, Harrow Chequers, Reigate Priory, ROYAL ENGINEERS, Upton Park, and the Wanderers.

The Royal Engineers faced the Wanderers (captained by Alcock himself) in the Final, which was played at the Kennington Oval in front of 2000 fans; Morton Peto Betts scored the only goal of the match (playing under the pseudonym A.H. CHEQUER) and Wanderers were the first winners of the FA Cup. Either Wanderers or the Royal Engineers figured in every one of the next six Finals, with Wanderers winning it no fewer than five times in all.

Among the many landmarks in the subsequent history of the Cup have been the 1882 win by the Old Etonians (the last time an amateur team won the competition), the 1883 win by Blackburn Olympic (the first northern side to win it), the unbroken run of successes by northern and Midlands clubs (notably Blackburn Rovers) that followed over the next 18 years, the theft in 1895 of the first FA Cup itself (*see* LITTLE TIN IDOL), Tottenham Hotspur's victory in 1901 (the last time a non-League team won), the celebrated WHITE HORSE FINAL of 1923 (when the Final was played at Wembley for the first time), the thrilling 1948 Final between Manchester United and Stoke City (won by United), the 1953 MATTHEWS FINAL, and the 1973 Final (in which Second Division Sunderland pulled off a giant-killing coup against Leeds United). Arsenal's victory over Manchester United in 1979 by a last-minute goal to bring the score to 3–2 ended another celebrated clash, prompting one newspaper to exclaim 'Has there ever been a final like this!'

The 100th FA Cup Final in 1981 was celebrated with a parade of some of the famous stars associated with the competition over the years, some going back as far as the early 1920s. 500 clubs now contest the FA Cup each year and around 600 matches are played before the victors are known. The only teams to have bettered the Wanderers' total of five wins are Newcastle United and Blackburn Rovers with six, Manchester United and Aston Villa with seven, and Tottenham Hotspur with eight. Only two clubs have contested the Cup every year since it was inaugurated: Maidenhead and Marlow.

The FA Cup has imitation tournaments in virtually every nation where football is played. See also CUP FEVER; CUP MAGIC; SCOTTISH CUP; WELSH CUP.

> Born on the streets, nurtured in the Public Schools and fathered by the Football Association, football owes its greatness and the rapid and sturdy growth of its youth to the principles of the Cup competition.
>
> Geoffrey Green, The Official History of the FA Cup (1949)

FA Sunday Cup See SUNDAY CUP.

FA Youth Cup FA competition for youth teams, which was founded in 1953. The first winners of the Cup were the Manchester United youth team, who included several of the BUSBY BABES.

Facchetti, Giacinto (1942–) Italian defender, who was a star of three World Cup campaigns (1966, 1970, and 1978). Playing at home for Internazionale, he won 94 caps and led Italy to victory in the 1968 European Championship.

Fair Play Award Award given by FIFA to the side that has displayed the best behaviour on and off the field during the course of a World Cup tournament. The bestowing of

the award to England in the 1990 competition was particularly valued by English officials, who had feared that the country's participation in international football after a lengthy ban following the Heysel Stadium disaster of 1985 would be marred by crowd violence and ill-feeling on the pitch; in all the English team averaged just one foul every 6.79 minutes and received only six of the 174 cautions of the tournament. See also BOBBY MOORE AWARD.

Fairs Cup See UEFA CUP.

Falcão, Paulo Roberto (1953–) Brazilian midfielder, nicknamed Il Divino, who was acknowledged to be among the best players in the world in the early 1980s. 'The Divine' Falcão rapidly built up a strong reputation in his home country in the 1970s but after failing to be selected – to the astonishment of many – for Brazil in the 1978 World Cup, moved to Italy in 1980, where he became a star with Roma and contributed to the club's victory in two Italian Cups and the Italian League championship in 1983. Suitably chastened by seeing one of their own sons acclaimed as a demi-god by Italian fans, Brazil invited him to represent the country in the World Cup competitions of 1982 and 1986, although injury prevented him from giving of his best in the latter tournament.

Falkirk Scottish football club, nicknamed the BAIRNS. Strip: dark blue shirts with white flashings, white shorts, and red socks. Founded in 1876, the Bairns joined the League in 1902 and passed their first milestone in 1907 when their total of 102 goals made them the first Scottish club to score 100 League goals in a season; a year later they were runners-up in the First Division, despite a fire that badly damaged their BROCKVILLE PARK home.

Success in the Scottish Cup followed in 1913 and in 1922 Falkirk became the first UK club to pay more than £5000 for a player when they bought Syd Puddefoot from West Ham for £5500. The investment was not rewarded with new titles and it was not until 1936 that the club claimed the Second Division championship. When on the verge of relegation in 1957, the new manager Reggie Smith restored their fortunes and also captured their second Scottish Cup victory.

Remarkable matches from the ensuing period included a meeting with Clyde in 1962, which ended with a 7–3 victory to Falkirk – all ten goals being scored by the same man, Falkirk's Hugh Maxwell. Further Second Division titles came in 1970 and 1975 and in 1991 the club claimed the championship of the First Division.

The Bairns enjoyed their biggest victory to date in 1893, when they beat Laurieston 12–1; their worst defeat came in 1951, when they lost 11–1 against Airdrieonians. John Markie holds the record for appearances for the club, having played with the Bairns on 349 occasions.

family enclosure See BOYS' STAND; SAFE.

Famous Five Nickname given to the forward line that brought success to the Hibernian team of the early 1950s. Comprising Gordon Smith, Peter Johnstone, Lawrie Reilly, Eddie Turnbull, and Willie Ormond, the Famous Five demonstrated their mastery of all aspects of the attacking game by carrying the side to victory in the Scottish First Division in 1948, 1951, and 1952. The original Famous Five were, of course, the fictional children made famous in the stories of Enid Blyton.

fan Fanatic, a follower or supporter of a particular football team (in the USA sometimes termed 'fannies'). The archetypal football fan as perceived by the popular imagination is uncultured, partisan (as displayed by the wearing of club colours and flags), drunk, noisy, and frequently given to violence. In reality, fans range from families to members of the peerage (prime minister John Major being an enthusiastic Chelsea supporter) and only a minority fit the stereotype. The quality of their support also varies from individual to individual: some would be hard put to name the members of the team they claim to support, while others know their birth dates, complete career details, and favourite foods.

It goes without saying that almost all fans pretend to know precisely what is wrong with their own team and are permanently aghast at the evident mismanagement of those in charge. The average fan's opinion of referees is also fairly unanimous – according to an old joke a fan may be defined as someone who can see the ball better several hundred feet away than the ref can when he is standing right next to it.

The press has always revelled in stories of the excesses committed by fans in pursuit of their beloved game. Tales of postponed weddings, children being named after entire football teams, and bets abound – some less true than others. Brighton and Hove Albion fan Bob Steer belongs to that select group of fans who have sacrificed personal pleasures for the good of his team – he elected to see his team's debut in the First Division in 1977 rather than attend his son's wedding (Albion lost 4–0). One man who would have sympathized with him was Hereford fan Kevin McCall, who cancelled his own wedding in 1991 when he realized married life might impinge on his obsession:

> I know it sounds awful, but it just hit me halfway through my stag night that I'd rather be going to the match with the lads than marrying Nicola.

Another marriage that was sacrificed for love of the game was that of Celtic fan Glenn Bonnell, who was given the ultimatum 'football or me' in 1984. Bonnell chose football (despite the fact that his home in Lancashire was a full 189 miles from the Glasgow base of his idols). He had to admit that he had only himself to blame:

> I can't really blame Carole. She never really understood my passion for Celtic and we had a lot of rows because I was always away. Following the lads takes nearly all my money and my mates say I'm crazy. But I don't care. I just can't give it up.

It has been calculated, incidentally, that if 10,000 football fans all cheered at the same time it would produce enough energy to boil three pints of water. See also HOOLIGANISM; TELEVISION.

> Watch against inordinate sensual delight in even the lawfullest of sports. Excess of pleasure in any such vanity doth very much corrupt and befool the mind.
>
> Richard Baxter, *A Christian Directory* (1678)

> Football, in itself, is a grand game for developing a lad physically and also morally . . . but it is a vicious game when it draws crowds of lads away from playing the game themselves to be merely onlookers at a few paid players.
>
> Lord Baden-Powell, *Scouting for Boys* (1908)

> As a boy I genuinely believed in the man who never ate bacon because its red and white stripes reminded him of Sheffield United – indeed in my blue and white Wednesday heart I applauded and supported his loyalty.
>
> Roy Hattersley, *Goodbye to Yorkshire* (1976)

> When more people are talking soccer topics from one Saturday to the next instead of 'H'

bombs, wars and politics, the country will be a better place to live in.

Henry Adamson, FA News (1962)

fanzine An unofficial pamphlet or magazine of the type that proliferated in the 1980s in connection with virtually every major football club in the UK. Modelled on similar publications associated with pop groups, cheaply produced, provocative, and usually the work of the fans themselves, fanzines often represent the genuine feelings of the terraces towards players, managers, and the football administration as a whole. Fanzines are typically completely unforgiving in their criticisms and are regarded with some mistrust by the football establishment, but continue to be sold in large numbers, with new titles replacing old ones with great rapidity.

The fanzine phenomenon has in part mushroomed as a response to the low priority given to the fans by clubs and football officials, with virtually no consultation taking place with supporters about such controversial issues as ground changes, the adoption of new team colours, and the development of a Super League. By the end of the 1980s it was estimated that the 200 existing fanzines were selling in total over one million copies each year. Some attributed their popularity partly to the low quality of much tabloid coverage of the game, in particular the use of flyers.

Many fanzines are notable for their unusual names if nothing else. Among the best known over the years have been Brighton's *And Smith Must Score!* (which refers to a missed goal opportunity involving Brighton's Gordon Smith in the 1983 FA Cup Final against Manchester United; Brighton lost), *Sing When We're Fishing* (Grimsby), *A Kick up the Rs* (Queen's Park Rangers), *Witton Wisdom* (Aston Villa), *There's Only One F in Fulham* (Fulham), *Dial M For Merthyr* (Merthyr Tydfil), *What a Load of Cobblers* (Northampton Town), and Shamrock Rovers' *Hoops Upside Your Head*, taken from the song by the Gap Band (particularly suitable in view of Rovers' strip of green and white hoops). Perhaps the most bizarre title of all though is Gillingham's *Brian Moore's Head Looks Uncannily Like London Planetarium* (a reference to a former director of the club). Other fanzines, notably *When Saturday Comes* and *The Absolute Game* (which takes its name from a song by The Undertones), cover the game as a whole.

The very first fanzines (a word coined by combining 'fan' and 'magazine') were printed in 1949 by science fiction enthusiasts.

Most players hate the fanzines. They tend to be critical of footballers and the way the game is run. Professional players are very wary of anything that makes fun of them.

Pat Nevin, Chelsea forward (1988)

far post The goalpost furthest away from the player with possession of the ball.

Fareham Town English non-League football club, nicknamed Town. Strip: red shirts, white shorts, and red socks. Founded in 1947 and based at Cams Alders, Fareham play in the Southern League.

Farnborough Town English non-League football club, nicknamed Boro. Strip: yellow with blue trim. Founded in 1967 and based at the John Roberts Ground, Boro reached the GM Vauxhall Conference for the first time in 1989, to be relegated again in 1993.

Faroe Islands The Faroe Islands joined FIFA in 1988 and are inevitably considered one of the less formidable European sides. Nonetheless, they enjoyed a moment of glory in 1990 when they pulled off a sensational 1–0 victory against Austria in the European Championship. Strip: white shirts, blue shorts, and red socks.

Farsley Celtic English non-League football club, nicknamed the Celts. Strip: all blue. Founded in 1908 and based at the Throstle Nest in Pudsey, Leeds, Farsley Celtic play in the Northern Premier League.

Fashanu, John (1962–) English forward, who spearheaded the Wimbledon side that became one of the dominant teams in the First Division in the late 1980s. He began his career with Norwich City and subsequently appeared for Crystal Palace, Lincoln City, and Millwall before joining Wimbledon in 1985. His strength and tenacity make him one of the most effective strikers in the League and a hero of Wimbledon's supporters.

Not blessed with talented feet, but put the ball in front of him and he'll knock people out of the way to get it. Dangerous.

Bryan Robson, England captain (1988)

His brother, Justin Fashanu (1962–), was also a noted striker, playing for Norwich

City and Nottingham Forest and attracting transfer fees of over £1 million. In 1992 he briefly became a player-manager of Fourth Division Torquay United. He caused a considerable stir in 1989 when he publicly revealed his homosexuality and subsequently found himself shunned by many top clubs.

fatalities *See* DEATHS.

Father of Football Nickname bestowed upon the football pioneer Ebenezer Cobb MORLEY.

Father of Italian Football Nickname of the great Italian manager Vittorio POZZO.

Father of League Football Nickname of the Scottish-born footballer William MCGREGOR, who helped to establish the Football League.

Fatty Nickname of the English half-back Billy WEDLOCK, who is still considered to have been the greatest player ever to appear for Bristol City. Fatty Wedlock, who was short and stocky rather than fat, played 413 games for the club and helped the team win promotion in 1906. He also won a total of 26 caps for England, winning particular praise for his ability to gain possession of the ball. He retired in the 1920–21 season.

Wedlock coped with his weight with no great difficulty, but the same has not been true of all keepers. Thomas Haylock of Greentown weighed in at 20 stones and decided to call it a day when his team mates took to calling him 'Cheesecake'. His manager, announcing he was dropping Haylock from the side in 1977, had to concede that 'top-of-the-net work upsets him'. *See also* FOULKE, WILLIAM.

Fédération Internationale de Football Association *See* FIFA.

Feethams The home ground of the English football club DARLINGTON. Situated next to the town's cricket pitch, Feethams was first used for football back in 1866 and first hosted Second Division soccer in the 1920s. Events in the ground's history have included a fire in 1960, which destroyed the old West Stand; the Stand was, however, rebuilt in 1961 exactly as it had been before.

Fellows Park The former home ground until 1990 of the English football club WALSALL. *See* BESCOT STADIUM.

Feltham and Hounslow Borough English non-League football club. Strip: blue and white hooped shirts, blue shorts, and white socks. Founded in 1991 and based at the Feltham Sports Arena, the team plays in the Isthmian League.

fences The metal mesh barriers that became a common feature of football grounds in the UK and elsewhere in the 1970s as hooliganism became an increasingly serious problem. Designed to prevent rioting fans spilling over on to the pitch, the use of fences was seriously reconsidered after the HILLSBOROUGH DISASTER of 1989 and alternative methods of crowd control were explored. In the immediate aftermath of Hillsborough the fences at Wembley were taken down for the so-called Requiem Cup Final, but the crowd invaded the pitch and the fences had to be re-installed.

Long before the first fences were put up in British grounds they had been seen in stadia elsewhere in Europe. In Sicily, where football crowds enjoy a particularly unenviable reputation for hostile behaviour, fencing was a common feature of grounds back in the 1960s. Refinements of fencing systems have included barriers fitted with vicious spikes (these were removed at the insistence of the Taylor Report) and experiments with electric fences – although these predictably met with a storm of protest:

What comes next – water cannon, guards, tanks, and consultant undertakers to ferry away the dead?

Simon Turney, Greater London Council (1985)

Fenerbahçe Turkish football club, who have long been the country's most successful domestic side. Strip: blue and yellow striped shirts, with white shorts and socks. Founded in 1907 and based at the FENERBAHÇE STADIUM in Istanbul, the club has dominated the League championship since it was established in 1959, winning it 12 times. The team also won the Cup in 1968, 1974, 1979, and 1983.

Fenerbahçe Stadium The home ground, in Istanbul, of the Turkish football club FENERBAHÇE. Nicknamed Priest's Marsh, the stadium stands beside the dried-up Frog River and was much used for the smuggling of arms by supporters of Kemal Atatürk in the days when Turkey was occupied by the Allies after World War I. As a result of this activity, the club was closed down several times by the authorities. Atatürk himself was said to be a supporter of the team and after independence was won the club was allowed to acquire its ground for the price of just one Turkish lira (1929). The venue was substantially redeveloped in the 1960s and 1970s.

Ferencváros Hungarian football club, nicknamed the Fradi or simply the Green and Whites, who are Hungary's most successful team. Strip: green and white striped shirts with white shorts and socks. Founded in Budapest in 1899, the Fradi have won the League championship and Hungarian Cup on numerous occasions and added the Fairs Cup in 1965. Star players with the side over the years have included Imre Schlosser, Gyorgy Sarosi, and Florian ALBERT. The Hungarian national side that reached the World Cup Final in 1938 included no fewer than four Ferencváros players.

Ferranti Thistle Former name of MEADOWBANK THISTLE. The club took its original name from the Ferranti works in Edinburgh, having started life as a works team there. The club's offices are, in fact, still to be found at the main Ferranti factory, though the team's name was changed under a directive from the Scottish League because of its commercial relevance.

Feyenoord Dutch football club, who rank among the top domestic teams in the Netherlands. Strip: red and white shirts, with black shorts and socks. Founded in 1908 with money from the mining tycoon C.R.J. Kieboom, the club has won 13 League championships and six Cup titles. In international competition, the team won the European Cup and the World Club Championship in 1970 and the UEFA Cup in 1974. Stars with the side in the 1970s included the great Johan CRUYFF.

Feyenoord Stadium Football ground in Rotterdam that is home to the Dutch football club FEYENOORD. The club opened its new stadium in 1937 and it has since been little altered. The adventurous functionalist style of the stadium attracted many admirers and it became the most prestigious international football venue in the Netherlands, although the fans who actually used it irreverently dubbed it The Tub. Events staged at the venue have included rock concerts, religious meetings, and even an ambitious dramatic spectacle in which events of World War II were re-enacted.

Fiancée of Italy Nickname of the Italian football club JUVENTUS.

Field Mill The home ground of the English football club MANSFIELD TOWN. The Stags played at two other grounds before settling in 1905 at Field Mill, which had previously been occupied by the Mansfield Mechanics club. Features of the ground include the huge West Stand, which was first erected at the Hurst Park racing course and was later moved to Field Mill in 1959.

FIFA Fédération Internationale de Football Association. The international organization that rules on matters relating to international football and also stages the World Cup tournament. FIFA came into existence in 1904, when the first meeting was held in Paris, with representatives of the game from France, Switzerland, Belgium, Spain, the Netherlands, Denmark, and Sweden. England chose not to get involved initially but finally joined two years later and the Football Association rapidly assumed a leading role in its affairs.

Based in Zurich, the organization has sometimes been the object of some controversy. The issue of playing matches against Germany after World War I led to British sides withdrawing from the organization from 1918 to 1922, while that of broken time led to all four UK international sides withdrawing once more in 1928. More recently there has been dissent concerning the introduction of the penalty shoot-out in 1982 and over rulings relating to the professional foul in 1990.

Presidents of the organization have included Jules Rimet and Sir Stanley ROUS. FIFA has some 165 member nations – more than even the United Nations.

Fifers Nickname of the Scottish football club EAST FIFE.

fifty-fifty ball A playing situation in which players from both teams are making equally strong challenges for possession of the ball (each thus having a 50 per cent chance of winning it).

Fiji Fiji joined FIFA in 1963 but have yet to make much impact in international competition. Strip: white shirts with black shorts and black socks with white trim.

Filadelphia The former home ground, in Turin, of the Italian football club TORINO. Opened in 1927 and named after the street on which it stands, the Filadelphia stadium witnessed the great era in the club's history before its famous side perished in the SUPERGA AIR CRASH in 1949. The tragedy is commemorated with a plaque at the ground, although Torino left the stadium in 1960; in 1989, on the 40th anniversary of the disaster the club purchased the old stadium and have since used it as a training ground.

Filbert Street The home ground of the English football club LEICESTER CITY. The club had several homes before moving permanently to Filbert Street in 1891, after a Miss Westland suggested the site in what was then called Walnut Street. Events in the ground's history have included a fire during World War II and the installing in 1971 of a huge plastic cover to protect the pitch (it proved of only limited value and was removed in 1982). Among the great games played there was one during the interwar period, when City's centre-forward Arthur Chandler scored no fewer than five goals (legend has it that as he scored his fifth five white swans flew low over the ground). A replica of the Statue of Liberty overlooks the ground from what was formerly the premises of Liberty Shoes.

Filberts Nickname of the English football club LEICESTER CITY, in reference to the club's ground, FILBERT STREET. *See also* FOXES.

films Few films have taken soccer as a central theme. The first film to do so was probably *The Winning Goal* (1920); among the films that followed were *The Ball of Fortune* (1926), *The Great Game* (1930), in which England international Jack Cock appeared, *The Arsenal Stadium Mystery* (1939), a vintage thriller with Leslie Banks as Slade of the Yard hunting down the murderer of a player (with members of the Arsenal squad making appearances as 'The Trojans'), *The Great Game* (1953), *Small Town Story* (1953), YESTERDAY'S HERO (1979), GREGORY'S GIRL (1980), and ESCAPE TO VICTORY (1981).

Soccer films from other countries have included the Swedish film *Stubby* (1974), a comic strip adventure about a six-year-old who plays for the Swedish national side, and the US movies *Boys in Company C* (1977), a Vietnam War film, and *The Longest Yard* (1974), which starred Burt Reynolds as a member of a prison football team. *See also* TELEVISION.

Finland The Finnish national team has a long history (the Finns were present in the Olympic tournament of 1912) but have rarely threatened to join the ranks of the top European sides. Strip: white shirts, blue shorts, and white socks.

Finney, Tom (1922–) English winger, nicknamed the Preston Plumber, who ranked alongside Stanley MATTHEWS as the outstanding English footballer of his era. Finney joined Preston North End on leaving school and emerged as a leading player after World War II, when English football entered a golden period. His skills covered every aspect of the game and included mastery of the art of dribbling and tackling as well as tremendous bursts of speed.

Finney was much in demand as an international and won 76 caps for his country between 1946 and 1958, scoring 30 goals and playing in every position in the forward line. His most memorable internationals included his role in stunning 10–0 and 4–0 victories over Portugal (1947) and Italy (1948) respectively. He was also the first player to be made Footballer of the Year in two seasons (1954 and 1957). He was often begged to lend his services to other teams, but he remained loyal to Preston, turning down, for instance, the offer of £10,000 with a car, a villa, and a huge salary if he joined the Italian club Palermo.

Finney's playing career finally ended after 569 first-class matches at the end of the 1959–60 season and, remarkably for such a great player, he never received a Championship or Cup winners' medal (although Preston did reach the FA Cup Final of 1954 and only missed the 1953 Championship title on goal average – they were runners-up again in 1958). His last game, at Deepdale in 1960, was marked by the presence of a huge crowd, who joined in singing 'Auld Lang Syne' as the great player made his farewell; deprived of Finney's presence, Preston soon went into decline and were relegated a year later.

He made a brief comeback in 1963, as a member of the Distillery side that drew 3–3 with Benfica in the European Cup.

Finney would have been great in any team, in any match and in any age – even if he had been wearing an overcoat . . . he had the opposition so frightened that they'd have a man marking him when they were warming up before the kick-off.

Bill Shankly

Fiorentina Italian football club, which emerged as a leading Italian side after the war. Strip: all violet. Founded in 1926 and based at the COMUNALE STADIUM in Florence, the club won its first League championship in 1956 and another in 1969 as well as enjoying victory in the Cup in 1940, 1961, 1966, and 1975. On the international stage, the team was winner of the European Cup Winners' Cup in 1961. In 1993 they were relegated to Serie B.

Fir Park The home ground of the Scottish football club MOTHERWELL. Motherwell first occupied Fir Park, then a pleasantly wooded area, in 1895. Curious features of the ground include the unfinished Main Stand, which ends in a bare steel skeleton; work on the stand in the 1960s had to be halted after a neighbouring resident won a court order protecting his property from being overshadowed by any new stand. When the owner finally sold up, the money available to finish the stand had long since run out.

Firhill Park The home ground in Glasgow of the Scottish football club PARTICK THISTLE. The club had a number of homes before settling at Firhill Park in 1909. They had used Meadowside, on the banks of the Clyde, from 1891 to 1908 and their eventual eviction to make way for a new shipyard was bitterly resented by many fans:

> A small group of spectators gathered around the flagpole and, as the Union Jack was being hauled down for the last time, one of the band pulled it away from the steward and wrapped it around his body. He then started singing Will Ye No Come Back Again, and the rest of the group took up the chorus.
>
> Ian Archer, The Jags

The opening of Firhill Park on what had been wasteground was a badly bungled affair, with the first match being cancelled at the last moment on the orders of the Office of Public Works; another month passed before the ground was passed fit for actual play. Happier times followed, with internationals and victory in the Cup; subsequent events included the arrival of greyhound racing and, in the 1980s, the sharing of the venue with Clyde.

firm Slang for a gang of football hooligans who take part in co-ordinated outbursts of violent criminal behaviour. Such firms were first identified by the popular press in the 1980s, when their activities led to much disquiet and threats from the authorities that the game would have to be much more rigorously policed. *See* HOOLIGANISM.

Firs Park The home ground in Falkirk of the Scottish football club EAST STIRLINGSHIRE. The club moved to Firs Park in 1921, having failed to find a ground in the Bainsford area they had resided in before. The proximity of Brockville Park, the Falkirk ground, has always militated against Firs Park ever becoming a prestigious venue; an attempt to relocate the club in 1964 culminated in one of the most notorious legal battles in football history.

Fisher Athletic English non-League football club, nicknamed the Fish. Strip: black and white striped shirts and socks with white shorts. The club was founded in 1908 and named after the John Fisher Catholic Society, which aimed to provide an opportunity for the deprived youth of Bermondsey to play football. Based at the Surrey Docks Stadium since 1982, Fisher Athletic joined the GM Vauxhall Conference in 1987. After relegation, the club now play in the Southern League.

Fishermen Nickname of the English non-League football club FLEETWOOD TOWN, in reference to the area's long history as a centre of the fishing industry.

Five Violins Nickname of the celebrated forward line-up that spearheaded SPORTING LISBON with great success in the 1940s and 1950s.

fixture congestion A perennial problem faced by the football authorities, whereby the increasing number of matches played by clubs makes the task of finding dates teams can agree on a formidable task. Such problems exercise the minds of many in the modern game – the foundation of the new Premier League in 1992 was greeted by some as a step in the right direction with its limits on the number of games played (of particular value to those attempting to bring together strong national teams).

However, the difficulties faced by today's administrators pale beside those faced by their predecessors in the early history of the game. On several occasions luckless teams found themselves with such a backlog of games to play that drastic solutions had to be called for. In the 1915–16 season, for instance, Celtic were obliged to play two League games on the same day, beating Raith Rovers 6–0 at home before travelling to Fir Park to overcome Motherwell 3–1. The same pressures were repeated even at international level and on three occasions in the 1890s England themselves were forced to play two internationals on the same day (against Ireland and Wales); remarkably enough they won all six games.

In more recent times Queen of the South were concerned when two separate teams arrived to play them on the same afternoon in 1981 (one had a wasted journey) while Glasgow Rangers recorded an apparently impossible feat when in 1987 they played two matches simultaneously, one at home against Hamilton Academical and one away at Dundee. In fact, the away game had been postponed due to bad weather and the away win was an invention of the Pools panel.

Similar pressures once caused the downfall of two teams in the York and District League – Heslington and Moor Lane Youth Club. Faced with a serious backlog of matches to make up, the two teams secretly agreed to drop a fixture involving the two sides and fabricated match reports, complete with a 0–0 scoreline and comments on the ref's handling of the game. Inevitably, they were found out and both sides were fined and relegated by the League.

FK Austria Austrian football club (also called Austria Memphis after their sponsors), nicknamed the Violets. Strip: violet shirts, white shorts, and violet socks. Founded in Vienna in 1911, FK Austria are second only to Rapid Vienna among the domestic sides and have a long list of home honours to their credit. The club had its origins in the Vienna Cricket and Football Club, which was formed by British exiles in Vienna during the 1890s and belonged very much to the aristocracy of the city, in contrast to Rapid, who were an essentially working-class club. One contemporary observed rather sourly: 'Rapid work, Austria play'.

Given their current name in the 1920s, FK Austria won the League championship title in 1924, 1926, 1949–50, 1953, 1961–63, 1969–70, 1976, 1978–81, and 1984–86. The club also enjoyed success in the Austrian Cup in 1921, 1924–26, 1933, 1935–36, 1948–49, 1960, 1962–63, 1967, 1971, 1974, 1977, 1980, 1982, 1986, and 1990. In 1978 they won the European Cup Winners' Cup.

The club's home ground since 1982 has been the FRANZ HORR STADIUM; before that the club often appeared at the huge PRATER STADIUM and a host of other venues. Stars with the club have included the Czech striker Matthias SINDELAR, who spearheaded the attack in the 1930s.

Flackwell Heath English non-League football club. Strip: red shirts, white shorts, and red socks. Founded in 1907 and based at Wilks Park in High Wycombe, the Heath play in the Isthmian League.

Flamengo Brazilian football club, nicknamed the People's Club. Strip: red and black hooped shirts, white shorts, and red and black socks. Founded in 1895 as a rowing club (taking up football in 1911) and based at the Gavea Stadium in Rio (though important matches are usually played in the MARACANA Stadium), the People's Club claim to be the oldest football club in Brazil. They emerged as a powerful side with the arrival of a number of dissatisfied Fluminense players and the two clubs have since been arch-rivals. The team has won the Brazilian League 20 times over the years, among other major honours. They were winners of the South American Cup in 1981, in which year they also became World Club Champions after beating Liverpool 3–0. Stars of the side have included Domingo da Guia and LEONIDAS DA SILVA in the 1930s and ZICO and Socrates in the 1970s and 1980s.

Flaminio Stadium The home ground, in Rome, of – at various times – both AS ROMA and Lazio. Opened in 1928 and named after the district in which it lies, the Flaminio Stadium began life as the Partido Nacional Fascista stadium and became the home of Lazio in 1931. Subsequently they were joined by their arch-rivals AS Roma in 1940 and the ground remained their shared home until 1953. The stadium was completely rebuilt and given its current name in 1959, since when both teams have returned on an occasional basis.

Fleet Nickname of the English non-League football club GRAVESEND AND NORTHFLEET.

Fleetwood Town English non-League football club, nicknamed the Fishermen. Strip: red and white shirts, white shorts, and red socks. Founded in 1977 when Fleetwood disbanded, the club are based at Highbury Stadium in Fleetwood and play in the Northern Premier League.

floodlights The first floodlit match of all was played at Bramall Lane on 14 October 1878 in front of a record crowd of 10,000 people (of whom 8000 entered in the blackness around the gates without paying). However, the first official League match under floodlights was not played until 1956, when Newcastle United beat Portsmouth 2–0 at Fratton Park.

Strangely, the idea of floodlighting (which

facilitated the development of many new competitions and meant fewer postponements) was strongly opposed for many years and the UK was behind many other countries in the introduction of such systems; the FA in particular refused to accept the benefits of floodlighting and remained against it for over 80 years, banning member clubs from playing in such conditions after 1930.

Doubts about such innovations were confirmed in the early days by such incidents as occurred at Kilmarnock in 1878, when two players were so badly injured after three lights failed that they had to retire permanently from the game. Further demonstrations of floodlighting (using oil rather than electricity and thus resulting in acrid fumes and an added fire risk) were seen in the 1880s, but the novelty soon wore off and such experiments were not taken up seriously until after World War I, when Herbert CHAPMAN was among those to press for such changes (Chapman having been won over to the idea when he saw a game in Austria played in the light of the headlamps of 40 cars).

By then floodlighting had been a feature of many stadia in the USA and South America for a good number of years, while Europe's first set of permanent floodlights had been erected at the Olympic stadium in Amsterdam in 1934 (being first switched on for a game between an Amsterdam XI and Stoke City).

In the UK Chapman's Arsenal and Tottenham Hotspur led the calls for the introduction of efficient floodlights in the 1930s while many more joined the cause after World War II. An exhibition match played at Southampton in 1950 furthered the cause, although much of the action went unseen by the crowd of 10,000 (who were allowed in free) after a heavy fog descended and the players themselves had difficulty seeing the ball when it was kicked above the level of the lights; the *Daily Telegraph* voiced the doubts of many when it reported the match under the headline 'Floodlit play needed infra-red glasses'.

Among the opponents of floodlighting even at this late stage were many players themselves: evening matches meant longer working days and travelling late into the night. Their doubts were eventually silenced by the offer of extra pay for matches played under artificial light. The first FA Cup match to be staged under floodlights took place in 1955, between Kidderminster Harriers and Brierley Hill Alliance. The last League club to invest in floodlights were Chesterfield, who finally acquired a set in the 1968–69 season.

> *Clubs cannot do just as they like – even if they desire floodlight football. That may be in the future. I cannot easily predict an era when the sorcerers of science may easily turn night into day as they now talk to a man on the other side of the world.*
>
> Sir Frederick Wall, FA secretary (1935)

Fluminense Brazilian football club, nicknamed White Powder, who rank as one of South America's most successful sides. Strip: red, green, and white striped shirts, with white shorts and socks. Founded by English immigrants in 1902, Fluminense were identified as the club of Rio de Janeiro's aristocracy (while Flamengo represented the common masses). Playing their most important games at the MARACANA Stadium and others at the Alvaro Chaves Stadium, the team have won the Brazilian League title some 28 times. Stars of the side over the years have included Ademir de Menezes, DIDÌ, Roberto RIVELINO, and Julio Cesar Romero.

Fontaine, Just (1933–) French inside-forward, born in Morocco, who was the inspiration of the French national team in the late 1950s. Fontaine's prolific performances as a goalscorer were invaluable to every team he played with and in 1958 his tally of 13 goals set a new record for the Finals of any World Cup (he scored 30 goals for France in just 21 matches). Capable of producing powerful shots with either foot and also competent in the air, he proved one of the most formidable strikers in the history of French football despite the fact that his career was twice disrupted after he suffered leg injuries. At home, he played for USM Casablanca, Nice, and Reims.

Football Association The senior authority governing the game of football in England and the oldest footballing organization in the world. The FA was founded in 1863, specifically at the suggestion of Ebenezer Cobb MORLEY, although others had also proposed the founding of a regulatory body to decide some of the contentious issues then dominating the game.

The organization came into being during the course of a meeting between representatives of a number of clubs at the Freemason's Tavern in Great Queen Street in Lincoln's Inn Fields, London; the clubs involved were BARNES, the War Office club, Crusaders, Forest of Leytonstone, the

No Names club from Kilburn, CRYSTAL PALACE, Blackheath, Kensington School, Percival House, Surbiton, BLACKHEATH Proprietory School, and the public school team Charterhouse. Charterhouse alone declined to become a member of the new organization, nervous of what the other public school teams would make of such a move.

Morley became the FA's first secretary and went on to draft the first set of laws to be adopted. Of the 14 rules he suggested none was more controversial than that forbidding hacking. The first match under the new rules was played between Barnes and Richmond late in 1863.

Under such respected secretaries as Charles Alcock (1870–95), Sir Frederick Wall (1895–1934), and Sir Stanley ROUS (1934–61), the FA's influence over the game grew steadily and inspired the formation of similar organizations around the world. The modern version of the FA presides over international matches involving the England team, the various FA competitions, and all aspects of the domestic game, from coaching to discipline and clarification of the rules.

There have been troubled times in the FA's history, however. Particularly contentious issues have included the long-running conflict with the Football League over the question of professionalism and the related problem of broken time payments, which led to the four home countries withdrawing from FIFA in 1928. Friction with the League has been a recurrent problem, culminating in 1972 with all 92 clubs in the League temporarily resigning from the FA. The introduction of the Premier League in 1992 was also the cause of disagreement between the two bodies.

The modern FA boasts 42,000 clubs and 2,250,000 players. Similar associations have been established in all the major footballing nations; the Scottish Football Association began life in 1873, while that of Wales was founded in 1876. The two halves of Ireland are represented by the FA of Ireland and the Irish FA (founded in 1880). See also AMATEUR CUP; CHARITY SHIELD; FA CUP; LANCASTER GATE; SUNDAY CUP; TROPHY, THE; VASE, THE; FA YOUTH CUP.

Football Capital of Europe Nickname of the Italian city of Milan, in reference to the domination by the city's two teams AC Milan and Internazionale of European competitions in the 1950s and 1960s.

Football League, The English football organization, which was founded at a meeting at the Royal Hotel, Piccadilly, Manchester, on 17 April 1888. The league competition established by the Football League was to provide a model for the hundreds of leagues that were subsequently founded in every footballing nation of the globe.

Prime mover behind the foundation of the organization was the redoubtable Scotsman William MCGREGOR (dubbed the 'Father of League Football'). The original members of the Football League (a title contributed by Preston's manager Major William Sudell) were all professional clubs from north and central England: Accrington, Aston Villa, Blackburn Rovers, Bolton Wanderers, Burnley, Derby County, Everton, Notts County, Preston North End, Stoke City, West Bromwich Albion, and Wolverhampton.

With McGregor as its first elected chairman, the League staged the first programme of (five) League matches on 8 September 1888, when a record attendance of 6000 was established for a game between Preston North End and Burnley. The most remarkable match that day was between Bolton Wanderers and Derby County – Derby winning the game 6–3 after Bolton had been 3–0 ahead after just six minutes. Jack Gordon of Preston North End was the scorer of the first League goal (his team went on to claim the first Championship title without losing a single match in a glorious year that also brought them the FA Cup).

The League prospered and a second division was added in 1892 from what was the old Football Alliance; both divisions subsequently grew in size until they reached a combined total of 40 clubs in 1905.

Perhaps the most exciting close to any League season in its early history was that of 1908–09, when the Second Division title and various relegation battles remained undecided until the very last day.

There was a break in the League's history during World War I, after which a third division (subsequently divided into Northern and Southern Sections for a time) was added (1920–21). World War II brought another interruption, after which the League reached its long-time total of 92 clubs.

The one millionth League game was played in 1971, when Hartlepool United drew 0–0 with Brentford; that same year also saw one of the most thrilling finishes in the history of the Football League, when Arsenal clinched the Championship with a goal by Ray Kennedy just three minutes before the end of the last game – giving the Gunners a League and FA Cup double. 18 years later Arsenal were once again the last-minute winners of the League when Michael Thomas scored a vital last goal against favourites Liverpool in the last match of the 1988–89 season (Liverpool remain the most successful club in the League's history, with 18 Championships).

Other recent landmarks have included the first commercial sponsorship of the League (by Canon in 1983). One of the most pro-found periods of change in the English League system came in 1992 with the for-mation of the Premier League for the top 22 clubs. The Fourth Division (introduced in 1958) vanished but it remained possible for clubs from the old First Division (now effec-tively the Second Division) to gain promo-tion to the upper rank, while new clubs could gain League status by promotion from the Conference, the most senior of various subsidiary leagues.

For many years the headquarters of the English Football League was at Starkie Street, Preston, but in 1959 the orga-nization moved to Lytham St Anne's in Lancashire.

I really believe that the game would have received a very severe check, and its popularity would have been paralysed once and for all, if the League had not been founded.

William McGregor

We cling to the myth that our Football League is the best in the world. There are others: the West German and South American leagues for example are as good. But it is the toughest in its demands on players and it is destructive of national football in its drain of players' energy and in denying them time for national commitments.

Sir Stanley Rous (1978)

See also SCOTTISH LEAGUE.

Football League Trophy British football competition open to teams in the lower divisions, which was founded in 1983. Previously the Trophy was known as the Group Cup; in 1984 it was renamed again, being retitled the Associate Members Cup. Subsequent names for the cup have included the Freight Rover Trophy and the Autoglass Trophy.

Football Spectators' Bill Proposed British Government legislation that was announced in 1989 in an attempt to rid football of the violence that had by then reached epidemic proportions. Largely instigated at the wish of prime minister Margaret Thatcher in the wake of the HEYSEL STADIUM DISASTER and other violent events, the bill proposed a compulsory national membership scheme and the establishment of new bodies to oversee the national game and inspect grounds as well as measures to prevent known hooligans from travelling to matches overseas.

The FA and the League bitterly opposed the bill but the Government insisted that the return of English clubs to international competition was contingent on acceptance of the bill by the football authorities. The Taylor Report, however, rejected the idea of a national membership scheme and the government eventually agreed to a new set of reforms partly funded by the state through tax cuts on the Pools.

Football Supporters' Association British organization formed to represent the inter-ests of fans following the upheavals facing the national game since the 1980s. The Association was established in the wake of the 1985 HEYSEL STADIUM DISASTER.

Football Trust Organization that was founded in 1979 by the various Pools businesses to provide financial support for worthy projects connected with both pro-fessional and semi-professional football. Funded out of the profits made from the Pools themselves, the Trust promotes such programmes as football for the disabled, work by the Sports Turf Research Institute, and improvements to grounds. In the wake of the upheavals of the 1980s the Trust's resources were boosted in 1990 by changes in the tax laws governing the Pools and by amalgamation with the Football Grounds Improvement Trust as The Football Trust 90. Members of the organization represent the clubs, the fans, and all the associated parties, including the police.

Football War See SOCCER WAR.

Footballer, The Humorous satirical bal-let on the theme of football, that was choreographed by Igor Moiseyev in 1930, with a score by V. Oransky. See also GOLDEN AGE.

Footballer of the Year Informal title given to the holder of both the Football Writers' Association Footballer of the Year trophy (founded in 1948) and to the holder of the Professional Footballers' Association Players' Player of the Year award (founded in 1974). The same accolade also goes to the winner of equivalent awards in Scotland and other footballing countries. Winners of the English awards have included among others Stanley MATTHEWS, Billy WRIGHT, Tom FINNEY, Danny BLANCHFLOWER, Bobby MOORE, Bobby CHARLTON, George BEST, Kevin KEEGAN, Kenny DALGLISH, Ian RUSH, and John BARNES and in Scotland Billy MCNEILL. In Austria, Gerhardt HANAPPI achieved the remarkable distinction of being named his country's Footballer of the Year every year between 1954 and 1960. *See also* EUROPEAN FOOTBALLER OF THE YEAR.

Footballers' Battalion Nickname of the 17th Service Battalion of the Middlesex Regiment in World War I, whose ranks included a number of celebrated footballers drawn from professional sides (the largest single contingent coming from Leyton Orient). Professional players who joined the regiment after its foundation in 1914 when war was declared were allowed leave on Saturdays in order to play for their clubs.

> *Do you want to be a Chelsea Die-Hard? . . . Join the 17th Battalion Middlesex Regiment . . . and follow the lead given by your favourite football players.*
>
> World War I recruiting poster

The fact that football continued for some time after war was declared in 1914 was a subject of some contention, as many believed that the recruitment effort would suffer as a result:

> *We view with indignation and alarm the persistence of Association Football clubs in doing their best for the enemy . . . every club that employs a professional football player is bribing a much needed recruit to refrain from enlistment and every spectator who pays his gate money is contributing so much towards a German victory.*
>
> Letter to *The Times* (1914)

In the event, many young players and fans answered the call by joining the Middlesex Regiment and other regular regiments and football played its part in the war. Nearly half of all professional players joined up in the first few weeks of the war and by Christmas 1914 the game had provided over 100,000 men, all too many of whom were destined never to return.

Opportunities to play the game in the trenches of northern France were rare, although the poignant kickabout that took place between British and German troops during the Christmas Day truce of 1914 (a brief respite before they resumed the grisly business of killing one another the next day) remains one of the great legends of the war.

The 18th London Regiment gave attacking play a new meaning when they went 'over the top' on 25 September 1915, kicking a ball between them as they charged towards the German lines during the First Battle of Loos. The 8th Battalion of the East Surrey Regiment also took their footballs into battle with them, dribbling balls through No Man's Land as they attacked German positions under heavy fire on the Somme on 1 July 1916. Captain W.P. Nevill, who provided the four balls used, was among the many casualties, but the attack was a success and the regiment won no fewer than 15 decorations for the day's work:

> *On through the hail of slaughter,*
> *Where gallant comrades fall,*
> *Where blood is poured like water,*
> *They drive the trickling ball.*
> *The fear of death before them*
> *Is but an empty name*
> *True to the land that bore them*
> *The Surreys play the game.*
>
> 'Touchstone', *Daily Mail* (1916)

Of football's many war casualties, Second Lieutenant Donald Bell, a former Bradford Park Avenue defender, became the only Football League player ever to win a Victoria Cross (posthumously on the Somme in 1916). *See also* KHAKI CUP FINAL.

Football's Godfather Nickname of Alan HARDAKER, the celebrated football administrator who was head of the Football League for many years.

Forest *See* NOTTINGHAM FOREST.

Forest Stadium The home ground of the German football club EINTRACHT FRANKFURT. Set in woods near Frankfurt, the Forest Stadium was first opened in 1925 on what had formerly been an army shooting range and was intended from the start to be one of Germany's most prestigious sports venues. The ground, with its colonnaded stands and grand entrance-way, remained largely unchanged until 1974, when it was substantially rebuilt in advance of the World Cup. The refurbished stadium has staged many major matches, including the 1988 European Championships.

Forfar Athletic Scottish football club, nicknamed the Sky Blues, and the Loons. Strip: sky blue shirts, navy blue shorts, and sky blue socks. Forfar were founded in 1885 and have played at Station Park in Forfar throughout their long history.

The club joined the League in 1921 but had to wait until relatively recent times for their golden era (picking up a single Division C championship in 1949 along the way). A resurgence of fortune was signalled in the 1977–78 season when the club got as far as the semi-finals of the League Cup, before narrowly losing to Rangers in extra time. In 1982 they had a similarly successful campaign in the Scottish Cup, again reaching the semi-finals, while in 1984 they celebrated their centenary by winning their first major honours by capturing the Second Division title by a record 63 points. Another meeting with mighty Rangers in 1985 went to a penalty shoot-out before Forfar finally conceded defeat.

The club enjoyed their record victory in 1988, when they beat Lindertis 14–1; they suffered their worst defeat back in 1930, losing 12–2 against King's Park, with eight of their opponents' goals being scored by John Dyet who was making his debut for King's Park. Alex Brash holds the record for League appearances with the club, having played in 376 games between 1974 and 1986.

Forthbank Park *See* ANNFIELD PARK.

foul An infringement of the rules, specifically one in which a player has tripped, held on to, or kicked an opponent. Other infringements in this category include charging from behind, playing the ball with the hand, obstruction, or indulging in dangerous play.

Many critics have detected a decline in behaviour on the pitch over recent decades, but it is arguable that the game has always had its villains. Back in 1890 the centre-forward of Royal Oaks, a team comprising fishermen from Shieldfield in Tweedmouth, was reputedly given to threatening to kill any goalkeeper who attempted to block his shots. Even the golden age of English football in the 1950s had its bruisers:

There was plenty of fellers who would kick your bollocks off. The difference was that at the end they'd shake your hand and help you look for them.

Nat Lofthouse

Players with a notorious reputation for 'hard play' have included such luminaries as Frank Barson (Barnsley, Aston Villa, Manchester United, Wigan Borough, and England), who was sent off on numerous occasions in the 1920s, Norman BITES YER LEGS Hunter, Harry CRIPPS (*see also* DOG, THE), Nobby STILES, and more recently Vinny JONES. *See also* INJURIES; PROFESSIONAL FOUL.

Angels don't win you anything except a place in heaven.

Billy McNeill

Tardelli's been responsible for more scartissue than the surgeons of Harefield hospital.

Jimmy Greaves

Foulke, William (1874–1916) Formidable English goalkeeper, nicknamed Fatty or otherwise known facetiously as Little Willie, who kept goal for his country in the late 19th century. Weighing in at his heaviest at 23 stones, he was a star with Sheffield United, contributing to the side's victories in two FA Cup campaigns and one League championship.

Numerous legends surround Foulke's gargantuan figure; among other feats, he was reputed to be able to carry a man under each arm and to punch a football as far as the halfway line. On one occasion a match had to be stopped after he snapped the crossbar. During another game he was injured but proved too large for the stretcher and had to be carried off the field by no fewer than six men. His agility made him a great keeper, however, and he was famed as a specialist in saving penalties (although cunning opponents learnt to aim at his ample stomach).

Foulke was also very well known for his mercurial temper, which often led him to give away penalties in the most remarkable fashion. On one occasion he picked up the Liverpool centre-forward George Allan, whose persistence had become irritating, and planted him headfirst in the mud outside his goal, giving the Reds the penalty they needed to win the match. Foulke's subsequent meetings with Allan were much relished by the crowds, notably the series of replays of their semi-final match in the 1898–99 season that eventually ended with victory going to Sheffield United.

On the one occasion that Fatty Foulke was on a losing FA Cup Final side the celebrated goalkeeper took particular exception to the decisions made by referee Tom Kirkham and the linesman and determined, as he lay in the team bath after the match, that he would have to put things right. A few moments later a steaming, naked 23-stone keeper was sighted scouring Crystal Palace for the luckless officials. Kirkham was obliged to evade the irate keeper by hiding in a boot cupboard, the door of which Fatty Foulke then set about wrenching off until restrained by various onlookers, who included the Secretary of the FA himself.

In 1905 Fatty transferred to Chelsea (as keeper and captain), where his enormous appetite created more legends. On one occasion he got into the dining-room before the rest of the team and polished off all eleven breakfasts. In response to the remonstrations of his team mates he only replied: 'I don't care what you call me, as long as you don't call me late for dinner.'

Fatty Foulke once excused himself for his notorious antics, explaining: 'Ask the old team if a bit of Little Willie's foolery didn't help chirp them up before a tough match.'

Chelsea made the most of the psychological advantage of having such a huge obstacle in their goalmouth by positioning two small boys behind the goal to emphasize Fatty's bulk (the original ballboys). He ended his career with Bradford City (making a career total of 347 League appearances) and finished up somewhat sadly earning small change saving penalties from holiday-makers on Blackpool Sands. Ultimately he caught a chill while doing this and died of pneumonia, aged 41.

A football wonder is Willie, the most talked-of player in the world. A Leviathan (22 stone) with the agility of a bantam. The cheeriest of companions and in repartee as difficult to score against as when between the posts.

William Pickford and Alfred Gibson, *Association Football and the Men who Made It* (1906)

four-three-three *See* CATENACCIO.

four-two-four Tactical formation that was frequently seen in the 1960s. The formation, first developed by Brazil in 1958, hinged on the use of a deep-lying forward and an attacking wing-half who acted as a link between defence and attack; however, the formation only worked if the team concerned had two effective wingers – when Alf RAMSEY's 1966 World Cup squad proved weak in this regard he reverted instead to a four–three–three configuration (*see* WINGLESS WONDERS).

Fowlers Nickname of the English non-League football club SOUTHALL, from the name of a past president of the club.

Foxes Nickname of the English football club LEICESTER CITY, in reference to the area's tradition of fox-hunting.

Fradi Nickname of the Hungarian football club FERENCVÁROS, being a derivation of Franzenvorstadt, the German-speaking area in which the club originated.

France The French national team has a long history in international competition and was one of the participants in the very first World Cup tournament in 1930. The French enjoyed their first golden period in the 1950s, when prolific goalscorers Raymond KOPA and Just FONTAINE spearheaded the attack (Fontaine's achievements with the team included a record tally of 13 goals in the 1958 World Cup Finals). With Fontaine and Kopa as their inspiration, the French side reached the semi-finals of the 1958 World Cup and eventually finished in third place; they made the semi-finals again in 1982, when they went out to West Germany after a penalty shoot-out (the first in World Cup competition) and once more in 1986. The resurgence in the team's fortunes in the 1980s was the work of a new generation of star players, notably Michel PLATINI, who led the team to victory in both the European Championship and the Olympic competition in 1984. As manager, Platini relived the triumphs of 1984 when he guided the team to the finals of the European Championship in 1992 (though the side failed to progress much further, despite the contribution of striker Jean-Pierre Papin). Strip: blue shirts, white shorts, and red socks.

Francescoli, Enzo (1961–) Uruguayan-born schemer, who established himself as one of the most formidable European footballers in the late 1980s. Having begun his career in Uruguay with Wanderers, he transferred to the Argentinian club River Plate (1983) and thence to the French teams Racing Club Paris (1986) and Marseille (1989) and to the Italian side Cagliari (1990). He has also made many international appearances, attracting much praise for his performance in the Uruguayan squad in the 1986 World Cup and inspiring his country's victories in the South American Championship in 1983 and 1987. He was South American Footballer of the Year in 1984.

Francis, Trevor (1954–) English forward, who earned the nickname Superboy as one of the most precocious young footballing talents of the early 1970s. Having made his debut for Birmingham City at the age of 16 (scoring 15 goals in his first 15 games), Francis subsequently established himself as one of the most effective strikers of his day, playing for Nottingham Forest (who became the first British club to pay a £1 million transfer fee in the process), Manchester City, Sampdoria, Atalanta, Rangers, and Queen's Park Rangers as well as for teams in the NASL. He also notched up a tally of 52 caps for England.

Subsequently he served as player-manager of QPR for a short time before moving to Sheffield Wednesday, where he raised the team to the very top rank, winning the League Cup in 1991 and reaching the finals of both the League Cup and the FA Cup in 1993.

Franz Horr Stadium The home ground, in Vienna, of the Austrian football club FK AUSTRIA. The club settled there in 1982, eight years after the ground was purchased by the Viennese FA, who named it in honour of their own president.

Fratton Park The home ground of the English football club PORTSMOUTH. The team acquired the ground (previously a market garden next to Fratton railway station) on their formation in 1898; the famous mock-Tudor decoration of the main entrance dates from 1905 when the ground was further developed. Events in the ground's history have included the very first League match to be played under floodlights (1956). Physical features of the venue include the 'Boilermakers' Hump', a vantage point once popular with workers from the shipyards nearby.

free kick A kick that is awarded to one team after their opponents have transgressed the rules of the game. A free kick is taken from where the offence took place and, according to the nature of the infringement, may be either a direct free kick, in which a shot at goal is allowed, or an indirect free kick, in which such a shot is not permitted. Members of the penalized team must stand at least nine metres away from the player taking the kick. When, in the USA, the National Professional Soccer League was established in the late 1960s free kicks were orchestrated by referees in order to create breaks in the action so that the television companies could screen commercials at regular intervals during the match.

Freeing of the Slaves Popular description for the removal of the maximum wage and retain-and-transfer regulations that until the 1960s severely restricted the freedom of players to negotiate salaries and have a say in their own transfers. Unrest among players went back a very long way, to the early days of professionalism in fact, but pressure for change became irresistible in the late 1950s when Jimmy HILL (chairman of the Professional Players' Association) was among those to argue that players should be able to defend their own interests with a freer hand. Before the old system was dropped in 1961 players could expect to earn little more than £20 a week in season and £17 in the summer and support among players for change was almost universal, with a strike threatened if nothing was done.

The maximum wage was finally lifted and Fulham quickly announced that their star Johnny HAYNES would be taking home £100 a week, setting a new precedent. Ironically, Hill himself retired as a player before he could enjoy the pleasures of negotiating his contract and, somewhat perversely, found himself in his new role as a manager having to find extra money to pay his own recruits.

> When I first played for my village side I was rewarded with a bag of vegetables and sixpence. At seventeen I was paid £5, and I counted it a dozen times on the way home, thinking I was in the big money.
>
> Joe Mercer, *Soccer the British Way* (1963)

> Some people tell me that we professional players are soccer slaves. Well, if this is slavery, give me a life sentence.
>
> Bobby Charlton (1960)

Freemason's Tavern Public house formerly in Great Queen Street, off Drury Lane, in central London, where the Football Association was founded on 26 October 1863. The site of this historic building is now occupied by the Connaught Assembly Rooms (which have themselves occasionally been used for meetings by the football establishment).

Freight Rover Trophy See FOOTBALL LEAGUE TROPHY.

French Stanley Matthews See KOPA, RAYMOND.

Frickley Athletic English non-League football club, nicknamed The Blue. Strip:

blue and white shirts, with blue shorts and socks. Founded in 1910 as Frickley Colliery and based at Westfield Lane in South Elmsall, West Yorkshire, the side play in the Northern Premier League.

Friedenreich, Artur (1892–1969) Brazilian centre-forward, who was a star of South American football for some 26 years (1909–35). Playing at home for Germania, Ipiranga, Americano, Paulistano, São Paulo, and Flamengo, he also made 17 appearances for the national side (scoring nine goals). In all he was credited with scoring a career total of 1329 goals.

Friedrich Ludwig Jahn Stadium The home ground of the German football club DYNAMO BERLIN. Named after a gymnast who promoted sport in the early 19th century, the stadium was opened in 1951 and rebuilt in 1987; the dreaded no man's land bordering the Berlin Wall formerly ran immediately behind the stadium, which was one of the most prestigious venues for football in what was East Germany.

friendly A match that is not played as part of a competition but purely for its own sake or a specified cause. The word friendly has proved a misnomer on too many occasions in the past and most teams consider good results in friendlies as important as wins in regular competition, providing players another opportunity to shine and managers a chance to experiment with new tactics, etc. The fact that the outcome of such matches has no direct influence upon a side's subsequent campaigns is no guarantee that the game will be played with any less passion and commitment than usual and there is an equal chance of outbursts of bad behaviour. In 1971, for instance, the entire team representing Portuguese champions Benfica were reported to UEFA after they attacked referee Norman Burtenshaw when they lost a friendly against Arsenal 6–2.

> The struggle between defence and attack – the basic contest in football – is really, and always, the chief interest in any football: that is why a 'friendly' match never quite rings true.
>
> John Arlott, *Association Football* (A.H. Fabian and Geoffrey Green, 1960)

Friuli The home ground of the Italian football club Udinese, in the city of Udine. Opened in 1976 and named after the region in which Udine lies, the stadium began its life in tragic circumstances: with the local population still recovering from an earthquake in which a thousand people had died earlier in the year, the rugby match with which the stadium was inaugurated was marred when a player was struck by lightning and killed. The dramatic arch that dominates the stadium became one of the most famous landmarks of the area, however, and the ground has since staged World Cup matches and many other prestigious games.

Fulham English football club, nicknamed the Cottagers. Strip: white shirts and socks with red and black trim, with black shorts. The club, based at CRAVEN COTTAGE, began life as Fulham St Andrew's Sunday School FC in 1879 and went on to win the West London Amateur Cup in 1887 and the West London League title in 1893, finally going professional in 1898, when the club acquired their current name. Fulham joined the Second Division in 1907, and spent much of their later history in that division, although they spent three seasons in the First Division after World War II and again in the 1960s, when stars with the team included Johnny HAYNES, George Cohen, and Alan Mullery. Other stars to appear with the side over the years have included Jimmy HILL, Bobby ROBSON, Bobby MOORE, George BEST, and Rodney MARSH. One aspiring Cottager who was rejected by the club but who later found fame in a different sporting sphere was the great decathlete Daley Thompson.

Fulham have a reputation for unpredictability and eccentricity – partly through the well-publicized association of the comedian Tommy Trinder with the side (he was chairman of the club for many years). Other celebrities to have joined the club's board over the years have included the singer Alan Price. Famous fans include the actress Honor Blackman.

In 1987 a threatened merger with Queen's Park Rangers was narrowly avoided when a consortium headed by Jimmy Hill bought up the club's name and the players' contracts although Fulham fans still fear they will one day be obliged to share grounds with Chelsea, their long-term rivals, at Stamford Bridge.

The club enjoyed their record victory in 1963, beating Ipswich Town 10–1; they suffered their worst defeat in 1986, losing 10–0 against Liverpool. Haynes holds the record for League appearances, having played in 594 matches between 1952 and 1970.

The club can boast one of the most

devoted fans in modern history – Yorky Whiting, a dustman from faraway Devon, who not only vowed to leave everything he had to the Cottagers in his will but also painted his house (called 'Craven Cottage' of course) in Fulham's colours. A set of goalposts stood at the entrance to his garage and much of the interior was decorated with hundreds of Fulham programmes.

> *Oh this year we're going to win the Cup,*
> *Hey, viva El Fulham,*
> *Then next year you know we're going up,*
> *Hey, viva El Fulham,*
> *Alan M. is a wonder, that's for sure,*
> *Hey, viva El Fulham,*
> *And Bobby – well, do we need say Moore?*
> *It's Fulham por favor.*

Supporters' song, to the tune of 'Y Viva España'

full-back A defender, usually one of two, whose prime role is to block attacks by the opposition (especially down the wing) and to return the ball to his own team's attack. On rare occasions, however, full-backs have made the most of their opportunities and completed the job themselves by scoring a goal: there are several instances of full-backs scoring from powerful shots from within their own half of the field.

funny old game, it's a Cliché often heard in situations where events have taken an unexpected turn. Its particular association with the game of football has been consolidated by constant repetition and is reflected by Jimmy GREAVES's adaptation of it for the title of his second volume of autobiography, *It's A Funny Old Life* (1990).

Futre, Paulo (1965–) Portuguese forward, who emerged as the most talented Portuguese player of his generation in the 1980s. Futre began his career with Sporting Lisbon at the age of 12 and five years later became the youngest player ever to make an appearance in the national side. In 1984 he transferred to Porto and there inspired some of their greatest successes, in particular their European Cup victory of 1987. As an international, he shone in the 1986 World Cup and a year later was bought by the Spanish club Atlético Madrid for £2 million.

G

Gable Endies Nickname of the Scottish club MONTROSE, after the nickname of the inhabitants of the town (referring to the gable-ended design of many houses in the High Street).

Gabon Gabon joined FIFA in 1963 but have yet to make much impact in international competition. Strip: green, yellow, and blue shirts, blue and yellow shorts, and white socks with green, yellow, and blue trim.

Gainsborough Trinity English non-League football club, nicknamed the Blues. Strip: royal blue shirts with white trim, white shorts, and blue and white socks. Originally members of the Second Division of the Football League (which they joined in 1892 and left in 1912), Blues are based at the Northolme ground and now play in the Northern Premier League.

Galatasaray Turkish football club, regarded as one of the three strongest sides in the country. Strip: yellow shirts, with red shorts and socks. Founded in 1905 and based at the ALI SAMI YEN STADIUM in Istanbul, the team have won nine League titles since 1962 as well as eight Cup victories but have yet to make much impact in European competition.

Gallacher, Hughie (1903–57) Scottish centre-forward, who was a key figure in the celebrated Wembley Wizards side that cowed England in 1928. Gallacher was one of the most gifted players of his era and was recruited by Queen of the South, Airdrieonians, Newcastle United, Chelsea, Derby County, Notts County, Grimsby Town, and Gateshead at various times in his career. As captain of Newcastle, he led the team to victory in the League in 1927. In all, he scored 387 goals in 541 League games. As an international, he scored 22 goals in 19 matches with the Scottish team. Though biting in his criticism of weaker players and often involved in controversy off the pitch, he has been described as the best centre-forward ever seen in British foot-

ball. His life ended in tragic circumstances when he committed suicide on a railway line after being accused of maltreating his son.

Gallagher, Patsy (1909–) Northern Ireland-born inside-forward, nicknamed the Mighty Atom, who was a star with such teams as Celtic and Sunderland in the 1920s and 1930s. A formidable attacker despite his small size, he enjoyed his most celebrated moment in 1925, when he was a key member of the Celtic side that appeared in the Scottish Cup Final against Dundee. Celtic were trailing by a single goal when Gallagher launched himself at the Dundee goal from deep within his own half. He successfully evaded the challenges of a number of defenders and got close to the Dundee goal before being brought down. Undaunted he locked the ball between his feet and somersaulted backwards over the line and into the goalnet. The goal was allowed and Celtic went on to win the game 2–1. Later in his career he also appeared for Falkirk. On the international stage he won 15 caps for Northern Ireland and one for the Republic of Ireland.

Galloping Major Nickname of the great Hungarian footballer Ferenc PUSKAS, reflecting his strong leadership of HONVÉD (which had close links with the Hungarian army).

Galston Former Scottish football club, which dropped out of the League in 1925, after just two years. The team played at Portland Park, outside Kilmarnock.

Gambia Gambia joined FIFA in 1966 but have yet to distinguish themselves in international competition. Strip: white shirts with red trim, white shorts, and white socks with red trim.

gambling See POOLS.

game of two halves Football cliché, meant to indicate that the fortunes of the two teams or patterns of play are radically different before and after the interval.

Commentators have long since learnt to be cautious in using the phrase.

One match in which its use would have been particularly unwarranted was that played at Sunderland in 1894 between Sunderland and Derby County; the late arrival of the referee after the deputy referee had already presided over 45 minutes of play led to the game being restarted and the two teams playing what is still remembered as 'The Game of Three Halves'. Sunderland, who had been winning 3–0 at the end of the first half, scored a further three goals in the second half and another five in the third half; the final scoreline was Sunderland 8, Derby County 0 (Sunderland went on to win the League championship that season). The restarting of the game created a particular headache for pressmen at the match – at the point that the game began again they had already sent off their first half match reports.

On other occasions two halves have been more like three-quarters and a quarter. In 1955, during a match between two army sides in Gravesend the referee's watch stopped and the teams completed a first 'half' of no fewer than 70 minutes.

Garibaldi Reds Nickname of the English football club NOTTINGHAM FOREST, after the bright red colour of their shirts (*see* REDS). The original Garibaldi Reds were the military forces who fought to liberate Italy in the 1840s. Garibaldi's men adopted a distinctive 'uniform' of red shirts after a stock of them were bought up by the Uruguayan government in 1843 and donated to Garibaldi, who was then in Montevideo to form his Italian Legion. When the Legion arrived in Italy in 1848 they brought their red shirts with them. Coincidentally, the black and white strip of Nottingham's other team, Notts County, provided the inspiration for the team colours of one of Italy's most famous clubs, Juventus. *See also* ARSENAL.

Garrincha (Manoel Francisco dos Santos; 1933–83) Brazilian wing-forward, nicknamed the Little Bird, who during the 1950s and 1960s was hailed as one of the most talented players ever to appear on the world stage. Born into a poor family in Pau Grande, Garrincha suffered badly from polio while still a child and had to overcome the drawback of a twisted right leg as a result. He made his first appearance for the Rio de Janeiro club Botafogo in 1952, where he rapidly attracted attention with his attacking ability (despite his short stature and disfigured leg).

In 1955 he won the first of a total of 51 caps with the Brazilian national team and three years later he played a key role in the country's victorious World Cup campaign. In 1962 he was central to Brazil's World Cup triumph once more, although his presence in the Final (won 3–1 by Brazil against Czechoslovakia) was only made possible after the president of Brazil intervened, the Little Bird having been sent off (and indeed hit by a bottle thrown from the crowd as he left the field) in the semi-final with Chile. Botafogo won the Brazilian Championship in 1964 and a year later Garrincha contributed to another Championship title, this time with Santos.

A bad car crash in 1965 hindered Garrincha's career somewhat and his performance in the 1966 World Cup was less remarkable than in the previous two tournaments (Brazil going out in the first round). Subsequently he transferred to Corinthians, Flamengo, Bangu, Portuguesa Santista, and Olaria, but his troubles both on and off the field multiplied and he retired. Brilliant on the pitch, he was unable to bring his private life under control and he finally died of alcohol poisoning in 1983, one of football's most regretted casualties.

Gascoigne, Paul (1967–) English forward, nicknamed Gazza, who became one of the most talked-about players of the late 1980s. Born in Gateshead, Gascoigne attracted attention for his skills while still with his school team and was subsequently signed for his local club Newcastle United. His progress there led Tottenham Hotspur to pay £2 million for him in 1988 and to his first appearances in the England team.

Already lampooned for his love of Mars bars (which he admitted he ate at the rate of three a day) – and his somewhat generous frame – he became a major media star in 1990 after he burst into tears during England's semi-final defeat at the hands of West Germany in the World Cup. It was not the first time a player had been seen to cry in a match (back in 1966 both EUSÉBIO and Bobby CHARLTON burst into tears during the World Cup) but the media treated it as though it was the first time it had ever happened.

The popular press launched the emotional, fun-loving Gazza as an icon of his time, following events both on and off the field with avid attention. Such was the strength of popular interest in Gascoigne's activities that his agent went so far as to register his nickname as a trademark, realizing its potential in the commercial market.

Gazza responded to all this with blundering good humour and even enjoyed a brief career as a pop star on the strength of his new-found celebrity. In 1992, however, he transferred (after delays due to injury) for a record fee to the Italian club Lazio, where it was presumed he would get some respite from constant press comment. The challenge of settling into a foreign League left Gazza unmoved, and he commented: 'Coping with the language shouldn't be a problem. I can't even speak English yet.'

Tottenham's Terry VENABLES had his own thoughts about the move: 'I had mixed feelings – like watching your mother-in-law drive over a cliff in your car.'

Opinions about the talented, cocky Gazza have gone from one extreme to the other. Some critics have accused him of immaturity both as a player and as a person, while others have pointed to his undoubted abilities and have compared him with great names of the past. Gianni Agnelli, the owner of Juventus, described him as 'a soldier of war with the face of a child' while Stan Seymour, chairman of Newcastle United, less flatteringly called him 'George Best without brains'. BEST himself once commented that he thought Gascoigne's shirt number (10) referred not to his position but to his I.Q., but on another occasion reflected: 'He is accused of being arrogant, unable to cope with the press, and a boozer. Sounds like he's got a chance to me.'

See also JONES, VINNY.

Gate Nickname of the English non-League football club MARGATE.

gate The number of supporters attending a match. The size of the crowd is a crucial barometer of a club's health in terms not only of its performance on the field but also with regard to its public image, facilities on offer, etc. Even in the early days of the game crowds of several thousand would gather to see matches involving their local teams, although official records were not kept for League matches on a regular basis until after World War II.

The peak period for attendances in British football came in the years immediately following the war, when over a million fans turned out to see their local teams every Saturday. The popularity of the game was such that factories regularly closed down when home matches were played, most of their workers absenting themselves with such excuses as family bereavement:

In order that the management may have knowledge of the numbers intending to be absent on Wednesday afternoon, will those whose relatives are to be buried on that day please apply by Tuesday for permission to attend.

Notice posted in a Barnsley colliery in advance of a local match (1945)

The Government finally found a way to alleviate the problem of absenteeism by introducing staggered working hours. In the 1948–49 season of 1848 games in the four divisions, 41,271,414 spectators were recorded. In contrast, in the 1985–86 season of 2028 games, only 16,488,577 fans went through the turnstiles; between 1976 and 1986 alone overall attendances fell by a third. There has been a similar decline in figures outside the League, although an increase in attendances was noted throughout the UK at the end of the 1980s, when the game was at its lowest ebb.

The record for a single day remains 1,272,185 spectators at 44 League matches on 27 December 1949. The record for a single match in the English League was set at Manchester City's Maine Road on 17 January 1948, when 83,260 witnessed a game between Manchester United and Arsenal. In Scotland the record for a League match stands at 118,567 for a meeting between Rangers and Celtic at Ibrox Park on 2 January 1939. The record for a Second Division League match stands at 48,110 for the crowd attending a game between Aston Villa and Bournemouth in 1972.

The record attendance in the FA Cup is 126,047 (plus another 70,000 who got in through an open gate without paying) for the memorable 1923 WHITE HORSE FINAL between Bolton Wanderers and West Ham at Wembley, the first occasion that the Final was played there. On this occasion the size of the crowd (which, if it really did reach 200,000 was an all-time record) and the calm efforts of a mounted policeman on a white horse to clear the pitch made national headlines (*see* BILLY). In the end the ground was so crowded that the spectators formed a solid wall on the very edge of the touchlines. The Scottish Cup record stands at 146,433 for a match between Celtic and Aberdeen at Hampden Park in 1937.

The European Cup attendance record stands at 136,505 for a semi-final played at Hampden Park between Celtic and Leeds United in 1970. An even larger crowd of 146,433 turned out to see Celtic play Aberdeen at the same ground in 1937, but the all-time record for the proven attendance at a single match goes to the game between Brazil and Uruguay at the Maracana Stadium, Rio de Janeiro in 1950, when 199,589 spectators were present.

At the other end of the scale the record for lowest attendance must be shared by a number of clubs who have recorded totals of 500 and less, usually when playing 'behind closed doors' on the orders of the football authorities (there were no paying spectators at all for matches between West Ham and Castilla in 1980 and between Aston Villa and Besiktas in 1982 as a result of disciplinary action by the European Football Union). Back in 1921 an official gate of 13 watched a game at a neutral venue between Stockport and Leicester (though another 2000 were allowed free admission).

In international competition, just 983 fans watched a European Championship match between the USSR and Finland in Moscow in 1976 (the temperature was 10 degrees below freezing and the players wore tracksuits and woolly hats). The 'crowd' of 469 who turned out to watch the short-lived Thames Football Club on 6 December 1930 is thought to be the smallest attendance recorded for a Saturday afternoon League game; the record for the lowest ever attendance at a League match is 450 for a game played on a Tuesday afternoon between Rochdale and Cambridge United in 1974:

We were disappointed we couldn't play on Saturday because we had supporters travelling from all over the country. There was one coming from London, one from Newcastle, one from Brighton . . .

David Kilpatrick, Rochdale manager (1986)

Gateshead English football club, nicknamed the Tynesiders. Strip: white shirts and black shorts. The original Tynesiders were a prestigious League football club, who were founded back in 1899, as South Shields Adelaide. Based at the now-dismantled Redheugh Park ground in Gateshead, the club joined the League in 1919 but rarely escaped the lower reaches. It all came to an end in 1960, when the club (somewhat harshly) were denied re-election to the League after finishing third from bottom and lost their place to Peterborough United. The current reincarnation of the team were formed in 1977 and play at the Gateshead International Athletics Stadium, in the Conference.

Gay Meadow The home ground of the English football club SHREWSBURY TOWN. Town settled at Gay Meadow in 1910,

before which it had been a popular recreation area dating back several centuries. Before Shrewsbury arrived, notable events in Gay Meadow's history over the years included a ceremony greeting the arrival of Sir Henry Sidney (father of poet and soldier Philip Sidney) in 1581 and a tragic acrobatic stunt attempted by one Thomas Cadman in 1739. Cadman's aim was to cross the icy River Severn via a tightrope stretched from the spire of the neighbouring church of St Mary's to the meadow itself; the outcome of his venture is recorded on a plaque at the church:

Let this small Monument record the name
Of CADMAN and to future times proclaim
How by'n attempt to fly from this high spire
Across the Sabrine stream he did acquire
His fatal end. 'Twas not for want of skill
Or courage to perform the task he fell:
No, no, a faulty Cord being drawn too tight
Hurried his Soul on high to take her flight
Which bid the Body here beneath good Night.

Feb. 2nd 1739 aged 28

The meadow was also the venue for touring productions by Sir Frank Benson's famous theatre company in 1903 (to mark the 500th anniversary of the Battle of Shrewsbury) and for various festive occasions such as haymaking parties, until the football club moved in.

Features of the modern ground include the Wakeman End (named after the Wakeman Technical School nearby), a row of tall trees between the stands and the river, and a set of ornate cast-iron Victorian turnstiles. The proximity of the River Severn has led to various problems, notably flooding (particularly bad in 1948 and 1967). Balls are also regularly kicked into the river; until his retirement in 1986 these were retrieved in a coracle by one Fred Davies, who was paid 25p for every ball he managed to bring back. (Fred has subsequently been re-employed following the failure of his son – who took over in 1986 – to control the coracle.) According to legend, as he reached for a wayward ball on one occasion he grasped hold of a swan by mistake.

Gayfield Park The home ground of the Scottish football club ARBROATH. The Red Lichties settled at Gayfield Park (previously a rubbish dump on the seashore) in 1880, although the original pitch (often referred to as 'Old Gayfield') was less than ideal with a narrow playing area and no room for spectators along one side. After witnessing such memorable events as the famous 1885 victory over Bon Accord by a record scoreline of 36–0, the ground was extended at the so-called 'Tuttie's Neuk End' and then shifted 60 yards to the south-west. The new 'Greater Gayfield' was opened in 1925 by the Earl of Strathmore; events in its subsequent history have included a fire in the Main Stand in 1958 and the destruction of a boundary wall by heavy seas in 1962 (Gayfield being closer to the sea than any other ground in the UK).

Gazza Nickname of the English forward Paul GASCOIGNE.

General, The Nickname of the England manager Sir Alf RAMSEY, who led the national team to triumph in the 1966 World Cup. *See also* CLASS OF '66.

Gentle Giant Nickname of the celebrated Welsh forward John CHARLES.

Gentleman Jim Nickname of James HOWIE.

Gentleman John Nickname of the Irish footballer and manager Johnny CAREY.

Gento, Francisco (1933–) Spanish outside-left, who was a star with Real Madrid and Spain in the 1950s and 1960s. He established his reputation playing for Nuevo Montana, Astillero, Rayo Cantabria, and Real Santander before joining Real in 1953 and subsequently rising to the post of captain of both the club and national teams. Described as the world's fastest winger, he played a key role in Real's long succession of European Cup victories in the late 1950s and notched up a total of 43 caps for his country.

Geoffroy Guichard Stadium The home ground of the French football club ST ETIENNE. It was opened in 1931 and named after the late grocer whose firm sponsored the club in its early history (the Guichard family remain closely linked with the team). The stadium was extensively redeveloped in the 1950s, 1960s, and again in the 1980s, making it one of the best appointed in Europe. Each stand is named after a prominent member of the club.

Gerets, Eric Belgian defender, who emerged as one of the most talented and controversial footballers anywhere in Europe

in the 1980s. He began his career with Standard Liège and subsequently distinguished himself for his country in the 1980 European Championships. In 1982 he led Standard to the runners-up position in the European Cup Winners' Cup, after which he was transferred to Milan. A match-fixing scandal dating from his days at Standard threatened to end his career in 1984, when he was suspended and dismissed by Milan – but he rebuilt his reputation with MVV Maastricht and then with PSV Eindhoven, with whom he won winner's medals in the Champions' Cup, the League championship, and the domestic Cup all in one season (1988). He also won back his place in the Belgian national team and played a key role in their 1986 World Cup campaign; by the time of his retirement from international football in 1990 he had collected 84 caps in all.

Gerhard Hanappi Stadium The home ground, in Vienna, of the Austrian football club RAPID VIENNA. It was opened in 1977 (as the Weststadion) to replace the old Rapidplatz ground, which had been the club's home since 1912. Gerhard HANAPPI was the architect who had designed the ground; he had also been one of the team's greatest stars, winning the Austrian Player of the Year title seven times between 1954 and 1960. The stadium was named in his honour just three years after it opened, when Hanappi himself died of cancer at the age of 51.

Germany Germany, in its various forms, has a long and very distinguished history in international competition as one of the great footballing nations. The team first took part in the World Cup in 1934, reaching the semi-finals, and reappeared in 1938 when leading players with Austria were obliged by the Nazis to play in the German team – though without much success. The German team was split into two in 1948, when East Germany and West Germany became separate states. Germany qualified for the 1994 World Cup in America.

East Germany, wearing a white and blue strip, first took part in the World Cup Finals in 1974 and two years later won the Olympic football title.

West Germany, wearing black and white, resumed football in 1950 and rapidly established their status as one of the leading European teams. They went on to win the World Cup in 1954 (Sepp HERBERGER's team overpowering Hungary in the Final), 1974 (defeating Holland in the Final), and

1990 (when their victims in the Final were Argentina) as well as the European Championship in 1972 and 1980; they were runners-up in the World Cup in 1966, 1982, and 1986, came third in 1970, and finished fourth in 1958.

The two teams were brought together in 1991 and looked set to continue to maintain their standing as one of the world's greatest football nations. Strip: white shirts, black shorts, and white socks.

Gers Nickname of the Glasgow football club RANGERS.

Gerson de Olivera Nunez (1941–) Brazilian midfielder, who masterminded Brazil's 1970 World Cup triumph. Winner of 78 caps with Brazil, Gerson played a minor role in the 1966 World Cup, inheriting the midfield role in which DIDÌ had excelled, and created many of the goals that took Brazil to the Final in 1970 – as well as a goal of his own in the climactic last match. At home, he played for Flamengo and Botafogo, helping the latter side to victory in the League in 1967 and 1968, before moving to São Paulo.

Ghana Ghana joined FIFA in 1958 but have yet to make much impact in international competition though they are considered one of the more promising African nations. Strip: all white.

ghosts See BOUNDARY PARK; CELTIC PARK; HIGHBURY.

giant-killer A lowly, often non-League, side that confounds all expectations by toppling a mighty opponent who would otherwise have been considered certain to win any match between them. Such surprise results are particularly associated with the FA Cup, the structure of which can bring teams from extreme ends of the League into contact.

Every major club has suffered its moment of embarrassment at the hands of opponents from a lower division, but humiliation of First Division giants by non-League clubs – the most feared (and most relished) form of giant-killing – is more rare. The following selection of scorelines involving non-League clubs and respected members of the League belong to the mythology of football and are still discussed in hushed whispers by supporters of the teams involved:

Celtic 2, Arthurlie 4 (1896–97)
Sheffield Wednesday 0, Darlington 2 (1919–20)
Blackburn Rovers 0, Corinthians 1 (1923–24)
Arsenal 0, Walsall 2 (1933)
Sunderland 1, Yeovil Town 2 (1948–49)
Dundee 0, Fraserburgh 1 (1956–57)
Liverpool 1, Worcester City 2 (1959)
Tottenham Hotspur 0, Norwich City 1 (1959)
Newcastle United 1, Bedford Town 3 (1963–64)
Arsenal 1, Swindon Town 3 (1969)
Leeds United 2, Colchester United 3 (1971)
Newcastle United 1, Hereford United 2 (1972)
Burnley 0, Wimbledon 1 (1974–75)
Leicester City 0, Harlow Town 1 (1979–80)
Birmingham City 1, Altrincham 2 (1985–86)
Coventry City 1, Sutton United 2 (1988–89)
West Bromwich Albion 2, Woking 4 (1990–91)
West Bromwich Albion 1, Halifax 2 (1993–94)

On the international stage memorable instances of giant-killing have included:

Romania 1, Cuba 2 (1938)
England 0, USA 1 (1950)
Czechoslovakia 1, Northern Ireland 2 (1958)
Italy 0, North Korea 1 (1966)
Mexico 1, Tunisia 3 (1978)
Spain 0, Northern Ireland 1 (1982)
Argentina 0, Cameroon 1 (1990)
Austria 0, Faroe Islands 1 (1990)
England 0, USA 2 (1993)

See also CORINTHIANS; DIDDY MEN; GRANDAD'S ARMY; USA.

Gigg Lane The home ground of the English football club BURY. The Shakers have played at Gigg Lane since they were founded back in 1885. Formerly part of the Earl of Derby's estate, the ground witnessed the club's great successes of the first decade of the 20th century, although it has rarely played host to large crowds since. Events in the ground's history have included gale damage in 1952, the arrival of the first floodlights in the northwest in 1953, and the staging of the first floodlit cricket match (a complete failure).

Gigi See RIVA, LUIGI.

Giles, Johnny (1940–) Irish inside-forward, who was a pillar of the highly successful Leeds United team that dominated

English football in the early 1970s. Renowned for his committed tackling and tactical skill, he began his career with Manchester United before moving to Leeds in 1964 and there forming a brilliant partnership with Billy BREMNER. Subsequently he became one of the most famous players of his day and also established a regular place in the Republic of Ireland squad, winning 60 caps. Later in his career he worked as player-manager of West Bromwich Albion, Shamrock Rovers, and Vancouver Whitecaps.

Gillingham English football club, nick-named the Gills. Strip: royal blue shirts with white trim, white shorts with blue trim, and white socks. The club were founded under the name Excelsior in 1893 in the wake of the success of another local club, the Royal Engineers. A year later the club turned professional as New Brompton, changing to Gillingham in 1913 and joining the Third Division in 1920. Based at the PRIESTFIELD Stadium, the club have had a somewhat chequered history, dropping out of the League in 1938 and not winning re-election until 1950 (at one point they were actually liquidated). Their single major honour remains the Fourth Division title won in 1964, achieved by virtue of a run of 52 unbeaten home matches (a record that was not broken until 1981, when Liverpool completed a run of 85 unbeaten home games).

Among the few famous players to join Gillingham has been the Irish international Tony Cascarino. Brian Yeo made a rare foray into the headlines in 1974, however, when his 31 goals made him the top League goalscorer of the 1973–74 season. Goalkeeper Fred Fox remains the only Gills player to be capped for England (he played in just one game, in 1925, and at the same time was transferred to Millwall).

The club enjoyed their record victory in 1987, when they beat Chesterfield 10–0; they suffered their worst defeat in 1950, losing 9–2 against Nottingham Forest. John Simpson holds the record for League appearances, having played in 571 matches between 1957 and 1972.

We ain't Jack and Jill,
We ain't Bill and Ben,
We ain't Ken Dodd or his Diddy men,
We ain't Looby Loo with all her toys,
We are the Gillingham Boot Boys.

Supporters' song, to the tune of 'Just one of those Songs' (1970s)

Gingerbreads Nickname of the English non-League football club GRANTHAM TOWN, in reference to the traditional Grantham gingerbread that was served to coach-travellers pausing at the town in the 18th century.

Giraffe, The *See* CHARLTON, JACK.

Giuseppe Meazza Stadium The home ground, in the San Siro district of Milan, of the Italian football clubs AC MILAN and INTERNAZIONALE. One of the most famous of European football venues, the stadium opened as home to AC Milan in 1926 and was even then one of the best-equipped grounds in the country. It rapidly established itself as Italy's main international venue and the Italian national team made regular appearances. World Cup games were staged at the stadium in 1934, after which a programme of improvements was embarked upon with the aim of increasing the ground's capacity.

Internazionale arrived to share the venue in 1947 and have remained in happy co-existence with AC Milan ever since. Further expansion followed in the 1950s when the stadium took on the unique appearance it still has today, with sloping access ramps wrapping tightly all around the tiered inner shell (the upper tier being dubbed by fans the 'Giraffe', because it extended so high up).

The stadium was renamed in honour of Giuseppe MEAZZA in 1979. Subsequently, the stadium was a centrepiece for the 1990 World Cup tournament, in preparation for which it was fitted with a breathtaking roof and a third tier of seating.

Gladiators Nickname of the English non-League football club MATLOCK TOWN, reflecting the area's history as a centre of the Roman occupation.

Glanford Park The home ground of the English football club SCUNTHORPE UNITED. Until 1986 Scunthorpe played at the Old Show Ground, which was bought by the club in 1924. Briefly the home also of Grimsby Town during World War II, the Old Show Ground claims a particular place in the history of football ground architecture, being the site of the country's first cantilever stand (erected in 1958). The Old Show Ground was finally bought by a supermarket company in 1986 and the club moved to their new home at Glanford Park just a mile away.

Glassboys Nickname of the English non-League football club STOURBRIDGE, in reference to the town's glassmaking industry.

glasses Few players in the modern game opt to keep their spectacles on during play because of the obvious dangers. In the past, however, a number of players kept their glasses on and still managed to join the ranks of the great. Sketches accompanying match reports as far back as the 1870s indicate that players even at international level were known to go on to the field wearing glasses and even monocles. Notable bespectacled players since those days have included the respected Alex Raisbeck, who is thought to have been the first first-class player to appear regularly wearing his glasses: he made over 340 League appearances for Liverpool in the early years of the 20th century. Goalkeeper J. Mitchell of Preston is the only bespectacled player to have appeared in an FA Cup Final (in 1922). On the international stage, Belgium's J. Jurion made 64 appearances for his country complete with spectacles and became a major star with Anderlecht, Ghent, and Lokeren in the 1960s.

In 1970 the entire Arsenal squad were tested for colour blindness (they were all able to see perfectly well). According to fans it is usually the ref who would benefit most from bringing his glasses with him on to the field of play. At least one player, however, has been suspended for voicing such an opinion on the pitch – in 1957 Leicester City's Johnny Morris received a two-week suspension after openly suggesting the referee needed spectacles.

> *Then my eyesight started to go, and I took up refereeing.*
>
> Neil Midgley, referee (1987)

Glaziers Nickname of the English football club CRYSTAL PALACE, in reference to the side's connection with Joseph Paxton's steel and glass Crystal Palace, where the modern club had its origins.

Glebe Park The home ground of the Scottish football club BRECHIN CITY. City settled at Glebe Park, in picturesque surroundings among market gardens and lawns, in 1906; features include a long hedge running down half the length of the North Side – the only one at a League ground in the UK.

Glentoran Northern Ireland football club, nicknamed the Cock and Hens. Glentoran (based at the OVAL) have long been the bitter rivals of fellow-Protestants LINFIELD, based like them in Belfast. They have won the Irish League championship on a total of 19 occasions. Stars with the Cock and Hens in recent years have included the forwards F. Roberts (who scored a record 96 goals in the 1930–31 season) and Terry Conroy.

> *We'll shout at the Oval, we'll shout at the Oval,*
> *We'll shout 'Come on the Glens',*
> *For there's not another team in the League,*
> *As good as the wee Cock and Hens.*
>
> Supporters' song

Glossop North End Former English football club, which dropped out of the League in 1915 after 17 years. The team joined the League in 1898 and in their first season caused a sensation when they, and Manchester City, became the first clubs to win automatic promotion to the First Division, thus making the town of Glossop the smallest ever to produce a First Division side. Based at the North Road ground, they dropped out of the top rank after one year, having won only four of their 34 matches. Stars of the side at their peak included ex-Woolwich Arsenal inside-forward T.T. Fitchie. They were known simply as Glossop from 1903.

Gloucester City English non-League football club, nicknamed the Tigers. Strip: all yellow. Founded in 1883 and based at Meadow Park in Gloucester, the Tigers play in the Southern League.

Glovers Nickname of the English non-League football club YEOVIL TOWN, with reference to the town's history as a centre for glove manufacture.

GM Vauxhall Conference See CONFERENCE, THE.

goal (1) The area into which the ball must pass for the attacking team to score a point, as delineated by a pair of vertical goalposts and a horizontal crossbar. The size of the goal (eight yards wide by eight feet high) is dictated by the laws of the game although there is from time to time discussion about possible changes (in recent years including pressure from the US footballing authorities for a larger goal to make for higher scorelines).

A number of variations have been tried over the years: in the ancient Chinese version of football called tsu-chu the goals were thirty-feet high but only a yard wide. In the

Eton Wall Game of the early 18th century the goals consisted of a door in a garden wall at one end and an elm tree at the other, while at Winchester there is a record of a boy standing with his legs apart to form a goal on at least one occasion.

Vertical poles became the usual form of goal early in the 19th century although the distance between them varied; at Harrow, if a replay was required the distance was doubled from 12 feet to 24 feet to make a result more likely. The Cambridge Rules stipulated goals with a width of 15 feet, while the FA finally decided upon a width of eight yards in the 1860s, since when there has been little variation. In the early history of the game, teams changed ends every time a goal was scored.

The modern goal is usually constructed out of Douglas fir, which will withstand a lot of punishment, but many clubs routinely renew the structure at the end of every season. The goals at Wembley, like those in some other countries, are made of aluminium.

(2) A shot in which the whole of the ball passes over the goal line into the goal itself, resulting in the attacking team scoring one point (provided no law of the game has been broken in the process). Among the many statistics concerning the scoring of goals the most interesting include the following:

First English League team to score double figures away: Sheffield United (10–0 against Port Vale, 1892).

First Scottish League team to score double figures away: Dundee (10–0 against Alloa Athletic, 1947).

First English League team to score 100 goals in a season: Sunderland (1893).

First English League team to score 1000 goals: Aston Villa (1904).

First European to score 1000 goals: Franz Binder (1950).

Scorer of the fastest goal in a League game: Jim Fryatt (Bradford City), after four seconds (1964).

Scorer of the fastest goal in the World Cup: David Gualtieri (San Marino), after 28 seconds (1993).

Only British footballer to average a goal a game throughout his first-class career: James McGrory (Celtic).

Scorer of record number of League goals in a single season: Dixie DEAN, with 60 goals in 1927–28.

Scorer of the biggest career total of League goals: Arthur Rowley (West Bromwich Albion, Fulham, Leicester City, and Shrewsbury Town), with 434 goals between 1946 and 1965.

Scorer of the biggest career total of first-class goals: Artur FRIEDENREICH (Brazil), with 1329 goals in 26 years.

Scorer of record number of goals in a first-class match: Stephan Stanis (Racing Club de Lens), with 16 (1942).

A small number of games have entered the mythology of football by virtue of the number of goals scored during them. The two highest-scoring games in the history of British football belong to the 19th century. The record in England stands at 26–0, achieved by Preston North End against Hyde in an FA Cup match in 1887. The record for Scotland is even more remarkable, with a scoreline of 36–0, achieved by Arbroath against luckless Bon Accord in 1885 – still the record for senior football anywhere in the world (see DEFEATS). According to one of the press reports of this latter game 'after the 20th goal, Bon Accord played like a team with no hope'.

Other contenders for the record have included a crushing victory by Manchester United's Busby Babes over Nantwich Town in the 1952–53 FA Youth Cup, when the Red Devils won 23–0; the total would have been greater but for heroic efforts by the much-pressed Nantwich goalkeeper, who was later signed by Manchester United.

In women's football, Milton Keynes reserves crashed 40–0 to Norwich Ladies in 1983, Norwich's Linda Curl netting no fewer than 23 goals. North of the border, in the Scottish Ladies' League, Edinburgh Dynamos beat Lochend Thistle 42–0 in 1975.

Elsewhere in the world records for high scores, some achieved under highly dubious circumstances, have reached ludicrous levels. An Argentinian side of the 1950s, for instance, notched up a win of 71–0 after their opponents, the Wanderers, staged a sit-down strike on the pitch, while the Indian Boys Athletic Association of Calcutta averaged a goal every 37 seconds of a 70-minute game in 1983 to attain a final scoreline of 114–0. The all-time record would go, however, to a Yugoslavian club for their tally of goals in a crucial end-of-season match in 1979, had it not been for the fact that they had quietly struck an illegal deal with the other team shortly before the game took place: they won the game 134–1. See also BONUS; CORNER KICK; DOUBLE HATTRICK; HAT-TRICK; OWN GOAL; PENALTY; TEN-GOAL.

I am a firm believer that if you score one goal the other team have to score two to win.

Howard Wilkinson

We don't use a stop-watch to judge our golden goal competition now. We use a calendar.

Tommy Docherty, when manager of Wolves (1985)

I would have thought that the knowledge that you are going to be leapt upon by half-a-dozen congratulatory, but sweaty team mates would be inducement not to score a goal.

Arthur Marshall

goal kick A shot taken by the goalkeeper from within the six-yard area after the ball has crossed over the byline (having been last touched by a member of the opposing team). The goal kick was introduced officially in 1869, before when a 'kick-out' rule was observed. Very rarely goalkeepers have actually scored from goal kicks, the first instance of such a feat dating back to 1900, when Manchester City's C. Williams scored from a goal kick against Sunderland. More recent examples include a goal scored from within his own penalty area by Spurs' Pat JENNINGS in a Charity Shield match in 1967. When the Premier League was established in 1992 new laws meant that a goal kick could be taken from either side of the six-yard box.

goal net A meshed net enclosing the rear and sides of the goal. The first goal nets were the invention of J.A. Brodie, who took out a patent for his invention in 1890. The first official use of nets dates from 1891, when they were used in a match at the Old Etonians' ground in Liverpool and were subsequently given another trial in a game between representative teams from the North and South of England at Nottingham Forest's Town Ground. In 1892 they were used in an FA Cup Final for the first time. There were, however, teething problems – particularly in relation to the tautness of the mesh, which often caused balls to rebound. In the 1908–09 season West Bromwich Albion failed to press home their attack after they thought a goal had been scored but the ball rebounded and the referee, thinking it must have hit the crossbar, allowed play to continue; the missed goal cost Albion the fraction of a point they needed to secure promotion to the First Division that year. As recently as 1970,

Aston Villa were relegated to the Third Division after a similar incident.

The deepest goal nets in Europe are probably those at La Romareda Stadium in Zaragoza, where they extend a full four metres back from the goal line.

goal post One of the pair of vertical wooden beams used to support the crossbar of the goal. Although the crossbar was a later addition, the goal posts themselves date from the earliest days of the modern game in the mid-19th century, although initially they were often little more than long sticks. All goal posts are not the same: north of the border Scottish clubs have traditionally favoured squared posts as opposed to the elliptical English variety.

It is a little known fact that though goal posts are almost invariably painted white, there is no rule about this and they could theoretically be painted in any colour.

On rare occasions games have been disrupted by a goal post breaking. Examples include a seven-minute break in play during a match at Molineux in 1957 (it took some time to extricate Bournemouth striker Reg Cutler from the netting) and a 45-minute delay at Lincoln in 1970; in 1981 at Chester the damage was so severe when the goal collapsed after Chester's goalkeeper Grenville Millington collided with the post the whole game had to be abandoned and replayed at a later date.

goal posts, to move the To make some fundamental change to the parameters of a situation under discussion, usually resulting in the frustration of negotiations so far completed. This idiom, in general use for many years, clearly derives from football, where such a strategy would obviously have the effect of frustrating an opposing team's attack. In 1987 Rangers were accused by Dynamo Kiev of moving not the goal posts but the touchline for a match between the two clubs in the European Cup.

goal side The area between the goal and the ball.

goalkeeper The player who is assigned to the goal, with responsibility for preventing the opposing team from scoring. Goalkeepers – initially called 'net-minders' – were first mentioned in the rules of the Football Association in 1871; subsequent landmarks in the development of the role have included the change in the rules in 1912 that forbade handling of the ball outside the penalty area (first permitted in

1878). A campaign to allow goalkeepers to wear helmets, pursued by the US football authorities, failed to influence FIFA in 1983.

Notable goalies over the years have included Scotland's R. Gardner (who in the 1870s became the first goalkeeper to captain his country), the extraordinary William FOULKE, Dumbarton's James McAulay, John Doig (nicknamed the Prince of Goalkeepers), Liverpool's Sam Hardy, Walter Scott of Grimsby Town, who became the first keeper to save three penalties in a single match (against Burnley in 1909), the amateur goalie Howard Baker (who also held the British high jump record for 26 years), Ricardo ZAMORA of Spain, Czechoslovakia's Frantisek PLANICKA, Liverpool's Elisha SCOTT, Birmingham City's Harry Hibbs, Frank SWIFT of Manchester City (who was the first goalkeeper to captain England), Bert TRAUTMANN also of Manchester City (the first goalkeeper to win the Footballer of the Year award, in 1956), Roque Maspoli of Uruguay, Lev YASHIN of the Soviet Union, Hungary's Gyula GROSICS, GYLMAR DOS SANTOS NEVES of Brazil, Antonio Carbajal of Mexico, Gordon BANKS, Italy's Dino ZOFF, Uruguay's Ladislao Mazurckiewicz, West Germany's Sepp MAIER, Northern Ireland's Pat JENNINGS, who became the first British goalkeeper to win 100 caps, England's Peter SHILTON, and Wimbledon's Dave BEASANT (the first keeper to save a penalty in an FA Cup Final at Wembley).

It is not always, however, the most spectacular keeper who is necessarily the greatest, as once observed by Everton's Warney Cresswell: 'Good goalkeepers never make great saves.'

Several goalkeepers have claimed their place in history for their activities at the other end of the pitch, by scoring goals themselves. In 1910, during a match between Third Lanark and Motherwell both goalies managed this feat, though the fact that the existing rules allowed them to handle the ball as far as the halfway line undoubtedly helped. The record for the number of goals scored by a goalkeeper in a single season in the English League is held by Chesterfield's Arnold Birch, who scored five goals (all penalties) in the Third Division (South) in 1923–24. Chesterfield's Jim Brown is thought to be the only goalkeeper to have scored more than one goal in open play in top level football, scoring for the US team Washington Diplomats in 1981 and subsequently for Chesterfield in 1983.

Back at their own end of the pitch, few goalkeepers have approached the record held by Chris Woods, who in 1987, for Rangers, ended a run of 13 games without conceding a goal. Atlético Madrid's keeper Abel Resino set a new record in 1991 when he completed 1275 minutes of football without conceding a goal.

Goalkeepers can, however, be too good. In 1981 Bury's goalkeeper Neville Southall was so effective at stopping practice shots in training that he was banned from the sessions so that the strikers could rebuild their shattered confidence (their form rapidly improved).

Many goalkeepers are included among the great characters to have graced the game. Among the most remarkable was the Welshman Leigh Richmond Roose, a doctor and amateur footballer who kept goal for his country on no fewer than 24 occasions in the early years of the 20th century. Roose was notorious for his eccentric habits, which included a reputation for practical jokes and a strong belief in superstition. The son of a Presbyterian minister, he refused ever to allow the undershirt he wore under his football kit to be washed, fearing this would bring him bad luck. He frequently hired a private train to get him to matches, would often leave the goal in order to play alongside the forwards, if he was bored would chat to members of the crowd during the game, and was even known to alarm the management by faking serious injury; nonetheless, he was one of the most valued custodians ever to man the Welsh goal until his death in action during World War I.

Other goalkeepers are better known for their achievements outside the game; these have included Pope John Paul II (goalie for a Polish amateur side) and the great French novelist Albert Camus, who kept goal for the Algiers University team and once confessed: 'All that I know surely about morality and the obligations of man, I owe to football.'

> The goal stands up, the keeper
> Stands up to keep the goal.

A.E. Housman, *A Shropshire Lad*, 'Bredon Hill'

God, Hand of See HAND OF GOD.

Godfather, The Nickname of the English player and manager Don REVIE, reflecting his autocratic regime while in charge of Leeds United. His management was characterized by an eye for detail and an insistence upon respect for his decisions – reminiscent to some of the menacing paternalism of the character played by Marlon Brando in the film *The Godfather*, which was a major cinematic success in the year United won the FA Cup.

Gola League *See* CONFERENCE, THE.

Golden Age Football ballet that was composed by Shostakovich in 1930, with choreography by Semyon Kaplan and Vasily Vainonen. The plot of the ballet traces the conflict that breaks out between Fascists and a Soviet football team on tour in the West: it climaxes in a dance by the footballers and the capitalist workers united in celebrating the joys of work.

Golden Ball Award bestowed upon the European Footballer of the Year.

Golden Boot International award given to the leading European league goalscorer of the season. The award (organized by *France Football*) was first bestowed in 1968, when EUSÉBIO received it, having scored 43 goals; he won it again in 1973 after scoring a further 40 goals in a single season. The first British recipient of the award was Ian RUSH in 1984. Subsequent winners from the UK have included Ally McCoist, who received the award in 1991.

Golden Boy (1) Nickname bestowed upon the much-admired Welsh forward Ivor ALLCHURCH, reflecting both his talent as a player and his fair hair, which made him an instantly recognizable figure on the field.

(2) Nickname of the celebrated Italian midfielder Gianni RIVERA.

Golden Head Nickname of the admired Hungarian forward Sandor KOCSIS, in reference to his skill in the air.

Goldstone Ground The home ground of BRIGHTON AND HOVE ALBION. The first residents at Goldstone Bottom (as it was then called) were Hove FC, who settled there in 1900; Hove left a year later and the Seagulls became sole occupants of the venue. The ground's name derives from the fact that a stone supposedly used by the Druids once stood there. A local farmer, however, lost patience with the droves of archaeologists who visited the site to see the stone and in 1834 had the offending article buried; the stone was finally unearthed in 1900 and re-erected across the road from the ground, in Hove Park.

Events in the ground's history have included its use as a drill ground in World War I, the erection of a temporary stand (nicknamed the 'Lego Stand') in 1979 after the team reached the First Division, a fire in the South Stand in 1980, and subsequently extensive alterations to meet safety requirements.

Good Old Arsenal Title of pop song released by the Arsenal squad in 1971 to celebrate their winning of the double. Following the tune of 'Rule Britannia' it reached number 16 in the charts.

Goodall, John (1863–1942) English forward, nicknamed Johnny Allgood, who was one of the most famous English players of the 1880s and 1890s. Born in London, he was the captain and leading star of the celebrated Old Invincibles side that represented Preston North End, as well as being captain of England. He won a total of 14 caps between 1889 and 1898 and was acclaimed 'the pioneer of scientific professional play'. Later in his career he played as captain of Derby County; he also played cricket at county level with Derbyshire.

Fishing and nature, especially birds, I have loved, although the one passion of my life has been football – the most exhilarating game I know, and the strongest protest against selfishness, without sermonizing, that was ever put before a thoughtful people.

John Goodall, *The Derby County Story* (Andrew Ward and Anton Rippon, 1983)

Goodison Park The home ground, sometimes nicknamed Toffeeopolis, of the English football club EVERTON. The club made their first homes at Stanley Park (1878), at Priory Road (1883), and subsequently at ANFIELD (1884–92), where they clinched their first Championship in 1891, before settling permanently at Goodison Park (then a patch of wasteland described as 'a howling desert') on the north edge of Stanley Park after failing to agree on a rent increase at Anfield.

Everton's new ground was hailed as the most advanced in England and witnessed the Toffees consolidate their reputation as one of the best clubs in the land. Events in the history of Toffeeopolis have included the staging of a single FA Cup Final (1894), a visit by George V and Queen Mary in 1913 (the first visit by royalty to a League ground), requisition of the venue by the Territorial Army during World War I, visits by baseball teams from the USA, the installation in the 1930s of the first dug-outs in England, a visit by George VI in 1938, severe bomb damage during World War II, the staging of international matches during the 1966 World Cup, and the erection of the UK's first triple-decker stand (1971). The ground's most famous feature is the church of St Luke the Evangelist, which juts into one corner of the stadium.

Appropriately enough, it was at Goodison Park that Everton's greatest star, Dixie DEAN, died in 1980 while watching a match between his old club and Liverpool.

> *When at thy gate my weary feet I turn,*
> *The gates of paradise are open wide,*
> *At Goodison, I know a man can learn,*
> *Rapture more rich than Anfield can*
> *provide.*

Anonymous

Goole Town English non-League football club, nicknamed Town, or the Vikings. Strip: blue and red shirts, blue shorts, and red socks. Founded in 1900 and based at the Victoria Pleasure Grounds in Goole, the club play in the Northern Premier League.

Goose Eaters Nickname of the Hungarian football club MTK-VM. The nickname (in Hungarian, *Libasok*) constitutes a reference to the club's traditional links with the Jewish community in Budapest.

Górnik Zabrze Polish football club, which dominated Polish football in the 1960s and 1980s. Strip: blue shirts, with white shorts and socks. Founded in 1948 and based at the Górnik Stadium in Zabrze, the team had its origins among the district's miners (*gornik* meaning miner). The side has captured some 14 League titles since 1957 and has enjoyed success in the Cup on six occasions. In 1970 Górnik Zabrze became the first Polish club to reach the Final of a European competition when they lost to Manchester City in the European Cup Winners' Cup. Stars with the side over the years have included Ernest POL and Wlodzimierz Lubanski.

Gosport Borough English non-League football club, nicknamed Boro. Strip: yellow and blue. Founded in 1944 and based at Privett Park, Gosport Borough were relegated from the Southern Division of the Southern League in 1993.

IFK Gothenburg Swedish football club, nicknamed the Angels, who are one of the country's strongest sides. Strip: blue and white striped shirts, with blue shorts and socks. The club are based at the ULLEVI stadium and can claim 12 Championship titles and three Cup victories as well as two UEFA Cup triumphs (1982 and 1987) to their credit. Their most glorious era to date was the 1980s, when they never dropped out of the top four Swedish clubs.

Graf Zeppelin Final Nickname sometimes bestowed upon the FA Cup Final of 1930. As Herbert CHAPMAN's Lucky Arsenal side beat his old club Huddersfield Town 2–0 the German airship *Graf Zeppelin* passed over Wembley in salute.

Graham, George (1944–) Scottish midfielder and football manager, nicknamed Stroller, who has established himself as one of the leading managers in the English game in the early 1990s. Having spent much of his playing career with Arsenal, he went on to serve as the club's manager from 1986 (after four years in control of Millwall). He took the Gunners to success in the League championship in 1989 and 1991, after which he consolidated his reputation as one of the leading managers since World War II by capturing for his club the unique double of the FA Cup and League Cup titles in 1993. *See also* SUPERSTITIONS.

Grand Old Lady Nickname of the great Italian football club JUVENTUS (in Italian, *La Vecchia Signora*), with reference to the club's status as one of the most senior teams in Italy.

Grandad's Army Nickname of the COLCHESTER UNITED side that created one of the biggest upsets in FA Cup history in 1971. Colchester United were in the Fourth Division at the time and had been quoted odds of 100–1 against winning the FA Cup that year. Undaunted, the team – called Grandad's Army because seven of the players in the side were over 30 – battled their way through to the fifth round of the competition, when it seemed that defeat at the hands of mighty Leeds United (favourites to win the Cup and the League championship as well as the UEFA Cup) was inevitable. Against all expectations, however, REVIE's classic side collapsed in the face of an onslaught from Colchester and Revie's team left the field 3–2 losers, victims of one of the most daring giant-killing acts of all time.

> *On the morning of the match I went down*
> *to the waterfront . . . it was beautiful, just*

like a summer day, with blue sky and a calm sea. And as I looked out I knew, beyond all shadow of doubt, that we were going to beat Leeds. I can't tell you why – I just did. It wasn't wishful thinking. It was total conviction. I knew we were going to win.

Dick Graham, Colchester United manager

Grantham Town English non-League football club, nicknamed the Gingerbreads. Strip: white shirts with black shorts and socks. Founded in 1874, Grantham Town are based at the South Kesteven Stadium in Grantham and play in the Southern League.

Grasshoppers Swiss football club, who rank as the most successful domestic side in Switzerland's football history. Strip: blue and white halved shirts, white shorts, and white socks with blue trim. Founded in 1886 and based at the HARDTURM stadium in Zürich, the Grasshoppers have won 21 League championships as well as 17 Cup victories. Their most glorious moment in European competition came in 1978, when they reached the semi-finals of the UEFA Cup.

Gravesend and Northfleet English non-League football club, nicknamed The Fleet. Strip: red shirts and socks with white shorts. The club were established when Gravesend United and Northfleet United merged and are based at the ground in Stonebridge Road. The Fleet play in the Southern League.

Grays Athletic English non-League football club, nicknamed the Blues in reference to the team colours. Strip: royal blue and white. Founded in 1890 and based at the Recreation Ground in Grays, Essex, since 1894, the club were the first champions of the Corinthian League and in 1985 the first team to win the Division Two (South) title.

great. The boys done great Football cliché often heard in parody of the 'typical' unlettered coach, manager, or commentator (notably the television pundit Mick Channon whose catchphrase it became). The habitual use of the ungrammatical phrase by fans, players, and managers alike was lampooned in *The Guardian* in 1986 in the wake of the World Cup that year, when a correspondent attempted to conjugate the phrase 'done great': 'I done great. He done great. We done great. They done great. The boy Lineker done great.'

The phrase also inspired the title of a humorous fanzine of the 1980s, *The Lad Done Brilliant*.

Great Dictator Nickname of the FA Secretary Alan HARDAKER.

Greaves, Jimmy (1940–) English forward, who was a prolific goalscorer of the 1960s for both Tottenham Hotspur and England. Born in East Ham, Greaves made his debut in 1957, demonstrating his talent by scoring in his first match for Chelsea, and transferred to Spurs in 1961 after a brief period with AC Milan. He earned the first of 57 England caps in 1959 and subsequently won acclaim as one of the most effective and popular strikers of his era.

Highlights of his international career included a hat-trick against Scotland in 1961, two goals in the European Cup Winners' Cup Final in 1963, and his part in the early stages of the victorious England World Cup campaign of 1966.

Afflicted by hepatitis in 1965 and increasingly by his dependence on alcohol, he retired in 1971 and subsequently created a flurry of press interest when he went on to talk openly about his fight against alcoholism (*see* ALCOHOLIC). His ebullient nature and natural good humour enabled him to overcome the threats of alcohol and in 1980 he embarked on a new career as a television sports commentator.

He was always very calm, very collected and, where scoring goals was concerned, he was a Picasso.

Clive Allen, *There's Only One Clive Allen* (1987)

He was the Fagin of the penalty area; the arch-pickpocket of goals.

Geoffrey Green

See also GROVES, JACKIE.

Grecians Nickname of the English football club EXETER CITY, in reference to the Greek community traditionally centred on nearby St Sidwell's. A Greek market formerly took place on the land now occupied by ST JAMES' PARK, the features of which include a 'Grecian Gate' which was paid for by funds raised by supporters.

Greece Greece joined FIFA in 1927, although enthusiasm for international football had been somewhat diminished back in 1920, when the national team lost 9–0 to Sweden in their first-ever international. Subsequently the side built up a reputation for being hard to defeat at home and in 1980 achieved their greatest moment of glory to date by qualifying for the European Championship Finals at the expense of such noteworthy opponents as the Soviet Union, Hungary, and Finland. They also performed respectably in the European Championships of 1984 and 1988. Strip: white shirts, blue shorts, and white socks. Greece qualified for the 1994 World Cup in America.

Green Eagles Nickname of the national side representing NIGERIA (who play in a green strip).

Greenbacks Nickname of the English non-League football club BEDWORTH UNITED, in reference to the team colours.

Greens Nickname of the French football club ST ETIENNE, in reference to the team colours.

Greenwood, Ron (1921–) English manager, who managed England for five years (1977–82). A former centre-half with Chelsea, Bradford Park Avenue, Brentford, and Fulham, Greenwood began his career as a manager with Eastbourne United in 1957 and that same year took over as coach of the England youth squad. He moved as assistant manager to Arsenal and became coach of the England Under-23 team in 1958 and subsequently managed West Ham (1961–77), guiding the side to victory in two FA Cups and the European Cup Winners' Cup.

Greenwood succeeded Don REVIE as manager of England in 1977 and continued in the same quiet methodical style he had developed with the Hammers. The side qualified for the European Championships in 1980 and for the World Cup in 1982 but failed to progress far in either competition. Greenwood stepped down in 1982 to be replaced by Bobby ROBSON.

Gregory's Girl Film by the director Bill Forsyth, which is a loving depiction of a girl's progress in a Scottish boys' football team. Made in 1980, this naturalistic study of adolescent preoccupations, prejudices, and uncertainties is one of the more respected soccer movies.

A select number of women have, in fact, made their mark on the all-male professional game in real life, though usually in an administrative capacity. In the 1950s Crystal Palace were the first League club to enlist a female secretary – Margaret Montague, while in 1976 Pat Dunne became the first woman to referee an official game between male teams (in the Dorset County

Sunday League). In 1981 Liz Forsdick became the first woman to referee an FA Cup tie (between Burgess Hill Town and Carshalton).

As players, very few females have established themselves in male teams. Exceptions include Rose Reilly, who distinguished herself as a member of a Scottish boys' team before it was discovered that she was a girl; Scotland's manager Ally MacLeod was among her admirers, admitting: 'If she was a boy, I wouldn't have any hesitation at all in signing her. She has remarkable talent.'

Gren, Gunnar Swedish footballer, who was one of the celebrated Gre-No-Li trio of Scandinavians who took Italian football by storm in the 1950s. A highly effective provider of goal chances, he played for Garda, IFK Gothenburg, AC Milan, Fiorentina, Genoa, Örgryte, Gais Gothenburg, and Skogens as well as winning 57 caps playing for the Swedish national side.

Grenada Grenada joined FIFA in 1976 but have yet to make much impact in international competition. Strip: green and yellow shirts, red shorts, and yellow socks.

Gre-No-Li Nickname – derived from their surnames – of the famous Swedish trio of forwards Gunnar GREN, Gunnar NORDAHL, and Nils LIEDHOLM, who spearheaded the victorious Swedish side in the 1948 Olympics and subsequently made the Italian club AC Milan one of the strongest teams in Europe in the 1950s.

Gresty Road The home ground of the English football club CREWE ALEXANDRA. Crewe had a number of different homes before finally settling at Gresty Road in the late 1890s. Events in the ground's history have included a fire that destroyed the Main Stand in the early 1930s and modernization in the 1980s to meet safety requirements. Fans at Gresty Road are famous for the 'Gresty Clap', which refers to their habit of politely applauding good play.

Griffin Park The home ground of the English football club BRENTFORD. Brentford settled at Griffin Park in 1904 after playing at a number of venues around the town. Local tradition has it that the game of football itself was born in the vicinity of Griffin Park when Julius Caesar, on crossing the Brent, kicked the skull of a dead Briton.

Events in the ground's history have included plans for Queen's Park Rangers to take the venue over in the 1960s, a fire that destroyed much of the Main Stand in 1983, and the painting of what is thought to be the largest advertisement in the world on the roof of one of the stands (visible from jets flying to Heathrow Airport nearby). In the years before he found fame as a manager, Ron ATKINSON was once employed at Griffin Park painting names on the doors of the dressing-rooms, offices, and board-room. It is the only ground in the country that has a public house at each corner.

Grimsby Town English football club, nicknamed the Mariners. Strip: black and white striped shirts, black shorts with red trim, and white socks with red trim. Grimsby were founded in 1878 (as Grimsby Pelham – the Pelhams being a local land-owning family) at a meeting at the Wellington Arms. They changed to their present name a year later and joined the League in 1892 as a founder member of the Second Division.

They made their first appearance in the FA Cup in 1882 and in their first match crashed 9–1 against the Rotherham works side Phoenix Bessemer. After spells in both existing divisions, the Mariners failed to win re-election to the League in 1910 but returned a year later, since when they have made appearances in all four divisions (last leaving the First Division in 1948). Promotion from the Fourth Division in 1972 had unfortunate consequences for one supporter, who had vowed he would run naked round his firm's yard if the club went up: he duly honoured the promise and was presented with a special certificate from Grimsby manager Lawrie MCMENEMY.

The club's golden era was in the 1930s when the side reached the upper echelons of the First Division with contributions from such players as Jackie Bestall (who is commemorated by Bestall Street in Grimsby) and Pat Glover. Their only major honour remains the League Group Cup (won in 1982). Other famous names associated with the club over the years have included manager Bill SHANKLY.

Based at BLUNDELL PARK (which is actually not in Grimsby but in nearby Cleethorpes), the Mariners enjoyed their record victory back in 1885, when they beat Darlington 8–0; they suffered their worst defeat in 1931, when they lost 9–1 against Arsenal. Keith Jobling holds the record for League appearances with the club, having played in 448 games between 1953 and 1969.

Fans of the club are noted for their habit of performing a dance mimicking the energetic canoeists who enlivened the title shots of the hit television series 'Hawaii Five-O'. *See also* HARRY THE HADDOCK.

God rest ye, Merry Mariners,
Let nothing ye dismay,
A cup defeat at Blackpool,
Is just another day,
We'll save ourselves up for the League,
And never lose away,
Oh, tidings to Al and the boys, Al and the boys,
Oh, tidings to Al and the boys.

Supporters' song, to the tune of 'God Rest Ye, Merry Gentlemen' (1990)

Grobbelaar, Bruce (1957–) South African-born goalkeeper, who became a favourite with fans of Liverpool in the 1980s. Having arrived at Liverpool after serving in the Rhodesian army and subsequently playing in the USA for the Vancouver Whitecaps, Grobbelaar (whose surname translates as 'clumsy' in Afrikaans) began his career with the club somewhat falteringly and was treated as a joke by many residents of the Kop, who nicknamed him The Clown. Gradually, however, he overturned his unenviable reputation and distinguished himself as one of the best keepers of his day with a unique, even reckless style. He has often courted controversy, his eccentricities on the pitch including sheltering under an umbrella during a rainy match at Anfield.

Much underrated because of his tendency to clown around – and make occasional mistakes. What is often overlooked is the level of his moral courage. He tackles problems around the box that so many goalkeepers, including the best of them, shy away from.

John Giles (1989)

Grosics, Gyula (1926–) Hungarian goalkeeper, who is remembered as one of the greatest keepers of all time. As well as courageously blocking many strong attacking moves, he was also credited with the ability to set up spectacular counter-attacks in reply. He fulfilled the role of custodian of the national side's goal for many years in the 1950s (winning a total of 86 caps) and played at home for Dorog, Honvéd, and Tatabanya.

Group Cup The title under which the Anglo-Scottish Cup was played in 1982. The change in name was necessitated by the withdrawal of Scottish clubs from the competition; in 1983 the tournament was renamed again, this time as the Football League Trophy.

Groves, Jackie The hero of a series of soccer novels written by Norman Giller in collaboration with Jimmy GREAVES. Described as 'Soccer's Casanova', Groves is equally successful on the pitch and in the bedroom in such torrid tales as *The Final* (1979), *The Ball Game* (1980), *The Boss* (1981), and *The Second Half* (1981). Groves is a wayward US-born striker whose presence predictably stirs up considerable antagonism amongst his team mates. His sexual adventurism is explained as a consequence of the abuse he suffered as a child and of his pathological fear of homosexuality. Like most other soccer fiction, the books have (with reason) failed to excite critical interest.

Guatemala Guatemala joined FIFA in 1946 but have yet to establish a reputation in international competition. Strip: white shirts, white shorts, and white and blue socks.

Guinea Guinea joined FIFA in 1961 but have yet to make much impact in international competition. Strip: red shirts, yellow shorts, and green socks.

Guinea-Bissau Guinea-Bissau joined FIFA in 1986 but have still to establish an international reputation. Strip: all green.

Guiseley English non-League football club. Strip: all yellow with blue trim. Founded in 1909 and based at the Nethermoor Ground in Guiseley, the team play in the Northern Premier League.

Gullit, Ruud (1962–) Dutch footballer, who emerged as one of the finest players of his generation in the 1980s. Immediately recognizable with his dreadlock hairstyle, Gullit began his extraordinary career with Haarlem in 1979 and made his international debut two years later. He was transferred to Feyenoord in 1982 and played a key role as an attacking midfielder in the club's victories in the League and the Cup in 1984. A year later he left Feyenoord for PSV Eindhoven and in 1987 moved to AC Milan for a record fee of £6 million. That same year he carried off both the European Footballer of the Year and World Footballer of the Year titles before going on to play his part in winning Milan the 1988 Italian Championship, while at the same time helping Holland to secure the European Championship.

An injury to his right knee hindered his game over the next two years though he still managed to score two goals in the European Cup Final in 1989 and a year later still helped Milan to win another European Cup, the Super Cup, and the World Club Championship. One of the most dynamic of modern players, Gullit is a leading spokesman against racism in football, and is also known for his outspoken views, which have sometimes upset his superiors. In 1993 he moved on to Sampdoria.

Gulls Nickname of the English football club TORQUAY UNITED, in reference to their seaside location.

Gunners Nickname of the English football club ARSENAL, reflecting the team's origins among the workers at the Royal Arsenal in South London.

Guyana Guyana joined FIFA in 1968, but have yet to make much impact in international competition. Strip: green shirts, green shorts, and yellow socks.

Gylmar dos Santos Neves (1930–) Brazilian goalkeeper, who is considered the best Brazil has ever produced. Winner of 100 caps, he let in just 95 goals while manning the national side's goal and played a crucial role in the World Cup campaigns of 1958, 1962, and 1966. At home, he played for Jabaquara, Corinthians, and Santos.

H

hacking The kicking of an opponent's legs in an attempt to gain possession of the ball. Such behaviour would be enough to win the other team a free kick in the modern game and could lead to the offending player being booked, but in the early history of football such play was considered quite above board and was indeed hotly defended against critics who wished to see it outlawed.

In the days before rugby and football became distinct codes, hacking was an accepted feature of the game played at the leading English public schools – including Rugby School – and was considered a test of a player's resilience and courage. Others, however, saw hacking as a barbaric practice and pressed for its abolition when, in 1863, the FA drew up its first set of laws governing the game. The issue became the most contentious facing the new organization and threatened the break-up of the FA itself.

The Blackheath club described hacking as essential to the 'manliness' of football while A. Pember (first FA president) countered with the argument that such dangerous behaviour was 'likely to prevent a man who had due regard for his wife and family from following the game'. The Blackheath secretary scoffed that supporters of a ban on hacking were fonder of 'their pipes and grog or schnapps' than they were of football and that without hacking even the French would beat English teams after a week's practice. A young public schoolboy backed him up with a letter to *The Field*, protesting that although girls in the crowd 'squeaked a bit' when they saw their brothers injured through hacking ('it is in their nature to do so') 'you never hear a fellow squeak even if his leg is broken'.

It was all to no avail, however, and the FA outlawed the practice, precipitating Blackheath and other like-minded clubs into leaving the association and continuing on their own the development of what became rugby football (in fact they also banned hacking in rugby in 1871). Football's first great debate was settled.

Football is a gentleman's game played by hooligans, and rugby a hooligan's game played by gentlemen.

Unidentified chancellor of Cambridge University (late 19th century)

Haddicks Former nickname of the English football club CHARLTON ATHLETIC. Sometimes given as Addicks, it dates from the early history of the team when the players used a room over a fish and chip shop in East Street, close to a pub called 'The Lads of the Village', as their base. The owner of the fish and chip shop was a devoted supporter of the club and habitually arrived at matches armed with a haddock nailed on to a length of wood, which he waved enthusiastically during the match, thus inspiring the side's nickname.

Hagi, Gheorghe (1965–) Romanian midfielder, nicknamed the Maradona of the Carpathians, who emerged as the inspiration of the Romanian national side in the late 1980s. Although Hagi did not begin a serious career in football until he was 13, he rapidly built up a reputation in junior and youth football and soon captured a regular place in the national team, winning comparison with the great MARADONA himself. Formerly a star with STEAUA BUCHAREST, he transferred to Real Madrid after the 1990 World Cup.

Haig Avenue The home ground of the former English League football club SOUTHPORT.

Haiti Haiti joined FIFA in 1933 and made their first appearance in the World Cup Finals in 1974, when they rattled mighty Italy in a match that ended 3–1 in Italy's favour (Haiti's goal coming from centre-forward Emmanuel Sanon). Defeats by Hungary (7–0) and Argentina (4–1) finished their brave campaign. Allegations that voodoo witch-doctors have been recruited to help the national team have hit the headlines from time to time. Strip: black and red shirts, black shorts, and black and red socks.

Hajduk Split Croatian football club, which dominated Yugoslavian football back in the 1970s. Strip: red and blue striped shirts, with blue shorts and socks. Founded in 1911 and based at the POLJUD STADIUM in Split, the team won the League championship for the first time in 1927 and subsequently reclaimed it in 1929, 1950, 1952, 1971, 1974, 1975, and 1979 as well as winning the Cup in 1967, 1972, 1974, 1975, 1976, 1977, 1984, and 1987. In international competition, the side reached the semi-finals of the European Cup Winners' Cup in 1973 and of the UEFA Cup in 1984.

Halesowen Town English non-League football club, nicknamed the Yeltz. Strip: blue shirts, white shorts, and blue socks. Founded in 1873 and based at the Grove Recreation Ground in Halesowen, the club play in the Southern League.

half-back A midfield player who acts as a link between the defence and the attack in conventional tactical formations. For many years teams generally adopted a two–three–five system, first developed in the 1880s; in such a formation the centre-half attempted to dominate play down the centre of the pitch while the two wing-halves marked the attacking wingers of the opposing side.

half-volley A shot with the foot in which the ball is struck as it lands on the ground.

Halifax Town English non-League football club, nicknamed the Shaymen. Strip: sky blue and white shirts, white shorts, and sky blue socks. The club were founded at a meeting at the Saddle Hotel in 1911 and joined the League in 1921 as founder members of the Third Division (North). Subsequently they divided their time between the bottom two divisions, without winning any major honours (though they did reach the fifth round of the FA Cup in 1933 and 1953).

The 1931 season was even more traumatic than most, with directors resigning, creditors sueing, players being left unpaid, and an application for re-election being necessary at the close of their campaign. Their survival at all during the depressed 1930s was largely due to appeals to the club's supporters in the guise of SOS ('Soccer On Shay') drives.

It all came to an end in 1993, with the club – always in financial trouble despite help from the local council – losing its League status.

One of the few notable moments in the club's history was in the 1923–24 FA Cup when the team successfully drew twice with First Division Manchester City before finally going down in a second replay.

The Shaymen enjoyed their record victory in 1967, when they beat Bishop Auckland 7–0; they suffered their worst defeat in 1934, losing 13–0 against Stockport County (at one point in this latter disastrous match Halifax's Danny Ferguson asked team mate Hugh Flack what the score was; Flack replied 'I don't know, but I think we're losing'). John Pickering holds the record for League appearances, having played in 367 games between 1965 and 1974. *See also* DONKEY.

Hamburg German football club, originally founded as SC Germania in 1887, who have long been one of Germany's top clubs. Strip: white shirts with red trim, red shorts, and red socks. Under various titles, the club (based at the VOLKSPARKSTADION in Hamburg) have won six League championships, three Cup competitions, the European Cup Winners' Cup in 1977, and the European Cup in 1983. Stars with the side over the years have included Uwe SEELER and Kevin KEEGAN.

Hamilton Academical Scottish football club, nicknamed the Accies. Strip: red shirts with white hoops, with white shorts and socks. Founded in 1875 and based at DOUGLAS PARK in Hamilton, near Glasgow, the club was named after nearby Hamilton Academy, thus becoming the only senior club in the UK to be named after a school. The Accies' most important honours have included the Scottish League Division II championship in 1904 and the First Division title in 1986 and 1988; they were long-term residents of the First Division from 1906 to 1947. Notable players with the club have numbered amongst them David Wilson, who was the club's leading striker in the 1930s and who led the team to their second Scottish Cup Final in 1935 (the first was in 1911). More recently Hamilton inflicted a surprise defeat over Rangers at Ibrox Park in the 1988 Scottish Cup.

Other remarkable results in the club's history include their record victory against Chryston, whom they beat 11–1 in 1885, and a record defeat against Hibernian in 1965, when they lost by the same score. Like many other small clubs Hamilton face a perpetual struggle for survival; notwithstanding, Jimmy GREAVES once called them the friendliest club in Scotland.

Hamlet, The Nickname of the English non-League football club DULWICH HAMLET.

Hammers Nickname of the English football club WEST HAM UNITED, in reference to the team's origins in the East End docks (where the hammer symbolized the tools of the shipyard worker).

Hampden Park The home ground of the Scottish football club QUEEN'S PARK, which is also considered Scotland's national stadium. Queen's Park moved to what became the first Hampden Park in 1873, naming it after the neighbouring Hampden Terrace, which was in turn named after the English Parliamentarian John Hampden, who died at the Battle of Chalgrove Field in 1643 during the course of the English Civil War. This first version of Hampden Park included a clubhouse (built at a cost of £21) and a grandstand (built in 1876 at a cost of £306).

The club vacated the venue in 1883 to make way for a railway and in 1884 established the second Hampden Park on Mount Florida nearby. Cup Finals were staged here on a regular basis, while in 1884 it was the scene of the first all-ticket match (an international between England and Scotland). The need to improve facilities prompted Queen's Park to make one last move in 1903 to a new site close by.

Designed by Archibald Leitch, the third Hampden Park (the largest ground in the world until 1950) joined Ibrox Park and Celtic Park as one of the three best grounds then in existence. Events in the ground's illustrious history have included a fire in the Pavilion (1905), a riot between Rangers and Celtic fans in 1909, a fire in the press box (1945), another in 1968, and a further riot in 1980. It has also set numerous records for attendances, including the record crowd for a game between two club sides (over 145,000 for a match between Aberdeen and Celtic in 1937) and the highest official attendance ever recorded in the UK (nearly 150,000 for a match between England and Scotland in 1937).

Ironically as the home of Queen's Park this, the largest football stadium in the British Isles, regularly sees crowds of fewer than 1000 fans. *See also* HAMPDEN ROAR.

Hampden Roar The noise of the crowd at a major gathering at Scotland's HAMPDEN PARK. The volume of noise generated by huge crowds at internationals here is made all the more deafening by the action of the gusting wind that often courses through the stands, carrying the sound of chants and singing with it in powerful waves – a phenomenon remarked upon at other large grounds but nowhere as famous as here.

Hampton English non-League football club, nicknamed the Beavers. Strip: blue and red striped shirts, red shorts, and blue socks. Founded in 1920 and based at the Bevertree Stadium, Hampton play in the Isthmian League.

Hanappi, Gerhard (1929–80) Austrian footballer, who played in virtually every position on the pitch except goal and left-wing at the most senior level. Hanappi made a record 96 international appearances and was the match of the best players anywhere in the world. Having won his first cap in 1948, he played in two World Cup campaigns, often displaying his skills to the best advantage in the role of wing-half. In 1953 he won particular praise for his success at containing the great Stanley MATTHEWS in a game between England and the Rest of Europe in which he played at left-back. At home, he played for Wacker and Rapid Vienna, who eventually named their ground in his honour (in 1956 he very nearly became a player in the English Football League when Sunderland tried to buy him, but the deal was blocked by the Austrian FA).

hand ball An infringement of the rules in which a player other than the goalkeeper (or the goalkeeper out of his area) intentionally handles the ball. Such an offence is punished by the awarding of a penalty to the opposing team if it occurs within the offender's own penalty area. (Since 1912, the goalkeeper has been permitted to handle the ball only within his own penalty area, although before that he could handle it as far as the halfway line).

The issue of handling the ball was one of the most contentious in the early history of the game, when the rules of football overlapped considerably with those of what became the separate sport of rugby. The early public school versions of the game varied greatly in their approach to the issue, the Rugby School rules allowing handling at any time and those at Eton forbidding it completely; Harrow meanwhile permitted 'a fair catch off the foot'.

When the FA drew up its first set of rules it settled for a compromise position, permitting handling subject to certain restrictions, but the argument rapidly escalated in parallel with that concerning hacking. Everything came to a head at the fifth meeting of the FA in 1863 and shortly afterwards the member clubs split into two separate camps, those favouring handling developing the rugby code and those still affiliated to the FA confining it to the goalkeeper.

Some of the early clubs found the restriction harder to accept than others: records exist of at least one team obliging players to wear gloves while another went to the novel extreme of giving its players a florin to hold in each palm until they lost the habit of using their hands.

Hand of God The notorious handling incident involving the Argentinian striker Diego MARADONA that effectively put England out of the 1986 World Cup. England and Argentina met in the quarter-finals of the competition in an atmosphere of mutual hostility, this being the first occasion the two sides had played each other since the Falklands War between the two nations in 1982. Maradona, the controversial but supremely talented Argentinian captain (widely hailed as the finest footballer since PELÉ), was the focus of much of the attention.

When the big day against England came, Maradona scored two goals. There was no dispute about the second goal, which came at the end of a brilliant run through the English defence, but the circumstances of the first made him the most bitterly reviled footballer ever to appear in front of an English crowd. Slow-motion replays of the goal showed Maradona deliberately pushing the ball into the net with his left hand – although the referee, thinking the ball had been headed in – allowed the goal to stand.

The goal put the English team out of the tournament, which Argentina went on to win, and outraged English fans have never forgiven what seemed to them a blatant hand ball. Maradona himself failed to repair the damage when he attempted to pass off the controversy with the now-notorious comment: 'It was a little the hand of God and a little the head of Maradona.'

It has been suggested that he was trying to make light of the affair by punning on his own name (meaning 'Little God'), but his levity was not appreciated by the English public. Neither was a subsequent attempt to justify himself:

> Would an English player have gone to the referee and said: 'Don't award the goal – the ball hit my hand'? Of course not!

Maradona's dishonesty as a player was confirmed for many when in the 1990 World Cup he was once again seen to use his hand (this time his right hand) during a crucial match against the Soviet Union (as before, the referee failed to witness the manoeuvre although a television audience of millions saw it in detail).

Hapgood, Eddie (1911–73) English fullback, nicknamed the Ambassador of Football, who was one of the stars of the great Lucky Arsenal side of the 1930s. The future Ambassador of Football was always mad about the game, though early indications were that he was hardly going to prove a noble advertisement for it. As a boy of ten, he was regularly scolded for indulging his passion and even appeared before the bench in Bristol, where he was sternly warned by a magistrate: 'You really must curb this passion for kicking a ball about, otherwise it might get you into trouble.'

The advice was to no avail. Before joining Arsenal, Hapgood played for non-League Kettering (having turned down an offer to appear for Bristol Rovers, who tried to get him to accept a contract that meant driving a coal cart in the summer months). Bristol's loss was Arsenal's gain, for he was to win a grand total of five Championship medals and two FA Cup Winners' medals with the club.

Usually playing at left-back, he was widely admired for his mastery of the ball and for the elegance of his play, to the extent that other players accused him of conceit. A respected international, he made his debut for the national side in 1933 and captained England in the notorious Battle of Highbury (in which he suffered a broken nose) in 1934. He collected a record 30 caps in an international career somewhat shortened by the outbreak of World War II, but his diplomatic skills were never more severely tested than in the much-discussed 1938 meeting with Germany at the Olympic Stadium in Berlin.

With Germany already the masters of Austria and with an increasing awareness of the inevitability of war, England were anxious to avoid unpleasantness between the two sides. Accordingly, after consultation with the British ambassador to Germany, the decision was made that – as the German side had announced that they would stand to attention during the English National Anthem – the English team would have to give the Nazi salute, as demanded by the host nation, as 'Deutschland über Alles' played.

The resulting photographs of the England team with right arms upraised caused a furore in the British press, with opinion divided as to whether the German demand should have been acceded to. The game passed peaceably enough, England winning by the satisfying margin of 6–3. Hapgood, true to his reputation as a defender of football's good name, had been one of those players who had argued most strenuously against giving the salute, but gained consolation from the result, which he called 'one of the finest and most satisfactory' of his career.

When I go to see Herr Hitler I give him the Nazi salute because that is the normal thing. It carries no hint of approval of anything he or his regime may do. And, if I do it, why should you or your team object?

Advice given to England's footballers by Sir Neville Henderson, England's political ambassador

In contrast, at a game played between Aston Villa and a German team the following day, the English players refused to give the Nazi salute and instead 'honoured' their opponents by raising two fingers in the air.

Happy *See* STILES, NOBBY.

hard men Those players who have established a reputation for hard tackling and even dangerous play. The hard men of English football since World War II have included such daunting characters as the Savage Six who played for Bolton Wanderers in the 1950s, Dave MACKAY of Spurs, Ron CHOPPER Harris of Chelsea, and Tommy SMITH (*see* ANFIELD IRON) of Liverpool in the 1960s, Norman BITES YER LEGS Hunter and Johnny GILES of Leeds United in the 1970s, Stuart PSYCHO Pearce of Nottingham Forest in the 1980s, and Vinny JONES in the 1990s.

For as concerning football playing, I protest unto you it may be rather called a friendlie kinde of fyghte than a play or recreation, a bloody or murmuring practise than a fellowly sporte or pastime.

Phillip Stubbes, puritan (late 16th century)

Hardaker, Alan English football administrator, who was secretary of the Football League from 1957 to 1979 and one of the great characters of football. Nicknamed Saint Alan of St Anne's, The Great Dictator, Football's Godfather, Cagney of the League, and The League's Most Celebrated Enforcer, Hardaker was renowned and admired for his pugnacious and determined stance as secretary, which often made him a somewhat controversial figure. He is particularly remembered as the chief instigator of the League Cup.

I doubt if there is any football administrator who is better known or held in higher esteem.

Lord Westwood, League president (1974–79)

Hardturm The home ground, in Zurich, of the Swiss football club GRASSHOPPERS. Situated in the Hard district of the city, the original stadium was opened in 1929. Soon afterwards the main stand was destroyed by fire – one of a series of fires at Swiss football grounds that may have been the work of a single unidentified arsonist. Subsequently the stadium witnessed many of the club's greatest moments, although another fire in 1968 caused further damage. The stadium was extensively rebuilt in the 1980s.

Harefield United English non-League football club, nicknamed The Hares. Strip: red and white striped shirts, black shorts, and red and black socks. Founded in 1868, the club are based at Preston Park in Harefield and play in the Isthmian League.

Harem Girls Nickname of the Greek football club AEK ATHENS, reflecting the origins of the side among Greek refugees from the Turkish Republic in the 1920s.

Hares, The Nickname of the English non-League football club HAREFIELD UNITED.

Harlow Town English non-League football club, nicknamed the Owls. Strip: all red. Founded in 1879 and based at the Harlow Sports Club, the Owls play in the Isthmian League.

harpastum Name under which something akin to modern football was played in ancient Rome. According to certain historians this antique version of the game may even have been played in the UK by the Roman invaders, possibly influencing primitive ball games played by the indigenous population. Like the Greek *episkyros*, the *harpastum* code permitted handling and may more properly be considered a forerunner of rugby. *See also* GRIFFIN PARK.

Harriers Nickname of the English non-League football club KIDDERMINSTER HARRIERS.

Harris, Ron (1944–   ) English player, nicknamed Chopper, who acquired a reputation as something of a hatchetman while with Chelsea in the 1960s and 1970s. He was booked on a regular basis for hard tackles and became one of the most feared players in the First Division, although Harris himself protested that committed tackling was not his only skill: 'I like to think that apart from being a bit of a butcher, I've something else to offer.'

In fact, he proved he had other qualities by serving Chelsea as an effective captain, leading the side to victory in the FA Cup in 1970 and in the European Cup Winners' Cup the following year. After retiring from the game he bought a run-down golf club and made it a big success, becoming a millionaire.

Harrogate Town English non-League football club. Strip: amber shirts, black shorts, and amber socks. Founded in 1919 and based at the Wetherby Road ground, Harrogate play in the Northern Premier League.

Harrow Borough English non-League football club, nicknamed Boro. Strip: all red. Originally called Roxonian and based at the Earlsmead ground, Boro adopted their present name in 1967 and have spent most of their recent history in the upper reaches of the Isthmian League.

Harry the Haddock Nickname of an inflatable mascot that was adopted by fans of Grimsby Town in the 1980s. Hundreds of Harry the Haddocks were carried by crowds at the club's matches during the brief time that the fad lasted, the choice of a haddock being apposite for a town with such a long history as a centre of the British fishing industry.

Hartlepool United English football club, nicknamed Pool. Strip: sky blue shirts, navy blue and white shorts, and sky blue socks. The Pool were founded – as Hartlepools United (which name they retained until 1968) – in 1908 as a professional team to emulate the success of West Hartlepool, who had won the FA Amateur Cup in 1905. In 1916 the club, based at the VICTORIA GROUND in Hartlepool since its formation, earned the dubious distinction of being the first football club to have its ground bombed (by German Zeppelins that were subsequently shot down over the sea); demands for compensation from the German Government were never met.

Hartlepool joined the League in 1921 and have remained in the bottom flight of the League ever since – with the one exception of the 1968–69 season, when they reached the Third Division. The team's history is studded with repeated applications for re-election to the League (more than any other club) and by constant financial crises. Further humiliation has been suffered at the hands of lowly non-League sides (between 1927 and 1930 Hartlepool were knocked out of every FA Cup competition they entered by non-League clubs). There have been some happier memories, however: in 1957 they came within a whisker of beating the Busby Babes themselves in a match that ended 4–3 in Manchester United's favour (the Red Devils went on to win the League championship that year).

The club changed its name to Hartlepool in 1968 and added the word 'United' in 1977. Notable names to be associated with the side have included Brian CLOUGH, who was briefly manager in the 1960s.

The Pool enjoyed their record victory in 1959, when they beat Barrow 10–1; they suffered their worst defeat in 1962, when they lost by the same scoreline to Wrexham. Wattie Moore holds the record for League appearances with the team, having played in 447 games between 1948 and 1964. Arch-rivals of the club are Darlington.

> Me brother's in borstal,
> Me sister's got pox,
> Me mother's a whore down Hartlepool docks,
> Me uncle's a pervert
> Me aunty's gone mad
> And Jack the Ripper's me dad,
> La, la, la . . .

Hartlepool supporters' song

Hastings Town English non-League football club, nicknamed Town. Strip: all white. Founded in 1895 and based at the Pilot Field in Hastings, the club play in the Southern League.

Hatters (1) Nickname of the English football club LUTON TOWN, in reference to Luton's traditional hat-making industry (as reflected in their other nickname, the Strawplaiters).

(2) Nickname of STOCKPORT COUNTY, in reference to the area's history of hat manufacture.

hat-trick The scoring of three goals by a single player in the course of a match (originally three consecutive goals). The earliest hat-tricks in the FA Cup date from the 1874–75 season, when Oxford University's Parry and Wanderers players Kingsford and Wollaston all scored three times in the first round on the same day; it is very possible, however, that the honour of scoring the first FA hat-trick belongs to one or more unidentified players who contributed to a 7–0 victory by the Royal Engineers in 1873. The only player to score a hat-trick in an FA Cup Final remains Stan MORTENSEN, in the MATTHEWS FINAL of 1953.

The very first hat-trick scored in the history of the Football League was achieved by Walter Tait, who scored three times for Burnley in a 4–3 victory over Blackburn Rovers on the second Saturday of the first season (1888); the first hat-trick in the Scottish League was scored in 1890 when J. MacPherson of Rangers put in three goals against Cambuslang.

Argentina's Guillermo Stabile was the first man to score a hat-trick in the World Cup (1930), while Geoff HURST was the first player to score three goals in the Final of the competition (1966).

The record for the fastest hat-trick in British football goes to Blackpool's 'Jock' Dodds, who scored three goals in two and a half minutes against Tranmere Rovers in 1943 (subsequently Jimmy Scarth of Gillingham and Ian St John were also credited with three goals in two and a half minutes in 1952 and 1959 respectively). The fastest hat-trick in international football was recorded by England's Willie Hall, who scored three times against Ireland in just three and a half minutes in 1938. These achievements pale, however, beside the world record for the fastest hat-trick, which is held by the Independiente player Maglioni, who in 1973 netted three goals against fellow-Argentines Gimnasia in just one minute, fifty seconds.

Dixie DEAN retired with a grand total of 37 hat-tricks to his credit, a record that has yet to be surpassed in British football.

The hat-trick is so-called after the old cricketing tradition that a bowler claiming three wickets in a row is entitled to a new hat at the expense of his club (footballers sometimes claim the match ball). *See also* DOUBLE HAT-TRICK; TRIPLE HAT-TRICK.

Havant Town English non-League football club. Strip: yellow shirts, black shorts, and yellow and black socks. Founded in 1958 and based at Westleigh Park, Havant play in the Southern League.

Hawthorns, The The home ground in Birmingham of WEST BROMWICH ALBION. Albion had a number of home venues – notably Four Acres (a gift to the people of West Bromwich from the Earl of Dartmouth) and Stoney Lane (which included a small stand called 'Noah's Ark') – before settling permanently at The Hawthorns (so-called after the Hawthorns Hotel nearby) in 1900. Within the space of a month the bare, sloping meadow acquired by the club was a fully equipped ground (complete with the Noah's Ark stand transported from Stoney Lane) and able to accommodate large crowds; at 550 feet above sea level it is also said to be the highest ground in Britain.

Events in the ground's history have included the destruction by fire of Noah's Ark on Bonfire Night in 1904, the opening of the club's own railway station (called Hawthorns Halt) in 1931, the arrival in the late 1940s of the first electronic turnstile counters in the UK, the closure of the little-used railway station in 1968, and expensive damage caused by Leeds United fans in 1982. The arrival of bright multi-coloured seats in the East Stand led to it being rechristened the 'Rainbow Stand'.

Hayes English non-League football club, nicknamed the Missioners. Strip: red and white striped shirts, with black shorts and socks. Founded in 1909 and based at the Church Road ground in Hayes, the club play in the Isthmian League.

Haynes, Johnny (1934–) English inside-forward, who became England's first £100-a-week footballer in 1961. Haynes began his career with Fulham in 1952 and subsequently played a major role in winning the club promotion to the First Division in 1959. He made his debut for England in 1954 and became captain of the national side in 1960, though a serious knee injury sustained in a car crash two years later brought his international career to a premature end (with a total of 56 caps and appearances in the World Cup campaigns of 1958 and 1962). A one-club man, he resisted tempting offers to move to Italy or to Tottenham Hotspur among other clubs and was rewarded with an annual salary of £5200 at Fulham – to the outrage of many critics of the game who thought such high salaries immoral. His decision to remain with Fulham meant that he never won any of the top honours in the domestic game and many observers regretted that he never had a chance to display his skills as a ball-passer and goalscorer in a more distinguished club side. He finally left Fulham in 1970 and joined the South African club Durban City.

header A shot in which the ball is played with the head. The header has long been a legitimate manoeuvre, although such tactics were forbidden in the earliest versions of football, as played at the initial FA Cup Final in 1872. Players in the early history of the game (when balls were considerably more solid than the modern variety) risked serious injury playing the ball with their head. Even today, headers account for a large proportion of injuries – Fulham's Rodney MARSH, for instance, was left permanently deaf after heading a winning goal (and the post) against Leicester City in 1963. Wrexham's Stewart McCallum and Brazil's TOSTAO are among those players who have appeared on the pitch under strict medical orders not to head the ball as a result of previous injuries.

Undaunted by such risks, other players have recorded goals with headers from a considerable distance: no one, however, has bettered the spectacular headed goal scored by Aston Villa's full-back Peter Aldis against Sunderland in 1952 – he found the goal with a header from a full thirty-five yards away. Perhaps the most remarkable instance of a header in the history of the game is that credited to Arsenal's great star Eddie HAPGOOD, who was reported to have scored a penalty with a header during a match against Liverpool in 1935. (In fact, he had taken the penalty in the usual way and had scored with a header on the rebound from the goalkeeper).

A pass rising a yard above the ground should be a foul. A player receiving a pass has two feet and only one head.

Willie Read, St Mirren manager (1959)

Maybe it's because it's the only game in which players use their heads to propel the ball. Assuming that the fans of soccer also play the game, all that butting the ball with their heads might make their brains squishy.

Mike Royko, *New York Times* (1988)

Heart of Midlothian Scottish football club, nicknamed Hearts. The club's unusual and romantic name is derived from that of an old prison in Edinburgh – as immortalized in Sir Walter Scott's novel *The Heart of Midlothian* (1818); it was the club's first captain, Tom Purdie, who suggested the

name back in 1874 (50 years after the prison itself had been demolished). Strip: maroon shirts, white shorts, and maroon socks with white trim. Hearts were formed in 1874 and were founder members of the Scottish First Division in 1890.

Long considered one of the main rivals of the Old Firm though lacking the resources of Scotland's two most famous clubs, Hearts have never quite managed to emerge from the shadow cast by Celtic and Rangers, leading supporters to dub them The Nearly Men of Scottish Football. Nonetheless, they have a good record of success, having won the First Division title in 1895, 1897, 1958, 1960, and 1980, the Scottish Cup in 1891, 1896, 1901, 1906, and 1956, and the League Cup in 1955, 1959, 1960, and 1963.

Their home at TYNECASTLE PARK has seen such stars as striker Bobby Walker in the first decade of the 20th century, Tommy Walker in the 1930s, the TERRIBLE TRIO of the 1950s, and Dave McPherson and John Robertson in the 1980s; comedian Ronnie Corbett (whose cousin played for the first team) once had a trial for the club as a schoolboy. Their blackest period was in the 1970s when relegation threatened the club's very existence.

Hearts enjoyed their record victory in 1880, when they beat Anchor 21–0; they suffered their worst defeat in 1888, losing 8–1 against Vale of Leithen. Henry Smith holds the record for League appearances with the club, having played in 426 matches between 1981 and 1993.

This is our story, this is our song,
Follow the Hearts and you can't go wrong,
Some say that the Rangers and Celtic are
*   grand,*
But the Boys in Maroon are the best in the
*   land.*

Supporters' song, composed by Hector Nicholl in the 1950s

Hednesford Town English non-League football club, nicknamed the Pitmen. Strip: white shirts, with black shorts and socks. Founded in 1880 and based at the Cross Keys ground in Hednesford, the Pitmen play in the Southern League.

Helensburgh Former Scottish football club, that played in the Scottish League from 1923 to 1926. The club's home ground was Ardencaple Park.

Hellenic League English amateur league, that was founded in 1953. The League covers the Oxfordshire area and has two divisions. Distinguished members of the League have included Witney Town (holders of eight championship titles) and Abingdon Town (with four wins); in 1953–54 Princes Risborough created some kind of record for the League when they lost all of their 30 matches that season.

Hemel Hempstead English non-League football club, nicknamed Hemel. Strip: all red. Founded in 1885, Hemel are based at the Vauxhall Road ground in Hemel Hempstead and play in the Isthmian League.

Hendon English non-League football club, nicknamed the Dons. Strip: green shirts, white shorts, and green socks. Founded in 1908 as Hampstead Town and renamed Golders Green Town before settling on their present name in 1946, Hendon (based at the Claremont Road ground) have remained in the upper reaches of the Isthmian League since 1963.

Herberger, Sepp German manager, who led West Germany to victory in the 1954 World Cup. A former inside-forward who won three caps, Herberger was a brilliant tactician and worked as assistant manager to the team before being promoted to the top job in 1936.

here we go, here we go, here we go Widely sung supporters' chant that has been heard at grounds throughout the UK since the 1980s. Set to the tune of 'Stars and Stripes for Ever', this defiantly optimistic chant is usually heard when the team concerned has just scored or is emerging as the dominant side in a match. It caught on very rapidly and in 1985 was appropriated by Everton when they recorded it in an arrangement by Tony Hiller and Harold Spiro (which combined it with Offenbach's 'Can-Can' refrain); the single spent five weeks in the charts and reached number 14. The chant's popularity with crowds around the world was consolidated a year later when it was heard regularly during the World Cup.

Bands of fans often hurl the chant at one another both inside and outside grounds and it has since been heard throughout sport and in a number of nonfootballing contexts (by workers on strike etc.).

Hereford United English football club, nicknamed United. Strip: white shirts, black shorts, and white socks. United were formed in 1924 when several local teams were merged and played minor league football until 1972, when they were elected to the Fourth Division. Their promotion was in part a reward for a sensational match in the 1971–72 season that saw them join the ranks of famous giant-killers via a surprise 2–1 victory over a respected Newcastle United side in the third round of the FA Cup (the first time a non-League club had beaten a League team in 23 years).

Based at Edgar Street in Hereford, United (whose club badge depicts a Hereford bull) have spent just one season (1976–77) in the Second Division. They won the Third Division championship in 1976 and were winners of the Welsh Cup in 1990.

United enjoyed their record League victory in 1987, when they beat Burnley 6–0; they suffered their worst defeat in 1989, losing 6–0 to Rotherham United. Mel Pejic holds the record for League appearances for the club, having played in 412 games between 1980 and 1992.

> Hereford United, we all love you,
> We'll always support you,
> And will follow you through,
> Our supporters are the best and they do
>   their thing,
> When the lads take to the pitch, this is what
>   they sing . . .

Official club song (1979)

Herrera, Helenio Argentina-born manager, who developed the *catenaccio* defensive system in Italy in the 1960s. A naturalized Frenchman, Herrera was manager of Barcelona before moving to the Italian club Internazionale, where he remained for eight years. His employment of the *catenaccio* system brought the team two Championships, two European Cups, and two World Club titles.

Hertford Town English non-League football club, nicknamed the Blues, in reference to the team colours. Strip: all blue. Founded in 1908 and based at Hertingfordbury Park, the club play in the Isthmian League.

Heybridge Swifts English non-League football club, nicknamed the Swifts. Strip: black and white striped shirts, black shorts, and red socks. Founded in 1880 and based at the Scraley Road ground at Heybridge, the club play in the Isthmian League.

Heysel Stadium Belgian football stadium in the Heysel district of Brussels, that is now remembered as the scene of the 1985

Heysel Stadium disaster. The stadium was opened (complete with exhibition park and other sporting facilities) in 1930 to mark the country's 100th anniversary and subsequently staged more major European Finals than any other ground, with relatively little disturbance. Activities at the stadium have included football (it hosts the Belgian Cup Final), gymnastics, speedway, hot air ballooning, hockey, rugby, boxing, ballet, and cycling events as well as military tattoos.

The stadium was extensively modernized in the 1970s, although the extravagant neoclassical entrance to the main stand was retained in its original glory. Somewhat surprisingly there is no reference to the tragedy of 1985 at the ground and few changes were made in the wake of the disaster in the expectation that the whole stadium would be demolished and rebuilt from scratch, renamed the King Baudouin Stadium.

Heysel Stadium disaster Football disaster that took place during the European Cup Final between Juventus and Liverpool at the Heysel Stadium in Brussels in 1985, resulting in 39 deaths from crushing and suffocation. The events of 29 May 1985 initiated an international debate upon the issue of hooliganism and left an iradicable stain upon the reputation of English football fans.

The meeting between the two clubs was marked from the outset by mutual antagonism and violence and culminated in three mass charges by Liverpool fans against Juventus supporters in an area – Block Z – reserved for neutral spectators. In the ensuing panic 39 lives were lost (most of them Italian) and a further 454 people were injured, many of them after a retaining concrete wall collapsed under the pressure of the people crushed against it.

Subsequent investigations into the tragedy placed the blame squarely on the fans themselves, who had overpowered any attempt by the police to keep the sides apart and had behaved with complete disregard for others' safety; contributory factors included the availability of alcohol, poor segregation of the fans, and inadequate safety barriers. The match itself went ahead (the authorities fearing the consequences if it did not) but the fact that the horror had been witnessed by a worldwide television audience meant that the matter would have lasting repercussions on the sport:

> How can I forget those people? I saw them
> with my own eyes; violent, enraged. I saw

> them punching, spitting, throwing the
> passports of the dead and injured into the
> air to show their contempt.

Father of one of the dead at Heysel (1985)

All English clubs were banned by UEFA from taking part in European competitions (they had in fact already been withdrawn by the FA) and 14 Liverpool fans were imprisoned by the Belgian courts; the ban was finally lifted for all clubs except Liverpool in 1990 (Liverpool were finally readmitted in 1991). Three weeks previously English football had reeled when the BRADFORD FIRE had claimed more lives and thrown the national game into turmoil; with Heysel the very existence of the game in the UK came into question under pressure from prime minister Margaret Thatcher among others. Measures that came up for discussion in the wake of the disasters included national membership schemes.

> If this is what soccer is to become, let it die.

L'Equipe, editorial (1985)

HFS Loans League See NORTHERN PREMIER LEAGUE.

Hibernian Scottish football club, nicknamed Hibs or Hibees. Strip: green shirts with white sleeves, white shorts, and green and white socks (a scheme adopted in 1938 in imitation of the strip of all-conquering Arsenal). Founded in 1875 by Irish immigrants, Hibs (based at the EASTER ROAD ground in Edinburgh) joined the Scottish League in 1893 – after two years of inactivity – and have long been regarded as one of the main rivals of the Old Firm.

Their distinguished record includes the First Division championship in 1903, 1948, 1951, 1952, and 1981, the Second Division title in 1894, 1895, and 1933, the Scottish Cup in 1887 and 1902, and the League Cup in 1973. Their golden era was the 1950s when the team included the FAMOUS FIVE line-up of forwards; more recently financial crises have threatened the continued existence of the club with the possibility of a take-over by rivals Heart of Midlothian.

Hibs enjoyed their record victory in 1881, when they beat the 42nd Highlanders 22–1; they suffered their worst defeat in 1898, losing 10–0 against Rangers. Arthur Duncan holds the record for League appearances with the club, having played in 446 games.

Hidegkuti, Nandor (1922–) Hungarian centre-forward, who was one of the great talents that made up the MAGNIFICENT MAGYARS who represented Hungary in the early 1950s. He was much admired for his skill at splitting open opposing defences and in 1953 played a crucial role in the 6–3 victory over England at Wembley. Scorer of 39 goals in 68 internationals, he played at home for MTK Budapest.

Highbury Stadium The home ground, in north London, of ARSENAL. The Gunners moved to their new home in 1913 after taking the controversial decision to relocate the ailing club in north London, far from their roots in Woolwich. The site of the new ground was next door to the Gillespie Road Underground station (*see* ARSENAL TUBE STATION) on land owned by St John's College of Divinity; the Archbishop of Canterbury himself signed the agreement allowing the club to use the venue.

Archibald Leitch designed the stadium, which was large enough to stage internationals (the first played in 1923), but it was subsequently completely rebuilt in the 1930s when the club became the most famous in the land under the management of Herbert CHAPMAN (whose ghost is said to haunt the ground's corridors). One notable incident during the rebuilding of the North Bank was an accident involving a coal merchant and his horse and cart, who had arrived in response to calls for the public to bring their rubbish to the stadium to provide material for the banking. The horse and cart overbalanced and fell into the hole waiting to be filled – resulting in the horse being put down and becoming itself part of the foundations of Highbury's new stand (where it remains to this day).

The respected architect Claude Waterlow Ferrier designed the famous West Stand (complete with electric lift); it was opened in 1932 by no less a personage than the Prince of Wales (later Edward VIII). A matching East Stand was added a few years later, incorporating the celebrated marble entrance hall that quickly entered the mythology of English football in the oft-repeated phrase 'the marble halls of Highbury'.

> *The place was like a palace. You were immediately conscious of belonging to something really big, really important. Everyone at Highbury lived, breathed, talked, ate and drank Arsenal. Everyone believed in the club; everyone was proud to be part of it. It was just like playing cricket for Yorkshire.*
>
> Brian Close, *I Don't Bruise Easily* (1978)

The name of the stadium itself was changed to 'Arsenal Stadium' but the fans have continued to call it Highbury. Events in the ground's history have included the first radio broadcast of a football match (1927), the installation and subsequent removal (on the insistence of the FA) of a special 45-minute clock, the first match to be seen on television (1937), use as a first-aid station during World War II, several hits by German bombs during the Blitz, the installation of under-soil heating in 1964, and complete rebuilding of the North Bank in 1992. While work was carried out on this last improvement, the end of the pitch was screened by a huge mural depicting 8000 Arsenal fans. When it was pointed out that no black or female faces were to be seen in the mural the club hastily ordered it to be amended to provide a more accurate impression of the average Arsenal crowd.

The appearance of the ground in the 1930s is preserved in the 1939 film *The Arsenal Stadium Mystery*, starring Leslie Banks. Curiosities retained at the club include the club's own post box, Herbert Chapman's chapel seat from Yorkshire, busts of both Chapman and Ferrier, two small cannons (one of which was fired before each game in the club's early history), and a five-legged chair designed for a director who suffered from gout and tended to knock his chair over on getting up suddenly. Somewhat surprisingly, the pitch is the smallest League pitch in London.

Highfield Road The home ground of the English football club COVENTRY CITY. Formerly the property of Craven Cricket Club, Highfield Road became the permanent home of Coventry City in 1899. The ground was gradually developed as the years passed, suffered bomb damage in World War II, and witnessed little in the way of anything remarkable until the 1960s, when the extraordinary Sky Blue era began.

As the team stormed up to the First Division the ground was substantially improved with the addition of the prefabricated Sky Blue Stand, an ambitious electronic scoreboard, facilities allowing the closed-circuit televising of the team's away matches, and other innovative ideas that made the ground a model for other clubs.

Unfortunately the club then suffered setbacks with the resignation of manager Jimmy HILL in 1967 and a fire that destroyed the Main Stand and the Second Division championship trophy then in it. The innovations, however, continued with the ground becoming England's first all-seater stadium in 1981 (although a small standing area was reopened in 1983 to bolster falling gates and a further larger section became all-standing in 1985).

Hi-Hi's Nickname of the former Scottish football club THIRD LANARK.

Hill, Jimmy (1928–) English commentator and former player and manager, nicknamed The Chin in reference to his distinctive profile. Ridiculed as all commentators are for their attempts to reflect popular opinion, Hill deserves respect for his achievements as an administrator and manager in the 1960s. While still a player (he was a noted inside-forward with Fulham) he rose to prominence in the 1950s as chairman of the Professional Footballers' Association and played a key role in the negotiations to bring about the end of the maximum wage – finally achieved in 1961.

Subsequently he established himself as one of the most innovative managers in British football as head of Coventry City, where he presided over the so-called 'Sky Blue era'. After leaving Coventry he developed his career as a television personality and publicist for English football, carrying on his campaign for enlightened reform of the game in the UK. In the late 1980s he led a consortium to safeguard the future of his old club Fulham and of their home at Craven Cottage.

There are few roles in the game Hill has not fulfilled at one time or another: in 1972, during a match between Arsenal and Liverpool, he even vacated the commentary box in order to act as a linesman (being a qualified referee) when the regular linesman was injured (typically, he performed the role with considerable expertise).

Hill of Dung See PITTODRIE.

Hillsborough The home ground of SHEFFIELD WEDNESDAY, which in 1989 was the scene of the worst disaster in the history of British football (see HILLSBOROUGH DISASTER). Before settling at the Hillsborough site, Wednesday played at a number of different venues in the city, including Bramall Lane and Olive Grove (1887–99). Olive Grove is remembered as the venue in the 1898–99 season of an extraordinary match lasting just 11 minutes (that being the time remaining from an earlier fixture abandoned because of bad light).

The team moved to their new home in Owlerton in 1899 (a bold decision considering Owlerton was then outside the city of Sheffield itself) but prospered with the help of cheap transport by trams, which ferried fans from the centre of the city. Owlerton, as the ground was known, became Hillsborough in 1914 when the parliamentary constituency changed its name and it subsequently developed as one of the most important venues in the country. Events in the ground's history have included a much earlier disaster (when a wall collapsed in 1914, causing 80 injuries), the addition of a much-admired new North Stand in 1961, the hosting of four World Cup games in 1966, and visits by the Harlem Globetrotters basketball display team.

Hillsborough disaster The worst disaster in the history of British football, which took place at Sheffield Wednesday's home HILLSBOROUGH on 15 April 1989 and resulted in the deaths of 95 people and a further 170 injuries (relatives of another victim – Tony Bland – were given legal permission to disconnect the machinery keeping him alive in 1992).

Hillsborough was the venue that year for an FA Cup semi-final between Liverpool and Nottingham Forest and a huge crowd arrived to see the match. The Leppings Lane enclosure was swamped with Liverpool fans and spectators at the front of the overcrowded area were remorselessly crushed against perimeter fencing meant to prevent invasions of the pitch. Police horses were raised from the ground in the press of fans and in the confusion no one realized that a major disaster was taking place. The game was abandoned after just six minutes and attempts were made to extricate the still-living from a mass of corpses.

The footballing world was stunned by the enormity of the tragedy, which was seen by millions on television, and fundamental reforms of the game were demanded on all sides (see TAYLOR REPORT). The pitch at Anfield was covered with tributes to the dead and a chain of football scarves was laid between the homes of Liverpool's two great clubs, Anfield and Goodison Park. The name of Hillsborough itself became synonymous with what many perceived to be the decline of football in the UK in the 1980s.

Football is the one thing we did as a family and now we are not a family anymore.

Trevor Hicks, father of two girls who died at Hillsborough

It's all changed now, which is why it mattered to those young men from Liverpool that they should be there to support their team. What other group is going to troop their colours for them, present them with scarves and emblems? To what other section of society should they owe allegiance? Not to country; we're going into Europe. Not to community; we're all isolated, shut in little boxes, high-rise or low, watching another box. Not to God; science has got rid of him. Not to guilt; Freud shoved that out of the window.

Beryl Bainbridge, on the Hillsborough disaster (1989)

Hinckley Town English non-League football club, nicknamed the Eagles. Strip: white shirts, claret shorts, and sky blue socks. Founded in 1958 and based at the Leicester Road ground in Hinckley, the club play in the Southern League.

Hitchin Town English non-League club, nicknamed the Canaries. Strip: yellow shirts and socks with green shorts. Founded in 1865 and based at the Top Field ground in Hitchin, the club play in the Isthmian League.

Hoddle, Glenn (1957–) English footballer, nicknamed the King of White Hart Lane, who was a leading star of Tottenham Hotspur and England in the 1980s. Hoddle joined Spurs in 1975 and made his England debut in 1979, by which time he was gathering a reputation as a highly talented player – one of the most accurate passers of the ball in the modern game. He helped Spurs to win the FA Cup in 1981 and to retain it a year later but was criticized by some for his inconsistent performances and relatively weak contribution as a defender and his place in the England squad became increasingly insecure. His admirers, however, pointed to his evident skills and condemned England's management for not including him more often in the national side:

Hoddle a luxury? It's the bad players who are a luxury.

Danny Blanchflower (1981)

In 1987 Hoddle transferred to Monaco and helped the club win the French championship in 1988, in which year he made the last of 53 appearances for England. He suffered a serious knee injury in 1989 and in 1991 took the post of manager of Swindon Town, leading them into the Premier League for the first time in the club's history. In 1993 he took over as player-manager at Chelsea.

His announcement that he had become a 'born-again' Christian in 1988 provoked some ribaldry:

I hear Glenn's found God. That must have been one hell of a pass.

Jasper Carrot (1988)

Hogan, Jimmy (1882–1974) English coach, who had a profound influence upon the development of football in Austria and Hungary between the wars. Having played for Burnley and Fulham among other clubs, Hogan masterminded the much-admired Wunderteam that represented Austria in the 1930s, though he received little recognition for his achievements back in England.

hole, playing in the Expression much used by coaches in developing team tactics. Playing in the hole denotes the deliberate movement by attacking players into the no man's land between the strikers and the midfielders, where the opposition find it more difficult to mark their opposite numbers.

Holker Street The home ground of the former English League football club BARROW.

Holland See NETHERLANDS.

Holte End See VILLA PARK.

home It is generally accepted that any team that plays at its home ground enjoys an automatic advantage over its visitors, who may be disorientated by unfamiliar surroundings and lacking the full body of their home support. Nottingham Forest hold the record for avoidance of home defeats, managing not to lose a single one of 71 successive matches at the City Ground over a three and a half year period in the early 1950s. On 23 February 1926 and again on 10 December 1955 every one of the First Division clubs playing at home secured a win against their visitors.

Some clubs, in contrast, have found even a home advantage insufficient to secure victory on a regular basis: Arsenal, Notts County, Blackpool, and Loughborough Town all share the dubious distinction of having failed to achieve more than a single home win during the course of an entire League season.

Among other curious records concerning the home game is that involving Everton's Peter Farrell who in 1949 was selected to play for the Republic of Ireland against

England at Goodison Park: he scored a goal, thus becoming the only international to score an away goal at his home ground.

Several English League clubs never play at 'home' as their grounds are not situated in their home town. They include Manchester United (whose Old Trafford home lies on the border between Manchester and Salford), Nottingham Forest (whose City Ground lies in West Bridgford), and Grimsby Town (whose Blundell Park base is in Cleethorpes). *See also* AWAY.

Home International One of the matches that was formerly played between England, Northern Ireland, Wales, and Scotland in the course of deciding the British Home Championship, which was founded in 1884 and qualified as the oldest of all international contests. By the time of the last tournament in 1984, the Championship had been fought 88 times: England won 34 times, Scotland 24, Wales seven, and Northern Ireland three and there were 20 shared titles. Particularly memorable meetings in the history of the competition included Scotland's comprehensive 5–1 victory over England in 1928, which earned the Scottish players the informal title of Wembley Wizards.

In the 1950s the Championship was designated as a preliminary group for the World Cup Finals. The competition folded after England and Wales refused to play matches in Northern Ireland because of the political unrest there. Subsequently England and Scotland also refused to play both Northern Ireland and Wales. The tournament had by then already lost favour with both the fans and the players and had also become a focus of football violence, with Scottish fans mounting a damaging invasion of the Wembley pitch in 1977, resulting in the destruction of one of the goals. *See also* ROUS CUP.

Home Park The home ground of the English football club PLYMOUTH ARGYLE. For many years Plymouth had no permanent home, but they finally settled at Home Park (then surrounded by fields) in 1901 after it was vacated by the Devonport Rugby Club. The club's transition to professional status was marked with a series of exhibition matches at the ground and it soon proved a popular venue.

Events in the ground's history have included the demolition of the so-called 'Flowerpot Stand' after two fires before World War I, extensive bomb damage during World War II (with the Main Stand being completely destroyed), occupation by the US Navy (who played baseball there), rebuilding in the late 1940s, an influential court case in 1960 that resulted in a lowering of the ground's rateable value, and in 1977 the hosting of a European Cup Winners' Cup match between Manchester United and St Etienne (in order to lessen the likelihood of Manchester United fans going on the rampage as they had in France).

For many years after World War II temporary accommodation for spectators was provided by two trams, which replaced the bomb-damaged terraces; they remained in use (as the headquarters of the supporters' club and as a base for the groundstaff) until the 1950s.

One of the most remarkable matches ever played at Home Park took place in 1926 at the height of the General Strike between a team of strikers and the police. This curious affair was predictably interrupted by violence, with crowds attempting to prevent local transport getting anybody to the ground and repeated clashes between strikers and mounted police; the game itself ended – somewhat appropriately – with the strikers winning 2–1.

Honduras Honduras joined FIFA in 1951 and first hit the headlines in world football in 1969, when World Cup qualifying matches between the country and neighbouring El Salvador provided the spark for the so-called SOCCER WAR – although the reasons for the conflict were in reality deep-seated political issues. Fortunately peace was quickly restored and in 1982 both countries qualified for the Finals of the competition for the first time. Honduras made the most of their chance and drew 1–1 with the host country, Spain. They then registered another draw against Northern Ireland before going out with a 1–0 defeat against Yugoslavia. Strip: white shirts, with blue shorts and socks.

Honest Men Nickname of the Scottish football club AYR UNITED, which was inspired by a couplet in praise of the town in Robbie Burns's poem 'Tam o' Shanter':

Auld Ayr, wham ne'er a town surpasses,
For honest men and bonnie lasses.

Hong Kong Hong Kong joined FIFA in 1954 but have yet to make much impact in international competition. Strip: red shirts, white shorts, and red socks.

Honvéd Hungarian football club, which was widely acclaimed the best club side in the world back in the early 1950s. Strip: all white with red trim. Founded in 1949 as the army club, the team – based at the JÓZSEF BOZSIK STADIUM in Budapest – was built on the former Kispest club and rapidly established itself as the leading Hungarian side. Boasting several of the stars who made Hungary, in the 1950s, one of the strongest international squads ever seen (among them were Ferenc PUSKAS and Sandor KOCSIS), Honvéd won the League title in 1950, 1952, 1954 and 1955 before the Hungarian uprising of 1956 brought the great era to an end (several members of the team electing to remain in the West where they were playing an away fixture at the time of the trouble). Subsequently the team resurfaced to capture the League championship in 1980, 1984, 1985, 1986, 1988, and 1989 as well as Cup victories in 1964, 1985, 1989, and 1993. When Wolverhampton Wanderers beat Honvéd 3–2 in 1954 manager Stanley CULLIS said the victory meant his own side could rightly be called the Champions of the World – a remark that provided the spark for the foundation of the European Cup. On the collapse of the Communist regime the club reverted to its old title Kispest.

hooliganism Anti-social and often criminal behaviour, as perpetrated by a minority of football fans connected with virtually every major club throughout the world, though associated particularly with supporters of English clubs (*see* ENGLISH DISEASE). The very first hooligans were London's Hoolihan family, whose propensity for riotous behaviour in the 19th century was legendary:

> The original Hooligans were a spirited Irish family of that name whose proceedings enlivened the drab monotony of life in Southwark about fourteen years ago. The word is younger than the Australian larrikin, of doubtful origin, but older than Fr[ench] apache.
>
> Ernest Weekley, *Romance of Words* (1912)

See also FIRM; PITCH INVASION.

Hornchurch English non-League football club, nicknamed the Urchins. Strip: all white with red trim. Founded in 1923 and based at The Stadium in Upminster, Hornchurch play in the Isthmian League.

Hornets (1) Nickname of the English non-League football club HORSHAM, from the club's formal name.

(2) Nickname of the English football club WATFORD, in reference to the team colours.

Horsham English non-League football club, nicknamed the Hornets. Strip: green and amber shirts, green shorts, and amber socks. Founded in 1885, the club are based at the Queen Street ground in Horsham, West Sussex, and play in the Isthmian League.

Horwich RMI English non-League football club, nicknamed the Railwaymen. Strip: blue and white striped shirts with blue shorts and socks. Founded in 1896, the Railwaymen are based at the Ramsbottom Road ground and play in the Northern Premier League.

Howie, James (1878–1963) One of the stars of the Newcastle United side that was one of the most powerful teams in the League in the first decade of the 20th century. Howie, nicknamed Gentleman Jim, was particularly famous for his unique running style, in which he seemed to hop rather than run.

Huddersfield Town English football club, nicknamed the Terriers. Strip: blue and white striped shirts with white shorts and socks. The club were founded in 1908 as the result of a meeting at the Imperial Hotel two years earlier at which it was decided that a football club could be formed in what was recognized as a strong rugby area. Huddersfield joined the Football League in 1910 and spent ten years in the Second Division before rising to the top flight in 1920, at what proved to be the start of the side's golden era.

The man behind the extraordinary success of the club in the 1920s was manager Herbert CHAPMAN, who arrived at the club's home at LEEDS ROAD in 1921 and transformed the side between then and his departure for Arsenal in 1925. Forgetting their lack of First Division experience and the financial crises that had previously threatened amalgamation with Leeds United, the Terriers claimed victory in the FA Cup in 1922 and then stormed to triumph in three successive League championships (1924–26) under their highly talented captain Clem Stephenson. They were runners-up in the League in 1923 and subsequently in 1927 and 1928 before their trail of glory finally came to an end (significantly, their record-breaking unbeaten home run in the FA Cup that had lasted from 1913 was interrupted in 1932 by Chapman's Arsenal).

Huddersfield remained in the First Division until 1952, then divided their time between the top two flights for a further 20 years before ultimately dropping into the Third Division in 1973 and even spending some time in the Fourth Division (1975–80); they returned briefly to the Second Division in 1983 but fell back to the Third Division in 1988.

Famous names linked with the team since the 1930s have included Bill SHANKLY, who managed the club for a period before moving to Liverpool in 1959, Denis LAW, who played for the club in the late 1950s, and more recently manager Ian Greaves.

Famous fans of the club include former prime minister Harold Wilson, who claimed that he always carried a picture of the celebrated side of the 1920s in his wallet.

The club enjoyed their record victory in 1930, when they beat Blackpool 10–1; they suffered their worst defeat against Manchester City in 1987, losing 10–1.

Billy Smith holds the record for League appearances with the club, having played in 520 matches between 1914 and 1934.

Those were the days my friend,
We thought they'd never end,
We won the League,
Three times in a row,
We won the FA Cup,
And now we're going up,
We are the Town,
Oh yes, we are the Town.

Supporters' song, to the tune of 'Those were the days'

Hughes, Mark (1962–) Welsh forward, nicknamed Sparky, who emerged as one of the stars of the strong Manchester United side that won the FA Cup in 1985. He also featured in the side that won the FA Cup in 1990 and the Premier League title in 1993. Other highlights of his career with United have included the two goals he scored in the European Cup Winners' Cup Final in 1991, against Barcelona (who recruited him for a brief period in 1986). Other teams with which he has appeared include Bayern Munich (1987–88) and the Welsh national side. He is the only British player to have been twice voted the PFA Player of the Year (1989 and 1991).

Hull City English football club, nicknamed the Tigers. Strip: black and amber striped shirts with amber sleeves, black shorts, and black and amber socks. Hull began life in 1904 and defied the popularity of the rugby code in the area by using rugby grounds and attracting enthusiastic crowds, entering the FA Cup in their first season and joining the Second Division of the League just a year later.

Since 1905 the club – based at BOOTH-FERRY PARK – have experienced life in all three lower divisions without ever reaching the top flight. After reaching the semi-finals of the FA Cup in 1930 and claiming the Third Division (North) title in 1933, Hull enjoyed something of a golden era in the late 1940s and early 1950s, when players with the side included Raich CARTER, goalkeeper Bill Bly (who appeared for the club over a period of some 22 years), and Don REVIE.

They captured another Third Division (North) championship in 1949 but had to wait until their next outstanding era (the mid 1960s) for their next honour – the Third Division championship in 1966 – which was attained with the assistance of such admired players as Chris Chilton and Ken Wagstaff. The Terriers almost reached the First Division under manager Terry Neill in the 1970s but have since travelled regularly between the three lower divisions.

Their record victory came in 1939, when they beat Carlisle United 11–1; they suffered their worst defeat back in 1911, losing 8–0 to Wolverhampton Wanderers. In 1912 they met the Norwegian club Trondheim and District in a friendly and walked away with a 16–1 win (Steve Fazackerley scoring 11 of the goals). Andy Davidson holds the record for League appearances with the club, having played in 520 matches between 1952 and 1967.

I took my wife to a football match to see
Hull City play,
We waited for a trolley bus for nearly half
a day,
And when we got to Boothferry Park, the
crowds were rolling in,
The bus conductor said to me 'Do you
think that they will win?',
Shoot City Shoot! Shoot City Shoot!
The grass is green, the ball is brown and we
got in for half a crown,
Shoot City Shoot! Shoot City Shoot!
There ain't no guy as sly as our goalie Bill
Bly.

Supporters' song, to the tune of 'Sioux City Sue' (1940s)

Hun Nickname used by Catholics in reference to any supporter of a Protestant team (especially by Celtic fans in reference to Rangers). The nickname, more usually applied to Germans, is presumed to have had its origins in the Glorious Revolution of 1688, which saw the Catholic James II replaced on the throne by the Protestant William of Orange and his wife Mary.

> Can you see a happy Hun, no, no,
> Can you see a happy Hun, no, no,
> Can you see a happy Hun, I can't see a
> fucking one.

Cliftonville supporters' song, aimed at Linfield fans

Hungary The Hungarian national team has a long and distinguished record in international competition and in the early 1950s surpassed all other nations for their deeds on the pitch (see MAGNIFICENT MAGYARS). Early progress was made under the British coach Jimmy HOGAN, who boosted standards throughout the Hungarian game after his arrival in 1916, and the side made its first appearance in the World Cup Finals in 1934. With the inspiration of such players as centre-forward Gyorgy Sarosi, the team rapidly made its mark and over its first 29 World Cup fixtures averaged an extraordinary three goals a game (four or more on ten occasions). Austria stopped their progress in 1934, but four years later the team powered through to the Final, finishing 4–2 runners-up to Italy.

The golden era, however, began after World War II, when such talents as Ferenc PUSKAS, Gyula GROSICS, Jozsef BÓZSIK, Sandor KOCSIS, and Nandor HIDEGKUTI swept all before them. They captured the Olympic football title in 1952 and a year later cowed England 6–3, thus destroying the myth of English invincibility once and for all. An uncharacteristic defeat in the 1954 World Cup Final against West Germany robbed them of the supreme prize, but subsequently they re-established their standing as the best team in the world with further stunning victories.

It all came to an end in 1956 when the Hungarian Uprising signalled the break-up of the team. Later years have, however, seen Hungary take two more Olympic titles (1964 and 1968) and such highlights as a brilliant victory at the expense of mighty Brazil in the 1966 World Cup. Strip: red shirts, white shorts, and green socks.

Hungerford Town English non-League football club, formerly nicknamed the Crusaders. Strip: white shirts, navy blue shorts, and white socks. Founded in 1886 and based at Bulpit Lane, Hungerford Town play in the Isthmian League.

Hunter, Norman (1943–) English footballer, who was a much-feared defender with Leeds United and England in the 1960s and 1970s. Nicknamed Norman 'Bites Yer Legs' Hunter, he built up a reputation as one of the fiercest tacklers ever to play the game. One rare occasion on which his tackle failed to connect was in a World Cup qualifier in 1973; it proved crucial, Poland profiting by the mistake to score the goal that effectively put England out of the World Cup. In 1973 he became the first footballer to win the Player of the Year award.

> Norman Hunter telephoned me once to say that he'd gone home with a broken leg. I asked him 'Whose leg is it?'.

Les Cocker, Leeds United and England trainer

Hurst, Geoff (1941–) English forward, who is remembered as the scorer of the hat-trick that settled the Final of the 1966 World Cup in England's favour. Making only his eighth international appearance, Hurst entered the record books with the hat-trick (the first in any World Cup Final) – though there was much debate over whether the ball had actually crossed the line with the second goal. He made the argument academic in the dying seconds of the game, blasting in a long-range shot that was quite unstoppable. By the time of his retirement from the international game, he had notched up a tally of 24 goals in 49 fixtures; at home, he played for West Ham and Stoke City.

Hyde United English non-League football club, nicknamed the Tigers. Strip: red, white, and black shirts, white shorts, and black socks. Founded in 1919 and based at the Tameside Stadium, Hyde play in the Northern Premier League.

hypnotism The use of hypnosis in an attempt to improve a team's performance is a rare and desperate measure, but not unheard of within the professional game. In 1976 a hypnotist by the name of 'Romark' was called in to assist Millwall on their promotion to the Second Division and subsequently he worked with Fourth Division Halifax Town, allegedly contributing greatly to the club's victory over First Division Manchester City in the FA Cup in 1980. Previously the same hypnotist (really called Ronald Markham) had been called in by Spurs in 1975 to do what he could to help the side avoid relegation to the Second Division by beating Leeds United. Accordingly, he hypnotized Alfie Conn, Cyril Knowles, and Martin Chivers (three of the side's key players): all three men scored (Conn getting two) and the team's place in the First Division was secure. An offer by a local publican to hypnotize the entire Oldham Athletic team in the early 1950s was politely turned down with the excuse 'we're desperate, but not that desperate'. Barnet, however, successfully employed a hypnotist to help them overcome a disastrous start to the 1993–94 season.

Ibrox Park The home ground, in Glasgow, of the Scottish football club RANGERS. Rangers played on Glasgow Green and subsequently at Kinning Park among the shipyards of the Clyde before moving to Ibrox in 1887. The ground was inaugurated with a special match against the Old Invincibles (Preston North End), who were then the dominant team in England: Rangers lost 8–1 and the game ended early when Rangers fans (who apparently included a large number of women) invaded the pitch (the first of many such invasions the ground was to witness over the years).

The ground was soon playing host to internationals and Cup Finals and in 1899 the club decided to redevelop it, building an entirely new Ibrox Park on adjoining land. The second Ibrox Park began well but in 1902 was the scene of the first mass tragedy to affect the game when a stand collapsed (*see* IBROX PARK DISASTER). As a result of the disaster, Ibrox was redesigned by Archibald Leitch and its capacity reduced.

Subsequent events in the ground's history have included a royal investiture (1917), the erection of the largest stand at any contemporary ground (1929), the first six-figure attendance recorded anywhere in Europe (when 118,567 fans packed in to see the traditional New Year Old Firm fixture in 1939), and the first official floodlit Scottish League match (1956). In 1971 the stadium's reputation was once more blighted by tragedy when 66 people lost their lives in the second Ibrox Park disaster, after which the club embarked on a major rebuilding programme, with only Leitch's South Stand being preserved substantially intact – making it one of the best equipped stadia in Europe.

Ibrox Park disaster (1) The world's first major football disaster, which took place on 5 April 1902 at IBROX PARK. Six minutes after the start of a British Home International between Scotland and England the newly extended wooden Western Stand collapsed beneath the packed crowd that had turned out to see the game. Hundreds of spectators fell through a gaping hole in the structure and in all 26 people lost their lives; another 500 were injured. The match itself was resumed after a delay, other fans crowding round the broken section to see the game, as a shocked observer recorded: 'Not even the cries of dying sufferers nor the sight of broken limbs could attract this football maddened crowd from gazing upon their beloved sport.'

The game was subsequently discounted as a full international and was later replayed at Villa Park to raise money for the victims of the catastrophe. As a result of the disaster earth embankments were generally preferred to wooden terracing at other grounds in the UK.

(2) Scottish football disaster that took place on 2 January 1971 at IBROX PARK. Huge numbers of fans arrived at the stadium to see the New Year derby between Celtic and Rangers and there was a log jam of people as the crowd attempted to leave the ground at the end of the game. Many lost their footing on Stairway 13 (where two people had died back in 1961 and a further 32 had been injured in incidents in 1967 and 1969) and an avalanche of people poured down the steps. In the carnage that ensued 66 people were killed, mostly as a result of asphyxiation (some dying standing upright).

Early suggestions that the tragedy was caused by fans trying to get back to their places after Colin Stein scored a late goal were dismissed at the subsequent inquiry, which indicated that a possible trigger for the catastrophe may have been the interruption in the flow of the crowd when two boys bent to pick up dropped or thrown souvenirs. The tragedy, which was the worst witnessed in British football until the HILLSBOROUGH DISASTER of 1989, led ultimately to the Safety of Sports Grounds Act 1975, which limited ground capacities and established a licensing system for stadia in the UK.

Iceland The Icelandic national team has always been considered one of the minor sides in international competition, but has nonetheless enjoyed a number of notable moments of glory. Most celebrated of these

were two European Championship qualifiers in 1976 against East Germany (who
had participated in the World Cup Finals
just two years earlier): Iceland drew the first
leg 1–1 and won the second 2–1. Strip: blue
shirts, white shorts, and blue socks.

identity cards *See* MEMBERSHIP SCHEME.

Idrætspark The most prestigious venue
for football in Denmark. Opened in Copen-
hagen in 1911 and home to three local
clubs, the Idrætspark ('sports park') hosts
international football fixtures although
the stands offer little protection from the
elements. The huge 'Expensive Stand' is
decorated with an enormous mural based
on a painting of a football match by a nine-
year-old boy.

Ilford Former English non-League football club, once one of the most famous of all
amateur teams. Founded in 1881, they were
founder members of the FA Amateur Cup
competition and also appeared in the last
Final ever played in the tournament in
1974. They joined the Isthmian League in
1905 and remained in it for 61 years, winning the Championship three times. Other
honours included the FA Amateur Cup and
the London Senior Cup, both of which the
side won two years in succession between
1928 and 1930. They sold their ground and
merged with Leytonstone in 1979.

Imps Nickname of the English football
club LINCOLN CITY, in full the Red Imps.
The nickname refers to a grotesque carving
in Lincoln Cathedral (said to have been
a devil who was turned to stone after he
misbehaved in the Angel Choir); the Lincoln
Imp is now also the county emblem of
Lincolnshire.

Independiente Argentinian football club,
who have long ranked among South
America's strongest sides. Strip: red shirts,
blue shorts, and red socks. Founded in
1905 and based at the Cordero Stadium in
Avellaneda, Buenos Aires, Independiente
have won 11 League titles as well as the
World Club Championship in 1973 and
1984. One of the first South American clubs
to adopt the Italian *catennacio* strategy, the
team pulled off a sensational transfer in the
1930s when the great Paraguayan forward
Arsenio Erico joined the side for the equivalent of £1 and a £1 donation to the Red
Cross. The club's golden eras were the
1930s, when Erico inspired two League
triumphs, and the 1960s, when the team

established their dominance over the South
American Cup competition (with wins in
1964, 1965, 1972, 1973, 1974, 1975, and
1984).

India India joined FIFA in 1948 but has
yet to prove itself more than a minor player
in international competition. A 10–1 defeat
by Yugoslavia in 1952 demonstrated the
gulf in standards between the Indian sub-
continent and Europe. Strip: white and sky
blue striped shirts, white and blue shorts,
and sky blue socks with white trim.

indirect free kick A free kick from which
a goal cannot be scored directly. Indirect
free kicks are awarded for such offences as
obstruction within the penalty area.

Indomitable Lions Nickname of the
national team representing CAMEROON.

Indonesia Indonesia joined FIFA in 1952,
but have yet to make much impact in international competition. Strip: red shirts,
white shorts, and red and white socks.

inflatables The oversize inflatable mascots that became a popular fad among
fans at grounds throughout the UK in the
late 1980s. Inflatables sighted at various
grounds ranged from huge bananas (adopted
by Manchester City fans) and pink panthers
to black puddings and rainbow trout (mas-
querading as the Harry the Haddock
emblem of Grimsby Town). Interpreted
by some as a desperate attempt to revive a
sense of fun and lightheartedness in the
troubled modern game, the craze for inflatables had died down by the 1990s.

injuries The risk of serious injury is an
ever-present threat at all levels of the game
and all professional players expect to miss
games through injury at some point in their
careers. Back in the Victorian era, when
hacking increased the risk of serious injury,
Jack Harkaway's Journal for Boys even
went so far as to reassure young enthusiasts
of the game that the paper's publisher
Edwin Brett would pay £20 to the next-of-
kin of any boy killed playing football. The
first player to retire hurt in an FA Cup Final
was Lieutenant Cresswell of the Royal
Engineers, who broke a collar-bone during
the first Final in 1872.
  Serious injury has not always prevented
a player from completing the game in
progress: Manchester City's goalkeeper
Bert TRAUTMANN, for instance, remained
in goal for the rest of the match after

sustaining a broken neck in the course of the 1956 FA Cup Final (he attributed his ability to fall properly to his wartime training as a German paratrooper). Notable casualties in recent years have ranged from Dave MACKAY of Spurs, who broke his left leg twice in 1964 but continued to play for another eight years (often in great pain) and the same club's Paul GASCOIGNE, whose knee injury became a headline story when it threatened his transfer to the Italian team Lazio in 1992.

Leg injuries are among the most common suffered by players although they can vary widely in terms of severity; from superficial cuts to the catastrophically shattered leg suffered by Leyton Orient's Ledger Ritson in 1948, which resulted in amputation of the affected limb two years later.

In 1980 legal history was made when a player with Whittle Wanderers successfully sued an opponent in the courts after he suffered a broken leg in a late tackle and was awarded £4,900 plus interest and costs; a year later £20,000 was paid out of court to Dunfermline's Jim Brown, whose career had ended prematurely when he suffered a serious knee injury in a dangerous tackle in 1979. The first criminal prosecution relating to an injury resulting from alleged dangerous play reached the courts in 1992.

Some players are more injury-prone than others. Perhaps top of the list of casualties must come Hull City's keeper Billy Bly (with a career total of 13 fractures) and Stoke City's Denis Smith (with five broken legs, four broken noses, a cracked ankle, a broken collarbone, a chipped spine, and numerous less serious fractures and cuts).

Not every injury is sustained on the pitch, of course: in 1964 England's Alan Mullery missed a tour of Brazil after he ricked his back cleaning his teeth. Also embarrassing was the injury suffered by Manchester United keeper Alex Stepney in 1975: while shouting at a team mate he contrived to break his jaw. Even more humiliating was an incident during a match between the USA and Argentina in the 1930 World Cup; seeing one of his players was in need of assistance, the US trainer ran out to help but tripped – as he fell a bottle of chloroform in his bag broke, rendering the unfortunate trainer unconscious (attempts to rouse him were completely futile and he had to be carried off).

Sometimes faking injury has looked like a good tactical ploy; in 1984 Chile were disqualified from the World Cup and their goalkeeper Roberto Rojas was banned from international football for life after pretending he had been hit by a signal flare from the crowd during a qualifying match in Brazil (he even inflicted a minor injury on himself to make it look more convincing).

There was no faking about the injuries suffered by the Mexican striker Carlos Zomba of Atlanta after a match against Los Apaches in which he had scored four goals. An outraged fan shot him four times in the legs, bringing his career in football to a premature and decisive end and thus making him one of the 50 professional players who are forced to retire through injury each year. *See also* DEATHS; HEADER; MAGIC SPONGE; WEMBLEY.

injury time Time added on (at the discretion of the referee) at the end of normal play to allow for time lost during a game due to injuries to players. The phrase has long since passed beyond its original use in sporting contexts, being applied to extended industrial negotiations, for instance. *See also* EXTRA TIME.

Inlaws Nickname bestowed upon the US and Canadian teams that were members of the officially sanctioned United Soccer Association.

İnönü Stadium The home ground, in Istanbul, of the Turkish football club Beşiktaş. Spectacularly situated on the banks of the Bosporus, the İnönü Stadium was opened in 1947 and given its present name in 1973 in honour of the Turkish president Ismet İnönü ; neighbouring buildings include the former Emperor's harem.

Intercontinental Cup International club competition that was first held in 1985. It developed out of the Inter-American Cup, inaugurated in 1969 and played between the winners of the South American Cup and the Concacef Champion Clubs Cup.

international A match between teams representing two nations. The first international was an 'unofficial' match between England and Scotland played at the Kennington Oval in London in 1870. England won 1–0; players in the Scotland side included Lord KINNAIRD (FA president 1890–1923 and player in nine FA Cup Finals) and the celebrated philanthropist Quintin Hogg, subsequently founder of the Regent Street Polytechnic (he also played as a back for the Wanderers and for the Old Etonians). The English side included Charles Alcock (FA secretary 1870–95).

The first full international followed in

1872, when England and Scotland met in a goalless draw at Hamilton Crescent in Glasgow (it was another 98 years before an international between the two sides ended in the same score). The first international to be played by countries outside the UK took place in 1885, when sides representing Canada and the USA met. The first non-British fixture in Europe followed in 1902, when Austria and Hungary met in Vienna (Austria won 5–0). The international game took off in the early years of the 20th century and FIFA was established in 1904 to oversee future development, culminating in the first World Cup tournament in 1930. *See also* OLYMPIC FOOTBALL.

International Board The organization that exercises supreme authority over the laws of association football. Founded in 1886, the International Board has a long history of conservatism towards proposed changes in rules, and is credited by many with giving the game necessary stability. FIFA has four votes on the board, while the FAs of the four British nations have one each. Perhaps the most significant decision ever made by the board was that taken in 1925 to the effect that a player needed only two (rather than three) players between him and the opposite goal to avoid being offside.

International Cup International club competition that is contested between invited teams from Europe and Israel. Beginning life in 1962 and being variously known as the Rappan Cup and the Intertoto Cup, it is played in the summer months for the purpose of providing some results for the use of the football Pools.

Internazionale Italian football club, nicknamed the Black and Blues. Strip: black and blue striped shirts with black shorts and socks. The club was founded in 1908 as a breakaway from AC MILAN (then dominated by the British) and established a reputation for colourful, free-flowing football. Based at the ARENA and subsequently at the GIUSEPPE MEAZZA STADIUM, the club experienced Fascist suppression in the 1930s and 1940s, being obliged to play as Ambrosiana-Inter. The club's long list of triumphs includes 13 League championships, three Cup victories, two European Cups (1964 and 1965), and the World Club Championship (1964 and 1965). In the 1960s the club stirred up considerable controversy with its adoption of the *catenaccio* defence under manager Helenio HERRERA.

Invincibles *See* OLD INVINCIBLES.

Ipswich Town English football club, nicknamed Town or Blues. Strip: blue shirts, white shorts, and blue socks. Ipswich were founded back in 1878 at a meeting at Ipswich Town Hall but it was not until 1938 that the club was admitted to the Football League, as a member of the Third Division (South).

Ipswich remained in the Third Division until 1954, when the side won promotion after clinching the Third Division (South) title for the first time. A year later they were back in the Third Division but their fortunes were about to change, with the arrival at PORTMAN ROAD of Alf RAMSEY as manager. Ramsey revitalized the team, captured a second Third Division championship in 1957, and got them back to the higher level. There they stayed for a further four years before capturing the Second Division title in 1961, thus gaining promotion and incredibly going on to seize the League championship itself in 1962.

Ramsey's remarkable achievement, with a team whose defence (led by Jimmy Leadbetter) proved virtually impregnable, was eventually rewarded with him being given control of the England team (*see* CLASS OF '66). Ipswich, however, soon slipped out of the top flight without the assistance of their former manager and did not get back into the First Division until 1968 when they won another Second Division title.

A year later they found new inspiration under another future England manager, Bobby ROBSON. Robson led the side for 13 campaigns and saw his team win their first FA Cup in 1978 before going on to enjoy victory in the UEFA Cup in 1981, in which year they also finished runners-up in the League championship (a feat they repeated in 1982). The FA Cup victory of 1978 was a particular triumph for Roger Osborne, scorer of the only goal in the match; he was so overwhelmed by his achievement that he had to be replaced by a substitute for the last 13 minutes of the game. The side also reached the semi-finals of the Texaco Cup in 1973 and of the League Cup in 1982 and 1985, by which time Robson had moved to the England post. Stars of the Robson era included forward Paul Mariner and defender Mick Mills.

The club fell back to the Second Division in 1986 but battled their way back up, winning the Second Division title in 1992 and thus becoming founder members of the Premier League.

Ipswich enjoyed their record victory in

1962, when they beat Floriana 10–0; they suffered their worst defeat in 1963, losing 10–1 to Fulham. Mick Mills holds the record for League appearances with the club, having played in 591 games between 1966 and 1982.

> My name is Edward Ebenezer Jeremiah Brown,
> I'm a football supporter of Ipswich Town,
> Wherever they play you'll find me,
> I haven't missed a game since I was three,
> With my scarf and rattle and big rosette,
> Singing 'Where was the goalie when the ball was in the net?'
> Follow the Town, up or down,
> My name is Edward Ebenezer Jeremiah Brown,
> But everyone calls me Ted.

Supporters' song

Iran The Iranian national team has only played a minor role in international competition to date. The side first qualified for the World Cup Finals in 1978 but went out after two defeats, against Peru and Holland, and a draw with a demoralized Scotland. Strip: green shirts, white shorts, and red socks.

Iraq The Iraqi national team has played a relatively modest role in international competition but defied the odds in 1986 by qualifying for their first World Cup Finals. They performed well but still lost to Paraguay, Belgium, and Mexico and progressed no further in the tournament. Strip: all white.

Ireland The Republic of Ireland has a long and distinguished history in international competition. Teams representing Ireland have taken part in every World Cup competition except the very first and have featured in every European Championship to date. High points in the team's international career have included the World Cup qualifier in 1934 in which Paddy Moore became the first player to score four goals in a qualifying match, a 2–0 victory over England in 1949 (the first time the English team lost to a foreign side at home), and the extraordinary resurgence in the side's fortunes that has taken place since the late 1980s under the management of Englishman Jack CHARLTON. With Charlton at the helm, the team qualified for the European Championship in 1988 and for the World Cup Finals themselves in 1990 and 1993. In 1990 they only narrowly failed to progress to the semi-finals and could legitimately claim to be one of the eight top nations in the football world. The Republic of Ireland qualified for the 1994 World Cup in America. Strip: green shirts, white shorts, and green and white socks.

Iron, The (1) Nickname of the English football club SCUNTHORPE UNITED, in reference to the town's history as a centre of the steel industry.

(2) Alternative nickname of the English football club WEST HAM UNITED.

Iron Curtain Nickname of the celebrated RANGERS defence in the years immediately following World War II. Comprising George Brown, George YOUNG, Jock Shaw, McColl, Willie WOODBURN, and Cox, the Iron Curtain proved as impenetrable as the political barrier then being constructed between the communist East and the capitalist West.

Ironsides (1) Alternative nickname of the English football club MIDDLESBROUGH, in reference to the town's connections with the steel industry.

(2) Nickname of the former Welsh League football club NEWPORT COUNTY, in reference to the town's history as a centre of the steel industry.

Israel The Israeli national team has had a confused history in international football largely as a result of political tensions. The expulsion of the Israelis from the Asian confederation historically has meant that the team had to compete in a group with Australia and New Zealand in qualifying for the major international competitions – although it has now been admitted to the European fold. The team has made just one appearance in the World Cup Finals, in 1970, when they lost 2–0 to Uruguay, held Sweden to a 1–1 draw, and then pulled off a goalless draw against mighty Italy to create the sensation of the series. Strip: blue shirts, white shorts, and blue socks.

Isthmian League English amateur football league, which was founded in 1906. One of the most famous of all amateur leagues, the Isthmian League has been the launch pad for several celebrated sides, which in recent years have included Hendon, who in 1974 achieved a 1–1 draw with Newcastle United (FA Cup finalists that year); several teams from the League have captured the FA Amateur Cup.

The League was first contested by just six clubs but is now divided into four divisions, the winners of the Premier Division normally being promoted to the CONFERENCE. Notable members of the League during its long history have included Clapton and Ilford, Oxford City, Walthamstow Avenue, Dulwich Hamlet, Leytonstone, Wimbledon, Enfield, Sutton United, Woking, and Wycombe Wanderers. The League has been known by various different names over the years as its sponsors have changed; recent names have included Vauxhall and (from 1991) the Diadora League.

Italy The Italian national side are among the giants of international football and share with Brazil the honour of having won the World Cup on three occasions. Their first two victories in the competition, in 1934 and 1938, were largely a result of the inspired leadership of manager Vittorio POZZO, who also secured for his team triumph in the Olympics (1936). Subsequently the side espoused the catenaccio defensive system in the 1960s and captured the European Championship in 1968 – though defeat by lowly North Korea in the 1966 World Cup represented a low point in the team's record. Defensive tactics were replaced by more enterprising football in later years and in 1982 Italy collected their third World Cup under manager Enzo Bearzot. Italy qualified for the 1994 World Cup in America. Strip: green shirts, white shorts, and green and white socks.

Ivory Coast Ivory Coast joined FIFA in 1960 and are regarded as one of the more promising African sides. They were African Champions in 1992. Strip: orange shirts, white shorts, and green socks.

J

Jags Nickname of the Scottish football club PARTICK THISTLE, 'jag' being a Scottish dialect term for a thistle.

Jairzinho (Jair Ventura Filho; 1944–) Brazilian outside-right, who was one of the stars of the team that captured the World Cup in 1970, when he scored in every game Brazil played. At home he played for Botafogo and, after a spell with the French club Marseille, for Cruzeiro and then with the Venezuelan club Caracas (despite twice breaking his right leg). He was also included in the Brazilian squad that played in the 1974 World Cup, though not fully fit. In all he scored 37 goals in 98 international appearances.

Jamaica Jamaica joined FIFA in 1962 but have yet to make much impact in international competition. Strip: green shirts, black shorts, and gold socks.

James, Alex (1901–53) Scottish striker, nicknamed Wee Alex, who was the inspiration of the Lucky Arsenal side put together by Herbert CHAPMAN in the early 1930s. Born in Mossend, Lanarkshire, Alex James began his career with Raith Rovers in 1922 but went south of the border in 1925, joining Preston North End, and then Arsenal for a record £9000 in 1929. He played a key role in Arsenal's FA Cup victory in 1930 and subsequently received four Championship medals with the club, sometimes as captain. He won only eight caps for Scotland, probably because he was a player in the English League for most of his career, but made his mark nonetheless, notably in 1928, when he displayed his brilliance in the legendary 5–1 win over England that earned the side the nickname Wembley Wizards.

Wearing a pair of extra-long shorts that emphasized his short stature (he said they kept his knees warm), James dominated English football with his unrivalled skills and brash personality, though it was not unusual for disagreements between himself and his manager to reach the public ear. He retired as a player in 1937 and worked as a journalist and coach until his early death from cancer.

> *If his tongue went like a gramophone, so did his feet.*
>
> Hugh Taylor, captain of the Wembley Wizards

Jammies Alternative nickname of the Scottish football club HEART OF MIDLOTHIAN. Sometimes given as 'Jambos', Jammies is derived from 'Jam Tarts', rhyming slang for Hearts.

Japan Japan joined FIFA in 1929 but have yet to make much impact in international competition despite the recruitment of a number of top European stars to appear in the domestic league. Strip: white shirts, red shorts, and white socks.

Jennings, Pat (1945–) Northern Ireland-born goalkeeper, who was one of the most reliable keepers in the world over a period of some 20 years. Born in Newry, Jennings began as a player of Gaelic football before joining Newry Town in the capacity of goalkeeper in 1963. Subsequently he transferred to Watford and in 1964 made his international debut for Northern Ireland. That same year he moved to Tottenham Hotspur and in 1967 contributed to the team's victory in the FA Cup. Further honours with Spurs included two League Cup winners' medals and a UEFA Cup winners' medal (1972).

Having been made Footballer of the Year in 1973 and Players' Player of the Year in 1976 (in which year he also received an MBE), he moved to Arsenal in 1977 (Spurs wrongly assuming he was past his prime) and two years later won another FA Cup winners' medal. He went back to Spurs in 1985 (having become in 1983 the first British player to notch up 1000 first-class appearances) and in 1986 finished his long international career when he won a record 119th cap during the World Cup tournament.

Notable incidents in his long and celebrated career included the goal he scored from a goal kick in a Charity Shield match in 1967. Many admirers commented on the size of Jennings' hands (dubbed the Largest Hands in Soccer) and claimed they had much to do with his success, although others pointed to his undoubted courage and calm demeanour as more important factors in his playing style.

Somewhere in there the grace of a ballet dancer joins with the strength of an SAS squaddie, the dignity of an ancient king, the nerve of a bomb disposal officer.

Eamon Dunphy (1983)

JNA Stadium The home ground, in Belgrade, of PARTIZAN BELGRADE. The Jugoslovenska Narodna Armia (Yugoslav People's Army) Stadium was reopened in 1951 and until 1963 served as the country's national stadium; it is still a main venue for Cup Finals.

Johnstone Former Scottish League football club, which disappeared from the League in 1926. Based at Newfield Park in Renfrewshire, Johnstone first joined the Scottish League in 1912.

Johnstone, Jimmy (1947–) Scottish winger, who became one of the great stars to emerge with Celtic under the management of Jock STEIN in the 1960s. Johnstone's fiery temperament often got him into trouble, but combined with natural talent on the pitch to make him one of the most feared wingers in Scottish football (though some opposing teams learnt to provoke him into committing disciplinary offences that led to him being sent off). High points of his career included his performance in the 1967 European Cup Final. He won just 23 caps for Scotland because of his fear of flying.

Jones, Cliff (1935–) Welsh winger, who became a hugely popular star with Tottenham Hotspur in the 1960s and played a key role in the club's famous double in 1961. A courageous attacker and formidable in the air despite his relatively short stature, Jones – who hailed from a famous footballing family – began his career with Swansea Town in 1952 and made his debut for Wales in 1955. He moved to Tottenham in 1958 for a record fee of £35,000 and that same year helped steer Wales to the quarter-finals of the World Cup. After the double victory of 1961, he also contributed to success in the FA Cup in 1962, in the European Cup Winners' Cup in 1963 and once again in the FA Cup in 1967. A year later he joined Fulham and in 1969 collected the last of his 59 caps for Wales. He retired from League football in 1970 but remained active at a non-League level.

Jones, Vinny (1965–) English midfielder, who earned a reputation as one of the hard men of British football in the 1980s and 1990s. A former hod-carrier, Jones transferred from Wealdstone to Wimbledon in 1986 and subsequently established himself as one of the most notorious players in the League. He moved to Leeds United in 1989 and then went on to Sheffield United (1991) before returning to Wimbledon, via Chelsea.

Particularly controversial incidents involving Jones have included one in which he came literally to grips with Paul GASCOIGNE's private parts during a match in 1988; afterwards the two players are reputed to have exchanged gifts of a red rose and a lavatory brush. On another occasion he is said to have threatened to tear Kenny DALGLISH's ear off and spit in the hole. In his defence, Jones explained that 'I like to upset anybody I play against'.

Sent off six times in six years, he received his stiffest punishment to date in 1993, when he was fined £20,000 by the FA and given a six-month ban suspended over three years for bringing the game into disrepute after he featured in a video (entitled *Soccer's Hard Men*) giving advice on how to commit professional fouls. *See also* BAMBER.

I have been a great ambassador for this club.

Vinny Jones, on his disappointment at not winning the Wimbledon captaincy (1988)

Jordan Jordan joined FIFA in 1958 but have yet to establish a reputation in international competition. Strip: all white.

José Alvalade Stadium The home ground, in Lisbon, of the Portuguese football club SPORTING LISBON. The ground was named after the wealthy founder of Sporting and has played host to several leading Portuguese teams, including Benfica. The modern stadium was opened in 1956, at which time Sporting were considered by many to be the most powerful team in Europe. An extensive programme of refurbishment began in 1989.

José Rico Peréz Stadium The home ground, in Alicante, of the Spanish football club Hercules. Opened in 1974, it was named after the club's president and hosted games in the 1982 World Cup.

József Bozsik Stadium The home ground, in Budapest, of the Hungarian football club HONVÉD. Built in 1939, the ground became Honvéd's sole home in 1981, when the modest stadium was renovated. It acquired its present name in 1986, in honour of one of Honvéd's most illustrious players (subsequently president of the club).

Jules Rimet Trophy The trophy formerly awarded to winners of the World Cup tournament. The foot-high solid gold trophy featuring a winged seraphim was designed by the French sculptor Abel Lafleur and weighed nine pounds; it was named after Jules Rimet, the FIFA president who oversaw the inauguration of the competition in 1930.

The trophy led a perilous existence during World War II, being secreted in a shoe box under the bed of an Italian official in order to prevent it falling into the hands of the Nazis. After the war it had another adventure in 1966, when it was stolen just before the competition was due to get under way, but was recovered shortly afterwards (*see* PICKLES). One of the referees in the 1966 tournament, George McCabe, was so pleased at being selected that he went so far as to change the name of his house in honour of the trophy, calling it simply 'Jules Rimet'.

A new trophy – the 'FIFA World Cup' – was awarded to World Cup winners after 1970, Brazil having won the Jules Rimet Trophy outright after capturing the title three times. Unfortunately, the Cup later disappeared from the display case where it was kept at the headquarters of the Brazilian FA in Rio de Janeiro and has never been recovered (it is thought probable that it was melted down); a copy of the original trophy was then made by a West German goldsmith.

Juliska The home ground, in Prague, of the Czech football club DUKLA PRAGUE. Capable of accommodating 28,800 fans, the stadium is rarely full, bearing in mind the club's links with the military establishment.

Juventus Italian football club, variously nicknamed the Grand Old Lady, the Fiancée of Italy, and the Zebras (after the team colours). Strip: black and white striped shirts with white shorts and socks. The similarity between the Juventus strip and that of the English club Notts County is more than accidental, for Juventus adopted their strip in 1906 after one of their members brought back a Notts County shirt acquired during a trip to the UK.

Juventus were born in Turin in 1897 and are historically the country's most popular and successful club. Called Juventus ('youth') because of the youthfulness of the players and fans who were first associated with the side, the team have an impressive tally of victories in both the Italian League and the Italian Cup and players with the team are allowed to wear two stars on their shirts to signify the winning of 20 League titles.

In the 1930s, when the club was adopted by the Italian Fascists, the team notched up no fewer than five consecutive SCUDETTO titles. In 1947 ten of the Italian national team played for Juventus. The club's international honours include the Super Cup (1984), the European Cup Winners' Cup (1984), the European Cup (1985), the World Club Championship (1985), and the UEFA Cup (1977 and 1990).

The side that represented the club in the early 1980s was probably the best Juventus have ever produced, including such star names as ZOFF, Cabrini, SCIREA, Gentile, Tardelli, and ROSSI (all of whom played for Italy) as well as such celebrated imports as PLATINI and Boniek. This side won nine major trophies in just six seasons, although their triumph in the Final of the European Cup against Liverpool in 1985 was marred by the death of 39 fans (*see* HEYSEL STADIUM DISASTER). Since 1990 the club has been based at the NEW COMUNALE STADIUM in Turin.

It was a terrible season. I would not have wished it on my worst enemy.

Luca Di Montezemolo, vice-president of Juventus, after the club failed to qualify for a European tournament for the first time in 28 years (1991)

K

K's Nickname of the English non-League football club KINGSTONIAN.

Kaiser, The Nickname of the great German footballer Franz BECKENBAUER, a reflection of the complete control he enjoyed and of the respect with which he was treated by fellow-players and fans alike (although his cool demeanour never inspired great affection).

Kangaroos Nickname of the Czech football club BOHEMIANS. The club acquired the nickname after an early tour of Australia, during which the players were presented with a gift of two kangaroos as souvenirs of their visit.

Katmandu disaster Football disaster, which took place in March 1988 and resulted in the deaths of between 95 and 175 people and a further 700 injuries. The tragedy happened at the National Stadium in Nepal and was precipitated when the crowd of 20,000 panicked during a hailstorm; most of the dead were trampled to death or crushed against the locked doors of the stadium as terrified spectators tried to leave the ground.

Keegan, Kevin (1951–) English forward, nicknamed the Mighty Mouse, who was hailed as the leading English player of his generation. Keegan's career did not begin particularly auspiciously: he was passed over by Doncaster's schoolboy selection committee but was finally accepted by Scunthorpe United at the age of 17. He played there for two years before his big break came when he attracted the attention of Bill SHANKLY, who immediately recognized his prodigious talent. Shankly quickly acquired Keegan (through a transfer that he later described as 'robbery with violence') and his new recruit rapidly emerged as one of the Kop's favourites.

An inside-forward, he enjoyed a major role in Liverpool's fabulous run in the 1970s, helping the side to clinch three League championships (1973, 1976, and 1977), the FA Cup in 1974, the UEFA Cup in 1973 and 1976, and the European Cup in 1977. At the same time he began a distinguished international career for England in 1973, becoming captain of the side in 1976 (in which year he was also elected Footballer of the Year) and earning in all 63 caps between 1973 and 1982 (when his exclusion by Bobby ROBSON was the cause of some controversy). He made only one appearance in the World Cup Finals, however, playing for just 27 minutes against Spain in 1982 in what was to be his last international.

In 1977 he transferred to SV Hamburg – where he acquired his nickname – and two years later he helped the team to capture the German Championship, before returning to the UK to join Southampton in 1980 and subsequently moving to Newcastle United in 1982. He retired as a player in 1983 after completing his 500th League game and later went into management at Newcastle. He was voted European Footballer of the Year in 1978 and again in 1979 and in 1982 was awarded an OBE.

Described by Ron GREENWOOD as 'the most modern of modern footballers', Keegan made the most of the opportunities that are offered to players in the modern game to earn substantial amounts of money from commercial endorsements.

> *The Julie Andrews of football.*
>
> Duncan Mackenzie (1981)

kemari Primitive version of football that was played in Japan around 600 BC. The ball was kicked rather than thrown and the game was played on a pitch measuring approximately 14 square metres. *See also* TSU-CHU.

Kempes, Mario Argentinian forward, who was the hero of Argentina's successful World Cup campaign of 1978. Kempes established his reputation while playing for Rosario Central and his performance in the 1974 World Cup won him a transfer to the Spanish club Valencia, where he immediately claimed the honour of top scorer in the domestic league. Argentina's great triumph of 1978 was due largely to Kempes, who scored no fewer than six goals, including two in the final against Holland. Subsequently he fell out with his coach DI STEFANO and went into something of a decline, though he helped Valencia to victory in the European Cup Winners' Cup in 1980. That same year he returned to his native country, where he was recruited by River Plate and regained his place in the national side, playing in the 1982 World Cup. He ended his career in Austria, having collected a total of 51 caps.

Kendall, Howard (1946–) English football manager and former player, who emerged as one of the top bosses in English football in the 1980s. Having spent his playing career with such clubs as Birmingham City, Stoke City, and Everton, appearing in the FA Cup Final in 1964 and collecting a League championship medal in 1970, he moved into management as player-manager of Blackburn Rovers in 1979. Subsequently he was rewarded with two Manager of the Year titles in acknowledgement of his leadership of Everton (1981–87). He then moved to Athletic Bilbao and also took control of Manchester City for a short time before returning to Everton in 1990. He resigned after a disappointing couple of seasons in 1993.

Kenilworth Road The home ground of the English football club LUTON TOWN. Kenilworth Road is just a short distance away from the club's first ground, Dallow Lane, and became their home in 1905 after they had spent three seasons at a site on Dunstable Road.

Events in the ground's history have included the destruction by fire of their Main Stand (1920), the opening in 1931 of a 'Bobbers' Stand' (where admission cost just a 'bob'), repeated attempts to expand the ground over a railway line that runs close to one corner, plans in the 1970s to move lock, stock, and barrel to Milton Keynes, the installation of an artificial pitch in 1985 (later removed), and the highly controversial implementation of a members-only scheme in 1985, which was in part a response to a disastrous riot by visiting Millwall fans that year. It was this riot (just weeks before the HEYSEL STADIUM DISASTER) that led to increasing involvement of Margaret Thatcher's Government in British football.

Features of the ground include the Joe Payne Lounge, dedicated to the scorer of a record ten goals against Bristol Rovers in 1936 (*see* TEN-GOAL).

Kent League English football league that was founded in 1894. Suspended in 1959, the league was revived in 1968. Outstanding clubs in the long history of the league have included Maidstone United, who dominated the early years and won three Championships in a row at the turn of the century, Northfleet United, Millwall Reserves, and more recently such sides as Chatham Town, Ramsgate Athletic, Sheppey United, and Sittingbourne.

Kenya Kenya joined FIFA in 1960 but have yet to make much impact in international competition. Strip: red, green, and white shirts, with red, green, and black shorts and socks.

Kettering Town English non-League football club, nicknamed the Poppies. Strip: all-red. Founded in 1876 and based at the Rockingham Road ground in Kettering, the Poppies have played in the Conference since 1979 and have for many years been Northamptonshire's leading non-League team. They were runners-up in the FA Trophy competition in 1979 and reached the fourth round of the FA Cup in 1989 (when they finally lost to Charlton Athletic). Famous names linked with the team have included Eddie HAPGOOD who was recruited by Kettering from Bristol Rovers in 1925 and finally moved to Arsenal two years later.

Khaki Cup Final The FA Cup Final of 1915. Fought at Old Trafford between Sheffield United and Chelsea (United winning), the meeting was somewhat less exuberant than in other years, being settled against the background of World War I, which had begun a year earlier. The match was dubbed the 'Khaki Cup Final' in reference to the large number of uniformed men in the crowd. As the Cup was awarded, Lord Derby reminded the crowd that a more serious contest must now be fought:

> You have played with one another and against one another for the Cup. It is now the duty of everyone to join with each other and play a sterner game for England.

It was another four years before the FA Cup was staged once more. *See* FOOTBALLERS' BATTALION.

Khomich, Alexei Soviet goalkeeper, nicknamed Tiger, who attracted much admiration in the West in 1945 when he demonstrated his great talent while playing for Dynamo Moscow during their famous

English tour that year. He is considered, with Lev YASHIN, one of the two great keepers to emerge from Soviet or Russian clubs.

kick and rush A playing strategy that was particularly associated with Wolverhampton Wanderers and their manager Stanley CULLIS in the 1950s. The kick and rush tactic depended on the 'long pass', with the ball being kicked far into the opponents' defence at the first opportunity and the attacking team following at full speed. When Cullis coached the Wolves team in the strategy many observers of the game were highly critical, arguing that such play prevented the full exercise of individual skills and made for boring football. Nonetheless, Wolves – led by Billy WRIGHT – won three League championships and two FA Cups between 1954 and 1960 before new schools of tactics made the kick and rush look unsophisticated.

> *Our forwards are not encouraged to parade their ability in an ostentatious fashion.*
>
> Stan Cullis

In more recent times similar tactics were used by Wimbledon to great effect as they powered their way up through the divisions in the 1980s, espousing what manager Graham TAYLOR preferred to call the 'long pass'.

> *Football wasn't meant to be run by two linesmen and air traffic control.*
>
> Tommy Docherty (1988)

kick-off The initial kick, from the centre-spot, with which a game starts or is restarted after a goal has been scored. The ball is technically in play once it has travelled the equivalent of its own circumference into the opponent's half of the field (no opposing player may be within ten yards of it). It was once traditional for visiting celebrities to take the first kick at major fixtures; even members of the royal family were known to do the honours at Cup Final games. Queen's Park claim to have been the first club to adopt the traditional 3 p.m. kick-off time.

Kidderminster Harriers English non-League football club, nicknamed the Harriers. Strip: red and white halved shirts with white shorts and socks. Founded in 1877 as an athletics club, the Harriers are based at the Aggborough ground in Kidder-

minster and play in the GM Vauxhall Conference, which they joined in 1983. Past honours include six Birmingham League championships and the FA Trophy in 1987. Stars with the club over the years have included centre-forward Billy Boswell in the 1930s, who was described as the 'Dixie Dean of non-league football'.

killing the ball Bringing a moving ball under control at one's feet – an essential skill for any player wishing to make a premeditated, accurate pass.

Kilmarnock Scottish football club, nicknamed Killie. Strip: blue and white striped shirts with blue shorts and socks. Founded in 1869 (making them the second oldest club in Scotland) and based at RUGBY PARK in Kilmarnock since 1899, the club were one of the teams in the first Scottish Cup tie (1873), which they lost 3–0 to Renton, for reasons suggested in a newspaper report of the game:

> *Kilmarnock were at a disadvantage through not being thoroughly conversant with Association rules, having formerly played the rugby game, and being one man short.*

They joined the League in 1895 and won the Scottish Cup in 1920 and 1929, but had to wait until the 1960s for their golden era. In 1965 they captured the First Division championship for the first time by one of the narrowest margins ever recorded, beating Heart of Midlothian into second place by 0.04 on goal average. Stars during this heady era included Tommy McLean.

Kilmarnock enjoyed their record victory in 1930, when they beat Paisley Academical 11–1; they suffered their worst defeat in 1938, losing 9–1 to Celtic. Alan Robertson holds the record for League appearances with the club, having played in 481 games between 1972 and 1988.

> *As he lay on the battlefield dying,*
> *With blood pouring out of his head,*
> *He propped himself up on one elbow,*
> *And these are the words that he said,*
> *KILMARNOCK! KILMARNOCK!*
> *We are the champions!*
>
> Supporters' song, a version of 'Red River Valley'

King Kenny Nickname of the Scottish footballer Kenny DALGLISH.

King of East Anglia Nickname of the English manager Bobby ROBSON, in reference to his inspired leadership of IPSWICH TOWN in the 1970s.

King of Old Trafford Nickname of the Scottish inside-forward Denis LAW, who spearheaded the Manchester United attack in the 1960s.

King of Soccer Nickname of Sir Stanley MATTHEWS, more often dubbed the Wizard of Dribble.

King of White Hart Lane Nickname of the English footballer Glenn HODDLE, who played a key role in the strong Totteham Hotspur side of the 1980s.

King's Lynn English non-League football club, nicknamed the Linnets. Strip: yellow shirts with blue shorts and socks. Founded in 1876 and based at the Walks Stadium, King's Lynn play in the Southern League.

King's Park Former Scottish League football club, who dropped out of the League in 1939 after 18 years. King's Park were based at Forthbank Park in Stirling and went out of existence after their ground was damaged by the only bomb dropped on Stirling during World War II. Amid accusations of financial irregularities involving the club, King's Park were wound up and a new side – STIRLING ALBION – were established at ANNFIELD PARK. Players with King's Park included Alex Haddon, who in 1932 scored a remarkable series of five hat-tricks in consecutive matches in the Second Division.

Kingsbury Town English non-League football club. Strip: all white. Founded in 1927 and based at the Silver Jubilee Park, the team play in the Isthmian League.

Kingstonian English non-League football club, nicknamed the K's. Strip: red and white hooped shirts with black shorts and socks. Founded in 1919 (when Old Kingstonians and Kingston Town merged), the K's are based at the Kingsmeadow Stadium in Kingston-Upon-Thames and play in the Isthmian League. Past honours have included two Athenian League championships, the FA Amateur Cup in 1933, and the Isthmian League title in 1934 and 1937. For a time in the 1980s the club were without a home, hence the title of the club's fanzine *NHS* (short for 'No Home Stadium').

Kinnaird, Lord Alfred (1847–1923) English football administrator, who was one of the most influential pioneers in the early history of the Football Association. Tall and bearded, Kinnaird was highly respected as a player, taking part in an unsurpassed total of nine FA Cup Finals and winning five Cup Winners' medals (with Wanderers and Old Etonians). Subsequently he became a prominent member of the FA, rising eventually to the post of president. His unique contribution to the game was marked in 1911 when the second FA Cup itself was given to him.

Kippax The Kippax Street end of Manchester City's Maine Road ground where the most loyal of City's fans congregate.

Knowsley United English non-League football club. Strip: all red. Founded in 1983 and based at Alt Park in Huyton, Merseyside, United play in the Northern Premier League.

Kocsis, Sandor (1929–) Hungarian forward, nicknamed Golden Head, who was a star with the celebrated Hungarian national team of the early 1950s (*see* MAGNIFICENT MAGYARS). Kocsis, who played at home for Ferencváros and then for Honvéd, first appeared for his country in 1948 and in the 1954 World Cup won acclaim as the tournament's top scorer (with 11 goals). His high-scoring rate could be attributed to his unrivalled skill in the air. Having collected 68 caps playing for Hungary (in the course of which he scored 75 goals) he escaped the country during the troubles of 1956 and subsequently played for the Spanish club Barcelona.

Kop Nickname of several stands at British football grounds, and sometimes, by extension, of a team's most loyal supporters. The most famous Kop is, of course, that at Liverpool's Anfield home and fans of the club – who enjoy a reputation of being among the most passionate and intimidating bands of supporters in the world – are frequently dubbed 'The Kop':

> . . . *Spion Kop is one of Liverpool Football Club's prized possessions, and in all seriousness, I am certain matches have been won through the vocal efforts of its regular patrons.*

Matt Busby, *My Story* (1985)

The residents of Liverpool's Kop are particularly celebrated for their resilient sense of humour, which tempers their total commitment to their team. Other examples include the Kops at the Racecourse Ground, Bloomfield Road, Windsor Park, and that at Arsenal's former Manor Ground home, which vies with that at Anfield (first mentioned in 1906) as the earliest instance of a Kop.

Originally these Kops were simply mounds upon which the most committed fans congregated. The name Kop was taken from that of Spion Kop, the hill in South Africa that was the scene of a bloody engagement between British troops (mainly from regiments based in Lancashire) and entrenched Boer forces on 24 January 1900. 322 British soldiers (many of whom hailed from Liverpool itself) died in the assault on the hill as a result of bungling by their generals (commanded by General Sir Redvers Buller) who had intended a breakthrough of the Boer defences in order to relieve besieged Ladysmith.

That acre of massacre, that complete shambles.

Winston Churchill, reporting the original disaster

The Kop at Anfield was so called at the suggestion of a journalist, Ernest Edwards, in 1906 as a tribute to the city's fallen. Appropriately enough, 'Spion Kop' means 'look-out' in Afrikaans.

Kopa, Raymond (Raymond Kopazewski; 1931–) French forward, whose reputation as the finest French player of his generation earned him the nicknames Little Napoleon and the French Stanley MATTHEWS. Of Polish parentage, he proved an exceptionally talented centre-forward and played for Angers and Reims before transferring to Real Madrid, but returned to Reims (where he formed a brilliant partnership with Just FONTAINE) three years after he and his family became homesick. Highlights of his international career included his contribution to a 7–1 French victory over Greece in the 1958 European Championship and appearances in two European Cup Finals (with Reims and Real Madrid). He was voted European Footballer of the Year in 1959.

Krankl, Hans (1953–) Austrian centre-forward, who emerged as Austria's leading goalscorer in the 1970s. Krankl began his career with Rapid Vienna and became a pillar of the team, his achievements including a record-equalling 36 goals in the League championship in 1973–74. He became a regular choice for his country and shone in the 1978 World Cup. Highlights of his international career included the six goals he scored in a game against Malta in 1977. Krankl eventually left Rapid for Barcelona, where he was intended to inherit the role played by Johan CRUYFF, but he returned to Rapid three years later (though in the meantime he did score the decisive goal that won the Spaniards the European Cup Winners' Cup in 1979). After his retirement as a player, he became coach of the Viennese side Wiener SC.

Kubala, Ladislav (1927–) Hungarian-born forward, who had a long international career, occupying a place in the record books as the only man to play for three nations (Hungary, Czechoslovakia, and Spain). Having established his reputation with Ferencváros, he won six caps for Hungary before moving to Czechoslovakia, with whom he won another 11. In 1950 he defected to the West, joined Barcelona as a naturalized Spaniard, and went on to win another 19 caps with the Spanish national team. Later he moved to Espanōl, with whom he reached a European Cup Final, and also played for a time in the USA before taking up coaching, inheriting control of the Spanish national team in the 1970s and remaining in the job for 11 years.

Kuwait The Kuwaitis joined FIFA in 1962 and enjoyed their greatest success to date in 1982, when the team qualified for the World Cup Finals for the first time. They lost their first match, against France, 4–1 (confusion reigned as the team thought the game was over after someone in the crowd blew a whistle), but put up some stiff resistance to England before going down 1–0. Strip: blue shirts, white shorts, and blue socks.

L

Labruna, Angel (1918–83) Argentinian inside-forward, who was one of the star strikers who made River Plate a top South American club in the 1940s (*see* MACHINE). Labruna spent some 22 years with River Plate, resisting all attempts to lure him to Europe, and made 36 international appearances. After his retirement as a player (having scored nearly 500 goals) he served as coach to a number of clubs, including River Plate, who won six Argentine titles under his guidance.

laces, hitting the ball off the Technical term for a shot in which the ball makes contact with the top of the boot rather than the toe or sides. The shot is most often used for long passes out of defence or across the pitch.

Lambs Nickname of the English non-League football club TAMWORTH, in referance to their home at the Lamb Ground.

Lancaster City English non-League football club, nicknamed the Blues in reference to the team colours. Strip: all blue. Founded in 1905 and based at the Giant Axe ground, Lancaster City play in the Northern Premier League.

Lancaster Gate The home of the Football Association in west London. Features of the FA's headquarters at 16 Lancaster Gate include the Centenary Room, which contains such items of historical interest as a replica of the second FA Cup. The FA moved into the building in 1972 having previously (1929–72) had its home at 22 Lancaster Gate (a former hotel). Before that the organization was based from 1910 to 1929 at 42 Russell Square (which was reputed to have its own ghost), and before that at 104 High Holborn (1902–10), 61 Chancery Lane (1892–1902), 51 Holborn Viaduct (1885–92), and 28 Paternoster Row (1881–85). Until 1881 the FA had no permanent home but conducted its business at meetings at the Freemasons Tavern, the Kennington Oval, the offices of the *Sportsman* paper and at the Cricket Press, both on Ludgate Hill. Rulings enacted by the FA are often said to be handed down by Lancaster Gate.

Lansdowne Road The headquarters of the Irish Rugby Football Union, which in recent years has also served as the senior venue for Irish football internationals. With Ireland enjoying a new lease of life in such events as the 1988 European Championship and the 1990 World Cup, the national team has increasingly appeared at Lansdowne Road in preference to the more modest Dalymount Park.

As a venue for rugby, the stadium opened in 1878 and can claim to be the oldest surviving international rugby venue in the world; it is also, surprisingly, the second oldest venue still in use for international football, having hosted a visit by the England team back in 1900.

Laos Laos joined FIFA in 1952, but have yet to make much impact in international competition. Strip: red shirts, white shorts, and blue socks.

Largest Hands in Soccer Goalkeeping cliché particularly associated with the Irish keeper Pat JENNINGS.

late tackle Euphemism for a dangerous tackle, in which the attacking player challenges for the ball after the victim has already disposed of it. The challenger invariably claims it was a legitimate attempt to gain possession; the victim often has to nurse bruised shins (or worse). Such tackles became more common in the 1970s and 1980s with the coming of the era of the professional foul, although hard play was always a feature of the English game in particular.

Latics (1) Nickname of the English football club OLDHAM ATHLETIC, from an abbreviation of the word Athletic.

(2) Nickname of the English football club WIGAN ATHLETIC, from an abbreviation of the word Athletic.

Latin Cup International club tournament that was inaugurated in 1949. The Latin Cup was contested by clubs from a number of western European nations and was one of the first such competitions to prosper, with Spain, France, Portugal, and Italy all taking part. The tournament, which ran on a knock-out basis, was held every four years until 1957, by which time it had effectively been replaced by the European Cup. It was while en route to a Latin Cup match in 1949 that the FC Torino side representing Italy that year perished in the Superga air crash (Torino's replacement side still managed to reach the Final of the tournament before losing 3–1 to Sporting Lisbon).

Lato, Grzegorz (1950–   ) Polish forward, who achieved international fame in 1974 when he became top scorer in the World Cup that year (with seven goals). He established his reputation with Stal Mielec and made his debut for the national side in 1971. After the 1978 World Cup he was allowed to move to the Belgian club Lokeren and it was thought that his international career was over. He reappeared, however, for Poland in the 1982 World Cup, when he notched up his 100th cap, and played his last game for his country in 1984, after which he moved to the Mexican club Atlante.

Laugardalsvöllur The senior football venue in Iceland, which is also the most northerly football stadium in Europe. The Icelandic footballing tradition began in 1895 after a Scotsman brought the game to this icy outpost. Work on the Laugardalsvöllur stadium started after World War II and was completed in 1957. Since then it has hosted many international and domestic matches, although it is now home to only one local side, Fram.

Law, Denis (1940–   ) Scottish inside-forward, nicknamed the King of Old Trafford, who was one of the major stars in the classic Manchester United side of the 1960s and early 1970s. Born in Aberdeen, Law began his professional career with Huddersfield Town in 1957 and made his debut for Scotland in 1958, scoring in his first game. He was an unlikely star, frail and bespectacled, and when he first arrived at Huddersfield station officials sent to meet him failed to recognize their new acquisition. He soon established a reputation, however, as a resilient and aggressive player as well as earning a name for himself as a lively socialite.

In 1960 he moved to Manchester City

and a year later to Torino before being lured to Manchester United in 1962 by Matt BUSBY (for a record transfer fee). In 1963 he not only scored for United in the FA Cup Final but was also one of the players selected to play for the rest of the world against England to celebrate the 100th anniversary of the FA; playing alongside such fellow-greats as PELÉ, EUSÉBIO, PUSKAS, and DI STEFANO, he scored the side's only goal and turned in the best performance of them all.

He was elected European Footballer of the Year in 1964 and subsequently contributed to United's victory in two League championships and the European Cup (1968), forming a classic partnership with George BEST and Bobby CHARLTON and winning admirers for his flamboyance and cheery personality.

> We'll drink a drink, a drink
> To Denis the King, the King, the King,
> 'Cos he's the leader of our football team,
> He is the greatest centre-forward,
> That the world has ever seen.

Supporters' song, to the tune of 'Lily the Pink'

In 1973 Law returned to Manchester City and there had to undergo the trauma in 1974 of scoring the crucial goal against United that sent his old club down into the Second Division (the match ended early as fans burst on to the pitch); Law himself later admitted 'I have seldom felt so depressed as I did that weekend'. It was also the last goal he was to score in first-class football. That same year he notched up the last of his 55 international caps and retired to become a commentator, with a career total of 300 goals in 585 club games. His achievements as a player include a record five hat-tricks scored in European competition.

> Busby knew how important he was. When Denis was doubtful the boss would practically be on his hands and knees hoping he could play.

Harry Gregg, *The European Cup 1955–80* (John Motson and John Rowlinson, 1980)

> And when he's hurtling for the goal,
> I know he's got to score.
> Defences may stop normal men –
> They can't stop Denis Law.

Gareth Owen

> Denis Law could dance on egg-shells.

Bill Shankly

Lawton, Tommy (1919–   ) English forward, who ranks among the most distinguished players England has ever produced.

A centre-forward, he was considered a master in the air and was strong in every aspect of the game. Lawton made his League debut for Burnley in 1936 and shortly afterwards made the move to Everton. He made his England debut two years later, scoring against Wales in his very first game, and in 1939 played a key role in Everton's League championship triumph. After the war, he moved to Chelsea, while in 1947 he joined Notts County for a record £20,000. He won the last of his 23 caps in 1948 (having scored 22 goals in international competition) and in 1952 transferred to Brentford, where he served as player-manager. He signed for Arsenal in 1953 and two years later fulfilled the role of player-manager with Kettering Town. In 1957 he was appointed manager of Notts County, but was sacked a year later and retired from the game to run a public house.

lay off To pass the ball to a team mate who may then have a chance to score. Laying off the ball is one of the principal roles of the midfielders, who may receive the ball from the defence, control it, and then pass it to whichever forward is in the best position to shoot for goal.

Layer Road The home ground of the English football club COLCHESTER UNITED. The ground, formerly used by the army, became the home of amateurs Colchester Town in 1909 and of United on their formation in 1937. Spectators at the Layer Road End (the terracing of which is said to have been constructed by prisoners-of-war) get about as close to the action as it is physically possible anywhere in professional football, the back of the goal itself actually cutting into the stand. The capacity of Layer Road was drastically cut due to safety considerations in the 1980s, until only 4000 spectators could be accommodated.

Leafe Nickname of the English non-League football club WHYTELEAFE.

league The organization of eligible football clubs into a league, which operates on the basis that all member teams will play each other during the course of a season in pursuit of a championship title. The oldest league of all is England's Football League though several other minor British leagues are now around a hundred years old. Most centenaries of these leagues have been observed with appropriate celebrations. Not all have gone according to plan, however: in 1989 the Herefordshire Football

League had to cancel elaborate plans for a celebratory dinner-dance to mark the league's centenary when it was discovered that the organization was in fact only 90 years old.

The smallest league in the world is that in the Scilly Isles; the league has just two members, who play each other every week. Worldwide, Celtic, the Bulgarian club CSKA Sofia, and Hungary's MTK Budapest have all won nine successive League titles (CSKA Sofia have a record 26 postwar Championships to their credit).

League Cup English Cup competition that was inaugurated in 1960 at the instigation of the Football League Secretary Alan HARDAKER, although the idea of such a competition between members of the League had been voiced as early as 1892. The tournament had an ill-starred beginning, however, with six major clubs refusing to take part, arguing that their programmes were already full and that the competition was not worthy of serious consideration – hence the 'Mickey Mouse Cup' tag applied to the tournament by Liverpool in particular.

The first two seasons were remarkable for the fact that the absence of some of the strongest teams in the country allowed otherwise undistinguished sides to reach the later stages of what purported to be a national competition – Rotherham United and Rochdale taking the runners-up position in 1961 and 1962 respectively and Swindon Town winning it in 1963. Subsequently, however, the decision that the winners of the League Cup would qualify automatically for European competitions prompted the senior clubs to take the tournament more seriously, as well as attracting lavish sponsorship deals; entry became compulsory in the early 1970s.

The Cup became one of the most prestigious domestic competitions, being variously known as the Milk Cup (1982–86), the Littlewoods Cup (1987–89), the Rumbelows Cup (1990–92), and the Coca-Cola Cup (1993) in acknowledgement of the organizations providing finance for the tournament.

In the first 23 years of the competition it has been won by 23 different clubs. The most successful teams in the history of the League Cup are Liverpool, who have won it four times in succession (1981–84), and Nottingham Forest, who have also won it four times (1978, 1979, 1989, and 1990). Curiosities in the Cup's history have included the appearance of Forest's goalkeeper Chris Woods in the 1978 Final, when he became the first player to participate in a Wembley Final before making his League debut.

The trophy itself is one of the oldest cups competed for in football anywhere in the world, having been made by a celebrated Victorian silversmith back in 1895 for use in a competition between shipyard workers in the north-east and then put away in a locked cupboard, where it gathered dust for many years until being rediscovered.

If the FA Cup is football's Ascot then the League Cup is its Derby Day.

Alan Hardaker

League's Most Celebrated Enforcer
Nickname of the English Football League secretary Alan HARDAKER.

Leatherhead English non-League football club, nicknamed the Tanners in reference to the team's formal name. Strip: green shirts, white shorts, and green socks. Founded in 1946 and based at Fetcham Grove in Leatherhead, the club play in the Isthmian League.

Lebanon The Lebanon joined FIFA in 1935 but have yet to establish an international reputation. Strip: red and white shirts, white shorts, and red and white socks.

Lee, Francis (1944–   ) English forward, who was a star with Manchester City and England in the 1960s and 1970s. Lee earned a total of 27 caps for England and also turned out for such clubs as Bolton Wanderers and Derby County at different points in his career. Lee's recruitment to play football in South Africa in the 1970s was somewhat contentious but his contribution did not prevent the South African League being disbanded in 1978.

During his time with Manchester City he acquired the nickname 'Lee Won Pen' for the number of penalties he managed to 'win' for the team. It was even rumoured that he was being specially coached by manager Malcolm Allison to fake injury from foul play (*see* DYING SWAN). Whatever the truth behind the rumours, Lee certainly won more than his fair share of penalties (as many as a dozen in one season).

Leeds City Former English football club expelled from the League in 1919. City were formed in 1904 and moved into Elland Road where, in 1912, they were joined by their new manager Herbert CHAPMAN.

Before the great manager could establish himself at the club, however, proceedings were interrupted by World War I and the club's affairs were put in the hands of the receiver.

Soon after the war the revived club was rocked by a financial scandal in which it was alleged that certain illegal payments had been made to players during the war. When the club refused to hand over its accounts for inspection, City were found guilty of 'irregular practices' and summarily expelled from the League. The side's remaining fixtures that season were inherited by Port Vale and Leeds United was formed to succeed the disgraced club.

We will have no nonsense, the football stable must be cleansed.

John McKenna, League president, on City's expulsion

Leeds Road The home ground of the English football club HUDDERSFIELD TOWN. Leeds Road has been the home of Huddersfield Town ever since the club's formation in 1908; previously the site had hosted major local football matches as far back as 1899. At the time Huddersfield first occupied the ground, facilities were somewhat spartan and the players themselves were obliged to use an old tramcar for their dressing-room. Archibald Leitch designed new stands in 1910 and the ground was reopened a year later. Financial crises after World War I led to plans for the club to move to Leeds to share Elland Road but a campaign by fans to keep the team where they were was successful and the club found a new lease of life under their new manager Herbert CHAPMAN.

Events in the ground's history since then have included the destruction of Leitch's stand in a disastrous fire in 1950, the arrival and subsequent vandalization of the first electric scoreboard to be seen at a British ground, and the loss of two newly erected floodlights in a gale in 1962.

Leeds United English football club, nicknamed United or otherwise known as the Peacocks. Strip: all white (adopted under the management of Don REVIE in imitation of the strip worn by Real Madrid). United came into being in 1919 on the disbanding of Leeds City after the club, suspected of making illegal payments to players and refusing to allow the League access to its books, was expelled from the League. Initially, it was planned that Leeds United would merge with financially hard-pressed

Huddersfield Town, but in the event Leeds kept their separate identity and joined the League in 1920 as members of the Second Division.

Just four years later United captured the Second Division championship to win promotion to the top flight; they have never since dropped lower than the Second Division. Little of note occurred at the club's home at ELLAND ROAD between then and the late 1960s, when United entered their golden era – though John CHARLES was an inspiration with the team in the 1950s. With Don Revie as manager from 1961, the team returned to the First Division via the Second Division championship in 1964 and were subsequently transformed into one of the most formidable in the land, drawing on the talents of such players as Jack CHARLTON, Bobby Collins, Johnny GILES, Peter LORIMER, Allan Clarke, and the fiery Billy BREMNER.

Revie's restyled United won their first major honours in 1968 with victory in the League Cup and the European Fairs Cup; a year later they were League champions with a record total of 67 points (many of which were won during a run of 34 First Division matches in which they did not suffer a single defeat). They were also runners-up in the League in 1965, 1966, 1970, 1971, and 1972 and in the FA Cup in 1965, 1970, and 1973 (in fact, having battled to the final stages of no fewer than 17 competitions, they won just six major honours in these peak years).

In 1970 they underlined their status as the most powerful team in the country by threatening to achieve a remarkable treble of the European Cup, the FA Cup, and the League championship; it all went wrong at the last minute, however, with defeat in the semi-finals of the European Cup, against Chelsea in the FA Cup Final, and a runners-up position in the League behind Everton.

Critics accused Leeds of adopting a cynically aggressive style of play and their supporters were condemned as the worst behaved in the League, but no one could deny the effectiveness of their tactics on the field, which culminated in 1972 with triumph in the FA Cup (though they failed by the narrowest of margins to carry off the double with victory in the League championship as well). Other honours won under Revie included a second European Fairs Cup title (1971).

Revie left United to take over England shortly after and Brian CLOUGH – one of the critics of the side – stayed for only 44 days as his successor.

Despite the disruption, the club stormed to a second League championship in 1974 and a year later reached the Final of the European Cup, though a riot by Leeds fans after the game led to a three-year suspension from European football.

Subsequently the success came to an end and the club became more used to hitting the headlines through the violent behaviour of its fans. Facing severe financial difficulties, they dropped out of the First Division in 1982 but found consolation in the management of Howard Wilkinson, who saw them back into the top flight in 1990 and brought them their third League championship in 1992, after which they became founder members of the Premier League. Stars of the club in recent years have included captain Gordon Strachan.

Leeds enjoyed their record victory in 1969, when they beat the Norwegian club Lyn 10–0; they suffered their worst defeat in 1934, losing 8–1 to Stoke City. Jack Charlton holds the record for League appearances with the team, having played in 629 games between 1953 and 1973. *See also* MARCHING ON TOGETHER.

When I was just a little boy,
I asked my mother 'What should I be?
Should I be Chelsea?
Should I be Leeds?'
Here's what she said to me . . .
'Wash your mouth out son,
And go get your father's gun,
And shoot all the Chelsea scum,
Leeds are number one.

Supporters' song, to the tune of 'Que Sera, Sera'

Leek Town English non-League football club, nicknamed the Blues in reference to the team colours. Strip: blue shirts and socks and white shorts. Founded in 1945 as Abbey Green Rovers and later renamed Leek Lowe Hamil the club acquired its present name in 1951. Based at Harrison Park, Leek Town play in the Northern Premier League.

Leicester City English football club, nicknamed the Foxes, or the Filberts, after their ground. Strip: all blue. The club were founded in 1884 by old boys from Wyggeston School and other young footballers at a meeting in a house situated on the Roman Fosse Way, which inspired the team's initial name Leicester Fosse; members of the club paid 9d each as a subscription and another 9d to raise cash for a ball.

Leicester settled at their permanent home in FILBERT STREET in 1891 and have spent much of their history in the Second Division, with regular forays into the top flight. Honours collected by the club include the Second Division championship in 1925, 1937, 1954, 1957, 1971, and 1980. The only other major triumph was their capture of the League Cup in 1964, although they have appeared as runners-up in no fewer than four FA Cup Finals (1949, 1961, 1963, 1969).

Stars with the club over the years have included forwards Arthur Chandler (the first player to notch up 100 consecutive League and Cup appearances for the club and still remembered for scoring in 16 consecutive games in the 1924–25 season) in the 1920s and Arthur ROWLEY in the 1950s, goalkeeper Gordon BANKS and wing-half Frank McLintock in the 1960s, goalkeeper Peter SHILTON in the 1970s, and forwards Gary LINEKER and Alan Smith in the 1980s. Arthur Rowley, holder of a record for the greatest career total of League goals, established a record for the club when he scored no fewer than 44 goals in a single season.

The club's record victory stands at 10–0 against Portsmouth in 1928; their worst defeat was against Nottingham Forest in 1909, when they lost 12–0. Adam Black holds the record for League appearances with the club, having played in 528 games between 1920 and 1935. Fans of the club are known for their singing of 'When You're Smiling', first heard at Filbert Street in 1979, which is accompanied with synchronized hand waving.

Leicester Senior League English football league that was founded in 1896. Suspended between 1930 and 1934, it has been dominated by such teams as Leicester Fosse Reserves (winners of four titles), Hinckley United (holders of three titles), Leicester City's 'A' team, and Enderby Town.

Leicester United English non-League football club, nicknamed United. Strip: red and white striped shirts, black shorts with red and white trim, and black socks with two red hoops. Founded in 1898 and based at Winchester Road in Leicester, United play in the Southern League.

Leith Athletic Former Scottish football club, which disappeared from the League in 1953, having been a member since 1891. Based at Bank Park and subsequently at Beechwood Park and Old Meadowbank, Athletic finally went out of existence in 1955.

Lenin Stadium The home ground, in Moscow, of the Russian football club SPARTAK MOSCOW. The Central Lenin Stadium, opened in 1956, claims to be the largest and most popular sports complex in the world and comprises 140 separate sports installations. Named after the Soviet revolutionary leader, the stadium has frequently played host to international football as well as to such other events as the 1980 Olympics. Plagued increasingly by hooliganism in recent years, the stadium was the scene of one of the worst mass tragedies in football history in 1982 (*see* LENIN STADIUM DISASTER).

Lenin Stadium disaster Football disaster that took place at Moscow's LENIN STADIUM in 1982. The circumstances of the tragedy, in which at least 69 people and possibly as many as 340 lost their lives, remain shrouded in mystery and it was, indeed, not until 1989 that the Soviet press admitted there had been a substantial tragedy. It seems that the catastrophe occurred when crowds leaving just before the end of a match between Spartak Moscow and the Dutch side Haarlem tried to get back into the stadium via an icy ramp when a late goal was scored.

Leonidas da Silva (1913–) Celebrated Brazilian centre-forward, variously nicknamed the Black Diamond and the Rubber Man, who was the star of the 1938 World Cup, scoring four goals in Brazil's celebrated 6–5 victory over Poland that year. Although Brazil failed to win the competition (making the mistake of resting the Black Diamond at the semi-final stage), Leonidas – considered the finest Brazilian footballer of his generation – ended it as highest scorer in the tournament with a total of seven goals. He was particularly respected for his skill in the air and widely acknowledged to be the master of the spectacular bicycle kick. His clubs included Bonsucesso, Nacional, Vasco da Gama, Botafogo, Flamengo, and São Paulo.

Leppings Lane *See* HILLSBOROUGH DISASTER.

Lesotho Lesotho joined FIFA in 1964 but have yet to make much impact in international competition. Strip: blue, white, and green shirts, white shorts, and blue and white socks.

Letná Stadium The home ground (in English, the Summer Stadium) of the leading Czech football club SPARTA PRAGUE. The current stadium was built in the 1930s to replace an earlier venue, which was completely destroyed by fire in 1934 (with the loss of 10,000 sporting trophies).

Levski Gerena Stadium Bulgarian football stadium, situated in Sofia and home since 1959 to LEVSKI SPARTAK. Among the more remarkable scenes to be witnessed at the stadium was the 1985 Cup Final between Levski Spartak and CSKA when the players became involved in a mass brawl in the players' tunnel. The Government took a dim view of the affair and ordered both teams to change their names as a punishment; accordingly, Levski Spartak played as Vitosha for four years before reviving their old name in 1989 and CSKA became Sredec.

Levski Spartak Bulgarian football club. Strip: all blue. Founded in 1914 and based at the LEVSKI GERENA STADIUM, Levski Spartak are indisputably the most popular club in the country, with some 16 League championships and 19 Cup victories to their credit. In 1985, however, riots during the Bulgarian Cup Final brought the club into disgrace and as punishment the team were disbanded and obliged to adopt a new identity, playing as Vitosha. The old name was restored in 1989.

Lewes English non-League football club, nicknamed the Rooks. Strip: red and black hooped shirts, black shorts, and red socks. Founded in 1885 and based at the Dripping Pan ground in Lewes, the club play in the Isthmian League.

Leyton Orient English football club, nicknamed the O's. Strip: red shirts, white shorts, and red socks. The O's have their roots in the Glyn Cricket Club formed at Homerton Theological College in 1881, whose members played football in the winter months. The side subsequently attracted players who were employees with the Orient shipping line and thus the team became the Orient Football Club in 1888. Since then the team has been known as Clapton Orient (1898–1946), Leyton Orient (1946–66 and 1987–), and simply Orient (1966–87). Based at a succession of grounds in their early history, the side joined the League in 1905 and since 1937 have occupied the BRISBANE ROAD ground in Leyton.

Leyton have a relatively undistinguished record, though they captured Third Division titles in 1956 and 1970. During World War I players with the club formed the largest single contingent of football recruits in the Footballers' Battalion. They have twice survived severe financial crises (in the 1930s and again in 1967); the first crisis ended when Arsenal decided to make the club their nursery club for a time, while the second was overcome with the aid of a major fundraising effort.

The team's golden era was in the early 1960s, when they enjoyed a brief visit (1962–63) to the First Division, and again in the 1970s, when they did well in the FA Cup (reaching the quarter-finals in 1971 and the semi-finals in 1978).

Orient's record victory stands at 8–0, a score they managed against Crystal Palace in 1955, against Rochdale in 1987, and against Colchester United in 1988. They suffered their worst defeat against Aston Villa in 1929, when they lost 8–0. Peter Allen holds the record for League appearances with the club, having played in 432 matches between 1965 and 1978.

We're all mad, we're insane,
We eat Mars bars on the train.

Supporters' song

Liberia Liberia joined FIFA in 1962 but have yet to establish a reputation in international competition. Strip: red shirts, white shorts, and red socks.

libero Italian term, meaning 'free', for a player who operates as a sweeper. The term was first introduced by Karl Rappan, manager of the Swiss national team in the late 1940s, as he developed the concept of the *catenaccio* defensive strategy.

Libya Libya joined FIFA in 1963 but have yet to make much impact in international competition. Strip: green shirts, white shorts, and green socks.

Liddell, Billy (1922–) Scottish-born winger, who was renowned both for his sportsmanship and for his key role in the Liverpool team of the 1940s and 1950s. Described as 'a gentleman who scared defenders stiff', he was the side's star striker. Born in Dunfermline, Scotland, Liddell emerged as one of the most effective wingers of all time in the years immediately after World War II and played a key role in Liverpool's capture of the League championship in 1947. Subsequently Liddell – who was also capped 28 times for Scotland and was (with Stanley MATTHEWS) the only player to be called up to represent the Great Britain sides in both 1947 and 1955 – inspired the team over two decades, although the club had to wait until the arrival of Bill SHANKLY before the team's efforts were to be crowned with trophy success.

Liddell himself retired in 1961, having scored 229 goals in 537 games for Liverpool, and went on to become a youth worker, lay preacher, and Justice of the Peace. He is still considered by many to have been the finest player ever to represent the club.

Liddellpool Nickname of the LIVERPOOL team of the 1940s and 1950s, when winger (and later centre-forward) Billy LIDDELL was the side's star striker.

Liechtenstein Liechtenstein joined FIFA in 1974 but have yet to make much impact in international competition. Strip: blue shirts, red shorts, and blue socks.

Liedholm, Nils (1922–   ) Swedish forward, who was one of the celebrated Gre-No-Li line-up of strikers who played for Sweden in the 1948 Olympics and subsequently for AC Milan in the 1950s. He collected a total of 23 caps and played in the 1958 World Cup Final. After retiring as a player he embarked on a managerial career with several Italian clubs.

life. Football's not a matter of life and death. It's much more important than that The most famous of the witticisms associated with the legendary Liverpool manager Bill SHANKLY. Shankly's devotion to the game was undoubted and other famous figures have wholeheartedly endorsed his view. Manchester United manager Dave Sexton admitted in 1980; 'In a way, I see sport as being something even above real life', while Sunderland boss Alan Brown put it more strongly: 'Soccer is the biggest thing that's happened in creation, bigger than any 'ism' you can name.'

Other distinguished managers and players have seen the game differently. In the wake of the Hillsborough disaster Kenny DALGLISH said 'football is irrelevant', while Ruud GULLIT was quick to stress 'It's not my whole life', and Dundee United boss Jim McLean observed 'At the end of the day, it's not the end of the world'. France's Maxime Bossis echoed Shankly's famous comment even as he corrected it in 1986: 'Football is important but life is important too'.

> Then strip lads, and to it, though sharp be the weather,

> And if, by mischance you should happen to fall,
> There are worse things in life than a tumble on the heather,
> And life is itself a game of football.

Sir Walter Scott (1815)

> Football can be no more than a minor corner of any balanced life.

John Arlott

> Every dressing room should have a poster that says: 'There is more to life than just football and football management'.

Gerry Francis, Bristol Rovers manager (1988)

> I believe Bill Shankly died of a broken heart after he stopped managing Liverpool and saw them go on to even greater success without him. Giving your whole life to a football club is a sad mistake.

John Giles (1984)

Light Blues Nickname of a number of football clubs, in reference to their team strip, among them the Spanish football club Celta de Vigo. See also SKY BLUES.

Lilleshall Hall The site of the FA's main training centre and home of the Sports Council's National Sports Centre. Lilleshall Hall began its life as a sports centre as a result of a fundraising effort in South Africa in thanks for the UK's assistance during World War II, and was originally opened in 1951.

Lilywhites or **Lillywhites** Nickname of a number of British football clubs, in reference to their predominantly white strips. They include BERKHAMSTED TOWN, BROMLEY, DOVER ATHLETIC, MARINE, MOSSLEY, PRESTON NORTH END, RHYL, and TELFORD UNITED.

Lima football disaster Football disaster that claimed many lives in Lima, Peru, on 24 May 1964. The tragedy took place during a qualifying game for the Olympics between Peru and Argentina when, towards the end of the match, an equalizing goal by Peru was disallowed. A riot broke out at once and the police responded by firing into the air. In the ensuing panic 318 people were killed and another 500 seriously injured as the crowd rushed to leave the ground, leading to a stampede.

Lincoln City English football club, nicknamed the Imps. Strip: red and white striped shirts, black shorts, and red socks with white trim. Founded in 1883 (as successors to an older club dating back to 1861) and based since 1894 at SINCIL BANK, the club were founder members of the Midland League in 1889 and of the Second Division in 1892. They dropped out of the League in 1908–09, 1911–12, and in 1920 and subsequently joined the newly formed Third Division (North) in 1921.

They divided their time over the next 42 years between the Second and Third Divisions before dropping into the Fourth Division for the first time in 1962. In 1958 relegation from the Second Division to the Third seemed certain when it was realized that the Imps – then without a win in four months – had to win every one of their last six games to stay up; incredibly, they did it and avoided relegation by just one point. They won promotion from the bottom division in 1976 and 1981 but in 1987 became the first club to be automatically relegated to the Conference (*see* BRYN). A year later they returned to the Fourth Division at the first attempt.

Famous names at Sincil Bank over the years have included Graham TAYLOR, who was manager there in the 1970s. Another manager of the club, Willie Bell, attracted the headlines in 1978 when he resigned from Lincoln in order to take over the management of the US Campus Crusade for Christ, the team of a religious sect whose aim was to convert sportsmen to Christianity.

Lincoln enjoyed a record victory in 1951, beating Crewe Alexandra 11–1; they suffered their worst defeat back in 1895, when they lost 11–3 against Manchester City. Other memorable games have included a 9–1 thrashing administered to Halifax Town in 1932, when striker Frank Keetley knocked in six goals in just 21 minutes. Tony Emery holds the record for League appearances with the club, having played in 402 games between 1946 and 1959.

> Division Three, kiss my arse,
> Division Four, we're home at last!
>
> Supporters' song, on the club's relegation

Lineker, Gary (1960–) English forward, who became one of the most successful goalscorers of his generation. He began his career with his home club, Leicester City, in 1978 and just two years later helped the team win the Second Division title. Relegation followed a year later, but the 26 goals he scored in the 1983 season consolidated a growing reputation and in 1984 he was called up by England for the first time. A year later he transferred to Everton where his talent blossomed. In 1986 he not only won two Player of the Year awards and scored 30 League goals but also became the top scorer in the World Cup, with six goals (including three against Poland). The Spanish club Barcelona then acquired his services, for a fee of £2.75 million, though his time in Spain was somewhat affected by illness and injury. He returned to the UK, and Tottenham Hotspur, in 1989. A year later he led England on their fruitful World Cup challenge, which got the team as far as the semi-finals (scoring four goals). Having equalled Bobby CHARLTON's record of 49 England goals, Lineker – like Charlton a modest and likeable ambassador for the game – subsequently retired from international football after being controversially substituted in his final international appearance.

linesman An assistant to the referee, who follows play from the touchlines and signals when the ball has passed out of play, when a player is offside, etc. The duties of the linesmen were originally performed by the umpires who oversaw games before 1891, when the current system of two linesmen and a referee was introduced. Linesmen usually wear black, although complaints by referees that they could not make out their linesmen during floodlit games led to a shortlived experiment with luminous outfits in 1972.

Distinguished figures have sometimes undertaken the role of linesman in an emergency: in 1905 the legendary striker Steve BLOOMER played linesman during a match at Elland Road, while more recently the former player and television commentator Jimmy HILL donned the linesman's uniform at the last minute to help out when the regular linesman was unable to go on.

There have been occasions in the past when the job has proved more hazardous than it would at first appear. In one hot-tempered match involving an Argentinian side the entire team ended up in prison after a linesman was actually killed after daring to signal one of them offside.

Linfield Northern Ireland football club, nicknamed the Blues in reference to the team colours. The club was formed in 1886 by workers from the Linfield mill and has always been closely allied with the Protestant community in Belfast. Their long history of success has won them the accolade of Northern Ireland's leading club, with the stiffest opposition coming from Belfast Celtic until they disbanded in 1949 and from rivals Glentoran and more recently Portadown.

Based at WINDSOR PARK, Linfield have won the Irish League championship on no fewer than 40 occasions. The club has long-standing links with the Glasgow club Rangers.

Links Park The home ground of the Scottish football club MONTROSE. The original Links Park was home to the club back in the 1880s and was situated next to Dorward House. In 1887, however, Montrose moved into a new Links Park nearby although it was not until the 1920s that the club were able to erect their first grandstand (after a fundraising campaign that in its first year gathered the princely sum of just £7).

Linnets (1) Nickname of the Welsh non-League football club BARRY TOWN.

(2) Nickname of the English non-League football club KING'S LYNN, from the side's full name.

(3) Nickname of the English non-League football club RUNCORN, in reference to the birds often seen in the vicinity of the club's ground.

Linthouse Former Scottish football club, which disappeared from the League in 1900, having been a member since 1895. The side played at Langlands Park and Govandale Park in Glasgow.

Lion of Vienna Nickname of the great English centre-forward Nat LOFTHOUSE. He acquired the nickname after a celebrated encounter between England and Austria in 1952, during which Lofthouse scored two goals, one after a brilliant breakaway manoeuvre.

Lions Nickname of a number of football clubs around the world. They include the English club MILLWALL, the non-League teams ANDOVER and WEMBLEY, the Portuguese club SPORTING LISBON, and the Spanish football club ATHLETIC BILBAO (with reference to the local saint Mames de Cesarea, who was associated with lions).

Lion's Den Notorious section of the terracing at the GIUSEPPE MEAZZA STADIUM in Milan, where the most violent supporters of AC Milan gather. It was from the Lion's Den that a thunderflash was thrown on to the pitch during a game in 1987, threaten-

ing the life of Roma goalkeeper Franco Tancredi. *See also* DEN.

Lisbon Lions Nickname bestowed upon the CELTIC side that triumphed in the European Cup in 1967, beating Inter-Milan 2–1 in the Final in Lisbon. One of the most cherished of all the successes credited to Celtic, the victory led chairman Robert Kelly to describe his players as 'the greatest Celtic team of all time'. No one disagreed. Legend has it that a number of Celtic fans were so overwhelmed with the Portuguese experience that they settled permanently in Portugal, where they continue to honour the anniversary of the match every year.

Little Ant Nickname of the Brazilian footballer Mario ZAGALO.

Little Bird Nickname of the great Brazilian wing-forward GARRINCHA. He acquired the nickname early in his career, when it was allegedly as much a reference to his passion for 'little birds' as it was to his apparent physical frailty.

Little Napoleon Nickname of the celebrated French footballer Raymond KOPA.

Little Tin Idol Nickname of the original FA Cup, which was the first football trophy ever made. The Little Tin Idol, as it was popularly known throughout the game, was made by Martin, Hall and Company in 1871 for just £20 and was presented at the first FA Cup Final the following year. It was approximately 18 inches high, had two curved handles, and was crowned with the figure of a footballer on the lid. Won in its first year by Wanderers, it was presented 24 times in all.

The Cup did not travel far in its early years, being won exclusively by clubs from southern England, but in 1883 that all changed when Blackburn Olympic beat Old Etonians in the Final and took it north for the first time. Jubilant northerners called the arrival of the Cup in the north 'a triumph for the democracy', while Blackburn's captain Alf Warburton swore grimly: 'It'll have a good home, and it'll ne'er go back to Lunnon.'

Remarkably, he was right: it was not until 1901 that another London club (Tottenham Hotspur) claimed possession of the FA title – and by then the original Little Tin Idol had suffered an unexpected fate and had vanished from English football altogether.

On the night of 11 September 1895, while

it was on display in the window of the football outfitters William Shillcock in Newton Row, Birmingham (having been won that year by Aston Villa) the cherished trophy was stolen. Villa officials were mortified that the famous trophy should go missing while in their care and the shopowner himself was inconsolable, as he later recalled:

It was an incident which seemed to me at the time a great and unprecedented calamity. I pictured myself a ruined man. I seemed to see myself a hated individual – to see my business boycotted. What was this heinous offence of which I was guilty? Why, I was the man who lost the English Cup . . .

Despite intensive investigations and the offer of a £10 reward, the original Cup was never recovered. A successor (as close in design to the lost cup as possible) was rapidly commissioned by an embarrassed Aston Villa (using the insurance on the cup); the replacement cost £25 and Villa themselves were fined the same amount for their negligence by the FA.

Unfortunately lack of copyright in the Cup's design subsequently led to numerous replicas being made and in 1911 the second Cup was presented to the distinguished football administrator and FA president Lord KINNAIRD and a third Cup (the present trophy) was made in Bradford to a different design at the cost of 50 guineas; fittingly it was won in its first year by Bradford City.

The third trophy has not survived totally unscathed: in 1947 Charlton Athletic's manager Jimmy Seed dropped it and broke the lid (it was temporarily patched up by a local garage before being properly repaired by a silversmith).

It was not until a full 63 years had passed since the fateful night that the original Little Tin Idol disappeared that a little light was shed on its fate. In 1958 an 83-year old man was reported to have confessed to a Sunday newspaper that he had stolen the cup in order to melt it down to make counterfeit half-crowns.

Little World Cup (1) Nickname of the international tournament that was staged in Uruguay in 1981 to celebrate 50 years of the World Cup. The competition was fought out between all the previous winners of the tournament (except for England, who were unable to release players in the middle of the League season and were replaced by the Netherlands) and was eventually won by the host country, who beat Brazil 2–1 in the Final (at which the ball was kicked off by Nestor Mascheroni, the last survivor of the first Final in 1930). The Little World Cup itself was called the 'Copa de Oro' (Gold Cup) and was designed by the Uruguayan artist Lincoln Presno.

(2) Nickname of the international Mundialito tournament for women's football teams. Modelled on the World Cup itself, the Little World Cup has been won twice by England in recent years, in 1985 and 1988.

Littlewoods Cup *See* LEAGUE CUP.

Liverpool English football club, nicknamed the Reds. Strip: all red, with white trim. The Reds, one of the most celebrated of all British sides, owe their existence to an argument Everton had with the owners of their original ground, ANFIELD, in 1892. Everton failed to agree terms with the landlord, John Houlding, and finally left the ground for good, leaving Houlding to form a new club – initially also called Everton but later renamed Liverpool – to occupy Anfield.

The team played its first League game in 1893 (in which year goalkeeper Bill McOwen was the only Englishman in a side that included ten Scots) and has never since dropped lower than the Second Division. Liverpool are simply the most successful club in English football, with no fewer than 18 First Division championship titles (1901, 1906, 1922, 1923, 1947, 1964, 1966, 1973, 1976, 1977, 1979, 1980, 1982, 1983, 1984, 1986, 1988, and 1990). They have also captured the FA Cup four times (1965, 1974, 1986, and 1989), the League Cup four times (1981, 1982, 1983, and 1984), the European Cup four times (1977, 1978, 1981, and 1984), the UEFA Cup twice (1973 and 1976), and the Super Cup once (1977); no other British club has appeared in European competitions more often.

Stars with the side over the years have been many. They included in the early years such names as goalkeepers Sam Hardy and Elisha SCOTT, and winger Billy LIDDELL. Another recruit, the world champion heavyweight boxer Joe Louis also signed professional forms for the club in 1944 – but never actually appeared in a match.

The golden era, however, began with the arrival of the legendary Bill SHANKLY as manager in 1959. Under Shankly's direction the list of Liverpool stars grew longer and longer, with the inclusion of such players as Roger Hunt, Ron YEATS, Ian St John,

Tommy SMITH, Kevin KEEGAN, goalkeeper Ray Clemence, Emlyn Hughes, and John Toshack. Shankly's successor as manager after he surprised everyone by announcing his retirement in 1974 was Bob PAISLEY. Paisley added more names, among whom Kenny DALGLISH and Graeme SOUNESS were both destined to lead the club as manager (with yet more success). Stars of the side under their leadership in the 1980s included Ian RUSH, Peter Beardsley, John BARNES, and Dean Saunders. One curiosity of these highly successful times was the FA Cup side of 1986, which included only one English-born player (who himself qualified for the Republic of Ireland team).

For many years Liverpool were undisputed as the leading British side and the equal of the finest clubs anywhere in the world. Opponents despaired of beating them and Alan BALL, then manager of Portsmouth, spoke for many when he remarked in 1988: 'The only way to beat them is to let the ball down.'

Watford manager Graham TAYLOR was inclined to agree, stating: 'You get to wish that they would just occasionally pass the ball to the other team, like the rest of us do.'

Trainer Ronnie Moran admitted in 1980: 'If I told people that the secret of Liverpool's success is a dip in the Mersey three times a week, I not only reckon they'd believe me but I think our river would be full of footballers from all over the country.'

Fans relished their team's supremacy and were often heard to joke: 'For those of you watching in black and white, Liverpool are the team with the ball.'

The club's reputation suffered a terrible blow in 1985 when a minority of Liverpool fans was blamed for triggering the Heysel Stadium disaster. Liverpool felt the consequent ban on English sides in overseas football particularly keenly, as they would have qualified for several European competitions. Further heartbreak followed in 1989 with the Hillsborough disaster, in which nearly 100 fans – mainly Liverpool supporters – lost their lives, establishing for the club the almost unique status of having experienced the very best and the very worst in football in some 20 or so years.

Liverpool enjoyed their record victory in 1974, when they beat Stromsgodset Drammen 11–0; they suffered their worst defeat in 1954, losing 9–1 to Birmingham City. Ian Callaghan holds the record for League appearances with the club, having played in 640 games between 1960 and 1978.

Famous fans of the club include rock stars Rod Stewart and Elvis Costello, comedian Ted Ray (who once played for the third team), and disc jockey John Peel (who is only one of a relatively large number of fans to name one of their children after the entire Liverpool squad). Playwright Alan Bleasdale is another supporter; he once confessed to taking out a girl 'because she looked a lot like Ian St John'. *See also* KOP; RED ARMY; YOU'LL NEVER WALK ALONE.

> *Oh I am a Liverpudlian,*
> *From the Spion Kop,*
> *I like to sing, I like to shout,*
> *I go there quite a lot,*
> *I support the team that play in red,*
> *A team that you all know,*
> *A team that we call Liverpool,*
> *To glory we will go.*

Supporters' song

Lloyd George of Welsh Football Nickname of the great Welsh footballer Billy MEREDITH.

Lochgelly United Former Scottish football club, which disappeared from the League in 1926, having been a member since 1914. They played at the Recreation Ground in Cowdenbeath.

locomotives There is a long tradition of naming rolling stock after notable institutions and individuals, but until the 1930s football had not qualified for such recognition. In 1936, however, the first of a lengthy series of locomotives went into service carrying the name of a famous English club and over the next year many more sides were thus honoured. Representing clubs from Arsenal and Barnsley to Tottenham Hotspur and West Ham, the last of the class was scrapped in 1960. Coincidentally, the first of the series to go to the scrapyard was the locomotive named after Bradford Park Avenue (the only club thus honoured to lose its place in the Football League). Sir Stanley MATTHEWS had a Pullman railway carriage named after him in 1985 – while Brazil's striker DIDÍ could boast an entire station named in his honour. *See also* BOATS.

Lofthouse, Nat (1925–) English centre-forward, nicknamed the Lion of Vienna, who was a star with Bolton Wanderers and England in the 1950s. Born in Bolton, Lofthouse made his debut for the local side in 1939 and rapidly built up a reputation as an aggressive and courageous striker while still working as a miner (which entailed getting up at four a.m. and working an eight-hour shift down the pit before turning out for his team in the afternoon). Hailing from the same town as the celebrated Tommy LAWTON, he was destined to follow Lawton into the national side and benefited from his advice when they met after Lofthouse had just completed a schoolboy trial: 'Always try to bang in one or two Nat, and remember it's goals that count.'

Lofthouse made his debut for England in 1950, scoring twice against Yugoslavia. Subsequently he won the Footballer of the Year award in 1953 (in which year he scored in every round of the FA Cup, including the Final), became the top goalscorer in the First Division in 1956, and captained Bolton to victory over Manchester United in the FA Cup and scored the last of his 30 goals in 33 internationals in 1958.

His performance in the 1958 FA Cup was particularly controversial as in the second of the two goals he scored to clinch the game he physically forced the ball and the opposing keeper over the line. He retired as a player in 1960, due to injury, with a career total of 285 goals in 485 matches. In 1968 he took over as manager of his old club Bolton; he resigned the post in 1971 but resumed it briefly in 1985 and in 1986 accepted the post of club president.

Like a Centurion tank was our Nathan
Wi' a turn of speed like a bomb
Many a goalie's said sadly
'I wonder where that came from?'

Mr Kay, 'Lofthouse Saga' (1960)

Loftus Road The home ground, in west London, of the English football club QUEEN'S PARK RANGERS. Rangers had no fewer than 11 different homes (more than any other League club) before they finally settled at Loftus Road in 1917. Formerly the home of the amateur side Shepherd's Bush, Loftus Road was rapidly developed with the re-erection of a stand from the club's previous home at Park Royal but in the 1930s QPR played many of their matches at nearby White City, which was much larger. The low attendances the club attracted, however, prompted them to return to Loftus Road in 1932.

Events in the ground's history since then have included gradual development in the 1960s and 1970s, the installation of artificial turf (the first such pitch given the go-ahead by a British League club) in 1981, and its replacement by grass later in the decade. The same decade also saw plans to instal a retractable roof that would cover the entire stadium.

Lokomotive Leipzig German football club, nicknamed the Railwaymen. The team is based at the Bruno Plache Stadium in southeast Leipzig.

London Road The home ground of the English football club PETERBOROUGH UNITED. Peterborough have been at London Road since their formation in 1934, although it was formerly the home of another local club, Peterborough and Fletton United. The ground remained largely unchanged until the 1950s, when the club began a meteoric rise that ended in promotion to the League in 1960.

long ball game *See* KICK AND RUSH.

longest game A number of games over the years have been remarkable for the extent to which they overran the usual playing time of 90 minutes. From time to time concerted efforts have been made to establish a new record for the longest game on record, often for the purpose of raising money for charity. In 1980 the Irish club Callinafercy set a new record when they managed to keep playing for 65 hours, one minute. Four years later the record was comprehensively smashed when the US teams North Palm Beach Golden Bears and Palm Beach Piranhas of Florida – allowing themselves a break of five minutes every hour – played a game that lasted a grand total of 68 hours, 11 minutes (by which time several players had left the pitch suffering from exhaustion). *See also* EXTRA TIME.

Lorimer, Peter (1946–) Scottish forward, nicknamed Hot Shot, who was a star with Leeds United and Scotland in the 1970s (though he also spent short periods at York City and in the USA). He scored a grand total of 168 goals for Leeds and was capable of producing shots that reached 90 miles per hour. When Wimbledon's keeper Dickie Guy saved a crucial Lorimer penalty in the fourth round of the FA Cup in 1975 the achievement was enough to make Guy an instant hero with Wimbledon's supporters.

Loughborough Town Former English football club, which disappeared from the League in 1900, having been a member since 1895. Town played at the Athletic Ground in Loughborough, which was also used for cricket and once played host to the great cricketer W.G. Grace.

Louis II Stadium The home ground of the Monacan football club AS Monaco. The first Louis II Stadium opened in 1939 in the very shadow of Louis II's royal palace in Monaco. Although AS Monaco, who play in the French First Division, have only a small following in the principality, the club prospers with the support of the royal family (Prince Albert, heir to the throne, has even trained with the side). In the 1970s the stadium was completely rebuilt. At the time of its opening in 1985 it was one of the best-appointed venues in the world, with underground parking and a diversity of other sporting installations (including a swimming pool of Olympic dimensions). The pitch itself is laid on the top of the four-storey car park. Other features of this remarkable stadium include accommodation for 20 trainee footballers at one end of the ground.

Love Street The home ground, in Paisley, of the Scottish football club ST MIRREN. Love Street – officially St Mirren Park – became the club's home in 1895 and included amongst its original features a slaughterhouse next door and a cottage (which at one time was the home of the goalkeeper John Patrick). Supporters helped to construct terraces by bringing their rubbish to the ground and the Main Stand was added in 1911. An attempt to raise money for the club by hosting greyhound racing proved unsuccessful in 1932, as did an experiment with speedway in the 1970s. Features of the ground include Cairter's Corner, the traditional gathering place of a group of vociferous carters who supported the club. The ground also boasts the largest pitch in the League (120 by 80 yards).

Lucky Arsenal Nickname of ARSENAL during their golden era under manager Herbert CHAPMAN in the 1930s. It was during this period that the club achieved an extraordinary run of successes, winning no fewer than five League championships (1931, 1933–35, and 1938) and finishing runners-up in 1932 and third in 1937. For good measure Chapman's team also added the FA Cup in 1930 and 1936 and also appeared in the Final in 1932; other trophies included the FA Charity Shield in 1931, 1932, 1934, 1935, and 1939.

Arsenal's success ended the north's domination of English football and made Highbury Stadium the focus of the national game. The Gunners became the most loathed and envied team in the country and although many uncharitable opponents liked to pretend it was luck alone that had powered Chapman's sides, it was clear to everyone that the reforms he had introduced at Highbury were the way forward for all other clubs as well.

Lucky Arsenal were not, however, invincible and their 2–0 defeat by lowly Walsall in 1933 has entered the annals of football mythology (see GIANT-KILLER). Such humiliation was, though, rare.

Stars of the classic side forged with both cunning and money by Chapman included Cliff BASTIN, Alex JAMES, David Jack, Eddie HAPGOOD, Joe Hulme, Herbie Roberts (who was Chapman's highly effective stopper), Tom Parker, George Male, and Ted Drake. See also SMASH AND GRAB.

> At Highbury we went for results. Results meant getting goals so we cut the movements down from four passes to two. Our great ball was the long one and that opened the game up.
>
> Ted Drake (1960)

Luigi Ferraris Stadium Celebrated football stadium in Genoa, which is the home ground of the Italian football clubs Sampdoria and Genoa 1893 (so called in commemoration of the arrival of football in Italy when English businessmen first played it in Genoa and Turin). Genoa first played on the site of the current stadium in 1910, redeveloping the venue under its current name in the 1920s (Luigi Ferraris being a former Genoa centre-half who was killed during World War I).

Sampdoria arrived under a special sharing arrangement after World War II and improvements continued to be made until the 1980s when complete rebuilding of the venue to a revolutionary post-modernist design by the architect Vittorio Gregotti began.

Gregotti's design was breathtaking in its ingenuity, bearing in mind the lack of space available, and promised to make the ground instantly recognizable with four huge towers in what Gregotti called 'Pompeii red'. However, even before the work was half complete in 1988, the refurbishment became the subject of controversy when outraged sections of the crowd found that they enjoyed a very restricted view of the pitch from certain angles (causing the venue to be dubbed the 'Stadium of the Blind'). Adjustments were subsequently made to the upper tiers of seating and these, with other alterations, satisfied all but the most bitter of critics.

Luis Casanova Stadium The home ground, in Valencia, of the Spanish football club VALENCIA. Opened in 1923 and named after a past president of the club (no relation of the great lover), the Luis Casanova Stadium – which had to be largely rebuilt after damage in the Spanish Civil War – is remarkable for the huge early cantilever roof of the west stand (erected in 1954). The pitch itself was lowered by several metres in the late 1970s to allow the installation of extra seating.

Lurch Nickname of the English goalkeeper Dave BEASANT. This somewhat unflattering nickname likened him to the huge slow-moving butler in the 1950s US television comedy series 'The Addams Family'.

lure of the lira Journalistic cliché referring to the tradition of prominent British players being persuaded to leave their home clubs to play in the Italian League, which is often claimed to the best in the world. Bemoaned by the British press, such transfers have captured the headlines for many years now. Among the stars to make the move to Italy, where they stand to earn considerably larger amounts than domestic clubs can usually afford, have been the great John CHARLES (who became one of the lynchpins of the classic Juventus side of the 1950s), Denis LAW (who was briefly lured to Torino in the early 1960s), and more recently such luminaries as Paul GASCOIGNE, whose transfer to Lazio was the subject of much speculation in the early 1990s, and David Platt.

It is not only the British player who is in demand with Italian clubs, of course: in 1984 Napoli paid £4,800,000 to persuade MARADONA to succumb to the lure of the lira by transferring to them from Barcelona. *See also* TRANSFER.

It's like going to a different country.

Ian Rush, on his transfer to Italy (1988)

Luton Town English football club, nicknamed the Hatters (or more rarely the Strawplaiters). Strip: white shirts with navy blue and orange trim, navy blue shorts, and white socks. Luton were formed in 1885 when Wanderers and Excelsior merged at a meeting at Luton Town Hall (making the club the first professional side south of Birmingham) and were elected to the Second Division in 1897. Three years later, however, they failed to gain re-election and spent the next 20 years out of the League before finally returning in 1920 as a founder member of the Third Division.

Winners of the Fourth Division championship in 1968, the Third Division title in 1937, and the Second Division championship in 1982, the club has enjoyed three spells in the First Division (1955–60, 1974–75, 1982). Runners-up in the 1959 FA Cup, Luton won the League Cup in 1988 and were runners-up in 1989. Stars at their KENILWORTH ROAD ground over the years have included striker Joe TEN-GOAL Payne in the 1930s, Syd Owen, Bob Morton, Billy Bingham, and Allan Brown in the 1950s, Bruce Rioch in the 1960s, Malcolm MACDONALD and Ricky Hill in the 1970s, and Brian Stein in the 1980s.

The club's decision in the 1980s to refuse to admit away supporters, in the wake of hooliganism by visiting Millwall fans, was one of the most controversial moves in modern football and led to the club's exclusion from the League Cup in 1986.

Celebrities connected with the club have included the comedian Eric Morecambe, who was a director from 1976 to 1983.

The Hatters enjoyed their record victory in 1936, when they beat Bristol Rovers 12–0; they suffered their worst defeat back in 1898, losing 9–0 to Small Heath. Bob Morton holds the record for League appearances with the club, having played in 494 games between 1948 and 1964.

Luxembourg Luxembourg joined FIFA in 1910 but have remained very much one of the minnows in international competition. The national side, in fact, has not contrived to win a single match since a 2–1 victory in 1963. One result stands out, however, in the side's history – a World Cup qualifying game in which Luxembourg pulled off a startling victory over Portugal (complete with their great star EUSÉBIO). Strip: red shirts, white shorts, and blue socks.

M

Macao Macao joined FIFA in 1976 but have yet to make much impact in international competition. Strip: red and green shirts, with red or white shorts and socks.

McAulay, James (1860–1943) Scottish goalkeeper, nicknamed the Prince of Goalkeepers, who was one of the outstanding keepers of the 1880s. The first of a series of goalkeepers to win the accolade of 'Prince of Goalkeepers' he moved somewhat unusually into the goal after already establishing himself as a formidable centre-forward (he scored for his club Dumbarton in the Scottish FA Cup Final in 1881). As a goalkeeper, he occupied the Scottish national team's goal on eight occasions.

McCain Stadium Home ground of the English football club SCARBOROUGH. Scarborough were admitted to the League in 1987 as the first club to achieve automatic promotion into Division Four from the Conference. A year later, the Athletic Ground, which had been their ground since 1898, was renamed the McCain Stadium as part of a sponsorship deal with the McCain food company. The club had two former homes: the Scarborough Cricket ground from 1879, followed by a 12-year spell at the Recreation Ground (1887–98).

In an attempt to woo larger crowds the club announced in 1991 that they would build a crèche to increase their appeal to family audiences.

Macclesfield Town English non-League football club, nicknamed the Silkmen. Strip: blue shirts, white shorts, and blue socks. Founded in 1874 and based at the MOSS ROSE ground since 1891, Macclesfield play in the GM Vauxhall Conference.

McDiarmid Park The home ground of the Scottish football club ST JOHNSTONE. Opened in 1989 and nicknamed Mini-Ibrox after the famous Rangers ground on which it was modelled, McDiarmid Park replaced MUIRTON PARK as the club's home.

MacDonald, Malcolm (1950–) Eng-lish forward, nicknamed Supermac, who was a star with Newcastle United in the 1970s. Supermac's finest hour was in 1975 when he scored all five of England's goals against Cyprus in a European Championship qualifying game at Wembley. He eventually left Newcastle for Arsenal.

McGrain, Danny (1950–) Scottish full-back, who was one of the stars of the celebrated Celtic side managed by Jock STEIN in the late 1960s and 1970s. McGrain joined the team in 1967 and survived a fractured skull during a match against Falkirk in 1972, the diagnosis of diabetes in 1974, and a troublesome ankle injury in 1977. He triumphed over all the setbacks, however, to become captain of the side (and subsequently of the Scottish national team) in 1978. He played over 600 games for the club and played in no fewer than seven League championship sides. On the international stage he took part in the World Cup campaigns of 1974 and 1982, when he proved an inspiration. Having established himself as a folk hero and having collected every domestic honour, he ended his career with a brief stay at Hamilton Academical.

McGregor, William (d. 1911) Scottish-born football administrator, nicknamed the Father of League Football, who was the prime mover behind the foundation of the Football League in 1888, and became its first president. Born in Perth, McGregor joined Aston Villa after opening a drapery shop in Birmingham and subsequently emerged as a highly influential and respected figure in English football. At his suggestion the leading English clubs were invited to join together to play in the inaugural Football League season and the future course of the game in England was set:

I beg to tender the following suggestion . . . that ten or twelve of the most prominent clubs in England combine to arrange home-and-away fixtures each season . . .

MacGregor's letter to Bolton Wanderers, Blackburn Rovers, Preston North End, West Bromwich Albion, and Aston Villa

McGregor was a visionary who saw that the game badly needed a league similar to that familiar to the nation's cricketers if it was to prosper. Somewhat surprisingly, unlike the founders of the FA, McGregor himself was not a distinguished player of the game, as he readily admitted: 'I've never taken part in active football. I tried it once when I was very young and had to take to bed for a week.'

Machine, The Nickname of the celebrated forward line-up that spearheaded the Argentinian football club River Plate in the 1940s. Comprising José Manuel Moreno, Alfredo DI STEFANO, and Angel Labruna, 'La Maquina' became the most powerful force in Argentinian football and took the club to success in no fewer than four championships (1941, 1942, 1945, and 1947). At their peak in 1947, the players of The Machine were averaging nearly three goals every game.

McIlroy, Jimmy (1931–) Northern Ireland-born inside-forward, who led Burnley to victory in the League in 1960. Acquired by Burnley from Glentoran in 1950, McIlroy proved a brilliant schemer and the inspiration of the side for many years. Later, he moved to Stoke City and formed a devastating partnership with Stanley MATTHEWS. He ended his career with Oldham Athletic and then became a sports journalist. As an international, he won 55 caps and played a key role in the Northern Ireland campaign that took the team to the quarter-finals of the World Cup in 1958.

Mackay, Dave (1934–) Scottish half-back, who was widely recognized as one of the most talented players of his generation. Mackay, whose skills extended to virtually every aspect of the game, began his career with Heart of Midlothian in 1952 and won his first honour just three years later, when he was a member of the side that won the Scottish League Cup. Victory in the Scottish Cup followed a year later and in 1957 his contribution was rewarded with the first of 22 caps for Scotland.

After winning the League championship with Hearts in 1958 and again in 1959, Mackay finally made the journey down to Tottenham Hotspur, where he proved to be one of the best signings the club had ever made. He was one of the pillars of the side that achieved the double in 1961 and helped the club retain the FA Cup in 1962 before suffering a broken left leg twice the follow-

ing year. He recovered to assume the captaincy of the team and to lead them to triumph in the FA Cup for a third time in 1967.

In 1968 Mackay moved to Derby County and immediately helped to lift the club to the First Division. Voted joint Footballer of the Year in 1969, he accepted the post of player-manager with Swindon Town in 1971 and subsequently (1972) became manager of Nottingham Forest. He succeeded Brian CLOUGH at his old club Derby County in 1973 and two years later Derby won the League championship. He moved to Walsall as manager in 1977 and then became a coach in Kuwait for a number of years, finally returning to the UK as manager of Doncaster in 1987. He moved to Birmingham City in 1989, but left the manager's post in 1991.

McMenemy, Lawrie (1936–) English manager, nicknamed The Messiah, who won recognition as one of the most successful managers of his day when he transformed a hitherto undistinguished Southampton side in the 1970s. With McMenemy at the helm, the Saints (then in the Second Division) stormed to a 1–0 victory over Manchester United in the 1976 FA Cup Final. Boasting such talents as Alan BALL and Kevin KEEGAN, they won promotion to the First Division and remained one of the most promising sides in the League for several years, reaching the League Cup Final in 1979 and finishing as runners-up in the League in 1984. McMenemy himself won the undying gratitude of the club's fans before eventually moving to Sunderland as manager. His success at Southampton won him serious consideration as a possible England boss in 1977, though the post went eventually to Ron GREENWOOD; some years later, however, he was recruited to assist Graham TAYLOR in running the national squad.

McNeill, Billy (1940–) Scottish centre-half, who led CELTIC to glory in the European Cup in 1967, among other honours. He completed 17 seasons in all with Celtic, making 800 appearances and winning no fewer than 23 winners' medals (thought to be a world record). A cult figure to fans of the club, he continued his association with Celtic as manager from 1978 to 1983, when Celtic added another three League titles and the Scottish Cup and the League Cup to their tally. He then moved south of the border to manage Manchester City and Aston Villa before going back to Celtic in time to see them clinch the double in 1988, the club's centenary year.

Madagascar Madagascar joined FIFA in 1962, but remain a minor force in international competition. Strip: red shirts, white shorts, and green socks.

Maestro Nickname of the great English footballer Sir Stanley MATTHEWS.

magic sponge The proverbial sponge that is included in the essential equipment of every trainer's bag and which constitutes a symbol of his skill as an instant healer of every type of minor injury. The traditional tools of the trainer's art are the sponge and the bottle of smelling salts and most 'cures' are a question of shock tactics. Many a player has miraculously hobbled back into play after the application of the magic sponge – as much to avoid another dab of icy water from the sponge itself as to prove himself fully recovered. If the sponge does not work then the smelling salts are brought into play. These operate in a similar way, as Denis LAW once explained: 'These either lift the top of a man's head off, or at the very least take his mind instantly off all other pain.'

Magnificent Magyars Nickname of the classic national side – sometimes called the Marvellous Magyars or the Magical Magyars – that represented Hungary between the years 1950 and 1956. The Magnificent Magyars have a permanent place in the annals of international football and enjoyed enormous success against even the most prestigious opposition. Based around the army side HONVÉD and including such stars as Ferenc PUSKAS and Sandor KOCSIS among their ranks, the Hungarians caused a sensation in the UK in November 1953 when they thrashed a highly respected England side (then considered the best in the world and including such stars as Stanley MATTHEWS, Stan MORTENSEN, Tommy Taylor, Billy WRIGHT, and Alf RAMSEY) 6–3 at Wembley.

In the post mortem that followed the game the international careers of Ramsey, Mortensen, Harry Johnston, and Bill Eckersley all came to an end as the England management struggled to revive their team's reputation and address themselves to the challenge of the new tactics already adopted by other international sides. Nonetheless, the return match in Budapest six months later only served to deepen the gloom into which English football had been cast, with the Hungarians emerging victors in a 7–1 rout (the English team's heaviest defeat ever).

England were just one of the Hungarians' many notable victims. A year before, the team had been victorious in the 1952 Olympic tournament and in 1954 they were losing finalists (a surprise 2–3 defeat blamed on over-confidence) against West Germany in the World Cup – the only match they had lost in four years (during which time they had played 32 games). After this uncharacteristic defeat they resumed their unbeaten run, which lasted until 1956, when it all came to an end with the Hungarian uprising, as a result of which the team disintegrated. Even so, when Wales defeated Hungary 2–1 in Budapest in 1975 it was the first Hungarian home defeat for 30 years (and the first time a British team had won there since 1909, in which year England, inspired by Vivian Woodward, had beaten the Hungarians three times).

The team's stunning record at the highest level (with an average score of more than four goals a match) remains a subject of much admiration and in their day they were often described as the finest team ever assembled. *See also* CHAMPIONS OF THE WORLD.

> *The finest team ever to sort out successfully the intricacies of this wonderful game.*
>
> Tom Finney, *Finney on Football* (1958)

Magpies Nickname of a number of English football clubs, in reference to their black and white team strips. They include NEWCASTLE UNITED and NOTTS COUNTY and the non-League teams CHORLEY and DORCHESTER TOWN.

Maidenhead United English non-League football club, nicknamed the Tanners. Strip: white shirts, black shorts, and white socks. Founded in 1869 and based at the York Road ground, Maidenhead play in the Isthmian League.

Maidstone United Former English football club, nicknamed the Stones, which was a member of the League from 1989 to 1992. Strip: gold shirts, black shorts, and black socks with gold trim. The Stones were founded in 1897 as successors to Maidstone Invicta, who had been formed in 1891. They were professional until 1927 and then continued on an amateur basis until 1971, when they joined the Southern League. In 1979 they surprised many opponents when they battled through to the third round of the FA Cup.

The club, based at the WATLING STREET ground in Dartford, finally acquired League status in 1989 having won the Conference and in their first League season only narrowly missed promotion to the Third Division. Early results produced a record League victory of 6–1, against Scunthorpe United in 1990, and a record defeat of 4–1, against Colchester United in 1989.

It all came to end, however, in 1992 when the club was overcome by a financial crisis and lack of a home ground; a bizarre last-minute attempt to save their League status by moving lock, stock, and barrel to Tyneside proved unacceptable to supporters and the club went out of existence.

We are Maidstone, we are Maidstone,
Super Maidstone, from nowhere,
We are Maidstone, we are Maidstone,
Super Maidstone, from nowhere,
No one likes us, no one likes us,
The Council hate us, we don't care,
We are Maidstone, from nowhere.

Supporters' song, to the tune of 'Sailing'

Maier, Sepp (1944–) West German goalkeeper, who earned a record 95 German caps in the 1970s. He proved invaluable in his country's campaigns in the 1972 European Championship (which Germany won) and in three World Cups (1970, 1974, and 1978); he also won three European Cup medals (1974–76) with his home club Bayern Munich. He was forced into early retirement after a car crash.

Maine Road The home ground of MAN-CHESTER CITY. Maine Road replaced Hyde Road as the club's home in 1923 and opened as the second biggest football stadium – after Wembley – in England (the maximum capacity was estimated at somewhere between 80,000 and 100,000). New attendance records were regularly established at the ground in subsequent years and the venue was frequently full to the point of overflowing after Manchester United arrived to share the ground following bomb damage to Old Trafford during World War II. In 1946, 80,407 fans saw a semi-final replay between Birmingham City and Derby County, setting a new record for a mid-week fixture; that season also saw a record 2,250,000 spectators enter the turnstiles at the ground. The biggest crowd of them all was recorded at Maine Road in 1948, when 82,930 people saw

United play Arsenal (the largest ever League crowd).

The profits from these gates went towards such improvements as large seated areas (then a startling innovation) and the ground soon had more seats than any other in the UK. It also has the largest pitch in the Football League. Since United left in 1949 the main landmarks in the history of Maine Road have included the roofing over of the Kippax Street side (1956) and the installation of a distinctive white roof over the Main Stand (1982). Several streets close to the stadium bear the names of famous players with the club, among them Frank SWIFT, the former goalkeeper who died in the MUNICH AIR CRASH.

Major, The Nickname of the English football pioneer Major Sir Francis Arthur MARINDIN.

Major Soccer League US indoor football league, that was founded in 1978 (as the Major Indoor Soccer League). Members of the MSL include a number of former NASL teams. Curiosities of MSL rules include pitches with curved corners (as games are played on hockey pitches), the use of two referees (and an assistant not on the pitch), the division of play into four 15 minute intervals, and 'shoot-outs' (rather than penalties) in which a player is allowed five seconds in which to get the ball past the goalkeeper.

The organization has known much controversy and came close to disbanding in 1988. One particularly thorny issue was the League's refusal to release players for the national teams representing the USA and Canada.

The indoor game definitely provides more
what the American fan wants to see . . .
they like a winner and they like action . . .
they like the physical stuff.

Keith Weller (1983)

Malawi Malawi joined FIFA in 1967 but have yet to make much impact in international competition. Strip: all red.

Malaysia Malaysia joined FIFA in 1956 but have still to establish themselves as a major force in international competition. Strip: all yellow and black.

Malden Vale English non-League football club, nicknamed Vale. Strip: royal blue shirts with white trim, navy blue shorts, and red socks. Founded in 1967 and based at the Grand Drive ground in Raynes Park, London, Malden Vale play in the Isthmian League.

Maldives Republic The Maldives joined FIFA in 1986 but have yet to make much impact in international competition. Strip: green shirts, white shorts, and red socks.

Mali Mali joined FIFA in 1962 but have yet to establish an international reputation. Strip: green shirts, yellow shorts, and red socks.

Malta Malta joined FIFA in 1959 and remain a minor power in European football, though occasionally putting up respectable resistance to more distinguished nations. Strip: red shirts, white shorts, and red socks.

Man in Black Nickname of the almost legendary Spanish goalkeeper Ricardo ZAMORA, who regularly appeared in an all-black strip.

Man of Paper Nickname of Mathias SINDELAR, who was one of the great stars of the Austrian Wunderteam in the 1930s, despite his slender build (hence his nickname).

manager The club official who assumes responsibility for a team's performance on the pitch, wielding control over selection of players, choice of tactics, etc. The manager is usually a former player with an impassioned commitment to the game and is typically a resilient, often controversial character. The manager began as a purely administrative official – the first outstanding managers including Preston North End's Major William Sudell and Sunderland's Tom Watson in the 1880s – but it was not until the 1930s that he secured sole responsibility for the day-to-day running of his club.

Italy's Vittorio POZZO was one of the first men to establish the manager's influence over his team, while in England the most important figure was undoubtedly Arsenal's Herbert CHAPMAN.

Successful managers become part of football legend; less successful ones are vilified by all around them and vanish from the collective consciousness almost as soon as they are dismissed by their clubs. Some last longer than others: Charles Fowerraker managed Bolton Wanderers for 20 years between the two world wars while Willie Maley was manager of Celtic over a period of no less than 50 years leading up to World War II; Eric Taylor of Sheffield Wednesday holds the record for the longest-serving English League manager, having remained with the club in one managerial capacity or another from 1942 to 1974. By way of contrast, Steve Murray lasted just three days as manager of Forfar Athletic in 1980.

There are only two certainties in this life. People die, and football managers get the sack.

Eoin Hand, Ireland manager (1980)

Great teams don't need managers. Brazil won the World Cup playing exhilarating football, with a manager they'd had for three weeks . . . what about Real Madrid at their greatest? You can't even remember who the manager was.

Danny Blanchflower

All a manager has to do is keep eleven players happy – the eleven in the reserves. The first team are happy because they are in the first team.

Rodney Marsh

I think I have the best job in the country.

Bobby Robson, England manager (1985)

See also MANAGER OF THE YEAR; PLAYER-MANAGER.

Manager of the Year Annual award sponsored by Bell's Whisky, which goes to the most outstanding manager in British football. Several managers have won the award more than once since it was inaugurated in 1966, but no one can equal the record six awards won by Bob PAISLEY (1976, 1977, 1979, 1980, 1982, and 1983), though other Liverpool managers have also figured prominently. Bell's also established a monthly award for the best manager in each division, their role as sponsor being inherited by Barclays Bank in 1988. Similar schemes are also run in several other footballing nations.

Manchester City English football club, nicknamed the Blues in reference to the team colours. Strip: sky blue shirts, white shorts, and blue socks. Founded in 1887 as Ardwick FC, the modern club dates from 1894, when it was reformed under its present name. Manchester City – also nicknamed the Citizens – quickly established themselves as the leading club in Manchester, inspired by the playing of the great Billy MEREDITH. Having captured the Second Division championship in 1899 and

1903, the Blues won the FA Cup for the first time in 1904, when they also finished second in the League. A scandal over illegal payments, and consequently heavy fines and suspensions imposed by the FA, however, cast a considerable shadow over the club's progress and provided the opportunity for rival team Newton Heath (later to become Manchester United) to claim the role of the city's senior side – a situation that has remained much the same ever since.

Manchester City won the Second Division championship in 1910, and in 1923 settled at their permanent home at MAINE ROAD. The interwar years saw some of Manchester City's finest hours. A fourth Second Division title was won in 1928, while in 1934 the team captured the FA Cup for the second time (under their captain Matt BUSBY); the First Division championship followed in 1937. After World War II, City continued to share their time between the top two divisions, winning the Second Division title in 1947 and the FA Cup again in 1956, with a team including centre-forward Don REVIE.

Their 1957–58 season was noteworthy in that they became the only team in League history both to concede 100 goals and score 100 (actually 104) in a single season.

Another golden era opened in 1965 with the appointment of Joe MERCER as manager, assisted by Malcolm Allison. Over the next five years the club won the Second Division title (1966), the First Division championship (1968), the FA Cup (1969), the League Cup (1970), and – also in 1970 – the European Cup Winners' Cup. After achieving another League Cup victory in 1976 and finishing as runners-up in the 1981 FA Cup competition, the club reverted to their old habit of moving regularly between the two top divisions. In 1992 they were founder members of the new Premier League.

The club's record victory stands at 10–1, scored in 1930 against Swindon Town and in 1987 against Huddersfield Town; in 1906 they suffered their record defeat, losing 9–1 to Everton. Alan Oakes holds the record for the most League appearances for the club, having played in 565 games between 1959 and 1976. The Rodgers and Hart song 'Blue Moon' is famous as the anthem of City supporters (although it was first adopted by fans of Crewe Alexandra).

There are three types of Oxo cubes. Light brown for chicken stock, dark brown for beef stock, and light blue for laughing stock.

Tommy Docherty (1988)

Manchester North End *See* DARLINGTON.

Manchester United English football club, nicknamed the Red Devils. Strip: red shirts, white shorts, and black socks with black and white trim. This strip, like most others, has varied in detail over the years, but never more so than in the crucial last game of the 1933–34 season, when relegation threatened: in an attempt to change their luck, the team adopted shirts with cherry and white hoops for one match (against Millwall) and won 2–0 to keep their Second Division place (the traditional strip was restored for the start of the next season).

The Red Devils began life in 1878 as Newton Heath (a team formed by workers with the Lancashire and Yorkshire Railway) and continued to play under that title until 1902, when Newton Heath were declared bankrupt and Manchester United were formed. The club first joined the League (as members of the First Division) in 1892 and have never since dropped out of the top two divisions, earning a reputation as one of the most glamorous (and widely supported) teams in the world.

The side first distinguished itself towards the end of the first decade of the 20th century, when winger Billy MEREDITH played a major role in clinching the team's first major honour – the First Division championship – in 1908. The FA Cup followed in 1909 and another League title in 1911 but subsequently the club moved between the top two divisions and added nothing new in the way of honours until after World War II, which brought with it considerable damage to their OLD TRAFFORD home and temporary exile at Manchester City's Maine Road ground.

The man who engineered the great change in the club's fortunes was Matt BUSBY, who became manager in 1945 and set about reconstructing the team under captain Johnny CAREY. Featuring the talents of such players as Stan Pearson and Jack Rowley, the club enjoyed victory in the FA Cup in 1948 and another League championship title in 1952, after which Busby introduced a new generation of stars, who were popularly dubbed the BUSBY BABES and included such names as Bobby CHARLTON, Duncan EDWARDS, Tommy Taylor, and Roger Byrne. This second Busby team dominated English football, winning further First Division titles in 1956 and 1957, but it all came to a tragic end in 1958 with the MUNICH AIR CRASH, which claimed the lives of eight players.

Busby survived the disaster to rebuild, unbelievably, a third team, which established itself as one of the golden sides of English football history, incorporating as it did the formidable skills of Charlton, Denis LAW, and George BEST. At one point, during the 1966–67 season, every member of the side was a member of an international squad. This great side captured the FA Cup in 1963 and the First Division championship in 1965 and 1967 before crowning their achievements in 1968 with triumph in the European Cup.

Busby's successors included Tommy DOCHERTY, who added another FA Cup title in 1977, Dave Sexton, whose reign was celebrated in the song 'Onward Sexton Soldiers', and then Ron ATKINSON, who added FA Cup victories in 1983 and 1985. Alex Ferguson took over in 1986 and spent lavishly on new stars, before leading the club to success in the FA Cup (1990), the European Cup Winners' Cup (1991), the League Cup (1992), and the inaugural Premier League championship (1993). Stars of the side in recent years have included Bryan ROBSON, Lee Sharpe, Eric Cantona, Mark HUGHES, and goalkeeper Peter Schmeichel.

Manchester United enjoyed their record victory in 1956, when the Busby Babes defeated Anderlecht 10–0; they have suffered record defeats of 7–0 on three occasions, against Blackburn Rovers in 1926, against Aston Villa in 1930, and against Wolverhampton Wanderers in 1931. Bobby Charlton holds the record for League appearances with the club, having played in 606 games between 1956 and 1973. *See also* BRIGHT SIDE OF LIFE, ALWAYS LOOK ON THE.

We are the pride of all Europe, the Cock of the North,
We hate the Scousers, and Cockneys of course,
We are United, without any doubt,
We are the Manchester boys,
La, la, la, la . . . ooooargh!

Supporters' song, to the tune of 'Just one of those Songs'

man-for-man A defensive system in which each defender marks a specific member of the opposition.

Manor Nickname of the English non-League football club RUISLIP MANOR.

Manor Ground The home ground of OXFORD UNITED. The club moved to the Manor Ground just before World War I, before which the area had been used as a recreation ground for several amateur clubs (it was grazed by horses and sheep during the week). When Oxford (then called Headington United) turned professional in 1949 they became the sole tenants of the ground and set about developing it with the erection of stands and other facilities. These included a set of floodlights that were of considerable historical importance, being the first set to be installed at any ground in the UK (1950). The arrival of the lights at the Manor Ground (they were actually borrowed from various Oxford Colleges which used them to illuminate the college buildings) intensified the debate then going on about floodlit football and hastened the day when such matches received official approval.

United bought the ground in 1953 and continued to erect new stands in advance of joining the League for the first time in 1962. Events witnessed at the ground since then have included the sit-ins that greeted Robert MAXWELL's plans to merge Oxford United and Reading as THAMES VALLEY ROYALS at a new stadium in 1983.

Mansfield Town English football club, nicknamed the Stags. Strip: amber shirts with blue trim, blue shorts, and amber socks. The Stags, based at the FIELD MILL ground, were founded in 1910 as successors to Mansfield Wesleyans (formed in 1891). They were elected to the League, as members of the Third Division (South), in 1931 at the seventh attempt and remained in the Third Division until 1960, when they dropped into the Fourth Division. Subsequently they divided their time between the bottom two divisions with a brief break in 1977–78, when they tasted life in the Second Division for the first time.

Memorable moments in the club's history have included a surprise victory over Wolverhampton Wanderers in 1929 (which took them to the fourth round of the FA Cup), their defeat of West Ham in the Cup in 1969 (when they reached the sixth round), and triumph in the Freight Rover Trophy at Wembley in 1987 (under the management of Ian Greaves). Famous names associated with the Stags over the years have included managers Raich CARTER and Billy BINGHAM and strikers Ted Harston and Mike Stringfellow.

Mansfield enjoyed their record victory in 1952, when they beat Scarborough 8–0; they suffered their worst defeat in 1933, losing 8–1 against Walsall. Rod Arnold holds the record for League appearances with the club, having played in 440 games between 1970 and 1983. The club's local arch-rivals are Chesterfield.

Maracana The huge football stadium in Rio de Janeiro, which is one of the most famous football grounds in the world. Built in 1950 for the World Cup tournament that year, the Maracana was the largest football stadium in the world, accommodating crowds of up to 200,000. 173,830 people saw the 1950 World Cup Final there – but that total has been exceeded twice since, with 177,656 spectators flocking to the stadium to see a match between Flamengo and Fluminense and 183,341 attending a World Cup preliminary match between Brazil and Paraguay (1969). It has been estimated that over the first 20 years of its life the stadium played host to more than 58 million spectators in a total of 1823 games. The Maracana regularly hosts games featuring the Brazilian national side but by the 1990s was showing bad signs of wear.

Maradona, Diego (1960–) Argentinian footballer, who was widely hailed as the finest forward in the world in the 1980s. He began his career with the Argentinian sides Argentinos Juniors and Boca Juniors, but subsequently moved to Barcelona for a transfer fee of £4.2 million. In 1984 he moved again, this time to the Italian club Napoli for a record £6.9 million. Despite the drawbacks of injury, illness, and repeated clashes with the football establishment, he consolidated his reputation as the most deadly striker in the world on the international stage, inspiring Napoli to victory in two League championships and in the UEFA Cup and spearheading Argentina's attack in the World Cup campaigns of 1982, 1986 (when he became infamous to English fans for the Hand of God incident), and 1990. Following disappointment in the World Cup Final in 1990, Maradona suffered a further setback when he was banned for a year for drug offences.

The controversy attached to Maradona's name may cloud his memory in the future, but he has many distinguished admirers. Sir Stanley MATTHEWS called him 'The best one-footed player since Puskas' and Bobby ROBSON once quipped 'With Maradona, even Arsenal would have won the World Cup'.

Pelé had nearly everything. Maradona has everything. He works harder, does more

and is more skilful. Trouble is that he'll be remembered for another reason. He bends the rules to suit himself.

Sir Alf Ramsey (1986)

Maradona of the Carpathians Nickname of the Romanian midfielder Gheorghe HAGI.

Marching On Together Supporters' song, to the tune of 'Old Nell', which is associated with Leeds United. The song was first heard in 1972, when it was released as a pop single under the title 'Leeds, Leeds, Leeds', and was quickly adopted by the fans as their anthem.

Here we go with Leeds United,
We're gonna give the boys a hand,
Stand up and sing for Leeds United,
They are the greatest in the land.
Marching on together,
We're gonna see you win,
La, la, la, la, la, la,
We are so proud, we shout it out loud,
We love you – Leeds, Leeds, Leeds!

Margate English non-League football club, nicknamed the Gate. Strip: royal blue and white shirts with royal blue shorts and socks. Founded in 1880, Margate are based at Hartsdown Park in Margate and play in the Southern League.

Marindin, Major Sir Arthur Francis English football administrator, nicknamed The Major, who was an important figure in the early history of football as president of the Football Association (1874–90). Marindin was a respected soldier who was also one of the founders of the Royal Engineers football club, for whom he served as captain and full-back (appearing in two FA Cup Finals), and also of the Old Etonians (for whom he played in goal). When the two teams met in the FA Cup Final of 1875 he avoided offending either team by withdrawing from the game.

Subsequently he officiated as referee at no fewer than nine FA Cup Finals, earning much praise for his unruffled and always fair interpretation of the rules. As president of the FA in a difficult time, he protected the ideals of the amateur game and oversaw many important developments (not least the standardization of the laws governing the game in the four home nations). He finally stepped down when he saw that professionalism, which he had resisted, was inevitable.

Marine English non-League football club, nicknamed the Lilywhites. Strip: white shirts with black shorts and socks. Founded in 1894 and based at Rossett Park in Crosby, Liverpool, Marine play in the Northern Premier League.

Mariners Nickname of the English football club GRIMSBY TOWN, in reference to the town's long maritime tradition.

mark To dog the movements of an opposing player so as to prevent him receiving a pass or disposing of the ball.

Marlow English non-League football club, founded in 1870, nicknamed the Blues in reference to the team colours. Strip: royal blue and white. Originally called Great Marlow and now based at the Alfred Davis Memorial Garden ground, Marlow have spent most of their recent history in the Isthmian League.

Marseille French football club, formally titled Olympique Marseille. Strip: all white with blue trim. Founded in 1898 and based at the VÉLODROME in Marseille, the club have enjoyed their greatest era in relatively recent years, largely as a result of the presidency of millionaire Bernard Tapie, who provided the funds to acquire some of France's best players. Having won the League championship back in 1937, 1948, 1971, and 1972, they added to their list of honours further titles in 1989 and 1990 as well as their tenth victory in the Cup in 1989. In 1991 the team got as far as the Final of the European Cup, but lost 5–3 to Red Star Belgrade on penalties. Two years later, however, they realized their dream of European success when they appeared in another European Cup Final and this time won it – though the celebrations were somewhat clouded by a bribery scandal which subsequently erupted, threatening the club's suspension from European football.

Marsh, Rodney (1944–) English forward, who was renowned for his flamboyant talent in the 1960s and 1970s. A star with Fulham, Manchester City, and Queen's Park Rangers, Marsh was celebrated as one of the most entertaining players of his day (he also won nine caps for England). His recruitment by the US team Tampa Bay Rowdies in 1976 was a considerable boost to football in the USA. Subsequently he completed another three seasons with the Rowdies, as well as

re-appearing with Fulham. On his retirement as a player, he became a coach and eventually took over his old club Tampa Bay Rowdies in 1984.

> *In England, soccer is a grey game played by grey people on grey days.*
> Rodney Marsh, on US television (1979)

Martyrs Nickname of the Welsh non-League football club MERTHYR TYDFIL, after the name of the club.

Marvellous Magyars *See* MAGNIFICENT MAGYARS.

Marx brothers Nickname of the three England goalkeepers Gordon BANKS, Ron Springett, and Peter BONETTI, who shared the goalkeeping duties for the international side in the victorious 1966 World Cup campaign (*see* CLASS OF '66). As the English team steamed towards its finest moment in the Final that year the three keepers became firm friends and were virtually inseparable, enjoying as lively a rapport as the celebrated Marx brothers of the movies.

mascots Many clubs over the years have had an official mascot, typically a dog, which has graced home matches and team photographs with its presence. Such mascots date back to the very early history of the game and the lucky animals thus honoured were often treated with considerable care and kindness, the more superstitious believing that the team's luck rested on the mascot's welfare. As well as dogs, clubs adopted cats, sheep, goats, and even donkeys to perform the role.

Perhaps the most famous mascot of all, though, was human – a man by the name of Kenneth Henry Highett Baily (1911–93). A civil servant from Bournemouth, Baily made the decision to become his country's sporting mascot in the 1960s and subsequently attended as many international sporting contests as possible on behalf of his nation.

He fitted himself out with a traditional 'John Bull' outfit, complete with top hat, Union Jack waistcoat, and red hunting jacket, and became a regular figure at every England football match and at other sporting events both at home and abroad. Before the game started and at half-time he made a ritual tour of the stadium carrying a Union Jack flag, usually being greeted with a mixture of bemused applause and outright abuse from foreigners and home crowds alike. He featured regularly in televised coverage of England matches and was soon a national celebrity (his image was even used for the signboard of 'The Sportsman' public house in Pennington, Hampshire).

Where did you escape from?

Prince Charles, on being introduced to Baily

See also RUGBY PARK.

Masopust, Josef (1931–) Czech midfielder, who was a pillar of the Czech national side that featured in the World Cups of 1958 and 1962. A skilled dribbler, he formed a brilliant partnership in the national team with Svatopluk Pluskal and Jan Popluhar in the 1962 tournament, scoring Czechoslovakia's single goal in the Final. At home he played for Union Teplice, Dukla Prague, and finally with the Belgian club Crossing Molenbeek. He won a total of 56 caps in all and was voted European Footballer of the Year in 1962. After his retirement as a player, he served as manager of the Czech team for a number of years (1984–87).

Match of the Century A remarkable celebration match that took place between teams representing Great Britain and the Rest of Europe in May 1947. The game came about because of a financial crisis facing FIFA, the idea being that proceeds from the meeting would go to the troubled organization. Accordingly, the British selectors assembled an outstanding team that included such distinguished names as Stanley MATTHEWS, Tommy LAWTON, and Wilf Mannion, while those representing the Rest of Europe drew on the talents of such players as Johnny CAREY. The match was a huge success and Great Britain's convincing 6–1 victory consolidated the reputation of the home nations as the strongest footballing forces in the world. FIFA benefitted by £30,000.

Match of the Day The BBC television programme, which has built up a reputation as one of the most popular and enduring of all sports programmes since it was first screened (on BBC 2) on 22 August 1964. The very first 'Match of the Day' lasted 45 minutes and showed highlights of a game between Liverpool and Arsenal, which Liverpool won 3–2. The programme rapidly built up a big following (at its height being watched by an estimated quarter of the population of the UK) and two years after its launch it was transferred to BBC 1, where it became a standard feature of Saturday evening scheduling (its rousing theme tune being recognized by millions of viewers not even remotely interested in football).

Notable commentators who have worked on the programme include Kenneth Wolstenholme, David Coleman, John Motson, Tony Gubba, and Jimmy HILL. The programme has known its crises: in 1981, when Everton goalkeeper Jim McDonagh appeared (by mistake) in a shirt bearing the name of the team's sponsor the highly advertising-conscious 'Match of the Day' management settled for an uneasy compromise and filmed the action entirely from the side of the pitch so that the name could not be clearly seen. *See also* TELEVISION.

Good night – and don't forget tonight to put your cocks back.

Jimmy Hill, signing off on 'Match of the Day' on the evening before British Summer Time ended

Matlock Town English non-League football club, nicknamed the Gladiators. Strip: royal blue shirts, white shorts, and royal blue socks. Founded in 1885, the club are based at Causeway Lane in Matlock and play in the Northern Premier League.

Matthäus, Lothar (1961–) German midfielder, who became a pillar of the German national team in the 1980s. He established his reputation as a formidable goalscorer while with Borussia Mönchengladbach and Bayern Munich and made his international debut in 1980. Subsequently he played a key role in the World Cup campaigns of 1986 and 1990, when he led the team to victory as its captain. His achievement was reflected in his being voted European Footballer of the Year for 1990, among a host of other awards. He transferred to Internazionale in 1988, leading them to victory in the Italian League a year later and in the UEFA Cup in 1991 (when he was also top League scorer). In 1993 he returned to Bayern Munich.

Matthews, Sir Stanley (1915–) English forward, nicknamed the Wizard of Dribble, who became a symbol of all that was good in the English game in the years following World War II and who remains the most famous English footballer of all time. Born at Hanley in the Potteries, Matthews – the son of a boxer nicknamed the 'Fighting Barber of Hanley' – made his debut for Stoke City in 1932 and first played for England in 1934, scoring a goal in his first match. He quickly became a folk hero to the people of the Potteries and when he asked for a transfer in 1938 because of differences with the club management 3000 fans attended a public meeting to demand that he stay (which he did).

After the war he joined Blackpool (1947) and a year later was given the accolade of Footballer of the Year – an honour that was repeated a full 15 years later in 1963. His performance in the classic FA Cup Final of 1953, which Blackpool won 4–3, led to the match being immortalized as the MATTHEWS FINAL. He collected the last of his 54 caps for England in 1957 and in 1961 returned to Stoke City, playing a key role in restoring the side to the First Division in 1963.

He finally retired two years later, at the incredible age of 50, making him the oldest player ever to play First Division football (see AGELESS WONDER). His remarkable career was crowned with a knighthood that same year. Subsequently he served as manager of Port Vale for three years (1965–68) and of the Maltese team Hibernian (1969).

Usually playing at outside right, Matthews – a contender for the title of the most celebrated player of all time – was by far the most famous player of his era and won praise for his mastery of the game, which was bolstered by his physical fitness and unflurried, modest character. As a provider of potential goal chances he had no equal, although his own tally of goals was not huge (in the 1962–63 season he scored just one League goal). In fact, he scored only one hat-trick in his entire career (for England against Czechoslovakia in 1937).

His nickname reflected his unrivalled ball control, which enabled him to evade bewildered opponents and execute inch-perfect crosses:

> Playing Stanley Matthews is like playing a ghost.

Johnny Carey

Matthews himself gave few clues to the secret of his skills:

> Don't ask me how I do it. It always comes out of me under pressure.

He was so fast that a much-repeated joke of his era claimed that he could turn off his bedroom light and be under the bedclothes before the room became dark. Joe MERCER called him 'unique' and 'unplayable', Danny BLANCHFLOWER marvelled at the fact that though everyone knew the Wizard's repertory of tricks they still couldn't do anything about it, and Tommy LAWTON enthused

that Matthews 'used to put the ball on my centre-parting'. His other nicknames included The King of Soccer and The Maestro.

Matthews Final The FA Cup Final of 1953, which is uniquely associated with the name of the great English footballer Stanley MATTHEWS. 1953 was Coronation Year and the public looked to football to provide a fitting celebration of national pride and sportsmanship. Football was not wanting and in the Final between Matthews' Blackpool and Bolton Wanderers the scene was set for the making of football legend.

Matthews was 38 years old and considered a mythical figure by adoring crowds – but he had never been in an FA Cup-winning team (though he had been on the losing side twice previously). The whole country identified with his personal quest – but for much of the game it looked very much like he was destined for disappointment once more. However, with just 20 minutes of the match to go and with Blackpool trailing 3–1, Matthews suddenly came alive.

Treating the crowd to as fine a display of his skills that anyone had hitherto witnessed he outfoxed the Bolton defence time and again to lay on deadly accurate passes to centre-forward Stan MORTENSEN and the other strikers. Mortensen did not waste his chances and scored twice to complete his hat-trick. Then, with just a minute left to play, Matthews struck again and got the ball to Bill Perry, who scored the decisive goal (incidentally becoming the first South African player to win an FA Cup winners' medal).

Although it was the names of Mortensen and Perry on the scoresheet, it was Matthews who was the hero of the day and ever since then the match has been dubbed the Matthews Final, one of the classic meetings in FA Cup history. In fact, Matthews very nearly missed playing in the game altogether, having pulled a muscle during training just four days before.

> The last player to score a hat-trick in a cup final was Stan Mortensen. He even had a final named after him – the Matthews Final.

Lawrie McMenemy

> The '53 Cup Final was my most unforgettable match, but I did not win the game on my own. That's a myth. It was a great team effort.

Stanley Matthews

Mattress Makers' Ground Nickname of the VICENTE CALDERÓN STADIUM in Madrid, in reference to the use of red and white stripes as decoration throughout the venue.

mauling See PUBLIC SCHOOL FOOTBALL.

Mauritania Mauritania joined FIFA in 1964 but have yet to make much impact in international competition. Strip: green and yellow shirts, blue shorts, and green socks.

Mauritius Mauritius joined FIFA in 1962 but have yet to establish a strong international reputation. Strip: red shirts, white shorts, and red socks with white trim.

Maxwell, Robert (Robert Ludwig Hoch; 1923–91) British publisher, businessman, and Labour politician, born in Czechoslovakia, who became one of the more colourful personalities in the football world through his stake in Oxford United, Derby County, and other football clubs.

Variously nicknamed Captain Bob and the 'Bouncing Czech', Maxwell pursued his interest in football with much the same ambition and lack of scruples that characterized his dealings elsewhere in business and made many enemies within the game. He was in constant conflict with the football authorities over allegations that he was attempting to establish a monopoly of control over his clubs and fellow-directors were highly suspicious of his motives, though many were won over by his dynamism and wealth.

When Maxwell made a further acquisition in 1988 Tommy DOCHERTY quipped rather bitterly: 'Maxwell's just bought Brighton and Hove Albion, and he's furious to find that it's only one club.'

Plans to merge Oxford and Reading as Thames Valley Royals outraged members of both clubs and brought further conflict with the football establishment before the idea was eventually dropped. Having arrived at Oxford when it was on the brink of financial ruin in 1982, he left in 1987 when he acquired Derby County, installing his son Kevin as his successor at the Manor Ground.

After Maxwell's mysterious death while on his luxury yacht off Tenerife the tangled and dubious nature of his business enterprises finally came to light, though fortunately the clubs with which he had had dealings managed to avoid being drawn too deeply into the recriminations and legal complications that followed his demise.

I have played football since I was a toddler. Left wing, as you would expect. I was very fast.

Robert Maxwell (1985)

Mazzola Playing name of the Brazilian forward José ALTAFINI.

Mazzola, Sandro (1942–) Italian footballer, son of the celebrated Valentino Mazzola (who died in the Superga air crash), who was a star with Internazionale in the 1960s and 1970s. Playing initially as centre-forward but later as an attacking midfielder, Mazzola proved himself one of the most formidable players of his era and became a natural choice for the Italian national team. He played a leading role in the Italian World Cup campaigns of 1966, 1970, and 1974, scoring 22 goals in 70 appearances in all.

Meadow Lane The home ground of NOTTS COUNTY. The Magpies, the oldest surviving club in the Football League, played at Park Hollow next to Nottingham Castle, The Meadows cricket ground, Notts cricket club at Beeston, the Castle cricket ground, and Trent Bridge cricket ground, which was their home from 1883 to 1910, before finally moving to a permanent base at Meadow Lane.

Here they erected a Main Stand in just nine days (it is still standing), while another stand was floated across the River Trent from Trent Bridge (it was the oldest stand anywhere in the League prior to demolition in 1978). Because of the ground's proximity to a brook running from the river, a man with a long pole fitted with a cane basket was posted on the bank of the stream on match days to fish wayward balls out of the water.

Events during the ground's history have included occupation by the army in World War I, severe damage (traces of which can still be seen) from bombs during World War II (when a machine gun was positioned on the Kop), the use of prisoners-of-war to clear the pitch of snow, and the building of a new sports centre. A nearby road is named Iremonger Road after the club's celebrated goalkeeper Albert Iremonger. The ground was extensively redeveloped in 1993.

Meadowbank Stadium The home ground, in Edinburgh, of the Scottish football club MEADOWBANK THISTLE. For many years Thistle played at Crewe Toll and subsequently at City Park, the former home of Edinburgh City, but the club's controversial election to the Scottish League in 1974 meant that a superior ground was required and it was agreed that the club could use Meadowbank Stadium, which had been built in 1970 for the Commonwealth Games (which returned in 1986).

Often likened to the Crystal Palace complex in London, the Meadowbank Stadium (which is overlooked by Arthur's Seat) is also used for athletics among other events and is not suitable for the most important matches. Notable landmarks in the stadium's history as a football ground have included the decision taken in 1983 to admit women to matches free of charge, reviving a common practice of the previous century. Local fans have dubbed Thistle's home the Concrete Lavvy Pan.

Meadowbank Thistle Scottish football club, nicknamed Thistle or the Wee Jags. Strip: amber shirts with black trim, black shorts, and amber socks. Thistle have their origins in the Ferranti Thistle team that was founded in 1943 as the works team for the Ferranti company in Edinburgh. The club was reorganized in 1974, however, when it was unexpectedly and somewhat controversially elected to the Scottish League (the League obliged the club to find a new ground and to drop their old name as conditions of League membership).

Based at MEADOWBANK STADIUM, Thistle took several years to build up a strong side; they won their first major honour, the Second Division championship, in 1987.

Thistle enjoyed their record victory to date in 1985, when they beat Raith Rovers 6–0; they suffered their worst defeat in 1974, when they lost 8–0 to Hamilton Athletic. Walter Boyd holds the record for League appearances with the club, having played in 446 games between 1979 and 1989.

> Fisul, Fisul, I want a Fisul and I want one now,
> Not one, not two, but three goals in it,
> I wanna Fisul and I want one now.

Supporters' song, to the tune of the 'Banana Boat Song'

Meazza, Giuseppe (1910–79) Italian forward, nicknamed Peppino, who was a leading football celebrity in the 1930s. Handsome, unruly, charming, and a brilliant player who was especially renowned for his spectacular bicycle kicks, he made his debut for Internazionale in 1927 and rapidly attracted attention with his dazzling play both for his home team and for the Italian national side. He made 53 appearances for Italy and scored 33 goals, helping the side to victory in two World Cups (1934 and 1938).

His popularity with Italian crowds protected him from the wrath of the Fascists, who deplored his debonair behaviour and his reputation as a womanizer and gambler; on one occasion the Fascists sought to humiliate him by honouring every member of the national team but him (which only increased his popularity with the masses). He played for other teams (including AC Milan and Juventus) towards the end of his playing career and after his retirement continued to add to his fame for riotous living.

After his death the San Siro Stadium, home of Internazionale and AC Milan, was officially renamed the GIUSEPPE MEAZZA STADIUM in his memory.

medals Commemorative medals connected with football's prestigious events have been awarded since the earliest years of the organized game's history. Medals are awarded to players who appear in major finals and similar mementoes are handed out to successful managers and other staff.

Though many players can boast impressive collections of such medals won in the course of their career, it is unlikely that anyone will ever equal the achievement of Jimmy Delaney, who nearly managed to make a clean sweep of winners' medals from four national football association Cup Finals. He qualified for a Scottish Cup medal as a member of Celtic in 1937, for the English Cup medal as a player with Manchester United in 1948, for the Irish Cup medal with Derry City in 1954, and in 1956 narrowly failed to win an FA of Ireland Cup medal as a member of the losing finalists Shamrock Rovers.

Three players share the honour of having won five FA Cup medals, all of them prominent footballers of the 1870s and 1880s – James Forrest (of Blackburn Rovers), A.F. KINNAIRD (of the Wanderers), and C.H.R. Wollaston (also of the Wanderers). North of the border three players have been awarded no fewer than seven Cup Winners' medals in the Scottish Cup – Jimmy McMenemy (of Celtic), Bob McPhail (of Airdrieonians), and Billy MCNEILL (of Celtic), while Charles Campbell won a record eight medals between 1874 and 1886. Phil Neal of Liverpool holds the record for English League medals, having won eight in the 1970s and 1980s. J. Welford was the first man to receive winners' medals in both the English and the Scottish FA competitions, back in the 1890s.

Meisl, Hugo (1881–1937) Austrian manager, who led the spectacular Wunderteam that brought Austria much glory in the early 1930s. Assisted by the English coach Jimmy HOGAN, Meisl developed an elegant playing style based on an attacking centre-half and placed great emphasis on fast, accurate passing and technical skills.

Melchester Rovers The mythical football club for which the comic strip hero *Roy of the Rovers* played for so many years until his career ended in 1993. Strip: red and yellow. The club enjoyed virtually every honour the game had to offer thanks to the efforts of its great star and looked set to continue in business after 1993 as a monthly comic strip, with Race's son Rocky providing the goals. A real-life counterpart to the team was founded in 1993 and took to the field in the famous red and yellow strip to compete in Sunday league football.

membership scheme The admittance to football grounds of accredited club members only, which was suggested as a possible way forward in the late 1980s in response to the rising tide of violence at grounds throughout the UK. The idea was much favoured by the government of Margaret Thatcher but was opposed by the football establishment, the police, and other organizations who saw such a scheme as unworkable, expensive and an overreaction to the violence of a minority of fans. Civil rights groups also opposed the idea, fearing that the issue of identity cards could have menacing implications. Luton Town was one of a number of clubs to adopt such a scheme on a voluntary basis, but after five years' debate the concept of a national membership scheme was finally dropped after the Taylor Report came out against it in the wake of the Hillsborough disaster.

> *Until now they had to ask their victims: 'Are you one of us or one of them?' Now they'll just ask to see your ID card.*
>
> Denis Howell, shadow minister for sport, on football hooligans (1988)

Mercer, Joe (1914–90) English footballer and manager, who excelled in both roles and became one of the most popular figures in British football after the war. Mercer made his debut for Everton in 1931 and first appeared for England in 1938. A year later he played a key role in Everton's League championship victory – but the onset of World War II curtailed his international career (though not before he had risen to the post of captain and had collected five caps). After the war he moved to Arsenal and enjoyed a revival in reputation after switching from wing-half to the defence and becoming captain of the side that won the League title in 1948 and again in 1953 as well as the FA Cup in 1950 (in which year he was voted Footballer of the Year).

A broken leg spelled the end of Mercer's playing career in 1954 and he moved into management at Sheffield United in 1955. He transferred to Aston Villa in 1958 and led them to victory in the League Cup in 1960 before retiring through ill health in 1964. He returned to the game in 1965, as manager of Manchester City, and steered the team through one of their great eras, winning the League championship in 1968, the FA Cup in 1969, and the double of the League Cup and the European Cup Winners' Cup in 1970. Appointed manager of Coventry in 1972, he stood in as temporary replacement (for Alf RAMSEY) as manager of England in 1974.

Meredith, Billy (1875–1958) Welsh footballer, nicknamed the Welsh Wizard, who was considered the finest winger of his era. A coalminer from the Welsh town of Chirk (with whom he reached two Welsh Cup finals), Meredith began his professional career in 1894 and over the next 30 years excelled as a player for Northwich Victoria, Manchester City, Manchester United, and Wales.

Given to chewing on the toothpicks he always carried, he was one of the great characters of early 20th century football and the inspiration of the Manchester United side that won the League championship in 1908 and the FA Cup in 1909. Previously, as captain, he had already won an FA Cup (1904) with Manchester City (thus becoming the first player to appear in Welsh Cup and FA Cup-winning teams).

Meredith ranked alongside Steve BLOOMER as the outstanding British player of the prewar years and he was a regular choice for the Welsh national team, with whom he won 48 caps. By the time of his retirement at the age of 49 (at which age he made an appearance in an FA Cup semifinal) he had played some 1100 matches. After his retirement as a player he worked as a coach and scout as well as running a Manchester pub.

Merry Millers Nickname of the English football club ROTHERHAM UNITED, in reference to the town's many mills.

Merthyr Town Former Welsh football club, which was a member of the League from 1920 to 1930. Based at Penydarren Park, the club was eventually succeeded by MERTHYR TYDFIL.

Merthyr Tydfil Welsh non-League football club, nicknamed the Martyrs. Strip: white shirts and black shorts. Founded in 1945 as successors to MERTHYR TOWN and based at Penydarren Park, the club play in the Vauxhall Conference. They enjoyed a golden period in the late 1940s and 1950s.

Messiah, The Nickname of the English manager Lawrie MCMENEMY.

Metropolitan League Former English non-League football league, which embraced both amateur and professional teams in the London area. Founded in 1949, the League championship was dominated by such professional sides as Chelsea and West Ham United 'A' teams, who also figured in the history of the League's cup competition open to professional clubs. Sides that excelled in the League's amateur trophy competition included Newbury Town, who won it a record six times in succession in the late 1950s. The League went out of existence in 1971.

Metropolitan Police English non-League football club, appropriately nicknamed the Blues with reference to the team colours. Strip: all blue. Founded in 1919, the club are based at the Metropolitan Police (Imber Court) Sports Club in East Molesey, Surrey, and play in the Isthmian League.

Mexican wave The synchronized rising of the crowd at a football or other sports stadium, which creates the illusion of a wave running through the spectators. This novel effect depends upon people sitting in equivalent seats in every row rising at a given moment, raising their hands and then sitting down again as their neighbours follow suit. Most spectators give a hearty cheer when it is their turn to stand (or otherwise jeer those who decline to take part) and waves regularly travel around the whole stadium before petering out.

Such waves (which generally develop before matches begin or when the action on the pitch has become boring) were first seen during the 1986 World Cup tournament in Mexico (hence the name) and were rapidly imitated around the world (being seen even at the Wimbledon tennis championships). Mexican waves at British grounds almost invariably travel in an anti-clockwise direction, although in the southern hemisphere it has been observed that they generally travel in a clockwise direction (for no very apparent reason).

Mexico The Mexican national team has dominated central American football since the very beginning and Mexico itself has twice been the focus of international football as host of the World Cup (1970 and 1986). The Mexican side first took part in the World Cup Finals in 1930 but failed to prosper either then or in the series of 1950 and 1954 and it was not until 1958 that they managed to draw a game (against Wales). They registered their first World Cup win in 1962 and in 1970 rose to the challenge of playing before their home crowds by reaching the quarter-finals. The 1986 tournament began well for Mexico but again ended at the quarter-finals stage with defeat on penalties against West Germany. An appearance in the 1990 World Cup was ruled out by the authorities in punishment for the misrepresentation of the ages of three Mexican players in an international youth tournament. Strip: green shirts with red and green trim, white shorts with red and green trim, and red socks with white trim. Mexico qualified for the 1994 World Cup in America.

Mickey Mouse Cup Derogatory nickname that was applied to the League Cup in its early days, when many leading teams declined to participate.

Mid-Annandale Former Scottish football club, which played in the League from 1923 to 1926. The side was based at Lockerbie near Dumfries though the site of their pitch is unknown.

Middlesbrough English football club, nicknamed Boro or Ironsides (in reference to the area's heavy industries). Strip: red shirts and socks, with white shorts. Founded in 1876 as the result of a discussion during a tripe supper at the Corporation Hotel the year before, Middlesbrough first turned professional in 1889, then reverted to amateur status in 1892, and finally decided on permanent professional ranking in 1899.

The club had already taken possession

of the Amateur Cup in 1895 and 1898, winning the cup for the second time only after their semi-final against Thornaby had been played in the isolated hill village of Brotton in the Clevelands after fears of a smallpox epidemic then raging in Teesside meant that the scheduled venue at Darlington was unacceptable.

Middlesbrough joined the First Division for the first time in 1902 but got into trouble with the FA in 1910 over allegations that the club chairman (anxious to whip up local support in his campaign to be elected a member of parliament) had attempted to bribe the team's opponents to secure a win; both the chairman and the club's secretary-manager were suspended for life.

The club have returned to the top flight on several occasions, but have been denied any of the major prizes beyond the Second Division championship in 1927, 1929, and 1974 (when they won it by a record margin of 15 points). In 1992, the Boro qualified for the Premier League in the year of its establishment, but ended up being relegated at the end of the inaugural season.

There has been no shortage of stars at the club's home, AYRESOME PARK, with such players as Wilf Mannion, who won 26 caps in the post-World War II period, and Brian CLOUGH in the 1950s among those to bring inspiration to the side; other stars have included the formidable centre-forwards Alf Common in the early years of the century and George Camsell, scorer of a record 59 Second Division goals in a single season (1927–28).

The Boro enjoyed their record victory in 1958, when they beat Brighton and Hove Albion 9–0; they suffered their worst defeat in 1954, when they lost by the same margin to Blackburn Rovers. Tim Williamson holds the record for League appearances with the club, having played in 563 games between 1902 and 1923.

Middlesbrough Ironopolis Former English football club, that was a member of the League from 1893 to 1894. Based at the Paradise Ground in Middlesbrough, Ironopolis seemed set to eclipse amateur rivals Middlesbrough when they achieved League status. However, despite attracting large crowds and finishing their first season in eleventh place, Ironopolis disappeared from the League and their rivals gradually assumed their position as the town's foremost club.

midfield That part of the pitch that lies between the attack and the defence.

Midland Combination English non-League football league, founded in 1927 as the Worcestershire Combination, which is one of the most prestigious leagues in the Midlands. Oustanding teams in the league's history include Catshill Village, who won the Championship four times in the 1930s, and Evesham United, who won it a record five times after World War II; other distinguished sides include Alvechurch and Paget Rovers (both four times Champions).

Midland League Former English non-League football league, which was founded in 1889. Formally titled the Midland Counties League, it was long considered one of the leading minor leagues and several League teams (Barnsley, Chesterfield, Doncaster Rovers, Lincoln City, Rotherham County, Peterborough United, Scunthorpe United, and Shrewsbury) all played in its ranks before moving up to the League itself. The League disappeared in 1982 when it was merged with the Yorkshire League to form the Northern Counties Eastern League.

Mighty Atom Nickname of the much-admired Northern Ireland-born striker Patsy GALLAGHER, who was considered one of the most formidable forwards of his day, despite his slight build.

Mighty Mouse Nickname of the celebrated English striker Kevin KEEGAN, who established himself as one of the leading European stars of his day, despite his relatively small stature.

AC Milan Italian football club, nicknamed the Old Man, which is universally acknowledged to be one of the strongest teams in the world. Strip: red and black striped shirts, white shorts, and white socks. Founded in 1899 by the Englishman Alfred Edwards as Milan Cricket and Football Club, the club – whose earliest side included six English players – retains its English spelling of Milan (as opposed to Milano) in honour of its founders.

The team – sometimes dubbed the Aristocrats of European Football and the Red Devils after their strip – were based at a number of grounds before settling at their permanent home, SAN SIRO (renamed the GIUSEPPE MEAZZA STADIUM in 1979), in 1926. The club have a long list of victories to their credit, beginning just two years after the team's foundation with triumph in the Italian League in 1901; Milan have since won the League championship another 11 times (1906, 1907, 1951, 1955, 1957,

1959, 1962, 1968, 1979, 1988, and 1993). The club have also enjoyed success in the Italian Cup on several occasions, winning it in 1967, 1972, 1973, and 1977. Other honours include the World Club Championship in 1969 and 1989, the European Cup Winners' Cup in 1968 and 1973, no fewer than four European Cup titles (1963, 1969, 1989, and 1990), and the Super Cup in 1989.

Other landmarks have included the club's introduction of goal nets in 1906 (14 years before they were seen in England), a split in the club that led to the formation of rivals Internazionale in 1907, the arrival of new president Piero Pirelli (of the tyre company) in the 1920s, the temporary adoption by the club of the name 'AC Milano' under the Fascists in the 1930s, and the reopening of San Siro in 1955 (with further redevelopment for the 1990 World Cup).

Milan have known controversy during their long and distinguished history, however: in 1980 the club were forcibly relegated to the Second Division as a punishment for a bribe scandal, while in 1991 they were banned from all European tournaments after the club's players left the field without permission during a European quarter-final against Olympique Marseille. The team continues to command worldwide respect, however, and recent stars (attracted by the money of the club's multi-millionaire president Silvio Berlusconi and others) have included the Dutch trio Frank RIJKAARD, Marco VAN BASTEN, and Ruud GULLIT.

Milburn, Jackie (1924–88) Celebrated English footballer, nicknamed Wor Jackie (Our Jackie), who was a star with Newcastle United and England in the 1940s and 1950s. One of the most distinguished members of a famous footballing family, Wor Jackie (as he was dubbed by Newcastle fans) made his first appearance with the club in 1946 and three years later won the first of his 13 England caps (inheriting Tommy LAWTON's place as centre-forward and going on to score a total of 10 international goals).

Milburn rapidly emerged as the lynchpin in the Newcastle side that stormed to three FA Cup victories in the 1950s (1951, 1952, and 1955) and acquired the status of a cult figure in the north-east. Though a modest man himself, he proved the most formidable of strikers with a startling turn of speed and included among his many achievements the fastest Wembley FA Cup Final goal (after just 45 seconds in 1955) and a career total of 179 goals in 354 League matches.

Afflicted with fibrositis, he rarely headed the ball and occasions when he did so always raised a cheer from the crowd.

Milburn retired as a player in 1963 and was briefly manager of Ipswich Town (where he succeeded Alf RAMSEY) before taking up a second career as a journalist. His funeral was attended by tens of thousands of mourners; he is commemorated in Newcastle, the city where he is still accorded almost divine status, by a statue outside the city's main shopping centre.

> *Once he got going he was unstoppable. Whenever I think of Jackie I think of a greyhound going out of a trap.*
>
> Len Shackleton
>
> *The roar of the crowd told me he was exceptional. I could sense his pace, the dramatic presence. I didn't need eyes.*
>
> Gerry Brereton, blind entertainer (1988)

Milk Cup *See* LEAGUE CUP.

Millers Nickname of the English non-League football club AVELEY, in reference to the team's ground, Mill Field.

Millmoor The home ground of ROTHERHAM UNITED. Rotherham moved to Millmoor in 1907 and have remained there ever since, sandwiched between huge scrapyards. Features of the ground include the Railway End and the Tivoli End (named after the Tivoli Cinema that stands just outside).

Milltown The home ground, in Dublin, of Ireland's most celebrated football club, SHAMROCK ROVERS.

Millwall English football club, nicknamed the Lions. Strip: blue shirts, white shorts, and blue socks. Founded in 1885 and based from 1910 at the DEN in Cold Blow Lane, the Lions began life as Millwall Rovers (renamed Millwall Athletic in 1889), a team comprising workers (most of whom were Scottish) at the jam and marmalade factory Morton and Company.

Their first success was victory in the East End Cup in 1887 but subsequently they lived a relatively uneventful existence until the 1980s. The club joined the League in 1920 and then divided their time between the lower three divisions, winning the Third Division (South) championship in 1928 and 1938 and the Fourth Division title in 1962. Life was at times less than exciting – in the 1920s the club managed to finish in the same position in the division (fourteenth) at the end of no fewer than three successive seasons.

Millwall, whose home at the Den became one of the most daunting for visiting teams anywhere in the UK, finally reached the First Division in 1988, having captured the Second Division championship that year, and remained in the top flight for just two seasons before relegation in 1990. They finally left the Den for a new home (Senegal Fields) in the docklands in 1993. Over the years they have got as far as the semi-finals of the FA Cup on three occasions, becoming in 1937 the first Third Division side to progress to that round.

The club has been particularly prone to violent crowd disturbance and in the 1980s its fans were among the most reviled in the League, despite attempts by the club to improve their image as a home of 'family football' (even to the extent of installing crèche facilities). Stars with the side have included the exuberant full-back Harry CRIPPS (*see* DOG, THE) in the 1960s and Tony Cascarino and Teddy Sheringham in the 1980s.

Millwall enjoyed their record victory in 1927, when they beat Torquay United 9–1; they suffered their worst defeat in 1946, losing 9–1 to Aston Villa. In 1967 they enjoyed a remarkable run of home victories, winning 59 matches in succession before eventual defeat at the hands of Portsmouth. Barry Kitchener holds the record for League appearances with the club, having played in 523 matches between 1967 and 1982.

> We're regarded as a small club, but we're not. We're really a big club that had fallen into almost terminal decline.

Reg Burr, chairman (1988)

> We are Millwall, we are Millwall,
> We are Millwall, from The Den,
> No one likes us, no one likes us,
> No one likes us, we don't care,
> We are Millwall, super Millwall,
> We are Millwall, from The Den.

Supporters' song, to the tune of Rod Stewart's 'Sailing'

Mini-Ibrox Nickname of MCDIARMID PARK.

Minstermen Nickname of the English football club YORK CITY, in reference to York Minster.

Missioners Nickname of the English non-League football club HAYES, in reference to the club's origins as a boys' team called Botwell Mission.

Mitropa Cup International competition for European football clubs, which was the forerunner of the European Cup. Founded in 1927, the Mitropa Cup was contested by teams from several central European nations, making it the world's first multi-national club competition. It prospered in the 1930s but was eclipsed by other tournaments in the 1950s though it continued to be staged in a modest form. At various times it has also been known as the Zentropa Cup and the Danube Cup.

Molesey English non-League football club, nicknamed the Moles. Strip: yellow shirts, blue shorts, and yellow socks. Founded in 1950 and based at the Walton Road ground, Molesey play in the Isthmian League.

Molineux The home ground of the English football club WOLVERHAMPTON WANDERERS. Molineux began its life as a popular recreation ground, complete with boating lake, pleasure gardens, and athletics track. The football club arrived there in 1889 after vacating a ground at Dudley Road (where their 1893 FA Cup Final victory is commemorated in the names of several streets and by stone replicas of the cup in front of the houses that were built on ground's site).

The Molineux Grounds were named after the Molineux family who once lived at Molineux Hotel nearby. The site was gradually developed over the years as the team prospered (particularly under the management of Frank Buckley). Events in the ground's history have included the controversy that arose from Buckley's over-watering of the pitch in the 1930s (a tactic that favoured the home team), the celebrated 1954 meeting between Wolves and Honvéd, extensive redevelopment in the late 1970s (the cost of which brought the club to the verge of extinction in 1982), and a further financial crisis in 1986, in which year safety considerations led to all but the new cantilever John Ireland stand (named after a former club president) being closed to spectators. A deal with the council and commercial interests saved the ground and the club but its long-term future still remained in some doubt.

Relics that survived World War II include signs pointing to the air-raid shelters now buried beneath the stands.

monkey gland treatment *See* BUCKLEY BABES.

Montrose Scottish football club, nicknamed the Gable Endies. Strip: blue shirts, white shorts, and red socks. The club was founded in 1879 and later merged with Montrose United. Its first home was called 'Metally' as the pitch was next to the Metal Bridge; subsequently the club settled permanently at LINKS PARK, where the Gable Endies shared the pitch beside Dorward House with the local curling club.

Montrose never grabbed the headlines in the early years, but eventually attracted attention in the 1970s and 1980s with lengthy runs in the Scottish Cup (1973 and 1976) and in the League Cup (1975–76); more recently they captured the Second Division championship (1985) – their first major trophy in 106 years – and were runners-up in 1991, earning them promotion to the First Division for the second time in their history. Notable scalps collected by the club in recent years have included those of Hibs, who lost to Montrose in the course of their celebrated League Cup run, and of Hearts in the 1986–87 League Cup.

The club enjoyed their record victory in 1975, beating Vale of Leithen 12–0; they suffered their worst defeat back in 1951, when they lost 13–0 to Aberdeen.

moon, over the *See* OVER THE MOON.

Moonlight Dribblers Nickname given to EVERTON by some humorists in their early history. The nickname reflected the reputation the team had for training after dark, relying largely upon the light of the moon to illuminate their efforts. *See also* TOFFEES.

Moor Green English non-League football club, nicknamed the Moors, who were once one of the leading amateur teams in the Midlands. Strip: light blue and dark blue. Founded in 1901 and based at Sherwood Road in Hall Green, the Moors play in the Southern League and enjoyed a golden period in the 1930s.

Moore, Bobby (1941–93) English defender, who captained England to World Cup victory in 1966 (*see* CLASS OF '66). At home, Moore won an FA Cup winner's medal with West Ham in 1964 and led the Hammers team that captured the European Cup Winners' Cup in 1965 before enjoying his great moment of glory with the national team in 1966. He was renowned for his calm detached demeanour and this served him well both in 1966 and four years later when his reputation was threatened by scandal (*see* BOGOTÁ INCIDENT). His relaxed

manner concealed a gritty determination that few suspected, however. Geoff HURST once recalled:

> Bobby was great at that. Someone would come and kick a lump out of him, and he'd play as though he hadn't noticed. But ten minutes later . . . whoof! . . . he had a great 'golden boy' image, Mooro. But he was hard.

After leaving West Ham, he played with equal self-assurance for Fulham, reaching another FA Cup Final in 1975. He retired as a player in 1977, having amassed a total of 108 caps for England. Subsequently he managed Oxford City and Southend United and worked as a journalist until his early death from cancer in 1993.

Morecambe English non-League football club, nicknamed the Shrimps. Strip: red shirts, white shorts, and black socks. Founded in 1920 and based at Christie Park, Morecambe were founder members of the Northern Premier League in 1968.

Moreno, Rafael Spanish footballer, nicknamed Pichichi, who was one of the earliest stars with Athletic Bilbao. Immediately identifiable by the white skull cap he always wore, Moreno had the distinction of being the scorer of the first goal at the famous SAN MAMÉS stadium in 1913. He enjoyed enormous popularity with the home crowd and his early death in the 1920s was much regretted; his memory is preserved at the club's ground by a bust (at the foot of which for many years teams making their debut at the stadium placed flowers) and by the annual Pichichi Award presented to Spain's top goalscorer.

Morley, Ebenezer Cobb (1831–1924) English football administrator, nicknamed the Father of Football, who was the prime mover behind the establishment of the Football Association and who laid out the first set of laws to be followed by FA members. Also nicknamed 'the grand old sportsman of Barnes', Morley was a solicitor who had been himself a respected player of the game, representing Barnes (a club he had helped to found); he had also rowed for the London Rowing Club at Henley, kept a pack of beagles and hunted with the Surrey Union Foxhounds and the Devon and Somerset Staghounds, and was active as a promoter of athletics events.

Born in Hull, he founded the Barnes club in 1862 and subsequently pressed for football to be run on a universal set of rules as cricket was. His suggestion led directly to the formation of the FA and the drawing up of a table of 14 laws, which among other things forbade hacking. He went on to become the first secretary of the FA (1863–66) and its second president (1867–74) and finally died at the age of 93 a year after the first FA Cup Final at Wembley.

Morocco The Moroccan national team was the first African side to establish a worldwide reputation, partly by virtue of becoming the first African team ever to reach the Finals of a World Cup (1970). This first campaign saw the side present West Germany with stiff resistance before going down 2–1, another brave performance against Peru, and a well-deserved 1–1 draw with Bulgaria. The side have qualified for the Finals once more in 1986, when they startled the experts by winning their group (which included Poland, England, and Portugal) and then restricting eventual runners-up West Germany to a 1–0 victory. The team's other honours include victory in the 1976 African Nations Cup. Morocco qualified for the 1994 World Cup in America. Strip: all red.

Mortensen, Stan (1922–91) English forward, who was a star with Blackpool and England in the 1940s and 1950s. Nicknamed the Blackpool Bombshell, or otherwise known as the Electric Eel or Electric Heels, he bewildered defences with his ability to weave through them and reach the goal. He made his international debut under unusual circumstances, turning out for Wales against his own country, England, in 1943 (he was invited to play for Wales at the last minute when the Welsh left-half was injured). In all he scored 197 goals in 320 League games for Blackpool and 24 goals in 25 games for England.

One of the leading players of his day, Mortensen's achievements were sometimes eclipsed by those of his team mate Stanley MATTHEWS; ironically the 1953 FA Cup Final, in which he turned in a sensational performance and scored a hat-trick, is still remembered as the MATTHEWS FINAL. Later in his career he also played for Hull and Southampton.

I got the ball in the middle of the field and a voice out of the centre stand shouted out, 'Give it to Taylor'. So I gave it to Taylor. Five minutes afterwards, I got the ball again in the middle of the field and the same voice shouted, 'Give it to Matthews'. So I gave it to Matthews. A couple of minutes later, I got the ball again, but this time there were three Arsenal players around me so I looked up at the stand and the voice came back, 'Use your own discretion'.

Stan Mortensen, *Blackpool Football* (Robin Daniels, 1972)

Morton Scottish football club, nicknamed the Ton. Strip: blue and white hooped shirts, white shorts, and blue socks. Morton were founded in 1874 and joined the League in 1893, three years before they became the first football club in Scotland to adopt the status of a limited company.

For many years the club, based at CAPPIELOW PARK, had only one major honour to claim as their own – the 1922 Scottish Cup, in the Final of which they overcame Rangers thanks to a goal by star player Jimmy Gourlay. They resurfaced with Second Division titles in 1950, 1964, and 1967 and subsequently added First Division championships in 1978, 1984, and 1987.

Celebrated names associated with the club over the years have included Scotland goalkeeper Jimmy Cowan, striker and later manager Allan McGraw, and Andy Ritchie.

Morton enjoyed their record victory back in 1886, when they beat Carfin Shamrock 11–0; they suffered record defeats of 10–1 against Port Glasgow in 1894 and against St Bernard's in 1933. David Hayes holds the record for League appearances with the club, having played in 358 matches between 1969 and 1984.

Morton, Alan (1893–1971) Scottish footballer, nicknamed the Wee Blue Devil, who was a star player with Rangers and Scotland in the 1920s and the first Scottish player to become a household name. Morton, a qualified mining engineer, began his career as an amateur with Queen's Park in 1913, eventually turning professional for Rangers in 1920 (in which year he also won the first of 31 caps for the national team).

Playing at outside-left, he proved far more formidable on the pitch than his nine stone, five foot four inches frame suggested and was capable of defying even the most resolute of defences. He was one of the leading players in the Wembley Wizards side that humbled England in 1928, providing the crosses for three of Scotland's five goals, and achieved almost divine status among followers of Rangers, who still consider him to have been their greatest player.

Having helped his club to no fewer than nine League championships and two Scottish Cups (1928 and 1930), he retired as a player in 1933 with a tally of 742 competitive appearances and was immediately rewarded with a seat on the Rangers board. His portrait hangs in the entrance hall at Ibrox Park.

Moss Rose *See* CHESTER CITY.

Mossley English non-League football club, nicknamed the Lilywhites. Strip: white shirts, black shorts, and white socks. Founded in 1903 and based at Seel Park in Mossley, the Lilywhites have played in the Northern Premier League since 1972.

Motherwell Scottish football club, nicknamed The 'Well. Strip: amber shirts with claret trim, claret shorts, and amber socks. Founded in 1886 and based at FIR PARK in Motherwell, The club joined the League as members of the Second Division in 1893.

The club's first great era was in the early 1930s, when players with the team included strikers George Stevenson, Bobby Ferrier, and Willie McFadyen, who spearheaded the side that captured the First Division championship in 1932 (as well as appearing as losing finalists in the Scottish Cup in 1931 and 1933). Motherwell made another Cup Final appearance in 1939 (again finishing as runners-up) but had to wait until 1952 to claim their first Cup victory (they also won the League Cup in 1951).

Motherwell picked up Second Division titles in 1954 and 1969 and then weathered financial difficulties to enter their second great era in the 1980s. Manager Tommy MacLean brought titles in the First Division in 1982 and again in 1985, while in 1991 the team won a second decisive victory in the Scottish Cup.

Motherwell enjoyed their record victory in 1954, when they beat Dundee United 12–1; they suffered their worst defeat in 1979, losing 8–0 to Aberdeen. Bobby Ferrier holds the record for League appearances with the club, having played in 626 games between 1918 and 1937.

motorcycle football A variant of conventional football, in which the players are mounted on motorbikes. First developed in the 1920s, the fad reached a peak in the 1930s and 1940s, when crowds of as many as 10,000 turned out to see such contests, which were fast and noisy. Games were generally fought out between two teams of six and individual riders often reached speeds of up to 60 miles per hour in pursuit of the ball. International tours were even staged (such as the British Motor Cycle Tour of Scandinavia, which took place in 1949). One of the motorcycles used in such games is preserved at the Cotswolds Motor Museum in Bourton-on-the-Water.

Motors Nickname of the English non-League football club Vauxhall Motors.

Mozambique Mozambique joined FIFA in 1978 but have yet to make much impact in international competition, though the country has produced a number of outstanding individual players (among them the great EUSÉBIO and Mário COLUNA). Strip: red shirts, black shorts, and black and red socks.

MSL *See* MAJOR SOCCER LEAGUE.

MTK Stadium The home ground, in Budapest, of the Hungarian football club MTK-VM. Opened in 1912, the stadium witnessed the club's extraordinary run of ten successive Championships in the 1920s (the star of the team, György Orth is commemorated by a bust at the ground). The stadium is also noteworthy for the fact that it lies immediately next door to another football ground – that of the less well-known BKV Elöre, making the two teams the closest neighbours anywhere in the football world.

MTK-VM Hungarian football club, nicknamed the Goose Eaters. Strip: white shirts with blue trim, with white shorts and socks. Based in Budapest, the club was formed with the help of a group of Britons in 1888 (as MTK – in English, short for Hungarian Circle of Athletes). MTK subsequently merged with Vörös Meteor in 1975. Based at the MTK STADIUM, the club can boast 19 League titles and nine Cup victories (mostly as MTK between the wars).

The golden era of the Goose Eaters was between 1917 and 1928 when the club won the championship ten years in a row under the management of the Englishman Jimmy HOGAN. Perhaps the most famous player with the club in this period was the great György Orth, who scored 138 goals in just 167 games and later became a respected international coach. The athletics branch of the club has collected nearly 50 Olympic gold medals over the years.

Muirton Park The former home ground of the Scottish football club ST JOHNSTONE. Muirton was home to the Saints from 1924 to 1989, when the club moved to MCDIARMID PARK. The ground was in financial difficulties for many years and schemes to introduce pony-trotting and other sporting activities there were often under consideration.

Müller, Gerd (1945–   ) West German striker, nicknamed The Bomber, who was hailed in the 1960s and 1970s as the greatest German forward of all time. He not only helped his club Bayern Munich to win three European Cups (1974–76) but also had a highly distinguished international career, scoring 62 goals in 68 appearances for West Germany. He was top scorer in the 1970 World Cup (with a total of ten goals) and played a key role in his country's victory in the 1972 European Nations Championship and the 1974 World Cup. In 1970 he became the first German to receive the European Footballer of the Year award.

Müngersdorfer The home ground, in Cologne, of the German football club IFC COLOGNE. The Müngersdorfer Stadium, opened in 1923, was the first enclosed stadium to be built in Germany and forms the centrepiece of a huge sports complex. The stadium's construction owed much to the efforts of Cologne's mayor (and later Federal Chancellor) Konrad Adenauer.

Munich air crash The catastrophic air disaster in which the Busby Babes side that represented Manchester United with great success in the 1950s was effectively destroyed. The crash traumatized the world of football and remains one of the game's worst memories.

The Babes had just drawn a European Cup quarter-final in Yugoslavia against Red Star and were on their way home, with the journey broken for refuelling at Munich. Their BEA Elizabethan aeroplane came to grief as it took off in a snowstorm at Munich airport at four minutes past three o'clock on the afternoon of Thursday, 6 February 1958 and 23 of the 43 passengers and crew lost their lives. The dead included eight players: Roger Byrne, Geoff Bent, Eddie

Colman, Mark Jones, Bill Whelan, Tommy Taylor, David Pegg, and the brilliantly talented Duncan EDWARDS, who died 15 days later in hospital. Among the other casualties was the former goalkeeper Frank SWIFT, who had been accompanying the team in the role of journalist, and another seven respected sports writers. Among the injured were Busby himself, who suffered serious chest, leg, and foot injuries.

The team that was almost certain to dominate English football for the next ten years was shattered – but incredibly Busby gradually put together a new generation of stars, building around the survivors of the air crash (who included Bobby CHARLTON), and maintained the standing of the the the club as a tribute to those who had died. Inevitably the side lost their semi-final in the European Cup in 1958 although UEFA offered the team a place in Europe the following season because of the tragedy. The Football League and the FA, however, barred the club from accepting and it was not until Busby's men claimed the European Cup in 1968 that it was felt the past could be laid to rest.

A year after that famous victory the official report into the accident was finally published in East Germany; a British inquiry had concluded that the crash had been caused by slush on the runway, although the Germans suggested that iced-up wings had been the major cause (a view hotly contested by the pilot).

At six o'clock, out of pure curiosity, I turned on my television set. As the news came on, the screen seemed to go black . . . I sat listening with a frozen brain to that cruel and shocking list of casualties that was now to give the word Munich an even sadder meaning than it had acquired on a day before the war, after a British Prime Minister had come home to London waving a pitiful piece of paper and most of us knew that new calamities of war were inevitable.

H.E. Bates, novelist, *FA Yearbook 1958–59*

Nacional Uruguayan football club, who rank alongside Peñarol as the country's most successful domestic side. Strip: white shirts with red and blue striped collar, blue shorts, and white socks. Founded in 1899 as the result of a match in which a squad was put together to represent the country against an Argentine side, Nacional were the first Uruguayan club to be formed by native Uruguayans as opposed to European immigrants. Based at the Centenario Stadium in Montevideo, the team have won some 35 League championships and were also winners of both the American Cup and the World Club Championship in 1971 and 1980; they added a third World Club Championship title in 1988 after beating the Argentine side Newell's Old Boys. Fans cherish memories of the early 1940s – the 'Five Golden Years', when the team's victories included an 8–0 thrashing of arch-rivals Peñarol.

Nantes French football club, nicknamed the Canaries. Based in the BEAUJOIRE stadium, the Canaries were founded in 1943 and reached the First Division in 1963, since when they have won no fewer than six Championship titles.

Napoli Italian football club, which entered its golden era in the 1980s after recruiting the great Argentinian star MARADONA. Strip: light blue shirts, white shorts, and light blue socks. Founded in 1926 and based at the SAN PAOLO STADIUM in Naples, Napoli won the League championship in 1987 and 1990 and the Cup in 1962, 1976, and 1987, as well as the UEFA Cup in 1989.

Narodna Armia Stadium See PEOPLE'S ARMY STADIUM.

NASL See NORTH AMERICAN SOCCER LEAGUE.

National Open Cup US Cup tournament of many years standing, which remains the closest US football gets to a national championship. Between 1951 and 1983 it was dominated by sides from the German-American and Cosmopolitan Leagues.

National Professional Soccer League US football organization that was formed in 1967. Unlike the rival United Soccer Association, the NPSL failed to win the approval of the United States Soccer Football Association and the Canadian Soccer Football Association (and through them of FIFA) but decided to press on anyway, despite the fact that member clubs (dubbed the Outlaws) were banned from contact with all other teams and associations. They rejected the idea of importing entire sides from Europe and elsewhere, as practised in the rival league, and instead built up ten teams based on established players from around the world (this led to certain practical difficulties and Philadelphia for one had to employ a full-time interpreter).

Notable recruits included Welshman Phil Woosnam, Englishman Dennis Viollet, Spaniard Juan Santisteban, West German Horst Szymaniak, Argentinian Cesar Menotti, and Hungarians Ladislav and Branko KUBALA.

Backed by their contract with CBS television, the NPSL began well but soon lost ground to the rival organization. Neither league was prospering at the end of the first season and the two organizations merged as the NASL in a desperate attempt to keep the concept of a nationwide league alive. Winners of the single NPSL championship were the Oakland Clippers.

National Soccer League Canadian football league, which has continued to remain in operation ever since 1926 in eastern Canada despite the development of the NASL and other rival leagues over the years. At its strongest in the Quebec area, the NSL had its heyday in the 1930s and revived to a certain extent in the 1970s but has languished in more recent years.

National Stadium A large stadium just west of Lisbon, which is used to host most Portuguese finals and internationals. The ground is unusual in that it is built into a thickly wooded hillside and the east side of the stadium remains a wooded gap (allegedly because the money ran out when the stadium was being built in the 1940s). Opened in 1944 with a match between Benfica and Sporting, the ground witnessed in 1949 the last performance of the Italian club Torino before the Superga air crash, which took place the following day.

Nations Cup *See* EUROPEAN CHAMPIONSHIP.

Nea Filadelphia The home ground, in Athens, of the Greek football club AEK. The stadium was opened in 1936 and was constructed with money provided by Greek refugees from Turkey. One memorable match at the venue was a UEFA Cup game with Cologne in 1982: when the floodlights failed enthusiastic fans stepped in to help by lighting fires on the terraces. When it became apparent during the replay ordained by UEFA that AEK were losing loyal fans chanted 'Turn off the lights!'.

near post The goalpost nearest the ball.

Nearly Men of Scottish Football *See* HEART OF MIDLOTHIAN.

Neckar The home ground of the German football club Stuttgart, which is ranked among the largest football grounds in the country. The stadium, designed by the modernist architect Paul Bonatz and comprising the main part of a large sports complex, was built in 1933 and was initially called the Adolf Hitler Kampfbahn. As well as football matches (which have included World Cup games in 1974 and the European Cup Final in 1988) the stadium has also hosted athletics events and boxing. In 1950 the first international match of the Federal Republic of Germany was played here. The venue was extensively redeveloped in the 1970s.

Nelson English football club that played in the League from 1921 to 1931. Based at the Seedhill Ground in Nelson (now covered by a motorway), Nelson were Third Division (North) champions in 1923 but spent only one season in the Second Division before relegation. The 1926–27 season was remarkable for the tally of 104 goals scored and 136 conceded (a record for the Third Division), while their last season in the League saw them lose every single away game (the only club to suffer in this way in a season of at least 21 games). When they

subsequently failed to gain re-election to the League in 1931 their place was taken by Chester.

Nepal Nepal joined FIFA in 1970 but have yet to make much impact in international competition. Strip: all red.

Népstadion The Hungarian national stadium, in Budapest. Translated in English as the People's Stadium, it was constructed with the help of a huge army of volunteers, who were said to include such star players as Ferenc PUSKAS and other members of the famed Magnificent Magyars squad. It opened in 1953 and has since staged the majority of Hungary's Cup Finals and international fixtures as well as other sporting events.

Nest, The The former home ground of the English football club NORWICH CITY. The Nest was the most remarkable of all League grounds, being situated in an old chalk pit and overlooked by a cliff-face that reached to within a yard of the pitch itself (spectators lined the top of the cliff on matchdays and shots that went wide of the goal bounced back off the 50-foot high concrete wall that lined the rockface). The barriers keeping spectators back at the top of the cliff broke in 1922, luckily without causing any injuries, and it was inevitable that the club would have to find a more suitable home in the long run.

In fact, the move (to CARROW ROAD) did not happen until 1935, when the collapse of one corner of the pitch as old chalk workings gave way prompted new urgency in finding an improved base. In their final season at The Nest the club had to warn players to take particular care when venturing over the temporarily shored-up pitch, especially when taking corners.

Netherfield English non-League football club. Strip: black and white striped shirts, black shorts, and red socks. Founded in 1920 and based at Parkside Road in Kendal, the team play in the Northern Premier League.

Netherlands The Dutch national team emerged as one of the world's leading sides for the first time in the 1970s, though they have still to crown their achievements with victory in the World Cup. They took part in their first World Cup Finals in 1934 but failed to make much progress then or in 1938 and it was not until 1974 that they next qualified for another Finals series.

Boasting such talents as Johan CRUYFF and perfecting the art of total football, the side stormed through to their first World Cup Final but then lost to West Germany. Another campaign in 1978 also culminated in a place in the Final, but this time defeat came at the hands of Argentina and they finished runners-up once more. Better fortune attended their European Championship campaign of 1988, however, with the Dutch squad – including such stars as Ruud GULLIT and Marco VAN BASTEN – carrying off the title with style. Netherlands qualified for the 1994 World Cup in America. Strip: orange shirts, white shorts, and orange socks.

Netherlands Antilles The Netherlands Antilles joined FIFA in 1932 but have yet to make much impact in international competition. Strip: white shirts with red and blue trim, white shorts, and red, white, and blue socks.

Netherton United English non-League football club, which hit the headlines in 1982 when, all other possibilities having been exhausted, the club applied to the International Monetary Fund for help. The IMF, more used to receiving such applications from national governments, explained that it could offer no such help, but a whip-round among the organization's staff produced the princely sum of £25, which was duly forwarded to the impoverished but resourceful Nottingham amateurs.

netminder Former name for a goalkeeper, widely used in the early history of the game.

New Brighton Former English League football club, which was a member of the League from 1923 to 1951. Based at Sandheys Park and at the Tower Athletic Grounds, New Brighton's place in the League was eventually inherited by Workington.

New Brighton Tower Former English League football club, which played in the League from 1898 to 1901. The team was based at the Tower Athletic Grounds.

New Comunale Stadium The home ground, in Turin, of the Italian football clubs JUVENTUS and TORINO. This breathtaking new stadium was opened in time to host the 1990 World Cup and was immediately hailed as one of the most beautiful in Europe, with a unique roof supported by 56 steel masts; it also boasts its own rail link.

New Double Nickname given to the combination of victories by the same team in both the League championship and the League Cup. The New Double became a possibility for the first time when the Cup tournament was introduced in 1961 but was not achieved until 1978, when it was won by Nottingham Forest. *See also* DOUBLE.

New Kilbowie Park The home ground of the Scottish football club CLYDEBANK. The original Kilbowie Park was home to Clydebank Juniors from which the present club is descended. New Kilbowie Park was opened in 1939; features of the ground included a set of rounded goal posts (a contrast to the square variety usual in Scotland). The ground survived heavy bombing of the area during World War II and the facilities were gradually improved in the 1950s and 1960s. One of the stands is called the Davie Cooper Stand, named in honour of a player whose sale enabled the club to build it.

Hitler one, Clydebank nil, hallelujah!

Meadowbank Thistle supporters' chant, to the tune of 'Michael Rowed the Boat Ashore'

New York Cosmos The NASL team that represented the city of New York between 1971 and 1984. The Cosmos side became the most famous of all the clubs that contested the NASL title, chiefly through its import of some of the most famous players in the world, of whom the most prestigious was PELÉ himself.

At their peak the Cosmos attracted crowds of 70,000 to the Giants' Stadium outside New York and had a strong international reputation. Having joined the NASL in 1971, the Cosmos won the Championship in 1972 (at a time when they had few world-ranking players) but subsequently failed to dominate the League until 1975, when Pelé was signed up. The addition a year later of the Italian international Giorgio Chinaglia – destined to become the most prolific goalscorer in the NASL's history – and the arrival of the German star Franz BECKENBAUER in 1977 made the Cosmos the most powerful side in the USA. Among subsequent imports were the English player Dennis Tueart, the Yugoslavian midfielder Vladislav Bogicevic, and the Paraguayan internationals Julio Cesar Romero ('Romerito') and Roberto Cabanas.

They won the Soccer Bowl in 1977, 1978, 1980, and 1982 and subsequently played for a season in the Major Indoor

Soccer League as the NASL collapsed in the mid-1980s. An indication of the fact that at their best the Cosmos ranked alongside more established leading clubs elsewhere in the world was their record in the Trans-Atlantic Challenge Cup, which they won in 1980, 1983, and 1984, overcoming such prestigious opposition as Manchester City, Roma, Celtic, and Napoli.

> *You can't impose a team from above with a bundle of money and a big ad campaign. That's what they did with the Cosmos: they invested a few million dollars and when they saw it wasn't working they dismantled the whole thing and walked away.*
>
> Takis Moutis, president of US Hellenic League

New Zealand The New Zealand national team has enjoyed only rare moments of fame on the international stage. The squad's greatest moment of glory to date was in 1982, when the team qualified for the World Cup Finals for the first time. They suffered three defeats but managed to restrict Scotland to a 5–2 victory, thus preventing the Scots from progressing to the quarter-finals. Strip: white shirts with black trim, with white shorts and socks.

Newbury Town English non-League football club, nicknamed Town. Strip: amber shirts with black shorts and socks. Founded in 1887 and based at the Town Ground in Newbury, the club play in the Isthmian League.

Newcastle United English football club, nicknamed the Magpies. Strip: black and white striped shirts, black shorts, and black socks. Founded in 1881, the club originally played as Stanley but changed their name to Newcastle East End a year later and acquired their permanent title in 1892, after the rival side Newcastle West End had been disbanded.

Based at ST JAMES' PARK since 1892, the Magpies were elected to the Second Division in 1893 and five years later began a lengthy stay in the First Division (1898–1934); subsequently they spent another 14 years in the Second Division before returning to the top rank in 1948. Building sides drawn from both sides of the border, the club were able to field a team of no fewer than ten Scotsmen for a match in the 1920s.

They were relegated once more in 1961, were promoted in 1965, relegated in 1978, promoted in 1984, and slipped back to the Second Division in 1989. A revival in fortunes saw them obtain a place in the Premier League in 1993, after winning the First Division championship.

The club's first golden era was in the first decade of the 20th century when they were the most powerful team in the land, capturing the League championship in 1905, 1907, and again in 1909 as well as winning the FA Cup in 1910 (they were runners-up in 1905, 1906, 1908, and 1911). Their mastery of the game was such that in 1910 they were fined for fielding a 'weak team' consisting of reserves against fellow First Division club Bristol City – an away game from which they had emerged easy 3–0 victors.

Subsequently they won the Championship once more, in 1927 (when they were captained by the formidable striker Hughie GALLACHER), and the FA Cup in 1924, 1932 (*see* OVER-THE-LINE GOAL), 1951, 1952, and 1955 (and were runners-up in 1974). Other honours have included victory in the Texaco Cup in 1974 and 1975, the European Fairs Cup in 1969, and the Anglo-Italian Cup in 1973.

The club's run of successes in the 1950s is fondly remembered and the achievements of the great star of the side in those days, Jackie MILBURN, are still recalled by grateful fans in hushed tones; his total of 178 goals for the side between 1946 and 1957 remains a club record. Other stars of this second golden era included wing-half Joe Harvey and winger Bobby Mitchell. Among recent stars have been such players as Jimmy Scoular, George Eastham (*see* RETAIN AND TRANSFER), Bobby Moncur, Bobby ROBSON, Malcolm MACDONALD, and in the 1980s (towards the end of his career) Kevin KEEGAN – who subsequently became manager – and his successors Chris WADDLE, Peter Beardsley, and Paul GASCOIGNE.

Newcastle enjoyed their record victory back in 1946, when they beat Newport County 13–0; they suffered their worst defeat in 1895, losing 9–0 to Burton Wanderers. Jim Lawrence holds the record for League appearances with the club, having played in 432 games between 1904 and 1922. Dedicated fans of the club include Cardinal Basil Hume.

> *We went to Blaydon Races,*
> *'twas on the ninth of June,*
> *Eighteen hundred and sixty-two,*
> *On a summer's afternoon,*
> *We took the bus from Bamburghs,*
> *And she was heavy laden,*
> *Away we went along Collingwood Road,*
> *That's on the road to Blaydon.*

Oh, me lads,
You should have seen us gannin',
Passing the folks along the road,
Just as they were standin',
All the lads and lasses there,
All with smiling faces,
Gannin' along the Scotswood Road,
To see the Blaydon Races.

'Blaydon Races', Magpies supporters' song

Newport Welsh non-League football club, nicknamed the Exiles. Strip: amber shirts with black shorts and socks. Founded in 1898 and based at Somerton Park in Newport, Gwent, the club play in the Southern League.

Newport County Former Welsh League football club, nicknamed the Ironsides. Founded in 1912 and based at Somerton Road, the club enjoyed two spells in the League (1921–31 and 1932–88). Highlights in the club's history include the 1980–81 season in which Newport reached the quarter-final stage of the European Cup Winners' Cup. Low points include the start of the 1970–71 season, when the Ironsides recorded the worst start ever made by a League club, playing 23 matches without a win.

Newport IOW English non-League football club. Strip: gold shirts, royal blue shorts, and gold socks. Founded in 1888 and based at St George's Park in Newport, Isle of Wight, the team play in the Southern League.

Newton Heath The original name under which MANCHESTER UNITED played before 1902.

Newtown Welsh non-League football club, nicknamed the Robins. Strip: all red. Founded in 1875 and based at Latham Park, Newtown play in the Konica League of Wales.

Nicaragua Nicaragua joined FIFA in 1950 but have yet to establish an international reputation. Strip: blue shirts with white trim, blue shorts, and blue socks with white trim.

Nice one, Cyril Catchphrase that swept the UK in the 1970s. Popularized by a television advert for Wonderloaf in 1972 (in which 'Cyril' was identified as a baker of the aforesaid loaf), the phrase was used in all kinds of contexts – including sexual ones – as a congratulatory or conversely a somewhat sarcastic reaction to another's efforts.

Thus, when, in the 1990s, the generously proportioned Liberal politician Sir Cyril Smith was pictured attempting to touch his toes in an advertisement for Access, the slogan ran: 'Nice one, Cyril – but Access is more flexible'. The phrase became particularly relevant to football around 1973, when it was chanted by fans of Tottenham Hotspur to the side's left-back Cyril Knowles (1944–91) – subsequently immortalized in a pop song released by the 'Cockerel Chorus':

Nice one, Cyril
Nice one, son
Nice one, Cyril,
Let's have another one.

'Nice one, Cyril' (1973)

Nicholson, Bill (1919–) English manager, who rose to the top of his profession as boss of Tottenham Hotspur in the early 1960s. A former player for Spurs who won a League championship medal in 1951 and one cap for England, Nicholson retired as a player in 1955 and accepted the post of coach at White Hart Lane. Three years later he accompanied England to Sweden as coach to the World Cup Squad, after which he was promoted to manager back at Tottenham. Under his leadership, Spurs achieved the sought-after double in 1961 (*see* SUPER SPURS), adding an FA Cup title in 1962, the European Cup Winners' Cup in 1963, another FA Cup title in 1967, two League championships (1971 and 1973), and the UEFA Cup (1972). Nicholson resigned from his job in 1974 after a decline in the team's fortunes and was recruited by West Ham for a time before he returned to White Hart Lane as a managerial consultant in 1976.

Niger Niger joined FIFA in 1967 but have yet to make much impact in international competition. Strip: orange shirts, white shorts, and green socks.

Nigeria Nigeria joined FIFA in 1959 and have since been recognized as one of the more promising African footballing nations, with a number of players establishing reputations in Europe. They were winners of the African Nations Cup in 1980. Nigeria qualified for the 1994 World Cup in America. Strip: green shirts with white trim, white shorts, and green socks with white trim.

92 Club Supporters' club, founded in 1978, whose members can all claim to have seen a competitive first team match at every one of the grounds belonging to the 92 clubs in the League (there having been 92 clubs since 1950). Outstanding among its members are two fans, Bob Wilson and Michael Jones, who made a complete tour of all 92 venues in the course of the 1968–69 season. They achieved the feat in 264 days, watching an average of three games a week and witnessing in all 8370 minutes of play (they also managed to squeeze in a quick trip to see Berwick, who play in the Scottish League). Honorary members of the 92 club include Alan Durban, who by 1976 had played at all 92 venues, Eric Northover (a director of Northampton Town), and Jim Smith (who had visited every ground in his role as manager by 1986).

Ninian Park The home ground of the Welsh football club CARDIFF CITY. Ninian Park was opened in 1910 and subsequently won recognition as the most prestigious international venue in Wales (though FIFA's stipulation in 1989 that such matches be played in all-seater stadia threatened to change things).

The site of Ninian Park was formerly a rubbish tip; initial plans were that the new ground would be called Sloper Park, but when Lord Ninian Crichton Stuart assisted in solving an early financial crisis connected with the building of the stadium it was quickly decided that the venue would bear his name in appreciation of his contribution. Ninian himself kicked off at the first match (against Aston Villa). Early games carried the peril of injury to players who fell on the grass, which still threw up shards of glass and other debris from the rubbish tip it had been built on.

Events in the ground's history since then have included a fire in 1937, which destroyed the Main Stand; this came about as the result of an attempted burglary when some thieves tried to blow up the club safe (wrongly thinking it contained the takings from a recent match). Among other landmarks in the ground's history have been various memorable internationals (with the Welsh national team using the ground as their base for many years), a considerable reduction in capacity on safety grounds in the 1970s, and experiments in recent years with both Rugby League and American Football. In 1985 Jock STEIN died of a heart attack at Ninian Park moments after watching Scotland qualify for the 1986 World Cup Finals.

Features included the Bob Stand, where spectators formerly paid a shilling to watch a game.

Nithsdale Wanderers Former Scottish League football club, which was a League member from 1923 to 1927. The team was based at Crawick Holm in Sanquhar, near Dumfries.

Nordahl, Gunnar (1921–) Swedish centre-forward, who was one of celebrated Gre-No-Li trio of forwards who enjoyed enormous success in Italian football in the 1950s. Nordahl played for the Swedish sides Hornefors, Degerfors, and Norrköping until 1949, when he moved to Italy to play for AC Milan and subsequently for Roma. Having scored 473 goals in 518 games (including 44 goals in 33 internationals), he returned eventually to Sweden to serve as player-manager of Karlstad.

Nordic Cup International cup competition that is contested between Sweden, Denmark, Finland, and Norway. Founded in 1924, the Cup runs over four years with each nation playing each of the others once every year.

North American Soccer League Nationwide football league that was established in the USA in the late 1960s. The formation of the NASL was a determined attempt to organize a nationwide football network in the USA, where the game thrived in local pockets of support but lacked a high national profile ranking it with such mass sports as baseball and American football.

Spurred on by the popularity of the World Cup when it was televised throughout the USA in 1966, the movement towards the establishment of the NASL gathered pace in 1967, when the United Soccer Association and the rival unofficial National Professional Soccer League were set up. A year later the two leagues – which included sides from Canada as well as from the USA – were amalgamated as the NASL.

The League's first season was a disaster, with small crowds and very mixed standards of play and it took a concerted effort by enthusiasts to keep the five clubs remaining committed to a 1969 season. The NASL gradually grew in strength (particularly after the arrival of such guest players as PELÉ – who was recruited in 1975 – and George BEST) and by 1979 there were 24 member clubs.

Crowds of 70,000 flocked to such venues as Giants Meadow outside New York City to see the New York Cosmos and it seemed that at last US soccer had achieved the acceptance it had long sought. In 1977 no fewer than 3 million people passed through the turnstiles to see NASL games. Secretary of State Henry Kissinger even agreed to accept the post of NASL chairman.

The NASL was, however, beset with problems ranging from finance (attendances too often failed to match the ambitious expectations with which the League had been launched) to lack of support from the television organizations (who fretted over the difficulty of slotting in the all-important commercials at regular intervals). Playing standards were often low, largely because many of the imported players who starred with the teams were well past their peak (in 1978 at least half of all the players in the NASL were British guests). Furthermore, the administrators were having trouble adapting the game to the expectations of an audience unfamiliar with the relatively slow pace of the game and frequently found themselves obliged to tinker with the laws in a way that was not calculated to find favour with other footballing nations:

> With such refinements as a thirty-five yard offside law, synthetic pitches which are not conducive to tackling, 'shoot-outs' to eliminate drawn games and bonus points, the country which gave the world Disneyland has provided a Mickey Mouse football industry.
>
> Jack Rollin, *Rothman's Football Yearbook 1979–80*

By 1981 the League had begun to contract and on 28 March 1985, after 19 seasons, the NASL was declared defunct, with clubs reverting to a series of regional amateur and semi-professional leagues (notably the Western Soccer Alliance and the American Soccer League in the USA and, in Canada, the Canadian Soccer League, which was set up in 1987). The hosting of the World Cup in 1994 may prompt the formation of another nationwide league (a poll suggested 49 per cent of US adults would be interested in going to a game if the World Cup was held in the country).

In the meantime soccer lags far behind such native American pursuits as baseball and American football and has its heartland in areas where there are large immigrant populations (in New York City it remains the biggest organized sport alongside softball).

> Soccer is a game in which everyone does a lot of running around . . . mostly, twenty-one guys stand around and one guy does a

> tap dance with the ball. It's about as exciting as Tristan and Isolde.
>
> Jim Murray, *Louisville Courier Journal* (1967)

> People think it's a soft touch in the North American Soccer League but it's hard out there, I can tell you. You travel from one side of the continent to the other, play the next day, fly back and play two days later. You have astroturf and grass and 90 per cent heat with 95 per cent humidity, all these things to contend with.
>
> Keith Weller, player with Fort Lauderdale Strikers (1983)

> It's an elephant's graveyard.
>
> Gianni Rivera, of US soccer (1978)

North Bank The stand that is the traditional home of the most loyal Arsenal fans at HIGHBURY STADIUM.

North Eastern League Former English football league, which was open to professional sides from the north-east. Founded in 1906, the league was finally disbanded in 1958. Throughout its history it was dominated by the reserve sides of Middlesbrough and Sunderland, who between them won the Championship 21 times. Other clubs in its ranks included Ashington and Blyth Spartans. The league was briefly revived for a single season in 1962–63.

North End Nickname of the English football club PRESTON NORTH END.

North Korea The North Korean national side exploded upon the international scene in 1966, when the extraordinarily talented 'Diddy Men' squad took on the flower of the world's footballers with notable success during the World Cup in England that year. In this, their first appearance in the World Cup Finals, the North Koreans proved the undoing of mighty Italy and made themselves the darlings of the series before inevitably bowing out of the tournament (after offering stiff resistance to EUSÉBIO's Portugal). Strip: all white.

Northampton Town English football club, nicknamed the Cobblers. Strip: maroon shirts, white shorts, and maroon socks. The club were founded in 1897 by a group of schoolteachers and turned professional in 1901; in 1920 Northampton were founder members of the Third Division. Since then the club (based at the COUNTY GROUND) has visited all four divisions, enjoying its heyday in 1965–66 when it scaled the lofty heights of the First Division, only to return to the Fourth Division (where it had started the decade) in 1969. Honours include the Third Division championship in 1963 and the Fourth Division title in 1987. Players over the years have included entertainer Des O'Connor, who played for the youth side during World War II.

In the late 1960s the club was one of the few to experiment with the idea of whipping up support with a troupe of female cheerleaders based on the US model. By the 1990s, however, the financial crisis facing the club was such that there were rumours that it might go out of existence altogether.

The Cobblers' record victory stands at 10–0 against Walsall in 1927, and Sutton United in 1907; in 1901 they suffered their worst defeat, losing 11–0 to Southampton. Tommy Fowler holds the record for League appearances with the side, having played in 521 matches between 1946 and 1961.

Northern Former Scottish League football club, which enjoyed just one season as a League member (1893–94). The team played at Hyde Park in Springburn, Glasgow.

Northern Alliance English football league that is contested by teams from the Northumberland area. Founded in 1890, the Alliance stages a league and a Cup competition. Winners of the league title have included Alnwick Town (nine Championships) and Amble (five victories), while Marine Park have established a record four wins in the Cup.

Northern Ireland The Northern Ireland team has a distinguished international history, particularly when their record is put in context with the province's size. The national squad, usually bolstered with many players from the English Football League, has made three appearances in the World Cup Finals, in 1958, 1982, and 1986. The 1958 campaign saw Northern Ireland – the sensation of the series – draw with West Germany and twice beat Czechoslovakia but go out after losing 4–0 to France. In 1982, the team beat Spain 1–0 and managed two other draws to come top of their group, but then lost 4–1 to France once more and failed to reach the semifinals. The 1986 campaign ended after a draw and two defeats in Mexico. They were also winners of the Home International Championship in 1980 and 1984 and shared the title on a number of other occasions. Stars with the side over the years have

included Danny BLANCHFLOWER, Jimmy MCILROY, George BEST, and Pat JENNINGS. Strip: green shirts, white shorts, and green and white socks.

Northern League English football league, which was one of the most prestigious of all amateur leagues and survived the 1974 ruling that abolished amateur football as such. Founded in 1889, the League has over the years included many famous clubs, among them Bishop Auckland, Blyth Spartans, and Spennymoor United. Bishop Auckland are the most successful team in the league's history, having won 19 Championships to add to their seven victories in the League Challenge Cup and their record ten wins in the FA Amateur Cup.

Northern Premier League English football league, which was founded in 1968 as a step in the development of the pyramid system. The Northern Premier League was formed from the amalgamation of the Cheshire County League, Lancashire Combination, Midland League, North Regional League, and the West Midlands (Regional) League and comprises two divisions of around 20 clubs. Champions in the Northern Premier League (which has variously been known as the Multipart League and the HFS Loans League after its sponsors) generally win promotion to the Conference. Both Scarborough and Wigan Athletic rose from the Northern Premier League to eventual stardom as full League members.

Northwich Victoria English non-League football club, nicknamed the Vics. Strip: green and white shirts, with white shorts and socks. Founded in 1874 and based at the Drill Field in Northwich, the club were founder members of the Second Division in 1892 but remained in the League for only two seasons before dropping out (they were subsequently founder members of another four competitions). Winners of the FA Trophy in 1984, they play in the GM Vauxhall Conference. Star names associated with the club in its early history included the great Billy MEREDITH.

Norway The Norwegian national side has a relatively undistinguished international record, though it can reflect upon a few isolated moments of glory at the top level. The Norwegians qualified for their first World Cup Finals in 1934 and only narrowly failed to upset eventual winners Italy, who scraped through 2–1 with an extra-time goal. Two years later a 2–0 Norwegian triumph against Germany in the Berlin Olympics infuriated the Nazis, who saw the Norwegians finish in third place overall. Another cherished moment followed many years later, in 1981, when the team pulled off a dramatic 2–1 victory against England in a World Cup qualifier; the result threatened England's elimination and sent Norwegian spectators into raptures. Norway again beat England 2–0 in the qualifying rounds for the 1994 World Cup Finals. This time, England's elimination was secured. Other highlights have included a 2–1 win over World Cup holders Italy (1984). Strip: red shirts, white shorts, and blue socks.

Norwich City English football club, nicknamed the Canaries. Strip: yellow shirts and socks, with green shorts. Founded in 1902 on the initiative of two schoolteachers who set up the inaugural meeting in the Criterion Café, the Canaries got off to a shaky start when two years later they were expelled from the FA Amateur Cup as a 'professional' club. In 1905 the club officially accepted professional status and eventually the Canaries became founder members of the Third Division when it was created in 1920. They were promoted to the Second Division in the 1930s and again in 1960, finally reaching the First Division in 1972, under the management of Ron Saunders.

Known for their flamboyant playing style, Norwich have been rewarded with few major honours besides their victories in the League Cup in 1962 and 1985 (in which year, nonetheless, they were relegated). Other titles have included the Second Division championship in 1972 and 1986 and the Third Division (South) championship in 1934 (a season that witnessed their best-ever run with only one defeat in their last 20 games). In 1992 the team were founder members of the Premier League.

The club's first home was in Newmarket Road, after which they occupied (1905–35) an unusual ground in Rosary Road (*see* NEST, THE); since 1935 their base has been at CARROW ROAD. Remote from the footballing heartlands, the club have had to survive a series of economic crises, usually by selling their best players. The late 1950s were a particularly fraught time financially, with – according to legend – the players' salaries being paid for a period by the local newspaper.

They have, however, often produced a surprise when faced with prestigious clubs.

Examples of giant-killing acts pulled off by the club include a match in 1959, when Norwich – then in the Third Division – toppled mighty Tottenham Hotspur (two years away from their famous double) with a scoreline of 1–0.

Norwich enjoyed record victories in 1930, when they beat Coventry City 10–2, and in 1989, when they beat Sutton United 8–0; they suffered their worst defeat in 1908, when they lost 10–2 to Swindon Town. Ron Ashman holds the record for League appearances with the club, having played in 592 games between 1947 and 1964. *See also* ON THE BALL, CITY.

> Score, Norwich, score, once we get one
> we'll get more,
> We'll sing you assembly when we get to
> Wembley,
> So score, Norwich, score.

Supporters' song

Nottingham Forest English football club, nicknamed the Reds. Strip: red shirts, white shorts, and red socks. Forest are one of the oldest football clubs in the world, having been founded (as Forest Football Club) at a meeting at the Clinton Arms in Nottingham in 1865 (members of the club had previously met to play a form of hockey known as 'shinney'). The name Forest, incidentally, was a reference to the Forest Racecourse, where the club were initially based. Soon after the move to football was decided upon in 1865, the players went out and acquired a set of red caps – hence the team colours.

Forest had several homes (including the cricket pitch at Trent Bridge) before finally settling at the CITY GROUND in 1898. They played their first game in the League in 1892, as members of the First Division, and – apart from a grim period in 1949–51 when they visited the Third Division (North) – have never played outside the top two divisions. Honours were slow in coming, however, and until relatively recently the club could only boast two FA Cup victories (1898 and 1959) and two Second Division titles (1907 and 1922).

It all changed, however, in 1975 when Brian CLOUGH (assisted by Peter Taylor) became manager and subsequently led the team rapidly to the top, winning the League championship in 1978 after a run of 42 consecutive First Division matches without defeat and two European Cups in successive seasons (1979 and 1980). Under Clough's inspired direction, Forest also captured the League Cup in 1978, 1979, and later in

1989 and 1990. Star players of the Clough era, which finally ended in 1993 (when Forest lost their place in the Premier League at the end of the opening season and Clough retired) included John Robertson, goalkeeper Peter SHILTON, Viv Anderson, Nigel Clough (Brian Clough's son), Des Walker, and Stuart 'Psycho' PEARCE.

Somewhat earlier, the club tried hard to sign a youth player called David Frost, but he opted for a career in the media instead.

Surprise results involving Forest have never caused more astonishment that their 12–0 victory over Leicester Fosse in 1909. Forest were in danger of relegation at the time and their triumph was so unexpected that an inquiry was held to look into it; it transpired that their success probably had less to do with the skill of the Forest players than it had to do with the fact that the previous day several of the Fosse players had participated rather too enthusiastically in the wedding celebrations of one of their team mates. The 12–0 scoreline remains a record for a win in the First Division.

The club enjoyed their record victory back in 1891, when they beat Clapton 14–0 (a goalscoring record for an away game in English first-class football); they suffered their worst defeat in 1937, losing 9–1 against Blackburn Rovers. Bob McKinlay holds the record for League appearances with the club, having played in 614 games between 1951 and 1970.

Perhaps the most unusual of all Forest supporters was the jackdaw that in the immediate postwar years was reputed to catch a bus from Council House Square to the City Ground in order to see the match on days when the first team was playing.

Hello, hello, we are the Trent End boys,
Hello, hello, we are the Trent End boys,
We are the best in England,
That no one can deny,
We all follow the Forest.

Supporters' song, to the tune of 'Marching Through Georgia'

Notts County English football club, nicknamed the Magpies. Strip: black and white striped shirts with amber sleeves and trim, black shorts with white trim, and black socks with white and amber trim. The club (initially called Notts Football Club) is the oldest in the English Football League, claiming to have been founded back in 1862 (although the side was not properly organized until 1864 at a meeting at the George IV Hotel).

Notts County were founder members of the League in 1888 and have since spent periods in all four divisions. They have never won the Championship, but did enjoy victory in the FA Cup in 1894 (and are the only club to have entered the FA competition every year since 1877). Their victory was doubly remarkable for the fact that it made them the first Second Division team to lift the famous trophy.

Based at MEADOW LANE in Nottingham since 1910, Notts County have known both good times and bad and too often have found themselves languishing in the shadow of neighbouring Nottingham Forest. Stars with the side over the years have included the great Tommy LAWTON, who played with the team in the late 1940s. The team's record since then has been somewhat less distinguished and the club chairman himself rather nonsensically admitted in the 1980s that: 'Most of the people who can remember when we were a great club are dead.'

The Magpies enjoyed their record victory in 1885, when they beat Rotherham Town 15–0; they have lost by a record margin of 9–1 three times, to Aston Villa in 1888, to Blackburn Rovers in 1889, and to Portsmouth in 1927. Albert Iremonger, the celebrated goalkeeper who helped the side win the Second Division title in 1914 and 1923, holds the record for League appearances with the club, having played in 564 games between 1904 and 1926.

I had a wheelbarrow, the wheel fell off,
I had a wheelbarrow, the wheel fell off,
I had a wheelbarrow (ad infinitum)

Supporters' song (1990)

Nou Camp The home ground of the Spanish football club BARCELONA, which ranks among the finest stadia in the world. This huge three-tiered stadium was opened in 1957 and replaced the smaller Les Corts ground where the club had played since 1922. The ground's remarkable facilities include a museum, an indoor sports hall, and an Ice Palace (for ice hockey); the club's second team, moreover have a stadium all to themselves a short distance away (opened in 1982). Many changes were made in advance of the 1982 World Cup, when the stadium hosted the opening ceremony. Visitors to the stadium over the years have included the Pope and Michael Jackson.

NPSL *See* NATIONAL PROFESSIONAL SOCCER LEAGUE.

NSL *See* NATIONAL SOCCER LEAGUE.

numbers Football shirts were never numbered in the early history of the game and it was not until around 1928 that the idea was first experimented with. Shirts were numbered for the first time in an FA Cup Final in 1933, although the numbering did not follow the conventional method of both teams using numbers from 1 to 11, but instead numbers from 1 to 22 were used. It was not until 1939 that the numbering of shirts (which aids identification of players by referees, spectators, and commentators) became compulsory in England. When Scotland followed suit (with Airdrieonians claiming to have been the first club north of the border to number their players) Celtic defiantly refused to comply, but eventually (in 1960) settled on a compromise of numbering their players' shorts.

Much later, Don REVIE tried out an alternative method of numbering his men when he issued them with numbered sock tie-ups, which were thrown into the crowd for souvenirs at the end of the game. Other variations have included an experiment tried by Aberdeen, who put their players' numbers on the fronts of their shirts in the 1967–68 season, and matches in which the players' names have also been written on their shirts. This idea was first tried by Scotland in a 1979 international against Peru, and later adopted by the English Premiership in 1993, combined with the allocation of squad numbers.

The numbers themselves refer to the position each player is playing in, though on occasion teams have used this assumption to their advantage; when Liverpool met Wolverhampton Wanderers in 1952 they switched the left-winger and centre-forward as play began and in the ensuing confusion snatched two goals before the Wolves defenders realized they were marking the wrong men. Other managers to use similar ploys on a regular basis included Doncaster Rovers' Peter Doherty.

The system is somewhat different in the USA, where players are usually allotted a shirt number under which they play throughout the season (regardless of which position they actually fulfil). *See also* PELÉ.

Nuneaton Borough English non-League football club, nicknamed Boro. Strip: blue and white shirts, white shorts, and blue socks. Founded in 1937 and based at the Manor Park ground, Boro play in the Southern League.

IFC Nuremberg German football club, nicknamed The Club. Strip: red and white shirts, white shorts, and red socks. Founded in 1900 and based at the NUREMBERG STADIUM, The Club acquired its nickname in the 1920s, when it was the most powerful side in the German League, winning the Championship in 1920, 1921, 1924, 1925, and 1927. Since that golden period the side has added a further four Championships and Cup titles in 1935, 1939, and 1962.

Nuremberg Stadium The home ground, in Nuremberg, of the German football club IFC NUREMBERG. The stadium was opened in 1929 and subsequently acquired a degree of notoriety for its use by the Nazis, who staged huge parades close by (where traces of swastikas can still be seen). The ground was much improved in the late 1980s.

nutmeg To pass the ball between an opposing player's legs and then to retrieve it successfully after running round him. Defenders caught out this way are invariably horribly embarrassed. The word itself was probably inspired by the slang term 'nuts' (for testicles).

Nuts and Bolts Nickname of the English non-League football club ASHFORD TOWN, in reference to local industry.

O

O's Nickname of the English football club LEYTON ORIENT.

obstruction A playing offence that results from a player attempting to hinder an opponent not in possession of the ball or challenging for possession by standing in his way.

Oceania One of the six qualifying groups for the Olympic football tournament, presently including Australia and New Zealand. *See* ISRAEL.

Ochilview Park The home ground, on the outskirts of Falkirk, of the Scottish football club STENHOUSEMUIR. Ochilview Park (which commands a good view of the Ochil mountains) was opened in 1890 and was largely developed after 1921, when the club joined the League.

Events in the venue's history include a fire in 1928, which destroyed the Main Stand, and, in 1951, the first use of floodlights at any ground in Scotland (for a match between Stenhousemuir and Hibernian). Curiosities of Ochilview Park include the two external staircases leading up to the Main Stand: these were added as an afterthought after the architect forgot to include internal stairs in his original design. The pitch at Ochilview is the largest in Scotland, at 112 by 78 yards.

Ocsi *See* PUSKAS, FERENC.

Ocwirk, Ernst (1926–80) Austrian centre-half, nicknamed Clockwork, who demonstrated his skill before English fans in 1951, when Austria recorded a famous 2–2 draw against England at Wembley. Ocwirk, a star of the 1954 World Cup, was particularly admired for the precision with which he created new attacking moves and has since been described as the last great centre-half before the introduction of the sweeper dictated a change in tactics. On the domestic front, he played for FK Austria and later for the Italian club Sampdoria; he won a total of 62 caps in all.

offside The stipulation in the rules of football that there must be a certain number of the opposing team between an attacking player in the opposition's half of the pitch and the opposition's goal when the attacker receives a forward pass (or otherwise interferes with play). This rule prevents football from degenerating into a free-for-all in which both teams spend all their time lobbing the ball into a packed goalmouth and effectively concentrates play in the middle of the pitch.

The laws surrounding the offside rule in football have long been among the most contentious and hotly debated in the history of the game. The most significant change to existing offside rules was made back in 1925, when it was decided that a player remained onside if there were only two opponents between him and the other team's goal (rather than three as had previously been the case since an alteration in the rules in 1866). This change in the law was forced by the extraordinary success of right-back Bill McCracken, of Newcastle United, Distillery, and Ireland, who turned the practice of springing the offside trap into a fine art (making him the most controversial footballer of his era).

Unfortunately McCracken's activities starved crowds of exciting attacking play and caused frequent breaks in play, leading to a growing chorus in support of reform. The effect of the highly controversial change was to open up the chances for attacking players to score and new goal records of all kinds were rapidly set throughout the game (to the delight of most spectators, who generally agreed that the game had become much more exciting to watch). During the final season played under the old offside law a total of 4700 goals had been scored in the League; under the new arrangement the tally rocketed to 6373.

Not everyone was in favour, however, and many traditionalists perceived a distinct decline in tactical play, as a writer in *Gammage's Assocation Football Annual* observed:

The change did not improve the quality of first-class football . . . as the new rule tended to eliminate skill and to make pace a bigger fetish than ever, it was almost as common to see goals scored from bad play as from brilliant movements.

Such managers as Herbert CHAPMAN responded to the change by developing the role of the stopper and a fundamental change in team tactics was complete. In 1990 another adjustment in the rules allowed an attacker to remain onside when level with the last outfield defender.

There was an interesting experiment with the rules in the US game in the 1970s, when a 35-yard line similar to the 'blue line' used in ice hockey was added to reduce the area in which a player could be offside (the international football authorities eventually insisted upon the line's removal). In 1965 Heart of Midlothian and Kilmarnock participated in an experimental match in which no offside rule was observed: Hearts won 8–2.

The offside law seems to me to be like the bunker shot in golf; it causes an interesting and infuriating hazard in the course of play, and creates healthy argument about the game.

Danny Blanchflower

Fair enough, he was in an offside position, but I don't think he was offside.

Jimmy Greaves

offside trap The manipulation of the offside law to foil an attack by the opposing team. Typically, the offside trap is worked by the defence moving forward down the pitch together, forcing the opposing strikers to play the ball back to avoid being caught with fewer than two defenders between themselves and their target goal.

The offside trap is a risky tactic relying upon good co-ordination of the defenders and is generally used sparingly to unsettle opposing strikers. The idea was first perfected by Newcastle United's fullback Bill McCracken in the years before World War I and resulted in teams growing more and more cautious as they tried to spring offside traps on one another. McCracken's skill at working the trap frustrated even the most distinguished of opponents and on at least one occasion provoked infuriated fans into invading the pitch. It was quite a regular occurrence for games to be interrupted by as many as 30 free kicks for offside offences brought about by the working of such traps.

The FA finally intervened in 1925 by staging a series of experimental friendlies, in which the two options considered were adding a 40-yard line to reduce the area in which the offside rule applied and reducing the number of defenders needed to keep a player onside from three to two (the Two-for-Three Scheme that was eventually selected). This change greatly reduced the chances of springing such traps and many teams averaged as many as three or more goals a game. One side, however, continued to present a tight defence that stifled the attack: Hull City – whose manager was none other than Bill McCracken himself.

oggi, oggi, oggi, oi, oi, oi! Ubiquitous, meaningless, chant that was heard regularly at football grounds in the UK in the 1970s. Shouted with enthusiasm, this aggressive chant seemed designed equally to give voice to the confidence of those chanting it and to cow the opposition. It has since been heard in a wide variety of contexts, from trade union pickets to children's games, and among crowds at a range of sports attracting mass support. Variations on the theme have included 'Maggie, Maggie, Maggie, out, out, out!', which was taken up by opponents of Margaret Thatcher's Conservative government in the 1980s.

It has been suggested that the chant is of Cornish origins, 'oggy' being a dialect term for a Cornish pasty (Cornwall itself is sometimes referred to as 'Oggyland'). It is also thought to have been a warning cry used by crooked watermen on the Thames to advise their confederates of the presence of the police.

In football, an early application of the chant was 'Ogley, Ogley, Ogley, oi, oi, oi!', which was heard at matches in which Darlington's goalkeeper Alan Ogley was participating.

Old Boys Former pupils of various English public schools, who banded together in the latter half of the 19th century to form some of the most famous early English football clubs. These groups of Old Boys generally considered the playing of football purely in terms of a healthy pastime that was quite compatible with respectable Christian society (hence the links many clubs had in their early years with the Church). The most celebrated Old Boy clubs included Blackburn Rovers, Old Etonians, and Old Carthusians. One Argentinian team still play under a similar title to this day, as Newell's Old Boys.

Old Carthusians English amateur football club that comprised Old Boys from Charterhouse public school. One of the strongest early English sides, they won the FA Cup in 1881 and the Amateur Cup in 1894 and 1897 (constituting a unique double). Members of the side included four full international players, of whom Wreford Brown is remembered as the man to coin the word soccer.

Old Etonians English amateur football club, which comprised various Old Boys from Eton public school. This famous club was founded in 1865 by future FA president Alfred KINNAIRD and emerged as one of the first teams to dominate English football, appearing in no fewer than six FA Cup Finals between 1875 and 1883 and winning two of them. Their victory over Blackburn Rovers in the 1882 Final was particularly relished and prompted Kinnaird himself to celebrate by standing on his head in front of the pavilion at the Oval.

Old Firm Glasgow's two celebrated football clubs CELTIC and RANGERS, whose traditional rivalry reflects the cultural, religious, and historical differences between Scotland's Catholic and Protestant communities. The mutual antagonism of the two sides dates back to the foundation of the two teams and is among the fiercest such rivalries anywhere in the world of football.

The rivalry is based on a number of fundamental principles: Celtic are historically the team of the oppressed Scottish Catholic community (which included many poor immigrants from Ireland), while Rangers have their roots in the better-heeled indigenous Scottish Protestant tradition. The differences between them are religious, political, cultural, and emotional. Fans of Celtic, for instance, cherish their links with Ireland and share the same pride in Irish independence from the 'auld enemy' England, singing the anthems that were sung by Irish revolutionaries in 1916 – whereas Rangers fans identify with the cause of Protestant Unionism in Northern Ireland and celebrate their patriotism with various Protestant battle hymns.

The Old Firm has dominated the history of Scottish football. The first 'Old Firm' Cup Final was as early as 1894, when Rangers won 3–1; subsequently they have met in the Final many times – most notoriously in 1909, when the fourth Old Firm Final was abandoned without a result because of rioting between the two sets of supporters, who were furious that extra time would not be played (the Cup was not awarded that year, at the request of the two clubs). A hundred people were injured, goalposts were destroyed, parts of the stadium were set on fire, and the pitch was cut up:

> *Among the minor incidents of the day was the exhibition of the craze for souvenirs. The cross-bar of one of the goalposts was carried from the field into Somerville Road in front of the burning pay-boxes, and a crowd of men and boys hacked at it with pocket-knives and pocketed the chips. Among the* debris *littering the ground were a number of policemen's helmets, which had been lost in the day's struggle. These were also the objective of the souvenir-hunter, being cut into strips and carried away.*
>
> The Scotsman, report of the riot (1909)

The first Old Firm Final in the Scottish League Cup was, surprisingly, not until 1957, when Celtic trounced Rangers 7–1 (the highest total at any major British Final). Generally speaking, Celtic emerged as the stronger half of the Old Firm in the period before World War I, while Rangers had the upper hand between the wars and for 20 years after World War II – until Celtic's manager Jock STEIN oversaw a revival in his club's fortunes and captured nine successive Scottish League championships among many other honours. The late 1980s, however, saw Rangers once more in the ascendency.

As an illustration of the importance of the religious and cultural divide between the two clubs, it was not until the early 1950s that Rangers signed their first known Catholic player (Laurie Blyth) and as recently as 1989 the signing of former Celtic player and Catholic Maurice Johnston stirred up considerable controversy; Alfie Conn has the very rare distinction of having won Scottish Cup-winning medals for both teams in what were to prove two Old Firm Finals (1973 and 1977).

The antagonism between the two clubs is not confined to the terraces; as recently as 1987 tempers flared in an Old Firm match and four players were subsequently called before the Sheriff's Court in Glasgow to explain themselves. It is a standing joke that referees of meetings of the Old Firm are asked for the names of their next of kin before they go on the pitch.

> *Do you know where hell is?*
> *Hell is in the Falls,*
> *Heaven is the Shankhill Road,*

And we'll guard old Derry's Walls,
I was born under a Union Jack,
A Union, Union Jack.

Rangers fans song, to the tune of 'Wandrin' Star'

I am a merry ploughboy and I plough the
*   fields by day,*
'Til a certain thought came to my mind that
*   I should run away,*
Now I've always hated slavery since the day
*   that I was born,*
So I'm off to join the IRA and I'm off
*   tomorrow morn.*

Celtic fans song, 'The Merry Ploughboy' (Irish
revolutionary song)

Old Invincibles Nickname of the classic
PRESTON NORTH END side that dominated
the early history of the English Football
League and is still considered the world's
first 'great' football team. When the League
was founded in 1888 it was a player with the
Old Invincibles – Jack Gordon (or possibly
Fred Dewhurst) – who was credited with
the very first League goal and it was Preston
North End who powered through to take
the first title (remarkably without losing a
match). One game in the 1888–89 season
set a record for the First Division that has
only once been equalled, with Preston's
J.D. Ross scoring no fewer than seven goals
in a match against Stoke City.

The side's pre-eminence in the English
game was confirmed that same season with
their convincing success in the FA Cup,
which they claimed as their own after a campaign in which they did not concede a single
goal. They had also been runners-up in the
Cup the year before and had been so confident of winning that they asked to be
allowed to have their photograph taken
with the Cup before the Final was even
played (the referee refused and in the event
they lost 2–1 to West Bromwich Albion). A
year later the side retained the League title
and for the next three seasons they finished
as runners-up to create a record of success
that is unlikely ever to be equalled.

The team, managed by the brilliant
Major William Sudell, was hailed as the
finest in the history of the game and certainly Preston North End have never since
approached the achievements of their celebrated forefathers. Over the 80 matches
that the Old Invincibles played in the first
five years of League history they drew 14
and lost only 28 games, scoring 307 goals
themselves and conceding 138. Perhaps the
most famous of their victims were Hyde,
who crashed 26–0 to the Old Invincibles in
the FA Cup in 1887 (at one point in the

game the Invincibles scored six goals in just
seven minutes).

Among the star players was the enormously respected John GOODALL, centre-
forward for the national side, though the
emphasis was very much on team play
rather than individual talent. The side's
success underlined the superiority of professional teams over the old amateur clubs
(Sudell readily admitted he paid his players
and Preston were consequently ruled out of
the FA Cup for a single season) and added
to the heated debate over professionalism.
See also LILYWHITES.

Old Lady Nickname of the WEMBLEY
Stadium in London.

Old Man Nickname of the celebrated
Italian football club AC MILAN, which
reflects the club's status as one of the most
senior sides in Italian football – and indeed
arguably the finest team in the world.

Old Reds Nickname of the former English
League football club ACCRINGTON STANLEY,
in reference to the colour of the team strip.

Old Show Ground *See* GLANFORD PARK.

Old Trafford The home ground of the
English football club MANCHESTER UNITED.
United played at North Road and then
Bank Street, Clayton, until the side's FA
Cup Final victory in 1909 prompted a local
brewer to provide the funds for a massive
new stadium. When it opened in 1910, Old
Trafford (which cost £60,000 to build) was
hailed as the most advanced stadium of
its time and rapidly became the envy of
all other British teams, who marvelled at
such features as cushioned tip-up seats
and magnificent changing-rooms (which
included lavish bathing facilities) as well as
at the billiards room, massage room, and
gymnasium.

Huge crowds were attracted to the
ground on a regular basis – although only
13 fans paid to see a game between
Stockport County and Aston Villa in 1921
(another 2000 spectators stayed on to see
the game for free after seeing United play in
a game earlier in the afternoon).

The ground suffered more than any other
in the UK during World War II, however,
and had to be closed after severe damage
was inflicted (in 1941) by two German
bombs, which destroyed the Main Stand
and other terraces, as well as scorching the
pitch. The venue finally reopened in 1949
(United having shared Maine Road in the

meantime) and rapidly reasserted its reputation as the most popular venue in the north-west.

The existing stadium dates largely from the 1960s, when a massive and highly influential cantilever stand was added in preparation for the World Cup in 1966, along with the first private boxes to be installed at any British ground. Other features of the contemporary ground include a Manchester United museum, containing a telegram sent by Duncan EDWARDS shortly before the Munich air crash in 1958; those who died in the disaster are also remembered through a plaque and a clock dedicated to their memory. One part of the stands is reserved for families and no adult is admitted to it unless accompanied by a child.

Over the years the stadium has been variously described as 'A tabernacle of worship', 'A theatre of dreams', and 'A cathedral of football' and fans from all over the world go on regular tours of the terraces and other facilities. On match days the most fervent fans traditionally gather in the Stretford End, which is renowned throughout football as home to one of the most impassioned of all blocs of supporters. The ground is also said to have appeared in more feature films than any other in the country – among them *Hell is a City* (1960), *Billy Liar* (1963), *Charlie Bubbles* (1968), and *The Lovers* (1972).

oldest clubs The honour of being the oldest surviving club in the world is claimed by the English side Sheffield, which was formed in 1857. An historic match between Sheffield and Hallam in 1862 in order to raise money on behalf of the impoverished mill-workers of Lancashire is considered to mark the beginning of serious competitive club football (although informal sides representing schools, gentlemen's clubs, and villages had operated for decades before this). Hallam and Sheffield played their first match on Boxing Day 1860, Sheffield winning 2–0. 125 years later the two teams met again in a special anniversary match. In 1866 Sheffield played (and lost to) 'London' at Battersea Park in what was the first FA representative match; subsequently they also won the Amateur Cup in 1904. Hallam still play minor league football.

The first football club founded outside England is thought to have been the US club Oneida, which was formed in Boston in 1862 (football had in fact been played at nearby Harvard University since 1827). The oldest surviving Football League club is

Notts County, who were also founded in 1862. *See also* PUBLIC SCHOOL FOOTBALL.

oldest players The oldest player ever to participate in a First Division match is, of course, Stanley MATTHEWS. Matthews (who could boast the nickname 'The Ageless Wonder') played his last game in the First Division on 6 February 1965, when he turned out for Stoke City against Fulham at the age of 50 years five days.

He was not, however, the oldest player ever to play a League game. This honour goes to Neil MacBain, who played as emergency goalkeeper for New Brighton (of which he was then manager) in a match against Hartlepools United in Division Three (North) in March 1947 at the grand old age of 52 years four months (his side lost 3–0).

The oldest player to appear for any of the home countries at international level was Billy MEREDITH, who turned out for Wales against England in 1920 at the age of 45; at the age of 49 and eight months he was also the oldest player ever to take part in an FA Cup match.

None of the above, however, even approached the extraordinary career of Jack Wattam, who first started playing the game in his native Grimsby in the 1920s: he was still playing regularly for the Sunday League team Weelsby Rovers in the 1980s at the ripe old age of 74 (by which time he had appeared in a remarkable total of over 5000 matches). A model for younger players of today, Wattam (who was awarded the *Observer* Sports Nut of the Year award in 1983, in which year the Rovers lost all their 24 matches and let in 234 goals while scoring just 25) was never sent off or even booked in a career that lasted some 60 years.

Other players who have gone into the record books on account of their age include Eamon O'Keefe, who played for a Republic of Ireland Under-21 team in 1982 at the venerable age of 29. *See also* WALKING MATCHES.

I was an old player myself once.

Ossie Ardiles, when as manager he released some 'elderly' players from Newcastle United (1991)

Oldham Athletic English football club, nicknamed the Latics. Strip: all blue with red trim. Oldham were founded in 1895 as Pine Villa at the instigation of John Garland, landlord of the Featherstall and Junction Hotel. In 1899 they inherited the ground formerly used by the now-defunct

Oldham County and decided to adopt their present name. That same season the side needed only to win their final game to claim victory in the Manchester Alliance League; unfortunately only seven players turned up and they lost 2–0 and finished up in third place.

Oldham joined the League in 1907 (two years after moving into BOUNDARY PARK) and quickly distinguished themselves, reaching the First Division in 1910 and remaining in the top flight until 1923. During this halcyon period the club also reached the semi-final stage of the FA Cup (1913) and in 1915 missed the First Division championship by just two points. A turning point in the latter season may have been an incident involving the side's left-back W. Cook, who refused to leave the field after being sent off during a game against Middlesbrough; the game was abandoned (with Middlesbrough ahead) and Cook himself was suspended for 12 months.

Subsequently Oldham languished in the lower divisions for 60 years until manager Joe Royle supervised a revival in the club's fortunes in the 1980s and got them back into the First Division in 1991. A year later the team were founder members of the new Premier League. Royle's side also reached the League Cup Final and the semi-finals of the FA Cup in 1990.

Stars with the side over the years have included the former Manchester United player Charlie Roberts during World War I, the Scottish footballer Bobby Johnstone and Alan 'Iron Man' Lawson in the 1960s, Jimmy Fryatt in the 1970s, and in the 1980s, Mike Milligan, Andy Ritchie, and Graeme Sharp.

In 1967 Oldham conducted a tour of Rhodesia and were warned that a local witch doctor had cast a charm over the host teams' goal lines: it did not work and Oldham scored 45 goals in just 11 games, winning all but one of them.

The club enjoyed their record victory in 1962, beating Southport 11–0; they suffered their worst defeat in 1935, when they lost 13–4 against Tranmere Rovers. Ian Wood holds the record for the most League appearances with the club, having played in 525 matches between 1966 and 1980. *See also* HYPNOTISM.

Han we lost afore we'en started?
Han we heck! We'st win today!
We'en a team of gradely triers –
As they fund deawn Ashton road
An' fro' th' top o' th' League to th' bottom

We're noan as feeart as what they're coed.

Poem celebrating the Latics' first game in the First Division (1910)

Olympiakos Greek football club, which has long been the leading team in the country. Strip: red and white striped shirts, with white shorts and socks. Founded in 1925 and based at the Karaiskaki Stadium in Piraeus, Olympiakos have won 26 League championships and the Cup 19 times, but experienced a decline in fortune in the late 1980s.

Olympic football Football became an official Olympic sport in 1908 and has been included in the tournament every time it has been held (with the single exception of 1932 when it was dropped from the US Games that year over a dispute about the expenses of teams from South America). Even before 1908 (when a British team won the title – retaining it in 1912) football was staged as an unofficial part of the Games in 1896, 1900 (when the British team Upton Park won the tournament), and 1904 (when Canada – actually Galt football club – were presented with a gold medal). It was, in fact, largely because of the success of the Olympic competition in the 1920s that the World Cup came into being.

The Final of 1920 remains the most controversial in the history of the competition: fought by the host nation Belgium and Czechoslovakia it ended in confusion when the Czech players marched off the pitch in dissatisfaction at a decision by English referee John Lewis (the title became Belgium's by default – the last occasion on which it was won by the host country).

There was further trouble in the notorious 1936 Games held in Nazi Germany, with teams withdrawing and violence on the pitch involving a German referee and the national sides representing Italy and the USA erupting after an Italian player was allowed to play on after refusing to leave the field.

Between the 1950s and the 1980s the competition was dominated by 'amateur' sides from eastern Europe, which were comprised mostly of players from the armed forces of those nations (who thus qualified as amateurs even though many of them also appeared regularly for their national teams). Thus, winners of the tournament included Hungary (1952, 1964, and 1968), the Soviet Union (1956), Yugoslavia (1960 – and runners-up in 1948, 1952 and 1956), Poland (1972), East Germany (1976), and Czechoslovakia (1980). The

1964 competition was marred by a tragic riot that disrupted a preliminary match between Peru and Argentina and resulted in 328 deaths.

A major change was signalled by a FIFA decision that competing countries could not field players who had taken part in a World Cup tournament and in 1984 a non-eastern European side – France – took the Olympic title. The rule is now that players must be under the age of 23.

Olympic Stadium The name shared by a number of famous football grounds throughout Europe, most of which began life as hosts of the Olympic Games. The most notable of these venues include those in Athens (opened in 1982 in the hope that it would become a permanent home for the Olympics), Bruges (opened in 1975 and home of Clubbe Brugge KV and KSV Cercle Brugge), Helsinki (host of the 1952 Games and home of Helsingin Jalkapalloklubi), Amsterdam (built to house the 1928 Games and home to several clubs, including Ajax, over the years), Lausanne (opened in 1954 and home to Lausanne-Sports), Berlin (site of the notorious 1936 Games and used for the 1974 World Cup and since 1985 for Cup Finals), and Munich – a startling arena with an extraordinary tent-like roof that played host to the 1972 Games and which is home to Bayern Munich. Notable facts concerning these huge stadia include the information that the Helsinki venue is the only football venue to have appeared on a bank note (for ten Finnish markas), while the Olympic Stadium in Amsterdam witnessed the first installation of permanent floodlighting at any European stadium (in 1934).

Perhaps the most important of all the Olympic Stadiums in footballing terms is the ground in Rome, which is home to the Italian football clubs AS ROMA and LAZIO. Nicknamed the Stadium of the Cypress Trees, the venue was developed initially under the Fascists but remained unfinished until after World War II, finally opening in 1953 with a game between Italy and Hungary (the Hungarians won 3–0). It hosted the Olympic Games in 1960 and subsequently acquired the status of Italy's national football stadium, being used for the European Championships in 1968 and 1980 and for the European Cup Final in 1977 and 1984. Thirty years later it was substantially rebuilt in advance of staging the World Cup Final.

Oman Oman joined FIFA in 1980 but has yet to establish a reputation in international competition. Strip: red and white shirts, with red shorts and socks.

Omniturf *See* PLASTIC PITCHES.

On the Ball, City Music hall song that is traditionally associated with NORWICH CITY. The work of Albert T. Smith around 1890, the song was rapidly taken up by the team's supporters shortly after the club was founded in 1902 and is claimed to be the oldest football anthem still regularly heard at any football ground:

> *Kick-off, throw it in, have a little scrimmage,*
> *Keep it low, a splendid rush, bravo, win or die,*
> *On the ball, City, never mind the danger,*
> *Steady on, now's your chance,*
> *Hurrah! We've scored a goal.*

one-club man A player who spends his entire career with a single club. In these days of regular transfers, the one-club man is something of a rarity, but over the years many famous players have been uniquely associated with the fortunes of a single team, resisting all lures to move elsewhere.

Jimmy ARMFIELD spent the whole of his playing career with Blackpool (a total of 568 games), Tom FINNEY never left Preston North End, and Bobby CHARLTON remained with Manchester United throughout his playing career. Even more loyal to one club was John Trollope, who spent 20 years (1960–80) as a player for Swindon Town and appeared in no fewer than 770 games for them (second place goes to Roy Sproson who played 762 games for Port Vale between 1950 and 1972). In Scotland, Bob Ferrier completed 626 appearances for Motherwell between 1918 and 1937. Andrew Smailes, meanwhile, enjoyed an association with Rotherham United that lasted in all 29 years, during which he filled the roles of player, trainer, and manager. Charles Foweraker of Bolton Wanderers spent 50 years with the club, beginning as a part-time gate-checker in 1895 and ending up as secretary-manager.

one-two A move in which a player passes the ball to a team mate, who then immediately returns it to him. This basic tactic is also sometimes referred to as a wall pass (reflecting the similarity between the move and kicking a ball against a wall). Spurs manager Arthur ROWE was one of the notable tacticians who taught his players to develop complete attacks by stringing together a series of such 'one-touch' passes.

Ossie Nickname of the Argentinian midfielder and subsequently manager Osvaldo ARDILES.

Outlaws Nickname bestowed upon the US and Canadian teams who were members of the unofficial NATIONAL PROFESSIONAL SOCCER LEAGUE.

Oval, The (1) Famous English cricket ground, home of Surrey county cricket club, which was once also a celebrated venue for FA Cup Finals and other major football fixtures. The Kennington Oval was the setting for the very first FA Cup Final, in 1872 (when 2000 people paid a shilling each to see Wanderers beat the Royal Engineers 1–0), and subsequently hosted the Final annually from 1874 until 1892, by which time the Final attracted as many as 25,000 fans. Its adoption by the FA owed much to the fact that FA Secretary Charles Alcock was also Surrey's Secretary.

(2) The home ground, in Belfast, of the Northern Ireland club GLENTORAN. Occupied by the team since 1899, The Oval was badly damaged by bombs during World War II (swans enjoyed swimming in the craters left in the pitch) but was reopened in 1949 and remains one of the city's leading venues. Curiosities of the ground include a wartime bunker on the Kop End.

Over the Bridge Nickname of the English non-League football club ABINGDON TOWN, in reference to their location.

over the moon Football cliché, signifying great pleasure or relief at a result or any other item of good news. Quite where the much-derided expression came from remains a subject of some debate, though everyone seems united in their scorn for the phrase (and by extension, of those who are unwise enough to use it as a matter of habit). It began to be quoted on a regular basis by British footballers in the late 1970s and was rapidly picked up by the satirists, who thus unwittingly promoted its spread. By the 1980s the phrase was so prevalent and criticism of monosyllabic players and managers so intense that many within the football establishment called for conscious efforts to be made to improve the communication skills of young players. When a course to improve the linguistic capabilities of British footballers was instituted at a college in Sheffield, with the professed aim of

weaning people off 'soccer-speak', Jimmy GREAVES for one was delighted with the idea, saying: 'If the course had been around in my playing days, I'd have been over the moon.'

The phrase had, in fact, been associated with the world of football for some years before this, as evidenced by a comment made by Alf RAMSEY in 1962: 'I feel like jumping over the moon' – though, to be fair, he did protest, in 1973: 'I am not one to jump over the moon or off a cliff.'

The cliché's history before that belongs to non-footballing circles. Way back in 1857 Lady Cavendish recorded in her diary that her children were 'over the moon' at the news of the birth of another brother, and it has been suggested that the phrase was coined by young members of the family of the prime minister William Gladstone, who delighted in making up such colourful idioms. It seems plausible that the phrase ultimately derives from the nursery rhyme that runs: 'Hey diddle diddle, the cat and the fiddle, the cow jumped over the moon . . .'

Back in 1888 players in an international game between Wales and England had the opportunity to kick the ball literally 'over the moon', England's goalkeeper being one William Moon. *See also* SICK AS A PARROT.

Chris is on cloud nine. She is, how do you say in England, under the moon.

Colette Lloyd, mother of Chris Lloyd, on her Wimbledon victory (1981)

over the top or **over the ball** A dangerous tackle, in which a player challenges by going over the ball rather than attacking from the side. Such tackles became increasingly common in the 1970s when such teams as Leeds United developed the policy of the professional foul.

Overath, Wolfgang (1943–   ) West German midfielder, who was a pillar of the national team that fought the 1966, 1970, and 1974 World Cups. Winner of 81 caps, he spent most of his domestic career with IFC Cologne.

overhead kick A kick, usually a shot at goal, in which the player in possession keeps his back to the goalmouth and kicks the ball backwards over his head. Such shots are risky as the player has a poor view of the target area and can result in a charge of dangerous play, but can prove useful as a shock tactic when a high pass is received in the goal area; they are among the most spectacular shots in the game.

*It's all a matter of going for it. And not
minding too much if you get it wrong.*

Mark Hughes, on the overhead kick (1990)

overlap To move past a team mate in
possession of the ball into an attacking position (normally used by full-backs and other
defenders supporting the strikers).

Over-the-Line Goal The controversial
goal that settled the FA Cup Final between
Newcastle United and Arsenal in 1932.
Arguments about the validity of Newcastle's
goal raged for many years: basically, everything depended on whether the ball had
gone briefly out of play before it was passed
by United's Jimmy Richardson to Jack
Allen, who put it in the net. The referee
thought it had not; thousands of Arsenal
fans thought it had – and continued to do
so for a great many years afterwards.

Owls (1) Nickname of the English non-
League football club HARLOW TOWN.
(2) Nickname of the English football
club SHEFFIELD WEDNESDAY, in reference
to the original name of their Hillsborough
Stadium home – Owlerton (changed in
1914 when the parliamentary constituency
in which the ground lies changed its name).
The nickname is somewhat artificial as the
old name of the ground was generally pronounced 'Olerton'.

own goal A goal that is scored by a player
against his own team, usually as the result of
an accident (typically while attempting to
block an opponent's shot) or through a
misunderstanding with his goalkeeper. This
footballing phrase has long since entered the
general language, being used of any situation where someone (or something) has
suffered a setback through his own actions.
Examples of the phrase being adopted in a
non-sporting context include its use by the
military establishment in Northern Ireland
from the 1980s, who talked of terrorists
scoring an own goal when they were
destroyed by their own explosive devices.
    The very first own goal in Football
League history was not long in coming:
on the very first day of League football
(8 September 1888) George Cox of Aston
Villa became the first player to know the
embarrassment of appearing on the scoresheet as a scorer for the opposition when he
put in a goal on behalf of Wolverhampton
Wanderers. It is not only the incompetent
full-back who has fallen victim to such
self-inflicted humiliation: Lord KINNAIRD
himself, one of the founders of the modern

game, holds the distinction of being the first
man to score an own goal in an FA Cup
Final (while playing for Wanderers against
Oxford University in 1877). The 1877
season also saw the first own goal in the
Scottish FA Cup Final, scored by a player
called McDougall against his own team
Vale of Leven (who nonetheless won the
game 3–2).
    Few games have, however, equalled the
extraordinary meeting that took place
between First Division clubs Aston Villa
and Leicester City in 1976. The final scoreline was 2–2, which would have been
unremarkable but for the fact that all four
goals were scored by the same man – Villa's
defender Chris Nicholl, who headed two
goals for his own team and kicked in two for
his opponents. Nicholl's feat duplicated that
of Manchester United's Sam Wynne, who in
1923 also scored two goals for an opposing
Oldham Athletic side as well as two for
his own team (on that occasion, though,
another player scored to give Oldham a 3–2
victory). Robert Stuart of Middlesbrough
holds the dubious record of five own goals
in a single season (achieved in 1934–35).
    Few footballers have been more unfortu-
nate than the Democrata player Jorge Nino:
in 1982 he scored a hat-trick of own goals
in a humiliating 5–1 defeat against Atlético
Mineiro. Pat Kruse of Torquay United,
might though qualify as an equal for his
own achievement in the realm of the own
goal. In 1977 he became the scorer of the
fastest own goal in the history of senior
British football when he headed the ball into
his own net after just six seconds of a game
against Cambridge United. Both he and
Nino must have understood the feelings of
the unnamed Japanese player who, legend
has it, was so upset at scoring an own goal
that he burnt his boots and became a monk.

*There's never been a good time to score an
own goal against yourself.*

John Grieg

Oxford United English football club,
nicknamed the U's. Strip: gold shirts with
navy blue trim, with navy blue shorts and
socks. Although there was another Oxford
United, who played in the early years of
the 20th century, the modern club dates
back to 1893, when they played under the
title Headington (and later – until adopting
their present name in 1960 – as Headington
United).
    The club operated in minor leagues until
1962, when they were elected to the Fourth
Division as a replacement for Accrington

Stanley. Under manager Arthur Tanner and led by captain Ron ATKINSON, the U's – based at the MANOR GROUND – arrived in the Second Division in 1968 after winning the Third Division title and remained there for eight years before slipping back to the Third Division in 1976. Having survived a severe financial crisis in 1982, the club clinched their second Third Division championship in 1984 under manager Jim Smith and the following season added the Second Division title and won promotion to the top flight for the first time. The following season capped this sensational rise through the League with victory in the League Cup after a memorable 3–0 win in the Final over Queen's Park Rangers.

Oxford also have a proud record in the FA Cup, having progressed further in it than any other Fourth Division side back in 1964, when they reached the quarter-finals.

The successes of the 1980s were somewhat overshadowed by controversy surrounding owner Robert MAXWELL's plans to merge the team with Reading as Thames Valley Royals, but Oxford preserved their separate identity, despite slipping back to the Second Division in 1988.

The club enjoyed their record League victory in 1964, when they beat Barrow 7–0; they suffered their worst defeat in 1986, losing 6–0 to Liverpool. John Shuker holds the record for League appearances, having played in 478 games between 1962 and 1977.

At Oxford it took me weeks to convince the man on the gate that I was the manager. He always gave me the third degree before he let me in.

Jim Smith (1988)

P

Paisley, Bob (1919–) English manager, who succeeded Bill SHANKLY as manager of Liverpool and went on to become the most successful manager in the history of the English game. A former player with Bishop Auckland and Liverpool, with whom he won a League championship medal in 1947, he joined the coaching staff at Anfield in 1954 and subsequently became Shankly's right-hand man. He inherited the manager's job in 1974 and two years later saw his team collect both the League title and the UEFA Cup. Keeping to the principles set by Shankly and buying wisely, he led the team through their most glorious era, winning another five League titles, the European Cup in 1977 and 1981, and three League Cup victories. He finally stepped down in 1983 but remained at Anfield as an adviser to Kenny DALGLISH and took a post on the board.

Pakistan Pakistan joined FIFA in 1948 but have yet to make much impact in international competition. Strip: green shirts, white shorts, and green and white socks.

Paleface Nickname of the English forward Steve BLOOMER, who was one of the most celebrated English footballers of the late-Victorian and Edwardian eras. The nickname referred to his large, pale face, which generally bore a nonchalant, even careless expression during even the most closely fought matches.

Palmerston Park The home ground, in Dumfries, of the Scottish football club QUEEN OF THE SOUTH. Acquired by the club on its formation in 1919, Palmerston Park was developed steadily as the side prospered in the 1930s. After the war, German prisoners-of-war helped to restore the ground and in 1958 Palmerston Park became the first Scottish venue to boast its own pylon-mounted floodlights. The Main Stand was rebuilt in the 1960s after a fire.

Panama Panama joined FIFA in 1938 but have yet to establish a strong international reputation. Strip: red and white shirts, blue shorts, and red socks.

Panathinaikos Greek football club, which ranks behind Olympiakos as the most successful side in the country. Strip: green shirts, with white shorts and socks. Founded in 1908 – and thus the oldest surviving club in Greece – the team has won some 15 League championships and the Cup on 11 occasions. In 1971 they became the first Greek club to reach the final of a major European competition when they lost to Ajax in the European Cup.

Papua New Guinea Papua New Guinea joined FIFA in 1963 but have yet to make much impact in international competition. Strip: red shirts, black shorts, and red socks.

Paradise Nickname of CELTIC PARK, home of the now disbanded Northern Ireland football club Belfast Celtic. The site of the ground, now occupied by the Park Shopping Centre on the Donegal Road, is marked by a plaque.

Paraguay The Paraguayan national team have generally taken second place behind some of the other powerful South American sides, but have nonetheless enjoyed moments of international glory. The Paraguayans took part in the very first World Cup, in 1930, and in 1958 confounded many experts when they managed to take Uruguay's place in the Finals. In 1986 the Paraguayan team, which included star players Julio Cesar Romero and Roberto Cabañas, enjoyed their best World Cup campaign to date, fighting through to the second round before elimination against England. The team's other honours have included victory in the South American Championship in 1953 and 1979. Strip: red and white shirts, with blue shorts and socks. .

Parc Astrid The popular name by which the VANDEN STOCK STADIUM in Brussels, home of the Belgian club ANDERLECHT, is usually known (the original Parc Astrid being a public park next to the ground).

Park Avenue *See* BRADFORD PARK AVENUE.

parrot, sick as a *See* SICK AS A PARROT.

Pars Nickname of the Scottish football club DUNFERMLINE ATHLETIC. A number of explanations have been advanced concerning the origins of the nickname. According to one, it was coined when the club acquired League status, thus coming on a 'par' with other senior teams for the first time. Another has it that it was inspired by the black and white team strip, reminiscent of the colouring of a fish called a par, and yet another that it is short for 'Plymouth Argyle Rosyth Supporters', as seen on a banner unfurled by sailors from the Rosyth naval base nearby. A more jocular suggestion contends that par is short for 'paralytic' – a description of the team when they were going through a particularly unrewarding period.

Partick Thistle Scottish football club, nicknamed the Jags. Strip: amber shirts with red sleeves, red shorts with amber trim, and red socks. Founded in 1876, Partick Thistle joined the League in 1893 and have played at FIRHILL PARK since 1909. They won the Second Division title in 1897, 1900, and 1971 and the First Division championship in 1976. They have won the Scottish Cup just once, in 1921, and have also captured the Scottish League Cup a single time (in 1972). Stars with the side over the years have included Jimmy McMenemy, Alan Rough, and Maurice Johnston.

The club enjoyed their record victory in 1931, beating Royal Albert 16–0; they suffered their worst defeat back in 1881, losing 10–0 against Queen's Park. Alan Rough holds the record for League appearances with the club, having played in 410 games between 1969 and 1982.

> For years I thought the club's name was Partick Thistle Nil.
>
> Billy Connolly, comedian (1980)

Partizan Belgrade Serbian football club, which dominated domestic football in what was formerly Yugoslavia. Strip: black and white striped shirts, with white shorts and socks. Founded in 1945 as the Army club, Partizan are based at the JNA Stadium in Belgrade and have won some 11 League championships and five Cups since 1947. In

1966 they were losing finalists in the European Cup, making them the first Yugoslavian club to reach a major European final.

Paternoster Row The London street, close to St Paul's Cathedral, in which the Football Association had its first home. The Association moved into number 28 in 1881 and operated from little more than a single room for four years. The Row suffered badly from bombing in World War II. *See also* LANCASTER GATE.

> *An unpretentious, badly furnished little room.*
>
> J.J. Bentley, FA vice-president, of Paternoster Row

Peacocks Alternative nickname for LEEDS UNITED.

Pearce, Stuart (1962–) English defender, nicknamed Psycho, who established a reputation as one of the hard men of English football in the 1980s. He began his career with Wealdstone and subsequently transferred to Coventry City and (in 1985) to Nottingham Forest, where he became one of the most formidable obstacles to opposing strikers. He has also been capped many times, and under Graham TAYLOR became captain of England.

Peebles Rovers Former Scottish League football club, which was a member of the League from 1923 to 1926. The club continues in existence as a non-League side, still playing at Whitestone Park.

Peel Park The home ground of the former League football club ACCRINGTON STANLEY. Peel Park was first used by the team in 1919 and was subsequently developed by them into a substantial League venue. Like all grounds, it had its idiosyncrasies, which included a narrow sloping pitch and thin partition walls between the two dressing-rooms, which allowed teams to eavesdrop on their opponents. Events in the ground's history included an early televised match in 1955. League football at Peel Park came to an end in 1962, when Accrington Stanley were overcome by their debts, and there is now little trace left of what was once an established ground.

Pegasus The combined Oxford-Cambridge universities team that succeeded Corinthians as the most celebrated amateur club in the UK for a few years after World War II. In an age when the professional game was attracting record crowds the amateurs found new champions in Pegasus, who represented the very best traditions of fair play and sportsmanship. Pegasus captured the popular imagination, winning the Amateur Cup in 1951 and 1953, when they played at Wembley in front of crowds of 100,000.

Their stars (who were older than undergraduates in other decades because many of them had been called up for war service) included captain David Saunders (who played in every competitive game Pegasus turned out for), Mike Pinner (winner of 51 amateur caps for England), and Donald Carr, who was also a first-class cricketer who played two Tests for England and eventually rose to the post of secretary of the Test and County Cricket Board. The team's coach Vic Buckingham went on to manage several English League clubs. Founded in 1948 at the instigation of Harold THOMPSON (a champion of the amateur game who became chairman of the FA in 1976), the team was finally disbanded in 1963.

> To see Pegasus on this sunlit day was to admire the inner workings of some Swiss watch. Everything and everyone hung together. The mechanism worked perfectly.
>
> Geoffrey Green, The Times, reporting FA Amateur Cup Final (1953)

Pelé (Edson Arantes do Nascimento; 1940–) Brazilian inside-forward, nicknamed the Black Pearl, who is often described as the most talented footballer in the game's history. Born in Tres Coracoes, Brazil (where a statue of him now stands), Pelé was the son of a minor footballer nicknamed Dondhino. His mother, who had suffered the hardship of being married to a footballer who earned next to nothing, discouraged her son's enthusiasm for the game, but to no avail – he had already begun the love affair with football that was to make him famous throughout the world:

> Football is like a religion to me. I worship the ball, and I treat it like a god. Too many players think of a football as something to kick. They should be taught to caress it and to treat it like a precious gem.

In 1954 he won a place with the Bauru Athletic Club juniors in São Paulo – despite the opinion of several officials that he was too slightly built to make much impact in the game. Often hotheaded and reckless, he suffered a knee injury at the age of 16 that was to trouble him throughout the rest of his career, but gradually he learnt to control his temper and in time won praise as a symbol of and spokesman for the best in international football. One proud boast that he could fully justify was that he could apply his immense talent to any position on the field, including goalkeeper.

In 1956 he joined Santos, with whom he remained until 1974, finishing his first season as the club's top scorer and making his international debut the following year. The World Cup of 1958 confirmed his standing: he scored six goals in the tournament, including two in the Final (which Brazil won) – all at the age of just 17. Notable highlights of the career that followed included the scoring of his 1000th first-class goal in 1969 and a second World Cup victory in 1970; regretted by many was the tactic adopted by the Portuguese team in the 1966 competition when they deliberately attempted to kick Pelé out of the game, prompting him to threaten never to play World Cup football again.

Pelé retired in 1974 and Santos declined to hand his number 10 shirt to any successor, realizing the impossibility of finding anyone to equal their great star. Having lost the second fortune of his career, however, the Black Pearl came out of retirement and joined the New York Cosmos a year later for a contract worth $4,500,000. He was voted Most Valuable Player with the NASL in 1976 and in 1977 ensured Cosmos' victory in the Soccer Bowl. With a total of 1283 first-class goals, he then retired for good. He made his last appearance in a memorable match between Santos and Cosmos, playing one half with each team.

Since 1977 Pelé has maintained his status as a universally respected ambassador for the game, regularly meeting heads of state and on one occasion calling for and getting a two-day truce in a war between Biafra and Nigeria. He has devoted particular attention to promoting the game amongst poorer communities and has even been heard to express a desire to become president of Brazil.

> I was born for soccer, just as Beethoven was born for music.
>
> Pelé

penalty A direct free kick at goal from the penalty spot, which is awarded to the attacking team after some playing offence is committed by the defending side in the penalty area. The ball must be kicked forwards.

The penalty kick was not introduced for some 20 years after the FA Cup was inaugurated and even then was the subject of some controversy. Amateurs regarded the addition of such a law as a slur on their sportsmanship and for many years refused to use penalty kicks. Goalkeepers with Corinthians, for instance, pointedly stood by one of the goalposts until a kick against them had been taken. The change was inevitable, however, after an incident in a game between Notts County and Stoke at Trent Bridge, when a deliberate handball by a defender (County's Hendry) saved a goal and, indeed, prevented Stoke drawing level. Such flouting of the rules deserved stern punishment and so the penalty kick was suggested (it had recently been introduced in Ireland).

The very first penalty goal scored in the Football League was witnessed on 14 September 1891, when J. Heath of Wolves put the ball in Accrington's net.

The rules regarding the penalty kick were somewhat different in the early years, with goalkeepers being allowed to advance as much as six yards from their line. This practice was prohibited after 1905, when keepers were obliged to remain on their line until the kick was taken. Other refinements to the rules included one preventing keepers from moving about to distract the kicker (some keepers developed elaborate jigging routines) and another introducing the penalty arc, to keep other defenders a greater distance away from the penalty-taker.

Some matches are completed without a single penalty being awarded to either side, while other fixtures are dominated by action from the penalty spot. In a remarkable meeting between Crewe Alexandra and Bradford in 1924, no fewer than four penalties were given in just five minutes. Other matches that were distinguished by the awarding of four penalties included meetings between St Mirren and Rangers in 1904, Burnley and Grimsby in 1909, Northampton and Hartlepool in 1976, and Bristol City and Wolverhampton Wanderers in 1977, but the British record for penalty kicks was established in 1989, when a total of five penalties were given in a game between Crystal Palace and Brighton and Hove Albion (Palace won 2–1).

John Wark of Ipswich Town celebrated an unusual hat-trick when he scored with three penalties during a UEFA Cup match with Aris Salonika in 1980–81 – as did Herne Bay's George Evans in a game against Cray Reserves in 1980. Some players specialize in taking penalties. Of these the most notable include Francis LEE, who established a new record with the 13 penalties he scored in a single season (1972), and Burnley's Peter Noble, who scored with every single one of the 27 penalty kicks he took between 1974 and 1979.

Even more celebrated, of course, are the goalkeepers who save crucial penalties. Of these, the most famous must include Wimbledon's Dave BEASANT, who in 1988 became the first goalkeeper ever to save a penalty in an FA Cup Final at Wembley. Goalkeeper Willie Brewster of the Chelsea 'A' team also distinguished himself as a penalty-stopper in April 1955, when he saved four out of five penalties awarded to opponents Dunstable. Much earlier, Kettering's goalkeeper Fred Mearns saved no fewer than 19 penalties in the 1903–04 season.

Of Cup Finals settled by penalty kicks the most thrilling have included the FA Cup Final of 1938, which was decided in Preston North End's favour when George Mutch scored from a penalty against Huddersfield Town in the last minute of extra time (making it the first FA Final to be settled by a penalty).

On the whole, penalties tend to go in – but some teams find the taking of penalties is too daunting a challenge: in a remarkable League season (1934–35) almost exactly one-third (131) of the 394 penalties awarded were missed. On very rare occasions players have opted for the surprise tactic of passing the ball to a colleague rather than taking a direct shot at goal: in 1982 Johann CRUYFF did just that when he was given a penalty against Helmond Sport, passing the ball to a team mate, who returned it quickly to him to score (Cruyff's team Ajax won 5–0). *See also* HEADER.

A penalty is a cowardly way to score.

Pelé

penalty box The larger of the two rectangular areas that surrounds the goal, delineating the part of the field that must be vacated by all other players except the defending goalkeeper when the penalty-taker takes his kick.

penalty shoot-out A means of determining the winners of a game when both teams are level after a full 90 minutes play and extra time and a result is required from the match. The penalty shoot-out, in which the teams have five alternate shots at goal each, was used for the first time to produce a result in a first-class match in England when Hull City and Manchester United drew 1–1 in the semi-finals of the Watney Cup in 1970: United won 4–3. The device has since been used to get results at almost every level, including (since 1982) World Cup Final matches, but is not popular with either fans or players.

Contentious penalty shoot-outs that still rankle in the memory of many fans include that which led to England's exit from the World Cup Finals at the semi-final stage (against West Germany) in 1990.

In 1975 a marathon session of penalties was undertaken to settle the outcome of an Asia Cup semi-final between Hong Kong and North Korea. A nail-biting match had ended 3–3 after extra time and the ensuing penalty shoot-out also ended with both teams level. After that it was a case of first team to draw one goal ahead, but still no result was forthcoming, with alternate kicks all being either saved or both going into the net. Everyone in both teams had a go, then they had to start all over again. At long last Hong Kong missed and Kim Jung-min finished it with a fine goal, making North Korea 11–10 victors (they went on to win the Final against China); in all 28 penalties had been taken. The same figure of 28 penalties was reached in domestic British football in 1987, during a match between Aldershot and Fulham (Aldershot won 11–10).

One of the most unusual penalty shoot-outs that ever took place was a strange affair staged early in the 20th century, when the grandfather of the Burnley and Queen's Park Rangers player Dave Thomas figured in a penalty shoot-out with an elephant: the elephant lost 11–2. In another penalty shoot-out involving an elephant in the 1890s, however, an elephant (which belonged to Sanger's Circus) managed to cause some embarrassment to the professionals with Leicester Fosse. A challenge had been issued by the circus that their elephant (using an over-sized ball) could not be beaten in a shoot-out and Fosse responded by pitting four players against the creature. Three men failed to get the ball past the elephant and only William Keech, using a deceptive feint, managed to score. When Keech and the elephant ended up level at 2–2 a replay was ordered and this time Keech emerged the victor at 3–2. *See also* SHOOT-OUT.

penalty spot White marking indicating where penalties must be taken from. The first penalty spots were painted back in 1902.

Peñarol Uruguayan football club, which has long been Uruguay's most successful side. Strip: black and yellow striped shirts, with black shorts and socks. Founded in 1891 (as the Central Uruguayan Railway Cricket Club) by British immigrants, the club adopted its present name in 1913 (after the name of the district of Montevideo in which it has its home). Based at the Centenario Stadium, the side has won more than 40 League championships as well as the South American Cup in 1960, 1961, 1966, 1982, and 1987, and the World Club Championship in 1961, 1966, and 1982. The majority of the Uruguayan national squad that won the World Cup in 1950 were players with Peñarol.

Pensioners Nickname of the English football club CHELSEA, in reference to the Chelsea Pensioners (the veteran soldiers who occupy the Royal Hospital for old and disabled servicemen in Chelsea).

People's Army Stadium The home ground, in Sofia, of the Bulgarian football club CSFA. The Narodna Armia (People's Army) Stadium was opened in 1957 in the city's Liberty Park, which was created in 1880 to honour the liberation of Bulgaria from the Turks.

People's Club Nickname of the Brazilian football club FLAMENGO, reflecting its bedrock of support among the ordinary people of Rio de Janeiro (in contrast to the more aristocratic home crowd attached to archrivals Fluminense).

People's Game The game of football itself. This old cliché, cherishing the game's working-class image, dates back many decades but is still frequently heard when the interests of the ordinary fan appear to be in danger of being forgotten by the administrators of the game. Such complaints go back to the earliest years:

> I venture to suggest that the turn has come of the public who bring the grist to the mill. Why not covered accommodation for spectators, dry ground to stand on, and a reduced admission if possible? The profits will stand it. Many a wreath has been purchased by standing on wet ground on Saturday afternoons.

Birmingham Mail, letter (1892)

> If this can be termed the century of the common man, then soccer, of all sports, is surely his game . . . in a world haunted by

the hydrogen and napalm bomb, the football field is a place where sanity and hope are still left unmolested.

Sir Stanley Rous (1952)

People's Park Stadium *See* VOLKSPARK-STADION.

People's Stadium *See* NÉPSTADION.

Peppino Nickname of the Italian striker Giuseppe MEAZZA, who was one of the most famous Italian footballers of the 1930s.

Peru The Peruvian national team have often been overshadowed by other South American sides, but have nonetheless had a long history in international competition. Peru first participated in the Finals of the World Cup back in 1930, though it was not until 1970 that they qualified for a second time. They were back in 1978 when, coached by DIDÍ and inspired by Teofilo Cubillas, the team battled through to the quarter-finals before going out against Brazil. The highlight of the 1982 series was a draw with eventual winners Italy. Their other honours have included victory in the South American Championship in 1939 and 1975. Strip: all white with red trim.

Peterborough United English football club, nicknamed The Posh. Strip: royal blue shirts, white shorts, and white socks with blue trim. Founded in 1934 as successor to the disbanded Peterborough and Fletton side, the Posh spent many years as a non-League club, rising to dominate the Midland League in the 1950s (almost unbelievably, they lost just one game in a total of 103 matches between 1955 and 1960). Based at the LONDON ROAD ground, Peterborough acquired a reputation as formidable giant-killers and finally joined the League in 1960 after making no fewer than 20 applications over the years. Spearheaded by striker Terry Bly, they immediately claimed the Fourth Division title (with a record 134 goals in 46 games) and thus became the first club to win the Fourth Division title in the year of its election. Subsequent highlights included beating Arsenal in the FA Cup in 1965 and Newcastle United and Burnley in the League Cup a year later.

A financial scandal ruined everything in 1968, however, and the club were relegated as a punishment (as well as having to cope with a serious cash shortage). The club returned to the Third Division after winning the Fourth Division championship in 1974, were relegated once more, and made it back to the Third in 1991, to be promoted again to the new First Division in 1992.

The club enjoyed their record victory in 1969, when they beat Oldham Athletic 8–1; they suffered their worst defeat in 1946, losing 8–1 to Northampton Town. Tommy Robson holds the record for League appearances with the club, having played in 482 games between 1968 and 1981.

> *The Football League is upside down,*
> *The Football League is upside down,*
> *We're going up, with Colchester,*
> *The Football League is upside down.*

Supporters' song, heard in 1990, when Peterborough and Colchester were in danger of relegation

Petersfield United English non-League football club, nicknamed Reds. Strip: red and black shirts, white shorts, and red socks. Founded in 1889 and based at the Love Lane ground in Petersfield, the club play in the Isthmian League.

PFA *See* PROFESSIONAL FOOTBALLERS' ASSOCIATION.

Philippines The Philippines joined FIFA in 1928 but have yet to make much impact in international competition. Strip: blue and red shirts, blue shorts, and white socks.

Philips Stadium The home ground, in Eindhoven, of the Dutch football club PSV EINDHOVEN. PSV's links with the Philips electrical company are close and the modern stadium is well-equipped with sophisticated electrical devices (and lights) supplied by the club's patrons. Features of the ground include a massive new Main Stand (opened in 1988), well-appointed executive accommodation, and gas heaters, which are used to warm spectators from above during winter matches.

Pichichi Nickname (meaning 'nipper') of the celebrated Spanish footballer Rafael MORENO.

Pickles The young black and white mongrel dog who shot to fame in 1966, when he found the stolen World Cup. The Jules Rimet trophy had been taken on 20 March from a glass-fronted cabinet in Central Hall, Westminster, where it had been the star item in a stamp exhibition prior to that year's tournament in England. Uproar ensued and the FA and the police launched strenuous efforts to locate the missing trophy as the press of virtually every country in the world castigated the football authorities for their carelessness.

The top of the trophy arrived at the FA with a ransom demand and at the subsequent rendezvous a 47-year-old dock labourer was arrested. The Cup was still missing, however, and it was not until Pickles, out on a walk on Beulah Hill in south London with his owner David Corbett, sniffed at a mysterious bundle under a bush that it finally came to light.

The dog was showered with rewards, which included a film role at twice the usual rate, a medal from the National Canine Defence League, and a year's supply of treats from a dog food company, while his owner also enjoyed a large reward.

Pie Saturday The Saturday in 1901 on which Sheffield United met Tottenham Hotspur at Bolton in the FA Cup Final replay. The Final is remembered in Bolton not so much for the 3–1 scoreline in Tottenham's favour as for the fact that the game attracted the smallest FA Cup Final crowd (20,470) of the century. The fans stayed away in their thousands, fearing the crush and discouraged by the fact that the local railway company refused to offer cheap-day excursion tickets. The result was a commercial disaster for Bolton, particularly for the sellers of meat pies, who had assembled stocks of hundreds of pies; most of the pies were eventually given away (hence the fixture's nickname in the locality).

piggling *See* PUBLIC SCHOOL FOOTBALL.

Pilgrims (1) Nickname of the English non-League football club BOSTON UNITED, in reference to the US city of the same name, which was founded by English puritans (the Pilgrim Fathers) in 1630.
(2) Nickname of the English football club PLYMOUTH ARGYLE, commemorating the departure from Plymouth of the 102 Pilgrim Fathers who were the first English colonists of the Americas in 1620.

Pine Villa The former name (1894–99) of OLDHAM ATHLETIC.

Pirates Nickname of the English football club BRISTOL ROVERS, reflecting the city's maritime tradition.

pitch invasion The invasion of the playing field by fans, which inevitably interrupts play and leads to clashes with the authorities and damage to the game's public image. Though pitch invasions are usually thought of as a feature of the game in the last two or three decades, they are not, however, a recent invention. Back in 1881, for instance, a game between the Scottish clubs Queen's Park and Dumbarton witnessed the invasion of the pitch after a goal was scored and the whole game had to be replayed (making it the first result ever voided by crowd intervention). In 1888 an FA Cup tie was abandoned for the first time when the crowd came on to the field of play during a fifth round tie between Aston Villa and Preston North End. Another pitch invasion involving Villa fans in 1893 was even more serious, with the Hussars having to be called in to restore order and the club being barred from the FA Cup that year for failing to prevent such disruption.

One of the most notorious pitch invasions of recent times took place in 1974, when Scottish fans invaded the pitch at Wembley while celebrating their national team's 2–1 victory over England; goalposts were broken and the ground was much damaged before order was restored. It was the first such invasion of the pitch in the stadium's history and led quickly to the erection of fences to prevent fans escaping from the terraces (a measure also taken at many other major venues throughout the UK and indeed the rest of the world).

At their worst, pitch invasions have developed into full-scale riots. In 1974 a game between the Kenyan club Abaluhya and the Ethiopian side Asmara came to a premature end when the police opened fire on the crowd, leading to two deaths, while in 1964 a meeting between Peru and Argentina ended with a riot and 301 deaths. This latter incident was sparked off when referee Eduardo Angel Pazos disallowed a Peruvian goal two minutes from time. He admitted later: 'Maybe it was a goal. Anyone can make a mistake.'

1974 saw another controversial incident involving a pitch invasion, during the course of a crucial FA Cup tie between Newcastle United and Nottingham Forest. Forest threatened an upset when they took command of the game, leading 3–1, but then United fans came on to the pitch and assaulted Forest players. Play was halted as the violence escalated, with 23 people having to be taken to hospital and another 103 treated at the ground. When the match resumed, Newcastle assumed control and the final score was 4–3 in their favour.

A subsequent FA inquiry cancelled the

match result and the game had to be replayed on neutral territory (Newcastle won and went on to finish runners-up in the competition). The arguments rumbled on for some time, however, with critics pointing out that the invasion by Newcastle fans had effectively robbed Forest of their victory, providing an incentive for fans of other teams to launch similar invasions for the benefit of their teams. Years later Forest manager Brian CLOUGH was involved in an incident on the pitch when he manhandled fans who had mounted another invasion.

Pitch invaders come in all shapes and sizes – and, indeed, ages. In the 1980–81 season Ledbury Town supporter Sam Phillips was banned from his club's home matches after he assaulted the referee and tore his shirt; his age was variously estimated at between 77 and 82. Pitch invasions do not, however, always go as the offending fans intend: in the 1930s a pitch invasion launched by a sole supporter during a game between Southport and Blackpool ended ignominiously with the fan being tipped back over the railings by players and the only policeman on duty that day.

In the 1990s pitch invasions are more likely to reflect fans' deep-seated unrest at their treatment by the footballing authorities.

Pitmen Nickname of the English non-League football team HEDNESFORD TOWN, in reference to the area's traditional mining industries.

Pittodrie The home ground of the Scottish football club ABERDEEN. Translated from the Gaelic as Hill of Dung, Pittodrie (previously used as a dung heap for police horses) became home to Aberdeen in 1899 and within months was ready to host its first international (between Scotland and Wales). Opened for League football in 1903, the ground was substantially improved from the 1920s. Events in Pittodrie's history have included the installation in the early 1920s of the first dug-outs, use as an air-raid post in World War II, an explosion and fire in 1971 which damaged the Main Stand and threatened the welfare of the Scottish Cup on display at the club at the time, and conversion as UK's first all-seater stadium in 1978.

Plainmoor The home ground of the English football club TORQUAY UNITED. The club settled at Plainmoor in 1910 and gradually added various stands and other facilities over the years. A fire in 1985, just six days after the inferno at Valley Parade, caused some damage and hastened changes in the interests of safety. Hooliganism by visiting Wolverhampton Wanderers fans in 1987 led to the venue becoming a members-only ground. Under the terms under which the site was first developed Plainmoor has to remain open to the general public for recreation at all times, meaning that in theory at least anyone could insist upon being allowed to walk across the pitch, even during a game.

Planicka, Frantisek (1904–) Czech goalkeeper, who was renowned for his fast reflexes. Winner of more than 70 caps, he manned his country's goal in the World Cup campaigns of 1934 and 1938. His brilliant performance as captain in 1938 did much to ensure Czechoslovakia's passage to the Final (which they lost 2–1 to Italy). In 1938 he stayed on the pitch throughout the quarter-final match against Brazil despite breaking an arm three minutes before the end of the game (his last international).

plastic pitch An artificial playing surface, which has the advantage of remaining playable in weather that would mean postponements of matches scheduled for conventional grass pitches. Plastic pitches come in a variety of types and have their own distinct characteristics, with high-bouncing balls and sometimes blinding colours.

The idea of using artificial surfaces for football is not new and such a scheme was put forward as early as 1906 at Olympia in London (against the opposition of the FA), but in the event ended in complete failure. Indoor football on artificial surfaces was also played on an occasional basis before World War I, though no one saw such games as a threat to the traditional outdoor game. The technology to create reliable plastic pitches was, however, in place by the 1960s and the first such surface (tradenamed Astroturf) was laid at the Houston Astrodome in Texas, where the natural grass surface had withered and died due to lack of sunlight getting through the stadium's painted glass skylights. Within a few years 27 outdoor venues in the USA were equipped with artificial pitches and being used for a number of sports, including football. In 1976 a plastic pitch was used for the first time in World Cup football, for a match between the USA and Canada in Vancouver.

Traditionalists in the UK deplored the idea of replacing real turf with artificial surfaces when it was first put forward as a serious suggestion for British football grounds in the 1970s (in imitation of the US models), but nonetheless the first such pitch (tradenamed Omniturf) was eventually laid down in time for the 1981–82 season at Queen's Park Rangers' Loftus Road ground.

For a short time visionaries prophesied the end of the traditional grass pitch and QPR manager Terry VENABLES became co-author of a novel entitled *They Used to Play on Grass* (1971). Practical difficulties and emotional attachment to grass surfaces, however, meant that the plastic pitches (which were in any case expensive to install) failed to win wide approval. The artificial pitch at Loftus Road was finally taken up at the end of the 1987–88 season and grass was restored. Plastic pitches were outlawed under new Premier League guidelines. Oldham and Luton soon reverted to grass, leaving Preston's Deepdale as the only ground with an artificial pitch. In Scotland a plastic pitch was also installed at Stirling Albion's ground.

It'll never replace plastic.

Ray Harford, Luton manager, inspecting the grass at Coventry (1988)

Platini, Michel (1955–) French midfielder, who emerged in the 1970s as the most talented French player of his generation. Platini, the son of a football coach, made his debut for Nancy in 1972 and established his reputation immediately with 98 League goals in 175 appearances. He won the first of 72 caps in 1976 and in 1978 played a key role in Nancy's Cup triumph. St Etienne acquired his services in 1979 and two years later the team won the League Championship largely through his efforts. A year later Platini transferred to the Italian club Juventus and in 1983 he was top scorer in the Italian League, with 16 goals, and European Footballer of the Year. 1984 saw Platini win medals in the European Cup Winners' Cup and the Italian League championship and once more voted European Footballer of the Year. He also captained France to victory in the European Championship, scoring no fewer than eight goals in the process. The European Footballer of the Year award was his for the third time in a row in 1985, when he also collected a European Cup winners' medal.

Platini retired as a player in 1987 and was appointed manager of the French national team, with whom he had starred in three World Cup Finals series. He resigned in 1992 after a disappointing string of international results.

player-manager A player who also undertakes the management of a side. Player-managers are common enough in non-League teams, but relatively scarce in the upper echelons. The first man to fulfil both roles for a First Division side was Andy Cunningham, who managed Newcastle United in the 1929–30 season. The first player-manager in First Division football after World War II was not seen until the 1968–69 season, in fact, when Les Allen took both roles for Queen's Park Rangers.

Kenny DALGLISH established himself as the most successful of all player-managers in 1986, when he led Liverpool to victory in both the League championship and the FA Cup. Other notable player-managers of recent years have included Rangers' Graeme SOUNESS, Manchester City's Peter Reid, and Swindon and Chelsea's Glenn HODDLE . . . Apart from Dalglish, another seven men have played in and managed League championship teams: Ted Drake, Bill NICHOLSON, Alf RAMSEY, Joe MERCER, Dave MACKAY, Bob PAISLEY, and Howard KENDALL.

Player of the Year Annual award given by the Professional Footballers' Association to the outstanding player (often referred to as the 'players' player') of the season. The first such award was given in 1973, when it was won by Norman Hunter. *See also* FOOTBALLER OF THE YEAR.

Players' Strike The threat of a players' strike has hung over the game on a number of occasions in football's history. One of the earliest instances was in the first decade of the 20th century, when the football establishment was having to come to terms with players' trade unions for the first time. The Players' Union was a focus (albeit a weak one) for demands for change concerning players' rights, and relations between the union and the administrators were often fraught. Clubs even went to the extent of assembling lists of players not supporting the union with the idea that if need be they would call on their services to ensure the 1909–10 season went ahead if a strike was called over the issue of the union joining the General Federation of Trade Unions, and thereby assuming the right to strike. A compromise was eventually reached and the strike was averted.

Years later, the threat of a players' strike proved a catalyst for reform when it was threatened as part of the pressure exerted to end the old retain-and-transfer system and the maximum wage in the early 1960s.

More recently the idea of a players' strike was seriously considered once again when it seemed players would lose out during the somewhat traumatic discussions that led to the formation of the Premier League in 1992. Gordon Taylor, secretary of the PFA, warned that a players' strike was inevitable if the livelihood of any of the union's members was threatened but worked tirelessly – and eventually successfully – to reach an agreement without the need for such disruptive action.

Players' Union Professional footballers' trade union that was founded in 1899 to defend the rights of players. The union had a difficult beginning and was largely ignored by the FA, the League, and the clubs themselves. Its fortunes improved somewhat after 1907, when the outspoken Manchester United captain Charlie Roberts took over, and in 1908 the FA recognized the organization – though rapidly fell out with it again when the union said it was considering calling a players' strike. Roberts' own international career (he won three caps) may also have been prejudiced by his unflagging championship of the union. The union had some success in improving salaries but it was not until the 1960s that players won greater control over their contracts and transfers. *See also* PLAYERS' STRIKE.

play-off One of a series of matches staged at the end of a season to decide such issues as promotion and relegation or even Championship titles. Play-offs are not a new idea, as similar Test matches were used back in the early history of the Football League, involving the bottom three teams in the First Division and the top three in the Second Division. Play-offs were re-introduced in the League in 1986 as a measure to create a First Division of 20 clubs and to readjust the balance between the other divisions but proved fairly successful and have been employed regularly ever since in various formats, with play-off Finals being staged at Wembley itself. Play-offs were also an accepted feature of the NASL, with a mini-season in which the leading teams all played one another for the game's top honours.

Plough Lane Former home ground of the English football club WIMBLEDON. The club settled at Plough Lane in 1912 and, as an amateur side, had no need to develop the

ground in a major way until the 1950s, when the management began to plan for a more ambitious future. The club acquired League status in 1977 and the ground's facilities continued to be improved, with the addition of various lounges, bars, and a gym. The home team's meteoric rise to the First Division prompted speculation that the side would move to a new base, but they opted temporarily for entering a ground-sharing agreement with Crystal Palace at Selhurst Park in 1992.

Plymouth Argyle English football club, nicknamed the Pilgrims. Strip: green and white striped shirts, black shorts, and white socks with green trim (they are the only English League side to play in a mainly green home strip).

The club were founded in 1886 as an offshoot of the Argyle Athletic Club and through the support of local servicemen football quickly replaced rugby as a popular pastime in the city. Plymouth were founder members of the Third Division in 1920 and have since spent their entire history in the Second and Third Divisions (Plymouth remains, after Hull, the largest English city never to have had a First Division side). Based at HOME PARK since their formation, the club won the Third Division (South) title in 1930 (after a wearying run of eight seasons in which they only narrowly missed promotion) and 1952 and added another Third Division championship in 1959.

The team regularly face long journeys to play their opposition, being situated in a remote corner away from the football heartlands. The club reached the semi-finals of the FA Cup in 1984 and of the League Cup in 1965 and 1974. Stars of the side over the years have included Sammy Black and Moses Russell in the 1920s, Johnny Williams and Wilf Carter in the 1950s, and Tony Book and Paul Mariner in the 1970s. Plymouth enjoyed their record victory in 1932, when they beat Millwall 8–1; they suffered their worst defeat in 1960, losing 9–0 to Stoke City. Kevin Hodges holds the record for League appearances with the club, having played in 580 games between 1978 and 1992. Exeter City are the team's arch-rivals.

> Oooh ah, ooh ah ah, ooh to be a
>   Southerner,
> Who's that man in the big fat nose?
> The more he eats the more he grows,
> If he eats much more he will explode,
> Plymouth, Plymouth, Plymouth!
>
> 'The Oggie Song' (1980s)

points The position of teams within a League is decided by the number of points won up to that time. For many years (from 1888) a victory was rewarded by two points – a system subsequently adopted throughout the world – but since 1981 three points have been given to prolong the excitement over promotion and relegation struggles. Since 1888 one point has also been awarded for a draw. A single point can decide a championship: the 1927–28 season ended with just 16 points separating the League champions Everton and the tail-enders Middlesbrough and the bottom nine clubs finishing the season just two points apart.

Pol, Ernest (1932–) Polish forward, who emerged as Poland's first great postwar star. He established his reputation playing for the army club Legia but subsequently transferred to Górnik Zabrze and played a key role in making them one of the most formidable European teams of the early 1960s. Scorer of 186 League goals, he also notched up a record 40 goals for the Polish national team between 1955 and 1965 (including the five goals he scored in a single game against Tunisia in 1960).

Poland The Polish national team first qualified for the World Cup Finals in 1938, when (inspired by striker Ernest Willimowski) they distinguished themselves in a close match against Brazil before going out with a scoreline of 6–5. They then had to wait until the 1970s before once more asserting their place among the best teams in the world, capturing the Olympic football title in 1972 and reaching the World Cup Finals in 1974, when they won third place (having put England out of the competition in the qualifiers). The team also made good progress in the World Cups of 1978 and 1982 (when they reached the semi-finals and again finished third) but made a disappointing showing in the 1986 tournament. Famous names connected with the team in the 1970s and 1980s included Kazimierz Deynar, Robert Gadocha, and Zbigniew Boniek. Strip: white shirts, red shorts, and white and red socks.

Policemen Nickname of the Russian football club DYNAMO MOSCOW, reflecting the side's links with the security forces.

Poljud Stadium The home ground, in Split, of the Croatian football club HAJDUK SPLIT. This spectacular stadium on the Dalmatian coast was opened in 1979 by President Tito and was much acclaimed for its two vast innovatory transparent roofs, which protected fans from the elements while still letting light through.

Pomegranates Nickname of the Italian football club TORINO, in reference to the club colours.

POMO Position Of Maximum Opportunity. The area (usually around the far goalpost) where the chances of getting a successful shot at goal are the greatest.

Pompey Nickname of the English football club PORTSMOUTH, after the name of The Pompey public house that stands immediately outside the main entrance to the club's ground in Frogmore Road.

Pompey Chimes The unique chant that is associated with the English football club Portsmouth. The Pompey Chimes are delivered to the 'tune' of a chiming clock – thus:

Play up Pompey, Pompey play up.

Fans repeat the chant over and over again when things are going well. It has been suggested that Portsmouth's link with chiming clocks may have something to do with the clock in the city's shipyards, or else have come about through confusion with the local name for Portsmouth's beaches – called the Portsmouth Chines.

Pool (1) Nickname of the English football club HARTLEPOOL UNITED.
(2) Alternative nickname for LIVERPOOL.

Poole Town English non-League football club, nicknamed the Dolphins. Strip: all blue. Founded in 1880 and based at the Poole Stadium, the Dolphins play in the Southern League.

pools The British system of gambling on the results of football matches, which has long been a national pastime with millions of fans being lured by the prospect of winning large sums of money by predicting an afternoon's finishing scorelines. The famous Littlewoods Pools organization was set up in 1923 by Bill Hughes, John Moores, and Colin Askham (who was born Colin Henry Littlewood but had changed his surname to that of the aunt who brought him up after the death of his parents). Moores bought out his partners within a few years and his business rapidly expanded until by the 1950s his company and such other leading pools promoters as Vernons Pools (founded in 1929) employed over 100,000 people and ranked among the country's top ten industries. In 1949 the scope of the pools was widened to include the results of Australian matches.

Though now an accepted feature of the game in the UK (and the source of much-needed revenue) the pools were a distinctly controversial innovation when they were first introduced:

> *Much as I admire and love the game, I would sooner football died out altogether than it should become the tool of the gambling fraternity.*
>
> Dean of Durham, letter to *The Times*

Relations between the pools organizations and the football administration have also gone through periods of crisis – in 1936, for instance, the Football League tried to disrupt the distribution of pools coupons by refusing to give advance details of fixtures until a mere day or so before matches took place. This subterfuge came unstuck after just three weeks, however, when the pools companies still managed to get their coupons out in time (the clubs and fans also made it clear that they could not cope with not knowing who was playing who till the last minute). Things improved somewhat after 1959, when the League established copyright over their fixtures and as a result won a substantial share in pools profits.

Cyril Grimes, a wages clerk, was the first gambler on the pools to collect a £500,000 payout when he won £512,683 on a 30 pence stake in 1972. Just 15 years later winners were receiving record amounts of well over £1 million. Other winners have included a former player, George Barlow of Huddersfield and Bolton Wanderers, who collected £150,000 in 1961.

Perhaps the most problematic season for the pools organizers was that of 1962–63, when the UK was in the grip of one of the worst winters of the century and most fixtures were postponed (some many times). In desperation, the pools companies appointed a panel of five experts (Lord Brabazon of Tara, Ted Drake, Tom FINNEY, Tommy LAWTON, and George YOUNG, whose job it was to decide the results of the imaginary games – thus allowing business to continue as usual).

At least one local newspaper, the *Forfar Dispatch*, was inspired by the innovation to write full reports of the fictitious matches, complete with details of the goals, the off-the-ball clashes, and even such minor incidents as the referee having to stop play while he attempted to defrost the pea in his whistle. Legend has it that one wily player, hearing his team had been 'awarded' an away win, applied to his manager for his usual win bonus; the manager was not to be fooled, however, and curtly informed the player that he must have forgotten that he had been dropped for that game. The pools panel has since sat many times to decide the results of postponed games for the purposes of the pools. *See also* BRIBE SCANDALS; SPEND, SPEND, SPEND!

> *During the between-war years the football pools did more than any one thing to make life bearable for the unemployed.*
>
> George Orwell

Pop Nickname of the English striker Bryan ROBSON.

pop songs Since the 1960s many pop songs have found their way on to the terraces, while some popular anthems have similarly been transported into the studios where they have been used as the basis of chart hits.

The link between the worlds of pop and football is not new: fans were purloining tunes from the music halls as early as the late 19th century. The arrival of commercial radio in the 1960s, together with the popularity of such television programmes as 'Top of the Pops' undoubtedly accelerated the exchange, however. Examples of hit songs that have been enthusiastically taken up by supporters include such classics as John Denver's 'Annie's Song' (Sheffield United), Bob Dylan's 'Blue Moon' (universally heard), Eric Idle's 'Bright Side of Life' (again, widely heard), Glen Miller's 'Chatanooga Choo Choo' (Crewe Alexandra), Phil Spector's 'Da do ron ron' (Bradford City), Tom Jones's 'Delilah' (Stoke City), Jeff Beck's 'Hi ho Silver Lining' (both Sheffield clubs), Right Said Fred's 'I'm Too Sexy' (Manchester City), Dolly Parton's 'Jolene' (Meadowbank Thistle), The Scaffold's 'Lily the Pink' (Manchester United and Halifax Town), Manfred Mann's 'Mighty Quinn' (heard at many grounds), Paul McCartney's 'Mull of Kintyre' (Charlton Athletic), Frank Sinatra's 'My Way' (Heart of Midlothian), Rod Stewart's 'Sailing' (Millwall and Maidstone United), the Beatles' 'Twist and Shout' (Coventry City), and the Righteous Brothers' 'You've Lost that Lovin' Feelin'' (widely heard).

Of the football songs that have been

adapted for the charts the most successful have been England's 'Back Home' (number one in 1970) and 'This Time' (number two in 1982), Liverpool's 'Anfield Rap' (a hit in 1988), Chelsea's 'Blue is the Colour' (number five in 1972), Scotland's 'We Have A Dream' (a hit in 1982), Tottenham Hotspur's 'Ossie's Dream' (a hit in 1981), Manchester United's 'We All Follow Man United' (number ten in 1985), and Leeds United's 'Leeds United' (number ten in 1972). Other musical efforts include 'Diamond Lights' by Glenn Hoddle and Chris Waddle, which reached number 12 in 1987, and New Order and England's number one, 'World in Motion'.

Not every football song has been a hit, however: a song specially written in advance to celebrate Brazil's expected victory in the 1950 World Cup failed to prosper after the Brazilians went out of the competition with a 2–1 defeat against Uruguay. England's official song in the victorious 1966 campaign, 'The World Cup Willie Song', is also rarely revived.

Crewe Alexandra are unique among professional British and Irish football clubs in never having issued a club record.

Football is the opera of the people.

Stafford Heginbotham, chairman of Bradford City (1985)

Poppies Nickname of the English non-League football club KETTERING TOWN, in reference to the team colours.

Popplewell Inquiry The official inquiry into the Bradford fire and a football riot that occurred in Birmingham on the same day. Headed by Mr Justice Oliver Popplewell, the inquiry was set up two days after the disaster in 1985 and provided a focus for the arguments that raged over the issue of safety at the UK's ageing football stadia. When the Heysel Stadium disaster followed, Mr Justice Popplewell included reactions to that in his findings and the inquiry was extended to cover football violence.

The report released in July 1985 made many recommendations, including better evacuation procedures, more regular inspections of venues, smoking bans in wooden stands, and removal of inflammable materials as well as a national membership scheme. Some measures became law; others, such as the controversial membership scheme were eventually discarded after much agonising.

One of the most telling statistics publicized by the inquiry was that fact that there had been no fewer than 86 fires at UK grounds between 1977 and 1983, indicating that a major overhaul of ground safety was seriously overdue.

Port Glasgow Athletic Former Scottish League football club, which was a member of the League from 1893 to 1911. The club was based at Clune Park, near Clune Brae.

Port Vale English football club, nicknamed the Valiants. Strip: white shirts with black trim, black shorts, and white socks with black trim. Port Vale were founded in 1876 and from 1884 to 1911 were known as Burslem Port Vale after they moved to that part of Stoke-on-Trent. (Port Vale was in fact the name of the house where the founders met to inaugurate the team).

Early campaigns resulted in the club featuring in the fifth round of the FA Cup, without the team having to play a single match after various opponents dropped out (Vale themselves scratched from the competition after the fixture went to a replay). The club were founder members of the Second Division in 1892 but failed to win re-election in 1896 and remained out of the League until 1898. Subsequently they resigned from the League in 1907 because of financial difficulties and did not return until 1919, when they replaced disbanded Leeds City. They have divided their time since then between all three of the lower divisions, their best period being in the early 1930s when they were among the strongest Second Division sides (they won the Third Division (North) title in 1930).

Based at VALE PARK since 1950, they made their best showing in the FA Cup in 1954, when they reached the semi-finals (though at the time a Third Division club). Their defeat at the hands of West Bromwich Albion was particularly galling as the deciding goal was scored by Albion's Ronnie Allen, a former Vale player. That same season they established a record run of 30 League matches without conceding a goal and clinched their second Third Division title (by a record margin of 11 points).

Winners of a Fourth Divisionship championship in 1959, the team continued to prosper in the 1960s, when the side were remarkable for their many young players: for a match in 1966 the average age of the team was just 18. Manager of the team for a period in the 1960s was no less a figure than Stanley MATTHEWS.

The club were actually expelled from the League in 1968 over an illegal payments scandal, but were soon re-elected. They were restored to the Second Division in 1989 after an absence of 32 years, to be relegated to the new Second Division in 1992.

Port Vale enjoyed their record victory in 1932, when they beat Chesterfield 9–1; they suffered record defeats of 10–0 against Sheffield United in 1892 (when they were hampered by snow and their goalkeeper losing his glasses) and against Notts County in 1895. Defender Roy Sproson holds the record for League appearances with the team, having played in 761 games between 1950 and 1972.

> Just about the only point worth remembering about Port Vale's match with Hereford on Monday evening was the fact that the attendance figure, 2744, is a perfect cube, 14 by 14 by 14.

> Evening Sentinel, letter (1979)

Portman Road The home ground of the English football club IPSWICH TOWN. Portman Road had been used for football and other sporting events for some years before it was acquired by Ipswich Town in 1888. It was developed relatively slowly and there were various setbacks, which included damage in severe gales and the wrecking of the pitch when the ground was requisitioned by the Army in World War I. The stands housed the groundsman's sheep, goat, and chickens and in 1926 a game came to a premature end after rats were discovered in the Main Stand.

Portman Road became a League venue in 1938 and prospered after World War II, when it was also used for American football and rugby. The ground was transformed in the 1960s and 1970s to emerge as one of the best-appointed in the country with what has long been claimed to be the best pitch in the whole League. It was also one of the first English grounds to be converted to an all-seater stadium.

Porto Portuguese football club, nicknamed the Dragons. Strip: blue and white shirts, blue shorts, and white socks. Founded in 1906 and based at the DAS ANTAS stadium, Porto are one of the three big clubs in Portugal and have captured the League championship on 13 occasions. They have also enjoyed ten Cup victories and in 1987 won a remarkable triple of the European Cup, the Super Cup, and the World Club championship (they also reached the European Cup Winners' Cup Final in 1984, but lost to Juventus). Much of the credit for the team's success in recent years belongs to coach Artur Jorge.

Portsmouth English football club, nicknamed Pompey. Strip: blue shirts, white shorts, and red socks. Portsmouth were founded in 1898 by the local solicitor A.J.E. Pink and some business colleagues, who also bought the land that became the site of the club's ground, FRATTON PARK.

The club was a founder member of the Third Division in 1920 and by 1927 – inspired by the attacking power of striker Billy Haines – had risen to the First Division where it remained for the next 32 years (1927–59). This period witnessed Pompey's finest era to date, with the team joining the select few to have won the League championship in successive years (1949 and 1950) and also clinching a surprise victory over Wolverhampton Wanderers in the FA Cup in 1939 (they had previously been runners-up in 1929 and 1934). Success in the 1939 FA Cup was attributed by many to the 'lucky' white spats worn by manager Jack Tinn (*see* SUPERSTITIONS). The advent of World War II meant that the Cup remained in Portsmouth's possession until 1946. Stars of this glorious period in the team's history included half-backs Jimmy Scoular, Reg Flewin, and Jimmy Dickinson, and wingers Peter Harris and Jack Froggatt.

The team's fortunes tailed off rather after the 1950s and the club declined through the divisions (even spending two seasons in the Fourth Division in the late 1970s). They clawed their way back into the First Division in 1987 under the management of Alan BALL, but had a disastrous season and were relegated once more the following year. Past presidents of the club have included Field Marshal Viscount Montgomery of Alamein.

The club enjoyed their record victory in 1927, beating Notts County 9–1; their worst defeat followed in 1928, when the side crashed 10–0 against Leicester City. Jimmy Dickinson holds the record for League appearances with the club, having played in 764 games between 1946 and 1965 (his 19 seasons with the club included seven in which he participated in every League game).

The club's arch-rivals are Southampton (who are commonly labelled 'Scummers' by the Portsmouth faithful). *See also* POMPEY CHIMES.

Portugal The Portuguese national side made its international debut in 1921 but for many years failed to make much impact among the leading European nations. The success of such domestic clubs as Benfica and Sporting in European competition in the 1950s and 1960s inspired the national side, however, and the 1966 World Cup saw Portugal storm through to the semifinals, beating such prestigious opposition as Brazil and Hungary on the way. Succeeding World Cups were disappointing and it was not until 1986 that the Portuguese team once more qualified for the Finals. The only other outstanding campaign came in 1984, when the team did well in the European Championships. Among the most famous players to appear for Portugal over the years have been EUSÉBIO and Mário COLUNA. Strip: red shirts, green shorts, and red socks.

Posh Nickname of the English football club PETERBOROUGH UNITED, which is thought to have been acquired by the team in 1934, when fans admired their smart new strip in a match against Gainsborough Trinity. The word 'posh' itself dates back originally to the days when wealthy passengers travelling by sea to India favoured a cabin on the port side on the way there and a cabin on the starboard side on the way back ('Port Out, Starboard Home') – thus avoiding the worst of the day's heat; the word later became identified with anything exclusive or simply smart.

postponement The delaying of a fixture because of adverse weather conditions or other unavoidable factors making play impossible on the intended day. The Scottish teams Inverness Thistle and Falkirk know all about postponements: their fixture in the 1978–79 season was postponed 29 times in all due to bad weather before they finally met (Falkirk winning 4–0). The severe winter of 1962–63 also has a place in the football record books, leading to 261 postponements in the third round of the FA Cup competition that year, with 16 ties being postponed ten or more times (a fixture between Birmingham City and Bury Town was postponed 14 times and another between Lincoln City and Coventry City was the subject of 15 postponements).

Potters Nickname of the English football club STOKE CITY, reflecting the importance of the pottery industry in the Stoke-on-Trent area – the 'Potteries' – since the 19th century.

Pozzo, Vittorio Italian football manager, nicknamed the Father of Italian Football, who laid the foundations of the modern Italian game while manager of the national team in the 1930s. Pozzo was a fan of the English club Manchester United before World War I and subsequently coached his teams in a similar style with enormous success, Italy winning both the 1934 and 1938 World Cups and an Olympic title under his management. Key features of his tactics were the use of an attacking centre-half and the employment of long passes.

Prater Stadium The popular name of the WIENER STADIUM in Vienna, which serves as Austria's national football stadium. The name refers to Prater Park, in which the stadium is situated.

pre-match entertainment The employment of marching bands and others to keep the crowd amused as they await the start of play. Such displays are an accepted feature of all major matches and are generally of a fairly conventional nature. On occasion, however, clubs have varied the usual diet with somewhat bizarre offerings that must sometimes have been more entertaining than the games themselves. One fan reported having seen on his travels an exhibition of karate skills (in Dublin), a yodelling display (in Czechoslovakia), a man dressed as an orange (before an Arsenal match), a full Highland band in a gale (before one of Chorley's games), and a novelty penalty competition fought out by a bevy of beauty queens (seen before an Everton fixture).

One man who delivered his own unique style of pre-match or half-time entertainment was Joey Goodchild, who was famous for the tapdances he performed on the roof of the main stand of Watford's former Cassio Road ground in the 1920s. His career ended somewhat prematurely when he fell off the roof in mid-performance and landed on a man and woman in the crowd (fortunately without injury to anyone concerned, though the club was obliged to pay £25 compensation for the incident).

Premier League or **Premiership** The controversial new league for top English football clubs that was founded in 1992 by the Football Association. The League came about after years of heated debate and owed its establishment largely to pressure from the leading clubs, who saw the opportunity to improve their financial footing and thus to improve the state of the game at the top level at least. With the intention of reducing the number of teams in the League to 20 from 1995, the new organization offered the chance to relieve over-crowded fixture lists (allowing the national team more time for preparation) and extra money to keep the best British players at home. Clubs in the lower divisions were particularly against the League, fearing that they would be starved of funds by the elite teams, though it was promised that funds would also be directed to less prestigious sides. Winners of the first Premier League championship were Manchester United. *See* BIG FIVE; BIG TEN; SUPER LEAGUE.

Prenton Park The home ground, in Birkenhead, of the English football club TRANMERE ROVERS. The ground was acquired by the club in 1896 and its subsequent development has always been restricted by lack of funds. Events in the ground's history have included the traumatic years of World War II, when Prenton Park was used as a base for producing black smoke clouds as a defence against German bombers and was disfigured by tank traps and bomb damage (after peace returned the tank traps were used to provide foundations for some new banking). A new Main Stand was constructed in the 1960s and in the early 1980s the club applied unsuccessfully to be allowed to install a plastic pitch.

Preston Ladies Pioneering women's football club, nicknamed Dick-Kerr's, that was founded in Preston in 1917 to raise money for a military hospital and subsequently developed as an extraordinary interwar phenomenon, attracting huge crowds in an otherwise male-dominated sport (*see* WOMEN'S FOOTBALL).

The side became the leading female team of the early 1920s, when crowds of up to 53,000 turned out to see them at Goodison Park among other major venues. Most of the proceeds of their matches – about £70,000 in all – went to charity, although the FA still refused to give such teams their blessing and in 1921 prohibited women from playing at League grounds, arguing that they were exploiting the game.

Highlights of the history of Preston Ladies included a tour of the USA (1922), in the course of which they played a dozen male sides and beat an all-male team from New Bedford 5–4, and a match against Bradford Ladies in 1924 that was notable for the successful use of floodlights. They finally disbanded in 1965, having played some 800 games and having represented England, as World Champions, for many years.

Playing in a black and white strip, complete with black and white knitted hats, stars of the side included French goalkeeper Carmen Pomies, centre-forward Florrie Radford, and wing-forwards Jenny Harris and Lily Parr (who was given to performing cartwheels on scoring a goal).

Preston North End English football club, nicknamed the Lilywhites. Strip: white shirts, navy blue shorts, and white socks (the 'PP' on the club badge stands for 'Proud Preston'). The club – sometimes nicknamed simply 'North End' – were founded in 1879 as an offshoot of North End Cricket and Rugby Club (established in 1863) and played football exclusively from 1881. They were founder members of the League in 1888 and immediately established themselves as the best team in the country (*see* OLD INVINCIBLES).

Led by Johnny GOODALL, the side captured the first Championship title without conceding a single defeat and retained it the following year, when they also won the FA Cup. The club also pioneered the use of paid players (*see* PROFESSIONALISM) and continued to dominate English football through the early 1890s. With the passing of the Old Invincibles, Preston – based at DEEPDALE – experienced more mixed fortunes over the next 30 years, dividing their time between the top two divisions (and collecting the Second Division championship in 1904 and 1913); prominent figures in the side over this period included centre-half Joe McCall and the brilliant Alex JAMES (famous for his baggy shorts).

Further success followed in the 1930s, however, with the club returning to the upper echelon of the League and carrying off a second FA Cup title in 1938 (despite the fact that their forward line at the time were all noticeably shorter than those of other teams). They maintained their place in the top rank after World War II with the assistance of the celebrated winger Tom FINNEY (later to become president of the club) and in 1953 missed winning the First Division championship by the narrowest of margins; they were runners-up once more in 1958.

The 1960s signalled a gradual decline in the club's position (despite an appearance in the FA Cup Final in 1964) and in 1970 they were relegated to the Third Division for the first time. (At one point in the mid-1960s the club had no fewer than 16 Scottish-born players on its staff). Subsequently they moved between the two divisions until in 1985 they sank down to the Fourth Division, where they languished for two seasons before battling back to the Third Division in 1987, only to be relegated in 1993.

The Lilywhites' record 26–0 victory

against Hyde in 1887 made football history; they suffered their worst defeat in 1948, when they lost 7–0 to Blackpool. Alan Kelly holds the record for League appearances with the club, having played in 447 games between 1961 and 1975.

Preston Plumber Nickname of the celebrated English winger Tom FINNEY, in reference to the plumbing business that he ran both during and after his playing career ended.

Priestfield The home ground of the English football club GILLINGHAM. Priestfield was acquired as the home of New Brompton (later retitled Gillingham) in 1893 and in the early years hosted a wide range of events, from smoking concerts and athletics to women's football. A number of stands were built before the end of the century and one of these (built by dockyard workers) was still in use in 1985, at which time it was oldest surviving stand at any League ground.

Priest's Marsh Nickname of the FENERBAHÇE STADIUM in Istanbul, which is home to the Turkish football club FENERBAHÇE. Situated beside the now dried-up Frog River, the nickname of the stadium reflects the waterlogged condition of the ground on which it stands (an enduring problem for the groundstaff).

Prince of Dribblers Nickname of the English forward Robert Walpole SEALY-VIDAL.

Prince of Goalkeepers (1) Nickname of the Scottish goalkeeper John Edward DOIG.
(2) Nickname of the Scottish goalkeeper James MCAULAY.

Prince of the Half-Backs Nickname of the English footballer N.C. Bailey. He was the first player ever to occupy the position of right-back with the England team.

Prince of Wingers Nickname of the great Welsh forward Billy MEREDITH.

Professional Footballers' Association The footballers' trade union, which was founded in 1907 to protect players' rights. The PFA came into its own in the early 1960s when, after many years of pressure, it finally won fundamental reform of the rules governing players' contracts and transfers (*see* FREEING THE SLAVES; PLAYERS' STRIKE; RETAIN-AND-TRANSFER). This suc-

cess was largely due to the inspired work of such figures as chairman Jimmy HILL.

The modern PFA advises players on such matters as pensions and other benefits, represents players in negotiating contracts, and also assists with retraining those members whose playing careers are over.

professional foul A deliberate playing offence that is committed for tactical purposes, such as preventing the opposing team from pressing home a strong attack. The professional foul, which is condemned by most critics (and many players and managers) as cynical play that harms the image of the game, came into its own in the 1970s when it became a tactical weapon in the arsenal of such clubs as Leeds United, who won many enemies as a result.

The first player actually to be sent off for such an offence in English League football was Leicester City's Eddie Kelly, who was found guilty of a deliberate handball in a match against Rotherham United in 1982. Three years later, Kevin Moran of Manchester United became the first player to be sent off for a professional foul (or any other offence for that matter) in an FA Cup Final.

Many referees confined themselves to awarding a free kick and a warning in punishment for such play but from 1990, under a ruling from FIFA, offenders who committed such fouls had to be dismissed from the field – though the ruling has proved difficult to apply in practice, with referees having to make their own interpretation of the intent lying behind what may or may not have been a blatantly deliberate foul. Hand ball offences and fouls in the penalty area in particular have led to conflicting opinions about the culpability of the players concerned (*see* HAND OF GOD).

The phrase has been adopted widely outside football, often in reference to dubious business methods. *See* LATE TACKLE; OVER THE TOP.

It was beautifully done. It was wrong, but it was necessary.

Jack Charlton, of a professional foul in a match between Barcelona and Dusseldorf (1979)

professionalism The playing of football by paid players, as opposed to amateur football, in which the participants gather together out of sheer enthusiasm for the game rather than for financial reward. The issue of professionalism was the most hotly debated argument to dominate the early history of the game and at its climax it led to a temporary break between the two camps (*see* AMATEUR SPLIT). Opponents of professionalism feared that the influence of money would lead to a decline in playing ethics and jeopardize the high ideals of many of the game's founders; proponents argued that the game could not develop without it and that in any case many clubs were already secretly paying their star players.

The FA threatened clubs that paid their players with fines and other punishments, but still the practice continued to grow. Northern teams like Blackburn Rovers led the way, paying such stars as Fergie Suter, H. MacIntyre, and J. Douglas, while not openly admitting to paying salaries as such. The argument really burst into life in 1879, when Darwen attracted the Scottish players Fergie Suter and Jimmy Love with promises of financial benefits (although these were indirect, in the form of better jobs and other perks). A veritable tidal wave of Scottish players subsequently travelled southwards to northern English clubs who were only too eager to fund their arrival and swept aside futile attempts by the FA to bar such paid players from taking part in the major competitions.

An FA sub-committee was formed in 1882 to investigate the problem and the FA itself took action in 1883 by expelling Accrington for paying a player. In 1884 Preston North End were accused of paying players and this time, instead of denying the offence, manager Major William Sudell openly admitted the club's guilt, excusing himself on the grounds that if his club did not pay players, then it would inevitably fare less well against the many other clubs also breaking the FA's rules. The amateur stalwarts were outraged, but repressive measures taken to stop all payments (including a ban preventing Preston taking part in the FA Cup competition) only provoked further resistance from northern clubs and in the end it was obvious that the FA would have to concede defeat.

Professionalism was officially sanctioned in England in 1885 at a meeting at Andertons Hotel in Fleet Street:

The first effect of the change will be to make the Rugby game the aristocratic one, and the Association game will probably almost die out in the South of England, where it is already declining in favour.

Manchester Guardian (1884)

Three years later the world's first professional league, England's Football League,

was established. Southern clubs hesitated for some time before accepting the new development themselves but when it became clear towards the end of the century that southern football was being left far behind that played by the professional clubs of the north, they too saw that payment of players was essential if they were to compete with the best sides in the game. Royal Arsenal (braving a ban by the London Association) led the way in 1891 and Millwall and Southampton were the first to follow suit and soon all but the most dedicated amateurs had accepted the development.

Reactions from foreign opponents where professionalism was not permitted was mixed: Scotland protested strenuously when England included their first professional player, James Forrest, in their squad for a match between the two sides in 1885 and Forrest was obliged to wear a different shirt to his team mates to mark him out (he received just £1 for the game). It was inevitable that other countries would follow England's lead, however: Scotland finally sanctioned professionalism in 1893 (by which time many clubs were already secretly paying their players). France permitted professionalism in the 1930s (leading to the import of several leading English professionals).

Earnings have escalated dramatically in recent decades. Paid players of the 1880s took home something in the region of £1 a week, while their successors at the turn of the century could expect £4 a week. The lifting of the maximum wage in 1961 ushered in a new age and Fulham's Johnny HAYNES became the first £100-a-week footballer, to the outrage of many observers – though even then his earnings lagged a long way behind those of players in other countries:

Italian players wonder how on earth players like Haynes live on such a salary! If anyone suggested that the Italians should play a whole season and bank only £5000, plus another £90 or so in bonuses, there would be a nationwide strike.

John Charles (1962)

Since the early 1960s salaries have seemed to rise almost without limit for top players, with the best in the game commanding fees running into six figures or more. *See also* LURE OF THE LIRA.

The biggest difference between playing for Forfar and playing for Glasgow Rangers? Probably about two or three hundred pounds a week.

Stewart Kennedy (1984)

programme Printed details of the players taking part in a game (and other information) that are sold at a match. The oldest surviving football programme is thought to be one from a fixture involving Preston North End and Derby County, the first match of the 1893–94 season. Surviving programmes from before World War II are particularly sought after and can command prices of several hundred pounds if in good condition. Oddities in the history of football programmes include an experiment with shared programmes that was undertaken by Liverpool and Everton in 1915.

promotion The transfer of a team from one division or league to a higher one at the end of a season in which it has performed well. How it should be decided which teams should be promoted and which relegated has varied over the years. Back in the 1890s, for instance, there were experiments with Test matches, which involved the top three teams of the Second Division meeting the bottom three sides of the First Division to sort out the placings for the following season.

These Test matches were a mixed success, however, and in 1898 became the subject of controversy after a notorious game between Stoke City and Burnley, when the two teams (whose places in the First Division depended upon getting at least a draw) secretly agreed that none of their players would attempt a shot at goal. Attacking runs ended in lame passes to the opposition or 'shots' towards the corner flags and the crowd of 4000 howled with disgust. When the ball was kicked into the stands the spectators refused to give it back – when replacement balls followed they kept those too. The farce signalled the end of the Test match system and subsequently promotions and relegations were decided automatically. A three-up, three-down (four, lower in the League) system was introduced in 1973, only to be frequently adjusted since.

Willie Carlin has an almost unrivalled knowledge of what it feels like to win promotion at the end of a season, having been promoted with his club no fewer than four times in the early 1970s (with Notts County, Carlisle, Derby County, and Leicester). *See also* PLAY-OFFS.

PSV Eindhoven Dutch football club, based at the Philips Stadium in Eindhoven. Strip: red shirts, white shorts, and red socks. Founded in 1913, PSV have profited greatly from their close links with the Philips electrical company and are one of the top Dutch teams. They won their first League championship in 1929 and have since won it again in 1935, 1951, 1963, 1975, 1976, 1978, 1986, 1987, 1988, and 1989. They have also won the Dutch Cup six times (1950, 1974, 1976, 1988, 1989, and 1990) and captured the UEFA Cup in 1978; success in the European Cup followed in 1988. Stars with the club in recent years have included twin brothers Rene and Willy Van der Kerkhof, Ruud GULLIT, and Ronald Koeman. England manager Bobby ROBSON was appointed manager of the club in 1990, before moving on to Sporting Lisbon.

Psycho Nickname of the English defender Stuart PEARCE.

public school football Much of the early history of the modern game of football is bound up with the sporting activities of England's leading public schools, where a number of variants of the game were played in the 19th century. The original idea for the FA Cup competition, for instance, was derived by Charles Alcock from a knock-out competition between the Houses of his old school, Harrow (the winner of the tournament was traditionally acclaimed 'Cock House'). Other public schools notable for their football included Eton (home of the ETON WALL GAME), Winchester, and Westminster Hall (where attempts were made as early as 1710 to stop boys playing football matches in the cloisters; the matches sometimes extended over two or three days).

Though many public schools subsequently favoured the rugby code at the expense of the association game, their impact upon the early development of the game cannot be overestimated. Pupils at Westminster and Charterhouse were especially creative, adopting a new style of play that put the emphasis upon dribbling skills rather than violent battles for possession of the ball. The emphasis in the public school version of the game though was still largely on the physical aspects and contests were characterized by various forms of thuggery identified by such names as mauling, piggling, shinning, and tagging (*see also* HACKING).

The variations in rules adopted by different schools made meetings between them problematic (in particular the different attitudes taken towards the issue of handling the ball). Ultimately it was Old Boys from various public schools who were to set about codifying the laws of football while at Cambridge University (in 1863).

Kensington School, Blackheath Proprietary School, and Charterhouse all have a special place in the history of the modern game, having been among the dozen clubs who met in 1863 to discuss the formation of the FA (which only Charterhouse declined to endorse).

> I challenge all the men alive
> To say they e'er were gladder,
> Than boys all striving,
> Who should kick most wind out of the bladder.

Charterhouse school song (1794)

See also GOAL; OLD CARTHUSIANS; OLD ETONIANS.

Puerto Rico The Puerto Rican national team became affiliated to FIFA in 1960 but have yet to make much impact on international football. Strip: red and white shirts, blue shorts, and blue and white socks.

pure football Tactical system in which teams are trained to rely upon 'one-touch' passes and shots and to respond as a unit, falling back together to stifle attacks and moving forward as one when possession of the ball has been gained. This old-fashioned style of play depends on having capable midfielders among other factors; practitioners of the 'purist' game in recent years have included Nottingham Forest, Tottenham Hotspur, and Ipswich Town.

Purfleet English non-League football club. Strip: green shirts, and shorts and yellow socks. Founded in 1985 and based at the Ship Lane ground in Grays, Essex, Purfleet play in the Isthmian League.

push and run A style of tactical play in which attacks are mounted on bursts of speed and short accurate passes. The technique was developed by Tottenham Hotspur's manager Arthur Rowe in the early 1950s and brought the club two Championship titles (1950 and 1951).

> Make it simple, make it quick.

Arthur Rowe

Puskas, Ferenc (1926–) Hungarian forward, nicknamed the Galloping Major, who spearheaded the indomitable Hungarian national team of the 1950s (see MAGNIFICENT MAGYARS). Born in Budapest and sometimes also nicknamed Ocsi (kid brother), Puskas made his debut for Hungary in 1945 while playing with the Budapest team Kispest. In 1948 he was the top goalscorer in the Hungarian League, with a total of 50 goals (he was to be top scorer in the League a further three times later in his career). A year later the Kispest side changed its name to Honvéd and consolidated its links with the Hungarian army. With Puskas leading the attack Honvéd won no fewer than four Hungarian League championships. In 1952 he also won a gold medal with the national side in the Olympic Games and in 1953 he captained the team in a classic meeting with England at Wembley.

It was one of the great matches of the decade, with Puskas confounding the English defence with his ball skills and inspiring a 6–3 Hungarian victory. He went on to captain Hungary in the World Cup in 1954, reaching the Final, but in 1956 left his homeland in the wake of the Revolution (when it was initially reported that he had been killed).

Subsequently he played in Austria and (1958–66) with Real Madrid, becoming a key factor in the club's capture of five Spanish League championships. He also scored four goals in the club's European Cup victory in 1960 and a further hat-trick in the Final of 1962 as well as making four appearances for the Spanish national team and being acknowledged top scorer in the Spanish League four times.

After his retirement as a player in 1966 (by which time he was second only to PELÉ with a total of 83 goals in 84 internationals for Hungary and another 35 goals in 39 matches for Real Madrid) he coached the Greek team Panathinaikos to the Final of the 1971 European Cup.

> His shooting was unbelievable and his left foot was like a hand, he could do anything with it. In the showers he would even juggle with the soap.

Francisco Gento, colleague at Real Madrid (1980)

> Look at that little fat chap there . . . we'll murder this lot.

England player, of Puskas prior to the 1953 match

Pyramid, The The network of minor leagues that feeds into England's Football League. Headed by the Conference, the pyramid is a complex arrangement of leagues and until measures were taken to simplify the requirements for promotion and relegation (including ground facilities) in the 1980s there was endless controversy over which league should feed into which (critics labelled the system 'Pyramuddle'). Since the 1986–87 season the winners of the Conference have been automatically promoted to the League (subject to ground requirements).

Q

Qatar Qatar was affiliated to FIFA in 1970, but the national team has yet to make an impact on international football. Strip: white shirts, maroon shorts, and white socks.

Qemal Stafa Stadium The home ground, in Tirana, of the Albanian football clubs Partizani, 17 Nëntori, and Dinamo, which is the most important venue for football in the country. Opened in 1946, the stadium is named after Albanian writer and Communist Party founder Qemal Stafa, who was killed in Tirana by the Italian invaders in May 1942, when he was just 22.

Quakers Nickname of the English football club DARLINGTON, reflecting the strength of the Quaker religious movement in the area since the 17th century (so-called because their founder George Fox (1624–91) once told a judge that he should 'quake' at the name of the Lord).

Quality Street Kids Nickname of the group of young stars that emerged from the triumphant CELTIC side of the late 1960s under the inspired management of Jock STEIN. They numbered amongst them Lou Macari, Kenny DALGLISH, and David Hay – all of whom were eventually sold to English clubs – as well as the admired full-back Danny MCGRAIN.

Queen of the South Scottish football club, called Queen of the South after the traditional nickname of their hometown Dumfries (though they are known colloquially as the Doonhamers). Strip: royal blue shirts, white shorts, and blue and white socks. Founded in 1919 when the Arrol-Johnson, Dumfries, and K.O.S.B. teams merged, the Doonhamers – based at PALMERSTON PARK – are geographically closer to clubs in England than they are to the other 22 clubs they play in Scotland. They joined the Scottish Third Division in 1923 and subsequently enjoyed a lengthy spell in the First Division from the 1930s to 1950; they captured the Second Division title in 1951 but have since failed to rejoin the top flight. Notable stars with the side have included strikers Hughie GALLACHER in the 1920s and Billy Houliston in the 1940s.

The club enjoyed their record victory in 1932, when they beat Stranraer 11–1; they suffered their worst defeat in 1962, losing 10–2 to Dundee. Allan Ball holds the record for League appearances with the team, having played in 619 games between 1962 and 1983.

Queen's Park Scottish football club, nicknamed the Spiders. Strip: black and white hooped shirts, white shorts, and black and white hooped socks. The Spiders are Scotland's oldest football club and, as occupants of the HAMPDEN PARK ground since 1903, are the unofficial custodians of Scottish football. They were founded in 1867 and have retained their amateur status throughout their illustrious history.

Their great years were in the last two decades of the 19th century, when their domination of the Scottish Cup was all but complete, with victory in 1874, 1875, 1876, 1880, 1881, 1882, 1884, 1886, 1890, and 1893 (as well as runners-up position in the FA Cup in 1884 and 1885). During this period the club enjoyed a run of seven years in which they went unbeaten, including five years in which they did not concede a single goal. In 1872 they also undertook the organization of what was effectively the first international between Scotland and England, Queen's Park selecting the Scottish squad almost solely from among their own players; the result was a goalless draw.

Their only honours since those heady days have been Second Division titles in 1923, 1956, and 1981, although they can claim to have been the first football club to have appeared on television and the first to instal x-ray equipment and to favour a 3 o'clock kick-off.

Star players of the Victorian era included Charles Campbell (winner of a record eight Cup winner's medals) and J.B. Weir.

Queen's Park enjoyed their record victory in 1885, when they beat St Peters 16–0; they suffered their worst defeat in 1930, losing 9–0 to Motherwell. J.B. McAlpine holds the record for League appearances with the club, having played in 473 games.

> *Surely the greatest of clubs . . . what pigmies some of our strictly modern clubs seem, how thin and poor their records, when a comparison is instituted between them and Queen's Park! What a halo of romance and glory surrounds the Queen's Park club! What a wealth of honourable tradition is theirs!*
>
> William McGregor (1906)

Queen's Park of England Proposed name under which a resident team at the Wembley Stadium was intended to enter the Football League in the 1920s. The idea was that the new club would be based on the existing Argonauts amateur side and would fly the flag for the newly opened venue – but the small crowds attracted by existing League teams visiting Wembley eventually persuaded the organizers against pressing ahead.

Queen's Park Rangers English football club, nicknamed Rangers. Strip: blue and white hooped shirts, white shorts, and white socks. Sometimes simply known as the R's, Rangers began life as St Jude's Institute, formed in about 1885 from the amalgamation of St Jude's with Christchurch Rangers. The club adopted their present name in 1887 (most of the players living in the Queen's Park district) and had a number of homes before LOFTUS ROAD, where they settled in 1917 (subsequently having two spells at White City). To date, Rangers have had 18 homes and four changes of team colours.

QPR joined the League as founder members of the Third Division in 1920 and had to wait until 1968 before they finally won promotion to the top flight, since when they have divided their time between the top two divisions and established themselves as one of London's leading sides. Star players who spearheaded the Rangers' assault at the senior level included the flamboyant Rodney MARSH and subsequently midfielder Gerry Francis (later manager), goalkeeper Phil Parkes, defender Frank McLintock, striker Stan Bowles, Paul Parker, and Ray Wilkins. Noted managers of the side in the last two decades have numbered amongst them Dave Sexton and Terry VENABLES.

Honours won by the club include the League Cup (1967) and runners-up positions in the FA Cup (1982) and the First Division (1976). August 1975 was a particularly memorable month in that it saw QPR defeat no fewer than three reigning League champion clubs: Derby County (5–1), Mönchengladbach (4–1), and Benfica (4–2).

Rangers have enjoyed record victories by a margin of seven goals on three occasions, against Tranmere Rovers in 1960 (9–2), against Bristol Rovers in 1937 (8–1), and against Crewe Alexandra in 1983 (8–1). They suffered record defeats of 8–1 against Mansfield Town in 1965 and against Manchester United in 1969. Tony Ingham holds the record for League appearances with the club, having played in 519 matches between 1950 and 1963.

> *Queen's Park is a clever team, there's not the slightest doubt,*
> *But Bristol City fairly knocked them out;*
> *They were determined to win, or at least to have a try,*
> *But now they have to wait till the sweet bye-and-bye.*
> *Never count your chickens till they are hatched.*
>
> 'In Memoriam' card circulated in Bristol after City drew with QPR in the FA Cup; QPR won the replay (1914)

quickest goal The record for the quickest goal in British football is shared by two men, both of whom were credited with scoring just four seconds after the start of play. Albert Quixall of Manchester United achieved the feat during a match against Bayern Munich in 1959, while Jim Fryatt of Bradford Park Avenue equalled it in 1965, four seconds after kick-off against Tranmere Rovers. Quixall scored with a shot from 58 yards, but Fryatt's goal was the end of a dazzling passing sequence involving no fewer than five players.

Records exist of a number of players scoring goals after just three seconds, though at less elevated levels. *See also* OWN GOAL.

R

R's Nickname of the English football club QUEEN'S PARK RANGERS.

Racecourse Ground The home ground of the English football club WREXHAM. The club originally played at a ground called Acton Park, first used for football in 1873 and the scene of the first Welsh Home International (against England in 1877). Wrexham was also the birthplace of the Welsh FA. The Robins settled at the Racecourse Ground in 1905, though it had previously been used as a venue for various sporting events as early as 1850. The ground was considerably developed after Wrexham joined the League in 1921 and again in the 1960s, when new facilities included the so-called 'Pigeon Loft' stand on the Kop; this small stand incorporated a frame and seating taken from the Majestic Cinema in Wrexham and was finally sold on to Wrexham rugby club. The ground was largely rebuilt in the 1970s and the Racecourse Ground once again became a Welsh international venue.

Racing Club Argentine football club, once dubbed 'The Academy', which is based at the Estadio Racing Club in Buenos Aires. Strip: sky blue and white striped shirts, with black shorts and socks. Racing were founded in 1905 by French immigrants who had previously been connected with the Racing Club de Paris. The team became the first Argentine club to win the World Club Championship (1967) and numbers among its other honours 15 League victories and the South American Cup (1967).

Racing Club Warwick English non-League football club, nicknamed Racing in reference to the club's Townsend Meadow ground at Warwick Racecourse. Strip: red shirts, white shorts, and black socks. Founded in 1919, Racing play in the Southern League.

Radcliffe Borough English non-League football club, nicknamed Boro. Strip: all blue. Founded in 1949 and based at Stainton Park, Manchester, Radcliffe Borough play in the Northern Premier League.

radio The first radio broadcast of a football match was heard in 1926, when the FA Cup Final between Bolton Wanderers and Manchester City was relayed to listeners in public halls in the two home towns. The first nationwide broadcast, however, was not until 22 January 1927, when a meeting between Arsenal and Sheffield United at Highbury Stadium was covered by the BBC (*see* BACK TO SQUARE ONE). A week later an FA Cup tie between Corinthians and Newcastle United was the second match to be covered on radio (the Scottish Cup Final was also broadcast to listeners later the same year just days before the English FA Cup Final was also covered).

The Football League, however, decided against allowing such broadcasts of their games, relenting from time to time in the 1930s and during World War II but imposing a complete ban (eventually rescinded) in 1951. The FA too imposed several bans, fearing an adverse effect on attendances.

Radio coverage of football has come a long way since its beginnings, resisting even the competition of television, though styles of commentary differ widely around the world with excitable South American or Italian broadcasters making British presenters seem a model of restraint and decorum.

> *We are the best in the world. We have beaten England. Lord Nelson . . . Lord Beaverbrook . . . Sir Winston Churchill . . . Sir Anthony Eden . . . Clement Attlee . . . Henry Cooper . . . Lady Diana. We have beaten them all. Maggie Thatcher, can you hear me? Maggie Thatcher, your boys took a helluva beating. Norway have beaten England at football!*
>
> Borge Lillelien, Norwegian radio commentator after England defeat (1981)

Rahn, Helmut (1928–) West German striker, who won 40 caps playing for West Germany in the 1950s. His great moment of glory came in the 1954 World Cup Final, when his two goals settled the match in Germany's favour despite the fact that they started out underdogs against Hungary.

Raich Nickname of the English forward Horatio Stratton CARTER, who was one of the most famous English footballers of the 1930s and 1940s.

Raiders Nickname of the English non-League football club SHEPSHED ALBION.

Railwaymen (1) Nickname of the English football club CREWE ALEXANDRA, reflecting Crewe's long history as a railway town.

(2) Nickname of the English non-League football club HORWICH RMI, in reference to the club's links with the railway industry.

(3) Nickname of the German football club LOKOMOTIVE LEIPZIG, reflecting the club's origins among the railway workers of Leipzig, which boasts the largest railway station in Europe.

Rainham Town English non-League football club, nicknamed the Reds. Strip: red and white shirts with red shorts and socks. Founded in 1945 and based at Ship Lane ground, the Reds play in the Isthmian League.

Raith Rovers Scottish football club, nicknamed Rovers. Strip: royal blue shirts, white shorts, and royal blue socks with red and white trim. Raith Rovers were founded in 1883 and took their name from the Laird of Raith and Novar, who leased a ground at Robbie's Park in Kirkcaldy to them. They moved to their present home, STARK'S PARK, in 1891 and finally joined the League in 1902 (as members of the Second Division). They won the Second Division championship in 1908 and again in 1910 (sharing it with Leith), 1938, and 1949 but have not otherwise figured in the major honours, although they were losing finalists in the Scottish Cup in 1913 and in the Scottish League Cup in 1949. Better things were promised, however, in 1993, when the team won promotion to the Premier Division.

The 1937–38 season was distinguished by the fact that the club's total of 142 goals remains the highest ever recorded by any British League club. Raith Rovers are also the only club ever to contrive to draw or lose every single one of their home matches without a win (in 1962–63) and one of the few teams ever to have been shipwrecked: the vessel, the *Highland Loch*, on which they were touring the Canary Islands in

1920 ran aground on a sandbank during a storm and the team had to be rescued by lifeboat.

Star players with the side over the years have included Alex JAMES, who later moved to Arsenal, and Jim BAXTER.

Raith Rovers enjoyed their record victory in 1954, when they beat Coldstream 10–1; they suffered their worst defeat in 1936, losing 11–2 to Morton. Willie McNaught holds the record for League appearances with the club, having played in 430 matches. Off the field, Raith Rovers were the first club to run their own lottery (1958).

Rams Nickname of the English football club DERBY COUNTY, in reference to the county emblem of Derbyshire.

Ramsey, Sir Alf (1920–) English football manager, nicknamed The General, under whom England won the World Cup in 1966. Ramsey began his career as a right-back in 1944 with Southampton and made his first England appearance four years later. Having moved to Tottenham Hotspur in 1949, he contributed to their Second Division championship in 1950 and their League title in 1951.

As a manager, Ramsey took over Ipswich Town in 1955 and saw them safely into the Second Division in 1957 and into the First Division in 1961, completing his work there with the First Division title in 1962. A year later he took over the England team and built up the side that was to win the highest honour of all in 1966. He was knighted in 1967 in recognition of his achievement but failed to retain the title in 1970 and was finally sacked as England manager in 1974 when the team missed qualifying for the World Cup altogether. Subsequently he served briefly as manager of Birmingham City in 1977.

Ramsey's determination to win the World Cup against all the odds and his ability to inspire the England team (all chosen personally) won him many admirers although critics accused him of having too cold and superior an attitude and he never became a great favourite of the public (who also detected a basic lack of self-confidence). His tightlipped responses to questions from the press did nothing to endear him to the nation and during the course of the 1966 campaign he got into further trouble when he remarked somewhat undiplomatically after a rough match against Argentina that England's best play 'will come against a team who come to play football and not act as animals'.

As manager of England he adopted a four-three-three formation to relieve pressure on his wing-forwards and won over the loyalty of his squad, despite the fact that the media continued to attack him for negative thinking and lack of imagination as a tactician. He never had any doubt, however, that he could pull off the greatest victory of all:

> Listen to them moan, but those people will be going mad if we beat West Germany by a goal in the World Cup Final.

Alf Ramsey, after an ill-received 1–0 win against West Germany, February 1966

England's success ensured 'Sir Alf' a permanent place in the history books; among the more unusual of the many tributes he received for his efforts was the naming of a pub in Tunbridge Wells in his honour in 1973 (the great man himself pulled the first pint). See also WINGLESS WONDERS.

> As a manager, Alf Ramsey is like a good chicken farmer. If a hen doesn't lay, a good chicken farmer wrings its neck.

Jackie Milburn

> Ramsey – tha's as much use as a chocolate teapot.

Unidentified fan during Southampton match in the 1940s

Rangers (1) Scottish football club, nick-named the Gers, who with their rivals Celtic form the OLD FIRM. Strip: royal blue shirts with red and white trim, white shorts, and red socks. Rangers were founded in 1873 by a group of rowing enthusiasts from the Garelock district of west Scotland; they played on Flesher's Haugh – an area of parkland in Glasgow – and then at Kinning Park before settling permanently at IBROX STADIUM. The club (whose motto is simply 'Ready') became a symbol of the Presbyterian Unionist community of Scotland in response to the rallying of the Catholic immigrant Irish community around Celtic and the team's turbulent and glorious history has been dominated by dealings between the two leading sides.

Although their record in the Scottish Cup has been patchy, with a total of 26 wins, Rangers have won the Scottish League more times than any other club (43 Championships in all). They have also won the Scottish League Cup 18 times and captured the European Cup Winners' Cup in 1972. This latter victory, over Dynamo Moscow in Barcelona, was somewhat marred by rioting by Rangers fans, which led to the

side being temporarily banned from the competition; manager Willie Waddell had to plead with a UEFA disciplinary committee before he was allowed to keep the Cup.

Stars with the team over the years have been numerous; among the most illustrious names are Alan MORTON, Bob McPhail, and Bill Struth, who was manager of the side between 1920 and 1957, presiding over 18 Championship and ten Scottish Cup wins. George YOUNG remains the most capped club player in Scottish football history, being capped 53 times while with Rangers between 1946 and 1957. Rangers can also boast the largest number of capped players in the UK, with over 100 representing their country as some point in their careers with the club.

Among the many landmarks in their history was the remarkable 1898–99 season, which saw the team win every one of their 18 League matches. More recently the club have maintained their standing after massive investment in new players from England and other countries under the successive managements of Graeme SOUNESS and Walter Smith; at the start of the 1990–91 season, in fact, the club could have fielded an entire team without a single Scot in it, prompting one wag to observe: 'It's brilliant – now we can beat Rangers and England at the same time.'

Contemporary stars include Ally McCoist, who in 1990 became the club's leading goal-scorer since World War II.

The club's record victory stands at 14–2 against Blairgowrie in 1934; they suffered their worst defeat back in 1886, losing 10–2 to Airdrieonians. John Grieg holds the record for League appearances, having played in 496 matches between 1962 and 1978. See also IRON CURTAIN.

> As I was walking down Copland Road,
>   I met a crowd of strangers,
> They said to me 'Where can we see the
>   famous Glasgow Rangers?'
> So I took them off to Ibrox Park, to see a
>   great eleven,
> Said I 'It isn't Paradise, but man, it's my
>   blue heaven'.

Supporters' song, to the tune of 'We're no awa' to bide awa' '

(2) Nickname of the English football club QUEEN'S PARK RANGERS.

Rapid Quarter Hour Traditional hand-clapping routine that is associated with the Austrian football club RAPID VIENNA. The Rapid Quarter Hour consists of Rapid fans keeping up a round of enthusiastic clapping that can last as long as 15 minutes; the device is employed as an encouragement to Rapid players when the team seems to be in a hopeless position.

Rapid Vienna Austrian football club, which has long been – with FK Austria – one of the country's two leading domestic clubs. Strip: all white with green trim. Founded in 1898 and based at the Hanappi Stadium in Vienna, Rapid established their dominance of Austrian football between the wars and can now boast some 29 League titles as well as 13 Cup victories. They were also losing finalists in the European Cup Winners' Cup in 1985. In the golden era of the 1930s the team supplied many of the Austrian national side dubbed the Wunderteam. When Austria was annexed by Nazi Germany, the club demonstrated their strength by capturing the German Cup in 1939 and the German Championship itself in 1941. Stars of the side since the war have included Hans KRANKL in the 1970s.

Råsunda Football ground in Stockholm, nicknamed Solna, which is home to the Swedish football club AIK (the Allmänna Idrottsklubben or General Sports Club). Known by the name of the district in which it lies, the Råsunda Stadium was constructed on a former lake bed in the years before World War I (though the site had been used for football as far back as 1898). The stadium was redesigned in 1937, using Arsenal's Highbury Stadium as its model, and was reopened by King Gustaf V (whose speech began 'I hereby pronounce this tennis stadium open . . .'). The venue rapidly established itself as the most important football ground in the country and in 1958 it hosted the World Cup Final. It has since staged many other international matches as well as rock concerts and boxing.

Rattin, Ubaldo Antonio (1937–   ) Argentinian centre-half, who acquired notoriety as the first man to be sent off during a World Cup Final. Rattin was one of the pillars of the Argentine national side and appeared in the 1962 World Cup Finals and was appointed captain of the side that met England in the quarter-finals of the 1966 tournament. He was ordered off the pitch after arguing with the referee but took 8 minutes to go as the match threatened to turn into a fiasco. On the domestic front, he was a distinguished player with Boca Juniors, making his debut with the team in 1956 and remaining with them until he retired due to injury in 1970.

rattle A wooden handheld device producing a loud clacking sound that many fans once carried to football matches. The rattle, which operated by means of a sprung lath of wood slapping against a notched wheel when the rattle was swung, was once an essential accessory for dedicated fans of all ages, along with the club scarf and rosette. The heyday of the rattle was in the immediate postwar period when thousands of rattles were taken to matches around the UK; by the 1960s, however, they had become a relatively rare sight and by the 1980s could more or less be assigned to football history.

Reading English football club, nicknamed the Royals (*see also* BISCUITMEN). Strip: navy and white hooped shirts, white shorts, and navy blue socks (though several other colour variations have been experimented with in recent times). The club were founded in 1871 and can thus claim to be the oldest League club in the south. They entered the FA Cup for the first time in 1877, in which year they merged with the Reading Hornets (subsequently they were also amalgamated with Earley in 1889).

Having settled at their permanent home at ELM PARK in 1896, they joined the League (as founder members of the Third Division) in 1920 and have spent most of their history since then (including a period of 40 years between 1931 and 1971) in the Third Division, with just two spells (1926–31 and 1986–88) in the Second Division and several trips down into the bottom level in the 1970s and 1980s. Their first visit to the Fourth Division was a double embarrassment, coming as it did in 1971, the club's centenary year. Winners of Third Division titles in 1926 and 1986 and of the Fourth Division championship in 1979, they reached the semi-finals of the FA Cup in 1927 (in which year they overcame such distinguished opponents as Manchester United and Portsmouth). The 1985–86 season was especially notable for the opening run of 13 victories (a record for any League club).

Notable names connected with Reading over the years have included manager Ted Drake in the 1950s and more notoriously Robert MAXWELL, whose ideas for the club's future included possible union with Oxford United (*see* THAMES VALLEY ROYALS).

Noteworthy achievements in the club's history include the period between 1933 and 1936 when the team were not beaten at home in 55 consecutive games.

Reading enjoyed their record victory in 1946, when they beat Crystal Palace 10–2; they suffered their worst defeat in the 1893–94 season, when they lost 18–0 against Preston North End. Martin Hicks holds the record for League appearances with the club, having played in 500 games between 1978 and 1991. Famous fans of the club have included cricket commentator John Arlott.

Real Title (meaning 'royal') of a number of Spanish football clubs, including REAL MADRID, Real Sociedad, and Real Oviedo.

Real Madrid Spanish football club, which dominated European club football in the late 1950s and which remains one of the world's leading clubs. Strip: white shirts with blue trim, with white shorts and socks. The title 'Real' (meaning 'Royal') was formally bestowed by King Alfonso XIII in 1920, in acknowledgement of the side's growing status.

Founded back in 1902, Real won two League championships in the 1930s and seven Spanish Cup titles before 1943, when the arrival of Santiago Bernabeu as president ushered in a new glorious era that was to see the side transformed into what may justifiably be claimed to be the most famous football club in the world.

Bernabeu (whose name is now preserved in that of the BERNABEU stadium) provided the conditions Real needed to realize their vast potential and the club rapidly established a stranglehold on domestic competitions, winning the League 23 times and the Cup nine times between 1946 and 1990. Among the many records they set in the 1950s and 1960s was a remarkable run that saw the team undefeated at home from February 1957 to March 1965 (a total of 114 games).

In international competition Real dominated the early history of the European Cup with a side that included such legendary names as Alfredo DI STEFANO and Ferenc PUSKAS. Other significant names associated with the side's golden era in the late 1950s include the brilliant winger Francisco GENTO, who made 88 appearances for the club and played with them in no fewer than eight major finals.

Incredibly, Real won every single one of the first five European Cup competitions, the most exciting final being their 7–3 victory against Eintracht Frankfurt at Glasgow in 1960. The Glaswegian crowd that witnessed the 1960 Final refused to leave the stadium until the Spanish victors had done a lap of honour and many critics consider that match to have been the finest ever seen in the history of the British game.

Real's right to the nickname Club Kings of the World was officially confirmed in 1961, when they beat the South American champions PEÑAROL in the first World Club Championship, but not even Real could maintain such a record of success once their great stars left and they have failed to win the European Cup again since their sixth victory in 1966 (though they did win the UEFA Cup in 1985 and 1986).

> We never had a blackboard, and hardly ever talked about our opponents, and this attitude helped us to turn games our way. In the days of di Stefano we just came to the stadium, put on our shirts, and played.
>
> Francisco Gento

General Franco himself was a regular visitor to the club in the postwar years. Current members of the club include King Juan Carlos and his wife.

> To be honest I was terribly pleased I wasn't playing. I saw di Stefano and these others, and I thought these people just aren't human. It's not the sort of game I've been taught.
>
> Bobby Charlton, of a Real–Manchester United match (1957)

Rebels (1) Nickname of the English non-League football club SLOUGH TOWN, in reference to their refusal to join a reformed Spartan League after World War II (preferring instead to become founder members of the Corinthian League).

(2) Nickname of the English non-League football club WORTHING.

Recreation Ground (1) The home ground of the English football club ALDERSHOT. Aldershot's ground was unique in that it was the only League ground located within a public park (making it one of the most picturesque of all venues). The club first played at the Recreation Ground in 1927.

(2) The home ground of the English football club CHESTERFIELD. The club arrived here in 1884; it was the last League ground to have floodlights installed (1967).

Recreation Park The home ground of the Scottish football club ALLOA. The club settled at the Recreation Park ground in 1895 and the venue has changed little since the 1920s, when the club first won promotion to the First Division.

Red and Yellows Nickname of the Italian

football club AS ROMA, in reference to the team colours.

Red Army Nickname of the supporters of virtually any football club that plays in a red strip. The name is particularly associated with fans of Liverpool, who adopted the title (recalling the Red Army tag of the former Soviet armed forces) during the celebrated SHANKLY era of the 1960s. Other teams whose supporters have also adopted the nickname include MANCHESTER UNITED, whose fans dubbed themselves 'Fergie's Red Army' after manager Alex Ferguson led them to victory in the inaugural Premier League season in 1993. One of football's least interesting but most widely heard chants consists of endless repetition of 'Red Army! Red Army!'.

red card The small red card carried by English referees for use in punishing playing offences. Under a regulation agreed in 1976, waving the red card signifies that a player is being sent off. The first player to be shown the red card was David Wagstaffe of Blackburn Rovers; the last before use of the red card was suspended in 1981 were Nigel Gray of Orient and Gary Stevens of Cardiff City. Approved of in many quarters, the red card was reintroduced at all levels in 1987. *See also* YELLOW CARD.

Red Devils (1) Nickname of the English football club MANCHESTER UNITED, in reference to the red team strip.
  (2) Nickname of the Italian football club AC MILAN, in reference to the team colours.

Red Imps Alternative nickname of the English football club LINCOLN CITY.

Red Lichties Nickname – anglicized as 'Red Lights' – of the Scottish football club ARBROATH and indeed the nickname of all inhabitants of Arbroath (which is famous for the Bell Rock lighthouse built by Robert Stevenson).

Red Star The name of a number of clubs around the world, particularly in the former Communist countries of the eastern bloc, where the red star was a symbol of communist political ideology. The most famous of all the Red Star sides is Serbia's RED STAR BELGRADE; others include the French club Red Star, which was once one of the leading Parisian teams. Founded in 1897 by Jules Rimet, this French side acquired its name not through its political sympathies but at the suggestion of the English governess with

the family of one of Rimet's colleagues, who liked the name.

Red Star Belgrade Serbian football club that has established itself as the most successful and popular Serbian club. Strip: red and white striped shirts, with red shorts and socks. Founded in 1945 and based at the RED STAR STADIUM in Belgrade, the club can boast nearly 20 League titles and 12 Cup victories. They also appeared as losing finalists in the UEFA Cup in 1979 and in 1991 captured the European Cup after beating Marseille in a penalty shoot-out. Red Star were Manchester United's last opponents before the Munich air crash that destroyed the Busby Babes in 1958. Star strikers with the team over the years have included Bora Kostic in the 1950s and more recently Darko Pancev.

Red Star Stadium Football ground in Belgrade, which is the home of RED STAR BELGRADE. The stadium was substantially renovated after the team arrived in 1945 and became Yugoslavia's main international venue. Highlights in the stadium's history since then have included the staging of the European Cup Final in 1973 and the Final of the European Championship in 1976.

Red-Blues Nickname of the Italian football clubs BOLOGNA and Cagliari, in reference to the team colours.

Redbridge Forest English non-League football club, nicknamed the Stones. Strip: red and blue striped shirts, royal blue shorts, and light blue socks. Founded in 1989 when Walthamstow Avenue (founded in 1900) and Leytonstone-Ilford (founded in 1979) merged, the club are based at the Victoria Road ground in Dagenham and play in the Conference. Their predecessors as the Stones, Leytonstone, had a distinguished record in the Isthmian League, winning the Championship eight times between 1938 and 1966 and on another two occasions as Leytonstone-Ilford (in 1982 and 1989). They also won the FA Amateur Cup in 1947, 1948, and 1968.

Redditch United English non-League football club, nicknamed Reds. Strip: all-red. Founded in 1892 and based at the Valley Stadium in Redditch, the club play in the Southern League.

Redheugh Park The former home ground of GATESHEAD, who were members of the

League from 1919 (when they were titled South Shields Adelaide) to 1960. Redheugh was once one of the major footballing venues in the north-east and witnessed appearances by many famous teams. The loss of League status in 1960, however, spelt doom for the ground and nothing now remains of this once popular venue (the club itself was reformed elsewhere in 1977).

Reds Nickname of a number of football clubs, in reference to their predominantly red strip. They include ACCRINGTON STANLEY, ALFRETON TOWN, BALDOCK TOWN, BARNSLEY, BOLTON WANDERERS (in the days when the team wore red and white quartered shirts), CLIFTONVILLE, CRAWLEY TOWN, CSKA SOFIA, LIVERPOOL, NOTTINGHAM FOREST, PETERSFIELD UNITED, RAINHAM TOWN, REDDITCH UNITED, UXBRIDGE, and WORKINGTON.

re-election The process by which clubs that finished the season at the bottom of the League were allowed to remain in it after winning an election, with votes cast by other League clubs and associate members. Under the rules laid down when the League began in 1888, the bottom four clubs in the League at the end of each season were obliged to seek re-election, though this number was subsequently reduced to three in 1896 and finally to two in 1909. With the creation of two regional Third Divisions in the 1920s the number again grew to four; with the arrival of the Fourth Division in 1958 the bottom four of that division faced re-election. The system was changed, however, in 1986–87 when automatic relegation of the bottom League club was introduced.

Some clubs never had to apply for re-election, while others were plagued with repeated appications. Hartlepool hold the record for having to apply for re-election, with a grand total of 14 applications (followed by Halifax Town and Barrow with 12). Between World War II and the end of the re-election system in the 1980s, New Brighton (1951), Bradford Park Avenue (1970), Barrow (1972), Workington (1977), and Southport (1978) all lost League status after failing to win sufficient votes to avoid relegation.

referee The official who exercises authority over all matters on the pitch while a game is in progress, controlling discipline, ruling on fouls and offsides, etc., and also keeping time. Umpires who combined the duties of linesmen and referees were first used in foot-

ball around 1874, when they were first described in the rules of the game. Whistles were introduced in 1878 and in 1891 the umpires were reorganized into referees and linesmen, each with their own distinct duties.

For much of the early history of the game referees were recruited through their love of the game rather than by the lure of cash rewards and a popular saying had it that all a referee could hope from football was 'a small match fee, expenses, and a decent funeral'.

> *To regulate the game, to earn expenses and a guinea fee!*
> *Yes! There is great attraction in the name of Referee.*
>
> Anonymous (1893)

Payment for referees was standardized in 1938, with referees of League games receiving three guineas (while linesmen got one and a half guineas). This rate of pay contrasts sharply with that of the modern ref, who can command very respectable fees: the Brazilian ref Arnaldo Coelho, for instance, received £500 for refereeing the World Cup Final in 1982, making him the world's highest-paid ref of his day.

Such rewards are often well-earned and the modern official needs to keep very fit if he is to follow the course of play for a full 90 minutes or more. One referee was once kitted out with a pedometer so that it could be seen how far he travelled in the course of a match: the resulting reading was 6 miles 720 yards. In the 1930s, experiments were made with two referees dividing the work between them, each controlling one half of the pitch – trial games did not provide enough work for the two men, however, and the idea did not catch on.

Changes were made in the standing of referees with the inauguration of the Premier League in 1992. The retirement age was raised and it was also decided that referees would play in green shirts, rather than the traditional black in which they had appeared for many decades.

Good referees are usually those whose presence on the pitch is hardly noticed, as Alan HARDAKER once observed: 'Referees should arrive by the back door and leave by the back door.'

Some personalities have, however, inevitably emerged to make their impact on the game in the wider context. The outstanding referee in the early history of the game was Major Francis MARINDIN, who officiated at nine FA Cup Finals in the 1880s and rose to the post of president of the FA itself. The most illustrious of his successors since then have included Jimmy Howcroft, who brooked no nonsense in matches in the interwar period, and Stanley ROUS. Among the best-known refs of modern times have been Denis Howell (who became Labour's Minister for Sport) and the outspoken Clive THOMAS, who has favoured the continued development of the role of the referee and attracted controversy with his support for such future developments as radio link-ups to other officials and access to other high-tech tools.

British refs are traditionally considered the best in the world. Even so, they are (contrary to popular belief) only human and subject to the occasional error of judgement. One referee (Ivan Robinson) experienced the embarrassment of scoring the only goal of a game, between Third Division Plymouth Argyle and Barrow, in 1968. According to the rules of the game the ball remains in play after striking a referee: in this case, the ball was deflected off the referee's foot straight into the Plymouth goal – though the goal was credited to a Barrow striker to save the ref the further embarrassment of seeing his name on the scoresheet, it effectively took Barrow to top of the Third Division.

Cases of referees being deliberately biased in favour of one team are thankfully rare, but not unheard of – even at international level. One of the most notorious cases in recent times was that involving the European Cup Winners' Cup Final between Leeds United and AC Milan in 1973, during which referee Michas made a number of clearly unfair decisions against the English side; he was subsequently suspended by his national association and by UEFA, but the 1–0 result in Milan's favour stood.

Referees have never been popular on the terraces. Abuse and even physical assaults on officials are regrettably all part of the job and most referees endeavour to suffer in silence.

Sometimes, though, the referee fights back. In one oft-repeated joke (probably without foundation) an irate referee is taunted beyond patience by a critic in the crowd and yells at the offender: 'Who's refereeing this match – you or me?' Back comes the instant reply: 'Neither of us!'

Sympathy must go to all referees subject to such pressure, but perhaps most of all to the referee who presided over the 1878 FA Cup Final between Royal Engineers and the Wanderers, who must have been victim of more ribaldry than most of his colleagues

because of his name: Segar Bastard. In contrast, a Scottish referee of the 1950s was blessed, or cursed, with the name Charlie Faultless.

> *Referees have the most difficult job in the world ... we're wrong in expecting referees to be perfect when we're not perfect ourselves.*
>
> Don Revie, *World Soccer Referee* (1976)

Trevor Brooking has the distinction of being one of the few professional players ever to have floored a referee: a sudden change of direction resulting in a collision that left the official prostrate on the ground. Fellow team mate Bobby MOORE picked up the whistle and blew it to stop play: the ref was found to be quite unconscious and had to be helped off the field of play.

The risks attached to the role were never more clearly illustrated than they were back in 1912 following a match between the Welsh clubs Wattstown and Aberaman Athletic: a Wattstown player by the name of Hansford burst into referee William Ernest Williams's dressing-room and killed him in a rage. Hansford was subsequently imprisoned for manslaughter.

> *You British! You think I know damn nothing about the game! Let me tell you – I know damn all!*
>
> Hungarian referee during England–Scotland match

See also BOOKING; RED CARD; YELLOW CARD.

relegation The demotion of a club from a division or league to a lower one. Barring complete extinction, relegation is the worst fate that can befall any club and the spectre of such demotion adds spice to the closing stages of every league season. Relegation from the Football League itself is the most unwelcome prospect of all, bringing with it not only an inevitable loss in prestige but often severe financial hardship (with lost sponsors and reduced gates).

Originally movement between the divisions of the Football League was decided by 'Test matches' (*see* PLAY-OFF) in which the clubs involved in possible promotion or relegation played each other to decide which moved. A new system of promotion and relegation was introduced in 1898–99 and when a Third Division was formed only one team dropped out of each rank. This was the situation until 1957–58, when the Fourth Division was created and a new arrangement was introduced whereby four clubs exchanged places each season between the two lower divisions. From 1974 three teams were promoted or relegated in the top three divisions for the first time.

Virtually every club has experienced the shock of relegation a number of times, although some managed to delay their first relegation for a surprisingly long time: Aston Villa and Blackburn Rovers were strangers to relegation until as late as 1936, a traumatic season that saw both clubs drop into the Second Division for the first time.

Originally relegation from the League only happened if a club failed to gain re-election on a vote of all the other League clubs (a relatively rare event) but this system was eventually replaced in the 1980s by one in which the bottom club in the League was automatically replaced by the top non-League side. The dubious honour of being the first club to be automatically relegated from the League goes to Lincoln City, who were replaced by Scarborough (they regained League status one year later).

Some relegation battles are more exciting than others. Few seasons have been more thrilling than that of 1927–28, when nine teams were still in danger of relegation from the First Division on the very last day of the season (Middlesbrough and Tottenham Hotspur eventually went down). Few clubs know more about relegation than Bristol City, however, who in the 1980s dropped 86 places in the League and became the first team to suffer relegation in three consecutive seasons.

> *After three games this season, I know my club Birmingham City are going to be relegated. Is this a record?*
>
> Sunday People, letter (1977)

Renton Scottish football club, which was a prominent member of the League until 1897. Renton, who were based at Tontine Park from 1891, were one of the most enthusiastic of the 11 founder members of the Scottish League in 1890. Their inaugural season was, however, nothing if not controversial, with the team being suspended by the League after it allegedly played a professional side, St Bernards (Renton defended themselves on the grounds that the team they had played was not the same one – but failed to convince the authorities). They returned to the League the following season, but subsequently dropped out.

replay A repeat match that is arranged when a first meeting has failed to produce a result between two sides (as required in knock-out competitions such as the FA Cup).

Being forced to participate in a replay can result in a radical change in fortunes for both sides. Closely fought draws have turned into one-sided routs on a number of occasions, examples including meetings between Tottenham Hotspur and Worksop Town in 1923 and between Newcastle United and Southport in 1932, in both of which games the first club mentioned romped home with scores of 9–0. On one memorable occasion in 1932, after a match between Port Vale and Charlton Athletic was abandoned due to bad light the replay found one player, Jimmy Oakes, now appearing for the other side as he had since been transferred, making him one of the very few players to play for both sides in the same match.

The first FA Cup Final replay was as early as 1875, when the Royal Engineers finally beat the Old Etonians 2–0. The record number of replays involving League clubs in an FA Cup tie was established in 1955, when Stoke City and Bury had to meet four times before a result was reached (Stoke won 3–2). In non-League football, Mansfield House and Highfield played each other five times in 1970 before they settled their FA Intermediate Cup tie (amounting to very nearly ten hours of football). *See also* ABANDONMENT; ALVECHURCH; POSTPONEMENT.

representative A match in which players represent their country or region, etc., rather than their usual club. The first representative match of all was played back in 1866, when teams representing Sheffield and London met at Battersea Park (London won 2–0). Since then teams have been assembled to represent all manner of entities, from those representing local leagues to others playing under the title 'The Common Market' and the 'Rest of the World'.

Republican Stadium The home ground, in Kiev, of DYNAMO KIEV. The original stadium was built by youth brigades on the site of the last Tsarist Russian exhibition (1913) and dubbed the 'Red' stadium, opening in 1923. It was rebuilt in the 1930s and was due to reopen in front of a massive invited audience in 1941, but on the very day of the ceremony the Nazis invaded. The stadium was wrecked by the retreating Germans in 1943 and finally opened in 1945, by which time many of the original invitees had perished. It was briefly renamed the Khrushchev Stadium in the 1960s but most fans know it as the Central Stadium.

Requiem Cup Final Nickname bestowed upon the FA Cup Final of 1989, which was held in the wake of the Hillsborough disaster. The catastrophe at Hillsborough had happened as Liverpool prepared to meet Nottingham Forest in the semi-finals of that year's competition, but the match was inevitably put off when the scale of the disaster became known. For some days debate about whether the game should be reheld raged in the press but the football establishment quickly agreed that the tournament should continue, if only as a tribute to those who had died. Several of the papers condemned the decision and even the chief executive of Liverpool voiced his opposition to the idea, but the club finally agreed to participate. Some outraged observers continued to protest, saying the Final should at the very least be postponed until the following season and the trophy itself be given permanently to the people of Merseyside.

The remaining matches were highly traumatic and emotional, especially for Liverpool fans, who saw their team vanquish Nottingham Forest at Old Trafford and then go on to meet Everton in what was quickly dubbed the 'Requiem Cup Final'. Fittingly, Liverpool emerged champions with a 3–2 scoreline, but the atmosphere was sombre compared to other years and there was further unrest when hundreds of fans mounted a pitch invasion.

Rest of the World The remarkable team comprising players selected from a number of different countries that was assembled in 1963 to play England to mark the centenary of the FA, the world's oldest football organization. The match (witnessed by royalty and several heads of state among other VIPs) was the highlight of the anniversary celebrations at Wembley and many of the great names of postwar football were present.

The extraordinarily talented Rest of the World squad of 16, chosen by FIFA, consisted of Alfredo DI STEFANO, Hungary's Ferenc PUSKAS, Brazil's Djalma dos SANTOS, the Soviet Union's Lev YASHIN, West Germany's Karl-Heinz SCHNELLINGER and Uwe SEELER, Yugoslavia's Milutin Soskic, Chile's Luis Eyzaguirre, Czechoslovakia's Josef MASOPUST, Svatopluk Pluskal, and Jan Popluhar, France's Raymond KOPA, Spain's Francisco GENTO, Portugal's EUSÉBIO, and Scotland's Jim BAXTER and

Denis LAW, who turned out to be the star of the side, scoring the Rest of the World's only goal in what turned out to be a 2–1 England victory.

The final result owed much to the fact that the Rest of the World squad lacked experience playing together and the side is still remembered as the most individually talented side of players ever seen.

Another distinguished Rest of the World side was assembled in similar circumstances in 1988 to celebrate the centenary of the Football League.

retain-and-transfer The system by which football clubs were able to exercise almost unfettered control over the transfer of players on their payrolls, enabling them to retain a player even against his wishes at the end of his contract.

The system (together with the restraints on what professional footballers could earn from the game) was a source of much resentment over the years. The highly controversial retain-and-transfer practice was finally brought to an end in 1963 as the result of an important High Court case, which was brought by Newcastle United's George Eastham when his club refused him permission to transfer to another side (he had hopes of joining Arsenal). Eastham's clash with Newcastle resulted in him being forced to take a job outside football at the end of the 1960 season and, as no settlement of the dispute seemed imminent, he applied to the courts (with the support of the Professional Footballers' Association). A relatively unassuming character, Eastham himself had by the time the case came to trial already got his transfer to Arsenal, but he allowed the matter to go ahead as a test case. His demeanour at the hearing was typically quiet and reasonable, and the judge (Mr Justice Wilberforce) had to remind him to speak up: 'You are in rather an outside-right position. Would you speak up so that people on the left wing can hear?'

When the evidence had been heard the decision was decisively in Eastham's favour. The judge ruled that the retain-and-transfer system was 'an unreasonable restraint of trade' and since then players have enjoyed much more freedom in controlling their careers. *See* FREEING THE SLAVES.

I regard this as a system from the Middle Ages. It is really like treating men like cattle, and really the position is that they are paid slaves. The transfer fees paid are more than a player can earn during the whole of his playing life. It is rather like transferring shares in a company, or any other inanimate property.

Gerald Gardiner QC, for the plaintiff George Eastham

The worst contract I have ever seen.

Lord Walter Monckton, on Football League player's forms (1947)

Revie, Don (1928–89) English player and manager, nicknamed the Godfather, who made Leeds United the strongest club in England in the early 1970s. As a player Revie appeared for Leicester City, Hull City, Manchester City, Sunderland, and Leeds United during an illustrious career that was crowned with six games as a forward for England and the title Footballer of the Year in 1955. As one of the stars of Manchester City in the 1950s, he helped take the team to two successive FA Cup Finals (in 1955 and 1956), winning a Cup-winners' medal at the second attempt, when the team's success was attributed to the so-called Revie plan.

Revie joined Leeds United as player-manager in 1961 and subsequently put together a side that became one of the strongest in Europe, building around Jack CHARLTON and the dynamic midfield partnership of Billy BREMNER and Johnny GILES. Under Revie's direction, United – in danger of relegation to the Third Division when he took over – captured the League Cup in 1968, the European Fairs Cup in 1968 and 1971, the League championship in 1969 and 1974, and the FA Cup in 1972.

The ultimate promotion came in 1974, when Revie – already made Manager of the Year on three occasions – was appointed manager of England. The selection of Revie was not popular with everyone, however, and Alan HARDAKER for one expected the worst, commenting that the appointment of Revie (who had done little to assist Ramsey in his years as England boss) was 'a classic case of poacher turning gamekeeper'.

Revie threw himself into the task, trying to duplicate the close-knit teamsmanship that had worked the miracle at Leeds. Among other measures, he adopted 'Land of Hope and Glory' as the team's anthem and tried to ensure priority for the national side's fixtures over club dates. Initial success, however, turned into a long run of humiliating defeats and failure to qualify for the 1976 World Cup Finals.

Further controversy followed in 1977 when, instead of accompanying the England team on tour to South America, Revie travelled in secret to Dubai to negotiate a very lucrative deal to take over the Arab Emirates national side. When news of the deal broke and Revie's denials of such negotiations were made public, he was bitterly condemned by the FA and the press for deceitfulness. He gave up the England job and was banned from English football for ten years by the FA, although Revie succeeded in getting the ban overturned a year later. The judge at his appeal called his actions 'a sensational and notorious example of disloyalty, breach of duty, discourtesy and selfishness'. His friends, however, said he was basically a decent man who had been unable to cope with the frustrations of the job.

Loyalty and respect seem old-fashioned words nowadays, but, as far as professional football is concerned, these are still the most important qualities of all in my view.

Don Revie (1975)

Revie plan The tactic of deploying a deep-lying centre-forward that was developed in England by the Manchester City team spearheaded by centre-forward Don REVIE. The tactic was in fact copied from that used with great success by Hungary against England at Wembley in 1953, when their centre-forward was Nandor HIDEGKUTI. City's use of the Revie plan in the 1950s took the club to the FA Cup Final in 1955 and again in 1956, when they beat Birmingham City 3–1.

Rhine Stadium The home ground of the German football club Fortuna Düsseldorf. Opened originally in 1926, the stadium was transformed in the early 1970s into one of Germany's most spectacular football venues and now hosts many international sporting events.

Rhyl Welsh non-League football club, nicknamed the Lilywhites. Strip: all white. Founded in 1928 and based at Belle Vue in Rhyl, the Lilywhites play in the Cymru Alliance.

Riazor The home ground, in La Coruña, of the Spanish football club Deportivo. The current ground was opened in 1945 but was substantially redesigned in the early 1980s, incorporating nautical motifs to reflect the city's maritime history (these include a bronze model of the city's ancient lighthouse, reputed to be the oldest working lighthouse in the world). It was used as one of the World Cup venues in 1982.

ribbons According to time-honoured custom ribbons in the winning team's colours are always attached to the Cup or trophy presented at the climax of certain major football competitions. The tradition dates back to 1901, when members of Tottenham Hotspur festooned the FA Cup with ribbons in the team colours (blue and white) at a celebration dinner after they won the Cup that year (making them the only non-League club to do so since the League was founded).

Rijkaard, Frank (1962–) Dutch sweeper, who established himself as one of the most formidable stars of the Dutch national side in the 1980s. He emerged as a star with Ajax and subsequently transferred to Real Zaragoza and AC Milan, playing a key role in the latter team's European Cup victories in 1989 and 1990. On the international stage, he was outstanding in the 1988 European Championship, but was widely condemned for his behaviour in the 1990 World Cup. In 1993 he returned to Ajax.

Riva, Luigi (1944–) Italian forward, nicknamed The Rumble of Thunder or simply Gigi, who was a leading star with Legnano, Cagliari, and Italy. Despite breaking both his legs in the course of his career, he scored a total of 156 goals in domestic competition and another 35 goals in 42 appearances for the Italian national side.

Rivelino, Roberto (1946–) Brazilian footballer, who was one of the most flamboyant stars of the Brazilian national side in the 1960s and 1970s. Rivelino began his career with the Brazilian club Corinthians and subsequently made his international debut in 1968. Two years later he played a key role in Brazil's famous World Cup victory, scoring three goals and winning fans throughout the world for his buccaneering style. Playing on the left-wing and also as a midfielder, he was greatly respected for his powerful long-range shots at goal, which could beat even the most capable defences. He scored another three goals in the 1974 World Cup but failed to shine in the 1978 tournament and that year moved from Fluminense (whom he had joined in 1975) to the Saudi-Arabian club Al-Ahly. He collected a grand total of 120 international caps in all.

River Plate Argentinian football club, which ranks among the most distinguished anywhere in the world. Strip: white shirts with red diagonal stripe, black shorts, and white socks. Founded in 1901 by English residents, River Plate are based at the Estadio Monumental in Buenos Aires and have some 18 Argentinian League titles to their credit as well as three victories in the National Championship (1975, 1978, and 1981), a single win in the South American Cup (1986), and one World Club Championship title (1986). The club's dominance of Argentinian football in the 1930s was boosted by its wealth, which enabled it to attract the best players to its ranks, and the team of the 1940s was spearheaded by a now legendary combination of forwards, who were nicknamed The Machine. The greatest of all the stars to appear for the club was, however, the incomparable Alfredo DI STEFANO, who made his debut with the side back in 1944.

Rivera, Gianni (1943–) Italian midfielder, nicknamed the Golden Boy, whose spectacularly successful career began while he was still a teenager (he made his First Division debut at the age of just 15 and was immediately snapped up by AC Milan). Subsequently he made over 500 appearances, playing in four World Cup tournaments and winning the European Footballer of the Year award in 1969 as well as winner's medals in two European Cups and two European Cup Winners' Cups and in the World Clubs Cup. He won 60 caps for his country, scoring a total of 14 goals. His influence over the game by the mid-1970s was such that he could afford to buy out one of his great rivals at AC Milan and then to buy the club itself to forestall any attempt to sell him. He enjoyed some success as manager of the club before his reputation was dealt a severe blow in a bribery scandal in the early 1980s.

robbed. We wuz robbed Cliché that has been particularly associated with football for many years. Uttered by indignant players and managers after their team has lost a game they felt they deserved to win, the phrase has its origins in boxing, specifically a famous world heavyweight fight between Gene Tunney and Jack Dempsey in 1927. Dempsey floored his opponent but was slow to retire to a neutral corner, thus delaying the start of the count and allowing Tunney extra time to recover. Tunney got back to his feet and eventually won the fight on points, to the irritation of Dempsey (who would undoubtedly have won but for the delayed count), prompting him to complain: 'I was robbed of the championship'. Five years later his protest was echoed by Max Schmeling's manager Joe Jacobs when

Schmeling lost against Jack Sharkey, Jacobs seizing the microphone to yell 'We wuz robbed!'

The phrase was enthusiastically taken up throughout sport and especially by footballers in need of that succinct telling phrase when natural inspiration falters. Like 'sick as a parrot' and 'over the moon', however, it has long since passed into the realm of ridicule and is now generally heard in parodies of soccer-speak. Courses to encourage players and managers to avoid the use of such hackneyed phrases were once advertised in the *Sun*, which even attempted a somewhat jocular alternative to 'We wuz robbed' for use by the country's sportsmen:

We were humiliated by the vastly superior technical skills of the opposition.

Robins Nickname of a number of football clubs, in reference to the use of red in the team colours. They include ALTRINCHAM, BRACKNELL TOWN, BRISTOL CITY, BUCK-INGHAM TOWN, CARSHALTON ATHLETIC, CHARLTON ATHLETIC, CHELTENHAM TOWN, DUDLEY TOWN, NEWTOWN, SWINDON TOWN, and WREXHAM.

Robson, Bobby (1933–) English manager, who led England in the 1980s. Robson began his career as a player, occupying the wing for Fulham, West Bromwich Albion, and England (winning 20 caps). He retired as a player in 1967 and accepted the post of manager of the Vancouver Royals and then (briefly) of his old club Fulham. In 1969 he was made manager of Ipswich and set about building up a formidable side that eventually triumphed in the FA cup in 1978 and subsequently captured the UEFA Cup (1981) and runners-up position in the League two years running (1981 and 1982).

Nicknamed the King of East Anglia, Robson reached the top of his profession and in 1982 was appointed manager of England, in which post he succeeded Ron Greenwood. Robson had previously been considered for the job in 1977 and had in the meantime added to his experience by guiding the England 'B' team. The successes he had enjoyed with Ipswich were not, however, immediately followed by a run of victories with the national side. A rough start developed into a serious decline and Robson quickly became a scapegoat following humiliating defeat in the 1984 European Championships and subsequent competitions.

The criticisms cut home and made life difficult for the England boss, leading one paper to observe that 'his natural expression is that of a man who fears he might have left the gas on'. Resentful crowds poured scorn over him but Robson stayed in the post and in 1986 the team fared somewhat better on a tour of South America, beating mighty Brazil against all the odds. England's 1986 World Cup campaign, however, ended at the quarter-final stage and once more Robson found himself the target of the press's venom. Worse was to follow in 1988, with England suffering three humiliating defeats in a row in the European Championships.

The 1990 World Cup campaign, by contrast, was a resounding and unexpected personal success, with England heroically battling through to the semi-finals and unlucky not to reach the Final itself. His reputation somewhat restored, Robson finally stepped down and took over the management of the Dutch club PSV Eindhoven, leading them to the Dutch Championship in his first season. He later became manager of Sporting Lisbon.

In England we tend to internalize things. If something upsets us in a restaurant we don't complain; we go home, sprout an ulcer, and blame it all on Bobby Robson.

Helen Lederer, comedienne (1989)

Robson, Bryan English striker (1947–), nicknamed Pop, who was a leading player in the British game in the late 1960s and 1970s. Born in Newcastle-Upon-Tyne, Bryan Robson was a star with Newcastle United, helping them to victory in the European Fairs Cup in 1969, and subsequently with Sunderland (1976–78), Chelsea (1978–79), and Darlington (1981–83). After retiring as a player, he worked as a coach.

Robson, Bryan (1957–) English footballer, nicknamed Captain Marvel, who emerged as one of the most talented midfield players of the 1980s. Having begun his career in 1971 with West Bromwich Albion – with whom he had to undergo a bodybuilding course before ultimately rising to the role of captain – he transferred to Manchester United as captain in 1980 on the invitation of manager Ron ATKINSON, who had been advised by Bill SHANKLY: 'Pay whatever you have to, just make sure you get him.'

The fee of over £1 million made him Britain's most expensive player to date. Over the years that followed he played a major role in the side's victories in three FA

Cup competitions, the League Cup, and the European Cup Winners' Cup.

In 1982 he established a new record when he scored for England against France in their opening game of the World Cup competition after only 27 seconds. Subsequently he formed a profitable partnership with England manager Bobby ROBSON, captaining the national side in both 1986 and 1990.

Throughout his playing career he was troubled, however, by injury, leaving both the 1986 and 1990 World Cup tournaments at an early stage (back in 1976 he broke his leg three times in a single season). By 1991 he had made 600 appearances for Manchester United and had won 89 caps for his country, including 45 as captain, fully justifying the nickname that linked him to the superhero of US comics.

Rocha, Pedro (1942–) Uruguayan inside-forward, who played a key role for Uruguay in four World Cup campaigns (1962, 1966, 1970, and 1974), winning 62 caps. Rocha joined Peñarol in 1959 and participated in the club's victory in no fewer than seven League championships and in the World Club Cup (1966) before transferring to the Brazilian club São Paulo. After his retirement he became a coach in Brazil.

Rochdale English football club, nicknamed The Dale. Strip: royal blue. Rochdale came into existence in 1907 on the demise of Rochdale Town (formed in 1900) and have always had to contend with the area's reputation as a stronghold of rugby. The club joined the Third Division (North) in 1921 and have never escaped the bottom two divisions (although they came close on three occasions in the 1920s). Their one great moment of triumph came in 1962, when they met (and lost to) Norwich City in the Final of the League Cup, becoming the only Fourth Division side to appear in the Final of a major competition. In 1970 they took part in another notable clash when they beat First Division Coventry City 2–1, obliging the Coventry manager Noel Cantwell to regret his pre-match taunt 'Where's Rochdale?'

Their record in the FA Cup is less than glorious: between 1928 and 1946 they failed to progress beyond the first round. The club have been based at Spotland, the old home of Rochdale Town, throughout their history. Supporters include the comedian Tommy Cannon, who was also a director.

The Dale enjoyed their record victory in 1926, when they beat Chesterfield 8–1;

they suffered record defeats in 1929, when Wrexham beat them 8–0, in 1931, when Tranmere Rovers won 9–1 (in a season when Rochdale managed to lose 13 consecutive home games), and in 1987, when Leyton Orient enjoyed an 8–0 victory. Graham Smith holds the record for League appearances with the club, having played in 317 matches between 1966 and 1974.

Rocks Nickname of the English non-League football club BOGNOR REGIS TOWN, reflecting its seaside location.

Roker Park The home ground of the English football club SUNDERLAND. Sunderland had a number of homes before settling at Roker Park and arrived there in 1898 after vacating a pitch in Newcastle Road, which they had first occupied in 1886 and where they had prospered under the nickname Team of All the Talents. The first match at Roker Park was against Liverpool and resulted in a 1–0 victory in the home side's favour (after an official opening ceremony by the Marquis of Londonderry, Sunderland's president). The following year it was the scene for a memorable international between England and Ireland, which ended with a 13–2 English victory.

The ground rapidly acquired a reputation as one of the finest English venues, though it was plagued by hooliganism from the very start (one referee had to be smuggled out of the ground disguised as a policeman to protect him from a mob). Casualties of other violent clashes and pitch invasions in the early years included a stabbed police horse.

The facilities had aged somewhat by the 1920s and major improvements were made, with designs for new stands by Archibald Leitch. World War II brought bomb damage (with a policeman being killed outside the ground), while subsequent events included the arrival of lights in 1952 (making Roker Park the second First Division ground to be thus equipped), the staging of World Cup games in 1966, and radical alterations to meet safety requirements in the 1980s.

Rokermen Nickname of the English football club SUNDERLAND, referring to their home (since 1898) at Roker Park.

AS Roma Italian football club, nicknamed the Red and Yellows (*giallorossi*). Strip: red shirts with yellow trim, with red shorts and socks. Founded in 1927, Roma have two Italian League championships (1942 and 1983) to their credit and six Cup victories (1964, 1969, 1980, 1981, 1984, and 1986) as well as one win in the Fairs Cup (1961). Based at the OLYMPIC STADIUM in Rome, the club reached the final of the European Cup in 1984, but lost to Liverpool on penalties (the match also hit the headlines for clashes between supporters of the two clubs).

Romania The Romanian national team took part in the very first World Cup tournament in 1930, when King Carol himself selected the players and paid their wages (they were knocked out in the first round). The team participated in the tournament in 1934 and 1938 and subsequently in the Finals of 1970 and 1990 but have made only modest progress in the competition, though they qualified for the 1994 World Cup in America. Strip: yellow shirts, blue shorts, and red socks.

Roots Hall The home ground of SOUTHEND UNITED. Southend first played at Roots Hall (named after a house that once stood nearby) in 1906, but subsequently moved to the Kursaal ground (1919–34) and then to the Southend Greyhound Stadium, before finally returning to Roots Hall in the early 1950s.

The pitch (now 50 feet lower than it originally was) was restored from the rubbish tip it had become and the ground was developed by the supporters' club until it was ready to stage the first home game in 1955 (after being opened by the FA chairman Arthur Drewry, with music provided by the club's own band). Incredibly, the concrete terracing of the South Bank, laid down over the course of five years in the late 1950s, was the work of just three dedicated supporters, led by groundsman Sidney Broomfield (who was honoured with a testimonial match in 1974). Plans for the team to leave Roots Hall and relocate in Basildon did not meet with a happy reception with fans in the 1980s.

Rossendale United English non-League football club, nicknamed the STAGS. Strip: blue and white striped shirts, white shorts, and blue socks. Founded in 1898 and based at the Dark Lane ground in Rossendale, the club play in the Northern Premier League. Rossendale were relegated from the Northern Premier League in 1993.

Rossi, Paolo (1956–) Italian striker, who was the star of the 1982 World Cup. Rossi made his debut for Italy in 1977 and was included in the squad that finished fourth in the World Cup a year later. His career faltered when he was banned for two years

as a result of a match-fixing scandal, but his return to international football in 1982 culminated in six goals that effectively captured the World Cup for his country and won Rossi the title of European Footballer of the Year. In all, he scored 20 goals in 46 internationals. At home, he played for Juventus, Como, Vicenza, Perugia, and Verona.

Rotherham United English football club, nicknamed the Merry Millers. Strip: red shirts, white shorts, and red socks. The club had its origins in Thornhill United (founded in 1878, reorganized in 1884, and later retitled Rotherham County) and in Rotherham Town, who merged with County in 1925 to form Rotherham United. Rotherham Town joined the Second Division in 1893 but dropped out after failing to win re-election in 1896. Rotherham County made it into the Second Division in 1919 and subsequently the Merry Millers have divided their time between the bottom three divisions (most of their recent history being spent in Divisions Three and Four).

Their finest era at their MILLMOOR ground began in the 1950s when promotion to the Second Division ended 30 years in the Third Division; in 1955 they were denied a place in the First Division only on goal average. In 1961 they enjoyed another moment of glory when the team were finalists in the first League Cup competition (losing to Aston Villa). One record which the club was not anxious to claim became theirs on 22 December 1934, when they became the only club between the wars to fail to arrive at a League game, fog preventing them from making it to Hartlepool. Famous names associated with the side have included centre-half Dave Watson and managers Tommy DOCHERTY and Emlyn Hughes.

The club enjoyed their record victory in 1947, when they beat Oldham Athletic 8–0; they suffered their worst defeat in 1928, when they lost 11–1 to Bradford City (it was not their best season – some months later they also went down 10–1 to South Shields). Danny Williams holds the record for League appearances with the club, having played in 459 games between 1946 and 1962.

rouge In the earliest history of the game, a 'goal' scored by successfully aiming the ball at an enlarged 'outer' goal. Games could be settled by the number of goals thus scored when no shots passed through the 'inner' goal, but a single goal scored in the inner area cancelled out any number of 'rouges'.

Records of games played employing this system exist from the 1860s.

Rous, Sir Stanley (1895–1986) English football administrator, who is remembered as one of the most influential figures in recent football history. Rous had only a modest career as a player but was an outstanding referee, presiding over the 1934 FA Cup Final and devising the diagonal system of refereeing that is still used today. He was appointed FA Secretary in 1934 and later became president of FIFA (1961–74). Author of the simplified set of 17 laws under which football is played today, he was a champion of properly organized coaching and also active in promoting European and US competitions. He was knighted for his services to football in 1949. *See also* ROUS CUP.

> *He had vision, he could sway men and control meetings, he was an excellent speaker . . . if Stanley had been a politician he would very probably have become prime minister.*
>
> Alan Hardaker, *Hardaker of the League* (1977)

Rous Cup International cup competition that was inaugurated in 1985 and named after the great football administrator Sir Stanley ROUS. The cup was initially competed for by England and Scotland but was subsequently contested by England, Scotland, and an invited nation from South America. Scotland pulled out of the competition in 1990, effectively bringing it to an end.

Rovers Nickname of a number of football clubs, which have Rovers in their formal name (usually in reflection of the fact that they had a series of homes in their early history). They include BARTON ROVERS, BROMSGROVE ROVERS, DONCASTER ROVERS, RAITH ROVERS, and TRANMERE ROVERS.

Rowe, Arthur (1906–) English footballer and manager, whose association with Tottenham Hotspur had a major impact upon English football after World War II. Rowe made his debut for Spurs in 1929 and subsequently rose to the post of captain before injury forced his retirement as a player in 1939 (he was also capped once for England). He worked as a coach in Hungary and then as manager of the British Army team before moving to non-League Chelmsford City and then returning as manager to Tottenham in 1949. Under Rowe, Spurs captured the Second Division title in 1959 and a year later won the League championship itself, inspired by their innovative manager's push-and-run tactics. He retired from the job in 1955 but later served (1960–63) as manager of Crystal Palace.

Rowley, Arthur (1926–) English inside-forward, who established his place in football history by scoring a record 434 League goals. He played for West Bromwich Albion, Fulham, Leicester City, and Shrewsbury Town in the postwar era and ended his career as player-manager at Shrewsbury.

Roy of the Rovers The fictional footballing hero of a comic strip, whose adventures with MELCHESTER ROVERS provided absorbing reading for young fans for many years. Roy Race's extraordinarily long career was charted first in *Tiger* in 1954 and later continued in a comic devoted to him. He was an unusually talented striker and over the years picked up virtually every honour the game had to offer, including an FA Cup winner's medal in 1961. He married in the early 1970s and in 1980 saw the Rovers carry off the First Division championship (which must have surprised those Liverpool fans who thought their team had won it that year). His disciplinary record was exemplary and he was never sent off in a playing career that extended over four decades and only finally came to an end (in a typically dramatic helicopter crash) in 1993 (the underlying reason being falling readership). By the time of his final game he was credited with having scored some 5000 first-class goals.

Fans of the Roy of the Rovers stories pleaded for his return and the publishers suggested that the adventures might yet be continued, this time as a monthly serial centred around the exploits of Roy Race's son Rocky.

Royal Albert Scottish football club, which was a member of the League from 1923 to 1926. Royal Albert still play at their original ground at Raploch Park, Larkhall in Lanarkshire.

Royal Arsenal *See* ARSENAL.

Royal Engineers British army football club, nicknamed the Sappers. Strip: red and blue. The Royal Engineers were one of the great clubs in the early history of organized football in England. They were one of the dominant sides in the early years of the FA Cup, winning the tournament in 1875 and reaching another three Finals between 1871 and 1878 (including the very first Final of all – which they lost 1–0 to Wanderers after full-back Lieutenant Cresswell broke his collarbone – in 1872). Stars with the Sappers in these pioneering days included their captain Major Francis MARINDIN (destined to become president of the FA in 1874).

Subsequently they maintained their reputation by clinching victory in the Amateur Cup in 1908 and continued their footballing tradition through World War I, when they adapted their skills on the pitch for training purposes. In these so-called 'gas-mask' games, play was periodically interrupted for players (in full military uniform) to put on or take off a gas mask as quickly as they could before they were allowed to touch the ball once more.

The club have since captured the Army FA Cup on several occasions and were three times winner of the Army Quadrangle Cup in the 1980s. They are best remembered for their early emphasis upon teamwork and for their unfailing dedication to the highest standards of sportsmanship.

Royalists Nickname of the English non-League football club WINDSOR AND ETON, in reference to the royal family's ancient links with Windsor Castle, a royal residence since the 12th century.

Royals (1) Nickname of the English football club READING, reflecting the town's location in 'Royal Berkshire' (see also BISCUITMEN).

(2) Nickname of the English non-League football club SUTTON COLDFIELD (the town itself often being called 'Royal Sutton Coldfield').

royalty Football has never been considered a royal sport in the same way as horse racing or polo, etc., but has nonetheless been graced with the presence of royalty many times over the years (chiefly through the more or less obligatory presence of some member of the royal family at major finals). Historically, the British royal family tended to range itself very firmly against the game, with Edward II even outlawing the playing of the game in London in 1314:

> Forasmuch as there is great noise in the city caused by hustling over large balls, from which many evils may arise, which God forbid, we command and forbid on behalf of the King, on pain of imprisonment, such game to be used in the city in future.

The competition football presented to archery practice made it no favourite of subsequent monarchs, including Edward III and Henry IV, who acted to restrict the sport. Elizabeth I was also no lover of the game, as evidenced by a proclamation of 1572:

> No foteball player be used or suffered within the City of London and the liberties thereof upon pain of imprisonment.

James I also banned the sport:

> From this court I debarre all rough and violent exercises, as the foot-ball, meeter for lameing than making able the users thereof.

Charles II, however, proved a relative enthusiast after Count Albemarle popularized it at the English court after seeing a game of calcio in Florence. A match was arranged between a team representing the King and another under the Count: the Count's team won the game and Charles lost a wager of ten gold coins, but was sufficiently won over to lift the royal ban on the game.

Edward VII was the first royal patron of the FA, accepting the honour in 1901. A later patron of the FA, George V, was the first reigning monarch to attend an FA Cup final, when he witnessed the event and presented the Cup to Burnley in 1914, and subsequently he attended several more, including the memorable Final at Wembley in 1923, where his presence was said to have done much to promote public order and allow the game to go ahead.

The tradition that the monarch or a member of the royal family should attend Cup Finals and important representative matches has continued into modern times, and the 1966 World Cup tournament in England was opened with appropriate formality by Elizabeth II. Three years later she even went to the extent of naming two of her racehorses after the Charlton brothers.

A significant number of the great names in football have also been summoned in recent decades to Buckingham Palace to receive various honours, up to and including knighthoods, for their services to the game. In return, football has acknowledged its allegiance to the Crown many times; in 1937 a special Spode Loving Cup was given to each First Division club to mark the coronation of George VI and the clubs used them for a loyal toast each New Year's Day for many years (though the toast now more usually takes the form 'Football, Friendship, and the League').

Foreign royalty has on occasion shown a keener interest in the game. Prince Rainier of Monaco ordered shirts in Scotland's colours as gifts for his own family, while back in 1930 King Carol of Romania exercised the royal prerogative by personally selecting the Romanian World Cup squad (and excusing all outstanding playing offences); he even threatened to close down a British oil company in Romania when it was suggested that players working for the company would not be granted paid leave to represent their country.

Royston Town English non-League football club, nicknamed the Crows. Strip: red and white striped shirts with red shorts and socks. Founded in 1875 and based at Garden Walk, Royston play in the Isthmian League.

Rubber Man *See* LEONIDAS DA SILVA.

VS Rugby English non-League football club, nicknamed The Valley. Strip: sky blue shirts, navy blue shorts, and sky blue socks. Founded in 1956 and based at Butlin Road in Rugby, the club play in the Southern League.

Rugby Park The home ground of the Scottish football club KILMARNOCK. Kilmarnock settled at Rugby Park in the 1870s, though the pitch was moved to its present site in 1899. The venue was occasionally used for international games early in its history but suffered severely during World War II when it was used as a storage depot for oil and coal. The ground was restored after the war with the help of Italian prisoners-of-war and a new Main Stand was added in the late 1950s. For many years Rugby Park was also home to a sheep which fulfilled the role of club mascot. The first sheep so honoured was called Ruby, the second Angus, and the third Wilma; Wilma was the last of the line and died in 1966 a year after the club won its first Championship.

Ruislip Manor English non-League football club, nicknamed the Manor. Strip: white shirts with black shorts and socks. Founded in 1938 and based at the Grosvenor Vale ground, Ruislip play in the Isthmian League.

rules *See* CAMBRIDGE RULES.

Rumbelows Cup *See* LEAGUE CUP.

Rumble of Thunder, The Nickname of the Italian forward Luigi 'Gigi' RIVA.

Rummenigge, Karl-Heinz (1955–) West German winger, who emerged as one of his country's most formidable strikers in the 1970s and 1980s. Playing at home for Bayern Munich, he made his debut for West Germany in 1976 and played a major role in the German World Cup campaigns of 1978, 1982, and 1986, winning 95 caps. He was voted European Footballer of the Year in 1980 and 1981; he joined Internazionale in 1984 and ended his career with the Swiss club Servette.

run Unbroken sequences of victories or defeats are the stuff of legend and a favourite subject of the football statistician. Most teams have enjoyed outstanding runs of either triumphs or disasters that fans rejoice in recalling.

Some of the happier runs include Gillingham's sequence of home victories that lasted without a break for over two years from 1963 to 1965, Burnley's 30 games without defeat in the 1920–21 season, Reading's 55 home games without defeat between 1933 and 1936, and Nottingham Forest's 42 First Division matches without defeat between 1977 and 1978. Glasgow Rangers can claim two significant runs of victories, with a series of 18 wins that gave them a 100 per cent success rate in the 1898–99 season and a further sequence of 38 consecutive wins in 1928–29.

Since the offside rule was changed in 1925, the record for the longest run without conceding a single League goal goes to Port Vale, who kept an unblemished scoresheet over 30 matches in the 1953–54 season.

Few clubs can boast the run Peterborough United enjoyed in the late 1950s, when they were the dominant non-League side: they won 103 home games in a row without a single defeat (scoring 428 goals in the process). Back in the 1880s the Scottish club Queen's Park went for seven years without losing a game and in five of them goalkeeper Jock Grant did not let in a single goal. Most impressive of all, however, is the run that was enjoyed by Real Madrid between 1957 and 1965, during which time the side did not lose a single home game: they won 114 games and drew another eight between two defeats at the hands of Atlético Madrid.

Runcorn English non-League football club, nicknamed the Linnets. Strip: yellow shirts, green shorts, and yellow socks.

Founded in 1918 and based at the Canal Street ground in Runcorn, the club won the Cheshire League championship in its first season (1919), subsequently switched (1968) to the Northern Premier League, and in 1981 became members of the Alliance Premier League, winning the championship in their first season. They were losing finalists in the FA Trophy in 1993.

running off the ball Moving into an unmarked position so as to receive a pass from a team mate.

Rush, Ian (1961–) Welsh striker, who was one of the most formidable members of the Liverpool squad that dominated English football in the 1980s. Rush made his professional debut for Chester in 1979 and joined Liverpool in 1980, in which year he made his first appearance for Wales. A year later he won the first of four consecutive League Cup medals with the club, while in 1982 he enjoyed success in the first of five League championships. He played a key role in Liverpool's European Cup victory in 1984, scored two goals in Liverpool's FA Cup Final against Everton in 1986, and then moved to the Italian club Juventus for £3.2 million. The transfer was not a success and he was back at Anfield a year later. In 1989 he scored two goals in a victorious FA Cup Final against Everton (despite coming on as a substitute). He proved most effective in partnership with Kenny DALGLISH, Peter Beardsley, and John BARNES.

Rushden and Diamonds English non-League football club, nicknamed the Russians. Strip: all red. Founded in 1889 and based at Nene Park in Irthlingborough, the club play in the Southern League.

Rwanda Rwanda joined FIFA in 1976 and have yet to make much impact on international football. Strip: red, green, and yellow shirts, green shorts, and red socks.

S

Saddlers Nickname of the English football club WALSALL, in reference to the town's history as a centre for the manufacture of saddlery and other leather products.

SAFE Soccer As Family Entertainment. Specially designated part of a stand to which fans and their families are admitted at special concessionary prices. The first such SAFE enclosure was created at Wembley for the final of the Freight Rover Trophy in 1986; its success suggested a possible way forward for the game to lure back the missing millions frightened away from football by high admission prices and the sometimes violent atmosphere at major games. *See also* BOYS' STAND.

Saffron Walden Town English non-League football club, nicknamed the Bloods. Strip: red and black striped shirts, black shorts with red trim, and black socks with red trim. Founded in 1872 and based at Caton's Lane, the club play in the Isthmian League.

St Alan of St Anne's Nickname of Alan HARDAKER, in reference to his reign as secretary of the Football League (which is based at Lytham St Anne's).

St Albans City English non-League football club, nicknamed the Saints. Strip: yellow shirts with blue trim, blue shorts, and yellow socks. Founded in 1908 and based at Clarence Park, the club play in the Isthmian League. The fact that the Kuwaiti national team wear the same strip as St Albans is due to the fact that the club donated an entire first team strip to them in 1991.

St Andrew's The home ground of the English football club BIRMINGHAM CITY. The club – then called Small Heath – played at the now vanished Muntz Street, a substantial ground with a potholed pitch, until 1905, when they settled at St Andrew's. At that time the ground was no more than a patch of wasteground with a railway line running close alongside (for some years players had to contend with steam and smoke from the engines billowing across the pitch).

A Kop (uniquely situated along the side of the pitch rather than at one end) was constructed on a foundation of rubbish and a huge Main Stand was erected in time for the first match in 1906. The venue suffered badly during World War II, when it was hit by 20 bombs and was further damaged when a fire accidentally started by a member of the National Fire Service swept through the Main Stand (then being used as an auxiliary fire station). The ground was gradually restored in the 1940s and 1950s and further improved in the 1960s.

In 1986, on the same afternoon as the Bradford fire, the collapse of a wall resulting in the death of a young fan during a riot by visiting Leeds United supporters fuelled demands for a reassessment of safety and related matters at all English grounds. Features of St Andrew's include the Jeff Hall Memorial scoreboard, erected in tribute to a Blues right-back who died of polio in 1959 at the age of 30.

St Anne's The headquarters of the FOOTBALL LEAGUE, in Lytham St Anne's, Lancashire. The League originally had its base in Starkie Street, Preston, until it moved in 1959 to what had previously been a private hotel in Lytham St Anne's, which was acquired for £11,000.

St Bernards Former Scottish League football club that was a member of the League from 1893 to 1939.

St Domingo's *See* EVERTON.

St Etienne French football club, nicknamed the Greens (*Les Verts*). Strip: green shirts, white shorts, and green socks. Founded in 1920, St Etienne are based at the GEOFFROY GUICHARD STADIUM and enjoy close links with the massive 'Casino' retailing organization started by Guichard (the chain's shop colours of green and white were the inspiration for the team's strip).

The club enjoyed a golden age in the

1960s and 1970s, when they brought their tally of French League titles to eight (they have since won another in 1981). St Etienne also won the French Cup six times between 1962 and 1977 (winning the Double four times in just eight years) and were runners-up in the European Cup in 1976. It all went wrong in 1982, however, when the club was accused of making illegal payments to players and subsequently slumped into the Second Division in 1984. Great names associated with the club include that of coach Albert Batteux, who presided over the golden era of the late 1960s, when the team won four League titles in a row (1967–70). Notable players with the club have included Hervé and Patrick Revelli and Dominique Rocheteau.

St Jack Nickname of the English footballer and manager Jack CHARLTON, which was bestowed upon him by grateful Ireland fans for his deeds since becoming manager of the national team in 1986.

St James' Park (1) The home ground of the English football club EXETER CITY. The venue was home to Exeter United in the 1890s and first played host to Exeter City on their foundation in 1904. Events in the ground's history have included a fire (1925), in which all the players' kit with the exception of a single pair of boots was destroyed (along with the Main Stand), and the acquisition of the ground as a training base by the US Army during World War II. Features include the Cowshed stand, the Grecian Gate entrance, and the club's own railway station. According to local superstition the outcome of games at St James' Park can be predicted by observing the positions of the seagulls that habitually perch on the crossbars of the two goals.

(2) The home ground of the English football club NEWCASTLE UNITED. Originally called Town Moor, St James' Park was home first to Newcastle Rangers, Newcastle West End, and ultimately to United after the West End and Newcastle East End teams merged in 1892. The ground remained relatively undeveloped until injuries suffered by spectators during a game after the club reached the First Division in 1898 prompted major redesigning of the venue.

Subsequent events have included a riot between Newcastle and Sunderland fans in 1901, which attracted some notoriety to the ground's name, improvements to the stands in 1930, the arrival of floodlights in 1953, the addition of a grand new entrance in 1957, redevelopment in the early 1970s,

serious pitch invasions in the 1970s, the demolition of the huge West Stand in 1987 on safety grounds, and the staging of massive rock concerts by the likes of the Rolling Stones and Bob Dylan.

St John, Ian (1938–   ) Scottish centre-forward, nicknamed The Saint, who was bought from Motherwell in 1961 by the legendary manager Bill SHANKLY and subsequently became one of the pillars around which the celebrated Liverpool side of the mid-1960s was built. In the late 1970s he was one of the stars recruited to help popularize football in South Africa. In later years he has established himself as a television commentator on football.

St Johnstone Scottish football club, nicknamed the Saints. Strip: royal blue and white shirts, with royal blue shorts and socks. Founded by local cricketers in 1884 and based at MCDIARMID PARK in Perth (though previously for many years at MUIRTON PARK), the club joined the League in 1911 but have enjoyed their best times in relatively recent years. The club's formal name, incidentally, is a reference to Perth's long association with St John the Baptist (the area being originally known as Sanct Johns Toun of Perth).

Manager Willie Ormond established St Johnstone as one of the most formidable teams in Scotland in the late 1960s, when their achievements included an appearance as losing finalists in the 1969 League Cup. In 1971 they enjoyed considerable success at European level, their most significant victories including a 5–1 win over a respected Hamburg side.

The club's golden era, however, opened in the 1980s when St Johnstone rose to the top of the First Division, clinching the Championship in 1983 and 1990 under manager Alex Totten.

The Saints enjoyed their record victory in 1969, when they beat Partick Thistle 8–1; they suffered their record defeat in 1928, losing 12–0 against Cowdenbeath. Drew Rutherford holds the record for League appearances with the club, having played in a total of 298 matches.

St Lucia St Lucia joined FIFA in 1988 and have yet to make much impact upon international competition. Strip: blue and white shirts, black shorts, and blue socks.

St Mirren Scottish football club, nicknamed the Buddies. Strip: black and white striped shirts with black and white shorts and socks. Founded in 1877 by the cricket and rugby players of Paisley, the club – sometimes also nicknamed the Saints – played at a number of grounds before settling permanently at LOVE STREET in 1895, five years after they became founder members of the Scottish League.

The club's first major triumph came in 1926, when they captured the Scottish Cup; subsequently they won it again in 1959 and 1987, on each occasion overcoming formidable opposition against the odds. Other honours have included the Second Division championship in 1968 and the First Division title in 1977.

The club's record victory stands at 15–0 against Glasgow University in 1960; it suffered its greatest defeat back in 1897, losing 9–0 to Rangers. Tony Fitzpatrick holds the record for League appearances with the club, having played in 351 games between 1973 and 1988. In one match in 1986 Billy Abercromby had the distinction of being shown the red card on no fewer than three occasions – once for a playing offence and twice more for arguing the decision: he was banned, fined, and put on the transfer list but nonetheless went on to lead the team to victory in the Scottish Cup a year later.

St Ouen The home ground, in the St Ouen district of north Paris, of the French football club RED STAR. The club first occupied the small stadium in 1910 and it was initially France's most prestigious football venue, despite its relatively spartan facilities. The ground was given its official name, Stade de Paris, in 1922, when Red Star were enjoying a golden era, but most fans continued to identify the ground as St Ouen. It hosted Olympic football in 1924 and during World War II was used by the German invaders as a park for military vehicles. Red Star went into decline after the war and eventually the once-famous stadium was hosting minor league football until a revival in fortunes on the pitch saw a return to the Second Division in the 1980s.

St Vincent and the Grenadines St Vincent and the Grenadines joined FIFA in 1988 and have yet to make much impact in international competition.

Saints Nickname of a number of football clubs with the word saint in their formal title. They include CHALFONT ST PETER, ST ALBANS CITY, ST JOHNSTONE, and ST MIRREN. The English football club SOUTHAMPTON is also nicknamed Saints, in reference to the teams's original name –

Southampton St Mary's (St Mary's being the church that ran the young men's association from which most of the early members of the side came).

Salisbury English non-League football club, nicknamed the Whites. Strip: white shirts with black shorts and socks. Founded in 1947 and based at Victoria Park in Salisbury, the club play in Southern League.

Salop See SHREWSBURY TOWN.

San Mamés The home ground, nicknamed The Cathedral, of ATHLETIC BILBAO. A source of intense Basque pride, The Cathedral was opened back in 1913 and shortly afterwards was honoured with a visit by King Alfonso XIII; in 1921 it staged the first international played in Spain. The stadium was rebuilt in the 1950s and again in the 1980s and is now dominated by a huge white metal arch, a powerful symbol of regional pride and history.

San Marino San Marino joined FIFA in 1988 but have yet to make much impact in international competition. Strip: all light blue.

San Paolo Stadium The home ground of the Italian football club NAPOLI. The club had a number of homes before settling at the current site in 1959. Chief of these were the Giorgio Ascarelli and Vomero stadiums in the city. The Ascarelli stadium, named after a president of the club, was renamed the Partenopeo Stadium under the Fascists (Ascarelli being a Jew) and was finally destroyed by bombs in World War II. The Vomero stadium was relatively short-lived and was notorious for pitch invasions and violence.

Named after St Paul on the advice of the local archbishop, the club's present stadium became a host of major international matches, but continued to be plagued by pitch invasions and riots as its predecessor had been. Major refurbishment followed in the 1980s as Napoli entered their greatest era to date under MARADONA and the venue was prepared to host games in the 1990 World Cup. Legend has it that the noise generated by Napoli's dedicated fans when a home goal is scored causes such strong vibrations in the locality that household ornaments in neighbouring buildings are often damaged.

San Siro See GIUSEPPE MEAZZA STADIUM.

Sánchez Pizjuán Stadium The home ground of the Spanish football club Seville.

The club had a number of homes before finally constructing their present stadium in 1958, realizing the long-term dream of president Ramón Sánchez Pizjuán, after whom it was eventually named (unfortunately he died before its completion). It is now one of Spain's leading international venues and hosted two games in the 1982 World Cup Finals. Features of the stadium include a huge mosaic depicting the club badges of Seville and 60 other teams from all around the world.

Sandgrounders Nickname of the English non-League football club SOUTHPORT, reflecting its seaside location.

Sant'Elia The home ground, in Sardinia, of the Italian football club Cagliari. The club settled at the Sant'Elia Stadium (named after the Sant'Elia district of Cagliari) in 1970, in which year the team won their only Championship title. The stadium was substantially refurbished in 1989 in time for the 1990 World Cup, despite the problems caused when it was found that the new pitch laid that year turned out to be infested with huge numbers of glow-worms.

Santiago Bernabeu Stadium *See* BERNABEU.

Santos Brazilian football club, which emerged as one of the most formidable teams in the world in the 1950s and 1960s. Strip: all white. Founded in 1912 as a result of football demonstrations given by British sailors in the port of Santos and now based at the Vila Belmiro Stadium, Santos owed their rise to glory to their great star PELÉ. They have won the League championship some 15 times since 1935 and in the early 1960s recorded a brace of remarkable doubles, winning both the South American Cup and the World Club Championship in 1962 and 1963. The brilliance of Pelé led to the club making numerous trips abroad and made them one of the most famous teams in football history – but it all crumbled away after Pelé left in 1973, since when the club has captured only one further title.

Santos, Djalma dos (1929–) Brazilian right-back, who was a formidable defender with the great Brazilian national side of the 1950s and 1960s. Playing at home for Portuguesa, he made his international debut in 1952 and subsequently formed a brilliant partnership with Nilton dos SANTOS (no relation). He won 107 caps in all and took part in the World Cup campaigns of 1954, 1958, and 1962.

Santos, Nilton dos (1927–) Brazilian left-back, who was one of the pillars of the great Brazilian team that won two World Cups (1958 and 1962). Santos made his debut for Botafogo in 1942 and eventually rose to the post of captain of the team. He made his first appearance on the international stage in 1950 and rocked many opponents with his attacking runs out of defence (often in collaboration with the full-back Djalma dos SANTOS); his second World Cup medal was won at the ripe old age of 37.

São Paulo Brazilian football club, which has long been ranked among the best in the country. Strip: white shirts with red and black horizontal stripe, with white shorts and socks. Founded in 1930 as successor to Paulistano and AA das Palmeiras, São Paulo have won some 16 League titles since 1931, enjoying golden eras under the influence of strikers Artur FRIEDENREICH and subsequently LEONIDAS DA SILVA. They were also the first Brazilian club to adopt professionalism (1933).

São Tomé and Principe São Tomé and Principe joined FIFA in 1986 and have yet to make much impact upon international competition. Strip: all green and yellow.

Sappers Nickname of the British army football club the ROYAL ENGINEERS, after the traditional informal name for military engineers.

Saudi Arabia Saudi Arabia joined FIFA in 1959 but have to date only played a minor role in international football, though they qualified for the World Cup Finals in 1994. Strip: all white with green trim.

Savage Six Nickname of the formidable defensive line-up that was fielded by Bolton Wanderers in the 1950s. Comprising Roy Hartle, Derek Henning, Eddie Hopkinson, John Higgins, Bryan Edwards, and Tom Banks, the Savage Six were renowned as hard men throughout the English game.

save To block a shot at goal, the principal role of the goalkeeper. Goalkeepers were first allowed to use their hands to make saves in 1878, and until 1912 were allowed to handle the ball anywhere in their half of the field.

Paul Cooper, keeper with Ipswich Town, Manchester City, and other teams, is credited with having made more saves in the Football League than any other. Others on the roll of honour include Wimbledon's Dave BEASANT, who in 1988 saved a penalty from Liverpool's John Aldridge to become the first goalkeeper to save a penalty in an FA Cup Final.

Argument will continue endlessly over which keeper made the finest save of all time, though contenders would have to include England's Gordon BANKS, whose blocking of a powerful shot from Brazil's PELÉ in the 1970 World Cup verged on the miraculous, and Pelé himself acknowledged it as the best save he had ever seen.

On occasion outfield players have distinguished themselves after they have donned the keeper's gloves when their own guardian of the goal has been injured or otherwise removed from play. Niall Quinn of Manchester City is the only outfield player to have saved a penalty in a League game after City keeper Tony Coton was sent off for a foul against Derby's Dean Saunders in 1991.

Scarborough English football club, nicknamed Boro. Strip: red and black shirts, white shorts, and red socks. Founded in 1879 as Scarborough Cricketers' FC, the club finally won promotion to the Fourth Division in 1987, becoming the first club to benefit from automatic promotion to the League on winning the Conference. Glory has also come to the club's home at the MCCAIN STADIUM through Scarborough's four appearances over the years in the third round of the FA Cup.

Despite such successes, however, the club has suffered more from lack of support than virtually any other team in the League.

Scarborough's record victory in League and Cup competition stands at 6–0 against Rhyl Athletic in 1930; their worst defeat came in 1919, when the side went down 16–1 to Southbank in the Northern League. Steve Richards holds the record for League appearances, having played in 119 games between 1987 and 1990.

scarf The football scarf, in the colours of specific teams, has outlasted many other fans' accessories, such as the rattle and the rosette. They were first produced in their thousands in the years following World War II, when record crowds flocked to games all over the UK.

schemer A key player, usually a defender or midfielder, who initiates rehearsed tactical moves and identifies weaknesses in the opposition that can be exploited in attack.

Schiaffino, Juan (1925–) Uruguayan inside-forward, who was the key figure in Uruguay's surprise victory in the 1950 World Cup tournament. He played at home for Peñarol but subsequently moved to Italy, where he became a star with AC Milan and Roma and added four Italian caps to the 22 he won with Uruguay.

Schillaci, Salvatore (1964–) Italian forward, nicknamed Toto, who emerged as a major star with Juventus and Italy in the late 1980s. Born in Sicily, he joined Juventus in 1989 after leaving Second Division Messina and a year later made his debut for the national side, forging a brilliant partnership with Roberto Baggio in the 1990 World Cup and coming out of the tournament as leading goalscorer, with a total of six goals. His contribution was particularly rued by Irish fans, who saw him score the goal that put Ireland out at the quarter-final stage. He moved to Internazionale in 1991.

Schnellinger, Karl-Heinz (1939–) West German sweeper, who was a stalwart of the West German national squad in no fewer than four World Cups (1958–70). He began his career with Duren, but subsequently played for Cologne, Roma, Mantova, and AC Milan as well as winning a total of 47 caps for his country.

Schoen, Helmut (1915–) West German footballer and manager, under whom West Germany won the World Cup in 1974. An inside-forward, Schoen enjoyed a highly successful playing career with Dresdner FC, making his debut for the club in 1932 and subsequently collecting winners' medals in the German Cup (1940 and 1941) and in the German League championship (1943 and 1944). He also made 16 appearances for the national side, scoring 17 goals. He retired as a player in 1955 and was appointed assistant manager of the national side. In 1964 he was promoted to the post of manager and two years later he got West Germany into the closely fought World Cup Final won by England. Now recognized as one of the leading footballing powers, West Germany – whose stars included BECKENBAUER and MÜLLER – went from strength to strength under Schoen's courteous leadership and in 1972 captured the European Championship. The World Cup itself followed in 1974 and in 1976 the team only narrowly lost the European Championship to Czechoslovakia (after a penalty shoot-out). The team's showing in the 1978 World Cup was less happy, however, and Schoen retired.

School of Science Nickname that was applied to EVERTON in the 1930s in acknowledgement of the team's premeditated and precise style of play. The side established itself as one of the strongest of its day, carrying off Second and First Division championships in successive seasons (1931 and 1932). Stars of the School of Science included Joe MERCER and Cliff Britton.

schoolboy football Football played at school level has a long and glorious history, not least in the fact that the rules of the game itself were first formulated by Old Boys from some of England's leading public schools (*see* CAMBRIDGE RULES; PUBLIC SCHOOL FOOTBALL).

There are several long-established competitions for schoolboy players, run under the aegis of the English Schools' Football Association (and its equivalents in Scotland, Wales, and Northern Ireland). This organization was founded in 1904 and now has around 14,000 affiliated schools. Tournaments run by the English Schools FA include the inter-association trophy competition, founded in 1905, county championships, and a six-a-side tournament (the semi-finals and finals of which are played at Wembley).

At international level, the home countries are represented by teams of under-15 and under-18 year olds. The best schoolboy players often join senior clubs as associate schoolboys at the age of 14 and may be selected to attend the FA School of Excellence at Lilleshall. The first Schoolboy International to be played at Wembley took place in 1950, when stars of the England side included Johnny HAYNES.

scissor kick A shot in which the legs cross in the manner of a pair of scissors opening, usually employed on the turn in front of goal.

Sclessin The home ground, in Liège, of the Belgian football club STANDARD LIÈGE. Situated in an area of heavy industry, the Sclessin Stadium became home to the club in 1909, was substantially rebuilt in the 1920s, and was again improved after World War II, when Standard established themselves as the leading Belgian side.

Scotland The Scottish national team are, with England, the oldest international side in the world (the two sides having had their first meeting in 1872). Subsequently Scotland lost only one international between 1873 and 1888 and meetings with the 'auld enemy' have always been considered the most important fixtures in the calendar. A decline in the late 19th century lasted until the 1920s, when the team enjoyed a resurgence that was crowned in 1928 when the so-called Wembley Wizards thrashed England 5–1 at Wembley. Scotland did not qualify for the World Cup Finals until 1950 (and even then did not go) but subsequently qualified for five Finals series in a row (1974, 1978, 1982, 1986, and 1990), though – despite some brave performances – they have yet to progress to the late stages of the competition. Stars of the side since the war have included such names as Denis LAW and Kenny DALGLISH (each scorers of 30 international goals). Strip: dark blue shirts, white shorts with navy trim, and red socks. *See also* Tartan Army.

Scott, Elisha (1894–1959) Northern Ireland-born goalkeeper, who was one of the most respected keepers of the interwar years. He occupied the Liverpool goal for many years, notching up 430 appearances and playing a key role in the League championship victories of 1922 and 1923, and subsequently played for Belfast Celtic. He also won 31 caps for Northern Ireland.

Scottish Cup The Scottish FA Cup competition, which was founded under the aegis of the Scottish Football Association in 1874. Similar in form to the English FA Cup tournament, the Scottish Cup was first claimed by Queen's Park, who triumphed over 16 other teams in what proved to be the first of three successive wins. Controversial finals in the years that followed included that of 1879, when Vale of Leven refused to play because of injuries and illness among their squad (the Cup was awarded to Queen's Park after they ran the ball into the undefended goal), and that of 1909, when a riot between Celtic and Rangers fans led to the Cup being withheld that year. The Final is traditionally held at Hampden Park; the most successful teams in the history of the Cup are (predictably) Celtic and Rangers. East Fife are the only team to have won the Cup while in the Second Division (1938).

Scottish Football Association The SFA was founded in 1873, just weeks after the English Football Association had organized the first international between the two countries and thus promoted the foundation of a similar body north of the border. *See also* SCOTTISH CUP.

Scottish League The Scottish League was founded by 11 clubs in 1890 and has since prospered in parallel with the Football League in England. The original members were Abercorn, Cambuslang, Celtic, Cowlairs, Dumbarton, Heart of Midlothian, Rangers, Renton, St Mirren, Third Lanark, and Vale of Leven.

A Second Division was added in 1893 (being temporarily suspended during World War I) and in 1921 automatic promotion and relegation between the two divisions was introduced. A Third Division was created in 1923 but was disbanded three years later and not revived until 1946, when the League was reorganized into A, B, and C Divisions. In 1975 the top 10 clubs formed a new Premier Division while the rest were split into Division One and Division Two.

The most successful teams in the history of the Scottish League are Rangers (with over 40 victories) and Celtic (with 35).

Scottish League Cup Scottish cup competition for League clubs, which was renamed the Skol Cup after its sponsors in 1984. The Cup was first contested by members of the Scottish League in 1947, when Rangers won it; since then its history has been dominated by Rangers and Celtic. It failed to attract much interest until it was reorganized in 1977 on a strictly knock-out basis. The 7–1 victory enjoyed by Celtic at Rangers' expense in 1957 established a record scoreline for any major British Final.

scout The club official whose duty is to identify promising young players for possible recruitment by his own team. Many legends have grown up around these shadowy, secretive figures who often attend matches incognito and wield the power to make or break a player's career; in reality they are often methodical, friendly characters who think themselves lucky if they identify more than a few major players. Chief scouts work in close co-operation with managers, but much of the actual scouting is done by expenses-only 'stringers' who are somewhat closer to the traditional image of the trilby-hatted devotee who turns out regularly in all weather at even the most unappealing fixtures.

What you have to get across very quickly is that the chances of reaching the top are slim. It's my job to break the hearts of those who don't make it – but we try to soften the blow.

Jim Cassells, Oldham Athletic chief scout (1991)

screening See SHIELDING.

scudetto The Italian football Championship, the highest honour in Italian domestic football. The most successful clubs in the history of the Championship have included AC Milan, Juventus, and Internazionale. It is often claimed that the scudetto witnesses the best domestic football anywhere in the world and even Second Division teams rank alongside some of the best produced elsewhere in Europe. *See also* LURE OF THE LIRA.

Scummers Nickname applied to fans of SOUTHAMPTON by rival Portsmouth supporters.

Scunthorpe United English football club, nicknamed the Iron. Strip: claret and blue shirts with white shorts and socks with a claret trim. Founded in 1899 (when Brumby Hall merged with some other local teams) and based at GLANFORD PARK since 1988 (before which they played at the Old Showground), the club were first elected to the Third Division (North) in 1950. They rose to the Second Division in 1958 (when they won the Third Division (North) championship) but since 1964 have divided their time between the bottom two divisions.

Between 1910 and 1958 they were known as Scunthorpe and Lindsey United after amalgamating with the latter team. Back in 1950 Scunthorpe were behind the successful campaign to have the League expanded by two clubs in each of the two Third Divisions then existing. The same season saw them become the first League club to be eliminated from the FA Cup before the first round (they were scheduled to play in the qualifiers before news of their promotion to the League was confirmed). A year later they established a reputation as a particularly challenging team to play at home, conceding just nine goals in a total of 23 home fixtures.

Star names to appear with the club over the years have included full-back Jack Brownsword and striker Barrie Thomas in the 1950s and early 1960s as well as goalkeeper Ray Clemence and forward Kevin KEEGAN, who were both later to establish their reputations with Liverpool; other celebrities to play for the team have included the England cricketer Ian Botham, who played at centre-half. Brian Godfrey, however, was the first player for the club to win an international cap, appearing for the Welsh Under-23 team in 1962.

Scunthorpe enjoyed a record 9–0 victory against Boston United in 1953; they suffered their record defeat in 1952, losing 8–0 to Carlisle United. Jack Brownsword holds the record for League appearances with the club, having played in 595 games between 1950 and 1965.

> *Any old Iron, any old Iron,*
> *Any any any old Iron,*
> *You look sweet, walking down the street,*
> *Hammer in your hand and boots on your*
>   *feet,*
> *Dressed in style, always a smile,*
> *We sing up the Iron,*
> *Oh we don't give a damn,*
> *About Donny Rovers fans,*
> *Old Iron, old Iron.*

Supporters' song

Seagulls Nickname of the English football club BRIGHTON AND HOVE ALBION, in reference to the club's coastline location.

Sealand Road The former home ground of the English football club CHESTER CITY. Sealand Road was home to the club from 1906 until 1990, when they elected to enter a ground-sharing arrangement at MOSS ROSE in Macclesfield, leaving their old base to redevelopment by a property company. Events in the ground's history included an experimental match in 1935, when two referees were used.

Seals Alternative nickname for CHESTER CITY, in reference to their former home ground, SEALAND ROAD.

Sealy-Vidal, Robert Walpole English forward, nicknamed the Prince of Dribblers, who was a star of both Westminster and England in the 1870s. Admired for his skill in dribbling the ball, he was one of the key players in the Wanderers side that won the very first FA Cup Final in 1872 and laid on the pass that allowed Morton Peto Betts (*see* CHEQUER, A.H.) to score the only goal of the game.

Seasiders Nickname of several English football clubs, in reference to their seaside location. They include BLACKPOOL and BRIDLINGTON TOWN.

Seeler, Uwe (1936–) West German striker, who served as captain of his country in two World Cups. Seeler made his debut for SV Hamburg in 1952 and subsequently rose to the post of captain of the side, which he led to victory in the European Cup Winners' Cup in 1968. He first appeared for West Germany in 1954 and four years later

played in the first of his four World Cup campaigns. As captain he took the team to the World Cup Final in 1966, losing to England, and again fulfilled the role in 1970. He won 72 caps in all and scored in every World Cup Finals series that he took part in (as well as establishing a record for World Cup selections). He was Germany's Footballer of the Year in three seasons, including his last (1970).

Sekularac, Dragoslav (1937–) Yugoslavian inside-forward, who is remembered as much for his fiery temperament as for his footballing genius. He emerged as a precocious talent with Red Star Belgrade and made his international debut in 1956 at the tender age of 18. Subsequently he was a member of the Yugoslavian squad that finished second in the 1956 Olympics and excelled in the World Cup Finals of 1958 and 1962, when Yugoslavia finished fourth. Controversy surrounded his name on more than one occasion – in particular after he came to blows with a referee during a League game (resulting in a year's ban and his transfer to the German club Karlsruhe). He ended his career with OFK Belgrade and then with the Colombian clubs Santa Fe and Millionarios.

selectors The FA officials who, until the mid-1960s, had the job of selecting players for the English national squad. The FA's International Selection Committee comprised 14 members and exercised complete control over the choice of players, often demonstrating considerable bias towards clubs with which individual committee members had connections. Changes were frequent and little attention was given towards building up coherent combinations of players who would complement each other's skills.

The system was less than ideal and attracted much criticism over the years from such influential figures as Herbert CHAPMAN, but nonetheless remained in place until the 1960s. It was Alf RAMSEY who brought the old system of selectors to an end in 1966, by insisting that he have complete control over the selection of his team in the role of manager. The selectors were left wondering what they were supposed to do instead and one of them ventured to ask Ramsey their role while at a cocktail party. Back came the curt reply: 'Attend cocktail parties.'

See also ROYALTY.

Selhurst Park The home ground, in

London, of the English football club CRYSTAL PALACE. Crystal Palace came to Selhurst Park in 1922, after occupying several grounds, including Joseph Paxton's Crystal Palace, where the club was based from 1861 to 1915. Formerly a brickfield complete with two tall chimneys, Selhurst Park was transformed with designs by Archibald Leitch by 1924 when, still unfinished, it hosted its first match. Subsequent events in the ground's history have included an international between England and Wales in 1926, building work in the 1950s, a visit by Real Madrid in 1962, the erection of the new Arthur Wait Stand (named after the club's chairman) in 1969, and the sharing of the ground with Charlton Athletic for several years from 1986 and then with Wimbledon.

sell a dummy *See* DUMMY.

send off To order a player to leave the field of play after he has committed a serious foul or is guilty of violent conduct (usually after he has committed two bookable offences).

Some players (John CHARLES, for instance) end their careers without having been sent off on a single occasion; others have been sent off so many times no one has kept count. Jack Burns of Rochdale threw away the chance of ending his career with an unblemished record at the very first hurdle, being sent off on his League debut in 1921. John Ritchie of Stoke City established some kind of record in 1972 when he came on as a substitute against Kaiserslautern: 40 seconds later he was on his way back to the dressing-room after being sent off. Sunderland and Hartlepools United's Ambrose Fogerty, meanwhile, has the distinction of having been the first player to be sent off in three English domestic competitions, with dismissals in the FA Cup (1958), the League (1965), and the League Cup (1966). The first England international to be sent off was Alan Mullery, who was ordered off during a match against Yugoslavia in 1968.

If the number of sendings-off can be taken as a measure of prevailing standards of fair play, then there was never a 'dirtier' season than 1982–83, when a record 242 British players were sent off. The record number of sendings-off in a World Cup tournament was recorded in 1990, when a total of 16 players were thus disciplined. Perhaps the best occasions bring out the best behaviour: there was not a single sending-off in an FA Cup Final from its inception to 1985, when Manchester United's Kevin Moran was ordered off the field for a late tackle during the 116th Final.

Some teams have better records than others. For some unfathomable reason players against Crewe Alexandra seemed particularly tempted to commit playing offences and for many years more opponents of the Railwaymen had been sent off than opponents of any other English team.

Some referees have not been content with sending off players but have gone to the extent of ordering off club officials who have incurred their displeasure – there are a number of celebrated instances in which famous managers and coaches have been ordered out of their dug-outs and been obliged to watch the remainder of a match from the stands after incurring the ref's displeasure.

Most remarkable of all, however, was a special game between Sheffield and Glasgow in 1930 – when the ref realized that his shirt was similar in colour to the Sheffield strip he actually sent himself off.

Senegal Senegal joined FIFA in 1962 but have to date only played a minor role in international competition, though they are considered one of the more promising African teams. Strip: green shirts, yellow shorts, and red socks.

Serie A The top domestic football League in Italy, which is often hailed as the finest domestic League in the world. With just 18 clubs, the League is little troubled with fixture congestion, allowing both club sides and the national team ample time to prepare and thus to raise their playing standards. The success of Serie A and the subsidiary leagues in Italy inspired the development of similar super leagues in other countries (with England forming the PREMIER LEAGUE on much the same lines in 1992).

set-piece A tactical attacking move usually beginning with a free kick that has been previously rehearsed in training. Goals scored from set-pieces account for nearly half of all goals scored in professional football. Typically, tall defenders are moved up to join the attack, where their height will be an advantage in aerial challenges in the goalmouth, and passes are made according to a pre-arranged plan, culminating in a shot at goal. Set-piece moves that result in goals are doubly effective in that they discourage the opposition from committed tackling because of the risk of giving away another kick. Teams usually have a number of set-pieces at their disposal and communicate which is to be employed by whispering numbers or secret passwords.

Seychelles The Seychelles joined FIFA in 1986 and have yet to make much impact on international competition. Strip: red shirts, white shorts, and red socks.

Seymour, Stan (1893–1978) Nicknamed Mister Newcastle, Seymour's involvement with NEWCASTLE UNITED included service as a player, manager, director, and chairman of the club. He joined the club as a player in 1920 and in 1924 scored the goal that won the FA Cup. As manager in the 1940s and 1950s he led Newcastle through one of their golden eras, thanks largely to the contribution of such players as Jackie MILBURN and Len SHACKLETON. It was under Mister Newcastle that the side won the Cup in 1951 and 1952, making them the first team to win the trophy in successive seasons in the 20th century. Seymour's son, also called Stan, eventually carried on the family tradition by also becoming chairman of the club.

SFA *See* SCOTTISH FOOTBALL ASSOCIATION.

Shackleton, Len (1922–) English footballer, nicknamed the Clown Prince of Soccer, who was one of the great personalities of the game in the years following World War II. Born in Bradford, 'Shack' played for England Schoolboys in 1936 and then joined the ground staff at Arsenal. He made his League debut for Bradford in 1946 and was soon transferred for a large fee to Newcastle United, scoring no fewer than six goals on his debut in a match against Newport County; the final scoreline was 13–0 (prompting the Clown Prince to make the oft-repeated observation 'And they were lucky to get nil'). He signed for Sunderland in 1948, in which year he also won the first of his five England caps.

Occupying the position of inside-forward, Shackleton thrilled crowds with his unorthodox individual flair (particularly with his deceptive ball control), although critics considered him too wayward to make a good team player. After his retirement from the field he became a sports journalist and wrote an autobiography, entitled *Clown Prince of Soccer* after his nickname.

True to his Yorkshire origins, he was renowned for his outspoken disregard for officialdom:

> I've heard of players selling dummies, but this club keeps buying them.
>
> Len Shackleton, criticizing Newcastle United in the 1970s

Shakers Nickname of the English football club BURY, which is thought to have originated in a chance remark made by the club chairman in 1891 to the effect that he expected his team to 'shake' their opponents.

shamateurism Slang term (a combination of *sham* and *amateurism*) that came to be applied in the late 19th century to the pretence of amateurism when players were in fact receiving surreptitious payment and other rewards from their clubs.

The issue of shamateurism dominated the English game for many years, even after the legalization of professionalism in 1885. At one point the practice was so widespread that it was not uncommon for players to turn down offers of places with semi-professional sides such as those of the Southern League in order to play for avowedly amateur clubs, who were actually offering more lucrative terms. Feelings about shamateurism were so intense that the threat of it spreading even prompted the FA to decline the chance of taking part in the World Cup in 1930, purely because FIFA wanted amateur players to receive some sort of compensation for earnings lost while taking part in the tournament (*see* BROKEN TIME).

The concept of shamateurism was finally consigned to history in the 1970s, when recruits were no longer classified as amateur or professional but simply as 'players', who were paid if their clubs could afford it. *See also* AMATEURISM; AMATEUR SPLIT.

Shamrock Rovers Irish football club, undisputed as the most successful team in the Republic of Ireland. Strip: green and white hooped shirts, with white shorts and socks. Founded in 1899 and now based at DALYMOUNT PARK in Dublin, Shamrock Rovers have won 14 League championships as well as 24 Irish Cups.

Shankly, Bill (1919–81) Celebrated Scottish-born football manager, under whose leadership Liverpool emerged as one of the greatest teams in English football history. Shankly had a successful playing career as a wing-half with Carlisle United, Preston North End (with whom he won an FA Cup winner's medal in 1938), and Scotland – winning five caps – before taking his first managerial post (at Carlisle) in 1949. Subsequently he took control of Grimsby Town, Workington, and Huddersfield Town, before finally arriving at Anfield in 1959.

Shankly set about the radical reconstruction of the Liverpool team around the talents of such players as Ian ST JOHN, Roger Hunt, and Ron YEATS, and successfully lifted the club out of the Second Division in 1962. Two years later the team embarked on a remarkable hat-trick of victories, winning the League championship in 1964 and 1966 and the FA Cup in 1965. Not satisfied with these achievements, Shanks then announced that he would assemble an even more powerful Liverpool side: 'I want to build a team that's invincible, so they'll have to send a team from Mars to beat us.'

He constructed his new squad around such players as Kevin KEEGAN and in 1973 saw the club clinch both the League championship and the UEFA Cup. A year later the side also triumphed in the FA Cup – and then Shankly, by now endowed with almost divine status among the club's supporters – announced his surprise retirement. Devoted Liverpool fans predicted the end of a glorious era but Shankly's right-hand man Bob PAISLEY and his successors maintained the club as one of the leading European sides, prompting many to conjecture that Shankly himself must have lived to regret his controversial decision to quit.

Shankly is often recalled for his legendary dry wit and his many 'Shanklyisms' are part of the myth of the modern game. Examples of the most well-known include:

Me having no education, I had to use my brains.

We murdered them 0–0.

I don't drop players, I make changes.

He reserved many of his most caustic comments for arch-rivals Everton:

This city has two great teams – Liverpool and Liverpool reserves.

If Everton were playing down at the bottom of my garden, I'd draw the curtains.

See also FOOTBALL ISN'T A MATTER OF LIFE OR DEATH *under* LIFE.

Shay, The The home ground of the former English League football club HALIFAX TOWN. The club acquired The Shay in 1921 at the same time as they won League membership. Formerly a council rubbish tip, The Shay, which was probably named after the local area, Shay Syke, was always one of the more humble of League venues. Legend has it that managers of the club intercepted new recruits at the local railway station and got them to sign up there and then before they had a chance to see their unprepossessing new home. Events in the ground's history included various attempts at diversification, with the iced-over pitch being used as a skating rink in 1962–63 and the ground being briefly run by Jack CHARLTON as a golf-driving range in 1966. Speedway races were also staged there after World War II. In 1985 The Shay played host to the smallest-ever crowd ever to attend an FA Cup tie between two League clubs, when Halifax met Scunthorpe (just 1501 turned up to watch). The pitch itself was the smallest in the League, measuring a full 30 feet less in width and 30 feet shorter in length than the largest pitch of all, at BRISBANE ROAD.

Shaymen Nickname of the English football club HALIFAX TOWN, in reference to the team's home at The SHAY.

Shearer, Alan (1970–) English forward, nicknamed Smokey, who emerged as a leading star with Southampton in the late 1980s (despite a former Southampton manager observing of him that he 'couldn't trap a bag of cement'). He scored on every senior debut he made, for Southampton, England Youth, England Under-21s, England B, England, and Blackburn Rovers (to whom he transferred for a British record transfer fee of £3.6 million in 1992). He is also the youngest player ever to have scored a First Division hat-trick.

Shed, The The stand at Chelsea's STAMFORD BRIDGE home where loyal Chelsea supporters traditionally congregate. In recent decades the Shed has acquired a particularly unenviable reputation for violence.

We are the Shed, my friend,
We took the Stretford End,
We'll sing and dance and do it all again,
We live the life we choose,
We fight and never lose,
For we're the Shed, oh yes, we are the Shed.

Song sung by occupants of the Shed, to the tune of Mary Hopkins' 'Those Were the Days'

Sheffield Association One of the earliest of local football associations and a pioneer in the development of association football. The rules observed by the Sheffield Association differed in a number of aspects from those followed by the London Association and there was much debate over variant attitudes towards throw-ins and offsides. In the Sheffield version of the laws of the game the ball could be kicked into play at throw-ins and attackers were still onside if there was only one player between them and the opponent's goal. A compromise was reached between the two associations in 1877, after which the laws of the modern game were able to evolve more smoothly. *See also* OLDEST CLUBS.

Sheffield United English football club, nicknamed the Blades. Strip: red and white striped shirts, white shorts, and black socks. Founded in 1889 as an offshoot of York-shire Cricket Club, who saw football as a good source of revenue and a way of keep-ing their players fit during the winter, United were initially called the Cutlers (Sheffield being renowned for its cutlery manufacture).

Advertisements in the local papers for players for the new team at BRAMALL LANE were not very successful and for a time the side consisted of just three men; in the end players had to be recruited from as far away as Scotland. The team's first match was played in great secrecy, possibly in the expectation that it would be some time before the newly assembled side found its feet. Even so, the first encounter (a 3–1 defeat against Sheffield FC) was witnessed by a reporter and the captain of Sheffield Wednesday, who had succeeded in tailing the team to their away fixture.

The club joined the League three years later and in 1898 entered its golden era when it carried off the First Division cham-pionship. Victory in the FA Cup followed in 1899, with further wins in 1902, 1915, and 1925. Notable stars of the side in its heyday included the memorable combination of 'Fatty' FOULKE in goal and 'Nudger' Need-ham on the wing.

After World War II the club's fortunes faded somewhat, particularly in compari-son with the record of their neighbours Sheffield Wednesday, with lengthy spells in the lower divisions. More recent honours won by United have included the Second Division championship in 1953 and the Fourth Division title in 1982. In 1992 they became founder members of the Premier League. Famous names connected with Sheffield United in recent decades have numbered amongst them the England star Tony Currie, winger Alan Woodward, defender Len Badger, and manager Joe MERCER.

The club's records include a 10–0 victory against Burslem Port Vale in 1892, the first time an away team had achieved a double-figure score in the League; the scale of United's triumph may have had something to do with the fact that the Vale goalkeeper had lost his spectacles in the mud. Their record defeat came in 1890, when they lost 13–0 against Bolton Wanderers. Joe Shaw holds the record for League appearances with the club, playing in 629 matches between 1948 and 1966. *See also* AWAY.

> *You light up my senses,*
> *Like a gallon of Magnet,*
> *Like a packet of Woodbines,*
> *Like a good pinch of snuff,*
> *Like a night out in Sheffield,*
> *Like a greasy chip butty,*
> *Oh Sheffield United,*
> *Come thrill me again . . .*
> *La la la la la la la Ooooooaargh!*
>
> Supporters' song, to the tune of John Denver's 'Annie's Song'

Sheffield Wednesday English football club, nicknamed the Owls. Strip: blue and white striped shirts, black shorts, and blue socks. Wednesday are among the oldest surviving League clubs and can claim descent from Sheffield Wednesday Cricket Club (so-called because the players met on Wednesday half-holidays) that was formed in 1816. The football club was founded at a meeting at the Adelphi public house in 1867 and subsequently used a number of grounds – notably the Olive Grove (1887–99) – before settling in 1899 at Owlerton (renamed HILLSBOROUGH in 1914).

Having joined the League in 1892, the club quickly established themselves as one of the leading teams, causing several upsets in the FA Cup and finally winning the trophy for the first time in 1896 (with fur-ther wins in 1907 and 1935). They won the First Division championship for the first time in 1903, and a year later successfully defended the title; they won it again in 1929 and 1930 (they have also won the Second Division title five times). Wednesday's for-tunes have fallen off a little since the 1920s, when the side that included such players as striker Jimmy Seed, winger Ellis Rimmer, and full-back Ernie Blenkinsop was con-sidered the best the club had ever produced.

The lowest point of all came in the 1970s when Wednesday (whose reputation had already been tarnished by a bribes scandal involving several of their leading players) were demoted to the Third Division for the first time. The relegation shook the club's fans, of whom one of the most bitter was Ken Wood: unable to face the prospect of seeing the Owls playing the likes of South end United and Halifax, he announced his decision to emigrate:

> I've torn up my rosette in disgust, burnt my scarf and given my rattle away – there's nothing to keep me here.

A year later the side avoided relegation to the Fourth Division by a single point. Another disgruntled fan was Bob Montgomery who attempted (unsuccessfully) to take the club to court for their uninspiring performance in an FA Cup replay in 1983. Montgomery's argument ran that the game Wednesday had played had been so bad it was not football at all and thus an offence under the Trades Description Act, the club having obtained his entrance money (which he now demanded be given back to him) under false pretences.

By the mid-1980s, however, the team was back on form and in 1991 was able to celebrate winning the League Cup (which helped to restore spirits after the shock of the Hillsborough disaster in 1989). The 1992–93 season promised even better things, with the team reaching the Final of both the League Cup and the FA Cup – but ended in defeat in both competitions against Arsenal. Stars of the postwar era have numbered among them Derek Dooley, top goalscorer in the League in 1952–53 whose brief career ended with the loss of a leg after an accident on the pitch the following season, goalkeeper Ron Springett in the 1960s (eventually exchanged with Queen's Park Rangers for his brother Peter), and managers Harry Catterick, Jack CHARLTON, Howard Wilkinson, Ron ATKINSON, and Trevor FRANCIS. Famous fans of the club include Labour MP Roy Hattersley.

The side enjoyed their record victory to date back in 1891, when they beat Halliwell 12–0; their worst defeat was in 1912, when they were defeated 10–0 by Aston Villa. Andy Wilson holds the record for League appearances with the club, having played in 502 matches between 1900 and 1920.

> Hi, ho, Sheffield Wednesday,
> Anywhere you go, well, baby,
> I see my sun is shining,
> I won't make a fuss – though it's obvious.

Supporters' song, to the tune of Jeff Beck's 'Hi, Ho, Silver Lining' (also sung by Sheffield United fans)

Shelf, The The stand at Tottenham Hotspur's White Hart Lane ground which is home to loyal Spurs fans. Plans to demolish this part of the stands led to a heated conflict between the club and the fans in the late 1980s and resulted in an eventual compromise that allowed 3000 supporters to remain standing on The Shelf. The campaign to retain The Shelf even led to the creation of a fanzine dedicated to the struggle to keep it, aptly titled LOTS (Left On The Shelf).

Shepshed Albion English non-League football club, nicknamed the Raiders. Strip: red and blue striped shirts with red shorts and socks. Founded in 1891 and based at the Dovecote ground in Shepshed, the club now play in the Midland Combination League.

shielding Keeping the body between the ball and an opponent who is challenging for possession. More recently the term has been largely replaced by the word screening.

Shilton, Peter (1949–) English goalkeeper, who won acclaim as one of the finest keepers in the world during his long international career in the 1970s and 1980s. Shilton distinguished himself while still a schoolboy, winning the English Schools Trophy in 1965 with Leicester Boys and in the same year winning the first of four schoolboy caps for England. He joined Leicester City in 1966 as understudy to England goalkeeper Gordon BANKS and a year later inherited Banks's regular place in the team.

Highlights of his subsequent domestic career included an appearance in the FA Cup Final (which Leicester lost) in 1969, the winning of the Second Division championship in 1971, his transfer to Stoke City in 1974 and then to Nottingham Forest in 1977, his winning of the Players' Player of the Year award in 1978 (in which year Forest won the League championship), and an important role in Forest's two European Cup triumphs in 1979 and 1980. He continued his domestic career with Southampton (1982–87) and Derby County, to whom he transferred in 1987.

Shilton won his first full England cap in 1971 and went on to collect a record 125 caps before his retirement from the international game in 1990, after England's strong performance in the World Cup. He retired as a League player in 1992, when he became manager of Plymouth.

Shilton's record-breaking England career nearly ended at an early stage, when he said (after just 21 appearances in the national side) that he no longer wished to be considered for selection (the post of England keeper at that time regularly going to Ray Clemence).

Blessed with a pair of large hands that seemed capable of stopping any kind of shot, Shilton established a reputation as a particularly dedicated player, who trained rigorously and adopted a highly scientific approach to his role. *See also* BEST GOAL-KEEPER IN THE WORLD.

> *I've seen forwards get past me with all the confidence of a Pelé or a Johan Cruyff and then, faced by 'Shilts', suddenly lose their nerve. I mean, it's happened to me when I've tried to beat him in training. All he has to do is crouch a little bit, and he sort of spreads and fills the bloody goal up.*
>
> Larry Lloyd, *The Magnificent Obsession* (Jason Tomas, 1982)

shinguards Protective pads that are worn inside the socks to lessen the risk of injury to the legs from misdirected kicks. Sam Widdowson, who played for Nottingham Forest, is believed to have invented the very first shinguards (initially worn outside the socks) in 1874. In an age when hacking was an accepted feature of the game, players welcomed Widdowson's invention and shinguards soon became essential items in many kitbags. Edward Charles Bambridge of Corinthians and England used a single shinguard in a County Cup Final while recovering from a broken leg; the opposition aimed as many kicks as they could at the protected leg but failed to prevent Bambridge scoring a decisive goal – it was only after the game was over that they discovered that the wily Bambridge had fooled them by putting the shinguard on his uninjured leg.

Modern players almost invariably wear shinguards, although many players in the 1960s and 1970s – including George BEST – thought them unnecessary. In the 1940s Bolton Wanderers resorted to desperate measures when, on arriving at Middlesbrough railway station, the team's shinguards went missing: the trainer bought 22 paperback romantic novels from the railway bookstall to use instead.

shinning *See* PUBLIC SCHOOL FOOTBALL.

Shire Nickname of the Scottish football club EAST STIRLINGSHIRE.

shirts *See* COLOURS; NUMBERS.

shoot-out A controversial variation upon the conventional penalty shoot-out that was adopted by the NASL in the late 1970s.

According to the NASL's rules, a game that ended in a tie could be extended by 15 minutes sudden-death overtime; if this ended with both sides still equal then a single player, starting at the 35-yard line, faced the opposing goalkeeper alone, with just five seconds in which to score (the keeper was allowed to move off his line).

Shopkeepers Nickname of the Russian football club SPARTAK MOSCOW, in recognition of its links with the producers' co-operatives trade union, to which it was affiliated in the 1930s.

shorts In the earliest years of the game, players generally wore knickerbocker-style shorts though later a baggier style was adopted, with the legs reaching down to the player's knees. Shorts got shorter after World War II, partly in imitation of those worn by players in many warmer climates. Alex JAMES was especially famous for his extra baggy shorts; he adopted these after newspaper cartoonist Tom Webster drew him wearing such a pair to exaggerate his lack of height.

Shotputters Nickname of the US national side that participated in the first World Cup tournament (1930). The nickname was bestowed upon the US team by French players, who were duly impressed by the muscular appearance of several of the squad. In fact, the players concerned were all former-British professionals, mostly from Scotland, and it was their skill as well as their physical strength that carried the US team to 3-0 victories against both Belgium and Paraguay before finally going out against Yugoslavia. *See also* USA.

Shots Nickname of the former English League club ALDERSHOT.

Showbiz XI Football team comprising various celebrities, who play matches to raise money for charity. The great days of the Showbiz XI were in the 1950s and 1960s, when players with the side – which often appeared on television – included such names as Sean Connery (inside-left) and Des O'Connor (right wing). Some former professional players also made appearances with the side, among them England's Billy WRIGHT and manager Tommy DOCHERTY.

Shrewsbury Town English football club, nicknamed the Shrews. Strip: amber shirts with blue trim, blue shorts, and amber socks with blue trim. Also nicknamed Salop and simply Town, Shrewsbury were founded in 1886 but did not join the League until 1950, when they won election to the Third Division (North).

Based at GAY MEADOW, the club remained in the lower divisions until 1979, when they finally won promotion to the Second Division (where they remained until 1989). Their honours include the Third Division championship (1979) and six victories in the Welsh Cup (1891, 1938, 1977, 1979, 1984, and 1985); they also reached the quarter-finals of the FA Cup in 1979 and 1982 and the semi-finals of the League Cup in 1961.

Giant-killing achievements have included a victory over Wimbledon in the 1991 FA Cup. Notable players with the club have included striker Arthur ROWLEY, who became the highest goalscorer in the history of the League with 434 goals in 619 games in the 1950s.

The Shrews enjoyed their record victory in 1955, when they beat Swindon Town 7–0; they have suffered record defeats of 8–1 on two occasions, against Norwich City in the 1952–53 season and against Coventry City in 1963. Colin Griffith holds the record for League appearances with the club, having played in 406 games between 1975 and 1989.

> My old man said follow the Town,
> And don't dilly dally on the way,
> We'll take the Station End and all that's in it,
> All get your boots on, we'll be there in a minute,
> With bottles and spanners, hatchets and spanners,
> We don't care what the fucking coppers say,
> Cos we are the boys from the Gay, Gay Meadow,
> And the kings of football songs,
> The Shrewsbury! The Shrewsbury!
>
> Supporters' song, to the tune of 'My Old Man'

Shrimpers Nickname of the English football club SOUTHEND UNITED, in reference to the club's seaside location at Southend-on-Sea.

Shrimps Nickname of the English non-League football club MORECAMBE, reflecting the club's coastline location. The same nickname was also formerly applied to BRIGHTON AND HOVE ALBION for similar reasons.

Shrine, The Nickname of WINDSOR PARK, the home ground of the Northern Ireland football club Linfield.

Shrovetide football Primitive form of football that developed as a Shrove Tuesday tradition at a number of villages throughout England in medieval times, long before the codification of the modern game. Using a ball that might be a hog's head or anything else suitably shaped, huge crowds of enthusiastic participants (often representing neighbouring villages) battled to carry, kick, or otherwise transport the ball to their opponent's goal, playing on an unmarked 'pitch' that might include such features as streams, ponds, roads, and cottages. It was not uncommon for scores of injuries to result from the mayhem and deaths were reported from time to time as players strove to win the honour of scoring the vital goal.

The village of Ashbourne in Derbyshire is particularly famous for its tradition of Shrovetide football, which dates as far back as 217 AD. In the Ashbourne version there are no official rules or boundaries and the goals – a millwheel spindle and a stone plaque – are some two miles apart; features of the playing area include Henmore Brook, in which much of the fiercest play takes place. Players born above the brook are called Uppards, while those born below it are called Downards. The scorer of the winning goal is allowed to keep the ball (a heavy leather article made by a local craftsman). The tradition was threatened in 1860 when attempts were made to prevent any further games in the village, prompting an unknown writer to lament the 'Death of the Right Honourable Game Football' in a court circular that year:

> The deceased Gentleman was, we are informed, a native of Ashbourn, Derbyshire, at which place he was born in the Year of Grace, 217, and was consequently in the 1643rd year of his age. For some months the patriotic Old Man had been suffering from injuries sustained in his native town, so far back as Shrovetide in last year; he was at once removed (by appeal) to London, where he lingered in suspense till the law of death put its icy hand upon him, and claimed as another trophy to magisterial interference one who had long lived in the hearts of the people.

Though the case and the subsequent appeal went against the Ashbourne game, the tradition survived and boisterous 'matches' still take place each Shrove Tuesday, beginning at two o'clock in the afternoon and ending at 10 o'clock in the evening (in earlier years) it sometimes lasted until Ash Wednesday morning. Other homes of similar traditions include Alnwick in Northumberland, Sedgefield in Durham, Atherstone in Warwickshire, Corfe in Dorset, and Chester, where matches were staged on feast days between the town's shoemakers and the drapers.

> And nowe in the winter, when men kill the fat swine
> They get the bladder and blow it great and thin,
> With many beans and peason put within:
> It ratleth, soundeth, and shineth clere and fayre
> While it is throwen and caste up in the ayre,
> Each one contendeth and hath a great delite
> With foote and with hands the bladder for to smite;
> If it fail to grounde, they lifte it up agayne,
> But this waye to labour they count it no payne . . .

Medieval verse

sick as a parrot Cliché, meaning fed up or bitterly disappointed, that is particularly associated with football through its overuse by players and managers in the 1970s and 1980s. Together with its counterpart, 'over the moon', the phrase surfaced in football around 1978, when it began to be repeated in countless television and radio interviews. Among the first offenders to use the phrase was Liverpool's Phil Thompson, who quoted it after his team lost in the 1978 League Cup Final. Critics and comedians quickly learnt to ape footballers in general by adopting the phrase and it had acquired the status of cliché within two years.

Quite where the phrase came from is a matter for debate. Something very similar was being said as early as the 17th century, as evidenced by the dramas of the playwright and adventuress Aphra Behn, who used the phrase 'melancholy as a sick parrot'. The poet Robert Southey also used a similar phrase – 'sick as peeate' – in his dialect poem 'The Terrible Knitters e' Dent' (1834), using it to convey a sense of oppression that might be likened to a heavy turf of peat in the stomach. Links have also been suggested to the celebrated 'Dead Parrot' sketch performed by television's 'Monty Python' comedy team and to the spread of psittacosis (a virulent and communicable parrot disease that can be passed to man)

that was believed to be responsible for a number of deaths in West Africa in the early 1970s.

Another theory runs that the phrase was originally 'sick as a pierrot', a reference to the melancholy Pierrot character who was first developed in French theatre in the 18th century. Alternatively, the phrase may have been inspired by the activities of South American parrot smugglers of recent times, who are known to have drugged the birds with tequila to keep them quiet in transit.

Sierra Leone Sierra Leone joined FIFA in 1967 and have yet to make much impact on international competition. Strip: green, white, and blue shirts, white shorts, and blue socks with white trim.

Silkmen Nickname of the English non-League football club MACCLESFIELD TOWN, reflecting the town's history as a centre for the manufacture of silk.

Simod Cup English cup competition that was founded in 1987. The first winners of the Simod Cup were Reading, who beat Luton Town 4–1 in the 1988 Final. The Cup had trouble establishing itself as a popular fixture and at one time a joke ran to the effect that the only difference between the Simod Cup and the ears of 'Star Trek's' Mr Spock was that Spock's ears had a point to them. Before its demise in 1992 it was renamed the Zenith Data Systems Cup.

Sincil Bank The home ground of the English football club LINCOLN CITY. The club moved to Sincil Bank in 1894 from their previous home, called John O'Gaunt's or the Cow Pat (because cows were allowed to graze on the pitch). Named after Sincil Drain (a rivulet nearby), the ground proved popular with local fans. During World War I some matches had to be played behind closed doors after politicians blamed a shortage of shells at the front on workers who preferred to loiter in public houses and at football matches rather than get on with their duties at the munitions factories (one of which was situated near Lincoln's ground). Events in the ground's history since then have included a fire that destroyed a stand in 1924 and radical restructuring of the facilities to meet safety requirements in the 1980s (including the demolition of the Main Stand).

Sindelar, Matthias (1903–39) Austrian forward, nicknamed the Man of Paper, who was the inspiration behind the wunderteam that represented Austria in the early 1930s. Sindelar was a brilliant centre-forward who – despite his slight build – could evade the attentions of most defences and was also an excellent marksman. As well as winning 43 caps for his country, he also played for Hertha Vienna, Amateur, and FK Austria (with whom he enjoyed victory in two Austrian League championships and two Mitropa Cup competitions). He was of Jewish descent, and committed suicide by gassing himself after the Nazis took over.

Singapore Singapore joined FIFA in 1952 but have yet to establish an international reputation. Strip: all white.

Sitting On Top Of The World Title of pop song associated with Liverpool. It reached number 50 in the charts in 1986.

Sittingbourne English non-League football club. Strip: red and black striped shirts, with black shorts and socks. Founded in 1881 and based at the Roman Road ground in Sittingbourne, the team plays in the Southern League.

Sivori, Enrique Omar (1935–) Argentinian midfielder, who was one of the celebrated Trio of Death who transferred to Italy in the 1950s. Renowned for his attacking ability, Sivori was a star with River Plate before he moved in 1957 to Juventus, where he formed a brilliant partnership with John CHARLES – though his fiery temper sometimes got him into trouble. Having played 18 times for Argentina, he also made nine appearances for Italy and was a member of the Italian squad in the 1962 World Cup. He was acclaimed European Footballer of the Year in 1961 and went into management and television after his retirement as a player (playing his last games with Napoli).

six-yard box The small rectangle that surrounds the goal. Originally two six-yard semi-circles delineated the area from which goalkicks could be taken.

Skol Cup *See* SCOTTISH LEAGUE CUP.

Sky Blues Nickname of a number of football clubs which sport a light blue playing strip. They include COVENTRY CITY, famous for the 'Sky Blue' era of the 1960s, and the Scottish club FORFAR ATHLETIC.

Śląski Stadium The Polish national football stadium, in the Silesian city of Chorzów. Opened in 1956 with an international

between Poland and East Germany, the stadium is a huge superbowl with few distinguishing features. It is used for Cup Finals and other leading domestic fixtures as well as international matches. Crowds at the Śląski Stadium are noted for their vocal efforts, which are aided by the stadium's design to produce a Polish version of the Hampden Roar.

Slavia Prague Czech football club, which is the oldest surviving club in the country. Strip: red and white halved shirts, with white shorts and socks. Founded in 1892 and based at the Dr V. Vacka Stadium, Slavia Prague claimed 15 League championships between 1913 and 1947 and enjoyed their golden era in the 1930s and 1940s. The club also established an international reputation for its deeds in the Mitropa Cup competition. After the war, Slavia were briefly known as Dynamo, under pressure from the political authorities. Stars of the team back in the 1920s included the great Frantisek PLANICKA.

Slim Jim Nickname of the Scottish winghalf Jim BAXTER, in reference to his slender build.

Slough Town English non-League football club, nicknamed the Rebels. Strip: amber and blue hooped shirts with blue shorts and socks (a colour scheme that led to the team being called the Wasps in pre-war times). Founded in 1890 and based at Wexham Park Stadium in Slough, the club play in the Conference.

Small Heath *See* BIRMINGHAM CITY.

smash and grab Nickname of the playing style that was adopted by Arsenal under Herbert CHAPMAN in the early 1930s. In an era when the Gunners were without question the foremost team in the country, their tactics typically consisted of snatching possession as ruthlessly as necessary and then quickly launching a devastating attack before the opposition's defence had a chance to organize itself. It was the epitome of a new type of inspirational football which ran counter to the more traditional game in which players gave themselves space and time to deliver accurate passes that formed part of a thought-out plan of attack.

Smith, G(ilbert) O(swald) (1872–1943) Celebrated English centre-forward, who was one of the great amateur stars of the Oxford University, Old Carthusians, Corinthians, and England teams in the 1890s and described as the finest footballer of his generation and football's equivalent of cricket's W.G. Grace (who was also famous enough to be known by his initials).

As an international Smith scored no fewer than 12 goals in just 20 matches for England between 1892 and 1893. He had immense shooting power, and could dribble and pass accurately. In the great tradition of Victorian sportsmen he did not confine his interests to football alone and was much respected as a cricketer, playing at the top level for Surrey. Outside sport he was a headmaster and author.

> *A genius in football he was. Like all geniuses he rose on stepping stones of his real self by taking infinite pains in terms of his natural gifts . . . he was as straight and hard a shot as I have ever met except perhaps only Steve Bloomer of Derby County, on one of Steve's special days. G.O.'s was every day.*
>
> C.B. Fry

Smith, Jim (1940–) One of the most successful managers of the 1980s, nicknamed Bald Eagle, who has worked for such clubs as Oxford United (where he clashed with Robert MAXWELL), Queen's Park Rangers, and Newcastle United.

> *People think it's all the good life managing a First Division club. But it doesn't feel glamorous driving from Newcastle to my home at Oxford on a Saturday when we've just lost. The only stop is for fish and chips at Wetherby. Mind you, they're good fish and chips.*
>
> Jim Smith

Smith, Tommy (1945–) English footballer, nicknamed the Anfield Iron, who acquired a reputation as one of the hardest men in the First Division in the 1960s and 1970s. Born locally, he joined Liverpool at the invitation of Bill SHANKLY and became one of the pillars upon which the great manager built his team. His team mate Emlyn Hughes called him 'the king of them all . . . the best pro I've ever met'.

> *Tommy very nice man, very nice player.*
>
> Ossie Ardiles

Smokey Nickname of the English forward Alan SHEARER, in reference to his well-publicized weakness for smokey bacon-flavoured crisps.

Snatch of the Day (1) The controversial deal that was struck between the Football League and the ITV television organization in the late 1970s. Nicknamed in reference to the popular BBC programme 'Match of the Day', the deal threatened to give ITV exclusive rights to televise matches, thus establishing a virtual monopoly; fortunately for the BBC, the deal was eventually prohibited by the Office of Fair Trading.

(2) The commercial agreement that gave the BSkyB television company the rights to broadcast Premier League matches when the new League was inaugurated in 1992. The battle to televise Premier League games was hotly contested between BSkyB and ITV and there was a series of highly publicized personal clashes before the issue was settled (for a price in excess of £300 million).

soccer Alternative name for Association Football. Many British fans dislike the term and insist on preferring the word 'football', though the 'soccer' tag (derived from the word 'Association') does in fact date back to the earliest history of the organized game. Oxford University and England international (and subsequently FA vice-president) Charles Wreford Brown is credited (or blamed) for coining the word back in the 1880s, when in reply to a query as to whether he intended to play rugger one afternoon, he replied: 'No, I am going to play soccer'.

Wreford Brown's new word reflected the contemporary fashion at Oxford for words ending '–er' (others including 'swotter', 'mugger', and another synonym for football – 'footer') and quickly caught on. The term is in general use in the USA, where 'football' is understood to refer solely to American 'grid-iron' football (which evolved from much the same roots as rugby football).

Soccer Bowl Name given to the Final that decided the NASL championship when it was in existence from the late 1960s to the mid 1980s. Inspired by the better-known 'Rose Bowl' Finals of American Football, the Soccer Bowl was a showpiece for US soccer and many finals were closely fought. The most successful club in the history of the Soccer Bowl was New York Cosmos, winner of five Championship titles. Attempts to lure larger crowds to the ailing NASL in 1984 by splitting the Soccer Bowl into a best-of-three series of games failed to save the League.

Soccer Conspiracy Case Infamous trial that resulted in the imprisonment of three celebrated English footballers – Peter Swan, David Layne (holder of 19 caps), and Tony Kay – in 1965. The scandal began with allegations in the *People* newspaper that the three players, all stars of Sheffield Wednesday, had conspired to prevent their team winning a match in order to win money on bets made on the result of the game. The ensuing investigation blackened the image of English football and led many to wonder how many games were being rigged for financial gain. After the trial, on charges of conspiracy to defraud, all three players were suspended for life by the FA. Their careers were ruined and the chance Tony Kay clearly had of being included in Alf RAMSEY's World Cup-winning squad in 1966 (he would have taken Nobby Stiles's place) was lost. Another seven less well-known players were also found guilty of similar offences and were gaoled for terms ranging from six months to four years.

> *He has given up for £100 what has in fact been one of the greatest careers of any footballer. He was tempted once, and fell.*

Counsel for the defence of Tony Kay

Soccer War The four-day war between the Latin American countries of El Salvador and Honduras, which is popularly supposed to have been triggered by a series of clashes between the two countries in the 1970 World Cup. El Salvador and Honduras met in a sequence of three matches that year before El Salvador emerged with a strong chance of winning a coveted place in the Finals. The games were marred by crowd violence and much ill-feeling between both sides, which reflected long-standing tensions between the two states.

Three days before the final game diplomatic relations between the two countries were broken off and shortly after El Salvador won the play-off to carry on their World Cup campaign troops began border incursions. An air attack by El Salvador on the airport at Tegucigalpa signalled all-out hostilities, which continued for four days until international pressure led to a ceasefire.

In fact, the war was less the outcome of the three football matches than it was the result of repressive measures taken by the Honduran government against El Salvadoreans living in Honduras, which in turn were inspired by complex internal economic and social problems in both states, particularly involving land ownership. Nonetheless, the three football games were seen as the spark that ignited the inferno and the conflict has ever since been popularly dubbed the Soccer War. *See also* SUPERSTITIONS.

Socceroos Nickname of the national team that represents AUSTRALIA (through the amalgamation of 'soccer' and 'kangaroo'). The nickname was heard on many lips during the 1974 World Cup Finals campaign, the first for which Australia had ever qualified. To their credit, the Socceroos provided stiff opposition against East Germany, West Germany, and Chile before going out of the competition.

Solihull Borough English non-League football club, nicknamed Boro. Strip: all red. Based at Moor Green, Boro play in the Southern League.

Solomon Islands The Solomon Islands joined FIFA in 1988, but have yet to make their mark in international competition.

Solway Star Former Scottish League football club. Based at Kimmetton Park in Annan, Dumfriesshire, Solway Star were members of the League from 1923 to 1926.

Somalia Somalia joined FIFA in 1960 but have as yet played only a minor role in international competition. Strip: sky blue shirts, with white shorts and socks.

Somerset Park The home ground of the Scottish football club AYR UNITED. The club arrived at Somerset Park in 1888 and subsequently became its owners in 1920, after which they set about extensive redevelopment of the site. Ayr shared the venue with Morton for a period in the 1950s. The Main Stand at Somerset Park is none too substantial and has over the years attracted the derision of visiting fans, as illustrated by a chant heard from rival Kilmarnock supporters:

> *Who's the clown who built your stand,*
> *Lego! Lego!*
> *Who's the clown who built your stand,*
> *Lego, Legoland!*

Son of God (1) Nickname of the Italian footballer Renzo DE VECCHI.

(2) The former Hereford United goalkeeper David Icke caused a considerable stir in the media in 1990 when he claimed to be the Son of God and his career as a football journalist was abruptly curtailed.

Sons Nickname of the Scottish football club DUMBARTON, originally given as 'Sons of the Rock' (thought to be a reference to the hill on which Dumbarton Castle stands).

soule Primitive form of football that was played by the Normans. It is thought possible that the Normans may well have introduced their game of soule to England after the invasion of 1066.

Souness, Graeme (1953–) Scottish player and manager, nicknamed Champagne Charlie or otherwise known as Souey or The Boss, who emerged as one of the most talented and controversial personalities in British football in the 1980s. Born in Edinburgh, Souness became a schoolboy international in 1968, in which year he signed for Tottenham Hotspur. He transferred to Middlesbrough in 1973 and helped them win the Second Division title a year later. In 1975 he won the first of 54 caps for Scotland, eventually becoming the team's captain.

Souness began his celebrated association with Liverpool in 1978 after a record transfer and collected with them a grand total of five League championship medals, three European Cup winners' medals, and four League Cup medals. He became one of the great stars to appear with the club, but his ruthless behaviour on the field and his energetic life off it provoked mixed reactions. The press made much mileage out of his reputation for high-living and even his fellow players were moved to comment on his rather deliberate attempts to court attention of all kinds – Scotland's Archie Gemmill made the rueful observation: 'If he was a chocolate drop, he'd eat himself'.

For his own part, Souness denied the justice in his reputation as one of the hard men of British football in his autobiography *No Half Measures* (1985), arguing: 'There is black and white proof I'm not the killer I'm supposed to be. I've only been sent off twice.'

Manager Tommy DOCHERTY, however, was one of many who preferred the version given elsewhere, and claimed: 'They serve a drink in Glasgow called the Souness – one half and you're off.'

In 1984 Souness moved to the Italian club Sampdoria and two years later began his managerial career as player-manager of Rangers. As a manager he displayed the same toughness and determination he had shown as a player, provoking similar controversy on a regular basis. Under his leadership Rangers prospered, although his unexpected departure for Liverpool in 1991

was the subject of much bitterness north of the border.

He stirred up more controversy when he allowed the *Sun* newspaper to publish stories about his love-life but received somewhat more sympathetic coverage in the media in 1992 when he underwent a highly publicized heart bypass operation.

South American Championship International tournament between the countries of South America, which was founded in 1916. This prestigious competition has changed its form several times over the years and was nearly dropped altogether in the 1960s (when it was not contested for eight years) but is now held every four years. Argentina and Uruguay have won the Championship more times than any of the other ten competing nations.

South American Cup *See* COPA LIBERTA-DORES.

South American Gullitt Nickname of the Colombian footballer Carlos VALDER-RAMA.

South Korea South Korea joined FIFA in 1948 and have been present in three World Cup Finals (1954, 1986, and 1990) but have yet to progress beyond the opening stages of the competition. Strip: all red. South Korea qualified for the 1994 World Cup in America.

South Midlands League Junior league that covers the home counties. The League acquired its present title in 1929 and has been dominated over the years by such teams as Barton Rovers, winners of eight Premier Division titles, and Baldock Town, who have won the Championship four times.

Southall English non-League football club, nicknamed the Fowlers. Strip: red and white. Founded in 1871 and based at the Western Road ground, Southall play in the Isthmian League.

Southampton English football club, nicknamed the Saints. Strip: red and white striped shirts, black shorts, and white socks with red trim.

Southampton were founded in 1885 as Southampton St Mary's (a curate of St Mary's taking the post of first president of the club) and settled at their permanent home at the DELL in 1898 but did not join the League (as founder members of the

Third Division) until 1920. In the meantime they reached two FA Cup Finals (1900 and 1902). They won promotion to the Second Division as Third Division (South) champions in 1922 and remained there for 30 years before dropping down for another seven years in 1953. Star players of the postwar period included defender Alf RAMSEY and striker Charlie Wayman.

Third Division champions in 1960, the club tasted life in the First Division for the first time in 1966 with a side that boasted such talents as Terry Paine, Martin Chivers, and Mick Channon. Relegation to the Second Division followed under manager Lawrie MCMENEMY in 1974, but two years later he took them to victory in the FA Cup for the first time, beating Manchester United 1–0 thanks to a goal by Bobby Stokes (who was rewarded with the prize of a car, despite the fact that he could not drive). They returned to the First Division in 1978 and were subsequently losing semi-finalists in the League Cup (1979) and runners-up in the League championship (1984), at which time stars included Alan BALL, Kevin KEEGAN, and Peter SHILTON.

The Saints enjoyed record victory margins of six goals in 1961, when they beat Ipswich Town 7–1, and in 1965, when they beat Wolverhampton Wanderers 9–3; they suffered their worst defeat in 1971, losing 8–0 against Tottenham Hotspur. Terry Paine holds the record for League appearances with the club, having played in 713 games between 1956 and 1974.

The team badge, combining a halo, a football, and a tree among other details, was the result of a competition held in 1974 (the tree referring to the Dell's former status as a wooded hollow). See also ALE HOUSE BRAWLERS.

> Twas back in 1976, upon the first of May,
> We all went up to Wembley to see
>   Southampton play,
> We showed 'em how to drink the beer,
> We showed 'em how to sup,
> We even showed United how to win the
>   Cup . . .

Supporters' song, to the tune of 'The Wild Rover'

Southend United English football club, nicknamed the Shrimpers. Strip: blue shirts with yellow trim, blue shorts with blue trim, and blue socks. Founded in 1906, the Shrimpers (sometimes nicknamed the Blues after the team colours) were based at ROOTS HALL at their foundation and again from 1955. They joined the League in 1920 and remained members of one of the bottom two divisions until finally winning promotion to the Second Division in 1991. Their single title remains the Fourth Division championship won in 1981 in a season in which they established 17 club records, including 30 victories and a period of 985 minutes without conceding a goal.

The club has had a good disciplinary record over the years: between joining the League in 1920 and 1952 not one single player with the team was sent off in a total of 1027 Third Division (North) matches.

Southend have enjoyed record 10–1 victories on three occasions, against Golders Green in 1934, against Brentwood in 1968, and against Aldershot in 1990; they suffered their worst defeat in 1965, losing 9–1 to Brighton and Hove Albion. Sandy Anderson, one of the few star players to appear for the club, holds the record for League appearances with the team, having played in 451 games between 1950 and 1963.

Of all rivals, Southend found Swansea City to be among the most formidable, failing to record an away victory against them in a total of 17 games between 1920 and 1991, when they finally broke the jinx with a 4–1 win.

> Oh, we do like to be beside the seaside,
> Oh, we do like to be beside the sea,
> With our bucket and spades,
> And our fucking hand grenades,
> Beside the seaside,
> Beside the sea.

Supporters' song

Southern League One of the junior Leagues that feeds into the Conference and thus into the Football League itself. The Southern League (later known as the Beazer Homes League after its sponsors) was founded in 1893 as a counterpart to the Football League (which then consisted solely of northern clubs) and numbered amongst its members such clubs as Luton Town, Millwall, Swindon Town, and Tottenham Hotspur – who won the 1901 FA Cup as a Southern League side. The Football League gradually absorbed most of the leading Southern League sides and the organizers struggled to keep the numbers up (at one point, in 1907–08, they even enlisted Bradford Park Avenue, a full 130 miles north of the nearest Southern League rival, Northampton).

Eventually the clubs that fought in the Southern League were elected to form the Football League's Third Division and the League shrank somewhat, being dominated between the wars by reserve sides of the major clubs. It was reorganized after World War II as a leading semi-professional league and now has a Premier Division and two regionalized Divison Ones (Midland and South). The winning club usually exchanges places with the bottom-placed team in the Conference. League clubs that have emerged from the ranks of the Southern League have included Cambridge United, Oxford United, and Wimbledon.

Southport English non-League football club, nicknamed the Sandgrounders. Strip: gold and black shirts, black shorts, and gold and black socks. Founded as Southport Central in 1881 and based at the Haig Avenue ground in Southport, the Sandgrounders were founder members of the Third Division (North) in 1921 and remained in the League until 1978, after which they played in the Northern Premier League until 1993, when they won promotion to the Conference.

Soviet Union The former national team of the now defunct Soviet Union had a proud record in international competition. Honours won by the side included victory in the 1956 Olympics and in the very first European Championship (1960). In the World Cup, the team got as far as the quarter-finals in 1958 and 1962 and finished fourth in 1966. Stars of the side over the years included the near-legendary goalkeeper Lev YASHIN and centre-forward Nikita Simonian. When the Soviet Union broke up in the late 1980s the team – victors in the 1988 Olympics – was restyled the Commonwealth of Independent States and then split up into the various states of the former union. Russia qualified for the 1994 World Cup in America. Strip: red shirts, white shorts, and red socks.

Spain The Spanish national team has yet to match the achievements of such prestigious domestic sides as Real Madrid, despite the presence of such individual stars as Ferenc PUSKAS and Alfredo DI STEFANO. In terms of the World Cup, Spain has never done better than reach fourth place (achieved back in 1950) – though the team did win the European Championship in 1964. Hosting the World Cup itself in 1982 did nothing to boost the side's performance but Spain qualified for the 1994 World Cup in America. Strip: red shirts, blue shorts, and black socks with yellow trim.

Sparky Nickname of the Welsh forward Mark HUGHES.

Sparta Prague Czech football club, which is recognized as the most successful (and popular) of all Czech teams. Strip: red shirts, white shorts, and black socks. Founded in 1893 and based at the LETNÁ STADIUM in Prague, Sparta have won some 24 League titles as well as eight Cup victories, enjoying golden eras in the 1920s and 1980s in particular. They notched up doubles of League and Cup wins in 1984, 1988, and 1989. On the international stage, Sparta were one of the clubs to dominate the history of the Mitropa Cup, winning it the first time it was contested (1927) and again in 1935. For a time after World War II the team played under the title Spartak Sokolovo (a name change dictated by the political authorities).

Spartak Moscow Russian football club, nicknamed the Shopkeepers. Strip: red shirts with white hoop, with white shorts and socks. Founded in 1922, Spartak are one of the best-supported teams in the country. Based at the LENIN STADIUM in Moscow, the Shopkeepers have a distinguished history, having won 12 League championships and nine Cup titles. Their golden era was in the late 1950s and early 1960s, though they failed to clinch any of the major European honours. The club's fans have a somewhat notorious reputation as the worst-behaved supporters in Russian football.

Remarkable matches in the history of the team include occasions during World War II when two Spartak sides played football on an artificial pitch temporarily laid in Red Square, with commentary of the game being relayed to beleaguered troops at the front as a morale-boosting exercise.

special A specially arranged train that is laid on specifically to transport fans to a match. The very first football special ran as long ago as 1881, when a train took Dumbarton supporters to see the Scottish Cup Final against Queen's Park. In more recent times the provision of special trains has been threatened by vandalism from a minority of fans, which has led to many trains having to be taken out of service.

spectacles *See* GLASSES.

spend, spend, spend! The reaction of Viv Nicholson, a Yorkshire housewife married to a trainee miner, whose life was utterly changed when in 1961 she and her husband Keith won £152,000 on the Littlewoods football Pools. The Nicholsons' win is often recalled now as a modern morality tale on the ageless theme of the corrupting power of money. Though the Nicholsons welcomed their good fortune – Viv's 'spend, spend, spend' being quoted in national newspaper headlines – the dream soon turned sour. Keith Nicholson died in a car crash and Viv went through a series of husbands until all the money was gone. At the end of it all she was back in a small house in the Yorkshire town of Castleford and, having survived indulgence in alcohol and drugs, had found solace in religion as a Jehovah's Witness. She wrote a sobering account of her life after the big win under the title *Spend, Spend, Spend* in 1977, which was also used by playwright Jack Rosenthal as the title of a television play (1977) about her experience.

Spiders Nickname of the Scottish football club QUEEN'S PARK, in reference to the team colours.

Spion Kop *See* KOP.

Spireites Nickname of the English football club CHESTERFIELD, in reference to the town's famous twisted church spire.

spitting Instances of players spitting at one another or at officials have become all too frequent in recent years. Accepted stoically by many participants as a minor irritation that must be endured in silence, the habit does little to improve the tarnished image of football in the public mind and offenders are consequently sometimes sternly reprimanded. In 1972, for instance, two Italian players in the Canadian National League were punished for spitting at the referee – one being suspended for 18 months and the other for no fewer than four years. An official explained the discrepancy between the two punishments somewhat laconically: 'One spit missed, the other spit hit'.

> *Spitting is part and parcel of the game now.*
> George Graham (1991)

> *As one of my old managers said, you just have to swallow it.*
> Gary Lineker, on being spat at (1991)

sponsorship The injection of finance from commercial enterprises in exchange for promotion of a company's products or name. Sponsorship in football is not a new idea. Back in 1904, for instance, the construction of Tottenham Hotspur's White Hart Lane ground was greatly assisted by the proprietors of the neighbouring White Hart public house, who saw the opportunity for a major increase in sales. Similarly, match programmes carried advertisements by local businesses as early as the 1890s.

The concept really took off, however, in the 1970s, when football was in dire need of new sources of revenue. The first sponsored English League tournament was the Watney Cup, a pre-season tournament inaugurated in 1971; in Scotland it was the Dryborough Cup. In 1976 Kettering Town became the first English club to have advertising on their shirts (the FA subsequently demanded that this be removed, but a compromise was eventually reached with the shirts carrying a single letter rather than the full name of the sponsor). The first Scottish club to carry advertising on their shirts was Hibernian.

Soon teams were queuing up to sign sponsorship deals, notably with manufacturers of sports clothing and equipment, who expected players to wear and use their own products. This did not always suit the players themselves, who were known to resort to such tactics as painting the required logos on their old boots so as not to have to wear a different make.

It has also become customary to rename established tournaments after their sponsors. The League Cup, for instance, has been named after its sponsors since 1982 (being retitled the Milk Cup, the Littlewoods Cup, the Rumbelows Cup, and the Coca-Cola Cup). The Football League itself was first sponsored by commercial concerns in 1986 (its sponsors to date have been the Canon electronics company, the *Today* newspaper, Barclays Bank, and Endsleigh Insurance). Commercial arrangements have also been made with non-League football and in regard to the new Premier League.

Hackles were raised throughout football, however, when the FA hesitatingly approved a lucrative deal that would mean sponsorship of the FA Cup by the Australian Elders lager brewing company (who would have retitled it the Fosters Cup): in the end the deal foundered over the amount involved and the Cup remained free of commercial influence to the relief of most fans.

Other companies have sponsored the Manager of the Month and other awards and such related enterprises as annual football publications.

Virtually every professional club has its sponsor (as evidenced by the names of commercial concerns now emblazoned on team strips throughout the land) and even national teams receive similar assistance (the 1990 England World Cup squad, for instance, were sponsored by Trebor Mints). When England agreed to sponsorship by Admiral under Don REVIE in the 1970s the team went to the extent of abandoning their traditional black and white strip in favour of a red, white, and blue outfit bearing the company's logo – a move that found little favour with fans, who welcomed the return of the old colour scheme a few years later.

North of the border, a company wishing to support Celtic or Rangers solved the problem of partisanship by providing funds for both clubs.

One of the more unusual sponsorship deals was that struck between a computer company and Aldershot in 1991: under the terms of the agreement the players wore jock straps carrying the company's name. *See also* TEXACO CUP.

Sporting Nickname of many clubs around the world that have 'Sporting' in their full name (for instance, the Spanish clubs Sporting Gijón and SPORTING LISBON and the Belgian club ANDERLECHT).

Sporting Lisbon Portuguese football club, nicknamed the Lions. Strip: green and white hooped shirts, black shorts, and green and white socks. Founded in 1906, the club are famous for their long-standing rivalry with Benfica (and Porto, one of the two other leading Portuguese sides) and can claim to be Portugal's largest and most popular club.

Based at the JOSÉ ALVALADE STADIUM, the team had its origins among Lisbon's aristocracy and consists of not just the football team but also another 140 clubs devoted to a range of sports, with a combined membership of 100,000. The club have a glorious record in the Portuguese League, having won the Championship 16 times and have captured the Cup on 15 occasions. Other honours include the European Cup Winners' Cup in 1964.

Stars of the side over the years have included the celebrated line-up of five forwards nicknamed the Five Violins who led the attack during the side's most prosperous era in the late 1940s and 1950s. The club's recent history has, unfortunately, been somewhat marred by crowd disturbances and debts.

spot-the-ball Football competition that is run by the Pool Promoters' Association. Entrants in the competition must guess the exact position of the concealed ball in a photograph taken during a match. In recent years, funds from the competition have helped towards the cost of safety work and other improvements at grounds around the country.

Springfield Park The home ground of the English football club WIGAN ATHLETIC. A popular sports park where horse-trotting and other events were staged as far back as 1897, Springfield Park has played host to five separate incarnations of the football club (Wigan County, Wigan Town, Wigan United, Wigan Borough, and, from 1932, Wigan Athletic). Incidents in the ground's history have included a fire in 1953, the erection of the existing Main Stand a year later, and the arrival of floodlights in 1965.

Spurs Nickname of the English football club TOTTENHAM HOTSPUR.

square pass A pass in which the ball travels sideways across the pitch from one player to another.

Sri Lanka Sri Lanka joined FIFA in 1950, but have not as yet made much impact on international competition. Strip: maroon and gold shirts, with white shorts and socks.

Stadio Nuovo The dramatic new football ground in Bari, which was created especially for the 1990 World Cup. Home of Bari AS, the current stadium replaced the Vittoria Stadium, which had been built by the Fascists to celebrate Italy's role in World War I (in the hope that such acknowledgements of past military prowess would assist in motivating the country's armed forces). Mussolini himself opened the Vittoria Stadium in 1934 and Bari AS settled there three months later. The venue suffered badly from bombs during World War II, but was also used by the Allies for a match between Bari and a British army team whose manager was Matt BUSBY, then an army officer. It continued to be used by Bari and the Italian national team after World War II but was eventually superseded by the Stadio Nuovo in the district of Carbonara in 1990.

Designed by the leading Italian architect Renzo Piano, whose other works include the co-design of the Pompidou Centre in Paris, the breathtaking new stadium is a distinctive superbowl incorporating such features as an underground road for use in emergencies and by VIPs. Construction of the stadium was complicated by the uncovering of an ancient settlement on the site; the final designs were altered to prevent this being disturbed.

Stadium of Light Football stadium in Lisbon that is home to the Portuguese football club BENFICA. The Estádio da Luz (to give its Portuguese name) lies in the Luz (Light) district of Lisbon, hence the venue's distinctive title. Benfica had five different homes before finally settling at the Stadium of Light in 1954. Appropriately enough, the venue saw the first modern experiments with floodlit football in Portugal in 1958. With Benfica the dominant club of the 1960s and 1970s, the stadium was further developed with an extra tier of seating being added in the late 1970s, making it (in 1982) the largest football stadium in Europe (with a capacity of 120,000).

Features of the ground include a giant metal eagle over the west entrance, a museum holding no fewer than 15,000 trophies, a portrait gallery depicting past presidents of the club, and hundreds of tiles bearing the names of supporters who donated money towards the stadium.

Stadium of Pneumonia Nickname of the José Zorilla Stadium in Valladolid.

Stafford Rangers English non-League football club, nicknamed Boro. Strip: black and white. Founded around 1876 and based at the Marston Road ground, Boro played in a number of different leagues before and after World War II but have spent most of their recent history in the GM Vauxhall Conference. They captured the FA Trophy in 1972 and 1979.

Stags Nickname of the English football club MANSFIELD TOWN, in reference to the deer of nearby Sherwood Forest.

Staines Town English non-League football club, nicknamed the Swans, reflecting the town's location on the River Thames. Strip: gold shirts with royal blue trim, with blue shorts and socks. Founded in 1892 and based at Wheatsheaf Park in Staines, the club play in the Isthmian League.

Stair Park The home ground of the Scottish football club STRANRAER. The club settled at Stair Park (so-called because the park had been given to the town by the Earl of Stair) in 1907. The ground was substantially developed in the 1930s but continued until 1985 to have the smallest capacity of any League venue in Britain. In 1981 it became the last Scottish League football

ground to have floodlighting installed. Though Stranraer play in the Scottish League, Stair Park is actually closer to Ireland than it is to Glasgow and on the same latitude as Newcastle.

Stalybridge Celtic English non-League football club, nicknamed Celtic. Strip: royal blue. Founded in 1911 and based at Bower Fold in Stalybridge, Celtic were Football League members from 1921 to 1923, but now play in the Conference.

Stamford Bridge The home ground of the English football club CHELSEA. Stamford Bridge is unique in English football as the only ground to have been built before its occupying club was even founded.

Before the ground was built the land upon which it stood had been used as a market garden. In 1896 the land was bought by H.A. Mears, whose ambition was to create the best football venue in London. He and his brother, J.T. Mears finally gained possession of the site in 1904, but an offer for the land by the Great Western railway company, in search of a marshalling yard, looked too good to refuse. A friend defended the original football plan and was bitten on the leg by H.A. Mears's dog for his trouble – but his reaction to the incident was so reasonable that he got his way and the railway company was turned down.

The stadium – then the second largest in the country – was built in 1905 and, as no existing club could be persuaded to move to it, it acquired its own resident team – Chelsea – that same year (though initially it consisted of only directors and no players). As the banking was raised for the terraces workmen came across a hoard of old coins but, believing them to be valueless, they left them where they were; this cache of now prized spade guineas still lies somewhere beneath the West Stand.

The ground proved an immediate success and, prior to the opening of Wembley in 1923, hosted three FA Cup Finals. Curiosities of the ground at the time included a weather-vane depicting a ball and a footballer (supposed to be George 'Gatling-Gun' Hilsdon, who was crippled by mustard gas in World War I); local superstition had it that if the weather-vane ever came down so would the club's fortunes.

The ground became a leading greyhound stadium in the 1930s and also hosted speedway races (the last dogs raced here in 1968). Improvements were made in the 1960s and a massive new East Stand was erected. Down came the weather-vane – and, as predicted, so did the club's fortunes; a long run of success came to an abrupt end with relegation and declining crowds, which, combined with the cost of the East Stand, led to a financial crisis.

Ownership of the ground passed to a property company who planned a huge building development that would mean the club leaving its home for good. Chairman Ken Bates launched an appeal to save Stamford Bridge and finally, after much wrangling, he acquired a large stake in the company then owning the site, thus placing the future of the ground on a somewhat firmer footing. The club's luck on the field has also improved somewhat since a copy of the old weather-vane was reinstated on the top of the West Stand.

Features of the contemporary ground include the infamous South Stand, nicknamed The Shed, where the club's most dedicated (and sometimes violent) fans congregate; it was largely due to the activities of the occupants of The Shed that Stamford Bridge became in 1972 the first ground to be equipped with security fencing (for a time lined with electric wires until these were removed for safety reasons).

Standard Liège Belgian football club, which was the first Belgian side to gain an international reputation. Strip: red shirts, white shorts, and red socks. Founded in 1898 and based at the SCLESSIN Stadium in Liège, the club won the League championship eight times between 1958 and 1983 and can also boast five Cup wins (1954, 1966, 1967, 1981, and 1993). Standard have also reached the semi-finals of the European Cup (1962) and the Final of the European Cup Winners' Cup (1982). A bribery scandal in 1984 led to the president, coach, and captain of the team being banned.

Stans Nickname of the English football club BRADFORD PARK AVENUE, after the cartoon character of *Bernard of the Bantams*.

Stark's Park The home ground, in Kirkcaldy, of the Scottish football club RAITH ROVERS. Rovers settled at Stark's Park (named after a local councillor, Robert Stark) in 1891. Councillor Stark himself once restored order during a pitch invasion by letting loose a bull kept next to the ground. Events in the ground's history have included gale damage in 1911, a fire in 1918, the building of a new stand in 1922, and the arrival of floodlights in 1960.

Station Park The home ground of the Scottish football club FORFAR ATHLETIC. Forfar made Station Park their home in 1888. Events in the ground's history have included gales which did extensive damage before the venue even opened and again in 1893, the building of the first large stand in 1919, the loss of the roof of this stand in another gale in 1921, a visit by the future George VI and Queen Elizabeth, and after further gale damage in the 1950s the erection of a gale-proof stand (funds for which were raised by such ideas as cooking the largest 'bridie' pie – containing meat and onions – ever made). Further improvements were made in the 1970s and 1980s.

Steaua Bucharest Romanian football club, which is the team of the Romanian army. Strip: all red. Founded in 1947 and based at the STEAUA STADIUM in Bucharest, Steaua have won some 15 League titles and 18 Cup victories over the years but enjoyed their greatest moment of triumph in 1986, when they became the first Romanian side to capture the European Cup. They have also achieved the double of League and Cup titles three years in succession (1987–89).

Steaua Stadium The home ground of the Romanian football club STEAUA BUCHAREST. The Star Stadium, as it is translated from Romanian, was originally used for youth football until, in 1974, it was taken over by Steaua Bucharest. It remained a relatively modest stadium until the late 1980s, when an ambitious modernization plan was begun. Steaua Bucharest being the army team, the stadium is kept clean and tidy by troops from the barracks next door.

> *Steaua, don't forget we want victory!*
>
> Sign above players' tunnel at the Steaua Stadium

Steelmen Nickname of the English non-League football club CORBY TOWN, in reference to the town's former status as a centre of the steel-manufacturing industry.

Stein, Jock (John Stein; 1922–85) The great Scottish football manager, nicknamed the Big Man, who won fame for his leadership of Celtic in their golden era in the late 1960s. Admired for his honesty, toughness, and modesty, the Big Man – who worked as a miner while still a boy – began his career as a player in 1942, appearing for Albion Rovers and subsequently Llanelli (1950) and Celtic (1951–55). He led Celtic to the League and Cup double in 1954 before injury forced him to take up the role of reserve team coach in 1955.

After spells as manager with Dunfermline Athletic and Hibernian, Stein rejoined Celtic as manager in 1964 and immediately set about restoring the club's ailing fortunes. In 1966 the club won the first in an extraordinary series of nine consecutive Scottish Championships, adding the European Cup in 1967 (his most glorious moment) and a further League title in 1977; he also notched up eight victories with the club in the SCOTTISH CUP.

In 1978, after he was dismissed by Celtic, he took over the roles of manager of Leeds United and of the Scottish national team. It was as Scotland ended a 1–1 draw against Wales at Ninian Park, thereby qualifying for the 1986 World Cup finals, that Stein succumbed to a heart attack and died.

> Jock had everything. He had the knowledge; he had that nasty bit that managers must have; and he could communicate. On top of it all, he was six feet tall, and sometimes he seemed to get bigger when he was talking to you. He was the best.
>
> Graeme Souness, Jock Stein, The Authorized Biography (Ken Gallacher; 1988)

> John – you're immortal.
>
> Bill Shankly (1967)

Stenhousemuir Scottish football club, nicknamed the Warriors. Strip: maroon shirts with silver pinstripe, white shorts, and maroon socks with white trim. Founded in 1884 and based at OCHILVIEW PARK, the club joined the League as members of the Second Division in 1921 and have since had a relatively undistinguished history, having picked up no major honours.

Among the few occasions when the club has hit the headlines was a match-fixing scandal in 1925, when unsuccessful attempts to bribe the team's goalkeeper resulted in a much-publicized legal case. They were nearly lost to Scottish football altogether in 1964, when their League place was only saved by a court action to prevent reconstruction of the League itself.

Notable players with the club over the years have included winger Willie Ormond in the 1950s.

Stenhousemuir enjoyed their record victory in 1937, when they beat Dundee United 9–2; they suffered their worst defeat in 1930, losing 11–2 against Dunfermline Athletic. Harry Cairney holds the record for

League appearances with the club, having played in 298 games.

Stevenage Borough English non-League football club, nicknamed Boro. Strip: red and white striped shirts with white shorts and socks. Founded in 1976, Boro are based at the Stevenage Stadium and play in the Isthmian League.

Stiles, Nobby (1942–   ) English footballer, nicknamed the Toothless Tiger, who was one of the hard men of British football in the 1960s. Stiles – called Happy by his team mates – was one of the stars of the celebrated Manchester United side of the period and made his England debut in 1965. A year later, he figured in the England team that lifted the World Cup (see CLASS OF '66) and became in the process one of the most contentious names in international football. Foreign supporters condemned him for his brutal tackling (notably a challenge against France's Jacky Simon) and the press made the most of his unprepossessing appearance (he took out his false teeth before a game). Otto Gloria, manager of Benfica, labelled him an 'assassin' and the Argentinian press – stung by defeat in the 1966 campaign – gave him the nickname El Bandito. Alf RAMSEY, however, responded to pressure to drop Stiles from the squad with the ultimatum that if El Bandito went, he went too.

In fact, those who knew Stiles better protested that his reputation was simply a consequence of his committed style of play and competitive spirit:

> Nobby Stiles a dirty player? No, he's never hurt anyone. Mind you, he's frightened a few!
>
> Matt Busby

Denis LAW, a colleague at Old Trafford, blamed the occasional dubious tackle on Stiles's weak eyesight (he wore powerful contact lenses on the field), claiming that many a tackle that went in at waist or hip height had been intended to go in at the feet.

> A reporter asked me if I took my teeth out to make myself look more ferocious and frightening to opponents. I said, 'No, it's because I don't fancy swallowing my false teeth'.
>
> Nobby Stiles

Stirling Albion Scottish football club, nicknamed the Binos. Strip: red shirts with white sleeves, white shorts and socks.

Founded in 1945 in the wake of the demise of King's Park, the club owe their creation to the dropping of several bombs on Stirling by a Luftwaffe bomber in World War II. The bombs severely damaged the ground used by King's Park, precipitating the disbandment of the team and the foundation of a new one.

Stirling Albion joined the League in 1947 and went on to win the Second Division championship in 1953, 1958, 1961, 1965, 1977, and 1991. Their home ground at ANNFIELD PARK was the first plastic pitch in Scotland. Their 20–0 victory against Selkirk in 1984 established a record scoreline in the Scottish Cup; their record defeat stands at 9–0, sustained against Dundee United in 1967. Matt McPhee holds the record for appearances for the club, having played in 504 games between 1967 and 1981.

The game against Selkirk in 1984 is fondly remembered by many fans. In fact, Stirling had expected amateur Selkirk to prove tough opponents and were agreeably surprised at the ease with which they won. At one point towards the end of the game Selkirk officials on the touchline held up as many numbers as they could find, wryly indicating that they would like to substitute the whole team.

> I thought it was 19–0. I must have lost count.
>
> Alex Smith, manager, after 20–0 win against Selkirk (1984)

Stockholm Stadion Swedish football ground that is home to the Swedish football club Djurgårdens IF. The stadium was built in 1912 to host the Olympic Games that year and imaginatively mimicked a medieval castle in design, complete with turrets and battlements (still largely unchanged). The stadium hosted most of Sweden's major international fixtures between 1912 and 1937, when it became home to Djurgårdens IF. Curiosities of the ground include the copper awning originally used to shelter the seats where the King of Sweden and his royal party sat, Nordic carvings, decorations, and sculptures.

Stockport County English football club, nicknamed County and otherwise known as the Hatters in reference to the area's tradition of hat-making. Strip: blue, red, and white flecked shirts, white shorts, and white socks. The club was founded in 1883 (as Heaton Norris Rovers, after the name of their first home ground) by members of the Wycliffe Congregational Chapel, acquiring its current name in 1890 and joining the Second Division in 1900.

Stockport County moved into their permanent home at EDGELEY PARK in 1902, missed a season in the League in 1904 after failing to win re-election, and enjoyed their first taste of victory in 1922, when they won the inaugural Third Division (North) championship. They won the title again in 1937 but in 1959 began a lengthy stay in the Fourth Division. They returned to the Third Division for three seasons in the 1960s, urged on by their own team of dancing girls and their club slogan 'Go Go County' but eventually sank down once more and had to wait until 1991 for their next promotion. Their other honours include the Fourth Division title in 1967; they enjoyed good runs in the FA Cup in 1935 and 1950 and in the League Cup in 1972–73.

County enjoyed their record victory in 1934, when they beat Halifax Town 13–0; they suffered their worst defeat in 1902, losing 8–1 to Chesterfield. Bob Murray holds the record for League appearances with Stockport, having played in 465 matches between 1952 and 1963.

Stoke Nickname of the English non-League football club BASINGSTOKE TOWN.

Stoke City English football club, nicknamed the Potters. Strip: red and white striped shirts, white shorts, and white socks. It is claimed that Stoke were formed as early as 1863, though a more likely date is 1868, when workers at the local railway formed Stoke Ramblers; this makes the team the second oldest side in the League.

The club (based since 1878 at the VICTORIA GROUND) joined the League as founder members in 1888, dropped out for a season in 1890, were relegated in 1907 and a year later declared bankrupt and had to resign from the League. The reformed club re-entered the League in 1919 and have since spent most of their history in the top two divisions (with visits to the Third Division in 1926–27 and again in 1990). Fans of the club had to wait over one hundred years, however, for the team's first victory in a major competition, with success finally coming in the League Cup in 1972. Other honours won by the team include the Second Division (North) title in 1927 and the Second Division championship in 1933, 1963, and 1993.

One notable game from the early history of the club was that played against Liverpool in 1902, when several members of the team fell victim to food poisoning: seven players struggled on by themselves and managed to restrict their opponents to just seven goals.

Stars of the side over the years have included Stanley MATTHEWS and Freddie Steele – whose efforts made Stoke runners-up in the First Division in 1946. One fan expressed his enthusiasm for the pair by naming his new baby Stanley Frederick Steele – although somewhat ironically the child later became a professional footballer for rivals Port Vale.

Steele himself nearly gave up the game in 1939 after suffering from depression, but the club sent him to a pyschiatrist and on his return he proved he was back on top form, scoring ten goals in five matches. Matthews returned to the club towards the end of his playing career in the 1960s, when he appeared alongside such team mates as Jimmy McIlroy and Dennis Viollet. Among notable players with the club since then have been George Eastham, Jimmy Greenhoff, and goalkeepers Gordon BANKS and Peter SHILTON.

Stoke enjoyed their record victory in 1937, when they beat West Bromwich Albion 10–3; they suffered their worst defeat back in 1889, when they lost 10–0 to Preston North End. Eric Skeels holds the record for League appearances with the club, having played in 506 games between 1958 and 1976.

Stoke City are among the teams to have enjoyed some success as recording artists, their effort being entitled 'We'll Be With You'.

stoppages Interruptions to play caused by throw-ins, free kicks, corners, fouls, goal-kicks, etc. The amount of time lost in stop-pages is often under-estimated; timings of a match in 1984, for instance, revealed that 44 of the full 90 minutes play was taken up by 143 stoppages, during which no actual play took place. A FIFA decision that World Cup referees should not add on time for stoppages was the subject of much heated discussion in 1982. *See also* EXTRA TIME.

stopper A defender, sometimes described as a centre-back, whose job is to bolster his team's defence. The stopper became a common feature of the English game in the late 1920s, after Arsenal's manager Herbert CHAPMAN deployed a stopper to strengthen the Gunners' defence in the wake of the 1925 change in the offside rule, which had led to increased pressure on defences everywhere.

The idea was, in fact, not Chapman's but that of his player Charlie BUCHAN, who argued for some time that the team's centre-half (Jack Butler) should be used solely as a defender before Chapman agreed to try out the plan (partly in response to Buchan's threat to leave the club if things remained as they were). Arsenal first deployed a stopper against West Ham that same 1925–26 season and emerged 4–0 victors.

Under Chapman, the Gunners were the first to realize the potential of such tactics and quickly established themselves as the most formidable side in the land – although similar stoppers had in fact been experi-mented with by Newcastle United earlier that same season and even before that by Andrew Cunningham of Rangers. *See also* WM FORMATION.

Stourbridge English non-League football club, nicknamed the Glassboys. Strip: red and white shirts, white shorts, and red socks. Founded in 1876, the Glassboys are based at the War Memorial Athletic Ground in Amblecote and play in the Southern League.

Strahov, The The national stadium, in Prague, of the Czech Republic. Opened in 1935, the venue was originally named after the former Czech president Tomáš Masaryk but was later renamed after the athlete and journalist Evžen Rošicky, who died in a Nazi concentration camp during World War II. It was extensively improved for the European Athletics championships in 1978.

Stranraer Scottish football club, nick-named the Blues in reference to the team colours. Strip: royal blue. Founded in 1870 by the amalgamation of several local clubs, Stranraer are the third oldest club in the Scottish League, which they joined in 1949; they have never been promoted higher than the Second Division.

For 108 years after their formation, the club never had a manager; teams were selected instead by the twelve directors. The remoteness of their ground at STAIR PARK has added to the difficulty of the club ever breaking into the mainstream and Stranraer remain unique among sides of the same longevity in that they have never seen one of their players capped. Desperate measures taken by the club to improve their fortunes have included a major clear-out of players in 1967, when only two men stayed on for the next season.

Stranraer enjoyed their record victory in 1965, when they beat Brechin City 7–0; they suffered their worst defeat in 1932, when they lost 11–1 to Queen of the South. Ian McDonald holds the record for League appearances with the club, having played in 256 games.

Strawplaiters Nickname of the English football club LUTON TOWN (*see* HATTERS).

streaker A fan who strips off and invades the pitch. Streakers in football have been few and far between, never attaining the fame of rugby's Erica Roe, who conducted a televised streak to the delight of a capacity crowd at Twickenham. Rare instances of the practice in football include a teenaged girl who paraded bare-breasted in front of the stands at Peterborough's London Road ground in 1975 and another seen at Arsenal's HIGHBURY STADIUM in 1982.

street football Long before there were massive stadia to play in, enthusiastic footballers made themselves equally at home at all manner of venues, from downs and fields to squares and streets and any other relatively open space. The playing of football in the streets of England had obvious hazards, both for players, who ran the risk of being ridden down, and for passers-by who were all too often caught up in the mayhem. Back in the 17th century, the streets of London were regularly invaded by football players, as observed in 1665 by Samuel Pepys in his famous Diary: 'The streets were full of footballs.'

A contemporary of Pepys, the playwright William Davenant, was one of those who recorded how impromptu games were inclined to create havoc with normal life in the city:

Methinks I am stopt by one of your heroic games, call'd football, which I conceive not very conveniently civil in the streets, especially in such irregular and narrow roads as Crooked Lane.

The craze for street football reached its height in the early 19th century, when wild mobs pursued balls even in the busiest throroughfares, leading to considerable disruption. The practice was somewhat curtailed in 1835 by the passing of the Highways Act, which prohibited such games and imposed fines of up to 40 shillings for offenders. Since then street football has moved to quiet back alleys and green spaces specifically designated for such activity. *See* CALCIO; ROYALTY; SHROVETIDE FOOTBALL.

I'll take you to where I used to live in the north-east and show you where I headed a

tennis ball so many times against a brick wall near our house it's got a hole in it . . . now you won't see a single kid in the street. It's full of cars. It's amazing we produce any players at all.

Bobby Robson

Stretford End *See* OLD TRAFFORD.

striker A forward; a player who is used chiefly in an attacking role. Few object to this relatively recent coinage but many have reservations to the even more recent 'strike', an Americanism meaning 'a shot at goal'.

Stroller Nickname of the celebrated Scottish football manager George GRAHAM, which was acquired during his playing career.

Strongest, The Bolivian football club. Strip: black and yellow striped shirts and black shorts. Founded in 1908, The Strongest have proved on numerous occasions that they deserve their unique name, being holders of record number of Bolivian League championship titles, including the first one ever contested in Bolivia (in 1914). In 1969 the club had cause to prove its resilience in a new way when the entire first team squad lost their lives in an air crash.

Suarez, Luis (1935–) Spanish midfielder, who emerged as a leading European star in the early 1960s. Having made his first appearance for Spain at the age of 18, Suarez consolidated his reputation as a midfield tactician with the national team, playing in the 1962 and 1966 World Cup campaigns. At home, he appeared for Barcelona and played a key role in getting the team to the Final of the European Cup in 1961. Subsequently he transferred to the Italian club Internazionale, with whom he enjoyed victory in two European Cup and two Intercontinental Cup campaigns, and finally to Sampdoria. He was voted European Footballer of the Year in 1960 and some time after his retirement as a player served as manager of the Spanish team (1988–91).

Subbuteo Tradename of the famous table-top football game, which has long been a favourite among football fans. Complete with teams in the colours of real sides, pitch markings, goals, and even entire stadia, this miniature version of football gathered popularity in the 1960s and has remained a bestseller even with the advent of sophisticated video football games.

Liverpool's Bob PAISLEY was one of the managers who used Subbuteo sets to illustrate tactical movements to his team and to highlight the weaknesses in their opponents. Attempts to win the game approval as an Olympic sport met with failure in 1992.

substitute A player who is allowed on to the pitch in replacement for a team mate who has had to leave the field of play either through injury or at the manager's discretion. The first 'subs' were seen in British football in the 1960s, though many a team would have been glad of the idea in earlier years. Chelsea, for instance, were reduced by exhaustion to just six men during a game played in a blizzard in 1932 (they lost 4–0), while Manchester City were left with just five men when they met Woolwich Arsenal in blazing heat in 1906 (they lost 4–1).

Many traditionalists opposed the introduction of substitutes but the case for the idea was strong, as underlined by the result of the FA Cup Final of 1957, when the loss of a key player through injury effectively robbed Manchester United of victory against Aston Villa and thus of the chance of becoming the first club to achieve a League and Cup double in the 20th century.

After many years of heated debate about the idea, the first officially sanctioned substitutes were seen in English football in 1965, when the League decreed that injured players could be replaced in such a way. Keith Peacock of Charlton Athletic was the first player to come on as a substitute in League football, when he participated in a Second Division match against Bolton Wanderers on 21 August that year; that same afternoon Barrow's Bobby Knox became the first League substitute ever to score a goal.

The system would have worked reasonably well but for the fact that less scrupulous clubs saw the opportunity of making decisive changes by instructing players on the field to feign injury, thus allowing a tactical change to be made. It was quickly realized that managers would have to be allowed full discretion in bringing on replacement players and the rules were accordingly altered for the following season.

1966 also saw similar rules adopted in Scotland, where the first League substitute was Archie Gemmell, who came on for St Mirren in a game against Clyde.

Notable performances by substitutes over the years include that by Birmingham City's Geoff Vowden during a match in 1968: he became the first substitute to score a hat-trick.

Clubs have been allowed to field two subs since 1986. Some subs have played for virtually 90 minutes, while others have come on so late they have had no chance to influence play (in 1973 Arsenal sub Brian Hornsby was allowed on the pitch with just three seconds of play left). One man whose appearance as a substitute was memorable if brief was Motherwell's Steve Kirk who came on in a Cup tie with Aberdeen in 1991: he scored a goal with his one kick at the ball and was then booked for celebrating too enthusiastically.

Sudan Sudan joined FIFA in 1948 and enjoyed their greatest international victory to date in 1970, when they won the African Nations Cup. Strip: green shirts, white shorts, and green socks.

Sudbury Town English non-League football club. Strip: all yellow. Founded in 1898 and based at the Priory Stadium in Sudbury, the club play in the Southern League.

Summer Stadium See LETNÁ STADIUM.

Sunday Cup English cup tournament that was founded by the FA in 1964. Recent winners of the Cup, which is the most prestigious competition open to Sunday football teams, have included Nicosia (based in the north-east), who beat the newly established London club Ouzavich 3–2 in 1991; Ouzavich themselves were congratulated on reaching the Final of such a fiercely fought competition only nine months after playing their first competitive game. The trophy awarded to the winners of the competition was originally the gift of the Shah of Iran.

Sunday football The playing of professional football on Sundays is a relatively recent innovation and was formerly considered unthinkable in many circles. Records exist of fines being levied against enthusiasts who kicked a ball about on a Sunday as early as 1589, when Hugh Case and William Shurlock of Chester were fined two shillings for playing football on a Sunday; another pair of players were also fined for a similar offence in Bedford in 1610.

The FA was finally prevailed upon to approve amateur matches on Sundays in 1960, although the first FA Cup tie to be played on a Sunday did not take place until 1974, when Cambridge United met Oldham Athletic and drew 2–2. Regular Sunday matches were introduced by the League in 1981, although similar games had taken place before – notably during the power and transport crisis of 1974 (the first of these games being a meeting between Millwall and Fulham on 20 January 1974).

At an international level, the side representing Northern Ireland was instructed by their FA not to play in two of the group matches because they were scheduled for Sundays – the team refused to comply with the ruling and subsequently progressed to the quarter-finals.

Similar reluctance towards playing football on the Sabbath has been shown in a number of other countries. *See also* CLERGYMEN.

Lord, remove these exercises from the Sabaoth. Any exercise which withdraweth from godliness either upon the Sabaoth or on any other day, is wicked and to be forbidden.

Phillip Stubbes, *Anatomie of Abuses in the Realme of England* (1583)

Five days shalt thou labour, as the Bible says. The seventh day is the Lord thy God's. The sixth day is for football.

Anthony Burgess

Of course I'm against Sunday soccer. It'll spoil my Saturday nights.

John Ritchie, Stoke City centre-forward (1974)

Sunderland English football club, nicknamed the Rokermen. Strip: red and white striped shirts, black shorts, and red socks with white trim. Also known as the Rokerites, Sunderland were founded in 1879 (as the Sunderland and District Teachers' Association Football Club) by Scottish schoolmaster James Allan (of Hendon boarding school). This team soon opened its ranks to players outside teaching and a year later acquired its present name. A financial crisis in 1881 threatened the dissolution of the club, but the day was saved when one of the members sold his prize canary for £1, thus enabling the club to continue.

Sunderland joined the League in 1890 and immediately established themselves as one of the leading English sides, clinching the First Division championship in 1892, 1893, 1895, and 1902 (they were also runners-up in 1894, 1898, and 1901). Stars of the team in these fabulous early years, when the side (based at ROKER PARK from 1898) was commonly dubbed the Team of all the Talents, included many players brought from north of the border by manager Tom Watson. They included goalkeeper Ted Doig and centre-forward Johnny Campbell.

A new generation of stars, spearheaded by striker Charlie BUCHAN, consolidated the club's reputation in the first decade of the 20th century, taking the club to victory in a further League championship in 1913, in which year they also finished losing finalists in the FA Cup. Quieter times then followed until the 1930s, when Raich CARTER became the most admired player in another strong Sunderland side that was dubbed the Bank of England. With Carter establishing himself as one of the most effective centre-forwards in the land, the club clinched a sixth League championship in 1936 and went on to win the FA Cup for the first time a year later. Other stars of the era included forwards Patsy GALLAGHER and Bobby Gurney.

Further major honours failed to materialize after World War II despite the contribution of such distinguished players as Len SHACKLETON, Billy BINGHAM, and Stan Anderson and in 1958 the club's record 68 years in the First Division came to an end with relegation. Brian CLOUGH's prolific goalscoring activities helped lift the club out of the Second Division six years later, but the team were relegated once more in 1970. Nonetheless, manager Bobby Stokoe steered Sunderland to a famous victory in the FA Cup in 1973 when they triumphed as underdogs over mighty Leeds United, thanks largely to a brilliant performance by goalkeeper Jim Montgomery.

Promotion to the First Division followed in 1976, but the Rokermen failed to keep their place in the upper flight for long and subsequently continued to move between the divisions, even descending to the hitherto unplumbed depths of the Third Division in 1987–88 before climbing back up the First Division in 1990. Relegation soon followed in 1992.

Sunderland enjoyed their record victory back in 1895, when they beat Fairfield 11–1; they suffered record 8–0 defeats against West Ham in 1968 and against Watford in 1982. Jim Montgomery holds the record for League appearances with the club, having played in 537 games between 1962 and 1977.

Wise men say, only fools rush in,
But I can't help falling in love with you,
Wise men say, only fools rush in,
But I can't help falling in love with you,
Sunderland! Sunderland!

Supporters' song

Sunderland Triangle The combination of Charlie BUCHAN, Frank Cuggy, and Jackie Mordue, who led the Sunderland attack with great success in the years before World War I.

Super Cup International cup competition that was founded in 1971. The Cup was contested by the winners of the European Cup and the holders of the European Cup Winners' Cup with the aim of producing one undisputed European champion team. The Dutch club Ajax won the Cup in the first two years that it was held, while Liverpool became the first British winners of the trophy when they clinched a record 7–1 victory over SV Hamburg in 1977 (the first Scottish winners were Aberdeen in 1983). The Cup does not occupy a very high place in clubs' priorities and was not held in 1981 and 1985 after the clubs concerned could not agree dates to play the two legs.

Super League The tag given by the press to the plans that gathered pace for a new English League consisting of the country's top clubs that was eventually realized in the shape of the Premier League, inaugurated in 1992. The spectre of a Super League, which would milk the lion's share of football revenue at the expense of smaller clubs worried many people for a long time and the debate was often acrimonious:

> The FA is trying to diminish the Football League and, with it, most of the professional clubs in this country. Its blueprint is a way for the leading clubs to seize virtually all the money leaving the remaining clubs to wither and for some die.

> Gordon Taylor, chief executive of the Professional Footballers' Association

Proponents, seeing the chance to acquire the funds to improve their clubs, argued that the new structure would benefit everyone, with a reduced number of fixtures (the Premier League should have just 20 members from 1995) allowing teams to concentrate on raising playing standards – and for the management of the national side to give their players more time to work together as a team. Defenders of the traditional League system dismissed such claims with passion:

> We already have a Super League – it's called the First Division and we think that will still be in place in years to come.

> Bill Fox, president of the Football League (1991)

> The Super League idea has about as much

> chance of getting through as there is of Arthur Scargill admitting he needs a wig.

> Ernie Clay, Fulham chairman (1982)

A Gallup poll revealed that 68 per cent of fans were against the Super League, but the bandwagon – spurred on by the prospect of lucrative deals for television coverage among other factors – continued to gather pace and the Premier League was founded in 1992. *See also* BIG FIVE; BIG TEN.

Super Spurs Nickname of the celebrated Tottenham Hotspur team that in 1961 became the first English side of the 20th century to win the double of the FA Cup and the League championship. In the process the team demolished many existing football records, winning 31 games in all and at one point during that memorable season claiming victory in 11 matches in a row.

The remarkable achievements of Tottenham Hotspur in these years were largely due to the efforts of manager Bill NICHOLSON, building upon the work of his predecessor Arthur ROWE. The team Nicholson put together included such complementary talents as Danny BLANCHFLOWER, Bobby Smith, Dave MACKAY, John White, and goalkeeper Bill Brown, who combined sheer skill with physical strength and daring. Much of the success of the side depended upon close teamwork, which was promoted by Nicholson's deliberate refusal to experiment with a large number of team variations: just 17 players put on the white shirts of Spurs in a total of 49 games in the classic 1960–61 season and three members of the squad, including Blanchflower, played in every single game.

Of the 'Super Spurs' apellation, Nicholson once commented: 'It is a neat tag but is simply not true. I feel we could do so much better.'

The nickname was still being heard towards the end of the 1960s, by which time the Super Spurs had added two more FA Cup victories (1962 and 1967) and another in the European Cup Winners' Cup (1963) to the club record; the European triumph was particularly emphatic, coming after Spurs thrashed Atlético Madrid 5–1 in the Final.

Few of the players who had launched the Super Spurs era were still involved by the time it came to an end. One of them, acclaimed Scottish inside-forward John White, had little time to appreciate the achievements of the side in which he was one of the linchpins: he died after being struck by lightning while playing golf on a London golf course in 1964.

> The theory that the League and Cup double will never be done in modern times is nonsense. I realize no one has done it for sixty years, but there is a simple explanation for that. No club has been good enough.

Matt Busby (1957)

super sub A substitute who is recognized as a particularly strong player, but who is kept back as a substitute until a situation particularly suited to his talents emerges on the field of play. The first man to be identified as a 'super sub' was David Fairclough, who was often used in the role of specialist substitute for Liverpool, being brought on to produce decisive last-minute goals (he eventually moved to Lucerne, Oldham, Beveren, Tranmere, and Wigan).

> It's like Bradman coming out to bat with 500 already on the board.

Charlton Athletic fan on Ian Rush playing as substitute (1988)

Superboy Nickname that was bestowed upon the English footballer Trevor FRANCIS, when he emerged as a precocious young star in the early 1970s.

Superga air crash The air disaster that wiped out the entire first team of the Italian football club Torino on 4 May 1949. The loss of the team – considered by many the strongest in Europe – was a major blow to Italian football, for Torino had been the dominant domestic club throughout the 1940s, with a remarkable run of five League championship titles and triumph in the Italian Cup in 1943 to their credit. Records established by the club in the 1940s included a comprehensive 10–0 defeat of Alessandria in 1948, a margin of victory that remains unsurpassed in Italian First Division football to this day.

Torino were on the brink of clinching the 1949 League title when the airplane bringing them home from a testimonial match against Benfica crashed into the Basilica of Superga, with the loss of 28 lives, including that of manager Leslie Lievesely. Among the dead were such celebrated players as striker Ezio Loik and captain Valentino Mazzola and eight of the Italian national side. In tribute to the dead, Torino were awarded the Italian League championship that year by consensus, with opponents fielding youth teams against Torino's own youth

side. A replacement team managed to reach the Final of the first Latin Cup that same season, but finished runners-up to Sporting Lisbon after losing 3–1.

Italian football fans were stunned by the disaster and the memory of Superga remains in the collective consciousness in much the same way as Munich does in the UK.

Supermac Nickname of the English striker Malcolm MACDONALD.

superstitions Although the modern game really only dates back some 125 years, it has acquired a complex mythology of its own, with its own legends and superstitions. As far back as the first decade of the 20th century players in the successful Newcastle United side that dominated the League for several years were renowned for their superstitious belief that they would win if they saw a wedding on their way to a match and that they would lose if they caught sight of a funeral taking place. Much later in the century, Ipswich Town credited a run of victories in the 1953–54 season to a seven leaf clover given to the team by a US fan.

Many individual players observe their own personal superstitions and carry lucky mementos, or insist on wearing lucky shirts or boots. Some superstitions are actually plain good sense, as is the convention that Arsenal goalkeepers wash new jerseys before playing in them: this practice dates back to 1927 when Arsenal's keeper Dan Lewis blamed his slippery new jersey for his failure to save the goal that spelled defeat in the FA Cup Final that year. Some players have 'lucky' foods that they eat before each game – as in the case of Derby County's goalkeeper Jack Robinson, who in the 1890s was always provided with rice pudding before a game in response to his prediction: 'No pudding, no points'.

Managers are also prone to such superstitions. Portsmouth manager Jack Tinn sported a pair of lucky white spats to matches during a lengthy Cup run in 1939 and insisted that they were fastened before each game by winger Fred Worrall, who rapidly tired of the tradition (though himself carrying a lucky sixpence and a miniature horseshoe on the pitch). Other superstitious bosses have included Leeds United and England manager Don P.EVIE and Arsenal's George GRAHAM, who wears a lucky red scarf.

Some grounds have been credited with lucky or unlucky reputations (as in the case of Derby's cursed BASEBALL GROUND). WEMBLEY itself acquired a reputation as an unlucky venue when a series of FA Cup Finals in the 1950s were disrupted by crucial injuries – the most notorious being the broken neck sustained by Manchester City's goalkeeper Bert TRAUTMANN in 1956.

Fans also observe their own taboos, wearing 'lucky' rosettes and scarves or faithfully sticking to habits of behaviour that have 'proved' lucky for their team in the past. One elderly fan of the Italian club Napoli, for instance, always pours salt on the pitch for luck before a match, while another parades down the side of the pitch banging cymbals together and still others enlist the aid of magicians, who cast spells over Napoli's home ground (the players themselves kiss or touch a tile bearing the image of the Madonna set into the wall of the players' tunnel).

Many foreign clubs observe various arcane rituals which include such bizarre rites as anointing the boots and foreheads of new recruits with the blood of freshly sacrificed lambs.

The national side representing El Salvador in the 1970 World Cup, having already been embroiled in the Soccer War that year, had to contend with the influence of a witch doctor when they met Haiti for the second of two qualifying games. The witch doctor sprinkled a mysterious powder on the pitch, muttered an incantation, and Haiti stormed to an unexpected 3–0 victory. When the witch doctor turned up at the play-off game that was then arranged, El Salvador's coach Gregorio Bundi took no chances: he aimed a punch at him and effectively ended his involvement in the match, which El Salvador went on to win 1–0.

Such drastic action would have been understood by members of the Peruvian Melgar side who were victim of a curse by a former player in 1979: they plummeted down the table until someone had the bright idea of soaking the players' shirts in a magical potion that warded off evil spirits – the team then won their play-offs and survived the imminent threat of relegation.

The services of a local witch doctor were also called on by the opposition during a tour of Rhodesia made by Oldham Athletic in 1967: the goal lines of the host teams were protected by magical powers to ensure that Oldham would not score. On this occasion, however, superstition did not pay off – Oldham scored 45 goals in 11 games and lost just one game.

Omens are there to be broken.

Bob Wilson

I'm not a believer in luck . . . but I do believe you need it.

Alan Ball

With our luck one of our players must be bonking a witch.

Ken Brown, Norwich manager (1987)

Surinam Surinam joined FIFA in 1929 but have yet to make much impact in international competition. Strip: red, green, and white shirts, with white or green shorts and socks.

suspensions Suspensions of individuals and clubs have long been one of the options open to those involved in policing football at all levels and vary in terms of severity, ranging from one-match bans to lifetime prohibitions against further involvement with the game.

The most notorious suspensions of recent times have included the five-week bans imposed on Kevin KEEGAN and Billy BREMNER in 1974 for brawling, the two-year ban imposed on Italy's Paolo ROSSI for match-fixing in 1980, the eight-match ban put on Queen's Park Rangers player Mark Dennis in 1988, and of course the lengthy ban imposed on all English clubs that prevented them participating in European competitions for several years in the wake of the Heysel Stadium disaster.

Suspensions for life are rare, but not unheard of. Victims of such bans have included Manchester United player Enoch West, who was prohibited from ever taking part again after he was found guilty of attempting to fix the result of a game against Liverpool in 1915: the ban was finally lifted after it had run for 30 years in 1945, by which time he was 62 years old.

Severest of all, perhaps, was the ban imposed on Trinidad's Selwyn Baptiste after he was found guilty of playing in a match just one day into a previous two-year ban in 1955: he was suspended for 1000 years. *See also* WOODBURN, WILLIE.

They know on the Continent that European football without the English is like a hot dog without mustard.

Bobby Charlton, predicting the lifting of the European ban on English clubs (1988)

Sutton Coldfield Town English non-League football club, nicknamed the Royals. Strip: royal blue shirts, white shorts, and royal blue socks. Founded in 1879 and based at the Central Ground in Sutton Coldfield, the Royals play in the Southern League.

Sutton United English non-League football club, nicknamed the U's. Strip: all amber. Founded in 1898 and based at the Borough Sports Ground in Sutton, the club play in the Isthmian League, though they were members of the Conference from 1986 to 1991 (making them the first Isthmian League side to accept such a promotion).

Sutton United's greatest moment of glory came in 1989, when they pulled off a sensational giant-killing coup against Coventry City, beating them 2–1 in the third round of the FA Cup.

Characters connected with the club in recent years have included their articulate manager Barrie Williams, who was well-known for his habit of quoting Shakespeare, Kipling, and the Venerable Bede in programme notes; he eventually moved on to a sports insurance company and became manager of the England women's football team.

Swans Nickname of a number of football clubs, relating either to their formal title or to their riverside location. They include STAINES TOWN, SWANSEA CITY, and WALTON AND HERSHAM.

Swansea City Welsh football club, nicknamed the Swans. Strip: white shirts and shorts, with black socks. The club were founded, as Swansea Town, in 1912 and joined the League as founder members of the Third Division in 1920. Subsequently they divided their time between all three of the lower divisions until 1981, when they won promotion to the First Division for the first time under manager John Toshack, under whom they briefly ranked as a top club in the League. As it turned out, they remained in the top flight for just two seasons before slipping all the way back down to the Fourth Division in 1986.

Memorable moments in the club's history have included the 1926 FA Cup campaign, which lasted as far as the semi-finals (with a victory over Arsenal on the way), a 3–0 victory over Real Madrid in 1927, and another Cup run in 1964, which also ended at the semi-finals stage. Star players over the years at VETCH FIELD have included centre-forward Trevor Ford in the 1940s and Ivor ALLCHURCH, John CHARLES, and Cliff Jones in the 1950s (when the side boasted the entire forward line-up of the Welsh national team).

The Swans enjoyed their record victory in 1982, when they beat the Maltese team Sliema W 12–0; they suffered their worst defeat in 1938, losing 8–1 against Fulham.

Wilfred Milne holds the record for League appearances with the club, having played in 585 games between 1919 and 1937. The club's arch-rivals are Cardiff City:

> He's a Swansea Jack,
> He wears black and white like he's some
>   sort of queer,
> He can't handle women and he can't handle
>   beer,
> He's a Swansea Jack.

Cardiff City supporters' song, to the tune of 'My Liverpool Home'

Swaziland Swaziland joined FIFA in 1976 but have yet to make much impact in international competition. Strip: blue and gold shirts, white shorts, and blue and gold socks.

swearing The use of abusive language by players risks a charge of bringing the game into disrepute and many players are cautioned for colourful remarks made on the field. Protests at referees' decisions in particular are often distinguished for the invective used. Referees are generally unmoved by such verbal assaults, however. On one occasion a Scottish player, outraged at a sending off, directed a fusilade of swear-words at the French referee – only to receive the reply: 'It is too late now for your apologies.'

Another player, Bristol's Mike Bagley, literally ate his own words when the referee's decision to book him for bad language irritated him: he snatched the official's notebook and consumed it (he was subsequently suspended for six weeks). Another aggrieved player was the unnamed man who was sent off for abusive language during a match early in the history of the modern game: according to popular legend, he was dumb.

> If everyone who swore during games was sent off, there wouldn't be too many players left.

Terry Venables

> Now then my man, we want none of that. Thee! Thee fuck off!

Exchange involving A.G. Baiche Bower and Bill Ashurst in England-Wales international (1925)

Sweden Sweden first participated in the World Cup Finals back in 1934 and four years later finished fourth (after being given a bye to the quarter-finals when Austria were forced to withdraw from the competition by the Nazis). They were present once more in 1950, when they finished third, and

in 1958 acted as hosts of the tournament –
when they ended as runners-up to Brazil.
They did not qualify for the Finals again
until 1970, when they narrowly failed to
reach the quarter-finals, and reappeared
in 1974, 1978, and 1990. Sweden were
also Olympic champions in 1948, and
qualified for the 1994 World Cup in
America. Strip: yellow shirts, blue shorts,
and yellow socks.

sweeper A player who operates freely
across his own team's defence to intercept
any threatening attacking move that has
broken through and then to develop an
attacking move by his own side. He is
usually positioned behind the back four
defenders, but may on occasion be deployed
slightly in front of them. Variously called a
sweeper, *libero*, or *verroulleur*, such
defenders were first seen in the late 1940s
and were subsequently deployed with great
effect by such managers as Helenio HER-
RERA, manager of the Internazionale side
that captured the European Cup in 1964
and 1965. Franz BECKENBAUER revolu-
tionized the concept by turning the sweeper
into an attacking role, the first step in the
move towards total football. *See also*
CATENACCIO.

swerving pass A pass in which the ball
describes a curve, usually employed to get it
past an opponent standing between the
player with the ball and the team mate
waiting to receive it.

Swift, Frank (1913–58) English goalkeeper, nicknamed Big Swifty, who was one
of the best-loved soccer personalities of his
day. Big Swifty joined Manchester City in
1932 and kept goal for them during their
victorious FA Cup campaign of 1934 and in
their successful run in the League championship in 1937. Blessed with a pair of huge
hands (nicknamed the 'frying pans') he first
occupied the England goal in 1946 when he
also filled the role of captain (the first time
the national team had been led by its
goalkeeper) and finally retired in 1950 to
became a coach and journalist.

Frank Swift's efforts to improve the working conditions of players and his legendary
good humour endeared him to both colleagues and readers and his death, as one
of the press entourage accompanying the
Manchester United team in the Munich air
crash, was much regretted. His light-
hearted manner did not extend to the determination he showed on the field, however:
at the close of Manchester City's tense 1934

Cup Final victory he keeled over in a dead
faint as he bent to pick up his gloves.

Swifts Nickname of the English non-
League football club HEYBRIDGE SWIFTS.

Swindon Town English football club,
nicknamed the Robins. Strip: red shirts, red
shorts, and red socks. Swindon are thought
to have been founded (as Spartans) in 1881
by the Rev. William Pitt and began life as
the offshoot of a cricket club. The modern
name was arrived at in 1883 when the Spartans merged with St Mark's Young Men's
Friendly Society.

Based at the COUNTY GROUND since
1896, the club established their reputation
in the first decade of the 20th century when
they twice reached the semi-finals of the FA
Cup but subsequently failed to consolidate
these successes with any consistency. The
greatest star of this period was undoubtedly
Harold Fleming, the inside-forward who
won 11 caps for England.

They did not join the League until 1920,
when they became founder members of the
Third Division and enjoyed a spectacular
debut against Luton Town with a 9–1 victory. They remained in the Third Division
until 1963, when they finally won long-
awaited promotion under manager Bert
Head, whose star players included Mike
Summerbee and Don Rogers. Their best
season of recent times followed in 1968–69,
when they captured the League Cup (with a
surprise 3–1 victory over First Division
Arsenal in the final) and regained their lost
Second Division place. Unable to compete
in the Fairs Cup because of their Third Division status, Swindon were rewarded for
their League Cup success with a place in the
specially created Anglo-Italian Cup, of
which they became the first winners
(beating AS Roma 5–2 on aggregate in
1969); a year later they won it once more,
beating Napoli 3–0. Since those heady days,
however, they have moved between all three
of the lower divisions under such managers
as Lou Macari, Osvaldo ARDILES, and
Glenn HODDLE.

The club seemed set to taste life in the
First Division for the first time when they
won play-offs in 1990, but a sensational
financial scandal involving the Macari
management led to the club being forced to
stay down. They finally won promotion to
the Premier League in 1993. This was not
the first time the club had been involved
in controversy: back in the 1950s goalkeeper Sam Burton attracted notoriety when
he developed an arm-waving technique

designed to distract the opposition's penalty-takers.

The Robins enjoyed their record victory in 1925, when they beat Farnham United Breweries 10–1; they suffered their worst defeat in 1930, losing 10–1 against Manchester City. John Trollope holds the record for League appearances with the club, having played in 770 matches between 1960 and 1980.

> We went to Wembley Stadium on the
>   twenty-eighth of May,
> Heading for the play-offs, Swindon Town
>   to play,
> We didn't win a trophy and we didn't win
>   a cup,
> But what really riles the Geordies is we lost
>   and still went up.

Sunderland supporters' song, referring to the fact that they inherited Swindon's First Division place after the Macari scandal in 1990

Switzerland The Swiss national side made its first appearance in the World Cup Finals in 1934 and was present again in 1938, when they triumphed over a powerful German side after a replay before going out to Hungary. Postwar campaigns included that of 1954, when the Swiss side (then hosts of the competition) reached the quarter-finals and went down 7–5 in one of the most remarkable games ever played in the history of the tournament. However, from 1966 until 1994, managed by Englishman Roy Hodgson, they failed to qualify for another World Cup. Notable players with the team over the years have included Karl Rappan in the 1930s, Claudio Sulser in the 1980s, and Heinz Hermann of the 1990s. Strip: red shirts, white shorts, and red socks.

Syria Syria joined FIFA in 1937 but have yet to play more than a minor role in international competition. Strip: all white.

T

tackle To attempt to wrest possession of the ball from an opponent. Poor timing of tackles or deliberately dangerous play risks injury to both players. Kicking an opponent, tripping, charging from behind, and pushing are all outlawed under the laws of the modern game (though earlier versions of the rules were less strict).

> It's a man's game and men make tackles and I hope men accept tackles without bleating too much.
>
> Steve Coppell (1991)

tactical foul See PROFESSIONAL FOUL.

Taiwan Taiwan joined FIFA in 1954 but have yet to make much impact in international competition. Strip: blue shirts, white shorts, and red socks.

Tamworth English non-League football club, nicknamed the Lambs. Strip: red shirts, black shorts, and red and black socks. Founded in 1933 and based at the Lamb Ground, Tamworth play in the Southern League.

Tannadice Park The home ground of the Scottish football club DUNDEE UNITED. The club – then playing as Dundee Hibernian – first settled at Tannadice Park (then called Clepington Park and home to non-League Dundee Wanderers) in 1909, a daring and apparently foolhardy decision in view of the fact that it was directly opposite Dundee's Dens Park home (the two venues remain to this day the closest in British football at such a senior level).

Dundee United collaborated with the owner of Clepington Park to get Wanderers removed and then took the venue over themselves (though not before the outraged Wanderers had taken away from the ground everything that could be moved). The ground remained relatively undeveloped until the late 1920s and 1930s. Events in the ground's history since then have included the staging of an Empire bantam-weight boxing title match in 1941, replacement of old stands in the 1960s, and the erection of executive boxes and lounges in the 1970s.

Tanners Nickname of a number of English football clubs, usually in reference to local leather-working industries. They include LEATHERHEAD and MAIDENHEAD UNITED.

Tanzania Tanzania joined FIFA in 1964 but have yet to make much impact in international competition. Strip: yellow shirts with black trim, yellow shorts, and yellow and black socks.

Ta'Qali The leading international football venue in Malta. Opened in 1980, it was constructed on a former British airbase and replaced the much more spartan Empire Stadium in Gzira. All Malta's eight senior football clubs play at the stadium on a regular basis.

target man A player whose role is to receive passes from his own defence and then move it on to a member of his own team's attack.

Tarmac Nickname of the English forward John BARNES, an extension of the epithet 'the Black Heighway' which many fans used to liken him to former Liverpool star Steve Heighway.

Tartan Army Nickname of the tartan-clad hordes of fans that customarily accompany Scotland wherever in the world they are playing. Scotland fans have the reputation of being among the most dedicated in the world, with many stories of supporters selling their houses and sacrificing their marriages in order to continue to follow their heroes. In the 1970s they were recognized as being among the most hard-drinking and violent bands of supporters anywhere in world, reflecting the frequency of disturbances in the domestic game (see OLD FIRM).

Scotland's (brief) campaign in the 1978 Argentina World Cup, for instance, was witnessed by large crowds of native Scots, many of whom had hitch-hiked thousands of miles, braving both muggings and mass arrest on the way. The behaviour of Scottish fans at Wembley in 1977 after their team beat England led to condemnation of the Tartan Army from all quarters and hastened moves to act against hooliganism in the game throughout the UK (Scottish fans tore down the goal and did much damage to the pitch and fixtures of the famous stadium, even attempting to take large sections of goalpost by train back to Scotland).

Taylor, Graham (1944–   ) English football manager, who took over responsibility for the England team in 1990, as successor to Bobby ROBSON. Taylor's appointment as England manager was the culmination of a highly successful career at the top level of English domestic football. A former player with Lincoln City, he became manager of his old club in the mid-1970s and subsequently took control of such clubs as Watford, where he presided over the team's rise to the First Division, and Aston Villa before winning the England post. He resigned in 1993 following England's failure to qualify for the 1994 World Cup Finals in America.

Taylor, Gordon See ARTHUR SCARGILL OF FOOTBALL, THE.

Taylor Report The findings of the two-month official inquiry into the Hillsborough disaster of 1989, which was headed by Lord Justice Peter Taylor, a Newcastle United fan in his youth. The report summarized the problems of the contemporary British game, pinpointing outdated grounds, hooliganism, and drinking among the ills afflicting football as a whole. Of Hillsborough in particular, Taylor laid much of the blame at the feet of those responsible for policing the crowd but also criticized the behaviour of a few drunken fans. Taylor insisted that the only way forward was through major improvements 'both in bricks and mortar and human relationships'.

The government accepted all of Taylor's conclusions, even though he came out against their proposals for a national membership scheme. Specific recommendations included the introduction of all-seater stadiums, the expense of which brought into question the whole financing and structure of the existing Football League (compromises were subsequently agreed on the requirements that had to be met by clubs in the lower divisions).

The lesson here is that Hillsborough should not be regarded as a freak occurrence, incapable of happening elsewhere . . . Complacency is the enemy of safety.

Lord Justice Peter Taylor

Team of All the Talents Nickname of the extraordinarily successful Sunderland side that dominated English football in the early 1890s. The team was the work of manager Tom Watson, who is considered by many to have been the first great professional football manager. Watson constructed his side by looking north of the border and luring a number of skilled Scottish players to Sunderland; when the side captured their first League championship in 1892 there was only one native Englishman in the squad (himself a recruit from a Scottish team). The success Watson had in attracting some of the best players in Scotland did not go down well north of the border and some of his 'poaching' raids were conducted at the risk of his own personal safety.

Stars of Watson's side included the prolific striker Johnny Campbell, goalkeeper Ted Doig (nicknamed the Prince of Goalkeepers), captain Hugh Wilson, and Watson himself. Under Watson's leadership (1889–96), the Team of All the Talents triumphed over all opposition, remaining unbeaten in a single League home match from September 1891 to 1894 (when they lost against Blackburn Rovers) and then enjoying another run of 37 home games without defeat, which only finally came to an end in 1896 (a total of 82 League home games with just one loss).

Other records established during this period included the 100 League goals scored in 1893, making them the first team to reach this figure. On an individual level, Johnny Campbell scored a total of 83 goals in just 81 games in the three seasons in which the team won the League title (1892, 1893, and 1895).

The side's success did much to foster the popularity of football in the north-east but did not long outlast Watson's transfer to Liverpool in 1896: that same year they finished second from bottom.

Team of Boys Nickname of the highly successful West Bromwich Albion side of the early 1930s. The Team of Boys, all relatively young, enjoyed their hour of glory in 1931, when they achieved a unique double by winning promotion from the Second Division and the FA Cup.

Team of the Eighties Accolade that was afforded by the popular press to Crystal Palace around 1980. Having won the Second Division championship in 1979, the team was confidentally expected to have a major impact upon the First Division under the inspirational leadership of Terry VEN-ABLES. In fact, Palace spent much of the decade back in the Second Division, and it was not until 1989 that they got back into the top flight (under Steve Coppell) and went some way towards justifying the description by reaching the FA Cup Final in 1990 (only to lose the replay to Manchester United) and finishing third in the League championship (their best position ever). As things turned out, it would have been more appropriate to bestow the title upon Liverpool.

Tel, El Nickname of the English manager Terry VENABLES.

television The showing of football games on television has been a major factor in the development of the sport in all the leading footballing nations since World War II, bringing in huge revenue but also making its own demands upon the game.

For many years the football authorities blocked live coverage of games in the fear that such broadcasts would lead to a drop in attendances at matches. Probably the first time football was seen live on television was back in 1936, when such a broadcast was permitted of a game in Germany. That same year television cameras were present at a fixture involving Arsenal and Everton, while the first live transmission was sent in 1937 during a practice game at HIGHBURY STADIUM.

The 1937 FA Cup Final was the first major final to be covered by television (it was watched by an estimated audience of 10,000) and cameras began to appear at grounds all over the country in the years following World War II (the very first match other than a Final to be broadcast was an FA Cup tie between Charlton Athletic and Bristol Rovers in 1947). The first Scottish match to be shown live on television was the Scottish Cup Final in 1955, with commentary by Kenneth Wolstenholme.

The Football League finally gave in to pressure for television coverage of their fixtures in 1960, although it was not until 1983 that it permitted regular live coverage of League matches. The emphasis since then has been on live coverage rather than recorded games although quite what the television companies have been able to show has depended upon the different deals (for ever-increasing amounts of money) that they have struck with the football authorities. For part of the 1985–86 season no football was seen at all on television after the two sides failed to reach an agreement.

The agonizing process by which deals with the television companies have been reached in recent years have at various times threatened the destruction of the Football League itself and was a major factor in the formation of the Premier League (which BSkyB TV won the rights to televise the first five years for a fee of some £300 million). The needs of commercial US television, with its desire to appeal to a domestic audience brought up on other sports with more regular breaks and higher scorelines, has also threatened controversial changes in the most basic rules of the game at World Cup level.

FIFA estimated that 2.7 billion people (half the population of the world) watched the 1990 World Cup Finals on television. The future suggests larger audiences still, some of whom will have the technology to choose between camera angles, select their preferred commentary (or elect to have none at all), decide which part of the pitch to look at, and even listen in to comments between players and officials during the game:

> *The possibilities that are opening up are unbelievable. Two years ago I would have dismissed them as the drug-crazed dreams of a madman.*
>
> David Hill, head of Sky Sports (1992)

Alloa feature among the few football clubs to have participated in television drama, having appeared in an episode of 'Doctor Finlay's Casebook'. Less enthusiastic about appearing on television were Wolverhampton Wanderers in 1965, who considered taking the BBC to court over the fictional series 'United', which in the club's eyes was too close a parallel to their own troubled recent history.

Other television productions linked to football have included 'The Zoo', seen in the 1970s, 'The World Cup: A Captain's Tale', seen in 1982, and more recently such diverse magazine-style programmes as 'Standing Room Only'.

Some fans have found watching the game on television as intense an experience as actually being at the match. A Swedish viewer during the 1974 World Cup, for instance, threw his television set out of the window in disgust at his team's play (it fell four storeys and landed on the roof of his car), while in 1978 Italians incarcerated in Argentinian prison cells were provided with televisions with which to see the World Cup in order to forestall the possibility of a riot.

In 1982 Yugoslavian fan Marinko Janevski took exception when his wife turned off the television during a game and strangled her before switching the set back on to watch the rest of the game. At his subsequent trial for murder he attempted to defend himself on the grounds of provocation, explaining that 'I always get excited when watching football'. His plea was not successful.

> For better or worse, sport in the second half of the twentieth century has capitulated to the commercial speculator; a process accelerated by the international scope of television as a purveyor of instant play, inter-play, and re-play.

Doug Ibbotson, *Sporting Scenes* (1980)

> Don't tell those coming in the final result of that fantastic match, but let's just have another look at Italy's winning goal.

David Coleman, commentator

> And there'll be more football in a moment, but first we've got the highlights of the Scottish League Cup Final.

Gary Newbon, commentator

See also MATCH OF THE DAY; RADIO; SNATCH OF THE DAY.

Telford United English non-League football club, nicknamed the Lillywhites. Strip: white shirts, black shorts, and white socks. Founded in 1877 as Wellington Town and based at the Bucks Head Ground in Wellington, they spent their early history in the Southern League before joining the Conference and changing their name to Telford United in 1969. Honours won by the club have included the Cheshire League championship in 1946, 1947, and 1952 and three victories in the FA Trophy competition. The club is also renowned for its long history of giant-killing acts.

ten yards rule The stipulation in the rules of the game that opponents must be no less than ten yards away from the kicker when a free kick is taken. The rule, introduced in 1913, is so often bent that reformers have suggested that referees should adopt the practice followed in rugby by picking up the ball and advancing another ten yards as a punishment when a team fails to keep their distance.

Ten Years Stadium The huge superbowl football stadium that was opened in Warsaw in 1955 to commemorate the tenth anniversary of the foundation of the first Communist government in Poland. The stadium, which was constructed with rubble from the city's war ruins, actually opened 11 years after the event it was supposed to celebrate and has never proved popular with the fans, being completely featureless and entirely open to the elements. It was used for a variety of major sporting events including Cup Finals and internationals, though none since 1983.

Ten-Goal Nickname that was bestowed upon Luton Town's reserve wing-half Joe Payne in 1936 when he scored a sensational ten goals in a single match. Payne was playing as centre-forward (a position he had not tried previously) for the game against Bristol Rovers and scored ten goals in the course of Luton's 12–0 victory, thus establishing a new record in the Football League. After the match transfer offers flooded into the club, but Payne stayed with Luton long enough to score a club record of 55 goals the following season, before moving to Chelsea, West Ham, and Millwall, and retiring in 1948 (he also won one cap playing for England). Payne himself dismissed his feat as 'just one of those days'. His achievement is commemorated in a Joe Payne Lounge at Luton's Kenilworth Road ground.

terraces The staggered levels upon which fans stand to watch a game. The first terraces constructed at football grounds around the world either made use of natural features or were raised by piling up rubble and earth, often lined with cinders and old railway sleepers. Subsequently they were concreted over and embellished with crush barriers to prevent spectators losing their footing in a packed crowd. All kinds of debris lies beneath the terraces at even the most modern stadiums, ranging from dead horses (*see* HIGHBURY STADIUM) to heaps of rare coins (*see* STAMFORD BRIDGE).

Over the years fans have come to recognize the 'culture of the terraces', which in the popular mind represents the working-class soul of the game in the UK. The idea that clubs might one day be forced to replace their much-loved if exposed and less than luxurious terraces for all-seater stadia would once have been considered a figment of a diseased imagination, but the escalation of violence on the terraces in recent years and the spate of disasters that afflicted the game in the 1980s signalled a fundamental change in the tradition and marked a sea change in the nature of football as mass entertainment.

The Taylor Report following the Hillsborough disaster of 1989 spelt it out when it dictated that all major grounds should be converted to all-seating as soon as possible; the decision raised howls of protest among dedicated fans but little sympathy for their fondness for the old-fashioned terraces was forthcoming from outside the game and change became inevitable.

Even with this physical alteration to British grounds, however, they are still looked on with envy by fans of many clubs elsewhere in the world. What British grounds might lack in luxury they generally make up for in atmosphere, with crowds responding with passion in enclosed grounds where the terraces reach almost to the touchlines, in contrast to the vast and soulless 'superbowls' of the Continent, where spectators are all too often a considerable distance away from the action, across athletics tracks and behind security barriers.

> Blimey, the ground looks a bit different to Watford. Where's the dog track?

Luther Blissett, on arriving at the San Siro stadium in Milan (1983)

Terras Nickname of the English non-League football club WEYMOUTH.

Terrible Trio The renowned combination of Alfie Conn, Willie Bauld, and Jimmy Waudhaugh, who spearheaded the Heart of Midlothian attack in the 1950s. The Terrible Trio, aided and abetted by wingers Alex Young and Jimmy Crawford, were the key element in the club's golden era, during which they captured the League Championship in 1958, the Scottish Cup in 1956, and several League Cup titles.

Terrible Twins Nickname of the partnership that was forged by Brentford's Jim Towers and George Francis in the 1950s. The success the two men enjoyed led to them being transferred as a single unit first to Queen's Park Rangers and finally to Gillingham, where they continued to prove a major asset.

Terriers Nickname of the English football club HUDDERSFIELD TOWN, in reference to Yorkshire terrier dogs (as depicted in the club badge), which are renowned for their persistence and courage.

Terrors Nickname of a number of football clubs, among them the Scottish side DUNDEE UNITED and the English non-League club TOOTING AND MITCHAM UNITED.

test match *See* PLAY-OFF.

Texaco Cup Tournament between Scottish and English Football League clubs that was initiated in 1970 with financial support from the Texaco oil company. The first winners were Wolverhampton Wanderers, who beat Heart of Midlothian in the Final (16 teams from the four home nations took part). In 1976 the competition was reorganized as the ANGLO-SCOTTISH CUP, while in 1981 it was transformed once more as the GROUP CUP after the Scottish teams withdrew (the only winners from north of the border had been St Mirren in 1980). This in turn was renamed the FOOTBALL LEAGUE TROPHY in 1983 and replaced by the ASSOCIATE MEMBERS CUP in 1984 and the FREIGHT ROVER TROPHY in 1985.

Thailand Thailand joined FIFA in 1925 but have yet to make much impact in international competition. Strip: all red.

Thame United English non-League football club. Strip: red and black. Founded in 1883 and based in Windmill Road, Thame, the team play in the Isthmian League.

Thames Former English League football club, which was a member of the Third Division (South) for just two seasons (1930–32). Based at the West Ham Greyhound Stadium, Thames were replaced in the League by Newport after finishing bottom of the Third Division (South) and thus became the only London club to lose their League status. A game involving Thames and Luton in 1930 was attended by just 469 spectators, thought to be the lowest-ever crowd at a Saturday afternoon League match.

Thames Valley Royals The controversial football club that was proposed by millionaire Robert MAXWELL as a merged replacement for Oxford United and Reading in 1983. The new club would have played at a new stadium to be constructed somewhere between Oxford and Reading. The plan was greeted with outrage and scorn and fans staged sit-ins at Oxford's MANOR GROUND in protest at the idea. Maxwell himself was unimpressed by public hostility to his proposals and brushed aside the objections of the fans with typical firmness:

> I understand and sympathize with their strong feelings, but I cannot accept their conservatism or parochialism.

The whole enterprise was scuppered just weeks after it was first unveiled when Reading's new chairman came out against the merger.

Third Lanark Former Scottish football club, nicknamed the Hi-Hi's, which was based in Glasgow and began life as the team of the Third Lanarkshire Rifle Volunteers. Third Lanark, founder members of the Scottish FA in 1873 and of the Scottish League in 1890, were one of the leading Scottish sides in the early history of football north of the border, appearing in the Scottish FA Cup Final as early as 1876 and winning it in 1889; subsequent honours included the Scottish League championship in 1904 and another FA Cup victory in 1905.

Other highlights of the club's history over the years included a Scottish League Cup match against Alloa in 1953 when the Hi-Hi's became only the second club in the competition's history to record a double-figure score (and the first away from home), winning the game 10–0. Famous names associated with the club included George YOUNG, who was manager of the team between 1959 and 1962. Third Lanark finally disappeared from the Scottish League at the end of the 1966–67 season. The pitch alone remains of their base at Cathkin Park.

This Time (we'll get it right) Pop song recorded by the England World Cup squad in 1982. The record reached number two in the charts, but the team failed to relive the triumph of 1966 and went out after a disappointing 0–0 draw with hosts Spain.

Thistle (1) Nickname of the Scottish football club MEADOWBANK THISTLE.
(2) Former Scottish League football club, which was a member of the League from 1893 to 1894. Thistle were based at Dalmarnock, south of Celtic Park.

Thomas, Clive (1936–) Welsh referee, nicknamed The Book, who became one of the most controversial officials in the modern professional game. Overseeing games at all levels, he earned a reputation for toughness and saw that every match was played according to the book (hence his nickname). Among his most provocative actions was his decision to disallow a goal in a World Cup Final match between Brazil and Sweden in 1978: he allowed a corner kick to be taken by Brazil even though the full 90 minutes was up but, when Brazil subsequently scored, refused to let the goal stand as the game had, he said, ended at the moment the kick was taken.

He also stirred up controversy with his outspoken views, criticizing fellow-referees and pressing for reforms to allow the use of two-way radio communication with linesmen, video-headsets, and goal-line cameras. He retired in 1984 and became managing director of a property company but continued to voice his thoughts about the national game. When the Premier League was established he put himself forward as an authority for all top-level referees, arguing with typical ebullience: 'I'm the only chap with the qualifications and character to do it.'

Some of his decisions were greeted with indignant protests, but The Book never changed his mind, leaving players and managers to fume at his often idiosyncratic interpretation of the rules.

> He drives you spare sometimes . . . with Clive you are just playing to one man's rules and you don't know what's happening.
>
> Graham Taylor, manager of Watford (1982)

Thompson, Sir Harold English scientist who became chairman of the FA in 1976. Famed for his scientific work and as president of the Britain-China Society, as well as a Fellow of the Royal Society, 'Tommy' was also the founder of Pegasus and had himself played as a centre-half for Oxford University. No stranger to controversy, he witnessed as chairman the abolition of the amateur-professional distinction in 1972, the imposition of a record suspension on England manager Don REVIE in 1977, and the installation of Ron Greenwood as Revie's successor, among other significant changes.

Throstles Nickname of the English football club WEST BROMWICH ALBION. The club's emblem is a golden throstle (or thrush), which features on the team badge and recalls a caged bird that belonged to the landlady in whose premises (the Plough and Harrow public house) the club originally had its headquarters. The team adopted the thrush as their mascot and for many years a similar bird was kept in a cage in the Main

Stand at the Hawthorns; superstitious fans maintained that when the bird sang the team would do well.

through ball A pass in which the ball is kicked between two defenders to reach an attacker bearing down on the opposition's goal, thus splitting the other side's defence.

throw-in The throwing of the ball back into play after it has crossed the touchline marking the side edge of the pitch. Early rules allowed different interpretations of how a throw-in might be taken. Although the London Association's rules were not dissimilar to the modern version of events, the Sheffield Association dictated that the ball should be kicked from the touchline, and that the throw-in should be taken by the team who were first to touch the ball after it had gone out of play.

There were disagreements about how throw-ins should be taken even at international level. In 1882 England insisted before a match with Scotland that they be allowed to throw the ball in as they liked. The Scottish team reluctantly agreed to this and then found that the English players had perfected a one-armed throw that could carry the ball almost from one end of the pitch to the other (Notts County's William Gunn was particularly skilled in such throws, employing his experience as an England cricketer). The rules were hastily changed so that from 1882 only double-handed throw-ins were permitted.

Even so, there was still scope for occasional surprises: in 1938, for instance, Barnsley's Frank Bokas actually scored a goal against Manchester United from a throw-in (the goalkeeper just touched the ball as it went in). Even more remarkable was the extraordinary throw-in technique that Newcastle United's Steve Watson perfected in the early 1990s, which involved him turning a somersault before releasing the ball (the FA deliberated on his style but had to concede that it was a legitimate manoeuvre).

It has been calculated that there is on average about one throw-in every minute in modern first-class football (around 85 a match).

Tiger Nickname of the Soviet goalkeeper Alexei KHOMICH.

Tigers Nickname of several football clubs, usually in reference to the colours of the team strip. They include GLOUCESTER CITY, HULL CITY, HYDE UNITED, and WORKSOP TOWN.

Tilbury English non-League football club, nicknamed the Dockers. Strip: black and white striped shirts, black shorts, and white socks. Founded in 1900 and based at the Chadfields ground, the Dockers play in the Isthmian League.

Tipton Terror Nickname of the English striker Steve BULL, in reference to his birthplace.

Toffeeopolis Nickname of GOODISON PARK, the home ground of the English football club Everton.

Toffees Nickname of the English football club EVERTON, in reference to Ye Ancient Everton Toffee House, which was situated close to the hotel where the club was founded.

Togo Togo joined FIFA in 1962 but have yet to make much impact in international competition. Strip: white shirts, green shorts, and red socks with yellow and green trim.

Ton Nickname of the Scottish football club MORTON.

Tons Nickname of the English non-League football club CLAPTON.

Toothless Tiger Nickname of the English footballer Nobby STILES, in reference to his false teeth.

Tooting and Mitcham United English non-League football club, nicknamed the Terrors. Strip: white shirts, black shorts, and red socks. Founded in 1932 and based at the Sandy Lane ground in Mitcham, the club play in the Isthmian League.

Torino Italian football club, nicknamed the Pomegranates. Strip: red shirts, white shorts, and red socks. Founded in 1906 by players from Juventus and FC Torinese, Torino enjoyed their golden era in the 1940s, when they brought their total of League championships to six (1928, 1943, 1946, 1947, 1948, and 1949). It all came to an end, however, in May 1949 when the entire team perished in the Superga air crash; they still managed to win the Championship that year through the efforts of their youth team in the last few games of the season. Since those times, the club have added one more League title (1976). They have won the Italian Cup four times (1936, 1943, 1968, and 1971). Since 1960 the team has been based at the Stadio Comunale in Turin.

Torpedo Moscow Russian football club; one of the country's leading teams. Strip: white shirts, black shorts, and white socks. Founded in 1924, Torpedo were named after the first Soviet-made production car, which was manufactured at the Likhachev Auto Plant where the side first evolved. They are based at the Torpedo Stadium in Moscow and have won three League championships and six Cups; they achieved the League and Cup double in 1960.

Torquay United English football club, nicknamed the Gulls. Strip: yellow and navy shirts with navy blue shorts and yellow socks. The club were founded in 1898 after old boys of Torquay College and Torbay College agreed on the idea while listening to the band in the Princess Gardens. The team played as Torquay Town from 1910 to 1921, when they acquired their current name; they turned professional in 1921, by which time they had settled permanently at the PLAINMOOR ground. The club have never won a major title, although they enjoyed something of a golden era in the 1960s, when they won promotion to the Third Division on two occasions.

The Gulls enjoyed their record victory in 1952, when they beat Swindon Town 9–0; they suffered record defeats of 10–2 in matches in 1931 (against Fulham) and in 1933 (against Luton Town). Dennis Lewis holds the record for League appearances with the club, having played in 443 matches between 1947 and 1959.

The bestowing of an award to Gulls supporters as 'Best Behaved Supporters' in the late 1960s stung the recipients into devising their own version of 'She'll be Coming Round the Mountain', since adapted for use at numerous other grounds in the UK:

> We're the best behaved supporters in the land,
> We're the best behaved supporters in the land,
> We're the best behaved supporters,
> Best behaved supporters,
> Best behaved supporters in the land,
> Singing – I threw a bottle at the ref,
> I threw a bottle at the ref . . .

toss-up The flipping of a coin to decide such issues as which end a team is to defend and who is to kick off. It is rare indeed now that the result of a professional football match is decided by tossing a coin, but this was once accepted practice at all levels of the game. An FA Cup tie was decided in this way for the first time back in 1873, when Sheffield won the toss against Shropshire Wanderers to proceed to the second round of the competition after a 0–0 draw. More recently, in the 1964–65 Fairs Cup, a coin was used for the first time to decide which team should reach the quarter-finals. Furore surrounded the toss of a coin to decide who won a first round tie between ASK Linz and Dynamo Zagreb in the European Cup Winners' Cup in 1963–64 and subsequently the away-goals rule was employed.

In 1930 the outcome of an entire Cup competition was decided on the toss of a coin. The Glasgow Charity Cup Final that year had ended with both teams level; Rangers were unable to participate in a replay because of an impending tour of the United States and Celtic agreed to the result being decided by a coin: Rangers won.

Tostao (Eduardo Gonçalves de Andrade; 1947–   ) Brazilian striker, nicknamed the White Pelé, who was much admired for his leadership of the victorious Brazil team in the 1970 World Cup. As well as scoring 33 goals in 55 international appearances, he also played for the Brazilian clubs America (Belo Horizonte), Cruzeiro, and Vasco da Gama.

total football Modern free-flowing style of football, first perfected by the German star Franz BECKENBAUER in the early 1970s, which depends upon the use of an attacking SWEEPER. Other players are encouraged to combine roles in attack and defence, rather than being restricted to a conventional 'position'. As well as the German national side in which Beckenbauer was the leading player, other exponents of the system included the Dutch football club Ajax, who stormed to success after success in the early 1970s with the employment of such tactics by Johan CRUYFF and other star players (culminating in the 1972 season in which Ajax won the League and Cup double, the Champions' Cup, the World Club Cup, and the European Super Cup). *See also* CATENACCIO; LIBERO.

> People keep talking about Total Football, all I know about is Total petrol.
> Derek Dougan

Toto Nickname of the Italian striker Salvatore SCHILLACI.

Tottenham Hotspur English football

club, nicknamed Spurs. Strip: white shirts, navy blue shorts, and navy socks with white trim. The club had its origins in the Hotspur football club that was founded by some cricketers (mostly old boys of St John's Presbyterian School and Tottenham Grammar School) in 1882. The name Hotspur was inspired by the historical Harry Hotspur familiar from the plays of William Shakespeare (the Hotspur family being of the Northumberland aristocracy but also owning land around Tottenham in the 1880s). Harry Hotspur himself acquired his name from his frequent use of spurs when riding and it is thought that the team's ball and cockerel emblem is probably also related to this idea, as fighting cocks were once fitted out with miniature spurs.

The original Hotspur team lacked a headquarters so customarily held their early meetings under a gaslight on Tottenham High Road; they finally settled at WHITE HART LANE in 1898. Spurs remained in the Southern League for some years and in 1901 became the only non-League club of the 20th century to win the FA Cup. Their victory, which was only achieved after humbling no fewer than four First Division sides, established them as one of the most powerful teams in the South:

> Than the famous Spurs there is probably no more popular club in England. Did they not recover the Association Cup for the south? Did they not play pretty and effective football? Are they not scrupulously fair? Are they not perfectly managed?

William Pickford and Alfred Gibson, *Association Football and the Men Who Made It* (1906)

League membership finally followed in 1908 and their first season ended with promotion to the First Division, where they stayed until 1915. They returned to the top flight in 1920 after clinching the Second Division championship and a year later added a second FA Cup win, with a team that included such star players as Arthur Grindsell and Jimmy Seed.

Many years then lapsed before the club's next major honour, with the team dividing its time between the top two divisions. The breakthrough came in 1950, when the Second Division championship launched Spurs on a 27-year campaign in the top flight, during which time they won two First Division championships (1951 and 1961), three FA Cup tournaments (1961, 1962, and 1967), two League Cups (1971 and 1973), the European Cup Winners' Cup (1963), and the UEFA Cup (1972).

The man who engineered the beginnings of this long run of successes was manager Arthur ROWE, whose devastating push-and-run tactics took the club to the top of the League, though it was his successor Bill NICHOLSON who constructed the celebrated team of the early 1960s that clinched the double in 1961 and came to be known as Super Spurs. The European Cup Winners' Cup victory in 1963 was especially significant in that it was the first major European trophy to be won by an British side.

Relegation to the Second Division in 1977 was followed by a prompt return to the First Division a year later, since when the side has added to its tally of successes another UEFA Cup triumph (1984) and another three FA Cups (1981, 1982, and 1991) to establish a record of eight wins (they were also losing finalists in 1987), as well as runners-up position in the League Cup and European Cup Winners' Cup (both 1982). Their comparative failure in the League has underlined the club's reputation in recent years for attractive football, but lack of consistency in the League, though they did win a place in the Premier League when it was founded in 1992.

One of the most glamorous of British teams, the club found itself in some financial trouble after taking the step of floating shares on the Stock Exchange in 1983. Among the leading lights at White Hart Lane in recent years has been chief executive and former Spurs player Terry VENABLES (controversially sacked in 1993 in the course of wrangles with chairman Alan Sugar). Other star names associated with the team over the years have included defenders Alf RAMSEY and Ron Burgess in the late 1940s, right-half Danny BLANCHFLOWER, centre-forward Bobby Smith, and winger Cliff Jones in the 1950s, left-half Dave MACKAY, goalkeeper Bill Brown, and striker Jimmy GREAVES in the 1960s, goalkeeper Pat JENNINGS and forwards Martin Chivers and Martin PETERS in the 1970s, forwards Osvaldo ARDILES (successor to Venables as manager in 1993) and Glenn HODDLE in the 1980s, and strikers Gary LINEKER and Paul GASCOIGNE in the early 1990s. Famous fans of the club include England cricketer Mike Gatting and television personality Bruce Forsyth.

Spurs enjoyed their record victory in 1960, when they beat Crewe Alexandra 13–2; they suffered their worst defeat in 1978, losing 7–0 against Liverpool. Steve Perryman holds the record for League appearances with the club, having played in 655 games between 1969 and 1986.

The club can boast an honourable record for fair play, having gone from 1928 all the way to 1965 without a single player being sent off (Frank Saul ended this unequalled run when he was dismissed against Burnley on 4 December 1965).

> *Glory, glory, Tottenham Hotspur,*
> *Glory, glory, Tottenham Hotspur,*
> *Glory, glory, Tottenham Hotspur,*
> *And the Spurs go marching on.*

Supporters' song, to the tune of 'Battle Hymn of the American Republic'

> *Three cheers for Spurs!*
> *They beat Stoke!*
> *Glad I'm a football fan.*
> *Glad I'm a bloke.*

Wendy Cope, *Roger Bear's Football Poems*

> *I haven't just signed a player, I've rescued a lad from hell.*

Brian Clough, on signing Steve Hodge from Spurs (1988)

touchline The white line that runs down the length of the pitch on both sides, denoting the point at which the ball goes out of play. The origins of the term go back to the rule observed in the early years of the game that awarded the throw-in to the team who first touched the ball after it had crossed the line.

Toulouse French football club, nick-named the Violets. Founded in 1937, Tou-louse actually went out of existence in 1967, when their players were transferred to Red Star, but returned in 1981. They are based at the stadium in Toulouse.

tour A series of away matches, often tak-ing clubs to far-flung parts of the footballing world. The first tour of all was undertaken by the Royal Engineers in 1873, when they played against three teams in the north midlands (they won all three games). The first British club to conduct an overseas tour was Oxford University, who combined football with an educational tour of Germany in 1875. In 1897 Corinthians became the first British club to play outside Europe when they travelled to South America, where their skills boosted the development of the game throughout the continent. Memorable tours in the years since then have included the sensational visit of the Soviet club Dynamo Moscow to the UK in 1945 and the extraordinary world tour made by the US club Dallas Tornado in 1968, which took place before the team had played a single home match.

Town Nickname of a number of football clubs that have the word town in their for-mal title. They include BILLERICAY TOWN, BRIDGNORTH TOWN, CAMBERLEY TOWN, EDGWARE TOWN, EGHAM TOWN, FAREHAM TOWN, GOOLE TOWN, HASTINGS TOWN, IPSWICH TOWN, KINGSBURY TOWN, NEW-BURY TOWN, SHREWSBURY TOWN, WITHAM TOWN, and WOKINGHAM TOWN.

tracksuit manager A manager who con-centrates upon team tactics and other mat-ters on the pitch, rather than upon the financial business of a club and other related affairs.

trainee A young apprentice who is recruited by a club with a view to training him as a possible future first-team player. A traditional part of the trainee's duties is the cleaning of the first team's boots (they may also be required at some less wealthy clubs to do such menial tasks as clean out the public lavatories after a match – as Denis LAW often had to do when he was with Huddersfield Town). The current appren-tice scheme was inaugurated in 1960; in the ensuing 10 seasons over 2000 players joined the League clubs as apprentices (mostly as 'associated schoolboys'), of whom over 1100 eventually turned professional. Not all professionals go straight into the game on leaving school, however. Among those to have worked in other spheres before establishing careers in football in recent times have been Chris Waddle, who was employed making sausages in a factory in Newcastle, David Seaman, who was a baker's assistant, and Ian Wright, formerly a labourer and plasterer.

trainer The club official whose primary duty is to maintain the fitness of players. As well as overseeing exercise routines and con-sulting on diets, etc., he also provides basic first aid for injured players (*see* MAGIC SPONGE).

training The undertaking of various exer-cise programmes and practice games, etc., as preparation for a match. Conscientious training is a prerequisite of every modern professional player's life, though it was not always so:

> *The Corinthians of my day never trained, and I can safely say that the need of it was never felt. We were all fit and I think I could have played on for more than one and a half hours without being any the worse.*

G.O. Smith

Records of team training do, however, go back as far as the 1880s, when Blackburn Olympic became the first squad to train specifically for an FA Cup Final (that of 1883, which they won).

Modern training programmes extend much further than exercises on the training ground itself and the life of the contemporary professional is dominated by the instructions of the manager and his staff, who may seek to regulate his diet, his alcohol intake, and other aspects of his private life.

Most myths about training for football games (as well as other sporting events) concern the prohibitions laid down against players indulging in sex before an important fixture. In reality, many managers have proved themselves less than anxious about the issue. Bill SHANKLY made it clear that he for one was not about to put a blanket ban on such activity, as long as it was all in moderation:

Of course a player can have sexual intercourse before a match and play a blinder. But if he did it for six months, he'd be a decrepit old man. It takes the strength from the body.

By way of contrast, somewhat firmer views on the subject were expressed by another 'expert' in 1968, when sex symbol Brigitte Bardot was asked for some advice for members of the French Olympic team. She told them: 'Get there early, rest a few days, train carefully and cut out the romance until you get used to the altitude.'

See also LILLESHALL HALL.

Tranmere Rovers English football club, nicknamed Rovers. Strip: all white. Tranmere Rovers were formed (as Belmont) in 1884 and acquired their present name in 1885. They nearly went out of existence altogether in 1899 when all the players left to join another club, but went on to establish themselves as a leading Lancashire side, finally joining the League (as founder members of the Third Division (North)) in 1921.

Based since 1912 at PRENTON PARK, the club have generally languished in the shadow of the Merseyside giants, but have soldiered bravely on in the two lower divisions throughout their history, with brief spells in the Second Division in 1938–39 and again from 1991. Their few honours include the Welsh Cup in 1935, the Third Division (North) title in 1938, and the runners-up position in the Leyland Daf Cup in 1991. Their history has, however, been

enlivened by the presence of several great stars, who all began their careers at Prenton Park – the greatest being Dixie DEAN and Tom 'Pongo' Waring.

Curiosities of the team's history include the fact that in the 1977–78 season of 46 matches, the same 11 players appeared in all but five games.

Tranmere have enjoyed record victory margins of nine goals against Oldham Athletic in 1935 (13–4) – an aggregate total of 17 goals (nine scored by Rovers centre-forward Bunny Bell) that established a League record – and of 13 goals against Oswestry in 1914 (13–0); they suffered their worst defeat in 1953, when they lost 9–1 against Tottenham Hotspur. Harold Bell (who never played for anyone else) holds the record for League appearances with the club, having played 595 matches between 1946 and 1964, during which time he made a League record of 401 consecutive appearances.

Fans of the club are particularly sensitive to identification with their neighbours across the Mersey:

Don't be mistaken, and don't be misled,
We're not Scousers, we're from Birkenhead,
You can shove your cathedrals and shove
your pierhead,
We all follow Tranmere and that's in
Birkenhead.

Supporters' song, to the tune of 'The Wild Rover'

Trans-Atlantic Challenge Cup International cup competition that was staged between leading US and European sides visiting the USA and Canada. The first Trans-Atlantic Challenge Cup tournament took place in 1980, when New York Cosmos emerged as the winners, beating Manchester City 3–2 and AS Roma 5–3. Subsequently the Cup was won by the Seattle Sounders in 1981, Chicago Sting in 1982, and by the New York Cosmos in 1983 and 1984 (the last year the competition was staged).

transfer The commercial deal that is struck to allow a player to move from one club to another, usually for a cash sum, as part of an exchange of players, or more rarely in return for equipment or other material assets. Many players transfer many times in their careers, while others resist all invitations and stay with one side (*see* ONE-CLUB MAN).

Announcements of new record transfer fees have long been the source of much scandalized comment in the press. As far back as 1905, the transfer of Alf Common from Sunderland to Middlesbrough for the princely sum of £1000 (the highest transfer fee to date) created a furore and culminated in an FA investigation (only a year earlier he had been the first footballer to change clubs for the figure of £500 when he switched from Sheffield United to Sunderland for £520). As a result, it was decided that a maximum figure of £350 should apply to all transfers – an arrangement that held good for barely four months. Common effectively saved Middlesbrough's place in the First Division and the precedent was set.

Prices continued to escalate, although only recently have they reached the astronomical levels that have left observers gasping. Syd Puddefoot moved from West Ham to Falkirk for a record £5000 in 1922, while David Jack was the first British footballer to be sold for £10,000 when he was transferred from Bolton Wanderers to Arsenal in 1928. A new record was set in 1938, when Wolverhampton Wanderers paid £14,000 for Bryn Jones, a figure that one newspaper speculated would never be surpassed.

Prices continued to rise after the war, with Tommy LAWTON moving for a record £20,000 from Chelsea to Notts County in 1947. In the 1950s John CHARLES became the first British player to transfer to a foreign club (Juventus), for the respectable fee of £65,000. In 1951 Jackie Sewell became the first player to be literally worth his weight in gold (taking into account his body weight and the current state of the gold market) when he was sold for £35,000. 1958 also saw the first player to be sold on a hire-purchase basis (Cliff Holton, who moved in this way from Arsenal to Watford). Subsequently Denis LAW was the first British footballer to pass the £100,000 mark when he was transferred for that sum from Manchester City to Torino.

Trevor FRANCIS became the first British player to be the subject of a £1 million transfer when he was sold to Nottingham Forest by Birmingham City in 1979. The first player to be exchanged between Scottish clubs for the same amount was Ian Ferguson, who moved from St Mirren to Rangers in 1988. Bryan ROBSON transferred from West Bromwich Albion to Manchester United for £1,500,000 in 1981, while a scant 11 years later Blackburn Rovers paid Southampton a staggering £3.6 million for striker Alan SHEARER. A new British transfer record was set in 1993, when Rangers paid £4 million for Dundee United's Duncan Ferguson.

British transfer fees, high though they now are, pale in comparison with the amounts paid by various continental teams. Mark HUGHES of Manchester United and Gary LINEKER of Everton both moved to Barcelona for £2 million in 1986. The first British player to break through the £3 million barrier in a foreign deal was Ian RUSH, who transferred from Liverpool to Juventus for £3.2 million in 1987. Paul GASCOIGNE's subsequent transfer from Tottenham Hotspur to Lazio set the Italian club back a cool £5 million, while David Platt's transfer from Bari to Juventus for £8 million in 1992 made him the most expensive British player to date. Other players who have commanded similar fees in the foreign transfer market have included Ruud GULLIT, who cost AC Milan £5.7 million when they acquired him from Ajax, and MARADONA, whose two transfers (in 1982 and 1984) netted a total of £11,900,000.

By way of contrast, many players just starting out, nearing the end of their careers, or failing to make the grade have been transferred for free or have featured in bizarre exchanges of equipment and other assets. Moss End's Jock Spelton was transferred to Holt United for 30 sheets of corrugated iron, while William Wright joined Blackpool in 1951 for the price of a set of tangerine shirts and early in his career Ireland international Tony Cascarino once moved from Crockenhill to Gillingham for a set of tracksuits. In 1937 Gillingham also exchanged a player to Aston Villa for three used turnstiles, a typewriter, two goalkeepers' jerseys, an assistant trainer, and three jars of weedkiller.

Even more bizarre was the transfer fee paid by the Uruguayan club Rentistas to Central Español for Daniel Allende in 1979: the club had no money but through a director did have access to a slaughter house and paid for Allende with 550 beef steaks (handed over at 25 a week) plus a 'stake' in any later transfer fee earned for him.

On not dissimilar lines, Manchester United received wing-half Hughie McLenahan from amateurs Stockport County in 1927 for the price of three freezers of ice cream.

As an encouragement to impoverished clubs, however, it must be noted that of the 11 players who claimed the FA Cup for Bolton Wanderers in 1958, not one had cost more than the £10 paid as a signing-on fee.

See also LURE OF THE LIRA.

I am no longer a footballer. I am an industry.

Johan Cruyff, on his transfer from Ajax

Hey, son, the punters are all shouting that you're useless, daft and stupid. But don't worry son, you're not useless, daft or stupid. I am. I paid forty grand for you.

Bertie Auld, berating one of his Partick Thistle players

Trautmann, Bert (1923–) German-born goalkeeper, who became a great favourite with English crowds after World War II. Despite the drawback of his nationality in a time when wartime memories were still very fresh, Trautmann established himself as a popular successor to the great Frank SWIFT at Manchester City and is particularly remembered for his courageous performance in the 1956 FA Cup Final, when he remained at his post after breaking his neck.

Treble, The A combination of three titles, all of which are won by the same team in a single season. Recording victory in three major competitions in a single season is rare in senior football. One club who came close to claiming a classic treble were Leeds United, who in 1970 had reached the semi-finals of the European Cup and the FA Cup and were ahead in the League championship. Unfortunately, the prospect of a historic achievement vanished utterly with disappointment in all three campaigns with defeat in the European Cup semi-finals against Celtic, in the FA Cup Final replay against Chelsea, and only the runners-up position in the League (behind Everton). Everton themselves looked set to achieve a treble of the European Cup Winners' Cup, the League championship, and the FA Cup in 1985, but had to be content with a double after they lost to Manchester United in the FA Cup.

Teams that have actually managed to win three or more important titles in a single season include Ajax, whose tally at the end of 1972 included victories in the domestic League and Cup tournaments and in the Champions' Cup, the World Club Cup, and the European Super Cup. The only English club to manage a Treble of major titles in a single season is Liverpool, who captured the League championship, the League Cup, and the European Cup in 1984. North of the border, Rangers were the first team to win the Scottish treble of the Scottish Cup, the Scottish League Cup, and the League championship (in 1949). *See also* DOUBLE, THE.

Trésor, Marius (1950–) French centre-back, born in Guadeloupe, who was a pillar of the French national side throughout the 1970s. Playing at home for Ajaccio, Olym-

pique Marseille, and Bordeaux, he won particular praise for his brilliant performances in the 1978 and 1982 World Cups.

Tricky Trees Nickname sometimes applied to the English football club NOTTINGHAM FOREST.

Tring Town English non-League football club. Strip: red and white shirts, white shorts, and red socks. Founded in 1904 and based at Pendley Sports Centre, Tring Town play in the Isthmian League.

Trinidad and Tobago Trinidad and Tobago joined FIFA in 1963 but have yet to make much impact in international competition. Strip: white shirts, black shorts, and red socks.

triple hat-trick The scoring of nine goals in a single match is rare in the extreme, but has been known. The first man to score such a triple hat-trick in British League football was Robert 'Bunny' Bell of Tranmere Rovers, who scored nine times in a 13–4 win against Oldham Athletic in 1935 (he also missed a penalty). The few distinguished men to have achieved the feat since then include Hibernian's Joe Baker who scored nine goals against Peebles Rovers in 1961 and Bournemouth and Boscombe Athletic's Ted MacDougall, who netted nine goals in an 11–0 victory over Margate in 1971 (a record for the FA Cup). *See also* TEN-GOAL.

Trophy, The *See* FA CHALLENGE TROPHY.

Trotters Nickname of the English football club BOLTON WANDERERS, in reference to the fact that until they settled at BURNDEN PARK the players were constantly on the move from one temporary home ground to another.

Trowbridge Town English non-League football club, nicknamed the Bees. Strip: gold shirts with black shorts and socks. Founded in 1880 and based at the Frome Road ground, the club play in the Southern League.

tsu-chu Primitive form of football that was popular in ancient China during the Han dynasty 2000 years ago and which remains the earliest known version of the sport. Our knowledge of how the ancient Chinese played their game is sketchy and depends upon such vague accounts as the following written by the poet Li Yu, who lived in the first century AD:

*A round ball and an oblong space with two
    teams standing opposed
The ball flies across the moon at the full
Captains are appointed and take their
    places in accordance with regulation
    unchanging
In the game make no allowance for kith
    and kin and let not your mind be swayed
    by partialities
Be cool, determined, and show not the
    slightest irritation when you fail . . .*

Another contemporary explained the title of the game thus: 'Tsu must kick . . . Chu is stuffed leather ball.'

Records of the game go as far back as 206 BC, when it was played on the birthday of the Emperor Che'eng Ti, who participated both as a player and as a spectator. It is said that one of his successors as emperor was so enthusiastic about the game that he had critics of it summarily executed. It seems likely that skill at dribbling the ball was central to the game. The goal comprised two 30-foot high bamboo poles, which stood just a yard apart and supported a silken goal net. The two teams aimed to kick the ball between the posts and if they won were rewarded with a magnificent banquet. Losers were often put to death or flogged.

It is thought that the game may have evolved from similar kickabouts incorporated in Chinese military training as far back as the fourth century BC. The game of tsu-chu itself had more or less died out before the end of the first century AD, by which time several new variants had begun to evolve. *See also* KEMARI.

Tub, The Nickname of the FEYENOORD STADIUM in Rotterdam.

Tunisia The Tunisian national side are among the few African nations to have built up a considerable international reputation. The team made their first appearance in the World Cup Finals in 1978 and impressed observers by beating Mexico 3–1 and then giving a good account of themselves before losing 1–0 to Poland and holding reigning champions West Germany to a draw. Strip: red shirts, white shorts, and red socks.

Turf Moor The home ground of the English football club BURNLEY. The club first played at the ground, then literally a square of turf on the moors, in 1883 and have never left it since. Events in the ground's history have included what was probably the first visit by a member of the royal family to any football ground (by Queen Victoria's son

Prince Albert in 1886) – an honour which led to the team being dubbed the 'Royalites' for some years. One fan died in 1924 when a record crowd turned up for an FA Cup match against Huddersfield. Unusual events from the same era included one match played on a very windy day, when the Burnley goalkeeper Jerry Dawson saw one of his goal kicks result in a corner against the Clarets. Turf Moor was substantially redeveloped under chairman Bob Lord in the 1970s when it was described as one of the most modern in the country; a new main stand was named after Bob Lord himself.

Turkey The Turkish national side have a long history but have rarely threatened to join the ranks of the most prestigious international teams. They owed their entry in the World Cup Finals in 1954 to the drawing of lots after a play-off against Spain and subsequently performed respectably against West Germany (losing 4–1) and against South Korea (winning 7–0) but then lost a second match against a stronger West German side 7–2 and have not since reappeared in the Finals. Strip: white shirts and shorts, with white and red socks.

23rd August Stadium The Romanian national football stadium, in Bucharest. The stadium was opened in 1953 and named in memory of the date on which the Romanians rebelled against their German invaders in 1944 (a national holiday). As well as athletics and other events, the stadium hosts most of the country's international football fixtures.

Twerton Park The home ground (in Bath) of the English football club BRISTOL ROVERS and of non-League Bath City, who first occupied it in 1932. Twerton Park became Rovers' new home under a pioneering ground-sharing scheme in 1986, after the club vacated EASTVILLE STADIUM, partly due to a disastrous fire in 1980 and partly due to disagreements with the landlords. After rejecting a suggestion that they relocate in Gloucester, Rovers moved in with Bath City, bringing with them their goals, ten turnstiles, and a groundsman. Bristol Rovers were still there in 1990, when a fire severely damaged much of their temporary home.

Two-for-Three Scheme *See* OFFSIDE TRAP.

two–three–five Tactical formation in which five forwards are supported by three half-backs and two full-backs. The two–three–five formation was the classic system used by virtually all teams in the early history of the game. It first became universal in the 1880s and remained the standard formation at least until 1925, when the change in the offside rule opened the door to new systems. It was still the backbone of most team tactics up until the 1950s, when the arrival of the deep-lying centre-forward and other innovations prompted managers to experiment with different shapes (favourite alternatives being the four–two–four and four–three–three shapes).

Tykes Nickname of the English football club BARNSLEY, from the ancient dialect term for a native of Yorkshire (originally used to denote comical rustic characters or, as an insult derived from Old Norse, a dog or cur).

Tynecastle Park The home ground, in Edinburgh, of the Scottish football club HEART OF MIDLOTHIAN. Hearts opened the first Tynecastle Park in 1881 but subsequently moved to a new ground of the same name in 1886. The ground was substantially developed in response to the club's successes in the years before World War I and again in the 1950s.

Tynesiders Nickname of the English non-League football club GATESHEAD, reflecting their location near the River Tyne.

U

U's Nickname of a number of football clubs called 'United'. They include COLCHESTER UNITED, OXFORD UNITED, and SUTTON UNITED.

UEFA The Union of European Football Associations, which is the governing body of European football. UEFA was formed in 1954 and within a year of its foundation was given the task of launching what was to become the European Cup, now the showcase for the European game. Wielding authority over the national FAs, UEFA was modelled on its equivalent in South America and is ultimately responsible to FIFA. Based at Berne, the organization has ruled on some of the most contentious issues in contemporary football. In 1985 it imposed a lengthy ban on English clubs after the Heysel Stadium disaster; other rulings have included one which limited clubs participating in European competitions to just three foreign players each.

UEFA Cup International cup competition, run under the aegis of UEFA, which was founded in 1954 as the International Inter-City Industrial Fairs Cup (usually referred to simply as the Fairs Cup). After a hesitant start, the tournament gradually won interest, with both club sides and teams representing certain cities taking part. Reformed in the 1960s on the lines of an international tournament open to losing finalists in a number of domestic competitions, it acquired its present name in 1972. Spanish sides featured strongly in the early years of the competition, while English teams won it six years in a row between 1967 and 1973 (two victories going to Leeds United).

Uganda Uganda joined FIFA in 1959 but have yet to make much impact in international competition. Strip: yellow and black shirts, black and yellow shorts, and yellow and red socks.

Újpesti Dózsa Hungarian football club, which was named after György Dózsa, a nobleman of the 16th century who died at the stake after leading an uprising against the Turkish occupants of Hungary. Strip: lilac shirts, white shorts, and lilac socks. Based at the Dózsa Stadium in Budapest, the club was founded in 1885 and can now claim 19 League championships and 7 Cup victories to its credit. The club of the Ministry of the Interior and Police, the team (originally called simply Újpesti) dominated Hungarian football in the early 1970s and also did well in Europe (finishing runners-up to Newcastle United in the 1969 Fairs Cup).

Ulleval Norway's national football stadium, in the city of Oslo. The stadium was opened in 1926; more modern facilities include the Coca-Cola Stand opened in 1986. The stadium is the headquarters of both the Lyn Oslo football club and of the Norwegian Football Federation.

Ullevi The home ground, in Gothenburg, of the Swedish football clubs Örgryte IS, GAIS, and IFK GOTHENBURG. Named after the Scandinavian god of sport, the present Temple of Ull (as the name translates into English) is the second stadium to bear the name and was opened in 1958. Sweden's largest football ground, it hosted World Cup games in the year of its opening and has since been used for many more international fixtures, boxing matches, speedway, and rock concerts as well as for domestic football matches. The European Cup Winners' Cup Final was held here in 1982, while back in 1975 it witnessed the first game involving the national Swedish women's football team.

Üllöi Út The home ground, in Budapest, of the Hungarian football team FERENCVÁROS, the most successful in the history of the Hungarian game. The first Üllöi Út was opened in 1911 and was subsequently developed as one of the leading venues in the country, hosting many major matches, including international fixtures.

In 1947 the stadium was the scene of a disaster, when parts of the terracing collapsed as a capacity crowd flooded the ground for an international meeting with Austria. Miraculously, no one died (though one man – later provided with a job for 25 years by the club – was permanently disabled by his injuries). It emerged that the ground's capacity had been exceeded by far due to the issue of many forged tickets. The stadium was completely rebuilt in the early 1970s, retaining only a statue to the founder of the club.

umpire In the early history of the game, one of the two officials who undertook the role of the modern referee. Competing teams provided one umpire each, who exercised control over one half of the pitch, giving rulings after players made an appeal (as in cricket). Disputes between the two umpires were inevitably common and from the 1890s an independent referee was supplied to arbitrate between them, relegating the umpires themselves to the roles of linesmen.

undersoil heating The heating of pitches by electrically heated wires laid beneath the playing surface, in an attempt to stave off the effects of cold weather. The first such system was installed at Everton's Goodison Park in 1958 at a cost of £7000 (though early experiments with such equipment had taken place at the club's practice ground back in 1937). Although Everton's system did not prove a success, similar systems were subsequently installed elsewhere in the UK and in other countries where much playing time would otherwise be lost through cold weather. The first Scottish ground thus equipped was Hibernian's Easter Road in 1980.

United Nickname of a number of football clubs throughout the UK, including CAMBRIDGE UNITED, CHESHAM UNITED, HEREFORD UNITED, LEEDS UNITED, and LEICESTER UNITED.

United Arab Emirates The UAE joined FIFA in 1972, five years before Don REVIE made his highly controversial move to the UAE after giving up the post of manager of England. The team enjoyed its most glorious moment to date in 1990, when the side qualified for the World Cup Finals in Italy thanks largely to the efforts of manager Mario ZAGALO (they lost all three of their games). Strip: all white.

United Soccer Association Officially sanctioned US football organization that was formed in 1967. Approved by the United States Soccer Football Association and the Canadian Soccer Football Association, the USA comprised just twelve teams (nicknamed the 'Inlaws') but was (with the rival NPSL) virtually the first attempt to create a nationwide football network.

The haste with which the organization was established, however, meant that there were few home-grown sides ready to meet the challenge the Association offered. To solve the problem various celebrated European teams were invited to spend the summer months of 1967 playing in the USA in the colours of the US clubs while resident teams were trained in preparation for the 1968 season. Thus it was that Wolverhampton Wanderers (Los Angeles Wolves), Sunderland (Vancouver Royals), Stoke City (Cleveland Stokers), Hibernian (Toronto City), Aberdeen (Washington Whips), Dundee United (Dallas Tornado), Glentoran (Detroit Cougars), Shamrock Rovers (Boston Rovers), the Brazilian club Bangu (Houston Stars), the Italian club Cagliari (Chicago Mustangs), the Dutch club Den Hague (Golden Gate Gales), and the Uruguayan club Cerro (New York Skyliners) all made the journey to the USA to demonstrate their skills in front of US audiences; Wolves and Aberdeen (in their respective US incarnations) reached the grand Final in Los Angeles, Wolves taking the title after an extraordinary match that ended with a scoreline of 6–5. *See also* OUTLAWS.

upright A goalpost.

Upton Park The home ground, in London, of the English football club WEST HAM UNITED. Popularly known as Upton Park after the local district, the venue is formally titled the Boleyn Ground, after the name of a house that previously stood next door to the site. The house itself – built in 1544 – was named Boleyn Castle, after Henry VIII's wife Anne Boleyn (though she never lived there).

The ground, then a cabbage patch, became home to the Hammers in 1904 and was steadily improved over the ensuing years until the team won League membership in 1919. New stands – one of them rejoicing in the name the Chicken Run – were then built, but much was destroyed by bombs during World War II (together with the club records). The last vestiges of Boleyn Castle were demolished in the 1950s and subsequently the Chicken Run also went as the ground was substantially refurbished in the 1960s.

The smallest crowd seen for a major game at Upton Park was recorded in 1980 when West Ham played Castilla in the European Cup Winners' Cup. The match had to be played behind closed doors after crowd trouble at the first leg of the fixture in Spain (during which one West Ham fan died); just 262 people attended.

Urchins Nickname of the English non-League football club HORNCHURCH.

Uruguay The Uruguayan national team has one of the most distinguished records in the international game. The side first established its reputation on the international stage in 1924, when the team became the first non-European squad to capture the Olympic football title. They repeated the feat four years later and then confirmed their dominance with victory in the very first World Cup, which Uruguay hosted in 1930. Memories of those golden years were evoked in 1950, when Uruguay claimed their second World Cup victory, after defeating favourites Brazil. In 1954 the epic meeting of defending champions Uruguay and mighty Hungary led to a match of such breathtaking brilliance that many commentators described it as the best match of all time (Hungary won 4–2 in extra time). The team has also won 13 South American Championships. Strip: sky blue shirts with white trim, black shorts and socks with sky blue trim.

> *Other countries have their history. Uruguay has its football.*
>
> Ondino Viera, team manager (1966)

USA The United States of America are hardly renowned as a hotbed of football (*see* NASL), but the national team has on rare occasions had a considerable impact on the international game. With a team that included a number of imported players, the USA did in fact participate in the very first World Cup in 1930, when they got as far as the semi-finals, and were also present in 1934.

The most famous outing of them all was the shock defeat of England in the World Cup Finals of 1950, which remains the most embarrassing and inexpicable result in England's international football history. No one had any doubt that England, acknowledged to be the finest team in the world and entering their first World Cup tournament, would thrash the Americans, who were ranked 500–1 outsiders. The US team seconded this opinion, seeing no way that a motley crew of inexperienced players from several countries, led by a former Wrexham player (Eddie McIlvenny) and backed by a goalkeeper who was better known as a former baseball player, could possibly overcome a team that included players of the calibre of Wilf Mannion, Billy WRIGHT, Tom FINNEY, and Stan MORTENSEN (who had already cowed Chile 2–0 in the first round). Players with the US squad readily admitted their lack of confidence and several were reported to have spent the evening before the match drinking to their imminent humiliation.

But it all turned out very differently. England hit the bars and posts of the goal around a dozen times and just could not get the ball in the net, while at the other end the Haitian striker Larry Gaetjens (fated to disappear in highly mysterious circumstances in Haiti in the early 1970s) headed the only goal of the game in the 37th minute (some said he was actually trying to duck out of the way and the ball hit him on the left ear). The final scoreline of USA 1, England 0 caused a sensation and effectively ended the English campaign (which petered out with a 1–0 defeat against Spain).

> *Bloody ridiculous. Can't we play them again tomorrow?*
>
> Wilf Mannion, at the end of the fateful match

The defeat traumatized English football and the FA quickly set up a technical committee to look into all matters relating to the country's participation in future World Cup competitions. As Billy Wright observed: 'To be defeated by the United States at football was like the MCC being beaten by Germany at cricket.'

A degree of revenge was had three years later when England trounced the Americans 6–3 but the infamous defeat lived far longer in the memory than the subsequent victory did.

The USA failed to build on their extraordinary success in 1950 and it was not until 1990 that they qualified once more for a World Cup Finals series. Nonetheless they revived memories of their great surprise victory 43 years on when they inflicted another devastating defeat upon England in a friendly in 1993, winning the match 2–0. The USA's selection as host of the 1994 World Cup also promised the chance of a resurgence of interest in the game at home.

> *Where are we going? What the hell are we doing? Why the hell do these people keep paying me?*
>
> Alkis Panagoulias, US national coach (1985)

I can't teach lame ducks to fly any more.

Bob Gansler, departing US national coach (1991)

Strip: white shirts, blue shorts, and white socks. *See also* ASL; CSL; SHOTPUTTERS; WSA.

USSR *See* SOVIET UNION.

Uxbridge English non-League football club, nicknamed the Reds. Strip: red shirts, white shorts, and red socks. Founded in 1871 and based at the Honeycroft ground in West Drayton, Uxbridge play in the Isthmian League.

V

Valderrama, Carlos (1961–) Colombian footballer, nicknamed the South American Gullit, who emerged as one of South America's leading players in the late 1980s. Acclaimed for his supreme ball control and skill as a dribbler, he was voted South American Footballer of the Year in 1987 and was a star of the 1990 World Cup. He transferred to the French club Montpellier in 1988 and subsequently to Valladolid in 1991.

Vale Nickname of the English non-League football club MALDEN VALE.

Vale of Leven Former Scottish League football club, which was a League member from 1890 to 1926. Based at Millburn Park, Alexandria, the team was once one of the most formidable in Scotland, but is now confined to minor league football.

Vale Park The home ground, in Burslem, Stoke-on-Trent, of the English football club PORT VALE. Port Vale had big plans for Vale Park, which became their sixth home in 1950. In defiance of their modest performance since the war, the Port Vale directors agreed to construct the finest stadium in the north, with a top capacity of 70,000 spectators. Work began on the project in 1944 and was far from complete when Port Vale actually moved in (still to come were more stands and the stadium's own railway station).

Unfortunately the money ran out and it became clear that Vale's 'Wembley of the North' would remain a dream. Stands subsequently suffered from fire and decay and changes in ground capacities due to safety considerations meant that just 16,500 fans could be accommodated there in the late 1980s. Oddities of the existing stadium include a huge players' tunnel that was originally intended to disappear into a massive main stand (like the railway station, never built).

Valencia Spanish football club, nicknamed the Ché's. Strip: all white. Founded in 1919 and based at the LUIS CASANOVA STADIUM, the club enjoyed their golden era in the 1940s, when they won the League championship three times and the Cup twice. Subsequently they won the championship in 1971 and the Cup in 1954, 1967, and 1979; the European Cup followed in 1980 and the Fairs Cup in 1962 and 1963. They added the Super Cup in 1980.

Valiants (1) Nickname of the English football club CHARLTON ATHLETIC, in reference to the club's home ground, The VALLEY.

(2) Nickname of the English football club PORT VALE.

Valley, The (1) The home ground of the English football club CHARLTON ATHLETIC. Charlton set about constructing a new home called The Valley in 1919, after occupying a series of different venues. They chose an old chalk pit, which they then cleared and enlarged with banked terraces using earth from an excavation at a local hospital (which was found to contain many bones).

The ground prospered and within years had grown to be the biggest anywhere in the country and was being considered as a venue for FA Cup Finals. The first stand was completed in 1922 but just a year later the club decided to move, citing insufficient support in the local area as a reason. While the first team tried to settle at another ground in Catford the reserves played at The Valley, but the move was a failure and the Catford plan was dropped after a few months.

Against expectation, The Valley failed to attract international games and development of the ground was slow, even during the club's golden era in the 1930s. Minor bomb damage was suffered during World War II, when Charlton played host to bombed-out Millwall. Subsequently few changes were made to the ground, which fell into some disrepair.

The crisis came in the mid-1980s, when the club's financial problems coupled with the huge cost of repairs necessary to the terracing and an unexpected rift with Michael

Gliksten, owner of the site, persuaded the club to move on. The team relocated at distant Selhurst Park, and later, Upton Park, leaving disconsolate fans to complain that their interests had been sacrificed. The last game at The Valley, in 1985, was an emotional affair; there was a demonstration at half-time and at the end fans invaded the pitch and helped themselves to pieces of the treasured turf.

The Valley's history as home to Charlton seemed to be over and the ground quickly deteriorated as vandals moved in. The fans changed everything, however, with the passion and ingenuity of their protests (*see* VALLEY PARTY) and against all the odds the club were back at The Valley in 1991, with promises to restore their old home. The ground re-opened on 5 December 1992; Charlton beat Portsmouth 1–0.

Features of the ground include the Bartram gate, in honour of the club's famous goalkeeper Sam Bartram.

(2) Nickname of the English non-League football club VS RUGBY.

Valley Parade The home ground of the English football club BRADFORD CITY. Valley Parade was home of the club from their earliest history, when they played as Manningham Rugby Club. With the team's arrival in the First Division in 1908, the ground was rapidly developed until it compared with the best in the country. Of particular note was the Main Stand, which was to provide shelter for fans for 77 years before destruction in the tragic fire of 1985, with which the stadium is forever associated (*see* BRADFORD FIRE DISASTER). Sadly ironic was the fact that renovation of the stand had been due to start only one day later.

Events in the ground's intervening history included the erection of various other stands and the arrival of floodlights in 1954. In the aftermath of the fire it was suggested that the club move to a new stadium altogether. The decision was taken, however, to remain at Valley Parade, which would be extensively refurbished. A new Main Stand was opened in 1986. The fire is commemorated at the ground by a statue (and by another in Bradford Cathedral).

Valley Party English political party that was founded by fans of CHARLTON ATHLETIC in 1990. The party was created as a publicity vehicle for the gathering protest movement that had dedicated itself to persuading the club to return to its traditional home at The Valley (an aim fulfilled in 1991). The party came into being specifically in reaction to a decision by Greenwich Council to oppose the renovation of the stadium and stood in the council elections that year, winning an astounding 14,838 votes.

To go on and on the way they did . . . amazing. They deserved a result.

Lennie Lawrence, club manager

Van Basten, Marco (1964–) Dutch centre-forward, who became a star of Italian football in the 1980s. Van Basten began his career with the Dutch club Elinkwijk but subsequently moved to Ajax and then to Italy, where he and Ruud GULLIT were recruited by AC Milan (1987); he also established himself as a key figure in the Dutch national side. He was Europe's top goal scorer in 1985–86 and played brilliantly in the 1988 European Championship (when he scored a virtually impossible goal against the USSR in the Final) and in the 1989 European Cup Final – being acclaimed European Footballer of the Year in both seasons – although his game was disrupted several times by injury. With 25 goals, he was top scorer in the Italian League in 1992.

Van Himst, Paul (1943–) Belgian striker, who is considered by many to have been the finest player ever to represent Belgium. As captain of the national side, he led the team to third place in the European Championship of 1972 and scored a total of 30 goals in 81 appearances. At home, he was a star with Anderlecht in a period when the club dominated Belgian football. He left the team in 1975 to play for Racing White but returned in 1982 as manager and led the side to victory in the UEFA Cup a year later. He gave up the post in 1985 and was subsequently appointed manager of the Belgium team.

Vanden Stock Stadium The home ground of the Belgian football club ANDERLECHT. Popularly dubbed Parc Astrid, the stadium first played host to the club in 1918, when it was formally entitled the Emile Versé stadium, after one of the team's patrons. The venue remained relatively undeveloped until the 1930s, when an ambitious and innovatory cantilever stand and other facilities were added. The home team subsequently established itself as the strongest in Belgium and the ground continued to be improved after World War II, becoming the best-appointed football venue in the country. Nonetheless, in the 1970s the decision was made by the new club president (and former player) Constant Vanden Stock to launch a complete redevelopment of the stadium. Parc Astrid can now claim the title of most luxurious football ground in the world, boasting plush executive accommodation, new stands, lounges, restaurant, and bars.

Vanuatu Vanuatu joined FIFA in 1988 and have yet to establish a reputation in international competition.

Varela, Obdulio (1917–) Uruguayan centre-half, who was the captain and inspiration of the formidable Uruguayan national side that won the World Cup in 1950. Winner of 52 caps, he also distinguished himself in the competition four years later, when the team's victims included both England (4–2) and Scotland (7–0). At home, he played for Wanderers and Peñarol.

Vasco da Gama Brazilian football club, which ranks among the strongest in South America. Strip: black shirts with white diagonal stripe, with white shorts and socks. Founded in 1898 and based at the São Januario Stadium in Rio, Vasco da Gama won the League title at the first attempt in 1923 and subsequently added another 16 League honours as well as the National Championship in 1974 and 1989. Many of the players who represented Brazil in the World Cup of 1950 hailed from Vasco da Gama.

Vase, The *See* FA CHALLENGE VASE.

Vélodrome The home ground of the French football club MARSEILLE. The stadium was opened in 1937 after the team won the French Championship that year and subsequently staged World Cup matches in 1938. With a decline in the team's fortunes on the pitch the club left temporarily in 1965 but were back at the stadium and in the First Division just one year later. The cycle track that gave the stadium its name was built over in 1970 and various other improvements have been made in recent years. Games at the stadium traditionally end in a spectacular post-match entertainment, which might range from a firework display to a pop concert.

Venables, Terry (1943–) English player and manager, nicknamed El Tel in reference to his managerial experience in Spain in the mid-1980s (Tel being a familiar shortening of 'Terry'), who became one of the most prominent football personalities of the early 1990s.

As a player, Venables distinguished himself as a wing-half or inside-forward with Chelsea, Tottenham Hotspur, Queen's Park Rangers, and Crystal Palace and was the first man to play for England at all five levels (schoolboy, youth, amateur, under-23, and full). As a manager he took control of Crystal Palace (getting them back into the First Division in 1980), Queen's Park Rangers (returning them to the top flight in 1983), and Barcelona (with whom he captured the Spanish Championship in 1985) before ultimately taking the post of chief executive at Tottenham Hotspur.

His installation of an artificial surface during his time at Queen's Park Rangers' ground was just one cause of debate in what has been a career beset with controversy (which he has gladly invited with the apology 'I'm there to be disagreed with'). A consummate businessman with an eye for the main chance, Venables had capitalized on the furore in 1971 by publishing a novel (which he had written in collaboration with Gordon Williams) under the title *They Used to Play on Grass*. He has also designed a successful football game, called 'The Manager'.

El Tel's contribution at Tottenham Hotspur was equally full of incident and culminated in public conflict with chairman Alan Sugar in 1993. His eventual dismissal as chief executive of the club provoked fierce protest among his many devoted fans, but in 1994 he was appointed England coach.

I'm past the Kenny Dalglish stage. I've gone potty. I've been there and I'm coming back.

Terry Venables (1991)

See also TEAM OF THE EIGHTIES.

Venezuela Venezuela are relatively inexperienced in terms of international competition, being with Ecuador the only South American side never to have qualified for the Finals of a World Cup. Strip: dark red shirts, white shorts, and white socks with black trim.

Vetch Field The home ground of the Welsh football club SWANSEA CITY. The site was originally used as a field for the cultivation of vetch or tare (as described in a map dating from 1843) and was first developed as a sports ground in 1891. The Swans adopted it as their permanent home in 1912, despite the fact that in the initial season the pitch was laid with cinders rather than grass and the players were obliged to wear knee pads to save themselves from injury. Development of the ground was rapid in the 1920s with new stands and terraces. Further improvements followed in the 1970s and early 1980s with the club's arrival in the First Division.

Vicarage Road The home ground of the English football club WATFORD. Watford played their first match at Vicarage Road (formerly a recreation ground) in 1922, two years after joining the League. The ground was developed slowly owing to lack of resources, despite help from Benskins Brewery (who let their initial loan ride for 35 years and matched every pound raised by supporters). The players themselves helped to construct new terraces in the 1930s (when the stadium was also used for dog-racing for the first time).

Improvements continued at a very gradual pace after World War II, but came faster after the team's playing fortunes picked up in the 1980s. A game in 1961 was held up for a time after a two-foot hole unexpectedly appeared near one of the penalty spots in the course of a match against Grimsby Town (the hole had to be filled in with turf from the edge of the pitch). Expensive electric scoreboards were installed in 1978, dog-racing ended in 1979, and in 1986 the first stage of the ambitious Sir Stanley Rous Stand was opened (built with the assistance of a £1 million contribution from chairman Elton John). The Rookery End at Vicarage Road is named after the Rookery silk mill that once stood next to the site.

Vicente Calderón Stadium Football stadium in Madrid, nicknamed the Mattress Makers' Ground, that is the home of ATLÉTICO MADRID. Initially called the Manzanares Stadium until 1971, it was renamed in honour of the man who was the club president when the venue was opened in 1966. The official opening was celebrated with a match played in the presence of General Franco and the future King Juan Carlos. The stadium extends over the city's ring road to the banks of the River Manzanares and is decorated throughout with red and white stripes – hence the ground's nickname.

Vics Nickname of the English non-League football club NORTHWICH VICTORIA.

Victoria Ground (1) The home ground of the English football club HARTLEPOOL UNITED. The site was a rubbish tip until 1886, when it was transformed into a sports ground and named after Queen Victoria in honour of her approaching Golden Jubilee. Pool settled there in 1908, though little of interest occurred in the early years but for a raid by German airships during World War I. Coming under fire, the airships jettisoned their bombs, two of which fell on the grandstand at the ground (the two Zeppelins were then shot down over the sea). Claims for compensation for the bomb damage after the war were ignored by the German government, who had the effrontery to drop another bomb nearby during World War II.

A 'temporary' Main Stand was added in 1921 and remained until the 1980s. There were considerable improvements in the 1960s during the CLOUGH era, including the tardy installation of floodlights and the erection of the Mill House Stand (named after a local public house).

(2) The home ground of the English football club STOKE CITY. Stoke have been in residence at the Victoria Ground since 1878, longer than any other British League club at one ground. Named after the Victoria Hotel opposite, the ground has been steadily improved over the years, the current Main Stand dating from the 1960s (with the players themselves helping to lay concrete at the rate of one shilling an hour). Curiosities of the modern ground include a viewing area specifically given over to players' wives (the only one of its kind).

Vietnam Vietnam joined FIFA in 1964 but have yet to make much impact in international competition. Strip: red shirts, white shorts, and red socks.

Villa Park The home ground, in Birmingham, of the English football club ASTON VILLA. Villa moved to Villa Park in 1897, the year in which they won the double, and rapidly transformed what had been the Aston Lower Grounds (an amusement park) into one of the leading football grounds in the country, complete with cycle track, practice pitches, and (until 1966) bowling green.

The stadium was substantially redeveloped before World War I (when the cycle track was removed) and in 1922 the large Trinity Road Stand, with its grand staircase entrance, was added (opened by the future King George VI). The ground housed a rifle company during World War II, when the Trinity Road stand was used as an air raid shelter. Further improvements were made in the 1950s and 1960s in preparation for World Cup matches in 1966.

The building of a new North Stand with offices beneath in the late 1970s brought the club trouble in the shape of a financial scandal and a police investigation and resulted ultimately in the imprisonment of the former stadium manager and the architect of the stand itself. A sports centre and other facilities have been added in recent years.

The Holte End (the largest Kop in the country) is named after Sir Thomas Holte, resident of nearby Aston Hall in the 17th century.

Villans Nickname of the English football club ASTON VILLA.

Ville Nickname of the English non-League football club WATERLOOVILLE.

Violets (1) Nickname of the Austrian football club FK AUSTRIA, in reference to the club colours.

(2) Nickname of the French football club TOULOUSE, in reference to the club colours.

Virgin Soldiers Alternative nickname of the English football club CRYSTAL PALACE. The club acquired the nickname (recalling the war novel by Leslie Thomas) after businessman Richard Branson – head of the Virgin business empire – agreed to sponsor the team.

Vitosha The name under which the Bulgarian football club LEVSKI SPARTAK was forced to play for four years in the late 1980s.

Vogts, Berti (Hans Hubert Vogts; 1946–) West German right-back and manager, who was a key figure in the national side for many years before eventually succeeding BECKENBAUER as manager of the German team in 1990. He appeared regularly for the national side between 1967 and 1978, winning a total of 96 caps and a World Cup winners' medal in 1974. At home, he began his career with VfR Buttgen and then became a star with Borussia Mönchengladbach.

Volksparkstadion The home ground of the German football club SV HAMBURG. The stadium was opened in 1925 and was quickly established as one of the most important German football venues. Taken over by Allied forces after World War II, it was refurbished in the 1950s and has since hosted more international matches than any other German stadium. The stadium also houses a synchotron accelerator circuit used for scientific experiments.

volley A shot in which the ball is kicked before it touches the ground.

Vršovice Stadium The home ground, in Prague, of the Czech football club BOHEMIANS. Opened in 1914, the stadium boasted only a cinder pitch until 1951.

Vulture, The Nickname of the Spanish international footballer Emilio BUTRAGUEÑO. The nickname was derived from his surname, *buitre* being Spanish for vulture.

W

Waddle, Chris (1960–) English forward, who earned a reputation as one of the most talented English players of the 1980s while with Newcastle United. Having begun his career with Tow Law Town, Waddle eventually left Newcastle for Tottenham Hotspur and subsequently moved to Marseille for a record £4.5 million. A regular choice for the England squad, he played in the 1986 and 1990 World Cups. In 1992 he returned to Britain, signing for Sheffield Wednesday.

Wales The Welsh national team has comprised many of the most famous names in British football over the years, but has a comparatively undistinguished record in international competition. Though the team won six British international championships between the wars, it has qualified for the World Cup Finals only once, in 1958. Inspired by such players as John CHARLES and Ivor ALLCHURCH, the team beat Hungary 2–1 and drew a further three games before going out against Brazil. In the European Championship, Wales's best year was 1976, when the side won its qualifying group but was then put out by Yugoslavia. Stars with the side in recent years have included Ian RUSH and Mark HUGHES. Strip: all red.

walk To leave the pitch after being SENT OFF.

walking football A version of the game in which players are not permitted to travel at more than walking pace. Such games are particularly suited to elderly or invalid squads. Remarkable examples of such games include one played at Derby in 1937, when the Crewe Railway Veterans met the Derby Railway Veterans – all the players were over 65 years of age (they drew 0–0).

wall A line of defending players, who attempt to block shots at goal from a free kick. The wall cannot be nearer than 10 yards from the kicker. The goalkeeper is usually in charge of constructing such walls.

wall game *See* ETON WALL GAME.

wall pass Alternative term for ONE-TWO.

Walsall English football club, nicknamed the Saddlers. Strip: red, white, and black shirts, white shorts, and red socks with white hoops. The club were founded in 1888 when Walsall Swifts (founded in 1877) and Walsall Town (founded in 1879) merged, using the title Walsall Town Swifts until 1895. The club were based at FELLOWS PARK for many years before a move to the BESCOT STADIUM in 1990.

Walsall joined the League (as members of the Second Division) in 1892 but dropped out in 1895, gaining re-election a year later, losing League status again in 1901, and subsequently returning as members of the new Third Division (North) in 1921. The team remained in the lower divisions until 1961, when they tasted life in the Second Division for two seasons, and more recently enjoyed another brief spell in the Second Division in 1988–89. The club's sole major honour is the Fourth Division championship (1960).

The team has had its moments, however. In 1933 the club pulled off one of the most sensational giant-killing coups of all time when they astounded the experts by humbling Herbert CHAPMAN's mighty Arsenal at the peak of their glory by beating them in the FA Cup 2–0. Legend has it that the cheers of the Walsall fans could be heard two miles away and that Arsenal fans at HIGHBURY STADIUM, where the reserves were playing, greeted the announcement of the result with laughter, thinking it was a joke.

> On my way home to my lodgings that night, in the Underground Railway, I felt positively suicidal. Visions of the Arsenal goals that might have been rose up before my eyes; hopes that the events of the afternoon had been nothing but an evil nightmare would delude me for a brief moment, only to be banished away by the cold, grim reality. Walsall 2, Arsenal 0. Nothing could change those figures.
>
> Cliff Bastin, *Cliff Bastin Remembers* (1950)

This famous victory was echoed in 1984, when the Saddlers once more obstructed the Gunners' progress by beating them in the League Cup, enabling lowly Walsall to reach the semi-finals of the competition.

Star players with the club in the 1960s included Colin Taylor, Tony Richards, and goalkeeper Phil Parkes. In the 1972–73 season Walsall set a new record when they employed the services of no fewer than seven goalkeepers in their League games.

The side enjoyed their record victory in 1899, when they beat Darwen 10–0; somewhat perversely in 1896 Darwen were one of the two teams to inflict record 12–0 defeats on Walsall (the other being Small Heath in 1892). Colin Harrison holds the record for League appearances with the club, having played in 467 games between 1964 and 1982.

Walter, Fritz (1920–) West German midfielder, who was captain of the German team that won the World Cup in 1954. Having made his international debut in 1940, Walter won a total of 61 caps (scoring 33 goals in the process) and reappeared in the World Cup Finals of 1958 but an injury sustained in the semi-finals effectively ended his international career. At home, he played for his local club, Kaiserslautern.

Walton and Hersham English nonLeague football club, nicknamed the Swans, reflecting the riverside location of Waltonon-Thames. Strip: red and white shirts, white shorts, and red socks. Founded in 1896 and based at the Sports Ground in Walton-on-Thames, the Swans play in the Isthmian League.

Wanderers The semi-legendary English football club, which dominated the early history of the FA Cup competition. Strip: orange, violet, and black. The team were founded in 1859 as Forest FC, an Old Harrovian squad who were based at Snaresbrook near Epping Forest. Having changed their name to Wanderers in 1863 and adopted Battersea Park as their home ground, the team went on to win the FA Cup five times in the first seven years of the competition (1872, 1873, 1876, 1877, and 1878); the 1876 win meant they had won the Cup outright, but they sportingly gave it back to the FA for use in subsequent years.

Stars of the Wanderers included Lord KINNAIRD (later president of the FA for 33 years), C.H.R. Wollaston (the only man to appear in all five of the club's successful finals), and A.G. Guillemard (the 'father' of

rugby union). Their illustrious history came to an end in 1881, when the team disbanded after players defected to various Old Boys' clubs.

Wankdorf The most prestigious football ground in Switzerland, which is home to the Swiss football club BSC Young Boys. Named after the local district, it was opened originally in 1925 but was substantially redeveloped in the early 1950s. Though relatively basic in terms of facilities, the stadium has staged many important internationals and in 1954 was the scene of a World Cup Final between Hungary and eventual winners West Germany (days earlier it was also the scene of the notorious Battle of Berne quarter-final between Hungary and Brazil). It is also used for Swiss Cup Finals and other major domestic matches and in 1989 was used for the Final of the European Cup. Plans for further refurbishment were unveiled in the late 1980s.

War Cup The League War Cup, a special cup tournament that was organized by the Football League during World War II. Designed as a temporary replacement for the FA Cup proper, the War Cup was won by West Ham (1940), Preston North End (1941), Wolverhampton Wanderers (1942), and – after the competition was split into regional competitions – Blackpool, Arsenal, and Swansea in 1943, Aston Villa, Charlton Athletic, and Bath in 1944, and Bolton Wanderers, Chelsea, and Bath in 1945.

All teams suffered massive disruption during World War II, with grounds being damaged by bombs and both facilities and personnel being required for war service. Standards of play in the War Cup and parallel competitions inevitably suffered, though fans in such army towns as Aldershot were glad of the chance to see visiting celebrities stationed at nearby barracks don the shirts of their home clubs. 75 professional players (including Bolton Wanderers captain Harry Coslin, Liverpool full-back Tommy Cooper, and Luton goalkeeper Cohan) lost their lives in the course of the war.

Ware English non-League football club, nicknamed the Blues in reference to the team colours. Strip: blue and white striped shirts, blue shorts, and red socks. Founded in 1892 and based at the Buryfield ground, Ware play in the Isthmian League.

Warrington United English non-League

football club, nicknamed the Wires. Strip: yellow shirts, blue shorts, and yellow socks. Founded in 1961 and based at Common Lane in Warrington, the Wires play in the Northern Premier League.

Warriors Nickname of the Scottish football club STENHOUSEMUIR.

Warta The home ground, in Poznan, of the Polish football club KS Warta. Opened in 1928, this huge stadium acquired a grim reputation during World War II, when it was used as a concentration camp for labour slaves, of whom many thousands starved to death between 1940 and 1943.

Wasps Nickname of the Scottish football club ALLOA, in reference to the team colours.

Waterlooville English non-League football club, nicknamed The Ville. Strip: white shirts and blue shorts, with blue socks. Founded in 1910 and based at Jubilee Park in Waterlooville, the club play in the Southern League.

Watford English football club, nicknamed the Hornets. Strip: yellow shirts, black shorts, and black socks. Founded in 1891 (as Watford Rovers – although this link is debatable), the club have been based at the VICARAGE ROAD ground since 1922, two years after they joined the Third Division.

The team slipped down to the Fourth Division in 1958, returned to the Third in 1960, and then ascended to the Second in 1969. An advertisement for a new manager in 1971 drew an application from a 12-year old girl among others; she was not appointed and in 1972 the Hornets sank back into the Third Division, dropping into the bottom division in 1978.

At this point the club's fortunes improved dramatically after pop star Elton John, a former local resident whose uncle Roy Dwight had broken a leg playing for Nottingham Forest in the 1959 FA Cup Final, took over the chairmanship and invested a large sum from his personal wealth in the team. This money, together with the recruitment of Bertie Mee and future England boss Graham Taylor transformed the side and set it on a meteoric path up through the divisions, finally reaching the top flight in 1982. Earning a reputation for innovation (which included an emphasis on 'family football') and fostering such major new talents as John BARNES, Watford were

runners-up in the League championship in 1983 and reached the final of the FA Cup a year later.

Largely through Elton John's efforts, the club enjoyed a high public profile and such ventures as a tour of China in 1983 were widely reported. The team's golden era came to an end later in the decade, however, with Taylor leaving and the club being demoted to the Second Division in 1988.

Watford enjoyed their record victory in 1926, beating Lowestoft Town 10–1; they suffered their worst defeat back in 1912, when they lost 10–0 against Wolverhampton Wanderers. Luther Blisset holds the record for League appearances with the side, having played in 415 matches during three spells at the club between 1976 and 1992.

> *Wanted: Professional footballers, men (or women) aged 18–80. Preference given to applicants with two arms and two legs in working order.*
>
> The Times, advertisement on behalf of Watford (1983)

See also BREWERS.

Watney Cup English pre-season football competition involving the two top-scoring teams in each division, which was founded in 1970. The first sponsored Football League tournament, it was first won by Derby County and subsequently by Fourth Division Colchester United, who overcame West Bromwich Albion in the Final after penalties, Bristol Rovers, and Stoke City. The competition came to an end when the sponsorship did in 1973. It is remembered as the first tournament to make use of the PENALTY SHOOT-OUT to decide drawn matches.

Waysiders Alternative nickname of the Scottish football club AIRDRIEONIANS.

Wealdstone English non-League football club, nicknamed the Stones. Strip: white shirts with blue trim, white shorts, and blue socks. Founded in 1899 and based at Watford's VICARAGE ROAD ground, the Stones play in the Southern League. The club's finest hour was in the 1984–85 season, when they clinched victory in both the Southern League championship and the FA Trophy competition.

Wedlock, Billy See FATTY.

Wednesday, The Former name of the English football club SHEFFIELD WEDNESDAY.

Wee Alex Nickname of the Scottish forward Alex JAMES, in reference to his diminutive build.

Wee Blue Devil Nickname of the Scottish footballer Alan MORTON.

Wee Jags Alternative nickname of the Scottish football club MEADOWBANK THISTLE. 'Jag' is a Scottish dialect term for a thistle.

Wee Rovers Nickname of the Scottish football club ALBION ROVERS.

'Well Nickname of the Scottish football club MOTHERWELL.

Welling United English non-League football club, nicknamed the Wings. Strip: red shirts and shorts with white socks. Founded in 1963 and based at Park View Road in Welling, the club have played in the Conference since 1986.

Welsh Cup Welsh equivalent of the FA Cup in England, which is open to clubs either in Wales or in neighbouring English counties. The tournament was first held in 1877, when the Druids of Ruabon lost 1–0 to Wrexham (unfortunately the Cup itself was not then ready for the winners to receive). Among Wrexham's successors as winners of the competition have been Chirk (who won five times between 1886 and 1894) and Cardiff City (who won it in 1927 as part of a treble comprising the Welsh Cup, the FA Cup, and the Charity Shield and subsequently captured it 10 times between 1964 and 1976). Oswestry, winners of the competition in 1884, were the first team to take the Cup out of Wales. Since 1961 success in the Welsh Cup has brought with it a place in European competition.

Welsh Wizard Nickname of the great Welsh footballer Billy MEREDITH, likening his maverick genius to that of the Welsh-born prime minister David Lloyd George who was also known by the same nickname. Indeed, Meredith was also known as The Lloyd George of Welsh Football.

Wembley (1) England's prestigious international football venue, nicknamed the Old Lady, which is also the traditional venue for the FA Cup Final. Also dubbed the Venue of Legends, the stadium (originally called the Empire Stadium) was erected in north London in the space of 300 days at a cost of £750,000 in time for the celebrated 1923 Cup Final (dubbed the White Horse Final), when something approaching 200,000 fans flooded into the ground.

The initial impetus for the building of the stadium had been the need to find somewhere to house the British Empire Exhibition, which had been planned as a boost to national morale after World War I. The site in the Wembley district of London seemed ideal and the Duke of York (later George VI) cut the first turf in 1921. The construction, with its two distinctive domed towers and dazzling white interior, was completed with 25,000 tons of concrete, 600 tons of reinforcing rods, 1500 tons of steel girders, and 500,000 rivets; at its opening one official proudly described the stadium to be 'as big as the biblical city of Jericho' and all were agreed that it was without doubt not only the largest but also the finest football ground in the world. To prove the new structure's solidity just four days before the big game a battalion of infantry in full uniform were marched into the stadium and on to the terraces and ordered to stamp up and down in unison for an hour.

The huge crowd who turned out to see the first Final in 1923 vividly demonstrated the popularity of the new venue. The first international game to be staged at Wembley followed in 1924, when England met Scotland in a 1–1 draw (the 100th Wembley international took place in 1975, when England beat West Germany 2–0). The future of the venue was temporarily put in doubt at an early stage when in the wake of the Empire Exhibition a buyer could not be found, prompting one critic to write off the whole enterprise as: 'A vast white elephant, a rotting sepulchre of hopes and the grave of fortunes.'

A speculator finally bought the stadium (dismantling many stands used for the Exhibition and selling them for scrap) and the threat of demolition receded (though not before the speculator had committed suicide to escape his creditors). Arthur Elvin established a syndicate to take over the venue and subsequently oversaw the development of the ground until two years before his death in 1957; his ghost is said to haunt the place to this day.

Subsequently the stadium acquired further facilities through the construction of the Wembley Arena, which was opened in 1934, and many years later by the addition of a conference centre and other buildings. The restaurant, added in 1938, was designed to be completely removable to allow for extra seating at Cup Finals (though it has never been removed and is now permanent).

Some clubs have found that the challenge of appearing at Wembley has brought out the best in them; Newcastle United, in particular, enjoyed victory in three Cup Finals at Wembley in the 1950s. Other clubs dreaded their visits and individual players in the postwar era pointed to the number of injuries suffered in Cup Finals at the venue and said the stadium was jinxed. Victims of the jinx included Arsenal's Wally Barnes (who suffered a twisted knee in 1952), Bolton's Eric Bell (an injured leg in 1953), Jimmy Meadows (whose first-class career ended with a leg injury in the 1955 Final), Manchester City's Bert TRAUTMANN (who broke his neck diving at the feet of a Birmingham City forward in 1956), Nottingham Forest's Roy Dwight (a broken leg in 1959), Blackburn Rovers' Dave Whelan (a broken leg in 1960), and Leicester City's Len Chalmers (a leg injury in 1961).

The ground has a better record in terms of postponements, however: it was not until 1979 that a Wembley international was postponed for the first time (a meeting between England and Bulgaria being put off because of fog).

The original pitch was replaced in the 1960s, but this suffered from use for horse shows (one manager described the pitch as a 'cabbage-patch') and had to be replaced once more with turf from Ganton golf course in Yorkshire.

The most glorious moment in the venue's history came in 1966, when Wembley witnessed English football's finest hour with the national team's 4–2 victory in the World Cup Final (though the fact that the home team had been allowed to play all their games at Wembley was a cause of some dissent among the visiting nations). It has also hosted the Finals of several major European competitions.

In general the ground has an exceptionally good record of crowd behaviour at Finals, possibly because of the frequent presence of the monarch, but there have been some regrettable incidents. One of the most notorious events in the ground's distinguished history was in 1977, when Scotland beat England 2–1. Scottish fans went on the rampage, tearing down goalposts and cutting up bits of Wembley turf for souvenirs (Denis LAW reported seeing fans trying to get a severed crossbar into London's Underground, while imaginative entrepreneurs in Glasgow made a considerable amount selling what purported to be genuine Wembley penalty spots).

It is the dream of every English footballer to climb the 39 steps that lead to Wembley's royal box to receive one of football's top honours and a select few have realized this dream. One man who probably never dreamed he would do so was manager Bob PAISLEY, who became the first manager to be invited to climb the stairs when he collected the League Cup on Liverpool's behalf in 1984.

By the 1980s Wembley was showing its age rather badly and a complete facelift was carried out. The ground remains the most prestigious venue in British football and fans and players alike often talk of 'Wembley magic'. It is, however, a fact that the stadium only continues in business through the money it earns as a venue not for football but for greyhound racing, which is staged there several times a week. It is also much used for rugby, hockey, and rock concerts, and in 1982 played host to the Pope. Other Wembley events over the years have ranged from speedway to American football.

Curiosities of the ground include the Olympic torch dating from when the venue hosted the Olympic Games in 1948 and the fact that buried deep beneath the pitch is a train, which was left there during the stadium's initial construction.

(2) English non-League football club, nicknamed the Lions. Strip: red shirts, white shorts, and red socks. Founded in 1946 and based at the Vale Farm ground in Wembley, the Lions play in the Isthmian League.

Wembley of the North Nickname of PORT VALE's home ground VALE PARK.

Wembley Wizards Nickname of the Scotland team that pulled off a famous 5–1 victory over England at Wembley in 1928. The triumph is still cherished by fans north of the border, particularly in view of the fact that Scotland have never since scored more than three goals in any match with the 'auld enemy'. Remarkably enough, the 11 players who represented Scotland on that memorable day had never played together as a team before, and indeed never appeared in quite the same squad ever again.

Before the match Scotland knew that they would benefit greatly if the pitch was wet; their team talk before the game consisted of the instructions: 'Go to bed and pray for rain.'

Key players in the celebrated triumph included goalkeeper Harkness (an amateur), and forwards Alex JAMES, Alan MORTON, and Hughie GALLACHER. Curiously, not one of the celebrated Scottish forward line was over five feet, seven inches tall.

> *The success of the Scots was primarily another demonstration that Scottish skill, science and trickery will prevail against the less attractive and simpler methods of the English style . . .*
>
> Glasgow Herald

West Bromwich Albion English football club, nicknamed the Baggies, the Throstles, or simply the Albion. Strip: navy blue and white vertically striped shirts, white shorts, and blue and white socks. The club was founded in 1879 by workers at Salter's Spring Works in West Bromwich under the name West Bromwich Strollers and – having acquired their current name in 1881 – joined the League as a founder member in 1888.

The Baggies had a number of homes before settling permanently at the HAW-THORNS in 1900, since when they have spent most of their history in the top two divisions (tasting Third Division football for the first time in 1991). Glory came early to the club with victory in the FA Cup in 1888, the first of a total of five Cup triumphs (the others following in 1892, 1931, 1954, and 1968). The 1888 triumph was notable in that it was the first time an all-English squad had won the Cup (in fact, not a single Scot played for the team between 1907 and 1937).

The team's record in the League has been somewhat patchier, with a single First Division championship (1920) to their credit, although they were also runners-up in 1925 and 1954. Other honours have included Second Division titles in 1902 and 1911, the runners-up position in the FA Cup in 1886, 1887, 1895, 1912, and 1935, and victory in the League Cup in 1966 (with the runners-up position in 1967 and 1970).

Achievements of individual players with the club over the years have included the fastest 100 League goals, scored by Jimmy Cookson in 1927 in just 87 matches. Other stars with the side over the years have included winger Billy Bassett in the 1880s, defender Jessie Pennington in the 1920s, and strikers Billy Richardson in the 1930s, Ronnie Allen and Johnny Nicholls in the 1950s, Jeff Astle in the 1960s, Tony Brown in the 1970s, and Bryan ROBSON and Cyrille Regis in the 1980s, when the manager was Ron ATKINSON.

West Brom enjoyed their record victory back in 1892, when they beat Darwen

12–0; they suffered their worst defeat in 1937, losing 10–3 to Stoke City. A 4–2 defeat against non-League Woking in 1991 was felt especially keenly by the club: it was the first time they had lost to a non-League side since before World War I. Two years later non-league Halifax beat them 2–1 in the second round of the FA Cup. Tony Brown holds the record for League appearances with the team, having played in 574 matches between 1963 and 1980.

> *No thank you, when you've seen one wall, you've seen the lot.*
>
> John Trewick, Albion player, on being offered the chance to see the Great Wall of China during an Albion tour of the Far East

See also TEAM OF BOYS.

West Germany *See* GERMANY.

West Ham United English football club, nicknamed the Hammers. Strip: claret and blue shirts with white shorts and socks. West Ham (also nicknamed the Iron) began life as Thames Ironworks, a side formed in 1895 by workers at a shipyard of the same name at the suggestion of the owner, Arnold F. Hills. This amateur club, based at the Memorial Recreation Ground, disbanded in 1900 and West Ham United were established, retaining links with the shipyards for another four years.

The club moved into their permanent home UPTON PARK (formally called the Boleyn Ground) in 1904 and (guided by the still-revered managerial partnership of Charlie Paynter and Syd King) finally won election to the Second Division in 1919, since when they have divided their time between the top two divisions (joining the Premiership in its second season in 1993). They have never won the First Division championship but captured the Second Division title in 1958 and 1981 and won the FA Cup in 1964, 1975, and 1980; they also won the European Cup Winners' Cup in 1965.

West Ham enjoy a reputation as a friendly if unpredictable club given to 'exhibition' football although the supporters have been condemned for their predeliction towards violence on a number of occasions. The club has spawned a respectable number of star players, among them the 1930s striker Vic Watson, Malcolm Allison, Dave Sexton, Frank O'Farrell, Noel Cantwell, and John Bond in the 1950s, Bobby MOORE, Martin Peters, and Geoff HURST in the 1960s, and Trevor Brooking in the 1970s; pop singer David Essex was a schoolboy player with the club in his youth. Famous fans include the television character Alf Garnett (though ironically the actor who plays the role – Warren Mitchell – is a dedicated Spurs supporter).

The Hammers enjoyed their record victory in 1983, when they beat Bury 10–0; they suffered their worst defeat in 1963, losing 8–2 against Blackburn Rovers. Billy Bonds holds the record for League appearances with the club, having played in 663 matches between 1967 and 1988.

> Bow Bells are ringing, for the Claret and Blue
> Bow Bells are ringing, for the Claret and Blue,
> When the Hammers are scoring, and the South Bank
> Are roaring, and the money is pouring,
> For the Claret and Blue, Claret and Blue,
> No relegation for the Claret and Blue,
> Just celebration for the Claret and Blue,
> And one day we'll win, a cup or two, or three,
> Or four or more, for West Ham and the Claret and Blue.
>
> Supporters' song, to the tune of 'The Bells are Ringing'

See also BUBBLES, I'M FOREVER BLOWING.

Western Samoa Western Samoa joined FIFA in 1986 but have yet to make much impact in international competition. Strip: royal blue shirts, white shorts, and royal blue socks with white trim.

Western Soccer Alliance US semi-professional league that emerged as successor to the ill-fated NASL in the mid-1980s. Operating on the west coast of the USA, the WSA is seen by many as a natural starting point for a future nationwide league, in combination with the American Soccer League in the east.

Westfalenstadion The home ground of the German football club BORUSSIA DORTMUND. Opened in 1974, it succeeded the Red Earth Stadium next door and rapidly won over fans and players alike with its intimate 'English' atmosphere. The stadium is regularly used for international fixtures and attracts the largest average football crowd in the whole of Germany.

Weymouth English non-League football club, nicknamed the Terras. Strip: maroon shirts, sky blue shorts, and sky blue socks. Founded in 1890 and based at the Wessex Stadium in Weymouth, the club play in the Southern League. Notorious incidents in the club's history have included the 1982–83 season, when smooth progress in the Alliance Premier League was disrupted by a catastrophic players' strike.

whistle A whistle was first blown by a referee in 1878, when one was used in a game between Nottingham Forest and Sheffield Norfolk. The blowing of the ref's whistle has never been more crucial than it was at the end of an FA Cup semi-final between Sheffield Wednesday and Huddersfield Town in 1930. The whistle for full time was blown just as the ball was going into Huddersfield's net, denying Wednesday a 2–2 draw and getting Huddersfield into the Final.

In 1955 Arsenal left-back Dennis Evans had cause to rue the role of the whistle in a game against Blackpool: he casually rolled the ball into his own net after he heard what he thought was the full-time whistle – only to discover that the whistle had come from the crowd and he had given his opponents a goal (fortunately for him Arsenal still won the game 4–1).

In 1960, during a game between two Danish teams, the referee was about to blow the whistle for full time when his dentures fell out, giving one side time to equalize (somewhat redfaced, the referee refused to let the goal stand).

White Arrow Nickname of the celebrated Argentina-born centre-forward Alfredo DI STEFANO.

white boots White footwear was a passing fashion of the early 1970s, when a number of leading players preferred them to the more usual black variety. The fad was particularly associated with Alan BALL, the flamboyant English midfielder and manager, who became a national hero for his role in England's 1966 World Cup victory (at which time he was just 21 years old). Ball's white boots were a typical piece of showmanship by a player whose flair on the field was reflected in the high value placed upon him in the transfer market. Another prominent player to adopt white footwear was Peter Taylor of Tottenham Hotspur.

White City Former stadium in London, which was used for important football matches and other sporting fixtures until the 1980s. Erected for the Olympic Games of 1908, the huge White City complex (named after the white buildings in which the Franco-British Exhibition was housed there) became a greyhound stadium in 1927. Queen's Park Rangers were among the teams to use the stadium from time to time (they were resident for several months in 1962–63); other events ranged from speedway and show-jumping to cheetah racing. In 1966 the White City staged a World Cup Final match between France and Uruguay and also housed the administrative headquarters for the tournament. Dog racing at the stadium ended in 1984 and the complex was demolished and the land taken over by the BBC.

White Hart Lane The home ground, in north London, of the English football club TOTTENHAM HOTSPUR, which was named after a local thoroughfare after World War I (before which it was usually called the High Road Ground). The club arrived at White Hart Lane (then a nursery) in 1900, with the encouragement of the brewery that owned the White Hart Inn next door (who expected a big upturn in their profits through the custom of visiting fans).

Facilities were basic in the early years but improved rapidly after the team joined the Football League in 1908. Events in the ground's early history included a pitch invasion in 1904 (for which the club was fined) and the installation of the celebrated copper ball and cockerel emblem of the club above one of the stands in 1910 (rumour has it that the ball is a time capsule containing various mementos of the Edwardian period, among them the club's League registration papers).

The Army used the ground as a rifle range during World War I, after which the stands were further developed. Arsenal shared the ground for a time during World War II, when the venue also housed a gas mask factory and a mortuary for those killed in air raids. Matches played by Arsenal at White Hart Lane included an extraordinary meeting with Dynamo Moscow during their celebrated tour of 1945. Arsenal fielded a side that included such admired guests as Stanley MATTHEWS and Stan MORTENSEN, but in the event fortunes were decided as much by the weather as by individual skill. A dense fog restricted visibility to a matter of feet: complaints were made that the Russians had sneaked a twelfth player on to the pitch and that members of both teams were taking advantage of the conditions to commit all manner of foul play. Dynamo emerged 4–3 victors. Arsenal also featured in a memorable game in 1971, when their victory over Spurs at White Hart Lane brought them not only the League cham-

pionship but also decided the double.

A new pitch was laid in the 1950s but otherwise there were few changes until 1980, when the construction of the massive modern West Stand signalled the start of a planned major refurbishment of the ground. The spiralling cost of the West Stand – at £4.2 million the most expensive stand built at any British ground – led to financial difficulties, however, and other improvements were postponed as the club tried to grapple with its severe shortage of funds.

The favourite gathering place for home supporters is The Shelf, a standing area below the balcony of the East Stand. When the future of The Shelf was threatened by the club, fans united in opposing any change and won a reprieve for their popular haunt.

White Horse Final The FA Cup Final of 1923, which is forever associated with a white police horse called Billy. The Final, between Bolton Wanderers and West Ham United, was the first to be staged at the new Wembley Stadium and attracted a massive crowd of some 250,000, far more than the 127,000 the stadium had expected to accommodate. With people spilling on to the pitch and all the facilities comprehensively swamped by the sea of humanity, the authorities faced a seemingly impossible task and it looked likely that the game would have to be called off.

Mounted policemen, among them George Scorey and his mount Billy, strove to clear the playing area. The good humour of the spectators and the arrival of King George V to watch the match did much to help and miraculously the game was able to start, albeit 45 minutes late. The crowd lined the edge of the pitch and players had trouble making space for themselves when it came to taking corners and throw-ins (several times the ball stayed in play after bouncing off spectators on the line). Bolton won the game 2–0.

The fact that the day had not turned to tragedy had much to do with both the crowd's forbearance and the efforts of the many policemen and other authorities at the ground, but the newspapers the following day had eyes only for Billy, the horse who saved a Final. The FA learnt their lesson from the episode and subsequent Finals have been strictly all-ticket affairs.

George Scorey, who was also the subject of press interest, made light of the whole thing. When his girlfriend asked what kind of day he had had he replied 'Oh, just ordinary, lass. Just ordinary.'

Funnily enough, I didn't expect to be at the match and I wasn't bothered as I wasn't keen on football . . . I was thinking about my wedding . . . We arrived at kick-off time and were given orders to clear the pitch. Clear the pitch indeed! You couldn't see it. I felt like giving it up as hopeless because nobody seemed in charge and I didn't know where to start. Anyway, Billy knew what to do and it was the first time he really behaved himself. He pushed forward quietly but firmly and the crowd made way for him. He answered all my orders beautifully and, although it was hard work, the crowd (and they were good natured) seemed to respect the horse . . . In half-an-hour the job was done and the match started. I stayed, of course, but I can't remember much about the game. As I say, I wasn't very keen on football.

PC George Scorey

White Pelé, The (1) Nickname of the Brazilian forward TOSTAO.

(2) Nickname of the Brazilian forward ZICO.

White Powder Nickname of the Brazilian football club FLUMINENSE. It refers to the white face powder worn by fashionable aristocrats at the turn of the century, Fluminense being traditionally identified with the upper classes.

Whites Nickname of the English non-League football club SALISBURY, in reference to the team colours.

Whitley Bay English non-League football club, nicknamed The Bay. Strip: blue and white striped shirts with blue shorts and socks. Founded in 1950 (when Whitley Bay Athletic disbanded) and based at Hillheads Park, the club play in the Northern Premier League.

Whyteleafe English non-League football club, nicknamed the Leafe. Strip: green and white shirts, green shorts, and white socks. Founded in 1946 and based at the ground in Church Road, the Leafe play in the Isthmian League.

Wiener Stadium The Austrian national football stadium, popularly known as the Prater Stadium. Opened in Vienna in 1931, it was home to the classic Wunderteam side that dominated international football for several years. After the Anschluss of 1938 part of the stadium was used as barracks for German soldiers, though it also hosted

games involving the German national side during World War II before further use as a holding camp for Jewish detainees on their way to the concentration camps. Its use by the military made it a target for Allied bombers and it was hit 275 times during one raid alone. Restored after the war, it reclaimed its place as Austria's leading international venue, particularly after 1985, when a dramatic new roof was erected.

Wigan Athletic English football club, nicknamed the Latics. Strip: blue shirts and shorts with red and white trim, with blue socks. The club were founded in 1932 after a public meeting at the Queen's Hotel at which it was decided to establish a new club to attempt to regain the League place of disbanded Wigan Borough (who in 1931 became the first club ever to resign from the League). It was not, however, until 1978 that the team – based since their foundation at SPRINGFIELD PARK – finally won election to the Fourth Division.

Defying the rivalry of nearby Manchester and Liverpool and the area's traditional reputation as a rugby stronghold, the club consolidated their status by going on to win promotion to the Third Division in 1982, before relegation in 1993. Their honours over the years include the Freight Rover Trophy in 1985. Fans of the club are rumoured to include the former Soviet president Mikhail Gorbachov, who is said to have ordered an end to jamming of radio broadcasts from the UK so that he could keep up to date with Wigan's fortunes.

The club enjoyed their record victory in 1934, when they beat Carlisle United 6–0; they suffered their worst defeat in 1990, losing 6–1 to Bristol Rovers. Colin Methven holds the record for League appearances with the club, having played in 296 games between 1979 and 1986.

Wildcats Nickname of the Chilean football club COLO COLO (*colo colo* being Spanish for wildcat).

Wilkins, Ray (1956–) English midfielder, nicknamed The Crab, who began his playing career with Chelsea and later joined Manchester United (1979), AC Milan, Paris St Germain, Glasgow Rangers, and Queen's Park Rangers, often playing as captain. He is much admired for his leadership qualities and has won a total of 84 caps for his country.

Wimbledon English football club, nicknamed the Dons. Strip: blue with yellow trim. The Dons were founded – as Wimbledon Old Centrals – in 1889 by Old Boys from the Central School and subsequently soldiered on in minor leagues until 1977, when they were elected to the Fourth Division. Signs of coming greatness were first registered in 1975, when the club beat Burnley in the third round of the FA Cup and forced a replay against Leeds United in the fourth round.

Against all expectations, the club prospered after taking Workington Town's place in the Fourth Division and began a magical rise through the divisions, finally reaching the First Division in 1986, by which time they had earned a reputation for tough, committed play. Wimbledon finished sixth in the First Division in their first season and in 1988 beat Liverpool in the FA Cup Final.

The rapidity of the club's ascent meant that the Dons retained some of the non-League teamsmanship rarely seen in top flight football; star striker Alan Cork once observed of playing with the team, 'It's a bit like being at school with your mates', while manager Dave Bassett admitted that until the side reached the First Division players were expected to wash their own kit, provide their own towels, and clean their own boots. The club was a founder member of the Premier League in 1992. Stars at PLOUGH LANE during the club's startling rise to fame in the 1980s included John FASHANU, Vinny JONES, and goalkeeper Dave BEASANT; Wimbledon now share SELHURST PARK with Crystal Palace.

The side enjoyed their record victory in 1983, when they beat Newport County 6–0; they suffered their worst defeat in 1978, when they lost 8–0 against Everton. Alan Cork holds the record for League appearances with the club, having played in 430 matches between 1977 and 1992.

> Everyone says Wimbledon is a fairytale, a miracle. What fairytale? It was hard work and correct planning.
>
> Sam Hammam, managing director (1988)

> The borstal of football.
>
> Dave Bassett, manager (1987)

See also CRAZY GANG; WOMBLES.

Windsor and Eton English non-League football club, nicknamed the Royalists. Strip: red shirts with green piping, red shorts, and white socks. Founded originally in 1892 and re-established in 1902, the club are based at Stag Meadow in Windsor and play in the Isthmian League.

Windsor Park The home ground, nicknamed The Shrine, of the Northern Ireland football club LINFIELD. Situated in west Belfast, Windsor Park is also home to the Northern Ireland team and is regularly used for international fixtures. Opened in 1905, the venue includes such features as a Kop. Events in the ground's history have included a number of violent clashes between fans, which during one game in 1912 amounted to a pitched battle with supporters wielding knives and guns. Subsequent disturbances included the notorious riot of 1948 that resulted in the disbanding of the Catholic side Belfast Celtic and extensive damage caused by a terrorist bomb in 1972.

winger An attacking player who occupies a position on the extreme wing of the forward line. Though the winger's prime task is to provide crosses for forwards to score from, wingers often get the chance to score themselves. The record goal tally by a winger in League football was established by Stoke City's Neville Coleman in 1957, when he scored seven times during a match against Lincoln City. Perhaps the most admired wingers in British football since the war were Liverpool's Ian Callaghan and Peter Thompson, who were described as 'Ramsey's flirtation and Shankly's love affair' (curiously, they both won international caps but never appeared together in an England side). The day of the conventional winger came to an end in the 1960s, when a variety of new formations rendered the specialist winger obsolete.

Wingless Wonders Nickname that was bestowed upon Alf RAMSEY's World Cup-winning side in 1966. Although he had experimented with various team formations utilizing wingers in the qualifying games before the Finals, Ramsey was persuaded to adopt a four–three–three formation without wingers in the quarter-finals, when Geoff HURST was selected. His decision and the team's subsequent success convinced many managers to dispense with conventional wingers and to try further experiments with team formations. See also CLASS OF '66.

> We've all followed Ramsey. The winger was dead once you played four defenders. Alf saw that in 1966 and it just took the rest of us a little longer to understand.
>
> Dave Bowen, manager of Wales (1973)

Wings Nickname of the English non-League football club WELLING UNITED.

wins *See* DEFEATS.

Winsford United English non-League football club, nicknamed the Blues in reference to the team colours. Strip: royal blue shirts and socks and white shorts. Founded in 1883 and based at the Barton Stadium, the club play in the Northern Premier League.

Winterbottom, Sir Walter (1913–) English footballer and manager, who became the first manager of England in 1946. Winterbottom (a former player with Manchester United and Chelsea) is remembered more for his innovations as a football administrator than for the national side's modest achievements under his leadership (the team reached the quarter-finals of the World Cup in 1954 and 1962 but collapsed ignominiously in 1950 and 1958). As the FA Director of Coaching, he launched England's Under-23 team and set up a national system of coaching for the first time, innovations for which he won a knighthood in 1978.

Wires Nickname of the English non-League football club WARRINGTON UNITED.

Witham Town English non-League football club, nicknamed Town. Strip: red and black striped shirts with black shorts and socks. Founded in 1948 and based at the Spa Road ground in Witham, the club play in the Isthmian League.

Witney Town English non-League football club. Strip: yellow shirts with royal blue shorts and socks. Founded in 1885 and based at Marriot's Close in Witney, Town play in the Southern League.

Witton Albion English non-League football club, commonly nicknamed the Albion. Strip: red and white striped shirts, black shorts, and red socks. Founded in 1890 and now based at Wincham Park, Albion play in the Conference.

Wivenhoe Town English non-League football club, nicknamed the Dragons. Strip: blue shirts with white shorts and socks. Founded in 1925 and now based at the Broad Lane ground, the club joined the Isthmian League in 1986.

Wizard of Dribble Nickname of the great English footballer Stanley MATTHEWS.

WM Formation Playing formation, which was increasingly adopted by teams after the 1925 change in the offside law. Arsenal and other clubs re-invented the role of the centre-half (*see* STOPPER), leaving the full-backs to mark the wingers and the wing-halfs to play a more crucial role in midfield. The system acquired its name from the pattern adopted by the players, defenders lining up on the points of a W and attackers lining up on the points of an M.

Woking English non-League football club, nicknamed the Cards. Strip: red shirts with white trim with white shorts and socks with red trim. Founded in 1899, the club (based at Kingfield Sports Ground) now play in the Conference. In 1991 they pulled off one of the most remarkable giant-killing feats of modern times, defeating West Bromwich Albion 4–2 in the third round of the FA Cup at the Hawthorns. It was the first time Albion had lost to a non-League club since before World War I and the first time Woking had ever beaten a League side. The club deservedly received a standing ovation as they went down 1–0 against Everton at GOODISON PARK in the next round:

> We had 10,000 fans here, young lads were asking me for an autograph and old men wanted to shake my hand – who the hell am I?

> Adie Cowler, captain of Woking (1991)

Wokingham Town English non-League football club, nicknamed Town. Strip: amber shirts with black shorts and socks. Founded in 1875 and based at the Finchamstead Road ground in Wokingham, Town play in the Isthmian League.

Wolverhampton Wanderers English football club, nicknamed Wolves. Strip: gold shirts, black shorts, and gold socks. Wolves were founded around 1879 by players from two local teams (St Luke's and Wanderers). They were founder members of the Football League in 1888 and have since known life in all four divisions.

Based at MOLINEUX since 1889, their early history was relatively unremarkable, though they finished third in the first League championship and went on to enjoy victory in the FA Cup in 1893. Another FA Cup triumph followed in 1908, but the club spent 1906–23 in the Second Division and then dropped into the Third Division (North) for a season (1923–24) before recovering their Second Division place and then getting back to the First Division in

1932. They remained in the top flight for the next 33 years, a period that was to witness the team's great era.

Major Frank Buckley had some success with the team in the late 1930s, accompanying them as losing finalists in the 1939 FA Cup and making them runners-up in the League in 1938 and 1939, but it was manager Stanley CULLIS, who took over in 1948, who was to make the club the most powerful in the land. Under Cullis, who trained his players in the kick and rush 'long-ball' style, Wolves claimed their third FA Cup title in 1949 and went on to clinch three League championships in the course of the 1950s (in 1954, 1958, and 1959); they also won another FA Cup competition in 1960.

With such star players as Billy WRIGHT, Peter Broadbent, and Ron Flowers, Wolves showed themselves capable of beating the very best of both domestic and foreign opponents and after sensational victories against Moscow Spartak and Honvéd in 1954 Cullis was prompted to boast that his team were champions of the world (a claim that was to hasten the birth of the European Cup).

A decline in the early 1960s led to Cullis's departure and the side subsequently experienced mixed fortunes, winning the League Cup in 1974 and 1980 and reaching the Final of the UEFA Cup in 1972, but also tasting life in the Third (1985–86) and Fourth (1986–88) Divisions, before getting back to the Second Division in 1989. Their failure to add further honours to their tally prompted manager Tommy DOCHERTY to quip, in 1985: 'I just opened the trophy cabinet. Two Japanese prisoners-of-war came out.'

Of his defence he could only say: 'I'm glad I didn't have you four defending me when I had my court case. The judge would've put his black cap on.'

The club narrowly escaped total extinction in 1982 when a financial crisis threatened to overwhelm them; they were saved, however, through the efforts of former star player Derek DOUGAN and others and have since prospered on the pitch through the contribution of such players as Steve BULL (though further boardroom battles continued, notably around the figures of the Bhatti brothers, and the club actually went into receivership in 1986).

Wolves enjoyed their record victory back in 1886, when they beat Creswell's Brewery 14–0; they suffered their worst defeat in 1892, losing 10–1 against Newton Heath. Derek Parkin holds the record for League

appearances with the club, having played in 501 games between 1967 and 1982. *See also* BUCKLEY BABES.

> *There's basically no difference between the Wolves you see now and the Wolves who enjoyed the heady days of the Fifties. They just happen to be in the Third Division.*
>
> Gordon Dimbleby, chief executive (1985)

Wombles Alternative nickname for the English football club WIMBLEDON, in reference to the Wombles of Wimbledon children's television characters.

women's football Women football teams have participated in football for almost as many years as the men, though often in the face of considerable opposition from the authorities governing the male game. Women are not mentioned as such in the official laws of football, but can still be found guilty of ungentlemanly conduct, as can their male counterparts and are otherwise subject to the same rules.

Mixed football is not officially permitted by the FA, who banned it in 1902 after the women's game had experienced something of a boom in the late 1890s, organized by Nettie Honeyball (secretary of the British Ladies team) in England and by Lady Florence Dixie in Scotland. The women's game continued to grow, however, during World War I, when star teams included Preston Ladies. Outstanding players of the era included the Pioneer Ladies captain Ada Anscombe, who, it was rumoured, had been approached by a male side who offered two of their own male players in exchange for her.

Games between men and women footballers actually took place during the war years, chiefly in aid of charity. Records exist of the men compensating for any physical advantage by playing with their hands behind their backs (a game between convalescing Canadian soldiers – who kept their hands behind their backs – and a women's team in 1917 resulted in the ladies winning 8–5).

The Football League banned ladies' teams from using League grounds in 1921 but women's sides continued to flourish both in the UK and abroad. Leading British women players were lured to Italy and elsewhere in the 1960s, where they were able to claim professional status – a trend that revived in the 1980s just as it did in the men's game.

The Women's FA was established in 1969 and boasted 21 Leagues and 8000 registered players by the end of the 1980s. The 1921 ruling was rescinded and the FA allowed women to use FA pitches; full affiliation of the WFA followed in 1984. A Women's FA Cup was inaugurated in 1971, with Southampton beating Stewarton and Thistle in the Final. A Premier League was created in 1992, in parallel with that in the men's game. Top English sides include Doncaster Belles and Millwall Lionesses.

The WFA founded an England women's side in 1972, the team making its debut against Scotland and losing 3–2. A European Championship was started in 1982 and in 1984 England lost 4–3 on penalties to Sweden in the first Final of the Women's UEFA Cup. A year later England's women won the 'Mundialito' mini-World Cup, beating Italy 3–2 in the Final; they won it again in 1988. The first full-scale Women's World Cup was hosted by China in 1991, with the USA emerging as first champions. Linda Curl and Therese Wiseman have both won a record 60 caps playing for England.

More remarkable matches in the history of the women's game include an unusual meeting between Norwich Ladies and Milton Keynes Reserves in 1983: Norwich finished up 40–0 victors (22 of their goals being scored by Linda Curl). *See also* GREGORY'S GIRL.

Football is all very well as a game for rough girls, but it is hardly suitable for delicate boys.

Oscar Wilde

A tyme there is for all,
My mother often sayes,
When she, with skirt tuck't very high,
With girls at football playes.

Sir Philip Sidney (late 16th century)

Women should be in the kitchen, the discotheque, and the boutique but not in football.

Ron Atkinson (1989)

Wood, The Nickname of the English non-League football club BOREHAM WOOD.

Woodburn, Willie (1919–) Scottish centre-half, nicknamed Big Ben, whose career came to a sensational end in 1954 when he fell foul of a disciplinary tribunal. Woodburn was one of the great stars of the Rangers side of the 1940s and early 1950s and very much the cornerstone of the team.

Woodburn had begun his career with Rangers in 1938 and had soon won a reputation for hotheadedness despite his evident skills, which won him the accolade of 'greatest centre-half in the world'. After the war he was frequently in trouble for the physical nature of his play and in 1953 was banned for 21 days for a foul. Another ban, of six weeks, was imposed later in the year for a similar offence but still Woodburn was ruled by his touchpaper temper and in 1954 he was in trouble yet again after he punched Stirling Albion's inside-left Alec Paterson.

Woodburn's consequent appearance in front of the Scottish FA Committee, meeting in secret, lasted four minutes and everyone knew that the punishment would be severe. No one realized, however, just how severe it was to be: in what was the most punitive punishment ever handed down from such an authority to a famous player he was suspended from playing the game for life. Woodburn decided not to pursue the matter in the courts, believing that the ban would be lifted after a few months, but the SFA refused to relent until 1957, by which time Woodburn was too old to resume his playing career.

He was always a fierce competitor . . . but I think that basic determination was distorted by the mystique of Rangers. There is no doubt that in our time the very act of pulling that blue jersey over your head did something to you.

Willie Waddell

Woolwich Arsenal *See* ARSENAL.

Wor Jackie 'Our Jackie', nickname of the celebrated English footballer Jackie MILBURN.

Worcester City English non-League football club, nicknamed City. Strip: blue and white quartered shirts with blue shorts and socks. Founded in 1908 and based at St George's Lane in Worcester, City play in the Southern League.

Workington English football club, nicknamed the Reds. Strip: red shirts, white shorts, and red socks. Founded in 1884 and based at Borough Park in Workington, the club were for many years a League team, taking their place among the greatest sides in the land from 1951 to 1977, when they were replaced by Wimbledon. They now play in the Northern Premier League. Their record win in the League was in 1964, when they defeated Barrow 9–1. In 1966, when the team finished bottom of the Third Division, the club had more directors (13 in all) than it had full-time players.

Worksop Town English non-League football club, nicknamed the Tigers. Strip: amber and black shirts, black shorts, and amber socks. Founded in 1861 and based at Babbage Way in Worksop, the club play in the Northern Premier League.

World Club Championship International football competition, which is contested annually (in Tokyo) by the winners of the European Cup and the South American Copa Libertadores. The tournament was first held in 1961, when the Spanish side Real Madrid beat South American champions Peñarol. Winners since then have included Santos (1962 and 1963), Peñarol (1961, 1966, and 1982), Internazionale (1964 and 1965), AC Milan (1969, 1989, and 1990), and Independiente (1973 and 1984). The Championship has suffered from crowd violence over the years, both Manchester United and Celtic being greeted by riots on visits to South America, and is notable for the high number of dismissals of players from the pitch (no fewer than six players were sent off during a game between Racing of Argentina and Celtic in 1967). Winners of the European Cup have declined to take part on a number of occasions, leaving the runners-up in the Cup to take their place.

World Cup Prestigious international football competition, held every four years, which was founded in 1930. The World Cup tournament is the most senior of all international competitions and success or failure in it is a matter of great national pride or concern. Open to any country that is a member of FIFA, the tournament began with just 13 countries taking part but is now contested by some 100 nations, of whom just 24 go through to the final round.

The idea for such a competition was discussed as far back as 1904, when FIFA was formed, but it was not until the late 1920s, when Uruguay agreed to provide the stadium and pay the expenses of visiting teams, that the idea became a reality. The tournament has been spared most of the political difficulties experienced by the Olympic Games though there has been controversy from time to time (England, for instance, did not take part until 1950 due to their refusal to enlist as FIFA members). Brazil (1958, 1962, and 1970), Italy (1934, 1938, and 1982), and West Germany (1954, 1974, and 1990) have all won the Cup three times; the other winners have been Uruguay (1930 and 1950), England (1966), and Argentina (1978 and 1986).

Only Brazil have taken part in all 14 tournaments to date.

West Germany's Uwe SEELER appeared in more World Cup matches than anyone else, playing in 21 games in four tournaments, but never won a winner's medal; in 1986 his record was equalled by Poland's Wladyslaw Zmuda. Antonio Carbajal meanwhile, holds the record for participation in World Cup competitions, having turned out as goalkeeper for Mexico in 1950, 1954, 1958, 1962, and 1966. Gerd MÜLLER of West Germany has scored the most World Cup goals, with a tally of 28. The 1000th goal in the history of the World Cup was scored by the Dutch player Bobby Rensenbrink in 1978. The record highest score in any World Cup qualifier stands at 13–0, the score by which New Zealand beat Fiji in 1981.

Extraordinary incidents in the annals of the World Cup have included England's sensational defeat at the hands of the USA in 1950, the theft of the Jules Rimet Trophy in 1966 (see PICKLES), and the notorious Hand of God episode involving Diego MARADONA in 1986. See also BATTLE OF BERNE; BOGOTÁ INCIDENT: CLASS OF '66; DIDDY MEN; LITTLE WORLD CUP; SOCCER WAR.

> It's worse than losing a war, a national crisis of the highest magnitude.

Lord George Wigg, on England being knocked out of the World Cup in 1973

> The World Cup – truly an international event.

John Motson

World Cup Willie The cartoon lion who became the symbol of the 1966 World Cup tournament (see CLASS OF '66). Wearing a Union Jack football shirt, World Cup Willie appeared on all manner of merchandise associated with the World Cup and was adopted by the press in cartoons reflecting on England's preparations for the tournament. Skiffle star Lonnie Donegan also released a pop song under the title. Although the FA kept his origins shrouded in mystery, it was eventually revealed that the original 'World Cup Willie' was E.K. Willson, the FA's chief administrative officer, who was thus nicknamed by staff at the organization's headquarters.

World Youth Cup International football competition, held every two years, which is contested by teams of players aged under 18 (under 19 since 1991). Founded by FIFA in 1977, the tournament has been won twice by Brazil (1983 and 1985). Players in the competition are as keen to excel as their counterparts in the senior tournament. Back in 1981, one young Canadian enthusiast convinced his local paper that he had not only been picked to represent the Canadian team in a World Youth Cup competition in Australia but was also emerging as the star of the tournament, leading the side to ultimate victory. His home town went wild and the national press picked up the story before it was discovered that not a word of it was true: Canada had no youth soccer team and there was no competition taking place that year.

Worthing English non-League football club, nicknamed the Rebels. Strip: all red. Founded in 1886 and based at Woodside Road in Worthing, the club play in the Isthmian League.

Wrexham Welsh football club, nicknamed the Robins. Strip: red shirts, white shorts, and red socks. Founded in 1873 by local businessmen, the club can claim to be the oldest surviving football club in Wales. They joined the League in 1921, as founder members of the Third Division (North), and have spent most of their history in the bottom two divisions, with just one spell in the Second Division (1978–82). Their tally of honours includes the Third Division championship (1978) and a total of 21 victories in the Welsh Cup (in which competition they have also held the runners-up position 19 times).

Other landmarks in their history have included the signing of Graham Jones in 1967, who became the 100th player with the surname Jones to join the club since 1921. Another player with Wrexham, Eddie McIlvenny, went on to enjoy a brief moment of fame after emigrating to the USA when, as captain of the USA national team, he led his side to a sensational 1–0 victory over England.

Based at the RACECOURSE GROUND, Wrexham enjoyed their record victory in 1962, when they beat Hartlepools 10–1; they suffered their worst defeat in 1963, losing 9–0 to Brentford. Arfon Griffiths (manager of the club on their elevation to the Second Division) holds the record for League appearances with the club, having played in 592 matches between 1959 and 1979.

Here they come our mighty champions,
Raise your voices to the anthem,
Marching like a mighty army,

Wrexham is the name.

Supporters' song, to the tune of 'Men of Harlech'

Wright, Billy (1924–) English defender, who won fame as captain of England in no fewer than three World Cup campaigns (1950, 1954, and 1958). Wright began his career with Wolverhampton Wanderers in 1941 and recovered from a serious ankle injury a year later to make his international debut in 1946. He subsequently rose to the post of captain of the national team and went on to lead the side in a total of 90 matches (winning 105 caps in all). His skills as captain played a major role in Wolves' FA Cup victory in 1949 and in the League in 1954, 1958, and 1959 and earned him the accolade of Footballer of the Year in 1952. After his retirement as a player, Wright ventured into management at Arsenal (1962– 66) but had little success and eventually gave it up to work in television. He was also manager of the England youth and under-23 teams for a time. One of the most popular, if not naturally talented British players of the era, Wright was a great favourite of the home crowds and his marriage to pop singer Joy Beverley was a cause of national celebration.

WSA *See* WESTERN SOCCER ALLIANCE.

Wunderteam Nickname of the great side that represented Austria in the early 1930s and was almost universally acknowledged to be the most talented team in the world. Managed by Hugo MEISL and trained by the Scotsman Jimmy HOGAN, the side based its game on the short-passing style developed by Scotland and was soon humbling the most respected sides in Europe. Particular praise was reserved for the brilliant centre-forward Matthias SINDELAR.

The pre-eminence of the side was not best reflected in their tally of international honours, however; they did not participate in the inaugural World Cup competition in 1930 and lost to Italy in the World Cup semi-finals of 1934, by which time the team was already past its best. Chances of a reappearance in the 1938 tournament were ended by the Nazis, who insisted that the German team take Austria's place in the Finals (though several Austrians were included in the German squad).

Wycombe Wanderers English football club, nicknamed the Blues in reference to the team colours. Strip: light and dark blue. Founded in 1884 and now based at Adams Park, the Blues were long-term residents of the Isthmian League (1921–1985), winning the Championship seven times, until they won promotion to the GM Vauxhall Conference. Subsequently they enjoyed success in the FA Trophy in 1991 and again in 1993, in which year they also claimed automatic promotion to the Football League under manager Martin O'Neill.

X

X, Mister The name under which Morton billed their goalkeeper at a practice match in 1964, which inevitably led to much speculation about his identity. Mister X turned out to be the Danish keeper Eric Sorensen, who subsequently established himself as the first Scandinavian to make an impression in Scottish football.

Y

Yashin, Lev (1929–91) Soviet goaleeper, variously nicknamed the Black Octopus or the Black Spider, who was widely considered one of the greatest keepers of all time. Yashin was first seen on the international stage in the Olympics of 1956 and in the World Cup competition of 1958, when he was aged 29. Clad in his customary black strip, he made a series of brilliant saves and contributed to his country's successful passage to the quarter finals (and again in 1962); in 1966 he was part of the Soviet team that claimed fourth place in the competition won by England. His prowess in the Soviet goal, coupled with his dark good looks, contributed to the growth of a cult following around his name and he became one of the most popular players in the world.

At home he spent his entire career with Dynamo Moscow, with whom he won four Soviet League championship medals. Other honours included a European Championship medal in 1960, the title of European Footballer of the Year in 1963, and the Order of Lenin. In fact the Black Octopus was nearly lost to the world of football at an early stage in his career when he considered concentrating on ice hockey; it was as an ice hockey player that he first signed for Dynamo. He was noted for his superstitious carrying of two caps to every match he played: one cap he wore during the game, the other remained in the net for luck.

Yate Town English non-League football club, nicknamed the Bluebells. Strip: white shirts, navy blue shorts, and white socks. Founded in 1946 and based at the Lodge Road ground in Yate, Bristol, the club play in the Southern League.

Yeading English non-League football club, nicknamed The Dinc. Strip: red and black striped shirts with black shorts and socks. Founded in 1965 and based at the Warren ground in Hayes, Middlesex, Yeading play in the Isthmian League.

Yeats, Ron (1937–) English defender, nicknamed the Colossus, who was one of Liverpool manager Bill SHANKLY's most fruitful early signings. Shankly bought Yeats from Dundee United in 1961 at the same time he acquired Ian St John, and it was around these two enormously effective players that he constructed the classic Liverpool side that became a dominant force in the mid-1960s. Shankly had no doubts about the potential of his new recruit, proudly showing him off to the press with the words: 'He's a colossus. Come outside and I'll give you a walk round him.'

Also dubbed Rowdy Yeats after a television character, the Colossus – who was as big as his nickname suggests – acted as stopper and earned a reputation as a hard man to beat. He played on into the 1970s, remaining the pivot of the Liverpool defence, and then transferred to Tranmere Rovers, with whom he eventually rose to the post of manager.

> *With him at centre-half, we could play Arthur Askey in goal.*
>
> Bill Shankly (1962)

yellow card One of the two cards carried by referees for use in cautioning players. The yellow card is produced when a player commits a first playing offence. *See also* BOOKING; RED CARD.

Yeltz Nickname of the English non-League football club HALESOWEN TOWN. The origins of the nickname are somewhat obscure, but may lie in the tradition that workers in the nailshops of Quinton were formerly referred to as 'yellers' (as they called to one another from neighbouring shops). Another explanation suggests a link with an old man from Bourneville, who used to sell sweets at the ground.

Yemen Prior to unification of the Yemen Arab Republic and the Yemen People's Democratic Republic, the country was respresented by two teams in international competition. Yemen AR joined FIFA in 1980 and played in an all green strip; Yemen PDR joined in 1967 and played in light blue and white.

Yeovil Town English non-League football club, nicknamed the Glovers. Strip: white and green shirts, white shorts, and white socks. Founded in 1895 (as Yeovil Casuals), the club adopted the title Yeovil in 1908 and were known as Yeovil and Petters United from 1919 to 1945, when they adopted their current name. Playing in the Conference, Yeovil are based at Huish Park, which is notorious for its pronounced incline (popularly called the 'Yeovil Slope').

Over the years the club has built up a virtually unparalleled reputation as a non-League giant-killer, with over 20 League sides having come to unexpected grief at the hands of the Glovers and their infamous sloping pitch. The 1948–49 season in particular is still talked about. Despite the fact that the club was then near the bottom of the Southern League, the team battled their way through to the third round of the FA Cup and caused a sensation when they crushed Second Division Bury 3–1. The next round against Sunderland should have been a foregone conclusion, but Yeovil defied all expectations and defeated their illustrious opponents 2–1. The team subsequently went down 8–0 to Manchester United in the next round, but the side were already folk heroes, with a permanent place in the history of the national game.

Their remarkable success (perhaps not unconnected with the fact that the side included several highly experienced players once with major clubs) was attributed by some to the extraordinary diet of glucose, eggs, and sherry the team had followed.

Yesterday's Hero Football film released in 1979, which purports to tell how Leicester Forest won the FA Cup. It starred Ian McShane as a stereotypical fading striker with a weakness for drink, while other characters included a rock star chairman and a granite-hearted manager. Boasting a script by Jackie Collins and commentary by John Motson, the film failed, however, to make much impression at the box office.

York City English football club, nicknamed the Minstermen. Strip: red shirts, blue shorts, and red socks. Founded in 1922, the present club was the successor to an earlier York City founded in 1903 and disbanded during World War I. Based at BOOTHAM CRESCENT since 1932, York joined the Third Division (North) in 1929 and remained there until 1958, when they slipped down to the Fourth Division for a season. Their history since then has been split between the bottom three divisions, with their best times coming in the mid-1970s when they were briefly members of the Second Division.

They reached the semi-finals of the FA Cup in 1955, while still a Third Division side. That year witnessed what was perhaps the most remarkable triumph in the club's history – FA Cup victory against Blackpool (whose team included such illustrious names as MATTHEWS and MORTENSEN). At the other end of the scale they have been obliged to apply for re-election to the League on no fewer than six occasions. In 1971 there was some excitement when a group of local spiritualists predicted that the club would apear in an FA Cup Final by 1980; unfortunately for them the prediction came to nothing (though the team did reach the Second Division for the first time in 1974).

York enjoyed their record victory in 1957, when they beat Southport 9–1; they suffered their worst defeat in 1936, when they lost 12–0 to Chester. Barry Jackson holds the record for League appearances with the club, having played in 481 games between 1958 and 1970.

> Come on without, come on within,
> You've not seen nothing like a City win.

Supporters' song, to the tune of 'The Mighty Quinn'

You'll Never Walk Alone The classic football song that is associated with the English football club LIVERPOOL. A hit for the Merseyside band Gerry and the Pacemakers in 1963, it was adopted by the Anfield choir and achieved the status of club anthem. The song was re-released after the Bradford fire to raise fund for families of the dead.

> As you walk through the storm,
> Hold your head up high,
> And don't be afraid of the dark,
> At the end of the storm,
> Is a golden sky,
> And the sweet silver song of the lark,
> Walk on through the wind,
> Walk on through the rain,
> Though your dreams be tossed and blown.
> Walk on, walk on,
> With hope in your hearts,
> And you'll never walk alone,
> You'll never walk alone.

Young, George (1922–) Celebrated Scottish defender, nicknamed Corky, who led Scotland with great success in the 1950s. Young was one of the best-loved and formidable of postwar Scottish players, over six feet in height, and one of the most competent defenders of his era. He joined Rangers in 1941 and was made captain of Scotland in 1948, going on to make a record 34 consecutive appearances for the national side and acting as captain on a record 48 occasions. As captain of Rangers, he led the side to six League championships, four Scottish Cup wins, and two League Cup victories, completing the 'triple' in 1949. He was chosen Scottish Player of the Year in 1955 and retired as a player in 1957, subsequently managing Third Lanark (1959–62).

youngest players Many notable players began their careers at a precociously young age and some immediately made their mark (*see* DEBUTS). British record-breakers include Albert Geldard (1927) and Ken Roberts (1951), who at the tender age of 15 years and 158 days, share the distinction of having been the youngest players ever to appear in the Football League. Others are Ronnie Dix, who scored his first League goal at the age of 15 years and 180 days, Andy Awford, who became the youngest player to take part in the FA Cup when he came on at the age of 15 years 88 days, and Duncan EDWARDS, who became the youngest England international since World War II when he turned out at the age of 18 years and 183 days in 1955.

Yugoslavia The national team that represented the former state of Yugoslavia had a distinguished record in international competition, though it often failed to carry off the major honours at the last hour. The team captured the Olympic football title in 1960 but were runners-up another three times. Their best performances in the World Cup were in 1954 and 1958, when they reached the quarter-finals, and in 1962, when they finished fourth. They were runners-up in the European Championship in 1960 and 1968. Strip: blue shirts, white shorts, and red socks.

Z

Zaïre Zaïre joined FIFA in 1962 and are one of the stronger African footballing nations. Winners of the African Nations Cup in 1974, the team had the misfortune to lose 9–0 to Yugoslavia in their first World Cup Finals that year (though they managed to restrict Scotland to a 2–0 win). Strip: green shirts, with yellow shorts and socks.

Zambia Zambia joined FIFA in 1964 but have yet to make much impact in international competition. One of their strongest squads to date was destroyed in an air crash off Libreville, Gabon, in 1993 before it had a chance to realize its potential. Strip: green and copper shirts, white, green, black, and red shorts, and black and red socks with green, red, and yellow trim.

Zamora, Ricardo (1901–) Spanish goalkeeper, nicknamed the Man in Black, who was widely considered to be the finest keeper in the world in the 1920s and early 1930s and attracted a cult following. His clubs included Español, Barcelona, Real Madrid, and Nice. As an international, Zamora let in just 40 goals in 46 matches, in 21 of which Spain were undefeated. He played in the Olympic tournaments of 1920, 1924, and 1928 and subsequently in the World Cup in 1934. In England, however, he is often remembered for the much-anticipated clash when he had to defend his country's goal against England and the prodigious talent of Dixie DEAN in 1931: on this one occasion even he could not contain Dixie's skills and by the end of a memorable match had conceded seven goals. An award bestowed upon the best Spanish goalkeeper is called the Zamora Award in tribute to his achievements.

Zebec, Branko (1949–) Yugoslavian-born forward, who achieved fame as one of the most versatile and talented European strikers of the 1950s. Playing at both outside-right and centre-half at different stages of his career, he was a star with Partizan and Red Star Belgrade as well as making 65 appearances for the national team (highlights including the hat-trick he scored on his international debut in 1951). After ending his playing career with the West German club Alemannia Aachen, he became a successful coach, taking Dynamo Zagreb to victory in the 1967 Fairs Cup and guiding Hamburg to the final of the 1980 European Cup.

Zebras Alternative nickname of the Italian football club JUVENTUS, in reference to the club's black and white striped shirts. *See also* GRAND OLD LADY.

Zico (Artur Antunes Coimbra; 1953–) Brazilian striker, nicknamed the White Pelé, who established himself as one of the most formidable of PELÉ's heirs in the Brazilian side of the 1970s and 1980s. Born in Rio de Janeiro, Zico made his debut with Flamengo in 1969 and subsequently won his first cap with the national team in 1975 (scoring in his first game). Though plagued throughout his career by injury, he became a regular choice for the Brazilian national team and played in the World Cup campaigns of 1978 (when Brazil finished third), 1982 (when he proved one of the stars of the tournament), and 1986 (reaching the quarter-finals).

In all he scored 66 goals in 88 international games, as well as enjoying the title of South American Footballer of the Year in 1977, 1981, and 1982. He transferred to the Italian club Udinese in 1983 but returned to Flamengo – with whom he won three Brazilian Championships among other honours – two years later. He also played in Japan and accepted the post of Brazilian Minister for Sport.

Zigger Zagger Title of Peter Terson's play (1967) about football, taken from the chant of Stoke fan J. Bageley. A view of life from the terraces, it is a rare example of football being treated as a suitable subject for the stage and was written specifically for the National Youth Theatre. The action mixes football motifs with an examination of the bleak prospects facing a football-obsessed teenager in a society which appears to have failed him.

Zimbabwe Zimbabwe joined FIFA in 1965 but have as yet made little impact in international competition. Strip: green shirts, gold shorts, and green and gold socks.

Zito (José Eli Miranda; 1932–) Brazilian midfielder, who played a key role in the Brazilian World Cup campaigns of 1958 and 1962. Having made his international debut in 1955, he developed a particularly effective partnership with DIDÌ.

Zoff, Dino (1942–) Italian goalkeeper, who enjoyed almost unparalleled success as custodian of his country's goal over a period of 15 years and, with a total of 112 caps, became Italy's most capped player. Zoff's career was slow to take off and began with a disastrous debut in which he let in five goals for Udinese. Subsequently he transferred to Mantova (1963) and Napoli (1967) before making his international debut in 1968 in the team that won the European Championship. Things improved dramatically in 1972, when a move to Juventus coincided with the role of Italian keeper becoming his personal possession. He enjoyed a series of 12 international games (amounting to 1143 minutes of play) in which he did not concede a single goal (as well as another 903 unstained minutes in the League) and in 1973 was voted runner-up as European Footballer of the Year. He played a key role in Juventus's triumph in the UEFA Cup in 1977 and in 1978 helped Italy gain fourth place in the World Cup. In 1982 he reappeared in the World Cup as Italy's captain – though aged 40 – and led his side to victory with a 3–1 win over West Germany in the Final. Subsequently he became coach to the Italian Olympic team and to his old club Juventus and then to Lazio.

zonal defence A defensive system in which defenders block any attack that comes within their specified area, rather than concentrating upon marking an individual player. The tactic was adopted increasingly widely in the late 1960s.

Zorro Nickname of the Yugoslavian-born midfielder Zvonimir BOBAN, comparing his talent with the rapier skills of the dashing masked cowboy of numerous low-budget films made since the character first appeared in a strip cartoon in 1919.

Zubizarreta, Andoni (1961–) Spanish goalkeeper, who was acclaimed by many to be the finest keeper in the world in the early 1990s. Zubizarreta made his international debut in 1985 and subsequently made the role of keeper to the national team his own personal possession, rising to the post of captain. At home, he helped Athletic Bilbao to League victories in 1983 and 1984 (when the team also won the Cup) before moving to Barcelona for a record £1.2 million in 1986. In 1992 he was largely responsible for Barcelona's triumph in the European Cup.

Zulus Extraordinary football team that toured England in the wake of the Zulu War of 1879. Including such star players as Zulu warrior king Cetewayo and his brother Dabulamanzi, the squad overcame Sheffield, then one of the leading English clubs, 5–4 at Bramall Lane and subsequently acquitted themselves with honour against the cream of English teams without losing a single game.

The Zulus were in reality not the warrior chiefs of Zululand, but a collection of some of the finest British footballers of the day (including Scotland's Jack Hunter) who had been persuaded by a Mr Brewer to impersonate a Zulu squad in order to promote a charity in aid of the widows and orphans of soldiers killed in the recent Zulu Wars. The players entered into the spirit of the thing, disguising their faces with cork, dressing in feathers, beads, and black jerseys and stockings, and performing all manner of ritual dances and other antics.

The team attracted large crowds but it was not long before the Sheffield FA found fault with the enterprise – specifically when Hunter's involvement in a Zulu match north of the border made him ineligible to play in a North/South representative game. The fact that the players were being paid for their efforts also sealed the fate of the Zulu team, one of the more entertaining squads to grace UK grounds, and it was eventually disbanded (though the name was revived by a gang of football hooligans who terrorized visiting fans in the vicinity of Birmingham City's home ground in the 1980s).